MARKETS IN AFRICA

NORTHWESTERN UNIVERSITY AFRICAN STUDIES

NUMBER NINE

MARKETS IN AFRICA

EDITED BY

PAUL BOHANNAN AND GEORGE DALTON

NORTHWESTERN UNIVERSITY PRESS

Published 1962 by Northwestern University Press
Library of Congress Catalog Number: 61-12383

Published 1962 by Northwestern University Press
Library of Congress Catalog Number: 61-12383
Second Printing, 1965

This volume was prepared as part of The Human Environments
in Middle Africa Project, National Academy of Sciences–National
Research Council. It was financed by Quartermaster
Research and Engineering Command, under
Contract No. DA-19-129-AM-1309.

The ideas which are here expressed so laboriously
are extremely simple and should be obvious. The
difficulty lies, not in the new ideas, but in escaping
from the old ones, which ramify, for those brought
up as most of us have been, into every
corner of our minds.

JOHN MAYNARD KEYNES

PREFACE

BY MELVILLE J. HERSKOVITS

The essays in the present volume center on an important aspect of African economic activity. They make available fresh, first-hand substantive data from Subsaharan Africa that cannot but sharpen concepts to be used in the comparative study of economic phenomena. Subsaharan Africa is an area that in size and in differences in its ecological, historical, and cultural factors provides a laboratory setting for enquiry into questions of this kind. In the particular field of our interest, the range of complexity in its aboriginal economies, the characteristics of the systems with which African peoples came into contact, and the differing intensity of the impact of these systems upon the indigenous ones all provide rich resources. In essence, this vast area is one in which the student of human behavior can exercise the situational controls that are essential if he is to test his hypotheses, on the level of comparative data, in the tradition of scientific method.

The value of these studies thus goes beyond the new and detailed descriptive data in them. The facts having to do with the systems that existed before the colonial period, which they incorporate, make it clear that many of the questions raised as to the cross-cultural applicability of concepts developed by economists are essentially semantic. The extent to which the market concept has validity when applied to the economies of so-called "primitive" societies is a particularly relevant case in point. The significance of the controversy over this becomes materially lessened when we realize that modes of distribution through the exchange of goods and services, as culturally defined, are basic to any economy. Just as we find it useful, from time to time, to recall the truism that economic man is nonexistent, so we can advantageously bring to the fore-conscious of our thought the fact that no man is sufficient to himself alone.

Admittedly, it is not easy to discern similarities between rudimentary economic systems and the vast network of relationships that mark the great industrial complexes. Yet all societies, even those that are small, isolated, and technologically simple, have their areas of specialization. Their specializations may be restricted to sex, division of labor, and distribution in them may be a matter of intra-familial exchanges; moreover, the economic character of these modes of exchange may be distorted by ritual demands or kinship regulations. Yet when the basis of our consideration shifts from the classification of form to analysis of function, both the rudimentary and the complex forms, no matter how dissimilar their dimensions, turn out to be no more than extremes of a continuum, many of whose intermediate manifestations, indeed, are to be found in the various kinds of exchanges described in the chapters of this work.

On a somewhat different level, the point being made here has been well phrased by Miracle in the final chapter of this book, where he ends his discussion with this observation: "Perhaps a more fruitful question to ask than whether African economic behavior is normal is why do so many who generalize about the behavior of Africans so readily and uncritically accept evidence that superficially suggests African economic behavior is basically abnormal?" (p. 733). Miracle is here reacting to ethnocentric judgments based on the approach of the more conventional economists; but even when the ethnocentrism is deleted, it requires analysis in depth to see that African economic behavior is patently "normal," in the sense of being consistent with ends which are culturally defined as desirable. Africans, no less than other peoples, seek to fulfill their needs as they envisage them, whether these needs be biological or psychological. The means of solving the problem differs from society to society, in the light of the technological, historical, social, and psychological factors that are in play. But basically, the problem is the same wherever it may be treated.

The classification of market phenomena by the Editors is consonant with the position outlined in the preceding pages. We are given categories that describe a continuum based on "the role that the market place and the market principle play." At one end of this continuum we find societies without any formal centers of exchange—that is, without market activity, having what they term "multicentric economies." Toward the center are those in which marketplaces exist but where both the informal exchanges of less complicated systems and the "market principle" operate tangentially. Finally, at the other end, are the societies whose economies are dominated by the "market principle," where specialization of labor is so great that "the price mechanism functions as an integrative device" to dominate the economy (pp. 1–2).

That these categories must be flexible is made equally apparent in the chapters that follow, particularly where the acculturative factor enters, and the older principles of face-to-face exchange exist at the side of the impersonalities of the full pecuniary system. As categories, the degrees to which the factor of the market enters into non-European economies are paralleled by the three types of systems of exchange that have been delimited—barter, money-barter, and money. Such components as gift-exchange, or modes of acquiring prestige through the possession, display, or conspicuous utilization of valuable goods, and the geographical limits to trading operations, cut across these other categories, so that one or all of them may or may not be present. In East Africa, the economics of cattle is quite different from that of subsistence. Here we have dual economies, one of which is dominated by these valuables. Where the market principle is fully in play, the duality between prestige and subsistence sections of the economy or the nature of gift-exchange tends to be concealed, since both fall within the compass of a common denominator of value, money. Consequently, a grasp not only of the systems of exchange but of the nature and functioning of expressions of value that are employed is critical in any study of comparative economics.

In Africa, as elsewhere in societies moving into the world economy, the acculturative aspect complicates the analysis. The simultaneous presence of systems of exchange that fall into all the categories of marketing brings a dimension into play which blurs the lines drawn between our classes of phenomena even more than is the case where research is ordered in terms of a single time-plane. A simple schema may indicate key components in changing acculturative economies:

indigenous economies	differential media and variability in values of indigenous systems of exchange
acculturated market system	money dominant in systems of evaluation and exchange

In those African systems where values could be translated either into fairly standardized tokens such as cowries or manillas, the changes resulting from the acculturative experience have been less abrupt than where such tokens do not exist. On the other hand, the principle of cultural reinterpretation coming into play assured a carry-over of non-pecuniary modes of exchange, even into the full-scale "modern" economy. Gibson points this out for the changing economy of the Herero, where though money is known and the cattle conventionally used for bridewealth have been translated into English currency, "when we attempt to treat Herero bridewealth as an economic matter, we must assert emphatically that the laws of the market do not apply." That is, "the symbolic significance of the bridewealth animals outweighs their economic significance," so that, "in spite of the great desire for wives Herero men apparently do not compete for them by raising the amount of bridewealth offered to their parents" (p. 639).

The discussions of modes of exchange in this volume permit us to assess similarities and differences on a regional and even a sub-continental scale. Differences in the complexities of over-all systems and their technologies, between the economic organization of the cattle-keeping peoples of eastern and southern Africa and economies based on agriculture in the center and west, are to be seen in clear out-line in the presence or absence of markets in the pre-colonial epoch. It is equally clear, however, that even where markets were absent, Africans were not lacking in what might be called a "value-sense" in exchanges. This facilitated adjustment to the new situation in which money figured. The reinterpretations that came into play can be seen in many of the discussions of the non-pecuniary East African economies, where we find that money, rather than being accepted as a medium of exchange, was added to the list of exchangeable commodities.

Reining's discussion of Zande adaptation to the new system, where money is seen "primarily as a special item necessary to acquire in shops certain commodities that could not be manufactured in their subsistence economy," brings this out clearly. Thus, when an Azande woman was asked why she was selling flour in a market, she replied, "I am selling it for money." Psychologically, that is, money and flour are equivalent economic goods, one to be exchanged for the other. Nor, in this psychology, was money encouraged to enter into all sectors of the economy. "They believed it commendable to convert subsistence goods into money, but they did not want to reverse the process" (pp. 551–52). We also find this reinterpretation in con-temporary Bulu economic thinking, where, we are told, "The modern Bulu conceptualize cash as a commodity," to be distributed as surplus among kin and trade friends or used to obtain a position of prestige (p. 184).

Wherever markets exist, whether these centers are continuities of aboriginal economic organization or innovative, they are more than just means for achieving the circulation of goods. In part this is owing to the inherent character of the economic relationships they en-gender; in part to their extra-economic aspects. These latter are a function of their restricted local scope, and the degree of continued personal contact that marks the transactions of buyer and seller; moreover, market rituals validate and seal economic rights and contractual obligations. The market is a place to meet friends, to hear news, to contract alliances, to initiate sexual adventures. As one Mossi said to Skinner, "I must go to the market, and when I get there

I look for three persons: my girl friend, my debtor, and my enemy. If I do not know whether any of them are at the market, I am ill at ease. And when I go to the market and do not see them all, the market is not good" (p. 270).

We are struck by the variety of media of exchange that existed in pre-colonial Africa and the ways in which the mechanism of cultural reinterpretation has acted in shaping responses in this aspect of the acculturative situation. The cowry shell, most often cited for West Africa as a common form of money, and the somewhat different role of cattle in the east and south as repositories of value are well known. But in these pages we encounter many other forms of money and repositories of value. Thus Vansina, for the Kuba, in addition to cowries, lists standard-sized raffia-cloth squares, copper crosses imported from the Katanga, and certain green and white beads. Among the Wolof, Ames details the use of "cloth money" consisting of strips of cloth, as common denominators of value.

Other forms of what is well termed "commodity money," the media employed in the money-barter aspect of exchange transactions, are named. Ottenberg (p. 124) notes the use of brass rods and manillas by the Afikpo Ibo. Cloth was a subsidiary form of currency among the Mossi (p. 247). For the Bororo, Dupire reports a "complex system of reckoning exchange values" on the basis of a standard whose multiples are invariable, but the worth of which fluctuates in the exchange of commodities "according to the laws of supply and demand" (p. 346). This bears a striking resemblance to what obtains in Euroamerican systems where, for example, the dime is constant in relation to the dollar, or the shilling to the pound, but the value of a given unit fluctuates in real worth according to fluctuations in its purchasing power.

Another general characteristic of Subsaharan markets appears in the role of women as traders. The importance of women in the markets of the Guinea Coast has long been recognized, and it needs but a review of the literature of pre-colonial and colonial times, and no more than brief first-hand observation of the post-colonial scene, to establish their continued functioning in this capacity. The energy these women expend in carrying out these functions and the organized activity their work entails express the importance of their effort, both for themselves and for the economy as a whole. Preparing the cooked foods sold in the marketplaces, for example—pounding grain in the mortar, gathering and combining the necessary ingredients, and cooking the food—means that the sellers must call on a range of helpers, usually members of their families, but sometime extra-familial apprentices, in making available the products they offer for

sale. Hodder gives us some indication of the distances traversed by
these women in the course of their trading activities. He estimates
that, in a typical case, a woman who walks nine miles to various
markets will cover "some fifty miles or more a week . . . usually with
a basket or calabash of goods on her head . . ." (p. 109).

There can be little question but that the power of economic motivation traditionally found in these societies of western Africa accounts largely for the favorable economic position held by these
women. In much, if not all of the Guinea Coast countries of West
Africa, a woman's earnings belong to her. During the late colonial
and post-colonial period, in countries such as Nigeria and Ghana,
for example, this fact had significant ramifications into non-economic
spheres. Support for the nationalist movements that were the instruments of political independence came in considerable measure
from the donations of the market-women. It is also plain that their
traditionally sanctioned economic position made it possible for them
to adapt to innovations that were in the nature of continuities. Thus
they seem easily to have grasped how credit, in the banking sense,
could be a factor of importance in extending the scope of their
dealings, after European currencies became the universal medium
employed in effectuating exchanges. The extent of their adaptation
in this case becomes apparent when we examine the relations between
these women and the large European commercial enterprises, wherein
some marketers are reported as having monthly credit ratings with
these companies running into hundreds and even thousands of pounds
sterling.

It is interesting to speculate whether a comparable pattern may not
develop in those parts of Subsaharan Africa in which the market was
traditionally absent. Something of the sort seems to be taking place,
as is indicated by the descriptions of the economic role of women
among the Masai and to a lesser extent among the Arusha (p. 432),
and also among the Kipsigis (p. 510). On the Copperbelt, 40% of the
traders surveyed in the course of a study reported on in this volume
were women. We are also told that they predominate in the food-
selling sector of the Azande economy.

Should the new markets of eastern and southern Africa develop
lines of sex division in buying and selling comparable to those which
characterize the markets of the western and central parts of the continent, it seems likely that not only the economic position of women
but their place in the social order in general may undergo change. Certainly in the newly established markets of the regions where these
institutions were non-existent, the division of labor in market activities has seemed in a general way to follow that in the areas of Sub-

saharan Africa where markets have long existed. Everywhere in African markets, old or new, women tend to sell foodstuffs and related products and portable imported goods, while men are vendors of live-stock and dispose of their services where new instruments of production, such as the sewing-machine, must be used. With the growth of the African commercial sector, social implications of the persistence of these patterns of sex division of labor in the distributive process, or ways in which they may be strengthened, have implications that go far beyond the field of economics.

There are other widely-spread aspects of African market systems that reflect its economic importance. Especially in West Africa, markets rotate in accordance with the days of the week. That in many West African cultures they have the same names—that is, the name of the principal market of a given day—as the week-day on which they are held is evidence of the place they have taken in the conceptualizations of the people. Again, there is some evidence that this pattern of rotation, the "marketing ring," as Hodder calls this cyclical aspect of market operations among the Yoruba, is developing where the market is a new phenomenon. It may be conjectured whether this may not be a function of its economic effectiveness, something that goes beyond the African scene. That is, a large market provides a wider range of choice than a small one and, where there is a pattern of price manipulation, offers the buyer a better opportunity to purchase commodities to advantage. The factors of time and distance, both for sellers and buyers, also enter, especially where transport of goods is restricted to what can be carried by a single individual. The choice implied is between a single market at the center of a large district or a system of rotation whereby the advantages and disadvantages of distance can be more adequately partitioned between markets that move from one center to another on a fixed schedule.

Obviously, such a system does not meet all the problems of an effective distributive mechanism that fits the requirements of the ultimate consumer. This is implicit in the existence almost everywhere in Africa of what may be called "fringe" markets. In practically any African settlement, where money existed autochthonously or where the pecuniary convention has been introduced, one finds a few sellers of cooked foods or fruit or staples of one kind or another stationed at the intersection of well-travelled paths or along a motor road. In West Africa there are permanent small "night markets," where the wage-worker or the traveller can purchase hot food for his evening meal or where, for instance, a woman can buy staples in "broken bulk" lots that are small enough to tide her over until the "week-day market." Again, everywhere there is a gathering, whether

at a religious rite or a political rally or a funeral, there will be a few
sellers who set up an *ad hoc* market of bottled and locally prepared
drinks and cooked food.

In the restricted sense of face-to-face operations, it is clear that
Africans have been receptive to conventions of business enterprise.
This is not strange in those areas where the tradition of buying and
selling in the market strikes deep into the past; there seems, however,
to have been a degree of parallel receptivity where this complex was
not part of pre-existing patterns but has been an additive factor
acquired from the acculturative experience. Even in eastern and
southern Africa, the absence of a traditional base has not, to the
degree that might have been anticipated, inhibited Africans from
actively entering trade. The relevant chapters of this book are replete
with data which indicate that even where barter prevailed, extra-
familial and inter-tribal exchanges were to be found, while what
might be termed proto-markets, where particular kinds of goods
were bartered at particular times, did exist. If West Africa is at the
center of our continuum of market phenomena, ways of trading in
the eastern and southern parts of the continent provide us with re-
finements toward the non-pecuniary end of the scale.

The essays in this book document the fallacy of conceptualizations
which separate different levels of "the market" and concentrate only
on the "modern" sector because it is held to be different in kind rather
than in degree. For to disregard internal exchanges, which in some
African countries actually dominate the economies, is to distort the
reality of African economic processes, aboriginal or post-colonial.
Here the need to strike through the formal aspects of markets, whether
on a restricted local scale or in the sense of "the market" cast in impersonal terms of world movements of commodities and prices, to the
functional common factor of exchange, is critical. This is most
apparent when we consider implications for economic policy planning. Attempts to assess the factors of distribution in the new African
countries have most typically been based on the assumption that the
significant ones are those which appertain to the patterns of the
broad world economic system. The humble role of the local markets
is thus submerged in concern with the activities of large firms and
operations in the world market as shown by figures for export and
imports. What we have here is analagous to efforts to determine gross
national product for these same countries, wherein the contribution
made by the small farmer or artisan is ignored.

This is not to say that there are no important differences between
world industrial order and the inter-tribal or external trade of nonliterate societies, as the Editors of this book show. These are seen

not only in the differences between impersonal and face-to-face relations but also in the number and nature of the mechanisms of determining and establishing price—that is, expressions of value—and of the numbers of persons involved in the process. But these are differences of degree, not of kind.

This is true not only of the market. Money is a concept that lies on the level of form, and much of the controversary that has arisen in the study of the prestige economies of eastern and southern Africa could be assuaged if we thought in terms of denominators and repositories of value. Again, credit is regarded as an economic mechanism particularly identifiable with the working of business, operating under a price-profit system. Yet in the aboriginal economies of West Africa, the pawn was collateral for a loan. At least in Dahomey, the return to the lender, covering principal as well as interest, was in the labor of the member of the borrower's family who was pawned. The idea of re-insurance, that is, of distributing risk, is functionally implicit in the practice of East African owners of cattle decentralizing their herds. Such measures ensure against total loss in a raid or in a bovine epidemic. Perhaps the emphasis on numbers was traditionally established because the expectation of increase in those portions of his holdings thus preserved could be looked to to restore losses of raids and epidemics, not a rarity in the experience of the cattle-keeping peoples.

It goes without saying that under this approach to the economic data, the forms that are studied are to be placed as fully as possible in the context of their significance in the culture where they are manifest. One of the reasons for the need to hold this in mind is the distortion of perspective if a cultural pattern or an institutional arrangement be equated with an institution or point of view in another culture that resembles it sufficiently to be given the same name. Our basic data must derive from ethnographic facts we gather in the field. We were taught many years ago by the students of comparative linguistics that each cultural element can only be subjected to valid scientific study if it is analyzed in terms of the particular categories of the culture in which it functions.

How well the lesson has been learned is demonstrated in the chapters of this book. It is striking how often in these pages an English word in common use to describe a particular kind of economic phenomenon is found to be unsatisfactory, and recourse is had to the term in the native language employed by the people of the society under study. This frees the student from assuming a fit when the relevance of the designations generally used in economics is partial. He aligns his data by use of the native word, provides us with an explanation *in extenso* that makes resemblances to the common designation clear, while making explicit the differences that enter.

It is just here, however, that the importance of seeing through form for underlying function enters, since it is the forms that differ, the functions that provide the universals which give us a base for drawing our comparisons. If a given economic—or social, or political, or religious—institution is unique to the culture in which it is found, and we go no further than this, refusing to utilize any common nomenclature, classification and concepts will be ruled out, and the question arises as to the possibility of ever drawing comparisons. But without recourse to the method of comparison, we are left with no more than a series of discrete descriptions, from which generalizations cannot be drawn. This is why we must search for the functional unities that underlie the formal differences. That is, where terms in general use refer to the formal elements, we must be careful to refine their meaning when we employ them in cross-cultural analysis. But we must take care not to throw out the functional baby with the formal bathwater, just as we must be careful not to smother it in a blanket of social context.

EDITORS' NOTE

THE TIME

Most of the articles in this book refer to the 1950's; most were written in 1960. The "ethnographic present" is used throughout. This factor affects little of the information but does make obsolete those references to the colonial governments and colonial conditions which no longer apply in the independent countries of Africa.

REFERENCES

The references to printed books are inserted into the text by putting the author, year, and page in parentheses; complete references are to be found in the bibliography at the end of the volume. References to letters, personal communications, and archival materials are given in footnotes to avoid swelling the bibliography with generally unavailable material.

ACKNOWLEDGEMENTS

Quite literally dozens of our colleagues have given assistance in preparing this book. Special acknowledgement can be given only to Erna Thompson, who typed the manuscripts—some of them more than once—and to Susan Messerley, who assisted with proofs and made the Index.

CURRENCIES

The following currencies have been mentioned in the text. Their valuation with European or American currencies and their place in the currency system of the country concerned are noted briefly here.

East African shilling: par with the United Kingdom shilling; divided into one hundred cents.

West African shilling: par with the United Kingdom shilling, divided into twelve pence, each of which is divided into tenth-pennies (*nini* in Nigeria, other words elsewhere).

The Congolese franc: before independence was at par with the Belgian franc. First issued by the Banque du Congo Belge, later by the Banque Centrale du Congo Belge.

The C. F. A. (Colonies Françaises d'Afrique) franc: equals two

Metropolitan (old) francs. In 1956, 175 C. F. A. francs equaled $1 U.S.A.

The Ethiopian dollar in 1960 was equivalent to $ .40 U.S.A. The Maria Theresa dollar is no longer legal in Ethiopia but was the unit for evaluating livestock and other expensive items. The black market exchange rate varied from $1.25 to $2.50.

Since most of these studies were written, there have been changes both in the issuing agency and the value of some of the currencies.

CONTENTS

Preface by M. J. Herskovits vii
Editors' Note xvii
List of Maps and Figures xxi
List of Tables xxii
Introduction by Paul Bohannan and George Dalton . 1

THE GUINEA COAST AND THE CONGO

1. The Rural Wolof of the Gambia 29
   David Ames
2. African Traders in Central Sierra Leone . . . 61
   Vernon R. Dorjahn
3. Traditional Market Economy in the South Dahomey . 89
   Claudine and Claude Tardits
4. The Yoruba Rural Market 103
   B. W. Hodder
5. Afikpo Markets: 1900–1960 118
   Simon and Phoebe Ottenberg
6. The Bulu Response to European Economy . . . 170
   George R. Horner
7. Trade and Markets Among the Kuba 190
   Jan Vansina
8. Lele Economy Compared with the Bushong: A Study
   of Economic Backwardness 211
   Mary Douglas

THE WESTERN SUDAN

9. Trade and Markets among the Mossi People . . . 237
   Elliott P. Skinner
10. Social and Economic Factors Affecting Markets in Guro
    Land 279
    Claude Meillassoux
11. Exchange and Marketing among the Hausa . . . 299
    Michael G. Smith
12. Trade and Markets in the Economy of the Nomadic
    Fulani of Niger (Bororo) 335
    Marguerite Dupire

THE HORN OF AFRICA

13. Trade and Markets in Northern Somaliland . . . 365
    I. M. Lewis

14. The Abyssinian Market Town 386
    Simon D. Messing
15. The Konso Economy of Southern Ethiopia . . . 409
    Richard Kluckhohn

EAST AFRICA

16. The Evolution of Arusha Trade 431
    P. H. Gulliver
17. Livestock Markets among the Iraqw of Northern Tan-
    ganyika 457
    E. H. Winter
18. Economic Exchange in a Sonjo Village 469
    Robert F. Gray
19. Land Use, Trade and the Growth of Market Economy
    in Kipsigis Country 493
    R. A. Manners
20. Wealth and Power in Gusiiland 520
    Robert LeVine
21. Zande Markets and Commerce 537
    Conrad C. Reining
22. Trade and Markets among the Lugbara of Uganda . 561
    John Middleton

CENTRAL AFRICA

23. Rural Rhodesian Markets 581
    Robert I. Rotberg
24. Trade and Wealth among the Tonga 601
    Elizabeth Colson
25. Bridewealth and other Forms of Exchange among the
    Herero 617
    Gordon D. Gibson

CITIES AND INDUSTRIAL COMPLEXES

26. The Marketing of Staple Foods in Kampala. Uganda . 643
    A. B. Mukwaya
27. The Koforidua Market 667
    Daniel F. McCall
28. African Markets and Trade in the Copperbelt . . 698
    Marvin P. Miracle
    References 739
    Index 755

MAPS AND FIGURES

1. Location of Tribes and Areas Represented in this study   xxvi
2. Sierra Leone 63
3. Kolifa Mayoso (Temne) 72
4. Akinyele Area (Yoruba) 105
5. Olusun Village and Market (Yoruba) 107
6. Sketch Map of Eke Market (Ibo) 136
7. Average Length of Dry Season 212
8. Population Density (Lele and Bushong)
   Forest Cover (Lele and Bushong) 213
9. Age at Retirement from Work (Lele and Bushong) . 231
10. Period of Full Work (Lele and Bushong) . . . 231
11. Economy and Social Organization 232
12. Towns, Villages, Foreigners' Markets and Guro Markets 281
13. Tribal Settlements of the Guro 282
14. Relation of Markets to Forests (Guro) 284
15. Markets of Niger (Fulani) 355
16. Caravan Trails and Roads to Gondar 387
17. Koforidua and its Hinterland 668
18. Schematic Map of Koforidua, Showing Land Use . . 669
19. Koforidua Market 672–73
20. Koforidua Marketing Area 684
21. The Copperbelt and its Hinterland 699
22. Location of Tribes on the Copperbelt 704
23. Average Seasonal Variation in the Number of Sellers in
    Selected Rhodesian Copperbelt Markets . . . 709
24. Production and Net Imports of the Major Commodities
    Marketed in the Congo Sector of the Copperbelt . . 718
25. Proportion of Major Imports to Congo Copperbelt from
    Principal Zones of Supply 720–21
26. Conditions for Barter of Fish (Copperbelt) . . . 727

TABLES

1. Characteristics of the Market in Three Types of Economy 16
2. Equivalence of cloth (Wolof) 39
3. Equivalence of cloth to other items (Wolof) . . . 39
4. Expenditure of Wolof and Fula 51
5. Comparative Prices, Mayose-Magburaka (Sierra Leone) 73
6. Comparative Prices, Magburaka-Diamond Area . . 75
7. Liquid Measure and Value of Pots (Sierra Leone) . . 85
8. Solid Measure and Value of Pans (Sierra Leone) . . 85
9. Barter Equivalence (Sierra Leone) 86
10. Corn Prices in Mitro (Dahomey) 99
11. Analysis of Sellers in Three Yoruba Markets . . . 116–17
12. Products Sold in Upper Market (Afikpo Ibo) . . 148
13. Products Sold in Lower Market (Afikpo Ibo) . . 149
14. Occupation of Stalls in Upper Market (Afikpo Ibo) . 153
15. Cash Income in the Bulu Area (1956) 178
16. Estimated Cash Income from Cocoa (1951) (Bulu) . 178
17. Religious Preferences in the Bulu Area . . . 180
18. Cash Requirements for Bridewealth in the Bulu Area 181
19. Depreciation of the Cowry 198
20. Bushong Labor 202
21. Inventory of Houses (Bushong) 203–4
22. Regional Specialization and Trade (Bushong) . . 204–5
23. Products and Prices on the market Mwaak (Bushong) 206–7–8
24. Production and Value of Smithing (1954) (Bushong) . 208–9
25. Sample of Dealings on the market Mwaak (Bushong) . 209
26. Frequency of products sold on Mwaak (Bushong) . . 210
27. Value of Goods Offered for Sale on the market Mwaak (Bushong) 210
28. Annual Cycle of Work (Lele and Bushong) . . . 221
28a. Mossi Trade (1901–3) 246
29. Production, Trade and Export of the Mossi (1954) . 252
30. Markets near Nobere 258
31. Prices of Local Foodstuffs in the Markets of Sabon Gari, Zaria and Giwar, 1958–9. (Hausa) 321
32. Goods on Sale by Commodity Group (Hausa) . . 322
33. Commodities on selected market days (Hausa) . . 323
34. Composition of Giwa Market in 1949 and 1959 (Hausa) 327
35. Cash Revenue of Average Freehold Farmer (Amhara) 400
36. Commodity Prices; a General Average for a Medium-Size Konso Village 420

37. Absentee Rates for Lugbara Laborers 566
38. Cash Income per Head of Population (Lugbara) . . 567
39. Number of Vendors by Commodity (Northern Rhodesia) 588
40. Commodity by Price and method of Calculation (Northern Rhodesia) 590
41. Age of Market Vendors (Northern Rhodesia) . . 592
42. Educational Attainments of Market Vendors (Northern Rhodesia) 594
44. Duration of Vending Experience (Northern Rhodesia) 594
44. Duration of Vending Experience (Northern (Rhodesia) 594
45. Distance from Market Occupation (Vendors) in Miles (Northern Rhodesia) 596
46. Human and Animal Population of Sehitwa (Herero) . 628
47. Prices paid for Herero Cattle in 1953 628
48. Labor recruits from Herero as compared to other tribes 629
49. Herero Bridewealth and Premarital Status of Bride . 632
50. Value of Bridewealth and Premarital Status of Bride . 634
51. Inclusion of Sheep in Bridewealth 634
52. Equivalent Value of Bridewealth and Husband's Marital Order (Herero) 635
53. Bridewealth, Husband's Marital Order and Premarital Status of Bride (Herero) 636
54. Animals and Money in Bridewealth 636
55. Sheep and other Animals in Full Bridewealth (Herero) 637
56. Weekly Quantities of Foodstuffs in Katwe Market (Kampala) 644
57. Immigration into Bugerere 645
58. Reported Average Sales of Plantains for 22 Growers (Kampala) 649
59. Number of Lorry Loads Delivered in Katwe Market (Kampala) 651
60. Distribution of Market Sellers in Katwe Market (Kampala) by Commodities Sold 656
61. Percentages of Plantains delivered in Katwe by Sources (Kampala) 657
62. Quantities and Values of Three Principal Foodstuffs sold in Katwe Market (Kampala) 657
63. Average Retail Price of Three Types of Foodstuff (Kampala) 660
64. Range of Retail Prices on Different Days . . . 660
65. Range of Retail Prices in Five Markets (Kampala) . 661
66. Prices in cents per pound of Plantains and Sweet Potatoes (Kampala) 661

67. Cost and Profit of Plantains (Kampala) . . . 662
68. "Mark ups" (Kampala) 663
69. Percentage of Price of Plantains Received by Grower, Transporter, Wholesaler and Retailer 664
70. Number of Persons Entering Koforidua Market on Non-Marketing Days 674
71. Number of Persons Entering Koforidua Market on a Market Day 674
72. Use of Paths Approaching Koforidua Market . . 680
73. Number of Loads per Item per Road (Koforidua) . . 681
74. Number of Loads per Path per Hour (Koforidua) . . 682
75. Estimated Annual Purchases in Koforidua Area . . 686
76. Estimated Monthly Payrolls (Koforidua) . . . 686
77. Proportion of Crop Disposed of by Sale . . . 688
78. Types of Firms from which Commodities were Obtained (Koforidua) 689
79. Towns Supplying Produce to Koforidua Market . . 691
80. Monetary Value of Goods Sold per Day per Seller (Koforidua) 693
81. Estimated Tribal Size and per cent of Surveyed Rhodesian Copperbelt Vendors belonging to each Tribe . . 712
82. Experience of Market Vendors (Copperbelt) . . . 716
83. Middlemen Involved in the Marketing of Selected Commodities Sold in the Copperbelt, 1959 723
84. Fishermen and Buyers, Lake Mweru, 1958 . . . 725
85. Sales Price of Fish (Copperbelt) 725
86. Principal Commodities Appearing in Copperbelt Markets, 1959 733–34–35–36
87. Proportion of Major Imports to Congo Copperbelt from Principal Zones of Supply 737
88. The Principal Zones Supplying the Major Imports to the Northern Rhodesian Copperbelt, 1959 . . . 738
89. The Number of Sellers and Assistants Surveyed by Major Commodity Groups, Selected Rhodesian Copperbelt Markets, 1959 738

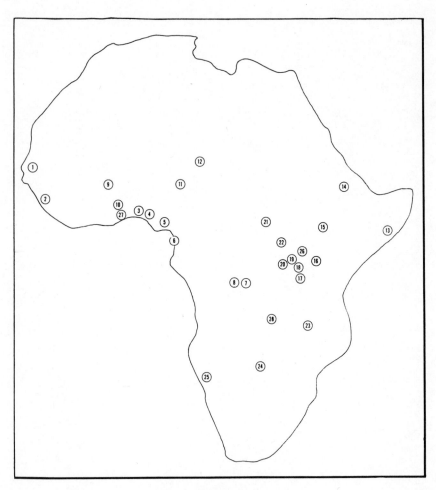

FIGURE 1

Location of Tribes and Areas
Represented in this Study

INTRODUCTION[1]

by Paul Bohannan and George Dalton

Because the papers in this volume contain much more information and many more viewpoints than could ever be dealt with in an Introduction, we are making this one brief. It contains three sections: one which examines the economic aspects of African markets, one which underscores the impression of many of our contributors that markets in Africa have many purposes beyond the economic, and finally one that deals with current changes in Africa as they affect markets.

THE MARKET IN AFRICAN SOCIETY

To study markets in Africa it is necessary that the distinction between the institution of the market place and the principle of market exchange be pointed up clearly. The market place is a specific site where a group of buyers and a group of sellers meet. The market principle[2] is the determination of prices by the forces of supply and demand regardless of the site of transactions. It is important to understand that the market principle can and often does operate outside the market place, as when a business firm hires labor, land is sold in the real estate market, or grain is sold on the "world market." When most of our contributors use the term "markets", they mean market places and not the diffuse interaction of suppliers and demanders whose activities determine prices. The two, of course, overlap in many instances, but not by any means in all.

We have classified the societies represented here on the basis of the role that the market place and the market principle play in each. A threefold arrangement has proved convenient. There are, first of all, societies that have no market places. The market principle, if it is

(1) All of the contributors save two had an opportunity to read an early draft of this introduction and make comments and criticisms. Over half availed themselves of the opportunity, and we have incorporated many of their suggestions. We want to thank them all, but must single out the assistance that has been given by Dr. Mary Douglas, who has influenced our thinking extensively in several matters.

(2) We have avoided saying "market mechanism" because "mechanism" is a word that anthropologists use for some types of institutional process. The term "price mechanism" does not encounter the same objection—that is, it is in accordance with the anthropological usage—and points up that in an economy dominated by the market principle, market prices serve to allocate resources, incomes and outputs. The market principle means price formation by impersonal forces of supply and demand; it does not imply any specific market situation such as pure competition or oligopoly.

present in such societies, is present in a few casual, interpersonal transactions. Traditionally, such "marketless" societies have been the concern solely of anthropologists, and it is the analytical categories of Malinowski, Thurnwald, Mead, Herskovits, Firth and Polanyi (only the latter not an anthropologist) that explain their organization and functioning.

There are, in the second place, societies in which market places exist and the market principle operates, but only peripherally; that is to say, the subsistence requirements of the members of the society are not acquired, to any appreciable extent, in the market place or through operation of the market principle. As in marketless societies, the test is a simple one: land and labor are not transacted by the market principle, and if the market—in either sense—were to disappear from such a society, inconvenience would result but no major hardship would necessarily follow because the basic necessities of life are acquired otherwise than by transactions in the market. Neither sellers nor producers depend on market sale for basic livelihood.

Finally, there are those societies (or social situations such as modern cities) in which market places may be (and usually are) present, but in which the primary source of subsistence goods for buyers and of income for sellers and producers is the market in the sense of transactional principle. In such a society, livelihood is acquired by first selling something, which means that not only products but the factors of production as well (particularly land and labor) come to be subject to the operation of the market principle. It is in such societies that the price mechanism functions as an integrative device to allocate resources, incomes and outputs.

In Africa, two different situations each characterize this market-dominated society. There is, on the one hand, dependence on the sale of a cash crop which makes the market of extreme importance to the producers of that crop; with the cash income they receive, they buy on the market not only the imported and luxury goods that they have come to demand, but also all or the major portion of their daily subsistence requirements. There is, on the other hand, a situation that we have come to associate with modern industrial societies, in which most people sell their labor "to the market" and buy their subsistence on the market. Both types of market dependence may occur together, as is indeed the case in the United States and in some African economies. In others, only cash crop or wage labor may appear.

The three typical situations can be summarized thus: (1) Societies which lack market places, and in which the market principle, if it appears, is but weakly represented; (2) Societies with peripheral markets—that is, the institution of the market place is present, but the market principle does not determine acquisition of subsistence or the allocation of land and labor resources; (3) Societies dominated by the market principle and the price mechanism.

The main questions that we are asking in the subsequent discussion are: do transactions in market places or by the market principle provide sellers and producers with the bulk of their material livelihood, or do they not? And what is the role of the market in each case?

Societies without Market Places.

Societies without market places are marked by a multicentric economy—a characteristic they share with societies having peripheral markets. A multicentric economy is one in which there are several distinct transactional spheres. Each sphere is distinguished by different material items and services, and may be distinguished by different principles of exchange, and different moral values.[3] As an example, the conventional classification of material items into subsistence goods and prestige goods usually indicates separate spheres (Veblen 1915; DuBois 1936; Herskovits 1938; Bohannan 1955, 1959). The Trobriands case, although the limiting one, is also the most widely known. One transactional sphere—the *kula*—contains only treasure items (arm bands and necklaces) and the principle on which they are exchanged is the principle of reciprocity: socially obligatory gift exchange. Another sphere of exchange, *gimwali,* contains some subsistence items—food, utensils, etc.—and the principle of exchange is the market principle. However, the bulk of subsistence in the Trobriands is not acquired through the market principle, but rather through gift-giving reciprocity based on kinship obligations—that is to say, *gimwali* is peripheral.

There is a further mode of transaction to be found in some marketless societies—the mode that Polanyi (1957) has called redistribution, entailing socially obligatory payments (tribute, *corvée,* tithe, tax, first fruits) of goods and services to an allocative center. The center— usually a king, chief or priest—distributes material items, feasts or military defense to the community at large, or else makes allotments to groups or individuals in accordance with their status. It may be,

---

(3) Our use of the word "moral" has been questioned by several of the contributors. We tried to change it and found ourselves capable of no shorter a phrase than "value judgment." We turned to the Shorter Oxford English Dictionary and found a long and complex entry under "moral," but believe that our meaning is found in the first definition: "Of or pertaining to the distinction between right and wrong, or good and evil, in relation to actions, volition or character; ethical." The French word does not distinguish *moral* from *morale,* and we include the latter meaning as well—something moral is something that is considered good both on grounds of social acceptance and participation and on grounds of ethics.

of course, that within a single society, one economic sphere utilizes the market principle, another the reciprocative principle and still another the principle of redistribution. It is common for several spheres to be present simultaneously in a single society, as indeed is so clearly the case in the Trobriands.

Firth (1958) has postulated that in many primitive economies, goods and services form separate spheres, and Thurnwald (1932) recognized the situation but said little about it. Malinowski (1922), who so clearly described separate transactional spheres, did not recognize that there are certain institutionalized means by which items are disengaged (Steiner 1954) from the *kula* cycle. That is to say, a man must give his sister's son a treasure at certain times in his life, treasures change hands on a non-*kula* basis at the time of marriage, and are indeed used for fines in some situations. There are even situations in which the *kula* valuables can be bought. In other words, even in the classic multicentric economy, with its separate spheres, there are prescribed means of transacting goods between the spheres. We have called such transactions "conversion," and they will be discussed below.

The movement of material goods in reciprocative and redistributive transactions cannot be understood outside the context of the social situations of which they form an integral part. The yams that change hands in the Trobriand Islands are material and therefore "economic" items. But one cannot understand why they change hands in recurrent patterns without considering the structure of kinship and political obligations. The market principle is set just as firmly into its social structure. The difference is that it may be institutionally distinguished by the society concerned from the kinship and political structures; hence—as the economist does— it can be analyzed as a self-contained unit, separate from the rest of the "social" situation.

In short, the social integument structures the material flows and accounts for the moral attributes, whether strong or weak, of any transaction including market transactions. To a Western observer, the moral attitudes toward redistributive and reciprocal movements seem to be stronger than those toward market transactions precisely because nonmarket moral attitudes are brought to bear on exchanges which, in our society, would be subject only to market, or economic, morality.

These moral—indeed, emotional—aspects of material goods transactions deserve emphasis for two additional reasons. We attach exaggerated importance to material subsistence goods and basic services despite the abundant evidence that transactions of prestige items in *marketless* economies are often regarded as vital, focal activities. We have long known that potlatch coppers and *kula* arm bracelets are treasure items largely divorced from daily livelihood. Nevertheless their transaction is an absorbing concern of primary social importance. It is not only the things involved which cause excitement, but also the preparation and organization for their exchange. The transactional process through which the things change hands is itself an activity of prime importance. Significantly, its importance is not derived from the quest for material gain. The potlatch and *kula*, both in items transacted and processes for transacting them, are special cases of spheres of economy whose counterparts are found widely (if less dramatically) in nonindustrial society. The Iraqw depend upon agriculture for subsistence livelihood, but their emotional concern is with cattle. Among the Sonjo the elders are concerned with the rank system in terms of which irrigation rights and disputes arising over their use are decided, in the same way that Trobrianders are concerned with *kula*: both are regarded as enormously interesting foci of activity—worthwhile pursuits for honorable men. In a word, transactions of goods necessary for biological survival need not on that account be regarded *socially* as important as are prestige item transactions.

Conversions.

Multicentric economies are, as we have seen, organized into independent spheres each transacting different material or intangible items; moreover, each sphere may (but may not) be characterized by a different transactional principle.[4] The importance of separate spheres of economy, their relation to social organization, and their permeation by moral values are all illustrated by the inter-sphere transactions we have called "conversions." To distinguish conversions from ordinary transactions *within* any sphere, we can call the latter "conveyances."

It seems to be universal in multicentric economies that the various spheres are hierarchically ranked on the basis of moral considerations. It further appears that in all such societies, especially those in which the market principle is not dominant, there are institutionalized situations in which the spheres are overridden, situations in which items are "converted" from one sphere to another. Conversions, rather than being skillful or unskillful, are regarded as morally good or bad. The concept of conversion—like that of price mechanism

(4) In the Trobriands, for example, fish-yam exchanges between inland and costal groups, *kula* transactions and obligatory gifts of foodstuffs to sisters, are all transacted by the same principle—that of reciprocity.

—may or may not be overtly recognized by the society that practices it, but because of the moral aspect of the hierarchy in which spheres are ranked, conversion always excites moral judgments.

In addition, for purposes of analysis, conversion can be divided into two sorts. There may be institutionalized conversion, such as that found among the Trobriands, the Tiv, or (within this book) the Sonjo or the Lele, in which he who manages to obtain more highly ranked items for lower is regarded as successful. On the other hand, there may be emergency conversion, a practice which seems to be widespread. The emergency may be war, drought, epidemic or epizootic. In order to survive, additional food must be obtained, and so highly ranked items must be sold off. In such situations, treasures are sold, slaves are given for food, children are pawned and voluntary debt bondage may be incurred.

Probably the main distinction between these two situations is that in institutionalized conversion, the man who converts "up" initiates the transaction. In emergency conversion, it is likely to be the man who converts "down" who initiates the proceedings, but it may be either. However, there is a further distinction: institutionalized conversion can be carried out by any of the three transactional principles (market, reciprocity or redistribution) because it is internally structured and sanctioned, both exchange partners usually coming from the same ethnic group. Indeed, institutionalized conversion is a socially approved form of wealth-getting. But in emergency conversion the exchanges are usually external to the group and always carried on by the market principle. The reasons why emergency conversion takes the form of an external, market transaction seem to be the following: emergency conversion is always a last resort, a desperate expedient used only when sufficient aid can be obtained in no other way. Therefore it is done externally with different ethnic groups—outsiders who have no social obligation to help the disaster-stricken group.[5] It is done between strangers, and hence without moral reaction.

Another characteristic of a multicentric economy with accompanying conversion should be noted. General purpose money—a money which, within a single sphere, carries out all the money uses—necessarily breaks down the spheres and creates a single sphere for "everything that can be bought with money;" everything—including labor and land—becomes a commodity. Hence, if there is any item which carries out any of the functions of money (and there may not be), the money item must vary from one sphere to another, or else it must

(5) Typically, a group suffering an emergency food shortage will first try to obtain outside supplies as gifts from distant kin or friends.

have a different money use in the two spheres. A single item used for the same money purpose in two spheres is either institutionalized so as to create a means of conversion or else it destroys the separation between the spheres. In Africa, this process has occurred by the expansion of the market into spheres formerly characterized by other transactional principles. The use of money earned in the market place or through the market principle for bridewealth or cult membership has sullied the brides and the cults with market morality.

Peripheral Markets.

Societies with peripheral markets differ from societies without markets in that the market place is present, but not necessarily in the sense that the market principle is more widespread. There is certainly no necessary difference in the multicentric aspects of the economy. That is to say, the market principle may be limited to the goods that appear within the market place. In such a situation all market sales are conveyances. Conversions still occur, but must take place outside the market place.,

Some distinguishing characteristics, both of the economies in which peripheral markets occur and of the market places themselves, appear to be the following: (1) from the viewpoint of the entire economy, market sales are not the dominant source of material livelihood. Either most people are not engaged in producing for the market or selling in the market, or those who are so engaged are only part-time marketers. Their livelihood comes largely from nonmarket spheres of economy. A common indicator of a peripheral market is the minute quantities transacted—it is on a pin money level. (2) Participants in peripheral markets are sometimes "target" marketers. This concept, first expressed with regard to "target labor," applies equally well to other ways of obtaining cash income in situations in which basic subsistence is acquired in nonmarket spheres. These "target marketers" engage in marketing sporadically to acquire a specific amount of cash income for a specific expenditure, such as a bicycle or tax payment, as is indicated in Colson's article on the Tonga. Typically, buyers in peripheral markets buy only a small proportion of their daily used material items; they too acquire the bulk of subsistence goods in other ways. However, it is common in peripheral markets for buyers to regard the market place as economically important because it is the only place to obtain some special item or import. There may also be present in peripheral markets foreign traders for whom the market is not peripheral, however much it may be so for the local attendants.

Two aspects of peripheral markets, of special interest to economists, concern the process of price formation and the role of market-made prices in the overall economy. With regard to price formation, supply and demand forces are operative, but are affected by a variety of social factors which impinge on price-making: kinship, clanship, religion or other status indicators of buyers, traditional norms of just price, eagerness of market women *not* to sell out quickly because the market place is a source of entertainment and social intercourse. In such markets one finds seasonal fluctuations in price, and predictable price changes, but within ranges not wholly determined by cost and demand; local institutional peculiarities impinge on price formation in varying degree. Moreover, sellers of home-produced items in peripheral markets frequently are unable to calculate money costs of production because they have bought no factor ingredients.

A unique aspect of economies in which peripheral markets appear is that prices made in the market place do not perform the function of allocating factor resources among alternative outputs. Here, we come to the essential difference between markets in so-called primitive economies and in Western economy: the peripheral market place is not integrated with production decisions. Although those products which enter the market are indeed apportioned by prices determined by supply and demand, there is absent that feedback effect on resource allocation which makes the interdependent formation of market prices—the market system—so crucially important in Western economy, and the price mechanism a central concern of formal economic theory. In this respect, prices in peripheral markets are like prices in antique auctions in our own economy. In both cases the prices do not affect future production of the things priced, although supply and demand forces determine the price in each market place. In a word, prices made in peripheral markets do not perform the economy-wide integrative function of the price mechanism in Western economy.

Where the market principle is dominant rather than peripheral, market prices integrate sectors of economy because all incomes are derived from the market price of output and all production decisions are guided by market cost of resource ingredients and the sales price of products. It is this fact that makes us emphasize as crucial the non-integrative role of market prices in peripheral markets as compared to Western markets. In economies containing peripheral markets livelihood does not depend upon market sale, and market place prices do not redeploy factors of production to those lines of output the market indicates as most profitable. If such peripheral markets were to disappear, the economy would not be seriously disrupted. Richard Kluckhohn has noted that, were Konso to forego markets, there would be a period of discomfort but no disaster. As consumption goods buyers, many of the peoples would seriously miss the goods that are now imported and distributed through markets, but even in those cases it is often the goods and not the institution of the market as the provider of livelihood that has become a near necessity. They would miss the market as a source of supply of consumption goods but scarcely as a place of sale, because the market is not the place where they get their primary income.

Market Economies and Market Societies.

Of the market situations discussed in this book, only three can be in any wise called "market societies," and all of them are located at points of great Western influence. Such societies are characterized by the dominance of the market principle and the price mechanism integrating all sectors of economy, and usually by the presence of a market-place complex. Moreover, the market principle—which is, seen from one point of view, the economic aspect of the social principle of contract—vastly supersedes in importance the actual, physical market place. The market principle, in becoming the integrative transactional principle, has come to determine not merely the economy, but a wider range of activity in the society (Polanyi 1944; 1947).

In an economy in which market exchange is the dominant principle, the "market place" takes on varied physical as well as organizational form: a place where outputs are sold, such as a bazaar, a retail store or a cluster of retail stores; a place where factor ingredients of production are sold or hired, such as a "labor market;" the "money market" in which loans are contracted; the "capital market" where titles to property are bought and sold, as well as finance for new ventures transacted. What these diverse markets have in common is decidedly *not* similarity in the institutional place of sale involved—the market place—but rather that the goods, services, and resources are bought and sold within a market-dominated economy: (a) sale at a money price is determined by impersonal supply and demand forces; (b) the buyers and sellers are dependent upon such market exchange for livelihood; (c) the market prices for finished goods crucially influence production decisions and therefore the allocation of resources, including labor, into different lines of production.

What we have called "peripheral" markets in Africa, function differently and are much less important in the total economy.[6] They

(6) A point of some interest, discussed below, is that the peripheral market place is often of great *social* significance as a place of entertainment, of political meeting, of juridical hearings and settlement of disputes. As such, it frequently takes on the aspect of a fair rather than of a commercial establishment.

refer to the institution of the market-place site where buyers and sellers meet to exchange a narrow range of products. In peripheral markets neither the market sellers nor producers from whom they may buy derive their livelihood from market sale. Moreover, changes in market prices do not redeploy factor resources in response to market profitability. When an anthropologist says that some African market operates like a Western market, he usually means simply that there are seasonal price fluctuations caused by changes in supply and demand; he does not mean that an interrelated set of market prices are formed which guide production decisions, or that the populace derives its livelihood through selling something to the market.

A related point also requires careful distinction between the market place as a physical site and market exchange as a transactional principle. As with our own economy, when the market principle comes to dominate an African economy, the traditional market place need not be the locus of the expanded market activity (United Nations 1954). For example, Hodder points out that the two most important cash crops of the Yoruba, cocoa and palm kernels, bypass the market place, which remains a pin money affair for women. Rotberg has found that in Central Africa it is cooperatives and not local market places that have expanded as more goods are transacted by the market principle. In sum, the dominance of the market principle is indicated by dependence for livelihood on sale for money at prices determined by diffuse suppliers and demanders, whether the commodity sold is labor, cattle, or agricultural produce, regardless of the physical site of the sale.

Money and Money Uses.

A similar point must be made about money and money uses in each of the market situations we have discerned—marketless economies, peripheral markets and market-dominated economies. In considering the role of money in non-Western economies there are two pitfalls to be avoided: the assumption that the most useful distinction is that between transactions with and those without money, and the assumption that money plays the same role in all economies as it does in our own.

The familiar dichotomy of barter versus money transactions does not reveal the *principle* involved in goods changing hands. The point is that both money itself as well as types of moneyless transactions take a variety of forms depending on the transactional principle involved. Some examples will illustrate the point. In the Trobriands both *kula* and *gimwali* are barter, i.e., carried out without the use of money. But the goods which enter each sphere of exchange, the transactional principle, and the moral reactions—all are radically different. *Kula* prestige items enter the sphere of reciprocal gift-exchange; they are not random transactions at bargained rates but carefully structured through gift-partners who exchange at traditional rates (all aspects of the transactions carried out within a code of etiquette). *Gimwali,* also moneyless, entails subsistence goods transacted in accordance with the market principle: random buyers and sellers haggle over price in the pursuit of material gain and utility. To call both *kula* and *gimwali* "barter" is correct but not analytically informative; to state that money is used in neither is not so important as to point out that each represents a different transactional sphere— that items transacted in one cannot normally be transacted in the other, that the terms of exchange are determined by a different principle, and that the social and the economic importance of each is entirely different.

The second obstacle to understanding the role of money in primitive economy is to assume that the distinguishing characteristic of money in all economies is the same as in market-dominated Western economy: its role as a means of exchange. In modern Western economy, the use of money as a means of exchange with which to acquire labor, raw materials, and finished products of all kinds is undoubtedly its most important use, but not its only use. Even in modern economy money has subordinate uses, such as means of payment (fines and taxes) and as a standard of value for transactions in which no "money" changes hands. Besides the fact that means of exchange is the most important money use in Western economy, there is a second distinguishing characteristic: just one all-purpose money is used to carry out all money functions. It should be emhpasized that these two prime characteristics of Western money are functionally related: because market exchange at money price is the dominant transactional principle, one kind of money must be used to make all material items, labor, and services available on the market. All-purpose money is a prerequisite for an economy in which market-exchange dominates: it makes labor, material resources and products commensurable commodities; it allows all items to be purchased and sold, and their market values to be compared. Because all material items enter market exchange, all must be purchasable with the same money. In sum, it is the dominance of the market exchange principle in Western economy which necessitates that one all-purpose money be used. Conversely, the use of all-purpose money can lead to the spread of the market principle to other spheres in which money enters, even when market exchange is initially restricted to just one sphere.

In those economies in which the market principle is either absent or peripheral, a single all-purpose money is necessarily absent. The absence of all-purpose money is an indicator of a multicentric economy in which the market principle is not dominant; i.e., labor, resources, goods and services change hands in accordance with different principles, the most important of them nonmarket principles. In such economies one may find one or more moneys in use, performing those money functions of payment and standard which are subordinate in our own economy. In Somaliland, for example, camels are the standard of value for calculating bloodwealth, but payment may be made (and usually is made) in another form. In Ethiopia, large livestock are valued in terms of Maria Theresa thalers but paid for in Ethiopian dollars, or goods valued in the latter.

When it is once seen that money uses in primitive economy are functionally related to transactional principles, several analytical points become clear: (1) In a marketless economy, one or more moneys may exist as special purpose money, each entering into a limited range of transactions. Frequently, such special purpose moneys are confined to prestige and ceremonial transactions—for example, bloodwealth and bridewealth. (2) Where the market principle is peripheral, market place exchange may be done without money, or by one or more types of special purpose money. Here, one must differentiate between peripheral markets as they functioned before and after European contact. Before contact, it was rare for money used as a means of exchange to have purchasing power outside the market place. For example, the purchase of land and labor were transacted in different spheres of economy—not by the market principle—and rights in people were transacted in still others. The introduction of European money into market-place transactions has had important repercussions on nonmarket spheres of indigenous economy which will be discussed below. (3) Where the market principle is the dominant and integrating mechanism of economy, all-purpose money of the Western type is in use. A unicentric economy exists in which the market activities of participants as well as the process of price formation are of those varieties familiar to Westerners.

Trade, Market and Surplus.

So far we have discussed only markets. It is necessary to enlarge our scope to include "trade" because there are some useful distinctions to be made between marketing and trading, and between marketers and traders.

One difficulty in analyzing trade is that the word is commonly used to mean several different types of activities: (1) any commercial transaction regardless of its site, the kinds of goods transacted, their destination or their personnel. (2) Those activities done only by professional specialists which provide them with their livelihood. (3) Any external transaction (foreign trade).

The first two uses of the word trade should be separated to signify two kinds of action. There is, on the one hand, selling one's own produce and buying one's needs, which we shall call "marketing." On the other hand, there is buying in order to resell. The French term *commercer* expresses precisely this latter meaning—that of professional trading.[7] Most anthropologists express the same idea by the term "middleman." To market and to "commercize" are not the same thing, and in Africa they are sometimes institutionally separated. Selling a portion of produce can be an integral part of subsistence farming. Buying for resale, however, is not. It is an additional activity.

External trade has special aspects which distinguish it from internal transactions of both the marketing and the professional trading varieties. Especially is this so for pre-contact Africa, in which much external trade was an activity of state—"administered trade," to use Polanyi's term—primarily in prestige or treasure items of elite circulation (Arnold 1957); or it was reciprocal gift trade of the types made familiar by the *kula* and the fish-yam exchanges of the Trobriands. In neither case was the market principle the mode of transacting nor, typically, was the market place the site of such transactions.

In post-contact Africa, the enlargement of the market economy has affected external trade as well as internal varieties. The separation between external trading and local marketing tends to disappear as enlarged imports and production for export entail transactions by the market principle. However, as noted below, it is still frequently the case that production for export bypasses the local market place.

With regard to the reasons for exchange, the view frequently expressed that marketing, buying for resale, or external trade arise from "surpluses" is much too simple and facile. Several of the essays in this book provide evidence for different views: external trade occurs among groups of people at all levels of material life, including those who by no stretch of terminology can be regarded as having a surplus of anything, including the items they trade. Too often the term surplus is used to mean simply that which is sold, or exchanged on the simplistic assumption that if something were needed it would not be sold or exchanged.

A special kind of external trade was induced by the exact opposite of surplus, namely an emergency shortage in which prestige items

(7) Marx (1867: Part II, Chapter 4) makes a similar distinction between marketing (C-M-C) and trading (M-C-M) but for different purposes.

(including slaves, children, and women) were traded off for subsistence goods. We have called such transactions emergency conversion because it is usually famine or war that induce such uncon-
ventional trade. Examples in this book are found among the Iraqw,
Guro, Kipsigis, and Lugbara and in the Copperbelt.

The essays also describe several instances in which neither external
trade nor local marketing arose, despite the potential material advantages attainable by so doing. On speaking of the Iraqw of Tanganyika,
Winter says:

> In aboriginal times, as well as today, the various ethnic groups in-
> habiting the region have exhibited great diversity in the fundamental
> nature of their economic modes of adaptation . . . it would seem that basic
> factors were present which would have led to the development of a large
> volume of trade and to the establishment of markets. Although a certain
> amount of external trade did take place, a large-scale system of intertribal
> exchange did not develop and markets failed to appear. Despite the
> differences between the various tribal economies, they did not become
> specialized parts of a larger interdependent regional economy . . . Most
> of the trade which did take place in the past occurred not because people
> were attempting to take advantage of their particular positions in relation
> to the factors of production as in a market-oriented economy, but because
> people were short of food as the result of crop failure.

The reasons that materially advantageous trade failed to arise
among complementary producers are illuminating. Despite the relative abundance of cattle and the scarcity of vegetable foods, the Masai
did not seek to trade off cattle for food. Such was unthinkable because
cattle were the essence of wealth—indeed, from the Masai point of
view, there could be no such thing as a "surplus" of cattle. Moreover,
when the Masai raided their neighbors, it was for more cattle, not for
vegetables. Similarly, Dupire tells us that the commercially minded
Hausa regard the Fulani as foolish for not taking advantage of seasonal
fluctuations in cattle prices and timing their sales to obtain the best
price for cattle. But the Fulani do not regard cattle as a regular cash
crop, so to speak, with which to acquire other goods. Other considerations override market price. The point of these examples is to
show that material gain is sometimes not considered as important as
other social ends, and therefore "surpluses" (meaning relative abund-
ances of one item) are often not exchanged, even when it would seem
to be materially advantageous to do so. In neither instance is potential
material return the reason for valuing cattle in the first place. A
related case of commercial transaction precluded by overriding social
values is provided by the Iraqw, who would not buy grain in an
impersonal market (despite the material advantage of so doing) be-

cause they would not use any item without being assured of the ritual purity of its producer.

Finally, there can be trade without material gain. Meillassoux points out that:

Toward affines or kinsmen ... Guro trading behavior was greatly affected by social considerations, as it was by the nature of the exchanged goods (guns, powder, woven cloth, cattle, *sombe*—used as matrimonial compensation) which involved prestige and not subsistence. Frequently, according to informants from this area, the terms of trade with the Baule were exactly repeated with the next Guro tribe, leaving absolutely no profit for the intermediary. All in all, trade was not what we would call in modern terms a "profitable business." It was, rather, that goods moved between people of pre-eminent status, on customary terms, until they reached the upper part of the country, whereupon they were traded at terms of exchange which profited the upper Guro.

The various characteristics that we have noted about market places and the market principle in the three typical situations can be summed up in tabular form. Undoubtedly, many other differences could be found, and other types may be isolated. But for the present, the ones we find most useful are summed up in Table 1.

NON-ECONOMIC ASPECTS OF MARKET PLACES

Market places provide regular meetings of fairly large numbers of people. The attendants at markets usually represent cross sections of the population, although there are exceptions—men attend markets only seldom and as buyers in South Dahomey, women never attend some cattle markets, and in several places markets are considered to be unwholesome places for children. Therefore it is to be expected (and it is certainly borne out by evidence) that the market place is utilized for purposes far beyond those for which nominally it was established. Market places can be utilized for almost every conceivable purpose that requires a large number of people brought together in a controlled situation. An exhaustive search through the essays of this book could lead to a very long list. Here we will limit ourselves to the statement of the principle that market places are (in sociological terminology) multi-functional institutions, and to a review of three or four social aspects most commonly found in the essays in this volume.

Probably the most common—because it is the most basic—non-economic function of market places is their roles as nodes in the network of communication. Undoubtedly one of the most important points for the dissemination of information is the market place, and that dissemination can take place either in an informal, more or less unrecognized manner or on a formal basis. Chiefs, priests, administrative officers and many others make announcements in the market. In most areas, to make an announcement requires the permission of the market authorities, and it may even require that the announcement be made by one of them to signify his approval.

Of even greater importance, perhaps, is that market places provide a place to meet one's friends and kinsmen, and exchange news and gossip. Women in particular (most of Africa is virilocal even when it is matrilineal) meet their kinsmen at markets and keep in remarkably

TABLE 1

Characteristics of the Market in Three Types of Economy

	Marketless Economies	Economies with Peripheral Markets	Economies in which the Market Principle is Dominant
Major Source of Subsistence Livelihood	Self-production and use; reciprocity; redistribution	Self-production and use; reciprocity; redistribution	Production for sale; factor resources for sale; marketing and trading as occupations
Price Formation for Goods and Services Changing Hands	Equivalency ratios; gift exchange	Supply and demand forces qualified by idiosyncratic social influences and controls; absence of factor markets	Supply and demand forces; market principle transacts factor ingredients as well as outputs
Market Price as Integrating Mechanism for Allocation of Resources, Incomes; Outputs	Absent	Absent	Present
Money and Money Uses	Standard Payment { special purpose moneys; moneyless transactions	Standard Payment { special purpose moneys; moneyless transactions	Exchange Standard Payment { one all-purpose money
External Trade	Gift trade; Administered trade	Market place exchange; Gift trade; Administered trade	Market trade

close touch with their natal villages by this means. Although it would be difficult to do, a study of markets (and perhaps other institutions) in their role of communications nodes would be extremely interesting.

The people at market provide not only listeners and gossip-mongers, but also provide an already gathered audience. It is not surprising that several of our contributors mention that performances of dancers or of entertainers take place in the market places. The festival aspect of markets is first pointed up by its frequent use as the place to drink beer. The market day—especially in West Africa—falls off into a beer drink.

Like any large collection of people, the gathering in a market place can be, and often is, used for recruitment of sexual partners. Many of our contributors speak of the market place as the place par excellence to form liaisons.

In a more organized fashion, the market places can be of political relevance. The reasons, obviously, are twofold: it can be politically advantageous to control the market place itself, and hence to some degree the people in it. On the other hand, it can be politically advantageous to control, in whatever degree, the produce which goes through the market place. We thus find throughout our essays (as in thirteenth century England) that control of market places is in the hands of the political authorities. In those parts of East and Central Africa where markets were introduced by the colonial administration, it has continued to control them: the size and shape of the market place, the type and arrangement of buildings, the conditions for selling and the composition of the sales force and the selection of goods—all are to a greater or lesser degree dictated by that administration. On the other hand, in West Africa, or anywhere else that the markets antedated European control, the market places still tend to be in the hands of indigenous authorities, either those recognized by the administration or, in a few cases, those not so recognized. Control of a market put a man at the hub of communications, where he could have immediate contact with people. It also gave him a recognized and approved *raison d'être* behind which he could hide any political chicanery which it was to his advantage to hide.

In return, the political authorities—indigenous and European—which control markets provide a "market peace," to use the old English term. This means that the markets were policed and that the safety of traders and customers was more or less assured. It may be that even the market place, or a portion of it, is used as a point of political asylum.

Obviously, it is also necessary, if the economic functions of a market are to be performed, for the market peace to be observed—this point has been made many times with reference to old European market places (Lipson 1931). Successful trade demands a minimal degree of political stability. The man who is responsible for the market peace thus must have a police force of some description at his disposal, and he must control sufficient power to maintain the peace. To police their markets, West African market officials can either call on their families, members of their clans or other social groups, or on the police force of the colonial administration. For those markets controlled by colonial administrations, a police force is at hand.

An extremely important political consideration is the fact that the market is often used as the center of juridical activities. In some areas the chiefs or other judges actually establish themselves as courts in or near the market place; in others their presence assures that when one finds one's adversary (easier at a market than any other place), the case can be laid before the officials informally. No African chief can refuse to hear a case brought to his attention at market (though he may postpone it until a regular court hearing). These courts may be the same as—but are often different from—the arbitrating facilities for settling disputes which arise among sellers and customers within the market place itself.

Markets are also often accompanied by religious activities, some of which may be connected with the market peace. The peace of the Ibo markets described by the Ottenbergs is kept primarily in the name of, and with the sanction of, certain shrines and the forces that they symbolize. Some African market places—particularly in those areas in which the market is indigenous—are founded with a religious ceremonial. Skinner's description of the religious aspects of the initiation of Mossi markets is perhaps the most elaborate description in this book. European markets of the Middle Ages were similarly associated with the Church and were often held in the shadows of cathedrals.

In summary, market places—particularly in areas in which the market is economically peripheral—fulfill many social and cultural needs of the population. Indeed, some markets are not regarded as primarily "economic" institutions by the people. They provide a meeting place where at least a certain minimum of security is assured and hence they can be used for political, religious, social and personal purposes. In a land in which collections of people on non-kinship bases or non-age-set bases may prove difficult, the market provides the skeleton for a very wide range of social usages.

A few words should also be said about the way in which markets fit together—in some parts of West Africa they form "rings," in other parts they do not. A market "ring" is a series of markets meeting on successive days. Among the Ibo there are four-day cycles; among Yoruba, Dahomey and Guro there are five-day cycles. In other areas there are seven-day cycles. In parts of East Africa, where the ring phenomenon is less highly developed (Le Vine describes it for the Gusii, but does not find it of great importance) the "ring" is little more than the series of markets attended by a group of traders. In areas of West Africa where the phenomenon is important, each market in the ring may develop an economic or even a noneconomic speciality, and the ring may be of very great local importance for the flow of goods, the settlement of disputes, or some other social activity.

Noneconomic activities may also be influenced by market rings, if for no other reason than that the movements of a large number of people follow along (and hence create) the rings, and that social activities follow (and are created by) people and their movements.

WESTERN IMPACT ON AFRICAN ECONOMY

The Nature of "Transition".

Europe has long been a factor in African economy. Cowrie shells and gunpowder, gold and slaves have gone in or out of Africa for thousands of years. But the nature of the role of Europe in Africa has undergone several climactic changes. In the middle decades of the fifteenth century, contact between Europe and sub-Saharan Africa became direct; trading ventures were established along the coasts, and in a few places there was an initial penetration of European ideas and indeed of Europeans themselves. Another drastic change occurred in the late nineteenth century, when European countries took over political control of most African areas. Again in the mid-twentieth century, with the emergence of independent African national states, the institutional features of the impact of Western economy on African economy have undergone pervasive change.

Probably the greatest change at present is the expansion of those economic activities organized on the market principle and the attenuation of the others. There are, so far as we know, three principles of transaction: market exchange, redistribution and reciprocity. It cannot be overemphasized that these principles are not mutually exclusive. All of them may be present simultaneously in any society. In our own society, subsistence transactions follow the principle of the market[8]; the services associated with education, welfare, military defense, and taxation follow the principle of redistribution; and we have a peripheral, left-over form of distribution on the principle of

(8) It should be added that in the United States, as indeed in all Western economies, the market principle and the allocative price mechanism have been institutionally

reciprocity in gift exchanges and the like. Other societies show the same principles, but they show them in vastly different institutional frameworks, and in significantly different proportions.

It seems clear, then, that the economic changes occurring in Africa today are of two sorts that must be analytically separated, even though they occur together. There are extensive changes in institutions. Such changes are taking place on one level. Concomitantly, but on another level, the "mixture" of the organizing principles of economic life is being changed. In this process, the area of the economy that is subject to the market principle is expanding while the areas of life subject to the principles of redistribution and reciprocity are shrinking.

It seems safe to predict that the process will continue, and that African economies are becoming like our own in the sense that the sector dominated by the market principle is being enlarged. It does not necessarily follow that the institutions of our society are bound to be duplicated exactly in Africa. We mean to imply no more than that some, but not all, products and factors of production have entered the market; more, but not all, people get their subsistence livelihood in producing for or selling in markets; multicentric economies are in the process of becoming unicentric. All-purpose money increasingly permeates nonmarket spheres of economy; external trade as well as internal becomes almost exclusively transacted on the market principle and (as with us) modified by such devices as marketing brands and redistributive taxation.

The questions, therefore, that we consider of greatest significance, and that can be illuminated by the articles in this book, are these: what sequential patterns of entrance into a more inclusively market-dominated economy can be discovered? What accounts for the marked differences in receptivity to organizational and technological change, which accompanies the increased importance of markets? What have the changes in institutionalization of the economy, which have accompanied the expansion of the market principle, created in the rest of the institutions of the societies?

Entrance into Market Economy.

Entrance into market economy is usually stated by anthropologists as "getting a cash income" or "entering the cash economy." However,

controlled by both governmental and private measures: labor legislation, unions, price supports, zoning laws, and oligopolization have reduced the range of price formation by purely competitive supply and demand forces. However, factor resources, including labor, as well as most goods and service outputs are still transacted by market purchase and sale; and the prices of such factors and outputs comprise the main source of income (livelihood) to the population. In a word, the United States is a controlled market economy. See, Robinson (1954) and Galbraith (1955).

getting a cash income always involves selling something on the market exchange principle. Broadly, there are three things that Africans have to sell to a market, in this sense. First, they can sell agricultural or pastoral produce—cash cropping. Such produce may be destined for local, regional or external consumption (United Nations 1954). Unless there are consumers, it is not possible for such sales to be made. One of the most important occurrences has been the willingness of European and other foreign firms to buy. In addition, transport facilities have been created in order to stimulate regional trade. Second, an African in search of cash can sell wage labor—industrial or agricultural. Most industrial wage labor and much agricultural wage labor is "sold" to European establishments, although particularly in West Africa there are large numbers of hired laborers on African farms. The third course by which a person can secure cash is to enter into commerce—usually petty commerce—as a market place seller, long distance trader, transporter, itinerant hawker or shopkeeper.

In short, (1) marketing of produce may increase, with direct repercussions on production, (2) labor may enter the market, and (3) buying for resale (as contrasted to marketing one's own product) may develop as a specialty. The greatest social changes have come where labor, entering the market, has moved geographically and occupationally in response to market demands, thus having repercussions in the rest of society. Almost as great a change occurs in the situation in which marketing and buying for resale have overlapped in a significant way, therefore increasing volumes of output and, concomitantly, changing work and consumption patterns.

Each African group makes a typical adjustment to its cash needs (United Nations 1954). That is to say, in the early stages of change resulting from Western impact, there is a greater or lesser specialization in one of these market activities. Each pattern of market entrance has, of course, different effects on social organization.

The pattern of entrance into market economy experienced by the Arusha is an especially good illustration because of the absence of indigenous markets. Traditionally, the Arusha were self-sufficient agriculturalists. They entered into market exchange in order to buy food and to earn cash with which to pay taxes. The need to buy food was traceable to a land shortage induced by population growth, colonial peace, and land occupation by European farmers. The ready accessibility of an urban market place allowed the Arusha to continue their agricultural ways by producing cash crops. Two important results followed the reluctant entrance of the Arusha into market economy. At first they sold to the market just that minimum of traditionally grown crops that would fetch them sufficient cash to buy

extra food and pay taxes. The Arusha did not at first rearrange production lines to suit market demand, or indeed even seek to specialize
in the most profitable crops. However, production for the market
increased in volume because the increasing shortage of land did not
permit most Arusha to cultivate sufficient food crops any longer
under the traditional economy. It was only after the reluctant acceptance of this necessity that the Arusha entered a market economy
more fully by changing production to take advantage of market
demands and prices. Moreover, all areas of Arusha culture felt the
impact of the market. Goats, beer and craft items became objects of
market exchange among the Arusha themselves. Secondly—and of
special interest to the anthropologist—is that the Arusha, in making
this change, found it necessary to denigrate Masai culture which
formerly they had venerated as ideal.

It is, in fact, no accident that foreign administrations have had to
do more than establish market places to create a market-dominated
economy—in many instances, production for the market has been
made mandatory, by separate and special legal means with heavy
sanctions.

The Kipsigis have had an even more dramatic entry into market
economy—indeed, their eagerness to enter market economy is only
the most striking of many examples which belie the view that Africans
have always been forced to change. Traditionally a people whose
values were pastoral in spite of their small patches of millet, Kipsigis
have become farmers and marketers with amazing alacrity and success. Perhaps their most striking achievement is the aplomb with
which they have handled the situation of land entering the market.
Their success may be explained by the fact that "land tenure" did
not really exist in their old system, so that when they settled and
changed their way of life, they had no traditional form of institutionalization for distribution of land or of labor which was relevant to the
new situation. They had nothing basic to unlearn.

Receptivity to Economic Change.

At the opposite pole from the Kipsigis, who have accepted economic and other social change, are the Lele who, in spite of contact
with the Bushong economy which they admit to be superior, have
consistently chosen to safeguard traditional social institutions at the
sacrifice of economic improvement. The question of receptivity to
economic change is a more general form of the commonly asked
question, what "social" factors limit economic growth (Higgins 1956).

This question actually harbors two problem areas that have commonly been confused. In economists' terms, they are: (1) Given the

social, economic, ecological and technological framework of some African society, why are continual increases in per capita output ("growth") not forthcoming within the *indigenous* system? (2) Given the indigenous framework above, why has European impact failed to induce greater institutional change ("growth")—organizational and technological change towards market industrialism—which would increase per capita output? Basic to both problems is the specific question of what constitutes "wealth" and the social importance and means of wealth-getting in indigenous African societies. Upon closer examination, it may be discovered that some indigenous economies do indeed "grow," but because the enlarged outputs need not pass through the market place nor be transacted via the market principle, the growth is either unperceived by Western observers or considered beside the point.

In Western market-economy wealth means income yielding property: an acre of agricultural land, a coal mine, a herd of cattle, an apartment house building, and a steel mill all have in common the fact that they produce output goods or services salable at a market price which yields their owners a property income (variously split up as profit, rent, or interest). Moreover, the wealth items—the acre of land, the buildings—are themselves salable for a money price on markets. Wealth, in our own economy, then, is material, income-yielding, quantifiable in money terms, and salable. These characteristics are dependently linked to the dominating organizational principle of market exchange.

Where indigenous wealth concepts and socially structured principles of wealth-getting in African society are radically different from those in market society, there is likely to be the most difficulty ("major obstacles") in transforming primitive to market exchange institutions. Two examples are the following.

Wealth in some African societies is composed of items that do not contribute to enlarging material output, but whose possession does yield material returns in the form of gift transfers. Among the Lele, rights in women and children are considered the highest form of wealth, and the path to material security and honorific status is not material accumulation but the creation of affinal dependencies which yield obligatory material gifts. Douglas contrasts the Lele path to high status with the Bushong:

He [a Lele man] will eventually marry several wives, beget children, and so enter the Begetter's cult. His infant daughters will be asked in marriage by suitors bearing gifts and ready to work for him. Later, when his cult membership is bringing in a revenue of raffia cloth, from fees of new initiates, his newborn daughter's daughters can be promised in marriage to junior clansmen, who will strengthen his following in the village. His wives will look after him in his declining years. He will have stores of raffia cloths to lend or give, but he will possess this wealth because, in the natural course of events, he reached the proper status for his age. He would not be able to achieve this status through wealth.

For the Bushong work is the means to wealth, and wealth the means to status. They strongly emphasize the value of individual effort and achievement, and they are also prepared to collaborate in numbers, over a sustained period, when this is necessary to raise output. Nothing in Lele culture corresponds to the Bushong striving for riches.

The pursuit of more highly ranked wealth items in Lele society is reinforced by technological considerations, such as the absence of storage facilities for perishables, as well as by the social obligation to share. The absence of monetary arrangements and capital markets also constrains the disposition of outputs. Currently produced items can either be self-consumed, given away, consumed in feasts, or used to obtain "superior" items or prerogatives via conversion. It seems clear then that one point of difference among African societies is that the structured means to high status have markedly different effects on indigenous output growth as well as on receptivity to organizational and technological change. In the Bushong (as in market society), individual material accumulation is the path to status. This is not so with the Lele, for whom status is the means to individual material affluence—not necessarily composed of enlarged outputs but often of gift transfers.

Wealth concepts differ in African societies in another way. There are some wealth items physically identical with those in Western society but regarded as wealth for reasons which make the African items of "social" rather than of economic significance. For example, cattle in parts of East Africa are wealth to their owners, for reasons other than the material yield of the herds. They are rarely slaughtered and eaten by their owners, who part with them only in emergency. Because the social valuation of cattle is so radically different from cattle as a regular market crop in Western economy, it would be uninformed for an outsider to regard East African cattle export as a potential wealth source of economic development. The change necessary to make it so is not "economic" at all—rather, it would have to be social and ethical (Herskovits 1952b : 108).

Dual Economy and Multicentric Economy.

We have now come to the point where we must consider the concept of the dual economy as it was set forth by Boeke (1953) and Furnivall (1939). To Boeke, the phrase "dual economy" means an economy, formerly "primitive," of which a portion has become "Westernized"—that is, some goods and services are transacted on the market principle, and cash income (all-purpose money) is received. The remainder of the economy, however, is said to lie in the "traditional" or "primitive" "subsistence sphere." In brief, the distinction is between "cash economy," which might better be called "the market," and "traditional economy," which is everything else.

The idea of "dual economy" in Boeke's sense incurs three objections. (1) It implies that the traditional portion of the economy is of one piece—a homogeneous sector or sphere. We find, rather, that several transactional spheres may be present within the traditional sector, each with a different principle for transacting goods and services (the Sonjo are the most obvious example in this book). Indeed, as noted above, the conventional labels of anthropology (subsistence goods, prestige goods, ceremonial goods) make this point clearly. Even in the traditional economy some items may be transacted by the market principle. In brief, the traditional economy itself may be multicentric. (2) The term "dual economy" implies a kind of gulf between the primitive and Westernized portions of the economy which in fact does not exist. It is rarely the case that some people in such a society are economically engaged wholly within the market sphere while others are wholly engaged within traditional spheres. (3) Lastly, the term "dual economy" implies a gulf between the market or cash sector and the traditional sector in another sense: that the market principle and money are new, and therefore were entirely unknown before Western incursion. Such may be true in a few cases, but decidedly not in most of them.

* * *

As we have proceeded with this analysis, we have come upon what at first appeared to be a paradox. Put briefly, it is this: the market place is a characteristic of economies in which the market principle is peripheral. The more pervasive the market principle, the less the economic importance of the market place.

African societies were marked by subsistence economies, with or without the presence of the peripheral market. The establishment of colonial status led in most areas to the enlargement or founding of market places. Items of petty trade, of European manufacture, entered these markets; produce entered these markets in newly large amounts. But as Western influence deepened and the market principle expanded, there were instances in which the market place was bypassed, as was the case with the export crops from parts of East Africa and the Copperbelt that have been marketed through cooperative societies. As the spheres of the economy merged and the multicentric economy tended toward the unicentric, labor and finally land entered the market but not, of course, the market place. The market principle has affected more and more institutions and has outgrown the market place because the essential ingredients of production—labor, land, machines—cannot be transacted in a market place. Where the market principle is dominant, it is inter-firm transactions which are all important, and not the petty transactions that occur in the market-place setting. Indeed, the very meaning of the market place changes from a bazaar to a group of buyers of something, wherever they may be located. The "market" for automobiles in the United States is everywhere, and the market for enamel basins becomes the collectivity of African housewives.

The market place and its institutional arrangement has undergone other, noneconomic changes. Just as its economic importance lapses with the "development of the economy," and it becomes merely a place of final sale, so its political importance lapses with the development of the polity, its religious significance with the acceptance of world religions, and its social significance with the adoption of the guitar, the radio, the "hoteli" and high-life.

THE GUINEA COAST AND
THE CONGO

CHAPTER 1

The Rural Wolof of The Gambia

BY DAVID W. AMES

The Wolof are a Negro Islamic people who occupy an area stretching from the Senegal River in the north to the Gambia River in the south and 150 kilometers eastward from the Atlantic Ocean. Population estimates vary a good deal but it is safe to say that well over half a million Wolof reside in Senegal and about 50,000 in British Gambia.

Most of the rural Wolof in the Gambia live in the Saloum districts on the north bank of the river where most of the material for this study was collected by me and my wife while making a general ethnographic study in 1950–51. Our work began in Njau, in the district of Upper Saloum, Central Division, a hamlet where it was easy to gain a view of the life of a community as a whole; further, the chief and his family lived there, and we could therefore observe the relations between him and the people of the surrounding communities. After working five months in the Njau area, we moved to Ballangar, in Lower Saloum, which is also the residence of a district chief and is a larger community than Njau. Every caste and occupational group in Wolof society is represented there. From both study centers, frequent trips were made to surrounding communities in both the Gambia and Senegal.

The traditional economy of the Wolof is much less complex than those of the famous kingdoms of the rain forests of the Guinea Coast. Wolof farming settlements in both Senegal and the Gambia average fewer than a hundred persons (Gamble 1957 : 14). In the nineteenth century, these hamlets were devoted primarily to the cultivation of subsistence crops, sorghum and millet. Abundance of food must have been rare because of the variable rainfall and the primitive, though ingenious (Gamble 1957 : 29–32), agricultural technology, which lacked even the typical West African hoe. Most families had a few goats and chickens and, perhaps, fattened a sheep for the Muslim feast of Ramadan; however, only the wealthy could afford cattle. Wolof farm communities were essentially self-sufficient. Part-time craft specialists—potters, weavers and blacksmiths—in each hamlet or in a group of hamlets provided the necessities, though meagerly, because of weakly developed technology and because of local warfare characterized by frequent pillaging, looting, and extortion.

It appears that traditional Wolof economy was carried on without the use of complex mechanisms of exchange. Markets, it seems, were absent, and the use of Western-type money and of cloth commodity money dates from the coming of the Europeans, though the use of commodity money seems to be a derivative invention of the Wolof. Most internal and external trade seems to have been carried on without money of any kind. Intertribal trade was sporadic and chiefly the concern of a few wealthy persons: warlike chieftains, powerful marabouts, and the like.

It is impossible to reconstruct the pre-contact trading patterns in any detail, but a good deal is known about the post-contact period and the present. Of all West Africa, the Senegambian region has the longest history of contact with Europe by sea, dating from the arrival of the Portuguese in the middle of the fifteenth century; of course, overland contacts with North Africa go back at least five hundred years before the arrival of the Portuguese.

The result is that there is an almost incredible mixture of ancient African, early European, and modern exchange mechanisms in use in the trade of the Gambia today: simple barter, money barter, the pawning of country cloth, the use of Western currency and credit mechanisms.

Space considerations do not permit a detailed discussion of "non-economic" exchanges such as bridewealth, although they are significant in the fabric of the non-economic aspects of Wolof life. For example, there are the gift exchanges frequently encountered in the *rites de passage* and the exchanges which are a part of a set of reciprocal rights and obligations between members of different occupational castes in Wolof society. Considerations of prestige are dominant in these "non-economic" exchanges though subsistence is a factor. Of course, these exchanges function in many other ways, such as cementing kinship and maintaining status.

EARLY TRADE PRACTICES

Reaching the mouth of the Gambia River in the middle of the fifteenth century, the Portugese initiated a trade in small quantities of gold for ivory, hides, wax and slaves. At this time, the Portuguese were interested in finding a sea route to the Far East, and Africa was viewed primarily as a geographical obstacle. Nevertheless, small missionary and trading stations were established along the banks of the Gambia.

Diogo Gomez, who explored the upper river as early as 1458, reported seeing a Moorish trader in a large town near the south bank of the river in a district called Kantora (Gray 1940 : 7). However,

Wolof contact with the Moors a little farther north began centuries before; chiefs in the region of the Senegal River were apparently being proselytized by the Moors in the eleventh century (Monod 1951 : 7–8). There are a few descriptions of the early trade with the Moors in the Gambia region. The manuscript of Valentim Fernandes, who visited the Senegambian region in the middle of the fifteenth century, refers to the Wolof trading with both the Moors and the Europeans for horses, and an entry on a margin states that fourteen or fifteen slaves were traded for a horse in 1455. According to Cadamosto, who visited Senegal at about the same time, Wolof warrior chiefs valued horses more than any other kind of wealth; and, in the trade with the Portuguese, they were said to have exchanged nine to fourteen slaves for a horse and its equipment (Astley 1745 : 587). Fernandes also speaks of the Portuguese exchanging clothing and cloth for hides, slaves and a little gold (Monod 1951 : 20–21). Everyday subsistence exchanges between native Africans also appear to have been carried out entirely without money.

Rather slight historical evidence suggests that in the region of the Senegal River there were some small native markets, but none farther to the south in the Gambian region. Markets may have developed in the Senegal from contact with Mauretanians living on the north bank of the river. Early observers of the Gambia, like Jobson and Moore, give many descriptions of the local scene but never refer to a market place like the one Cadamosto found on the Senegal River. Native Gambian market places seem to have developed long after the Europeans had established trading centers. It may not be unhistorical to note that all of my old Wolof informants concurred on this point; to their minds, markets were established by the Europeans. In any case, the following description is the only early reference I have discovered to an indigenous market. Astley (1745 : 587), describing the travels of Cadamosto, tells of one near the Senegal River:

... he went three or four times to see one of their markets, or fairs; which was kept on Monday and Fridays, in a meadow, not far from the place where he was lodged. Hither repaired, with their wares, both men and women, for four or five miles about; and those who lived at a greater distance went to other markets nearer them. The great poverty of this people appeared in the goods found in these fairs; which were, a few pieces of cotton-cloth, cotton-yarn, pulse, oil, millet, wooden tubs, palm mats, and every thing else for the use of life. Here also one meets with arms, and small quantities of gold. As they have no money or coin of any kind, all trade is carried on by way of barter, exchanging one thing for another, and sometimes two or three for one, according to the different values.

Diagne believes that this market was located at N'Dobe near Mouit
in the Senegal River area and that Wolof, Serere and Peulh procured
salt there from the mines of Gandiole (Diagne 1919 : 140), which
were under the control of the Wolof kingdom of Cayor, and the salt
was traded as far south as Fouta Jallon. Diagne (1919 : 141) notes
that it was known in the district of Saloum in the Gambia:

> Le sel de Gandiole était connu et chanté jusque les bords de la Gambie.
> Dans leur chant de guerre, les griots de Saloum parlaient de l'"effroyable
> vautour, Amady Goukane revenant de Gandiole avec sa bouchée de sel!"

Jobson, who explored the river Gambia in 1620, writes that a poor
grade of salt collected at the seaside near the mouth of the Gambia
was traded far into the interior for slaves (Jobson 1932 : 108). He
noted that the people of Setico, a Mohammedan village far up the
river near the Barrakunda Falls, sent slaves to the coast in exchange
for this salt, and took it far into the interior to trade for gold, perhaps
to one of the fabled "Wangara" gold fields where a silent trade was
said to have taken place (Bovill 1958 : 120). Though much of this
gold was retained and worked locally, early Portuguese traders were
said to have visited Setico to acquire gold (Gray 1940 : 12).

Until Portugal's power weakened and New World settlements
and plantations created a demand for slave labor, other European
nations did not interest themselves in Africa. The Senegambia was
one of the first regions in West Africa to export slaves. The traffic
in the Gambia was carried on first by the Portuguese, followed by
the Dutch, French, English, and Americans. It should be noted, however, that an intertribal trade in slaves and a trade with the Moors
has a much older history. Furthermore, the Moorish and native trade
was carried on in Senegal after the British abolished it along the
Gambia (Hewett 1857 : 515).

From the end of the fifteenth century, European traders operated
small factories along the coast and riverbanks or traded with the
Africans from their boats. In the early seventeenth century, one of
the earliest trading stations up the Gambia was established at Joar
(Ballangar, a few miles from Kaur), the river gateway to the Wolof
districts of Saloum. In the early eighteenth century "there were more
or less substantial houses at . . . Joar (near Kau-ur) which were built
in imitation of the Portuguese style of architecture" (Gray 1940 : 12).
The Royal Africa Company had its most important factory there
from the beginning of the eighteenth century, and the French traded
there too.

The settlement of Kaur was a famous center of trade close to
and almost one with Joar. Francis Moore (1730–35 : 72), an English

trader working up river in the early eighteenth century, observed that:

They (the people of Kaur) make exceeding good cotton-clothes here, very dear to purchase, and much valued by all the Women on the river. Here lives the old Man, so well known to all White Men, call'd Serin Donso, who exacts upon every Body very much, and has such great power over all the merchants who bring their Slaves here, that unless you see him, it is in vain to expect to Trade. This then is the chief Town of the whole River; and, as I hinted before, the best Place for Trade.

Local leaders, such as this Serin Donso, became wealthy and powerful as controllers of the slave trade with the Europeans from whom they received superior weapons. The native leaders imposed a tax on all European traders, paid in trade goods, called *namo*. According to elderly Wolof informants, this tax was still exacted from traders throughout the nineteenth century.

The British colony in Bathurst, at the mouth of the river, made mutually advantageous pacts with various African chieftains. A Wolof informant has described negotiations in the late nineteenth century with Governor Goudsbury in which administered trade is apparent, whether or not the historical details are accurate:

Governor Gouldsbury at Bathurst was the one who built a fort at Kataba for Seet Kani (a chieftain who controlled Ballangar). Seet Kani had an armory there. Governor Gouldsbury would send him guns and gun powder because Seet protected the traders in the river wharf trading centers. The Governor asked Biran Sise (another minor chieftain) to let him build a wharf and trading post in Kaur but Biran refused, so the Governor went to Seet Kani and he said, "Build in Ballangar, it is nearer the river and it is my town". Seet Kani had the bush cleared for the trading post and Governor Gouldsbury gave Seet an iron bed and a mosquito net.

Still Kaur had a reputation as a trading center in the early nineteenth century:

The natives who are a mixture of Jaloffs (Wolof) and Soosoos are a peaceable inoffensive race, and are chiefly engaged in trade, except when the approach of the rains summons them to the corn and rice grounds. (Gray and Dorchard 1825 : 46)

Kaur finally overtook Joar in importance with the increase in the groundnut trade during the last half of the nineteenth century, and all the Europeans moved there. As we shall see below, much of the basic economic exchange of the Wolof today in the Saloum districts takes place in Kaur.

After the British legally abolished the slave trade in 1807, their forces put a stop to shipping slaves from the Gambia (Gray 1940 : 333), and from 1816 on, a military garrison was maintained in Bathurst. Many traders established shops there, but for years afterwards, during its so-called anti-colonial period, the home government frowned on extending its territorial commitments upriver and Europeans traded there at their own risk (Gray 1940 : 369). Tribal wars, too, closed down factories upriver (Gray 1940 : 331). However, the temporary African wives of European traders often successfully continued the business after their husbands had returned to England or had died of the "fever." Furthermore, European traders in Bathurst got natives to maintain upriver trading posts for them and the Wolof, in particular had the reputation for being clever and industrious merchants (MacBriar 1861 : 6; Huntley 1850 : 142). Many Wolof in Bathurst built small craft for the river trade, and fishermen in the river or along the seacoast traded fish for commodities produced by the inland people.

> The Fisherman of Walo cut open the fish, dry it, and take it for sale to villages at a distance from the banks of the river; carrying on a very extensive commerce in this article. (Caillie 1830 : 31)

Shoberl writes that the inhabitants of this part of the coast (near Goree), in general, are much engaged in fishing, supplying those of the interior with considerable quantities of fish dried in the sun and receiving in exchange cotton cloths, indigo, and cotton wool, (Shoberl ca. 1800 : 69)

There was also considerable commerce between the people of Cayor and Saint Louis in Senegal, and items of both European and native manufacture were exchanged. F. Carrere and P. Holle in their *De la Sénégambia française* (p. 81), published in 1855, give us a detailed description of the items that were exchanged in this commerce:

> Les hommes du Cayor achètent à Saint-Louis des fusils, de la poudre, des balles, des sabres, du fer en barre, du tabac, des tissus imprimés, des liquides de toute espèce, du coton filé bleu et blanc, des verroteries, de la toile guinée, de l'ambre vrai et faux, du corail, etc. . . . Le Cayor fournit au Sénégal du mil, des boeufs, des moutons, des peaux, des volailles, du savon, des haricots, des fruits d'espèces diverses: *newe,* sort de pomme; *krewar,* cerises; *sidomm, soump; boui,* fruit du baobab; *dakrar,* fruit du tamarinier; *l'allo,* feuille du baobab, condiment nécessaire du couscouss; du vin de palmier, des patates, des melons et leur graine *(beraff),* du manioc, des ignames, du lait aigre, du beurre fondu, du coton en came, employé à la confection des pagnes, après avoir été filé par les négresses de Saint-Louis; des arachides et du sel.

In 1830, prior to the great imperialistic scramble for African territory, the first peanuts or groundnuts[1] were exported from the Gambia, and from 1848 onwards had become the dominant cash

(1) Peanuts were introduced two centuries earlier by the Portuguese and used chiefly for food.

crop. This was one of the earliest cash crops produced in tropical Africa; it indicates the economic adaptability of the Senegambian peoples, a characteristic which is encountered repeatedly. Gray is rightly struck by the unusual character of the development of this crop, though his description is marred by dubious reference to the "subconscious" origin of it.

The history of the Gambia groundnut crop is in some respects unique amongst the histories of economic crops in British tropical Africa. In some instances what is now a staple agricultural product of a tropical dependency was already being grown and exported, when the British assumed control of the country. In many other instances it was hardly grown, if at all, at the time of the advent of British rule and its growth has been promoted by the Government by means of official assistance and encouragement of the grower and by fostering and protecting the industry in the early days. Neither of these two things happened in regard to the Gambia groundnut crop. It was not grown for export in 1816 and, though from 1841 onwards large quantities have been exported from Bathurst and have contributed very largely to the colonial revenue in the shape of an export duty, yet for about half a century the crop was almost entirely grown on soil, which was not British, by natives of Africa, who were not under British rule or protection. It is one of the few instances in which the native of Africa has learnt more or less subconsciously that he has at his door a saleable product, which could fetch a good market price in Europe, and started to grow it with very little material instruction or encouragement from official sources. (Gray 1940 : 380)

The French in Sénégal were the chief purchasers of groundnuts and French currency remained legal tender in the Gambia until 1922. Some peanuts, as well as hides and cattle, were brought to Bathurst to exchange for English goods. A military officer stationed in Bathurst in the second half of the nineteenth century observed upcountry Wolof exchanging peanuts for trade muskets during the height of the native wars:

There is a colony of Jolloffs in Bathurst, but the majority of the people of that race that one sees in the town are traders from the interior, who bring down their ground-nuts to exchange for powder, muskets, and kola nuts. In the one street of stores, of which I have spoken, long lithe Jolloffs may be seen coming out of the shops with trade muskets, the stocks of which are painted red and the barrels made of renovated pieces of old gas-pipe. Into these unquestionably deadly weapons they pour two or three handfuls of powder, and then fire them off in the road to test them. The test frequently leaves nothing remaining but a fragment of barrel and stock, and the practice is one that is rather startling to strangers. (Ellis 1883 : 4)

During the latter half of the nineteenth century, intertribal trade was restricted by the native wars and only chiefs had enough wealth to purchase many commodities. Cloth[2] manufactured by the Wolof and grain were their chief commodities in these exchanges. Elderly Wolof most often recalled the following four intertribal exchanges: (1) Mandinko, Bambara or Serahuli traders in large parties brought gold to the Gambia from far inland to exchange for African cloth. They had weight measures made of iron called gɔrɔ, each valued at its equivalent in African country cloths. (2) Serahuli or Fulbe in large parties brought horses, cows, donkeys, and occasionally slaves to exchange for country cloth or grain. (3) The Wolof chieftains also acquired slaves from Jola traders by raiding villages in neighboring districts, especially the district of Fonyi. The chiefs often sold their slaves in order to purchase guns, gunpowder, horses, swords, alcohol, etc. (4) Coastal peoples, like the Serer and Lebu, came up the river in their canoes to barter dried fish and salt for African cloth and grain.

The British formally established a protectorate over the whole of the Gambian hinterland—a narrow strip of land on both banks of the Gambia river—in the year 1902. By this time European contact had already altered radically the traditional Wolof economy. A demand for goods of European manufacture had already been created and some items, particularly textiles (Gamble 1949 : 62), became necessities. The African farmer produced more peanuts to get European currency for purchasing these goods and for taxes. The traditional self-sufficiency of the Wolof hamlet had begun to break down, though enough of the traditional technology and skills had survived so that they could return to self-sufficient economy if they wished to. Increasing emphasis on cash crops led to reliance on outside sources of food,[3] and changes in the world market price of peanuts now had its repercussion on even the most remote hamlet. The farmer has become more dependent on the specialist in the river wharf town of Bathurst: for example, the tailor who sews clothing there with a Singer machine. The specialist in the commercial centers is in turn dependent on the farmer for cash income and for some food: women traders in the Bathurst market make annual trips upriver to buy guinea corn and rice.

In recent times certain craft specialties, such as cloth and pottery making, have declined because of the competition of cheap and plentiful European goods. However, some traditional specialists—blacksmiths who manufacture gold filigree jewelry and leather workers—have doubtless increased their production because of the *Pax Britannica,* improved transportation, and the increasing amounts

(2) The use of cloth as a form of money will be discussed separately below.
(3) Food had to be imported during the native wars in the late nineteenth century.

of European currency in circulation. Specialization generally has tended to shift from the household to some new occupation in an outside agency in the larger town controlled by Europeans in the fields of commerce, education, administration or health. In commerce, however, much specialization is seasonal, as jobs associated with the trade follows the fall harvest, such as truck driving, stevedoring at the wharves, clerking in the stores, petty trading in the market place, or hawking goods from village to village.

THE USE OF CLOTH-MONEY AS A MEDIUM OF EXCHANGE[4]

An interesting and complex form of transaction using commodity money, which played an important role in Wolof trade in the nineteenth century, deserves separate treatment here. I spoke with the oldest men I knew concerning the former use of cloth-money and their statements are corroborated for the most part by present-day Wolof practices and by European observers of the eighteenth and nineteenth centuries.

Cloth-money had close functional parallels with Western-type general purpose money, both in ceremonial exchange and in basic economic exchange. Although the Wolof no longer use cloth as money, they still weave it. Much of the bridewealth may be used to buy cloths (as many as fifteen) which are given to the bride. Wolof women card locally grown cotton and spin the thread. Wolof men, of a caste made up of the descendants of slaves, weave the cloth on the typically narrow West African loom in strips about five inches wide and cut (for most purposes) into lengths about seventy inches long. Several of these strips are sewn together by the women to make a piece which is often referred to by the English and French in this region as a *pagn* or *pagne* (skirt) and by the Wolof as a *malan*. This is then colored with indigo—formerly grown locally—and sometimes decorated with simple designs by the tie-dye technique.

Well into the latter part of the nineteenth century, native cloth in strips or in the form of *pagne* served as the principal medium of exchange. The functions of the cloth resembled those of the economists' conventional definition of Western-type, general purpose money: medium of exchange and standard denominator of value, having the characteristics of "homogeneity, divisibility, portability and durability" (Gregory 1933 : 601–2). It functioned also as a store of value. Its chief difference from money as we know it in Western culture was that the community or state did not formally control its

(4) Some of this discussion of cloth-money has appeared in a different form in Ames 1955.

quantity or purchasing power, but it was informally recognized as the standard of value and principal medium of exchange. Cloth-money also departs from our Western-type money in its being a product for use; as such it can be classified as a commodity money similar to those described by Herskovits as "money-barter" (Herskovits 1952 : 211–16).

Wolof cloth-money was an article of consumption, an economic necessity, and a hard-won product of manufacture. More than a symbol of wealth, it was real wealth of a most valuable kind—along with livestock, grain, and slaves. Some old men recall a time when it was difficult to find enough cloth to clothe the whole family properly. Of course, the unmechanized technology of the Wolof could have coped with the demand for cloth far more effectively if it had not been for religious and other ceremonial requirements. Their Islamic faith required that men wear long flowing robes and baggy pants. Every boy had to pay the ruler of his area sixteen strips of cloth before being circumcised. The fathers had to provide several garments for the use of the boys in the circumcision school. Before getting married a man had to pay the bride and her parents at least 30 χopa, the equivalent of 480 strips. Corpses were buried in large cloths. Cloth was used in other ceremonial exchanges and in miscellaneous gifts; to cross-cousins at naming ceremonies and marriages, to affinal relations at marriages, and to a caste of *gewel* (musicians) and *jam* (formerly slaves, now the descendants of slaves) who fulfil traditional ceremonial obligations.

That Wolof cloth-money was standardized and readily divisible is illustrated by the way in which it was equated with English currency. The terms seen in Table 2 were generally used by the Wolof in their economic exchanges. Costs of most goods and services were stated in terms of these units of cloth, and most often payments were made with cloth. Where the cloth was not available, it still functioned as a standard of value in economic exchanges.

The equivalents in Table 3 are not absolute; as in Western economies, the purchasing power of the money token varied from time to time. However, they represent an average of earlier scales of value as expressed by the informants. The terms most often used were the χasap (2 strips of cloth) and the χopa (16 strips), as indicated in Table 3.

Some commodities, like garden vegetables, were worth so little that they could not be paid for in cloth. Grain in small amounts, measured out in gourds, was the "petty cash" used in such payments. At the same time, a very expensive commodity like a fine horse, worth two slaves, was rarely bought with only cloth-money by other than chiefs. Where less wealthy people were making such purchases, whole granaries (worth 15 χ*opa*), livestock, or other objects of value entered the exchange, often in conjunction with cloth. Some exchanges, then, especially the "expensive" ones, were primarily or wholly moneyless, but even here most of the articles exchanged were valued in terms of cloth-money equivalent.

TABLE 2

Equivalences of Cloth

Wala wala or *sech*	1 strip of cloth	3 d.
	(slightly less than 2 yards in length)	
χ*asap*[a]	2 strips of cloth	6 d.
χ*asap* and a *wala wala*	3 strips of cloth	9 d.
Nyari (two) ϰ*asap*	4 strips of cloth	1 s.
Nyari χ*asap* and a *wala wala*	5 strips of cloth	1/3
Nyɛta (three) χ*asap*	6 strips of cloth	1/6
Nyɛta χ*asap* and *wala wala*	7 strips of cloth	1/9
Malan	8 strips of cloth	2/–
Malan and a *wala wala*	9 strips of cloth	2/3
Continuing on up to the largest individual unit of value:		
χ*opa*	2 *malan*	4/–

TABLE 3

Equivalences of Cloth to Other Items

3 large kola nuts	1 χasap
6 handfuls of unthreshed grain called a *sabarr*	1 χasap
8 sabarr	1 χopa
1 short-handled hoe	2 χasap
1 rooster	2 χasap
1 large goat	1 χopa
1 cow	15 χopa
1 young female slave about 14 years old	20 χopa
Bridewealth payment (approx.)	32 χopa
1 horse	50 χopa

(a) χ is a uvular fricative, ɛ, the short e as in English "set."

Like money in Western cultures, cloth-money was subject to fluctuations in value. When all the slaves were weaving during the dry season and cloth was more plentiful, its value as money went down. Then, for example, more strips were required to buy a farming tool from a blacksmith. During the rains, when the slaves stopped weaving and commenced work in the fields, the value of cloth went up. Frequently there was not enough cloth for trading purposes. During a period of cloth scarcity, families lacking cloth-money would have to sell property at a low price in order to get cloth (which was always acceptable) with which to buy necessities.

Cloth-money was used in external trade as well. The Wolof used it to buy horses, gold, and slaves from Bambara, Serahuli, and Fula traders, who took the cloth back to the east where, it is said, it was even more scarce and could be disposed of at a large profit. The inhabitants of the Wolof village of Kaur, on the north bank of the river Gambia, had a reputation for making especially fine cloth, much sought after by the foreign traders, and this village became an important trading center.

It is difficult to say just when and how the use of cloth as money developed among the Wolof. There are a few historical documents which have a bearing on the question; they show that the Wolof used cloth-money for at least several generations before the large-scale expansion of a cash-crop economy based on peanuts, around the first decade of the twentieth century. An early reference to cloth-money is found in the Gambia Annual Report of 1860, cited by Gamble (1949 : 62):

The king of Wuli compels the merchants of caravans passing from the interior with produce through his dominions to the banks of the river for trade to take a certain number of his country cloth at a fixed price, in exchange for any articles he or his court may fancy. These country cloth form a ready currency thruout the River Gambia, as well as in the adjacent rivers of Salum and Cassamance, amongst the natives and for all trade purposes they are as potent as the "mighty dollar".

The common people, as well as rulers such as the "king" just referred to, made purchases with cloth from the African traders—often Wolof (see below)—who were the bush representatives of European firms. The people also put their cloth in pawn with the traders. The *Annual Report* of the Gambia of 1865 (page 60) (Gamble 1949 : 69) mentioned this pledging system:

During the four rainy months of July, August, September and October, our native trader (the liberated African) is busy. He conveys rice and corn, the property of his European employer, articles at that time most in request up the river, receiving in exchange pagnes or country cloths, manufactured from cotton grown in the country in the native towns—in November he received ground nuts, hides and wax in exchange for these same pagnes, but his factory is now stocked by imports from home; the possession of guns, powder, Madras handkerchiefs and rum tempts the native to industry and the trade is very active till the rainy season came round when the pagn season again opens . . .

This practice continues in the protectorate to this day.

The independent invention of this system of exchange by the

Wolof seems unlikely, for there was no great need for money in economic transactions in a region where there were no markets. We find no mention of it until the nineteenth century, when there is considerable evidence that it developed out of more intensive trade contacts with the Europeans. Mollien writing in 1820 (page 60) mentioned the use of cloth as a measure of value in an account of his trip to the headwaters of the Gambia and Senegal Rivers. He writes, "The commodities which serve as standards for the value of others in their dealings by barter, are cotton cloths and millet..." Yet Durand (1806 : 34) writing several years earlier about the Wolof of the Kingdom of Cayor in Senegal, does not even mention cloth in his discussion of goods commonly exchanged in this region, nor do similar eighteenth century writings. Moore, telling of his trading experiences on the river Gambia, does not mention cloth-money, and it would seem reasonable to assume that he would have if it had played an important part in the economy. Likewise, the accounts of Adanson (1759) and of Saugnier (1791) omit all mention of the use of cloth-money, and so does Park (1799), who traveled in the Senegambian region toward the close of the century. It appears that, in the Gambian region at least, the use of cloth-money by the Wolof arose in the early part of, and continued through most of, the nineteenth century.

The Wolof, who traded first with the Portuguese, then with the British, Dutch and French, observed the European technique of evaluating goods with some commodity used as a standard, and later they saw European currency itself in use. In the Gambia, as in other parts of the West Coast of Africa, trade with the Europeans resulted in the use of a common standard of value—usually a trade good—wherever the indigenous population did not already have one of its own. One such standard widely used during the days of the slave trade in the Senegambian region and along the entire Windward Coast, was the "Iron Bar", a standard of value in which other goods were expressed. The trade became known as "the bar trade," and when Moore was in the Gambia he noted that a bar was equivalent to one pound of fringe, two pounds of gunpowder, one ounce of silver, or a hundred gunflints (Wyndham 1935 : 67). The price of trade goods stated in bars varied from one place to another, and some bars were worth more than others. Nevertheless, iron bars functioned adequately as a standard of value. Iron bars, as well as European cloth, gold dust, copper bars, and cowrie shells, were used in various parts of the coast, and as Wyndham (1935 : 70) says:

Whatever the measure of value was, whether bars, rounds, pieces, or any others, the prices of all the goods to be traded had to be reduced to one or more of them before trading could open.

Though a standard of value such as the "bar" served well during the eighteenth century, it apparently could not meet such varied needs as did cloth-money some years later among the Wolof. Cloth is obviously superior in that it could be used to purchase relatively inexpensive articles as well as expensive ones, it was more divisible and portable, and it was locally produced. It was therefore able to play an important role in non-European trade. Cloth-money seems to have been used along with European currency in trade in the early part of the nineteenth century. The large-scale use of European specie was introduced by migrant laborers, so-called "strange farmers," who came from French territory and lived as tenants within the compounds of the Gambian farmers. Gamble (1949 : 59) referring to the *Annual Report of 1853,* notes that:

One of the early results of the influx of strangers into the Gambia was the change in the medium of exchange. Most of the strange farmers came from territory in the French sphere of influence and for various reasons wanted cash. The French merchants apparently realized this earlier than the English and captured a good deal of the trade. The coin commonly in circulation was the five franc piece, known as the dollar, which was recognized as legal tender in 1843 and remained so until 1922. The demand for cash compelled British traders to import specie; this led to a decrease in the importation of duty paying goods and a considerable loss of revenue.

Moreover, the emergence of peanuts as an important cash crop export, from about 1835 on, made it easier for the farmer to obtain European specie to purchase trade goods. Thus, by the first half of the nineteenth century the Wolof of the Gambia region as well as neighboring ethnic groups had become acquainted with European currency.

Many Wolof became traders and undoubtedly thus learned a great deal about money. A statement made in 1842 before the Select Committee on West Coast of Africa (Paragraphs 8008, 8009, 8011) reveals that Wolof operating out of the European trading center of Bathurst ranged up and down the rivers of the Senegambia in small trading vessels and canoes, selling European goods. Many of the up-country Wolof, in turn, acted as middle men in trade with people living farther in the interior. The Wolof traders may well have been primary agents of "financial" acculturation.

Though the Wolof probably acquired the idea of a stable standard of value and money-token from trade with the Europeans, they used cloth rather than European coin as their medium of exchange. European currency was not plentiful even by the middle of the nineteenth century, and thus it is likely that cloth, relatively plentiful and well suited to serve as money, was substituted for European coin by the bush people. According to elderly Wolof informants, European specie was still scarce in the latter part of the nineteenth century, especially during the native wars before the British were effectively administering the protectorate, and much more time was devoted then to the cultivation of cereal crops than to the cash crop of peanuts. The amount of cash available was also reduced by the common practices of melting gold and silver coin to make jewelry (Mollien 1820 : 60) and of adorning the hair with coins. Locally woven cloth, then, was far more plentiful than European specie, though scarce enough for a small quantity to have a substantial value.

It appears that the use of cloth-money among the Wolof was a derivative invention. Similar innovations in other nonliterate societies are generally accounted for by contact with European traders and their money system. Herskovits (1952 : 215) suggests that the use of commodities as money (money-barter) in nonliterate cultures indicates an economic system in transition, and says that this change, in economic spheres which previously did not use money, was most often brought about by trade with Europeans. The Wolof development seems to follow this pattern, though it is different in some respects, i.e., many transitional commodity money uses were based on a European commodity as the standard of value.[5] The Wolof development is atypical in that the standard of value was an item of native manufacture, although the process was basically the same as that in commodity money used elsewhere. In another respect, the Wolof were clearly unusual: they used cloth-money extensively in trade among themselves and with inland tribes. In this they were unlike the Chukchee and other peoples who normally used no money at all for these internal transactions and used commodity money only when they were dealing with European traders.

CONTEMPORARY EXCHANGE PRACTICES AMONG THE RURAL WOLOF

Contemporary exchanges of the rural Gambian Wolof can be classed as follows: (1) Marketless transactions, effected outside the market place and the large European or Syrian-owned store; (2) exchange in the stores and market place of the wharf town or inland trading

(5) The iron bar appears to have preceded the use of cloth-money among the Wolof, but there is scant information on use in native transactions. Moore (1738 : 32) speaks of cattle and iron bars being used in bridewealth payments along the River Gambia. European trade salt may have served earlier as a sort of standard of value, since it was a popular commodity in the West African trade in the seventeenth century (Jobson 1932 : 108).

center; (3) transactions effected in noneconomic life—in the *rites de passage,* exchange between Wolof castes, and a variety of non-ceremonial gift exchange.

MARKETLESS EXCHANGE

(a) *Money purchases and moneyless transactions within the community and between adjoining communities.* Much of the year-round economic exchanges of the Wolof take place within the hamlet. Money purchases outnumber barter; however, when people do not have enough money to buy something they often make up the amount with grain, goats or cloth. Moreover, as money becomes scarce in the months preceding the trade season, money purchases are fewer and goods are most often purchased on credit, by barter, or by the sale of some commodity for cash. Gamble (1949 : 106), writing about the Wolof of N'jau in Upper Saloum in 1946–48, writes:

> During the rainy season from June to the end of August, the cash income was low and averaged only 14/– per man, coming mainly from the sale of goats, sheep, and native cloths.

I kept records of the daily expenditures of several married men and women in the hamlet of N'jau, and they indicate that small amounts of food (curdled milk, sugar, biscuits, vegetables, etc.) and kola nuts are purchased or bartered almost daily in dealings with neighbors or with local petty traders during the several months after the harvest when money is plentiful. And too, many items, especially kola nuts, are circulated as gifts. Though the vast majority of the Wolof exchanges are petty ones of this type, their value is probably no more than 15 percent of the total annual expenditures of the Wolof (Gamble 1949 : 104). The following is a typical record of the daily exchanges of a married woman, which I recorded during the trade season:

DECEMBER

15 – Went to a neighboring Fula village and bartered 4 cigarette tin cups of grain for a calabash of milk. Received a gift of a kola nut from a friend of her husband.
16 – Bought 2d of kola nuts from a petty trader. Gave a neighbor some peppers from her garden.
17 – Bought 3d of kola nuts. Gave tomatoes to two neighbor women.
18 – Bought 6d of curdled milk, 10d package of sugar, and 6d of palm oil.
19 – Received a gift of 1 kola nut from her husband's father.

20 – Received a gift of 2 handfuls of rice and 1 bottle of milk from her sister living in a neighboring hamlet.

21 – Bought 2 cups of groundnut oil for 1s and 1 package of sugar for 10d. Gave some peppers to a neighbor woman.

22 – Bought 2d of sugar. Received a gift of 3 kola nuts from one friend and 1 kola nut from another friend.

23 – Received a gift of 1 kola nut from one of the Chief's wives. Gave some cassava to a neighbor. Received some sweet potatoes from her husband's brother.

24 – Bought 10d of sugar. Received a gift of 3 kola nuts from her husband's mother.

25 – Went to a neighboring Fula village to barter 4 cigarette tins of grain for some curdled milk. Sold 2 cigarette tins of tomatoes for 6d. Gave a cigarette tin of peppers to a Fula woman friend. Received a gift of 1 kola nut from her husband's mother.

26 – Sold 2 cigarette tin cups of tomatoes for 6d and received an unspecified number of kola nuts from the Chief for helping to winnow his groundnuts.

27 – Bought 6d of palm oil. Gave 2 cigarette tin cups of rice to a lady visitor. She explained that it is Wolof custom to give rice to visitors.

28 – Bought 4d of kola nuts with money earned from the sale of tomatoes. Received a gift of 1 kola nut from friend of her husband.

29 – Received 3 shillings from the Chief for winnowing his groundnuts. Bought 6d of palm oil and 10d of sugar. Bartered grain for curdled milk. Sold 3d of tomatoes. Received a gift of some milk from a Fula shepherd and some kola nuts from her husband's paternal uncle.

30 – Bought an unspecified number of kola nuts.

31 – No exchange.

JANUARY

1 – Bought 6d of kola nuts and 10d of sugar.

2 – Bought 3d of kola nuts and 9d of bread baked by my cook. Bartered grain for curdled milk. Gave tomatoes to a friend. Received a kola nut from her husband.

3 – No exchange.

4 – Bartered grain for curdled milk.

5 – Attended a naming ceremony and gave the parents 1 s. and a calabash of grain, and after the ceremony she received some kola nuts from the hosts.

6 – Bought 3 cigarette tin cups of palm oil for 1s 6d. Bartered 3 tins of grain for 3 tins of milk.

The record above indicates that the Wolof have a kind of symbiotic relationship with the Fulani cattle-herding people, as exemplified by the regular exchange of grain for curdled milk. I have also recorded instances of the Wolof using money to purchase goats, beef, large grain storage baskets, and even magical charms and amulets from the Fulani.[6] During the dry season, Fulani shepherds bring their cattle down from Senegal to the Gambia River to water and pasture them. Wolof often house the Fulani in their compounds, and in return receive milk, and manure for their fields.

Some Fulani have settled in Wolof hamlets or founded hamlets of their own in Wolof territory, where they farm as well as tend their cattle. Some of the smaller Fulani hamlets are dependent on the larger Wolof communities for many things. A Fula, living in a hamlet consisting of only three compounds, remarked that if they want anything, they ask the Wolof for it and they usually get it, and vice versa:

When we visit the Wolof, they offer us kola nuts or snuff, and during the rains when we have no money to buy tobacco, some Wolof loan us money until the harvest. We don't have our own potters and leather workers, so we go to the Wolof. We Fulani have our own craftsmen, but this hamlet is too small to have any.

Anyone who has the money to buy a few items, e.g., a tin of cigarettes or a bag of kola nuts, can become a petty trader. Men are more often petty traders than women, perhaps because they usually have more money at their disposal. In the Saloum communities with which I was familiar, I observed that only the members of the slave-descent or blacksmith castes were petty traders. The freeborn worked for European trade establishments as truck drivers and the like, which they evidently considered to be work of greater prestige. The petty traders kept their goods in a locked box in their own huts, where their customers came to buy from them. Their merchandise ranged in variety (and quantity) from a tin of cigarettes or a few packages of sugar, to a larger variety of items including kola nuts, tobacco, matches, biscuits, peppermints, and soap. During the height of the trade season, some of them stocked other items such as women's head-ties and perfume. Some traded the year round, others only during the trade season when money was plentiful. A petty trader in a hamlet in Upper Saloum was also a money lender, and most of the adult men in the community were indebted to him at one time or the other. In a list of debts kept by this trader, loans ranged from 10s. to £6, the typical loan being about £3.

There was another type of trader in the Wolof hamlet, who might

(6) Wolof buy a type of medicine placed in a ram's horn called χar from the Fula. It is said to insure a big crop of sorghum or millet. The Fula medicine man asks his customer how much grain he wants and if the medicine brings the desired results, the customer is expected to give the Fula several handfuls of grain. In any case, he pays him 6d as a sort of down payment.

be called a "petty" entrepreneur. He did not keep a small store in his hut as the petty trader did, but from time to time would purchase some item outside the community and resell it to his neighbors for a small profit. For example, a young man obtained some little bottles of alcohol in Senegal which he sold to his Moslem neighbors as "medicine good for stomach trouble."

The biggest entrepreneur of all was the district chief. He speculated in grain, purchasing it when it was cheap and plentiful just after the harvest and holding it until the rains, when it sold for twice as much. However, the chief's large polygynous family and retainers of slave descent undoubtedly consumed a large portion of this grain. In addition, more grain was consumed in the ceremonies sponsored by him or a member of his family. Everyone in the district knew he could get ready cash from the chief in exchange for grain, and that he frowned upon their selling it to anyone else. He also used his large herd of cattle to obtain grain, bartering meat and curdled milk for it. Several instances were also noted of men slaughtering, butchering, and selling their own livestock—beef or goats—during the trade season.

As noted in the record of daily exchanges above, women also sell small quantities of garden vegetables locally. The women in Lower Saloum often sold rice which they grew and polished themselves and, as we shall see below, women sometimes sold their surplus garden produce to professional women vendors in the wharf town market place.

Part-time household craft specialists—blacksmiths, weavers, and potters—and musicians and praisers, can usually be found in the large hamlets or within a short distance from most communities. A customer can go to the craftsmen's compounds and purchase some cloth, some cooking pots, or ask the blacksmith to make him a certain farming tool. Women potters sometimes hawk their pots from hamlet to hamlet. Members of a caste of musicians and praisers do not have to be sought out, they often attend ceremonies uninvited. All these specialists living in the rural hamlets cultivate some crops during the farming season, though the blacksmiths and musician-praisers do not have fields as large as the others.

(b) *Itinerant Peddlers.* Much of the intertribal trade is carried on by the traveling hawker outside of the market place. The *Pax Britannica,* improvement in transportation, the widespread use of money, a more equal distribution of income than in the days of the robber baron chiefs—all have encouraged intertribal trade. Like other forms of trade, peddling takes place during the "trade season," after the harvest in the late fall and winter.

Since the end of the native wars, Mauretanians from Kifa have come down to the Gambia to sell sheep during the trade season. I observed one of these sheep hawkers driving before him a flock of very thin sheep; he explained that the sheep were thin because they had been constantly on the move for over two months. The sheep were sold to the Wolof for £2, £2 4s., and £3 according to size and condition. Only a few wealthy Wolof could afford to buy them. Such Mauretanians are said to buy green tea and black cloth to take back with them and to change their remaining English currency into French notes.

The Laube woodworkers, a low caste of Futa Toro Fulbe, also come during the trade season to sell mortars and pestles, wooden bowls, dippers and other household utensils. Though they are not Wolof in origin, the rural Wolof of the Gambia have been traditionally their overlords (as of the Fulbe cattle herders in their districts), but the Wolof regard them suspiciously, holding that they are notorious robbers and thieves.

Hausa medicine vendors come to the Gambia region every year. I met two of them in the Upper Saloum district of the Gambia who said they were from "Sokoto near Abidjan." They were selling medicine against headaches, stomach trouble, snakebite, and for success in love and increase of progeny. They also had medicine in the form of powder to be mixed with seed before planting in order to ensure a big crop. They use hocus-pocus to attract customers. For example, an informant told me that a Hausa vendor once asked for sand which he placed in a bag with some of his powder medicine; he then put his hand in the bag again and withdrew a handful of grain.

Some Serahuli, who weave large grass mats for fences and the sides of huts, visited Upper Saloum early in March. Mats nine yards long by two yards wide were sold for 5s. 6d., and mats five yards by two were sold for 3s. 6d. Bambara are said to weave such mats, and they were also observed cutting grass and wood for sale to Wolof during the trade season. A few Jola families had settled, at least semi-permanently, by the riverbank palm groves to make and sell palm oil and palm wine. A few other ethnic groups, who vend their wares in the large trade towns, will be discussed separately below.

Low caste Wolof women potters peddle their pots in surrounding Wolof, Fulbe and Mandinko communities (Gamble 1955 : 53). During the dry season, December to May, urban Wolof women from Bathurst go up river to the grain areas to barter palm oil, dried fish, peppers, salt, kerosene, tinned tomato puree, onions, and kola nuts for rice or millet (Gamble 1957 : 36, 53).

EXCHANGE IN THE TRADE STORES
AND MARKET PLACE OF THE WHARF TOWN

The largest volume of purchase and sale done by the Wolof in the Saloum districts takes place in the wharf town trade centers where the typical Wolof family head (the largest consumer) spends at least half of his income. The principal center is the old town of Kaur, and firms there have small branch stores in some of the surrounding hamlets. Kaur has a number of economic functions: (1) it has many stores, large and small, the larger ones being branches of French, English and Syrian firms which have their Gambian headquarters in Bathurst; (2) its large stores purchase groundnuts from the Wolof farmers and usually transport them from his field to Kaur; (3) it is a transit station—groundnuts sold in the region are brought to Kaur from other trade centers and loaded on small steamships which transport them to Europe; (4) it is an important link of commerce with Senegal; (5) it is the site of a small but active "native" market.

(a) *The wharf town trade stores.* A large part of the cash income of the Wolof men, the chief producers of the peanut cash crop, is spent in the stores of the trade towns, as indicated in the following record I kept of the income and expenditure of a young married man with two wives and two children. The record was kept during the height of the trade season in late November, December and January 1950—51, when the Wolof farmers in the district sold their peanuts and spent most of their cash income in the trade stores, though some local purchases, especially of meat, were substantial.[7]

NOVEMBER

18 – Journeyed to Kaur to purchase 9 yds. of European cloth to make dresses for his wives, £1. 7s. Paid two tailors, 2s. each to make the dresses—he explained that they did not charge him much because they were his friends.

20 – Bought 4s. worth of goat meat from a neighbor.

21 – Journeyed to Kaur to buy soap 6d., a sifter 1s. 6d., and matches 3s. 6d.

27 – Journeyed to Kaur to buy a blanket 13s., underwear for himself 3s., coffee and bread 1s. 6d. Gave friends tea and bread 9d., and pious alms to an old woman 6d. Sold 1s. of tomatoes from his garden.

28 – Journeyed to a small trade center called Panchang in the chief's lorry and bought a fish at the wharf for 1s. 6d.

(7) Petty local expenditures less than 1 shilling have been omitted. My informant traveled out of town more frequently than the typical Wolof family head because he was a messenger for the chief, a job for which he received a small monthly salary.

DECEMBER

5 – Only small local expenditures were recorded.

6 – Bought a shirt and 2 eating bowls at a trade store in Panchang (no price recorded).

7 – Bought a chicken from a neighbor 2s., palm oil from a petty trader 1s. Sold 1s. of sweet potatoes. (Note: he borrowed 4s. from my cook, promising to repay him when he sold his peanuts. All of his money from last year's harvest is gone, likewise his monthly badge messenger salary of £1.)

12 – While in Panchang arranging for a trader to send a lorry to his field for his groundnuts, he purchased the following on credit from the trader: 2 head-ties for his wives 10s.; 3 yds of cloth 10s. 6d.; a hat for himself 6s. 6d. Paid a tailor 1s. for making trousers from cloth.

13 – Sold 2^1/$_2$ bags of groundnuts for £5 7s. 6d.

14 – Trader's lorry picked up 2^1/$_2$ bags of his ground nuts which he sold to the trader for £4 6s. 1d. Paid the trader 3s. for transporting his groundnuts.

15 – Took his tenant farmer, who doesn't understand English money, to Kaur to buy cloth and shoes. While there he bought 3 yards of cloth 7s. 6d. and cloth for two ankle-length skirts for his wives for 17s. He also bought a large cat fish for 2s. 6d. and 1s. of palm oil. Gave a member of the gewel caste 2s. for praising him.

18 – Took two bags of groundnuts to Panchang and received £3 2s. with which he paid £2 6s. for rice supplied by the government and an additional 12s. 6d. for 2 bags of rice, his share of rice purchased by the village as a whole. He also bought 1 hen in a neighboring Fula hamlet for 2s. 6d.

19 – Went to Panchang to see a leather worker who was making an amulet for him. While there bought 1s. of fried meat, 1s. 6d. of biscuits and 1s. 4d. of sugar.

20 – Sold 2 bags of groundnuts in Panchang for £3 3s. 6d. He paid 1s. 6d. for transporting the nuts. He purchased a machete for 3s. 6d., and 2 loaves of bread for 1s.

JANUARY

1 – Went to Kaur and bought 2 yards of cloth for 8s. and paid the tailor 1s. Bought 8s. of grain in neighboring Wolof hamlet.

4 – Killed one of his goats and sold different cuts of it to his neighbors for 28s.

5 – Sold 1 bag of groundnuts in Kaur for £1 10s. Bought 2s. of butter fat and 1 bag of salt for 1s. 9d.

8 – Traveled to an up river trade town on messenger business and while there purchased a robe for himself for £1 5s. 6d., and European cloth and an African country cloth for his second wife for £2 6s.

10 – Gave a gewel who praised him 1s.

12 – Paid a Mauretanian £2 for a ram.

24 – Purchased 1 bundle of grass for 1s. 9d.

Comparative figures on the incomes and expenditures of both the Wolof and the Fula residing in the hamlet of Njau from 1946 to 1948 give some indication of the preference patterns underlying the consumption habits of the Wolof (Gamble 1949 : 106). The average cash income from groundnuts (£17.10.0) is practically the same for Fula and Wolof, but there are considerable differences in the way the money is spent.

TABLE 4

Expenditure of Wolof and Fula

	Fula 1947–48	Wolof 1946–47	Wolof 1947–48
Clothing	17 %	40 %	40 %
Cotton and yarn	11	—	—
Livestock	40	3.5	4
Marriage[a]	13.5	20	15
Debts	5	2.5	7
Tax	2	3	2
Sanke, etc.	2.5	2.5	6

(a) Marriage payments are less in the case of the Fula. The average marriage money is £8.10.0. contrasted with £14 with the Wolof.

Among the Wolof, apart from the subsistence function of cloth, clothing as a symbol of social status and religious respectability is very important.

During the trade season, the larger trade stores had one or more tailors on their premises working with Singer sewing machines. In addition to its chief commodity, cloth, the typical trade store offers the following goods for sale: cigarettes, tobacco, snuff, matches, headties, perfume, knives, iron cooking pots, charcoal braziers and other cooking implements, hurricane lamps, kerosene, rope, "power" pills, mentholatum and other patent medicines, blankets, flashlights and batteries, mosquito nets, canned milk, rice, grain, candy, sugar, biscuits, groundnut oil, canned sardines and beef, kola nuts, needles, thread, beads, sun helmets, sun glasses, sandals, tennis shoes, stocking caps, fezzes, men's underwear, and bicycles.

By March, the shelves in the stores were almost bare and most households had spent their money. Even in Njau, where the Wolof are more prosperous, sales in the branch store had dropped off markedly by March because of the dearth of money. By the time the rains came in late May or early June, many of the stores in Kaur had shut down. It was said that some of the traders left during the rains and did not return until shortly before the beginning of the trade season because they wanted to avoid lending money or selling food and clothing on credit.

There is an annual shortage of food as well as money during the rains, particularly in Lower Saloum.[8] The elder compound heads seek food, cloth, mosquito netting and cash from their wharf town trader friends in July and August, repayable with interest after the fall harvest. The young married men with fewer dependents than the compound heads more often borrowed cash than food. The French and English firms were not supposed to extend credit, though some of their agents did. In any event, the Syrian traders appeared to do most of the lending. The chief of the district of Upper Saloum also made loans of cash at the interest rate of 25 percent, which was comparable to the usual interest rate of the Syrian traders, though some asked 30 percent and, it was said, even 100 percent interest. However, it should be stressed that interest rates are for varying periods of time, generally less than a year. Many of the Syrian traders continued an old practice in using African country cloths as pawns or security on their loans. Wolof petty traders loaned smaller amounts of money at higher interest rates; as one informant put it, "The good ones make you pay back half again as much and the bad ones twice as much." If a trader does not have grain to sell on credit, he often lends a farmer cash to purchase it somewhere else.

Food is obtained on credit at high pre-harvest prices, which in many cases amounts to 100 percent interest. For example, Wolof informants state that they had to pay back two bags of grain for every bag obtained on credit. Gamble (1955 : 78) gives a similar example from Mandinko life which could describe the Wolof as well:

At harvest time rice is sold at 2d. a cigarette tin, but in the rains the price rises to 3½ d. The repayment of debts after the sale of groundnuts makes a considerable inroad into the average income; this leaves the people short of money; and the vicious circle is ready to be repeated.

A Wolof asking for credit had to be known as a groundnut farmer and he had to agree to sell his crop to the trader, though in actual practice the farmer sometimes did not live up to his end of the bar-

(8) Apparently this is an old pattern. A very old Wolof informant stated, "In the old days, our fathers insisted that we work very hard in the fields because we often ran out of food. In the years when we did not have enough food, the villagers would go up into Senegal, usually to Kaolak, to buy food. They took all of their possessions with them to exchange for food and they took their donkeys with them to carry back the food. If there was no food in Kaolak, they would go farther into Senegal. Sometimes the village would send several young men to Bathurst to buy food for them and would charter a boat to bring the food back. When they arrived there was great rejoicing." Even the young people today know certain edible wild plants and roots which they say the "old people" ate when there were food shortages.

gain. Anxious applicants for a loan of money were said to bathe in a magical solution with a piece of silver in it before visiting the trader so as to insure their success. The Wolof generally have the reputation for paying their debts, and traders often solicited their business by offering them credit. For example, Wolof customers were told they could expect a loan of food in the coming year. Traders drum up trade by hiring as their agents respected and well-liked persons who are "difficult to refuse"; especially those with many kinfolk. These agents, called *mɛt lango,* ingratiate themselves with potential customers by giving out kola nuts and other gifts supplied by the trader, and during the rains, the agents often arrange for the farmers to receive loans of cash, food and mosquito nets with the understanding that they must sell their groundnuts after the harvest to the employer of the *mɛt lango.*

Wolof farmers feel angry and impotent about their economic position. They complain about the price of groundnuts, which is fixed each year by the West African Produce Control Board, and they believe that the prices of trade goods are too high. They say that traders cheat them at the groundnut weighing scales and they feel frustrated because they have no way of checking the scales. A young married Wolof said typically:

The traders make us mad because we work so hard growing groundnuts and they rob us with their bad scales, and they do not call out the weight; just give you the money fast and you do not know whether or not it is the correct amount.

Another young man listening in on this conversation added,

Last year I was so sure that I would be cheated when I stood in front of their scales that I did not even go over to see my groundnuts being weighed.[9]

Again, an old Wolof man complained bitterly,

Before the holy wars we had plenty of grain. But now the Europeans get all the benefit of our labor. A farmer works hard clearing bush, planting, weeding, harvesting, and sells the fruit of his labor to the Europeans at a price he has no control over, and then he is cheated by the trader who weighs his groundnuts and sells him goods in his store. After a man buys a few things, he finds he has nothing left!

A kind of economic pragmatism of the people of the Gambia has had its impact on the economy of the region. The political boundary between the Gambia and the surrounding French territory is not an economic or social barrier to the Wolof. In making economic de-

(9) Gamble (1955 : 58–59) found that cheating by the traders was also a favorite topic of conversation among the Mandinko, and he gives considerable evidence based on his own observations to support their allegations.

cisions, their actions are based on a comparison of British and French conditions: the price of groundnuts; the price and quality of goods in the trade stores; the fertility of the soil; and opportunities for wage labor.

All these factors help explain the annual migrant farmer invasion of the Gambia by people from the surrounding French and Portuguese territories, and some of these "strange farmers," as they are called in the Gambia, work as stevedores in Kaur or some other groundnut transit center. A large minority of the migrant farmers are Gambians who, during the agricultural season, move to areas where the soil is both fertile and available. Wolof and Fula communities receive a larger proportion of the "strange farmers" than Mandinka communities (Gamble 1949 : 74), not only because the land is more readily available and fertile in their districts but because many of the "strange farmers" belong to the same ethnic group. In 1946 and presumably in subsequent years, they made up more than one-fifth of the adult male farm labor in Wolof and Fula hamlets. Their Gambian Wolof hosts provide land to farm, housing and food in exchange for two or three days' labor each week on his fields. Other features of the transaction vary: if the wife of their landlord has cooked for them, they may give her a gift before leaving; others give their landlords a portion of their crops.

French money is common and as acceptable as British money because of the frequent commercial intercourse between the Gambia and Senegal. Strange farmers and resident Gambian Wolof alike compare values in British and French trade stores with an experienced eye.

The Wolof have a fairly sophisticated understanding of many of the economic problems which confront them. I remember being surprised when the elders of a hamlet did not seem gladdened by the news that groundnut prices had been raised over those of the year before. Treating me like an ignorant child, they patiently explained that groundnut prices had gone up in the past but that prices of goods in the stores had gone up too, and that they expected this to happen again. One elderly informant stressed that their money could buy much more in the old days when groundnut prices were much lower. Another said:

> Money is more plentiful today, but it is useless because trade goods are so dear.

Still another showed that he understood the economic advantage of the producer processing his own raw materials when he stated, rather bitterly:

I think we like groundnuts better than you white men, but we must sell them to you to get money. We use them in our food and use groundnut oil to cook with. Now we sell our groundnuts to the white man and buy it back again in the form of oil.

(b) *The Kaur Marketplace.* The market place plays a subsidiary role in the economic life of the Wolof in the Saloum districts, though the market place at Kaur is one of the most active in the Protectorate. The Administration has built several additional ones on the north bank of the Gambia, and they have generally been more successful in the Wolof than in the Mandinka districts. As noted above, Kaur has a long history as a center of trade. The origin of the market place, however, is obscure. All my elderly informants felt certain that it was a fairly recent innovation, established long after the arrival of the European trader. Some informants can remember a small market place before the present one, consisting of several crudely constructed huts made of guinea corn stalks. One said that a Wolof district chief was responsible for its construction early in this century. Before then, apparently, exchange took the same form as does marketless exchange now. As an elderly informant remembers it:

There were no markets in the old days. People went about from compound to compound asking for what they wanted. Women stayed in the compound to sell their vegetables. There was no peddling of milk in the streets (it was scarce too); a person had to go to the compound of a cattle owner.

The Kaur market place is located in a small square adjacent to several trade stores, but farther inland from the river than most of them. It consists of two raised concrete platforms, with open sides and tin roofs, and includes a small screened-in room for the sale of meat. Women generally sold in one of the structures and men in the other, though there were a few men such as leather workers in a separate section of the women's building.

The Kaur market is particularly active on Saturday and Monday and, of course, during the trade season. During the rains, most of the market vendors, male and female, left altogether to work on their fields, though some, like the leather workers, had smaller fields which they cultivated for a while in the morning, returning to trading in the afternoon.

The social organization of this small market is not very complex compared to the large markets of the Guinea Coast. Several women vendors stated that there used to be more women than men selling in the market. Now the situation is reversed, but only for the trade season. The women sell agricultural produce: tomatoes, okra, peppers, limes, rice, cassava, dried fish, fermented locust beans, sweet potatoes, roasted groundnuts, small onions, beans, groundnut oil, coconuts, homemade ginger beer, and native salt. Many of their customers live and work in Kaur, often just for the trade season. Most Wolof women living in the rural hamlets have their own gardens and can purchase locally what they do not have. Very few of the market women grow their own produce. They buy their produce from women from the surrounding countryside who sell what they have and return home, or else they purchase it from Senegal or Bathurst. Sometimes the rural women sell their own produce in the market at lower prices, but usually the regular market women buy everything these women have. I was told by several of the women vendors that the eldest woman among them was their head, but this seems to be leadership only in the sense that the Wolof generally act with deference towards the senior member of any group. The eldest woman conceded that she was the "head" of the women vendors but stated that she had little control over them and that there was no formal organization or meetings. She said she could do nothing if a woman raised or lowered the price of her produce. Nevertheless, all the women keep their prices uniform by watching each other. There is no price cutting among the regular market women; they understand that it is not in their interest. I observed little haggling in the market except occasionally over the most expensive items. In the Bathurst market, there is reputedly an older woman to whom the younger women go for advice and with whom they meet to fix their prices. Comparing Bathurst with Kaur, one veteran woman vendor said:

We cannot have such an organization here because we are from different places and are not related in any way.

The men sell small items, most of which they buy from European stores, such as cigarettes, kola nuts, oranges, bread, dye, European thread, peppermints, aspirin, soap, onions, perfume, and native cloth. Some exchange French money for English. A man from French territory sold shells stuffed with herbs made by Serer medicine men for the prevention of snake bite and stomach pain. He also sold native thread spun by Mandinko women, and *mir* nuts to prevent dizziness, as well as different types of metal bracelets, and strings of glass beads or cloves which Wolof women wear around their waists. During the trade season, one man ran a miniature tea shop. He provided customers with table and stool and sold them bread and tea. Two men regularly slaughtered and butchered cattle to sell. Coastal Lebu and Serer came up the river in their canoes during the trade season to sell dried ocean fish and native salt, and fresh fish caught nearby in the river. Some were said to trade their fish and salt for grain as they did in the old days.

The leather workers were the only craft specialists who were observed regularly working and selling in the market place. They made men's leather slippers with pointed toes in the Muslim style, and women's sandals of brightly colored plastic; they covered amulets with leather or plastic, and placed leather trimmings on sun hats, fly whisks, etc. The Kaur leather workers are more formally organized than the other vendors in the market, perhaps to the extent that they can be said to have a craft guild in nascent form. The eldest member of any group of leather workers is the leader. He calls them together and suggests a program of action, subject to their approval. If one of the workers has a naming ceremony, he asks them to subscribe a small gift of money which he accepts in the name of the whole group. The groups are not necessarily made up of kin, but as the leader of the Kaur leather workers stated, "We are friends who work together, and thus we are related." The elders calls them together when others matters of common interest arise, such as a new Government trade regulation, or a member needs financial assistance to pay a heavy court fine.

There is no control of prices "because the work of the members of the group varies in quality and thus each person can ask different prices." There is no attempt to control the quality of goods: "this is something that nothing can be done about because the group varies in the extent of their learning and skill."

Leathers workers start teaching their sons the trade when the boys are ten or twelve years old. The boy is expected to take the money received from the first sale and buy kola nuts with it to give to his fellow workers as *sedaχ* (pious alms). It is believed that such an act will insure his success. He is also expected to give his earnings to his parents until he is married, except for the money he is allowed to keep for his personal expenses. The father instructs the son, who sits and works next to his father's market stall. If the boy's father dies, his maternal uncle teaches him.

CHANGING IDEAS CONCERNING MONEY AND TRADE

The gradual shift from subsistence economy to a mixed cash and subsistence economy and the widespread use of money has been reflected in a change in certain values and social patterns in Wolof culture. The process is cumulative: the new exists along with the old, sometimes in conflict. Money has now been added to the traditional indices of wealth, such as wives, slaves, cloth, livestock and grain. Muslim religious leaders and pious elders allege that the young people today are interested only in money, trade, and material possessions. Sons are said nowadays neither to need to work for their fathers nor to respect them because of the economic independence derived from new opportunities to earn money outside the hamlet. One commonly hears elders say something like:

> When we were young, things were done differently. Young men were not so lazy; they worked more for their fathers; they never missed any of the five daily prayers or broke the fast and they went regulary to the mosque on Friday; and they were more respectful to their elders and always obeyed them.

Though this is undoubtedly an idealized picture, there is some truth in the remarks. Observation of Wolof youth, however, indicates that there has been less change than the elders think—i.e., the infractions of tradition are not sufficient to justify saying that the Wolof have changed today from a sacred to a secular orientation. Though money is highly regarded today among young and old Wolof alike, they are all repelled by the acquisitive and avaricious orientation of the European. A young married Wolof, after asking me why the white man was so eager to acquire money, stated philosophically:

> God loves the truth,
> the white man money,
> and the African grain.

In the same vein, an old man remarked:

> If a person has a lot of money, it is like *setane,* because he always thinks about it.

The accumulation of large amounts of money *per se* is not highly regarded for the most part and, in any case, few acquire much of it. Money is generally desired only as a means to satisfy certain recognized needs. Wolof men uniformly stated that they grew groundnuts to purchase the following: food when their granaries were empty, clothing, money to pay the bridewealth and other marriage ceremonial expenses. Some added that they needed cash to pay for the hut tax, cattle, kola nuts, cigarettes, soap and other commodities. Bridewealth is now stated and paid chiefly in English currency. Plural marriages are desired by the Wolof men because they are thought to be productive of more children. In a society with a weakly developed technology, children were viewed as a major economic asset because of their labor potential.[10] A Wolof family head views children as a kind of insurance for his old age.

The money which married women earn by cultivating a small field of groundnuts or selling rice from their fields is deemed theirs to

(10) The economic significance of plural marriage is discussed at length in Ames, 1955 b.

use as they see fit. They use it chiefly to purchase items which their husbands often fail to supply in adequate amounts: food, clothing, jewelry, etc., and money to pay for some of their daughters' wedding expenses.

The extent to which money is used in present day exchanges and the extent to which it is in short supply is reflected in a large number of magico-religious practices designed to obtain money. Magical drawings of Islamic origin are made into amulets which are supposed to make one wealthy. There are charms to enable a person to become a trader, or if already a trader, to become rich. Wolof pray for money over the graves of their ancestors or of one of the famous holy men on Friday after attending the mosque. Kola nuts are left on the grave as *sedaχ* (pious alms), which is perhaps a reinterpretation of a pagan practice of leaving an offering to an ancestral spirit. It is also believed that a woman who works hard for her husband and pleases him in every way will have children who will grow up to be rich and respected in the community. This is referred to as "mother's luck" and is generally associated in the minds of the people with the "good" wifely behavior which insures that she will go to heaven.

Wolof pride themselves in their generosity; a penurious person is looked down upon and ridiculed. Prestige is derived from conspicuous consumption; for example, lavish gift-giving in the *rites de passage* and other situations, most commonly in intercaste exchanges.[11] The lowliest caste in Wolof society, the *gewel*, are professional minstrels and praisers who are usually wealthier than the members of higher caste groups, who often pay extravagantly for their services. Persons who refuse to give them gifts are publicly shamed by the *gewel* for their penuriousness, and it is fear of this as much as the prestige gained from paying and being praised by them that accounts for their being so well paid. Gifts of money and goods between other castes generally serve the same prestige function, as well as validating the caste position of the giver. An old man referred to the pride and generosity of the Wolof thus:

If the Wolof were animals, they would be the king of the beasts, the lion. They are very proud and thus very generous. They will give all of their money away over night!

Along with this prestigious consumption, however, the possession

(11) Wolof society has a rigid caste hierarchy. Membership in each stratum is inherited through the paternal line, and those who belong to the various castes are prohibited from marrying outside their own level. From high to low, these groupings are the *jambur* (persons of freeborn descent); the *jam* (descendants of slaves of *jambur);* the *tega* (black-smiths) and *ude* (leatherworkers) who can marry the *tega;* the *gewel* (minstrels) and lastly the *jam* of the *gewel.*

of wealth is increasingly a means for achieving power and status. The
white man is a symbol of wealth and power, and it is said if a Wolof is
called *tubop* (white man), it is because he is wealthy and someone is
trying to get something from him. An old man stated in a typically
disapproving manner:

Wealth is the cure for everything now; if you have wealth, you can
get anything.

A group of young men similarly said:

Money is the key to the world now, for example, people do errands for
you because of your wealth, they come to your house and tell you stories,
and you can hire people to work for you.

In former times wealth was acquired and maintained by freeborn
and royalty through the labor of their slaves on their fields, and by
warfare; now persons of all castes use money to hire farm laborers,
and seek wealth, and the persons best situated to do this more often
than anyone else are the salaried workers for the administration and
the trading firms. The abolition of slavery, together with wealth
derived from groundnut cash crops and from new opportunities for
employment, have acted as a social leaven. Freeborn informants
agreed that they act respectfully towards a wealthy person of slave
descent. Young freeborn men said:

Sometimes we work for wealthy *jam* and we do not say that they are
just slaves in public, though we do not really think they are our equals.

CHAPTER 2

African Traders in Central Sierra Leone

BY VERNON R. DORJAHN

This study[1] centers on the African trader in central Sierra Leone and his relationship with the world economy, which he encounters in the form of Syrian[2]-owned commercial houses and the European firms.

Trade in that part of Sierra Leone under consideration here focuses on Magburaka, with its representatives of Syrian and European commercial houses, its Native Administration market and its direct road and rail links with Freetown, the port and capital. In the Magburaka market and throughout the distribution area of which this town is the center, trade is largely in the hands of Africans, predominantly Temne, though nearly a dozen other tribal groups are represented. With improved transportation and the growing demand manifest in the lively, thriving Magburaka market, some traders specialize in dried fish, tomatoes, and a few other commodities. The activities of these entrepreneurs will be examined at some length.

The village trader with his stall or small shop is the most important commercial feature in rural areas, for markets are limited to the towns and are probably not indigenous. Of special concern are the questions of price determination, credit patterns between traders and the commercial houses in Magburaka, and the trader as buyer of local produce and pawnbroker. On the village level the mechanics of economic exchange must be considered, because goods may be obtained for money, by barter and through gift-exchange. Barter equivalences are fairly standardized, though bargaining does occur on the retail level as well as in transactions between trader and "wholesaler."

For all practical purposes Sierra Leone has only one port, the capital city of Freetown[3], though Bonthe handles a small trade, Sulima exports piassava in some years and iron ore is shipped from Pepel. Containing more than 75,000 people, Freetown is by far the

(1) The field work was done in 1954–55 under a post-doctoral fellowship of the National Science Foundation, with supplementary aid from the Program of African Studies, Northwestern University.

(2) Most "Syrians" in Sierra Leone came from Lebanon though the name is a general label. For an account of Lebanese migrations to, and activities in, West Africa see Hanna 1958.

(3) For further information, see Jarrett 1954, 1955.

country's largest urban center. It is a cosmopolitan city with a population that is linguistically and culturally heterogeneous, reflecting its position as hub of the rail and road transportation nets of Sierra Leone. Goods are imported by a number of trading firms, European, Indian and "Syrian" owned, and trans-shipped by road or rail to branches of these firms and other dealers in the many smaller urban centers of both Colony and Protectorate. Here, in turn, the goods are retailed directly by these branch outlets or wholesaled to other traders, chiefly African and Syrian. Most of the latter carry on retail trade but also wholesale to itinerant peddlers and traders who maintain small shops or stalls in their own villages. Each upcountry urban area, supplied with some goods directly from Freetown and one or more other nearby distribution centers, thus serves in turn as a distribution center for its own hinterland, an amorphous grouping of villages that changes from time to time.

The Sierra Leone Government Railway runs from Freetown to Pendembu, 227½ miles to the east. From Bauya Junction, 64¼ miles from Freetown, a branch line runs to Makeni, 83¾ miles to the northeast. The railway is narrow gauge, 2 feet 6 inches, and operates at a loss. Much of the equipment is obsolescent though new diesel engines are being acquired. Passenger service especially is criticized by Sierra Leoneans as slow, unreliable and expensive; occasionally complaints of various kinds are made about the freight service. Nevertheless, the railway makes a major contribution to the economic life of the country.

Regular launch service, passenger and limited freight, is maintained from Freetown north to the Great and Little Scarcies Rivers, the estuary islands and Port Loko, and south to Bonthe and the Sherbro area. Privately owned launches ply the major rivers when the water level is high enough; canoes operate above the rapids in some cases. "Bullom boats" (locally built sailing craft) ferry passengers and foodstuffs from the Bullom shore to Freetown.

The road network is extented each year, yet all but about 150 miles are dirt surfaced and inadequate for the growing volume of traffic. The Road Transport Department operates buses in the Colony area and maintains a limited service to some nearby Protectorate urban centers. Most freight and passenger movement upcountry is handled by privately-owned lorries. Most of those operating out of Magburaka are owned by "Syrians" and driven by Africans. Rough roads, overloading, hard driving and poor maintenance result in high transport costs.

Two banks are active in Sierra Leone: Barclays Bank D.C.O. and the Bank of West Africa Ltd. Both offer limited services in a few

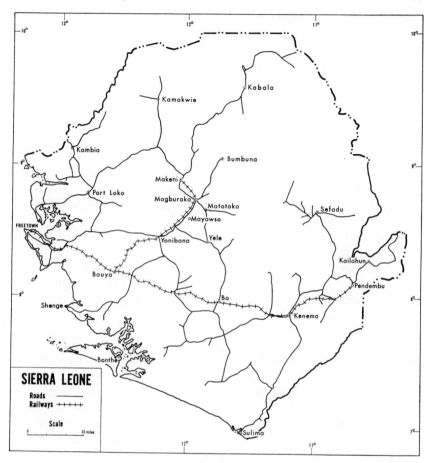

MAP 2

Sierra Leone

upcountry centers as well as Freetown. Currency is printed by the West African Currency Board in London. A Post Office Savings Bank provides savings account facilities wherever there is a post office. Few village traders, however, are aware that banking services exist, and these facilities are used by only a small number of Africans.

THE MARKET IN MAGBURAKA

Magburaka, a town of 5,000–10,000, served by the branch line of the railroad and by direct road links with Freetown, is an important distribution center. The United Africa Company Ltd., Paterson

Zochonis Co., Ltd., A. Genet Ltd., *Compagnie Française d'Afrique Occidentale* and *Société Commerciale de l'Ouest Africain* all have branch outlets here and nineteen Syrian traders have active shops, several rivaling the European firms in size of establishment and range of goods for sale. Generally the shops and stalls of the many African traders are smaller and less well stocked. In Magburaka, the European firms are essentially wholesale houses; the Syrians do some importing, sell wholesale to African traders and peddlers and at retail to the population of Magburaka and surrounding villages. The African traders are chiefly retailers having their own shops, selling in the Native Administration market or, less often, working as itinerant peddlers. To a lesser degree, some Magburaka peddlers supply goods "wholesale" to village traders, though the latter usually deal directly with the European or Syrian firms.

The market in Magburaka is controlled by the Native Administration. It is an open-sided, pan-roofed structure containing crude wooden benches and tables. Similar markets, also established by the government, are found nearby in Makeni, Matotoka, Yele and Yonibana; Temne refer to them as *romatila* ("place where they sell"), *japuwa* (a Mende word said to mean "farm where everyone buys") or usually, *makit,* a corruption of the English word. A Market Collector is in charge and collects ld. per day from each seller for each different commodity sold; an additional 6d. per basket of fish is charged. The Market Collector receives a salary from the Native Administration, and in some areas keeps whatever fees he collects above a certain set figure. The first sellers in the market building each morning select their own positions since there is no tenure or registeration of selling tables. Latecomers must sell seated on the ground outside of the structure, for there is insufficient space inside.[4] Most women sell two or three items though a few will stick to one.

Selling begins by 6:00 A.M. and 50 to 100 sellers are active throughout the morning. By 1:00 P.M. half this number remains; a comparative handful stays until 5:00 P.M. when the market virtually closes. There is no regulation of the hours or days the market is open; a few Christian traders do not sell on Sunday and most Muslims bypass Friday. Each seller determines his or her price. There is no agreement before the market opens on a standard price for any item. Temne traders regarded this suggestion as incomprehensible, saying that each must set his own price on the basis of what he paid for his goods and the profit margin he feels he must make. In order to get rid of odds and ends or to move goods rapidly, a seller will cut prices. There

(4) A new structure has since been erected (*Sierra Leone Trade, Industry and Travel* 1959 4 : 28).

is nothing other traders can do about this, and they reflect that on occasion they will do it themselves. In the course of a day, prices fluctuate somewhat but are generally stable. Nevertheless, price differences are such that customers shop around and haggle, often with moderate success. Traders consider it wise to keep prices down, sell for a small profit per item and try to increase the volume of sales. Their philosophy is aptly summarized in the oftenheard admonition: "Quick pennies are better than slow shillings." The lower the price, the earlier the trader sells out; and this is held to be desirable since it gets very warm in the market after midday. Then too, some sellers who live far from the market must get home in order to do farm work or prepare meals. Many are only part-time traders. One market regular stated that most business was transacted in the morning by people who return to the villages that same day.

The range of goods for sale in the Magburaka market is not large at any time. There is some fluctuation owing to seasonal shortages of perishable foodstuffs, but the following list from December is illustrative:

meat: beef, chickens	groundnuts
fish: tinned, dried, and on occasion, (relatively) fresh	cassava
	bananas and plaintains
bread: baked in Magburaka	palm oil: local produce
starch	and imported
matches	peppers: variety of red and green
sugar	tomatoes
salt	onions
tobacco: local produce	garden eggs
uncooked fou-fou	oranges
kola nuts	cigarettes
rice	kerosene

Most items, it will be seen, are produced in Sierra Leone if not in the Magburaka area; few imported goods are sold in the market. It is necessary, then, to consider local produce in terms of points of origin, transport and availability.

The tsetse fly and the virtual absence of good pasturage in the Magburaka area make the herding of cattle risky, if not impossible. Fortunately parts of Sierra Leone to the northeast and the Futa Jalon plateau of Guinée support pastoral Fula who find a ready market for beef in the urban centers of the rain forest. These Fula herdsmen drive small numbers of cattle from one town to another, selling one or two to be butchered locally. Lorry transport is rarely if ever used, though occasionally the railway is employed to ship cattle to Freetown. The one butcher in Magburaka was a Fula man who sold meat in the market. Beef prices per pound in 1954–55 were 2s. for "regular," 2/6 for liver, kidney and "fillet," the "choicer" cuts, 6d. for a "heap" of intestines, 12s. to 15s. for the head, depending on the size of the animal, and 10s. for the hide. While most hides were taken by shoemakers and sandalmakers, some sections were boiled and eaten by poorer people. Beef was purchased principally by the small European population, the Syrians, and wealthier Africans; few villagers could afford it. Little or no seasonal variation in supply or in price was evident.

Fish Sellers in Magburaka.

Most of the fish sold in the Magburaka market are caught along the Bullom shore, particularly that six mile strip between the villages of Mahera and Maiaia (Mayaia); a small amount also comes from Freetown, from Shenge[5] and from Tasso Island via Port Loko. From Port Loko and the Bullom shore, transport is used; from Shenge, water or road transport to the railway and thence to Magburaka; from Freetown fish are shipped by railway or lorry.

The fisherman of the Bullom shore include Bullom, Temne, Susu and a few Fula who work from canoes of various sizes with hook and line for larger fish and with seines and throwing nets for smaller species, particularly *bonga,* the most important kind of fish shipped upcountry. The relative abundance of any given fish varies from one part of the year to another, though at least on the Bullom shore some of the following are caught throughout the year: *krokos (krocoss),* snapper, *tenis, nguangua, bonga,* spanish barracuda, shark, and herring. Others less frequently taken are matchet-fish, whale, ladyfish, whiting, *kawaifu,* and *sak.* By far the largest portion of the trade is in dried *bonga* shipped upcountry.

Young men begin to fish when they are about eighteen years old since it is recognized that the profession demands both the intelligence and strength known to come only with maturity. A novice learns by hiring himself out as a paddler and observing the methods with which the nets are handled and the tide utilized, and by listening to the older fishermen swap stories. When confident of his own knowledge and skills, a man sets out independently. Initially, he may rent a large canoe and net at £3 per four- or five-day period, during which the owner sells the fish and holds the proceeds. At the end of the period, the owner divides evenly with the renter who may turn part of his share back to the owner if he is purchasing the boat. Canoes cost from £3 to £50, depending on the size; crew are hired at a flat wage per period.

(5) For an account of the *bonga* trade at Shenge and Bonthe, see Little 1951 : 281-8.

Upcountry traders usually deal with only one fisherman on the coast, for there is little opportunity to shop around and little purpose in doing so since all fishermen sell for about the same price. Purchasing is on a personal basis and a buying-relationship is set up between a given trader and a fisherman or fisherman's wife. When making nets, a fisherman is supported by his wives who also provide him with the necessary cordage; in return for this service the wives are given first priority to buy the *bonga* their husband brings in at 1/6 per dozen. After smoking them overnight, the wives sell the dried bonga at 2s. per dozen to the traders. Thus husband and wife receive separate incomes. Some traders buy fresh *bonga* directly from a fisherman, although such a practice creates doubts in the minds of the fisherman's wives if the trader is an attractive female. Conversely, some traders' husbands in Magburaka will not permit young and attractive wives to trade in fish, since they believe, with some justification, that such women will not be able to buy fish without granting favors to the fisherman.[6]

The smoke-curing of fish is done on the veranda of the fisherman's house or nearby in roofed, open-sided shelters. The *bonga* are placed on a platform of sticks and a fire is built beneath. An overnight smoking, 8 to 10 hours, ensures slight preservation only; traders who must travel far upcountry with large loads usually cure the fish for an additional seven days in the same manner. The fisherman's family permit the trader to use the same shelters, usually without charge, and for a nominal fee of 1s. may help tend the fires. The trader buys the wood and is responsible for his own food and lodging. It is more difficult to smoke-cure the larger fish, though *krokos* and snapper are dried and sold for £2.10.0 per dozen. The larger fish, however, keep longer when fresh and small amounts are taken upcountry a short distance and sold. To preserve them temporarily, the fishermen fillet, salt and dry them in the sun for several days; fish treated in this manner will last from a week to a month, depending on weather conditions.

On the beach, transactions between trader and fisherman are nearly always in cash, though some credit will be extended to old customers who are temporarily short of money. Such a situation might arise if a lorry overturned and the trader's load of fish spoiled; some fishermen would share such a loss. Some traders are permitted to take more baskets of fish than they can pay for after a particularly bountiful catch, though these extra baskets are credited at a higher price. A

(6) Upcountry Africans have a grudging admiration for the coastal fisherman, whose job they consider to be hazardous, but at the same time they characterize fishermen as "rough," "careless," "devil-may-care" and so on.

trader who fails to repay such an advance terminates the buying relationship. News of welchers spreads quickly among the fishermen and a defaulter is rather effectively "black-listed," thus finding it virtually impossible to buy fish anywhere along the Bullom shore until the debt is settled. Many traders bring rice and other consumer goods from upcountry but these must be sold for money since the fishermen refuse to barter.

At the Bullom shore, dried *bonga* cost £2 or more depending on the size of the basket used[7]; larger fish, such as barracuda, are cheaper by the basket since they cannot be packed so tightly as the smaller *bonga*. Transportation charges to Magburaka are 15s. per basket of fish and £1 per passenger. In Magburaka, the selling price varies from 3d. to 6d. per *bonga* (a reasonable markup considering the transport costs and the risk of spoilage). Assuming a 5d. selling price at Magburaka, a trader would have to sell at least two baskets to make any profit from one trip.

Whenever possible, traders will make definite arrangements with a particular lorry driver to eliminate costly delays in transport which take a toll in spoilage; a few wealthy traders charter lorries for their own use. Such prior arrangements for transport have drawbacks, for on occasion the trader will have to sell out stock hurriedly at a lower price to meet the transport schedule. The trader accompanies his dried *bonga* in transit whenever possible to guard against theft, for it is all too easy to slip a fish or two out of a basket. Those who send dried fish by way of the railway complain bitterly about theft of unattended goods.

Profits from the *bonga* trade depend not only on the markup but also on the volume. The elapsed time to travel and to obtain and dispose of a load of fish varies widely. The best a Magburaka trader can hope for is to leave home and travel to the Bullom shore the first day, procure the fish that night and early the following morning, return to Magburaka the second day and dispose of the *bonga* the third and fourth days. Thus, seven trips per month are possible if the schedule can be maintained consistently, but this assumes permanent standing arrangements with lorry drivers for transport and with fishermen and their wives for dried fish, no delays, and rapid sales in Magburaka. These are very unrealistic assumptions considering the rather frequent lorry breakdowns and other difficulties. In Magburaka it takes two to three days to sell out two baskets of *bonga,* even if one sells larger quantities to petty traders for resale rather than small quantities for home consumption. Overnight waits in Port

(7) The largest baskets used by Magburaka traders are 3 feet in diameter at the thickest part, and about 2 feet in height.

Loko, going or coming, are frequent, for lorries do not have a scheduled departure time, but leave whenever they are reasonably filled. Most Magburaka traders, as a result, spend seven or eight days per trip, which allows four trips a month. No generalizations can be made on the average number of baskets handled per trip, for this depends upon many factors: time of year, cash on hand, possible profit margin, demand upcountry, and so on.

Many women try *bonga* trading when they assemble sufficient finance, but the majority abandon it after a few trips and use the income to set themselves up in a less arduous, less aromatic, and more highly regarded profession. It is said that only those who have bounced over the "washboard" dirt roads, tended smoky fires in the wet season, and inhaled the variety of odors can properly appreciate the arduousness of the *bonga* trade. Then, too, a successful trader will sooner or later hear slurs on her character in the form of pointed remarks about what some women won't do to obtain fish when the catch is small. Those few who persist in the trade for some time make a lot of money[8], but the profession is not highly regarded and *bonga* traders have low status in the eyes of most Temne.

Vegetables and Produce Trade.

Some tomatoes are grown in the Magburaka area and brought in from surrounding villages as head loads, yet much of what is sold in the market is shipped in by lorry from the north and northeast, principally the towns of Kabala and Bumbuna. The tomatoes, usually the size of a golf ball, are in season from roughly December to April, a period in which traders from Kabala and Bumbuna sell in the Magburaka market. Prices in 1954–55 ranged from 8d. to 10d. for a one penny pan full (see table 5), or eight to twenty tomatoes for 1d., depending on availability. Bumbuna traders have the reputation of charging higher prices even though their costs are less. Transport charges are 11s. per box of tomatoes and 9s. per passenger from Kabala to Magburaka and 6s. per box and 5s. per passenger from Bumbuna, though purchase costs in Bumbuna are said to be greater. Tomatoes always sell out quickly in the Magburaka market since supplies are limited.

In some cases the trader is involved in both the *bonga* and tomato trades while the latter is in season. Baskets of *bonga* are taken for sale to Kabala, for example, and the proceeds are invested in tomatoes which are taken to Magburaka for sale. Rice, gari-dye or some other

(8) An official source states: "... it is generally accepted that the traders make excessive profits, ranging from 100 to 200 per cent." (Sierra Leone 1959 : 50). This estimate seems high with respect to the Magburaka traders.

commodity may then be purchased and taken to Port Loko or the Bullom shore and sold so that *bonga* can be purchased and the cycle begun once again.

Most of the remaining foodstuffs sold in Magburaka are brought to the market from surrounding villages either as head loads or by lorry; the only exceptions are palm oil, kola nuts, and less often, rice and groundnuts during local shortages. On occasion, palm oil is imported from Nigeria, and rice from other areas. Magburaka lies outside the dense oil palm zone of southern Sierra Leone, and much of what is sold there comes from Mende country to the South. Similarly, though some groundnuts are grown, production is insufficient for local needs, and is augmented by produce from northern Sierra Leone. In each case lorry transport is used; less often, the railway.

Palm wine is made locally by each ethnic group, though the Limba specialize in it and, since the establishment of the *Pax Britannica* made travel by individuals safe, Limba have migrated over most of Sierra Leone.[9] The Limba palm wine seller, with a calabash hung from each end of a balance pole, is a common figure at any railway stop or market; Magburaka is no exception. The palm wine seller is more often than not a peddler and, together with female traders who carry small amounts of foodstuffs as head-loads, he frequents railroad stations to sell to passengers. Palm wine sellers also make their beverages available at crossroads and lorry stops for those waiting to make connections. Some market traders will leave their stalls to meet an incoming train or lorry, though more often they will send a daughter to help her gain experience in retail selling.

An unknown number of tailors operate in Magburaka, while in most of the larger villages in the surrounding area, there are usually one or more. Sewing machines of varying vintage, the majority portable Singer models, are seen every day in Magburaka, where the tailors produce garments in both African and European models. Tailors work on an order basis for specific individuals, who more often than not supply the cloth, almost invariably of European manufacture.

Some dyeing of cloth is done by women, while others make baskets and mats which are on occasion sold, but the major industries and trades are those indicated above. Pottery is rarely made, having been superseded by goods of foreign manufacture, and "country cloth" likewise is seldom woven. Hunters and fishermen do not operate steadily near Magburaka, and therefore do not concern us here.

---

(9) Banton (1957 : 48–53) discusses outmigration from Limba chiefdoms in relation to the palm wine trade and other factors.

VILLAGE TRADERS

Turning from urban Magburaka, the distribution center, we move to the outlying villages to observe patterns of trade there. Some twenty miles south of Magburaka on the Freetown road lies Mayoso, a village of 491 people that served as chief's town for Kolifa Mayoso chiefdom before its amalgamation with Kolifa Mamunta-Rowala. The 1,780 people resident in Kolifa Mayoso are grouped into thirteen villages, several of which contain one or more traders: Robunki has four; Mayoso has four; Mamano, Masuba, Masang and Robis each have one. Nearly all goods handled by these traders come from Magburaka; two of them have on occasion obtained some articles directly from Freetown, while one, a recent Fula immigrant, gets all his wares from the capital; another, formerly resident in Makeni, continues to buy there and the Masang trader gets some goods from a Syrian in Kumbrabai Mamela. Before the completion of the direct (Okra Hills) road to Freetown, most traders in this area obtained their goods at Yonibana, and many continued to do so until the Kumrabai-Magburaka road was opened in 1946[10].

Usually these traders display goods on small stands in front of their houses, or on their verandas; only a few have separate buildings as shops. Of the twelve traders in Kolifa Mayoso in 1954–55, only one was literate and he was called upon by most of the others to take stock of their goods from time to time; he therefore could corroborate my direct observation of inventories. He himself had goods valued at £25, two other Mayoso traders £40 each, and the fourth, the Fula immigrant, £200–£300. The goods of the four Robunki traders together totaled less than £25, while the remaining traders in the chiefdom were on a similarly small scale. When one village trader ran short of cigarettes, matches or kerosene, he bought them from another and, as one trader phrased it, "thus we help each other." The literate Mayoso trader and a trader from Bonkolenken chiefdom (across the river Pampana to the east) shared salt and kerosene.

Of the twelve village traders resident in the chiefdom, all but three made rice farms in the spring of 1955, and even these three had gardens of cassava, yams and lesser crops. Nine of the village traders were thus largely dependent upon agriculture for subsistence while the remaining three, those with larger inventories of goods, supported their families, in part, by trading. To be sure, most of the traders did

(10) Before the railroad reached Yonibana (1912), trade goods were brought up the Rokel River from Freetown, and the various traders established on Bunce Island and at other spots in the estuary. How early trade goods found their way to the Magburaka area will not be known until adequate archeological excavations are carried out.

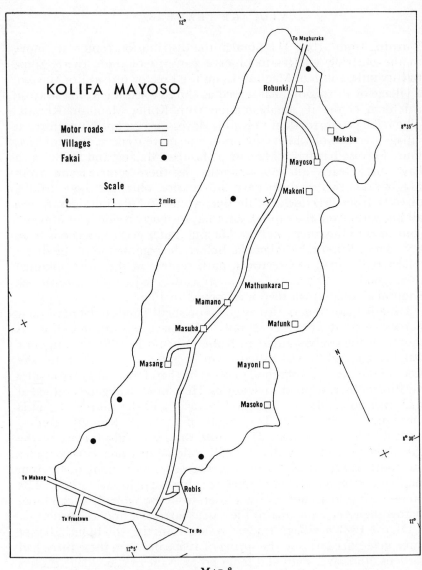

KOLIFA MAYOSO

Motor roads ═══════
Villages   □
Fakai   ●

Scale

0   1   2 miles

To Magburaka

Robunki ● □

Makaba □

Mayoso □

Makoni □

Mathunkara □

Mamano □

Masuba □

Mafunk □

Masang □

Mayoni □

Masoko □

To Mabang

To Freetown

To Bo

Robis □

12°
8° 35'
8° 30'
12°
12° 5'

N

MAP 3
Kolifa Mayoso

little of the physical work involved in farming or gardening themselves, but they were able, through their trading incomes, to secure
labor from various sources; not the least of these was that body of
villagers to whom the trader had extended credit. One of the ad-

vantages of trading, as the Temne see it, is that it frees one, at least in part, from the arduous physical tasks of farming.

As the figures for inventories cited above suggest, most village traders have only small stocks of imported goods. Their supplies of locally grown foodstuffs vary considerably. Nearly every trader, however, stocks matches, cigarettes, kerosene, salt, sugar, soap, soda pop, beer and moderately priced red wine produced in the Union of South Africa. In addition, the larger shops stock cotton, linen and silk cloth, caps of various materials, head-ties for women, "lappa cloths," men's shirts, needles and thread, a variety of tinned foods (especially fish, condensed milk, biscuits and cookies), toiletries (particularly perfumed soaps, talc and perfumes), medicines (such as aspirin, *Thermogene,* cod liver oil and other purgatives, *Mentholatum* and so on), laundry bluing, ink, pots and pans, and a variety of beverages. Rice is the staple food and, together with palm oil and groundnuts, comprises the basic stock of foodstuffs.

Price differentials between the Mayoso traders' shops and the Magburaka market are indicated in Table 5. Typically, local produce can be purchased more cheaply in Mayoso, near the farms, while non-local produce sells for less in Magburaka; transport costs seem to

TABLE 5

Comparative Prices, Mayoso, Magburaka–November 1954

Item and Amount	Mayoso £ s. d.	Magburaka £ s. d.
Rice: per bushel	2 2 0	2 3 0
per 1 penny pan	9	1
Cassava: 30 tubers	6	1 1
Groundnuts: per bushel	8 6	10
Palm oil: per *atulpitas*	4	4
Breadfruit: one	2	3
Oranges: 15	3	6
Bananas: 15	3	6
Pineapples: 1	1 6	2 6
Benniseeds: 1 cigarette cup	2	4
Okra: 30	3	6
Key Brand soap: chunk	3	3
Kerosene: bottle	9	7
Dried bonga: 1 fish	5	3
Cotton cloth: per yard	4 6	3 6

account for the differences. Yet there are exceptions, for in August and September when new rice first becomes available, old rice from the previous harvest or imported "polished" rice will be sold in the Magburaka market for 2d. less per one penny pan so that it may be sold before it spoils. In times of local shortages of rice, groundnuts, palm oil and other foodstuffs in Mayoso, these items may be priced lower in Magburaka where supplies are obtained by road and rail from more fortunate areas. Imported goods, however, almost invariably cost more in the villages.

Clearly the traders of Mayoso and other villages make some profit on this markup, though transport costs must also be reckoned, for the markup increases with the distance from the distribution center. Yet profits from such retail sales are small in view of the limited volume of sales and make up only a small portion of a trader's yearly income; indeed, some traders insist that they derive no income from retail sales of imported goods but stock them simply as a convenience for fellow villagers and to attract customers. Then, too, imported goods can be acquired on credit with payment in foodstuffs deferred until harvest; such practice assures the trader a supply of staples at low cost.

Because a number of factors enter into price determination, it would be well to summarize them before going on to consider how the village trader obtains his goods.

1) As indicated above, transport costs are important; usually, the farther the trader's shop from the source of his goods, the higher his prices.

2) The purchase cost of the goods, both imported and locally produced. The more he pays, the more he charges. This basic factor in price determination is important owing to fluctuations in supplies and prices of agricultural produce, and credit arrangements in the distribution center.

3) Considerations of supply and demand also enter; the village trader raises prices when the supply of goods decreases. Seasonal price fluctuations for basic foodstuffs can be explained largely in terms of relative quantity: prices are lowest just after harvest and rise steadily until they reach a peak high during the three months immediately preceding the harvest.

4) The necessity for keeping prices competitive so as to match other traders is a factor hard to assess. Wherever there are two or more traders in a village, each keeps close check on what the other charges. Similarly, the sole trader in a village must match the prices of his nearest competitors in surrounding villages lest people trade elsewhere. One difficulty in assessing the importance of this factor is that commodity prices are not standard; a trader charges one customer more than another depending on a variety of social factors, particularly kinship relations, the existence of debts between them, the need to improve relations with the chief, and so on.

5) The trader's need to obtain money or produce quickly may

force him to cut prices and accept a smaller profit. Such may be the case when his debts come due in Magburaka or when personal tragedy strikes the trader.

The operation of some of these influences can be seen in the case of the diamond mining area in Kono District.[11] This region has always been agriculturally poor, and with the immigration of thousands of outsiders seeking their fortunes, the food situation is even more acute and foodstuffs must be shipped in. High transport costs are one factor contributing to inflated food prices. Lorry loads of foodstuffs are brought in, sold to traders in the towns who resell to peddlers who in turn carry the food into the bush where the gangs work in the pits. The prices charged by these peddlers are high compared with those in Magburaka or even Freetown; one may speak of Kono as a "boom area." Supplies and prices fluctuate wildly; groundnuts usually sell for 6d. per cigarette tin, but if a peddler finds no competition, he will ask and get three times this price. Similarly, clean rice, ready for cooking, normally goes for 1/3 per cigarette tin, but in times of temporary shortage it will cost many times that. Table 6 illustrates the price differentials in the diamond mining area and in Magburaka.

TABLE 6

Comparative Prices, Magburaka, Diamond Area—November 1954

Item and Amount	Magburaka £ s. d.	Diamond Area £ s. d.	% Differential Using Magburaka as Base Price
Rice: per bushel	2 3 0	3 15 0	75
Bread: per loaf	3	1	300
Dried fish: per *bonga*	3	1	300
Palm oil: per bottle	1 6	3	100
Tinned fish: per tin	2	3 6	75

Before considering the question of profits, it is necessary to describe how the village trader obtains his goods. Few traders have much working capital, otherwise their shop inventories would be greater in order to increase volume of sales. In practice, goods are obtained on credit from the European and Syrian establishments in Magburaka. Such credit relations are complex, and must be considered in some detail.

Of the five European and nineteen Syrian firms in Magburaka,

(11) In 1954, mining by Africans was illicit as the Sierra Leone Selection Trust enjoyed a monopoly of diamond mining. In 1955 diamondiferous ground, excepting 450 square miles retained by the Selection Trust, was opened to Sierra Leoneans for alluvial mining.

almost all give credit to some village traders, although a given trader will rarely know more than three shopkeepers or factors well enough to obtain goods on credit. The literate Mayoso trader, referred to above, received credit from one European and one Syrian firm, although at some time in the past he received credit from all the other European firms and half a dozen Syrians. To establish credit relations and then to maintain them are constant problems for a village trader. Initially he must buy goods from one source for cash, hence the Temne observation that to trade one must be wealthy. However, as the trader buys rice, palm oil, palm kernels and other produce locally, he sells them only to his creditor firm, sometimes at no profit or even at a loss, so as to "make friends," as they put it, with a shopkeeper.[12] The maintenance of a good credit relationship depends upon the trader's ability to pay within the period stipulated. If the trader in turn extends credit to kinsmen and villagers and cannot collect in time (or if for any reason he cannot sell goods bought on credit quickly enough), he loses his privilege of buying on credit. This happens to most village traders repeatedly.

The factors of the European firms generally extend credit on a small scale, a few pounds sterling at a time, depending on the trader's reputation in settling his account before the firm's monthly inventory. Such advances must be repaid within a month or less, or else the defaulters must be "covered" by the factor from his own pocket. On the other hand, Syrians often give traders credit on a three to six month basis. Since they offer better terms, many traders prefer to deal with them even though their prices are usually slightly higher. In dealing with the European firms, the Syrians seem to have a marked advantage in that they can obtain goods in quantity on credit in Freetown, take delivery upcountry, and still get terms of six months to a year to pay. The African trader, on the other hand, works on too small a scale to deal directly with Freetown, and rarely gets credit terms of more than two months. These differences appear to Africans to explain in part why Syrians get richer while they themselves get poorer. One trader suggested that Syrians got better terms since it was difficult for them to hide or flee the country, whereas an African can (and many do) run off with borrowed money and goods and more easily hide out from law enforcement agencies. Most European firms try to discourage or forbid their factors the privilege of extending credit to petty traders. Yet most of them do so, covering the amounts loaned with their own funds and recording the transactions as "sales"

(12) The factor keeps the difference in such cases; this is a mild sort of extortion. The trader, usually illiterate, signs no note and the factor has no liens against the trader; all agreements are oral.

when stock-taking[13]. Those factors who grant credit *sub rosa* to many petty traders are highly regarded for their willingness to help others; in return, traders who receive goods on credit would not dream of selling palm kernels and other produce to anyone else so long as the price is standardized. Nevertheless, village traders grumble that factors charge them prices above list.

It is also generally recognized that Syrians can buy for less at the European firms; thus, as a case in point, one African trader bought a case of lump sugar for £2.7.6 and a quantity of cloth at 3/9 a yard while four days later he was present when a Syrian was charged £2.5.0 per case and 3s. per yard for the same items. Most traders reconcile themselves to the system and make no efforts to change it; occasionally some rebel and take their trade (in this case palm oil and palm kernels) elsewhere if they can.

A digression into the motives of factors for extending credit against the rules of their firms is in order. Obviously "illegal profits" can be made by selling above list prices, as noted above, even though there are risks involved. In addition, the extension of credit to African traders sets a virtual obligation on the trader to sell produce to the factor's firm, sometimes below the going rate if the factor has covered a delinquent payment or done some other favor. By so increasing his firm's business, a factor hopes for salary increments, more rapid promotion, and transfer to posts where opportunities are greater. Yet this is a dangerous game, for the factor gambles against discrepancies in his books, exposure by subordinates, and bankruptcy; his job and future are in the balance.

The village trader buys local produce which he sells to the European and Syrian firms; in this role he can be regarded virtually as an agent of these establishments. Chiefly palm oil, palm kernels, and rice are bought in Mayoso for sale in Magburaka; groundnuts are less often grown in quantity in the area. The palm kernels are usually sold to the European firms, while the oil is sold to Syrians who either store it for speculation on the seasonal rise in price or sell it in turn to the European firms at a profit on large quantities. Typically, kernels purchased in Mayoso cost £2 per bag in 1954–55 (roughly 12 fully packed bags weigh a ton). Transport from Mayoso to Magburaka was 2s. per bag and the firms paid a flat rate of £28.14.0 (1955)[14] per ton plus a commission of 5d. per bag. Thus a ton of

(13) The technique for recording such transactions is as follows: the amounts of credit extended by the firm's employee to the trader are not recorded as credit sales but as cash sales. The sales prices recorded are lower than the amounts actually paid by the trader when he settles his account.

(14) According to informants, the rate was £31.16.0 per ton and the commission, 2s. per bag in 1954.

kernels purchased in Mayoso and delivered in Magburaka cost the trader £25.4.0; he received £28.18.4, giving a profit of £3.14.4 per ton of kernels. This acceptable profit margin, however, seems to be realized only rarely. As indicated above, the firm's factor may actually pay something below the rate per ton if he has extended credit *sub rosa* to the trader in question and had as a consequence to cover a defaulted payment. The trader may willingly take less in the hopes of improving or establishing a credit relationship; some may even sell at a loss. It is possible also to get free transport from a Syrian firm if a trader sells to a European firm on behalf of the Syrian firm; village traders recognize that each Syrian gets a commission on what is sold in his name, though they do not know how much. Some European factors and Syrian firms will take an IOU for goods to be repaid in kernels or some other produce at harvest time.

Similarly, informal arrangements regarding palm oil, rice and groundnuts exist, though a trader who is in a financial position to do so will not sell all he buys but will retain quantities for later resale in the villages at a profit resulting from the seasonal rise in price associated with pre-harvest shortages, and from credit extended to impoverished villagers. In this regard the trader speculates, but the odds are in his favor. Palm oil is cheapest in March and dearest in August; rice and groundnuts become progressively more scarce and more expensive through the rainy season until the harvest, usually in September, October or November. Wealthy traders buy palm oil, rice and so on at harvest time when they are cheap, and sell when the price is higher before the next harvest.

It must be understood that few village farmers have savings of any size in cash or in readily salable assets. The annual tax in Kolifa Mayoso (1955) was 25s. per taxpayer (adult male, 16 years or over). Tax must be paid in currency, and to obtain money is difficult for most unless they sell farm produce; tax is usually due in March or April, some months after the harvest[15]. Most often the villager borrows tax money from a trader, unless he has a wealthy friend or relative who gives better terms, agreeing to pay it back in rice (or palm kernels and so on) at the following harvest. Loans are made at the rate of 5s. to 12s. per bushel of rice, depending upon when the transaction is made and on the bargaining powers of the trader; a number of social factors enter into each case. The trader in turn can sell the bushel of rice for £2, even shortly after harvest, realizing a sizeable profit. Various emergencies other than tax arise during a year—school

(15) The District Commissioner gives notice to the town headman, after January, as to when he will collect the tax, usually in March or April. As a headman gets a small remittance on each tax collected (9d.), he hurries his people to pay at once.

fees for children, a court case, a debt that is due and so on—and most Mayoso farmers had an account owing with one or more traders.

In the Mayoso area today a given piece of land is cropped more often than in the past; bush that has lain fallow for the ideal seven to ten years is rare, and most of this land is farmed again after only four years. Tropical laterite soils being what they are, yields per acre have decreased while even the modest improvements in sanitation and medical care and the existence of the *Pax Britannica* have led to population increase. The productive capacity of the land has decreased while the population has increased; harvests, say the farmers, are not what they once were. Consequently, many families are unable to grow sufficient food to last them from one harvest to another, especially when part of the yield must be turned over to traders in payment for loans. Those who are short of "good" land, who are inefficient farmers, or who are extravagant or unfortunate fall so far in debt that their entire rice harvest may be taken by traders for past debts. Such have no recourse but to borrow money or rice again from the trader in order to subsist; the trader willingly obliges, demanding two bushels for each bushel loaned, payable at the next harvest. The cycle perpetuates itself and can be broken only through a combination of good fortune, hard work, and self-denial; few Mayoso families ever succeeded. Clearly, village traders with working capital make sizeable profits here. Some will accept land in pledge or individuals in pawn if a family's harvest is insufficient; once entangled in these obligations, the farmer's position is nearly hopeless. On occasion, however, a trader overreaches himself, and when harvests are poor he cannot repay his own debts in Magburaka. Then he himself may face bankruptcy, even though he settles hurriedly with farmers on terms unfavorable to him and turns over rice, kernels and so on to Syrians and the firms at low prices. Nevertheless, speculation on the annual farming cycle and loaning at usurious rates yield the village trader most of his profits, though they may make him few friends.

To the northwest of Magburaka, in the groundnut country near Kambia and along the Great Scarcies River, traders buy groundnuts after the harvest in November at 7/6 per bushel, store them ten months until the rice harvest begins, when they are then bartered at par value, bushel for bushel. At this time, few people have groundnuts to add to the stew which sets off a good rice meal, and since new rice is plentiful, they eagerly seize the opportunity to get groundnuts. The rice collected by the traders is again stored to be resold, often to the same people for a higher price, or lent on the agreement that each bushel advanced will be repaid with two at the next harvest; the debt cycle is underway again.

Borrowing against next season's harvest is common, and though some chiefs and wealthy farmers will lend foodstuffs to kinsmen and friends if they have amounts above their own needs, it is the traders from whom most must borrow if their friends and kinsmen cannot or will not help them. Debtors who default are taken to court, and in most cases a man's siblings feel obliged to pay the debt though no court is empowered, under native law, to enforce either the transfer or inheritance of a debt. In Kolifa Mayoso, on two occasions, the Native Authority placed bankrupt individuals in Public Works Department jobs where they would have a chance to earn money to pay off outstanding debts. Formerly, such men would have pawned themselves and probably members of their families, but pawning is now technically forbidden. Nevertheless, several wealthy individuals took pawns and/or land in pledge in return for paying off bad debts.

In the decade of the 1950's a modified form of pawning was practiced as part of illicit diamond mining in Kono District. Bankrupt men went to certain traders who outfitted them with food, equipment and the funds which were demanded by the Kono chiefs for permission to dig in their chiefdoms. The miners, ideally, brought back all the stones they found to the trader who in turn sold them, keeping most of the profit for himself, and returning only a small percentage (minus the advance) to the miners. The diggers could then go out on their own or return under the same or slightly improved terms. The illicit diamond digging offered possibilities for acquiring great wealth in a short time and seemed providential to impoverished farmers. Food prices were inflated in the mining areas, however, and while a few struck it rich, most suffered from the unhealthful living and working conditions, the violence or dishonest middlemen and outfitters; some, of course, were apprehended by authorities.

Few Temne have personal property of sufficient value to use as security for loans, although in some cases it was observed that gold jewelry, bicycles, phonographs and so on were pawned. Generally the amount loaned was 50 to 60 percent of the recognized worth of the item; imported goods seemed to be valued in terms of purchase or replacement price. Traders accepting such security stipulated a period within which the loan had to be repaid and the amount of interest was agreed upon before witnesses at the time of the loan. A "friend," it was said, would not demand interest nor would he sell pawned property before he had issued several reminders; even then he would take the debtor to court. Traders, however, frequently had no such compunctions; they might sell the pawned item after time had run out whenever the opportunity presented itself for a cash profit, or retain it for their own use. To obtain a bicycle in such fashion, remarked one man, was cheaper than buying a new one.

In addition to the staple foods dealt with above, more perishable items are produced in the Mayoso area and shipped to Freetown or Magburaka for sale. Included here are oranges, bananas, peppers, kola nuts, benniseed, coffee and so on; a consideration of the first two is illustrative. A stem of bananas can be bought in Mayoso for 1/6 and sold for 4/6 or 5s. in Freetown. The cost of transport is 1/6 per stem and 10s. to 12s. per passenger one way. Similarly, oranges cost 5s. per bag in Mayoso and sell for 13s. to 14s. in Freetown but cost 5s. per bag to transport. Most of the bananas and oranges produced in Mayoso are purchased by a Freetown woman, a wife of a lorry driver who gets free transport; she makes good money and is envied by the Mayoso people. One of the Mayoso traders collects oranges for her and makes a small commission. Occasionally a Mayoso farmer takes his own produce to Freetown for sale, though invariably he loses money owing to the high cost of transport; nevertheless, it is an exciting trip and to see the new strange world of Freetown is felt to be well worth the expense. Simple arithmetic indicates that a person must go to Freetown with at least seven stems of bananas to break even, assuming no rotting or spoiling, a precarious assumption considering rough and uncertain transport.

It is impossible to generalize about the annual income of village traders if only because the great majority are illiterate and do not compute it. It may be well to summarize the ways in which a village trader derives his income:

1) by buying imported European goods in bulk and selling in small quantities for a higher price per unit;

2) as a buyer of local produce, by selling to the European and Syrian firms for a profit and a commission;

3) by buying local produce just after harvest and storing it for later resale, speculating on the seasonal rise in prices;

4) by advancing foodstuffs on credit to needy farmers and being repaid two for one at harvest time;

5) by serving as a "pawn broker," lending money or foodstuffs while taking movable personal property, an individual as a "pawn", or land in pledge as security for repayment.

That some traders become wealthy is evident from their personal possessions, property and style of life. Most village traders have a bicycle and many have a radio, a phonograph, European tableware, bedsteads with springs and mattress and so on. A trader dresses well, in either African or European modes (depending on the occasion), wears shoes part of the time, and frequently carries an umbrella. Traders' houses are usually larger, often roofed with iron pan rather than thatch, and boast more elaborate doors, window shutters and fixtures; some are whitewashed and a few are constructed partly of concrete or dried mud brick. More often than not a trader has several wives, themselves an index of wealth, who help him tend his shop and do most of the gardening and farming. Few traders do much physical labor; rather, they request those in their debt to help them or hire laborers.

As we have seen, however, a trader can lose money or become bankrupt in various ways, principally through poor management, lack of working capital and too slender profit margins. Lack of space precludes a detailed treatment of Temne kinship obligations, but it is sufficient to indicate that any person in economic difficulties turns first to his relatives; a trader's kinsmen are not exceptions. Canons of hospitality demand that a man feed those relatives who visit him, however long their stay, and in most circumstances this applies as well to friends who come to visit at mealtimes. More is expected of a trader, since he is felt to be a wealthy man, and guests look forward to the taste of tinned meat and salt in their rice and sauce, sugar in their tea and perhaps a bottle of wine or soda pop; that they partake of their host's kola nuts and tobacco goes without saying for the two are synonymous with hospitality. It is not by accident that hangers-on around the trader's shop often linger until mealtime or that relatives pay solicitous visits regularly. Furthermore, it is difficult for a trader to refuse a relative's request for a few cigarettes or lumps of sugar when a group of hangers-on are watching, all too ready to spread tales of his miserliness, and accuse him, at least behind his back, of behavior unbecoming a kinsman. In retaliation, all the trader can do is ask their help in small menial tasks or in assisting his wives to farm; even then some little gift ought to accompany the request. When a relative is to be married or falls ill, when a kinsman has a debt to pay off, when tax is due and in a multitude of other situations, the trader is asked to contribute, to advance credit, or at the least to sell at cost. A man cannot refuse every time without alienating his kinsmen and depriving himself of that emotionally supportive behavior that makes life worthwhile. Being wealthy, a trader is expected to give more than a poorer man.

Essentially, village traders live in a world of traditional Temne values where an individual has and needs little personal property and where he looks to his kin group for help in subsistence; what one is lucky enough to have he shares, and when one is in need, his kin group provides for him. Such a situation surely provides material and emotional support, but it makes it nearly impossible for a trader to accumulate sufficient wealth to expand his business; often it is difficult just to make ends meet, considering the continued drain on his stores and reserves. As Lewis[16] phrases it:

> The African trader, like the African doctor, lawyer, teacher, Government clerk, is leeched by his relatives ... if he has resources it is his duty to share. This prevents him from accumulating capital. When he does accumulate it, uncertainty often causes him to consume it hastily before someone else lays claim to it.

It is easy to understand how a trader can go bankrupt or barely break even when one sees that his creditors—the European and Syrian firms—have little patience with his excuses, honest and well-founded as they are. If they continue to extend credit to one who has defaulted in the past, it is on hard terms—terms which make it virtually impossible for a trader to improve his position. The risks inherent in the trader's position are known to all, and as one informant stated, "If you are going to open a trading shop, you should move far away from your people for they 'eat' your profits." Yet to estrange one's self from the kin group and the village and chiefdom one has known since childhood is a high price to pay for material profits—higher, in fact, than most Temne traders seem willing to pay.

CURRENCIES AND MEASURES

The history of trade in central Sierra Leone is bound up, in large part, with salt. "Native salt," produced by boiling sea water on the coast, was insufficient to meet the demand and, from early times, trade salt of European manufacture was brought up the Rokel River by canoe as far as Magburaka (then Makump) and then by headloads to areas away from the river. Salt was purchased at 1/6 per bag in Freetown, and from one bag the trader packed eight *tasaŋkər*[17], each of which sold upcountry for 4s; for each bag of salt taken upcountry, the trader realized £1.12.0 in currency or the equivalent in foodstuffs. Transport costs and the payment to Pa Suba[18] for rights of portage

(16) Lewis, (1954; 220–1). Perhaps this is one reason why African laborers and traders are so often "target workers." As one Temne trader phrased it: "A man works to get money that he may enjoy it, and if he dies without enjoying it, he is a fool; for he will not profit handing it on to his descendents."

(17) *Tasaŋkər* (pl.), *kasaŋkər* (sing.). This is a conical container, some 3′ to 4′ in length and 6″ in greatest diameter, shaped like *kayuŋ*, the fish trap.

(18) The Rokel River, the boundary between what were formerly Marampa and Masimera chiefdoms, has various rapids. Those between the villages of Malimera and Makabin are virtually "falls," and necessitated a portage. One of the chiefs of Marampa realized the possible revenue and sent a brother, Sesay Kabia, to supervise the collection of tribute from traders. Sesay and his followers examined all loads and took a varying percentage

around the Marampa rapids cut into profits, but the trade was rewarding. The *kasaŋkər* of salt came to be used as one form of traditional currency in payment of society initiations, bridewealth, buying medicine and so on[19]. This situation continued until the branch line of the railway reached the Magburaka area (Yonibana in 1912, Magburaka in 1913) when the price of salt fell and a kind of inflation of the *kasaŋkər* set in. The use of salt in general trade ceased almost at once, though the *kasaŋkər* still retained its old value of 4s. in ceremonial payments and is still so used today.

It is impossible to determine either when coins were first introduced into the Magburaka area or when they came into general use. Whenever it was, however, we can be sure that barter continued because an elaborate set of equivalences is remembered and in most areas was used extensively as late as 1930. Three leaves of tobacco were worth 3d., a mat 6d., and the *kasaŋkər* of salt 4s. Country cloth came in two sizes: the large size *(aŋlaŋkɔnɔ agbali)* was worth £1, the small size *(aŋlaŋkɔnɔ aŋmɔŋdema)* was worth 10s. Palm oil was worth 1d. per bottle[20] though it was usually sold in iron pots of various sizes. The names of the pots ware taken from their cost "in the early days" and, from the cost of the palm oil it took to fill each, these costs apparently were at one time equal.

The name are still in use today even though the pots themselves and their measures of palm oil both cost far more. Today the small sewing machine oil bottle, the *atulpitas,* the quart beer bottle and various gallon containers are rapidly replacing pots for liquid measure. The ubiquitous "tin" of palm oil equals 4 gallons. The volume relation between the new and old measuring containers is not always grasped by village Temne. The larger pots are rarely seen today; some old ones have become virtual heirlooms.

For solid measure, rice, groundnuts and other commodities were heaped in flat pans or basins. These are used today along with the cigarette tin (7 or 8 to the two-penny pan), the bushel, the box, the bag and a number of others. There are about 22 two-penny pans in

for themselves and the Paramount Chief. The traders and the people living in the area began to call Sesay, "Pa Suba Kemebot" (Mr. Stretches-out-his-gown), since he always held up the folds of his gown to receive tribute. Subsequently this man was moved to the growing town of Magbele and became a subchief of this section; the name "Pa Suba" then became a title assumed by each succeeding subchief.

(19) Salt served, at least upcountry, as the basis for a "money-barter" economy. Herskovits (1952: 215) and Ames (1955) have suggested that "money-barter" is indicative of an economy in transition, the change stemming from trade with Europeans. [Money-barter resembles what economists call "commodity money." Eds.]

(20) This "bottle", known as *atulpitas,* is that in which *Atwood Bitters* is sold. Such a bottle of palm oil cost 7d. in Mayoso in 1959.

the kilo, a measure formerly used by traders, and this equals the "box" of today. There are about 24 two-penny pans in the bushel, which equals one *kolonai* or "four kettle;" a bushel of rice weighs

TABLE 7

Liquid Measure and Values of Pots

Name	"Traditional" Cost of Pot	1955 Cost of Pot	Volume in Units
αηbɔt	3d.	4s.	1
αηsispɛns	6d.	8s.	2
αηshiliη	1s.	16s.	4
αηwαnα	1/6	?	6
αηα ɛyɛrɔn	2s.	?	8
αηdαlα	4s.	?	16
αηα eshiliη tɔfɔt	10s.	?	40
αηbɔlα	£1	?	80

84 pounds. Kola nuts were usually measured as follows: 6 two-penny pans equal 1 kettle which weighs 22 pounds. There are about 700 nuts in the kettle and 8 kettles equal 1 "measure," a "double bushel."

Older informants supplied barter equivalences with consistency for the period 1920–1930. A brief outline of these is as follows:

Trade goods could be acquired in the past either with British currency or by barter in terms of the equivalences indicated in Table 9. Any of the items listed, with the exception of salt and tobacco, could be bartered for trade goods[21] priced at the values indicated. All the foodstuffs including salt and tobacco, could be exchanged for one another at about the equivalences indicated.

TABLE 8

Solid Measure and Values of Pans

Name	"Traditional" Cost of Pan	1955 Cost of Pan	Volume in Units
(one) penny pan	1d.	6d.	1
two penny pan (pan fokɔpɔ)	2d.	1s.	$2^{1}/_{2}$
αyαgbawa[a]	8d.	4s.	15
αηkolmαn[b]	?	4s.	15
αηkitɔl	?	?	15
αpɛrcαη	1/4	8s.	30 (approx.)
kolonαi (αηfokitɔl)	?	?	60 (1 bushel)

(a) Said to be a Mende word.

(b) Corruption of "gold-man" or "gold-mine;" the pan was introduced during the 1930's when the panning of gold along the Pampana River was prevalent.

(21) The charges for various trade goods, as remembered by older informants ran as follows: satin, 6d. per yard, cotton cloth, 9d. per yard, khaki drill, 1/6 per yard, head-ties, up to 1s. each, sardines, 3d. per tin, *Gordon's* gin, 5s. per bottle, cube sugar, 3d. per package, pocket knife, 6d. each, matches, ½ d. per box, cutlass or machete, 9d. each.

Today, even in the villages, the small transactions of traders are usually carried out on a cash basis, although those who have no cash can still effect exchanges on a barter basis. During August in Mayoso, for example, the direct exchange of a two-penny pan of palm kernels for a cigarette tin of rice was common, as was 2 two-penny pans of groundnuts for a leaf of tobacco. Throughout most of the year, at least when the commodities are generally available, 1¹/₂ bushels of rice may be bartered for 1 to 1¹/₂ tins of palm oil[22]. Numerous other examples could be given, but these are sufficient to indicate that

TABLE 9

Barter Equivalences, Magburaka Area, 1920–30

1d.	— 1 cigarette tin of salt, 25 kola nuts, 1 leaf of tobacco, 1 two penny pan of rice, palm kernels or groundnuts[a], 4 eggs, 1 *atulpitas* of palm oil.
3d.	— three times any entry for 1d. or 1 *aŋbɔt* of palm oil.
6d.	— six times any entry for 1d. or 1 *aŋsispɛns* of palm oil, 1 mat, 1 chicken.
1s.	— twelve times any entry for 1d. or 1 *aŋshiliŋ* of palm oil.
1/6 to 3s.	— 1 bushel of rice, palm kernels or groundnuts depending upon the time of year, 1/6 just after harvest to 3s. during July and August, or 1 *aŋwana* of palm oil.
4s.	— four times any entry for 1s., 1 *andala* of palm oil and 2 or almost 2 bushels of rice, palm kernels or groundnuts depending on the time of year.
10s.	— ten times any entry for 1s., 1 ten shilling pot of palm oil, 1 small country cloth *aŋlaŋkɔnɔ aŋmɔŋdema*
£1	— twice any entry for 10s., 1 *aŋbɔla* of palm oil, 1 large country cloth *aŋlaŋkɔnɔ agbali*

(a) It should be noted that before 1925 groundnuts were relatively scarce; the better bearing varieties grown today had not been introduced. Before 1925 a given measure of groundnuts was worth more than the equivalent measure of rice or palm kernels.

bartering occurs; it should be mentioned again that some barter transactions entail deferred payment (until harvest). No village trader, to my knowledge, ever refused to exchange imported goods for local produce, though the equivalences are less well recognized here today and haggling enters.

The presence of barter does not necessarily indicate the existence or bargaining or haggling, as Herskovits (1952 : 88) for one has indicated, but in central Sierra Leone the two are present together. As has been indicated above, prices at any village trader's shop are flexible, depending on his relationship to the customer, which gives rise to bargaining and price variation on the retail level. The previous account of how the village trader established and maintained credit relationship in the distribution center suggested the presence of bargaining at that level as well.

It is difficult to assess the role of gift and ceremonial exchange in

(22) A "tin" is a 4-gallon container.

the total distribution of goods. Among the Temne of central Sierra Leone, ceremonial exchange takes place in a variety of situations: offerings to spirits, fines paid to the Paramount Chief for violation of taboo *(məsəm)*, life-crisis payments at birth, marriage (bridewealth and counterpayment), initiation into the *Poro* or *Bundu* societies, death, and many others (McCulloch 1950 : 68–70; Dorjahn 1959). These involve more than the exchange of food and other common items possessed by everyone. Traditionally, the goods involved in such exchanges included trade salt, "country cloth," hoes and so forth—things that were economically important. In more recent times, payments have been made largely in currency, though there existed the feeling, present at least before 1915 (Thomas 1916 : 95), that "if a man pays cash only, his wife will not sit long in his house." In 1955, most bridewealth consisted of coins and traditional items, such as salt and country cloth. It is impossible to indicate to what degree such ceremonial exchanges affect the circulation of goods in central Sierra Leone—it is probably not great today—but it is a type of economic exchange that is still practiced, which must be considered in any future studies.

CONCLUSIONS

In conclusion, several aspects of trade and marketing in this area should be stressed. Commercial relations are on a particularistic face-to-face basis. Such contrast with our own economic system is analogous to that which exists in the political sphere (Fallers 1956 : 238) where nonliterate peoples characteristically lack the impersonal bureaucracy of our own governmental system. Thus in the *bonga* trade, the upcountry tradewoman forms a buying-relationship with a particular fisherman or his wives. When possible, this trader will make arrangements for freight and passage with a particular lorry driver. Again, the village trader establishes a credit-relationship with a particular European or Syrian firm in order to obtain goods on credit. Finally, in the villages, a farmer buys from, sells to, and receives credits from a particular trader.

In the second place, social factors influence economic behavior, and operate on different levels. With respect to retail sales, a trader often charges kinsmen, close friends and important people, such as chiefs, less than his usual prices and presents them with small gifts from time to time. A man in debt to a trader, or a stranger, will be charged more.

Third, most African traders do only a small volume of business, and since they are short of working capital, can rarely expand. A number of difficulties are involved here, as we have seen. Kinship obligations become more costly when one has greater wealth. Prestige is acquired in part by the conspicuous consumption and distribution of wealth in the form of goods of European manufacture. Acquired tastes, expensive to satisfy, are all too easily added. The amount of goods which can be obtained on credit is limited, and the factors just considered make it difficult for the trader to save and reinvest in his own business. At least with respect to village traders, the poverty of material asset holdings makes it impossible for them to secure commercial bank loans, even if they should attempt to do so in the future.

CHAPTER 3

Traditional Market Economy in South Dahomey[1]

BY CLAUDINE AND CLAUDE TARDITS

INTRODUCTION

In Dahomey, it is usually considered that the provinces of Cotonou, Porto-Novo, Ouidah, Ketou, Abomey and Athieme differ from the northerly regions by their geographic as well as their human features and that they present a certain unity acknowledged in the expression "South Dahomey." This area is subject to equatorial seasonal variations, though moderate rainfalls have made possible the growth of extensive palm groves. The population is relatively dense and today reaches twenty to thirty inhabitants per square kilometer.

Two ethnic groups occupy this area: the Adja, including among others the Fong from Abomey and the Gunu of Porto-Novo, and the Yoruba, who form minority groups known locally as Nagots. The population figures for both groups exceed one million and represent about two-thirds of the total population of Dahomey. Some of the subgroups have long known a centralized form of political organization constituted by a hierarchy of patrilineages. Both Abomey and Porto-Novo kingdoms have had contacts with Europe for centuries and have played an important part in international trade from the seventeenth century down to colonial occupation and the foundation, in 1893, of the French "Colony of Benin." The slave trade dominated commercial relations for two centuries; at the end of the nineteenth century, trade in oil products replaced that in men. Dahomean economy has thus long been affected by international exchanges.

Southern Dahomey is a low plateau divided by large valleys cut out by streams flowing from north to south—Oueme, Couffo, Mono. It is one of the richest agricultural areas of West Africa, and to the resources of the soil can be added that of fishing in rivers and coastal lagoons. Cassava, yams, groundnuts, beans, corn, palm oil and fish supply the basic diet. These products, which are commercialized on a large scale, are exchanged between the different geographical units of the southern areas: plateau and valleys, coast and inland. They are sent to the city markets of the old urban centers—Abomey,

(1) Data used in this text were gathered during field work carried on in Dahomey in 1954 and 1955. The figures are given in old French metropolitan francs.

Ouidah, Porto-Novo—as well as to the modern port of Cotonou.

International trade gave intense stimulation to local exchanges, especially when the slave trade, which was a royal privilege, was replaced by trade in palm *(elaeis guineensis)* products, which interested the whole farming population. Nowadays, the value of palm products sent abroad represents two-thirds of Dahomean export trade. For years middlemen have operated between European firms and farmers; they "prospected" the bush in order to buy palm nuts and oil and in so doing they spread everywhere such European goods as textiles, hardware, kerosene and drugs.

Trading centers have developed in villages as well as in cities, and one can walk scarcely five or six miles without coming across a market place. The large number of people professionally interested in trading accounts for such a density. Moreover, the male population—that is, about half of the inhabitants—are farmers or fishermen while the women sell the products of men's activity. In the cities, modern primary and secondary economic sectors grew out of private and public European action, but factory workers, store clerks and civil servants represent only a small fraction of the population, not exceeding a few thousand people.

We shall give here a description of market economy based on observations gathered through all parts of South Dahomey. The figures are taken from a more detailed investigation carried on in a local rural market, which supplied us with a more vivid and accurate picture of the mechanism of traditional marketing activities. The village, called Mitro, is located about eighteen miles north of Porto-Novo, on the border of the plateau which rises over the Oueme river valley. It has 1,000 inhabitants and is an active market place where people of the valley exchange goods with the farmers of the upland.

GENERAL CONDITIONS OF TRADE

In South Dahomean society, the man is a stable element who, unless he emigrates (which is frequent nowadays), spends his life on the land which belongs either to his patrilineage or, more recently, to himself. He clears the bush, tills the ground, takes part in sowing and harvesting, cares for the palm trees; a woman seldom interferes with cultivation though she helps in sowing and may give a hand in harvesting. The husband provides his family with food, sells the harvest surplus in order to get cash, but seldom appears in market places except as a buyer.

Woman is a mobile element in the social group. When she marries, she leaves her father's compound where she grew up, and goes to live

with her husband. Domestic duties are numerous and tiresome during
the first years of her married life, for a new wife is responsible for all
the heavy and unpleasant tasks of the household—she fetches water,
grinds condiments, cooks meals, washes the garments, cleans the
houses not only for her husband but also for members of his family.
House commitments decrease after a woman has borne her first child
or when a new wife has been brought in. After a few years, a woman,
apart from raising her children, has all the time she needs for outdoor
work, and she has a good incentive to carry on business since she has
an exclusive right on her gains. She may buy goods for sale from her
husband but, in such cases, this aspect of their relationship will
remain no more than that between buyer and seller.

The following figures recorded in the village of Mitro show the
importance of women's marketing activity: among 201 women who
were questioned—about two-thirds of the total female population of
the village—176 (86 per cent)—carried on business at the time of the
investigation. Among the remaining 24, fourteen had temporarily
ceased to sell on the market place for various reasons and nine of the
remaining ten were too old. The tenth was a chief's wife whose husband was prejudiced against his wife's going from one market place
to another. Some of the women momentarily inactive were newly
married; others had just had a child, or were in mourning for a
kinsman.

We shall here underline how social and religious duties may
interfere with women's activities. For instance, a newly married
woman waits three months before leaving the compound, and though
the custom is not compulsory it is widely respected. Moreover, in
Moslem families, a woman frequently does not work outside the
home before the birth of her first child; were she to do so, her husband's reputation might suffer. A woman who has borne a child will
not likely go back to the market until the birth ceremonies are performed; neither will a woman who has lost a relative go to market
before the end of all death rituals. In this last case, some heavier
prohibitions interfere with trading activities, for a woman in mourning is forbidden to prepare food containing salt as well as to make
akasa, a corn starch paste[2] daily consumed by all south Dahomeans.
However, she is not obliged to cease all trade, she still has a right to
sell wood, flour, condiments or smoked fish outside of the market
place. One woman explained her situation by saying, "Death has

(2) The corn is left two or three days in jars of water; the starch comes out and settles
to the bottom. It has no taste save that of the banana leaves in which it is wrapped, and is
eaten with hot meat sauces. Dahomean students in France substitute prepared corn
starch (*maizena*) for this product.

taken *akasa* away from me and filled my hands with wood." Such practices simply show how economic and religious domains are linked in an African society in transition.

TRADE SPECIALIZATION

What is the range of commercial activities? As one could expect, specialization is tied to the diversity of regional production. Moreover, it is significant that another type of differentiation emerged, based on the nature of transactions carried out between production and consumption, so that we had to distinguish wholesale from retail trade.

Wholesalers get their supply of goods directly from the farmer and pay cash. They buy large quantities, from one to two hundred pounds of goods—fifteen to twenty full enameled basins— and sell smaller stocks to other women. These latter are the retailers who will later bring the goods, either raw or converted, to the market place for the consumer. Retailers could obtain goods from the farmers but they prefer to deal with wholesalers who sell them the quantities they need and give them credit for several days, whereas they could purchase from the producers only what the latter want to sell, and without any credit facilities.

The distinction made between wholesalers and retailers is obviously linked to the scale of the trade; it lies in the fact that most women can invest but small amounts of capital—a few hundred francs—and that a few more successful or better experienced dealers acquire stocks of goods worth a few thousand francs and from them enlarge their traffic. Besides, the boundary between wholesale and retail can easily be stepped over: women are quite willing to take risks and, as soon as they have enough money, they start speculative buying.

In villages, women speculate mostly on corn; the shrewdest buy and store corn in March and April and sell it during the period of scarcity in June and July before the new harvest, when the prices are at their highest. In the head town of Porto-Novo or the port of Cotonou, if they hear a ship will be delayed, women may agree to buy all the stocks of sugar and cigarets from the stores. Once in possession of the goods, they control the prices. The pound of sugar then may climb from 40 to 100 francs, the package of cigarets from 30 to 110 francs. The rise in the prices will often be felt in village markets two or three weeks later.

There are few wholesalers at the village level. There were 15 in Mitro out of 176 traders. Most of them were women between the ages of 30 and 40, familiar with market needs and able to invest 3,000 to 4,000 francs at once. Wholesalers deal mostly in staple crops: corn, cassava, yams, groundnuts, beans and palm products.

Retailers are more numerous and sell a larger range of goods. One may find in market places raw products gathered in the bush, such as medical plants, vegetables, condiments, fruits, wood, packing leaves. Available also are prepared foodstuffs, such as flour, cooked meals and imported European goods.

Gathered products are sold by women who begin business without the money required for a more lucrative trade or by old and tired women. A large number of women are always engaged in this branch of trade since it is easily carried on. Among 160 retailers in Mitro, 38 (25 per cent) were selling gathered products. The traffic in medical plants is specifically reserved to old women and forbidden to the young.

Commerce in cooked food assumes a peculiar aspect in South Dahomey. One finds on Dahomean markets all the products that may be seen along the coast: flour, grilled groundnuts, smoked fish, palm oil, "mustard," etc. Trading centers look like open restaurants where one finds all the local dishes. Husbands left alone because of their wives' business commitments are obliged to feed themselves at markets. Trade, taking women's time, has thus stimulated new commercial development which gives Dahomean markets their modern and lively aspect.

What is to be found on the merchants' trays? One can get boiled dishes such as *akasa* (a corn paste consumed at every meal), *abobo* (mashed beans with pimento and palm oil), *acra* (mashed sweet potatoes); fried food: *masa* (corn fritters, a delicacy eaten as a breakfast, with sugar), *klaklu gbado ton* (corn croquettes), *klaklu fenie ta* (cassava croquettes), *doko* and *atakre* (beans and sesame croquettes); and also stewed dishes generally eaten during scarcity periods before the new harvest: pastes made of beans *(moi moi)*, corn or cassava *(abla)*, sesame *(avruda)*, cassava flour *(ablo)*.

Other goods are also prepared for the markets: oil and soap made with palm oil and potash salts. The latter is locally consumed but palm oil is the most important product sold in Dahomean markets. Buyers are either consumers or middlemen collecting oil and nuts in the villages for the commercial firms in the cities. Local marketing in these products leads to international business. Today, however, old commercial channels are threatened, for shortly after the war, oil factories were built in the country. They buy directly from the producers.

The women who prepare and sell cooked food are the youngest, most active and most numerous agents in the market. They were 83 in Mitro (47 per cent) out of 176 traders—this figure includes 62 women selling *akasa*. Sooner or later every Dahomean woman prepares and sells *akasa*. She learns how to prepare it when she is a child; every home has the required outfit to make it, and it is always a profitable business since everybody needs *akasa*.

The last specialized branch of retail trade is that in imported European goods. Western products are now found on every bush market: in Mitro, six women were selling them. The products include food (canned meat and fish, salt, sugar); perfumes and cosmetics (toilet water, hair oil); drugs (talcum powder, quinine, laxatives); chemicals (sulfur, copper sulfate, antimony, chalk—eaten by pregnant women—alun, resin bars); hardware (enameled basins which have taken the place of the old earthen cooking pots, nails, needles, tools); kerosene; and miscellaneous items ranging from buttons and hooks to jerrycans filled with pebbles used as percussion instruments or empty tins topped by metallic bottle corks to replace the earthen oil lamps.

All these goods are bought either directly from the stores in the cities of Porto-Novo, Cotonou, Ouidah or from African middlemen in village markets.

TRAINING A TRADER

Such facts necessitate comments. These often complex businesses cannot be carried on without training and experience; besides, many trades require equipment and more or less capital. How does a woman acquire training, experience, capital and equipment?

A future saleswoman learns her job early. In Dahomey, when a girl is five years old, her mother sends her to the market to buy fruit or spices and gives her the money to pay for them; when she is seven years old, a girl helps her mother in her business; she picks fruit in the bush, gathers wood, prepares food, goes with her mother to the market. Later on, she will carry a little tray on her head and walk from house to house selling a few goods her mother has given her.

Some decades ago, a girl was not allowed to go trading on her own before she had her first menstruation or was married, but the custom is today disregarded. A young girl may presently sell goods on her own account, but her mother keeps the money she earns. It is kept till she marries, to complete the trousseau given by the bridegroom. Most of the time the young girl sells the same goods as her mother, for she has been trained to do so. Sometimes her father will help her with a small gift of money or goods so that she can sell cooked dishes that will bring in more money than the sale of fruit and vegetables. Once married, her husband may, according to custom, give her money to start a business of her choice. If he cannot afford it the woman may get funds from her family or from a friend, less often from a co-wife. Otherwise, she may buy goods on credit or, as we already mentioned, sell fruit, vegetables or wood from the bush.

Let us imagine that a woman has a sufficient capital—a few hundred francs— and that she has chosen to sell *akasa*. First, she observes the market conditions carefully. She buys *akasa* from several women, noticing the quantities and prices. She then buys two or three basins of corn. She discovers rapidly where to find the best quality of corn, the lowest prices in the village or on other markets, and will try to make good bargains. She knows her cost prices and manages to keep steady profits by decreasing the quantities of food sold when corn prices go up so as to avoid any change in the market prices. An experienced woman knows in advance how much gain she will derive from a market day, and if she finds that her trade is tiresome or unprofitable, she gives it up for a more lucrative one. We asked a number of women if they had changed trading activities during their lives: 79 out of 100 had made a change, and among the 21 who had not, there were 7 young girls.

The funds required to begin the various branches of business are as follows (approximately). To prepare cassava, corn (except *akasa*), sweet potatoes or beans, a woman needs from 100 to 400 francs to buy the basic products. An *akasa* merchant needs from 500 to 1,300 francs, according to the size of the basket she brings to the market. Women selling oil and soap invest 1,400 to 1,500 francs at a time in their goods. Sellers of imported goods have a weekly turnover amounting to 2,000 francs. The required funds for wholesalers reach 4,000 or 5,000 francs if they want to run their businesses efficiently.

Equipment is necessary, especially for women who sell cooked food. It consists first of baskets, trays, and basins used for presenting the food in the market place, which have an average value of 500 francs. The outfit used to prepare boiled and stewed dishes—earthen jars, enameled basins, sieves—is worth 700 to 1,500 francs; the rasp, jars and hemp bag used to prepare cassava cost about the same price. To make *akasa*, a woman must have utensils costing about 2,000 francs which include a grinding stone, several jars, wooden blades. This is the most expensive equipment, and formerly a husband had to include with the bridewealth the grinding stone and the two or three earthen jars necessary to make *akasa*. Today, however, earthenware has been replaced by enameled basins. Besides, the new bride's sisters-in-law give her a portable earthen stove, wooden spoons and

cooking pots for paste and gravy with which she will cook her first
meal under the critical supervision of her husband's family.

To prepare palm oil, a woman may use the pit dug by her husband; a vat is also needed by women making soap from local products.
Cans (worth 400 or 500 francs) belong either to the wife or the husband.

These figures show how much time and effort must be invested
before women can achieve or hold any position in business. It also
explains, in part, the distribution of professional activities, for some
branches of trade appear as necessary steps before more rewarding
commercial ventures.

PLACES OF TRADE

Market spots—places laid out with shelters and sometimes shops—are
the most important trading centers. However, a foreign observer will
be surprised to meet saleswomen widely scattered all over the country,
along small as well as large roads, at the crossing of paths, outside and
around the market places. Some women sell their goods walking from
one house to the other. There are several reasons for this: women often
prefer to stay near their own homes, others who are in mourning are
forbidden to enter the market place before the death rituals are over.
It may also happen that a woman who has worked in the market the
whole morning calls later on at the neighboring houses to sell what
remains of her goods.

Nevertheless the market place is the most suitable location for
transactions. It is a meeting center regularly attended by a large
crowd of customers. Village markets are held every other day, a great
market day *(awaya)* alternating with a small one *(awandu)*, the
difference lying in the number of buyers and sellers who attend it.
The regional trade calendar is set so that a village's great market day
corresponds to a small market day in the neighboring settlements.

Palm roofed shelters called *apatam* and held up by wooden posts
are erected in the market places; underneath and around the space
occupied by the merchants, a small earthen wall a few inches high
protects the women and their trays against running water and floods
during the rainy season. *Apatam* are built either by the men of the
village or by the women's kin. The sellers who have no private shelters
take places in the large public *apatam* as they arrive in the morning.
In the more important centers, market shelters are made of concrete
and covered with corrugated iron.

On great market days sellers and buyers come from about twenty
villages, as much as seven or eight miles away from Mitro. On other

days a few women come to the market from the nearest places while the active traders go to buy in other market centers or prepare their goods for the next important market.

Mitro is particularly well located to stimulate exchanges between women from the lacustrine villages or the valley who sell fish bought from their husbands and the uplanders who sell wood and staple food.

SELLING TECHNIQUES

Competition is hard in Dahomean markets. Merchants sell either the same goods or products for which there are ready substitutes. The appearance of the goods is the first factor that will be taken into consideration by the customers. Sellers will insist on the fact that the food offered had just been made. They advertise "crispy fritters," "freshly made *akasa,*" "nicely cooked mashed beans" or "juicy croquettes."

Bargaining is the rule. Prices asked by sellers as well as buyers are always higher or lower than those which are finally agreed upon. Long debates ensue in which praise and insults have their place. The merchant seldom loses money since she may always refuse a disadvantageous bargain, whereas a buyer may be unaware of the market prices or become impatient and lose money.

Prices of all goods are at their highest early in the morning. Sellers, though they know at which prices they will agree to sell, wait to see what the clients look like. The first customers make proposals, the merchants watch their colleagues and, after a few sales, prices tend to be set. Around nine o'clock, the market comes to a peak. An *akasa* seller told us: "If by eight, half of my basket of *akasa* has been sold, it is going to be a good market day; if not, it looks bad." When sales are slow, women will extend some credit or give bonuses rather than reduce the prices. Nevertheless, the prices fall slightly at the end of the day unless the balance between demand and supply remains favorable to the sellers.

We shall describe, for example, how fish is bought. A customer looks at a fish tray; the merchant asks 425 francs for forty fish; the customer offers 350 francs. After a short discussion, the merchant is ready to sell. The customer then withdraws the offer and proposes 300 francs; the discussion goes on till the seller has accepted; the buyer thinks it over a second time and says: "Two hundred seventy-five francs." The merchant finally agrees but the customer drops the proposed price down to 200 francs. At this point the merchant refuses to sell. Discussion starts again until at last the bargain is concluded for 225 francs. Customers who might have watched the scene could also have bought fish at the last price. In this case, there were none and the next customer to come along undertook bargaining anew and finally paid 235 francs for forty fish.

Besides bargaining, which leaves the buyer with the feeling that he obtained the most interesting prices, the merchants know how to impress their customers by using different measuring devices such as baskets, basins, and bowls, the sizes of which are rarely standardized. For instance, a corn merchant will prefer to use a narrow vessel: the customer helps herself, fills the vessel with corn, then surrounds it with her arm, piling up corn with the feeling that she has received more than her due. Salt merchants have similar practices: they sell salt in cigaret tins, of which the bottom is filled with paper; the salt is stacked above and over the edges of the tin. Oil merchants dig their fingers in the bowl while filling it; then add a small quantity of oil as if they were giving their customers a bonus. Groundnuts are heaped in small boxes so that some of them fall aside when the seller quickly throws the content of the box into the buyer's hands who afterwards is generously given some extra nuts. Fish are sold in bundles of forty and prices vary according to the size; the merchant will slip in among middle size fish a few small ones to increase her gains and one or two big ones to attract the customers. Buyers are not always fooled, but are easily convinced they were particularly well treated. This technique, which is more commonly used for food, is based on the general principle that it is more profitable for the dealers to reduce the quantities than to raise the prices and is part of the means through which the traders adapt themselves to price fluctuations.

PRICE FLUCTUATIONS

Several factors affect market prices. Some are accidental: for instance, prices may go down when a ceremony occurs in villages where markets are held because, on such occasions, housewives prepare huge quantities of food. Others are linked with seasonal variations of the agricultural production and the general movement of supply and demand.

Corn prices recorded in Mitro between July 1, 1954, and April 11, 1955, will give an idea of the price movement of a staple crop (see Table 10):

The first corn is harvested in July during the rainy season. The new corn called *sikiti* appears on the market together with *xuxu*, dried corn harvested several months earlier. The scarcity is such that both qualities—although *xuxu* is preferred by customers—reach their highest prices (in our data, 60 francs on July 7) of the year. With increasing supply, prices tend to fall until the beginning of August

(65 Frs. on August 8) and then to rise slowly afterwards. Farmers who need cash immediately sell part of the harvest but keep their stocks after their immediate needs have been fulfilled. Prices fall again with the second harvest in November. Fresh corn, *sikiti,* is

TABLE 10

Corn Prices in Mitro[a]

Date	Prices for Different Qualities of Corn		
	Xuxu[b]	*Sikiti*[b]	*Sankpo*[b]
July 1 (small market day)	80 Frs.	65 Frs.	
July 5 (s.m.d.)	75	60	
July 7 (great market day)	90	65	
July 9 (s.m.d.)	70	60	
July 11 (g.m.d.)	75	60	
July 13 (s.m.d.)	75	60	
July 15 (g.m.d.)	80	60	65 Frs.
July 19 (g.m.d.)	70	50	65–60
July 21 (s.m.d.)	70	50	65
July 25 (s.m.d.)	70	50	60
August 8 (g.m.d.)	65	45	
August 20 (g.m.d.)	70	50	
September 7 (g.m.d.)	85		
September 21 (g.m.d.)	80		
September 25 (g.m.d.)	80		
October 9 (s.m.d.)	75		
November 4 (g.m.d.)	65		
November 20 (g.m.d.)	50		
December 2 (g.m.d.)	50		
December 6 (g.m.d.)	50		
December 18 (g.m.d.)	40		
January 23 (g.m.d.)	35		
January 25 (g.m.d.)	40		
January 31 (g.m.d.)	25		
February 2 (s.m.d.)	30		
February 12 (g.m.d.)	50		
March 14 (s.m.d.)	50		
April 11 (s.m.d.)	60		

[a] Prices are given for one "measure" of corn (ten to fourteen pounds).

[b] *Xuxu* is a dried corn stored since the last harvest; *Sikiti* is the newly harvested corn of a poor quality since it has not been dried; *Sankpo* is a mixture of both qualities and its price depends on the proportion of dry and new corn.

brought no more to the market since farmers have less urgent need of money and keep the corn for drying. Prices fall further as the supply remains large; they increase again in January and February when farmers sell to pay their taxes, which also dimishes purchasing power. Prices from there on climb till the next harvest, reaching their maximum in June and July.

Cassava is the second important item of the native diet and is largely consumed during scarcity periods, replacing corn. Prices reach a maximum in December, January, February during the dry season when tubercles are hard to pull out of the hardened soil. The curve of cassava prices is the inverse of that of corn prices. The price of the basket of cassava, called *tagban,* varies from 150 to 400 francs.

Production of beans follows the same seasonal rhythm as corn. Beans grow in smaller quantities and may completely disappear from the market during August and September, before the new harvest. They are considered a delicacy and the price of a full basin varies between 150 and 400 francs.

Palm nuts cost from 120 to 150 francs per basin. They are gathered during the dry season. A large number of women treat the fruits and sell oil and nuts. However, since oil plants have been built in the country, women are losing the palm products trade. Fish is more abundant during the rainy season, and consequently prices reach their maximum during the dry months.

CREDIT PRACTICES

We have already mentioned the means used to stimulate transactions: credit and bonus. Producers, we said, sell when they need money and want to be paid cash but wholesalers allow payment facilities for five, seven or nine days, especially when business is slack, for they never feel sure they will be repaid. The price of the unit of goods is then raised from 10 to 20 francs as interest. Fishermen's wives extend no credit, but sometimes allow retailers whom they have known for a long time to pay them at the end of the market day. Retailers extend no credit since they only sell small quantities of goods and do not want to run the risk of losing money. Rather, they prefer to attract trade by small rewards in goods.

How well do women succeed in collecting their accounts? Dealers settle such matters between themselves without refering them to the village chief, but one often hears quarrels and threats uttered on the thresholds of houses, more seldom in the market place. The creditor warns her debtor that he or she will suffer from stomach aches or cramps. However the creditors more often appeal to the debtor's good will and remain patient. "I praise and encourage my debtor," said one woman. "If I quarrelled, she might get angry, talk badly about me all around, and I might lose customers. I would rather lose some money." Another merchant said: "I tell my friends and colleagues that so and so pays badly; then people may cease to sell her goods and she may be compelled to buy at other market places."

One also sees occasionally an old man in rags walking in the market place. He shouts insults accompanied by threatening gestures. This man is a town crier who, for a few francs, will publicly curse the debtors who have been designated to him.

PRICE CONTROL

According to our observations, prices are related to supply and demand. This is obvious when one reads the corn price movement. We have already drawn attention to the custom of reducing the volume of the goods rather than increasing market prices, which thus remain apparently stable.

At the scarcity period, in June and July, shortly before the harvest, production prices reach levels which might be heavily felt on the market prices. A market control is established then which is worth describing. The agency responsible for the price control operation is a men's secret association called *zangbeto* which is found among the Gunu of Porto-Novo and the Fong of Abomey.

Akasa is commonly sold in small portions packed in banana leaves, the weight of which varies with corn prices and seasons. From June on, the prices of corn suddenly climb up during two months; from then on, *akasa* merchants are obliged to reduce stringently the volume of the parcel sold at an unchanged price. Before doing so they send the doyen of the *akasa* dealers to the head of the *zangbeto* association. She gives the chief a bottle of palmwine spirits and money collected from all the *akasa* sellers. On the following night, members of the *zangbeto* walk through the village blowing horns; women must stay indoors and are even forbidden to glance out of the window. They are warned that the *zangbeto* accepts the fact that the parcels of *akasa* be modified on account of the price rise. Later on, after the harvest, corn prices fall but most of the dealers still use the corn bought before the harvest and go on selling *akasa* as usual until *zangbeto* gives the signal to decrease the prices. The night before a market day, *zangbeto* members go out again, dance around the market place while horns are blowing and, in the center of the place they put a parcel of earth packed in a banana leaf; this represents the quantity of *akasa* which should thenceforth be sold for one franc. *Zangbeto* watches the merchants and if they find that a woman trespasses the law, the members of the association walk through the village for seven nights, cursing the woman who disregarded the custom. Within a week the offender will have to obey the *zangbeto* orders and pay a fine of 1,000 francs, half a jerrycan of palmoil, two basins of corn and a bottle of palmwine spirits. If she does not comply, *zangbeto* will come out again, curse her for sixteen more nights and carry through the village a banana tree branch wrapped in a white cloth representing a corpse in a shroud. On the last night, the branch is buried and members of the *zangbeto* guard the "tomb" for seven more nights. The tradition says that the lawbreaker dies shortly afterwards.

We have but little information about commercial gains. Retailers selling raw goods earn from 50 to 200 francs per market day; women selling food other than *akasa,* from 50 to 150 francs every two days. Earning *on akasa* sales probably amount to 200 francs every two or three days. Women preparing soap can earn from 600 to 800 francs every five or six days. Speculation on corn, which is made possible as the crops ripen earlier on the plateau than in the valley, may bring 400 francs per deal every three or four days. The most advantageous trade is that of palm oil: gains may reach 1,200 to 1,800 francs for two or three days work each week.

However, a woman will seldom spend the entire month at markets. Tending her children, fatigue, sickness, and mourning frequently keep her away from business. We therefore doubt that the earnings of women exceed a few thousand francs per month with the possible exception of the time when the palm oil trade is flourishing.

Commercial gains are a woman's own property and she spends her money free of all control. Traders frequently reinvest part of their gains in their dealings and spend the rest to cover domestic and personal expenses, since spouses have to keep the house in good condition, replace old cooking utensils and buy their own clothes. A woman may own over twenty different cloths, some of which were given her by her husband when they got married, others bought by herself. A young woman seldom hesitates to buy expensive clothes and jewelry, especially when festivities occur. The husband gives money for food, pays for children's garments and school expenses, buys drugs and sees that the walls and roof of the house are kept in good condition. Trade gives to women a partial economic independence, and if their business is profitable they might even be able to lend some money—a few thousand francs—to their husbands against their future crops.

This happens frequently, since men have to face heavier expenses than women. Besides farm expenditures and family taxes, which are regular charges, they have to pay bridewealth for their sons' first wives and to meet funeral and cult expenses. The flow of money which comes from the development of market transactions has opened up new possibilities for market women to become money lenders. Traditional market economy ends up in what we might call banking operations.

CHAPTER 4

The Yoruba Rural Market

BY B. W. HODDER

In the literature on southwestern Nigeria, a fair amount of attention
has been given to the large-scale internal and external exchange
sectors of the economy: to trading and marketing in cocoa, kola nut
and oil-palm products. Very little, however, has been written on the
functions and characteristics of local market institutions.[1] Yet for
the bulk of the population, both in rural and in urban areas, it is
through the local markets that goods from abroad and elsewhere are
absorbed; and it is through these same markets that most local agricultural and cottage industrial products enter the economy.

The importance of the local markets is indicated by their large
number and by an almost bewildering variety of types. One possible
classification can be made on the basis of function, and in particular
on the place of any particular market in the wholesale and retail
distributive chains for (a) local foodstuffs (b) cottage industrial products, and (c) imported goods. Such a classification, however, is of
limited value because there is as yet insufficient data of the kind
needed to make possible anything more than a superficial analysis
along such lines. Another classification of local markets in Yorubaland is based chiefly on location and periodicity, and is put forward
here as the most useful classification for the purposes of this essay.
This tentative classification distinguishes five main types:

  i. *the urban daily market,* which takes place every day, and is
     characteristic of the larger towns, like Ibadan.
 ii. *the urban nightly market,* which is held every evening, begin-
     ning soon after dark and continuing to about 10 P.M. It is
     common in the smaller towns, such as Oyo or Fiditi, which seem
     unable to support a regular daily market. It occurs also in the
     larger towns which have daily markets as well. The Yoruba
     believe this to be a peculiarly Oyo Yoruba institution.[2]

---

(1) Some useful comments are made in Galletti, Baldwin, and Dina (1956 : 53 ff.) also
Nigeria Federal Information Service (annual) gives a list of a few, chiefly urban, markets,
and the days on which they occur.

(2) See Lloyd 1952 : 20. I am indebted further to Dr. Lloyd for his helpful criticisms
throughout this essay.

   iii. *the rural night market,* occurring at regular intervals, as at
       Ikereku.
   iv. *the rural daily market,* which is often primarily for fresh meat.
       Moniya is an example of this type.
    v. *the rural market.* This takes place at regular intervals of several
       days, as at Akinyele.

As defined here, the rural market is perhaps the most important single type of local market in Yorubaland which, though highly urbanized by West African standards, is yet predominantly rural and has a density of rural population averaging some 180 persons to the square mile. To avoid being too generalized, this essay deals specifically with the rural market and makes but incidental reference to other types of local markets in Yorubaland. Moreover, this essay is based largely upon field work in the country lying between Ibadan and Oyo in the Western Region of Nigeria; consequently, it is not claimed that the observations made and the conclusions drawn are in any way necessarily typical of other parts of Yorubaland.

There is little doubt that rural markets in Yorubaland are indigenous, though they have undergone some changes in form and function since the time of the earliest European contacts. Pre-contact trade was chiefly of two types: local petty trading in the hands of women; and long distance trading by men. This later type, as observed for instance by Clapperton, involved long journeys to the coast where slaves were sold for gunpowder, spirits and cloth (Clapperton 1829). Today, however, European firms or their agents have come into most parts of Yorubaland to sell their products either direct to the consumer or to traders, most of them women, who buy in bulk and sell in very small quantities in local markets. Furthermore, as will be shown later, present-day rural markets in Yorubaland are deeply affected by one important factor which has been operative only since the late 1920's: the introduction of cocoa farming on a large scale.

The distribution of rural markets show little correlation either with the distribution, or with the size, of rural settlements; this despite the fact that the rural population lives chiefly in compact villages or hamlets. Several of the largest rural markets are not in villages at all; and many settlements of considerable importance have no markets.[3] The bulk of the rural population, indeed, lives away from the actual market sites. This supports the contention that the village *per se* is not at all an important unit of economic organization in Yorubaland, however important a role it may play in the social

---

   (3) Hence the use of the term 'rural market' in preference to 'village market' or 'market village' in this essay.

organization (Galletti, Baldwin, Dina 1956 : 58). The rural markets are generally evenly spaced out, largely irrespective of settlements, at distances from each other averaging about seven miles. In the Akinyele area, shown in *Fig. 4*, no hamlet or settlement of any kind is more than five miles from a rural market. It is tempting to compare the resulting network of rural markets to patterns of market centers described in Europe and America by Cristaller (1933), Dickinson (1947), and Brush (1953 : 380–402), but closer examination reveals

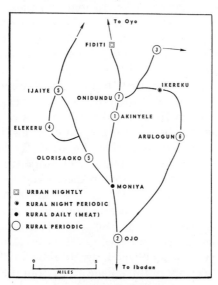

FIGURE 4

Markets in Akinyele Area

any comparison to be only superficially valid. In splite of the seven-mile average distance similarity, which is presumably associated with the average maximum convenient walking distance, the evenly spaced pattern of markets in parts of Europe and America is quite different in that it is clearly and causally related to the pattern and hierarchy of settlements.

In their location, rural markets are most clearly related to ease of access at varying periods of time. Accepting this, there arises an apparent contradiction in the lack of correspondence between the location of market sites and the location and hierarchy of village or hamlet settlements. For it would appear that villages themselves are to some extent determined locationally by accessibility factors. The explanation of this paradox lies in the difference in area over which these factors operate as between markets on the one hand and village settlements on the other. The location of the larger village settlements depends more on the wider considerations of position, whereas a rural market site is determined by often exclusively positional considerations. The main consideration in siting a rural market is ease and convenience of access from all settlements, however small, within a radius of only a few miles.

Some markets have been simply established in clearings in the bush, often at the junction of paths; others lie athwart a motorable road, sometimes near to or in a village. In many of these latter cases, the market has in fact created a village, often at the expense of a neighboring settlement. The way this has occurred is well illustrated at Akinyele. The permanent parent settlement of Akinyele lay some five hundred yards away in the bush. This original site is nowadays deserted except for two families, though over thirty ruined houses can be distinguished. Most of the population moved away after 1905 when the road between Ibadan and Oyo was built. The inhabitants moved down to the road near to the already existing village of Olosun, and established a market alongside the road. Today, though geographically Akinyele is one settlement, Olosun still retains its own administrative autonomy in some respects and reveals a distinct pattern of house distribution *(Fig. 5)*. In a great many other cases, too, the market site and any associated buildings are separated from the rest of the village. Thus at Ojo, the two primarily residential sections of the original settlement of Ojo lie well away from the road where Ojo market was established, again about 1905. Whereas the houses in the two sections of the village away from the road are mostly inhabited by farming families (many of whom have their family compounds and houses in Ibadan), most of the houses alongside the road are in fact simply stores of one kind or another or are inhabited by non-farming families: carpenters, blacksmiths, tailors, barbers, and laborers. There are also produce buyers, notably for cocoa and palm kernels. These produce buyers operate quite independently of the rural market or indeed of any other general trading market; they are normally located in a settlement of some local importance.

Many of the wider changes in the distribution of rural markets have also been determined by road building since the early years of the century. Cartographical and oral evidence confirms this in the Ibadan-Oyo area. Similarly, in the extreme southwest, near the Dahomey border, there has been a striking decline in the number of rural markets along the formerly much more important waterways of the lagoons and creeks and an increase in the number of rural markets further inland on the better drained and more densely farmed areas where the modern road network has been developed.

Rural markets in Yorubaland operate on a ring system.[4] Within each ring, markets occur in such a way that, in most cases, each market takes place on a day on which it is the only market operating within the ring. These rings are by no means self-contained; for each rural market ring impinges upon and is itself impinged upon by adjacent market rings. The timing of markets within each ring is normally on a four-day or multiple of four-day cycle. In local terminology the terms five-day or nine-day cycles are common, but the periods referred

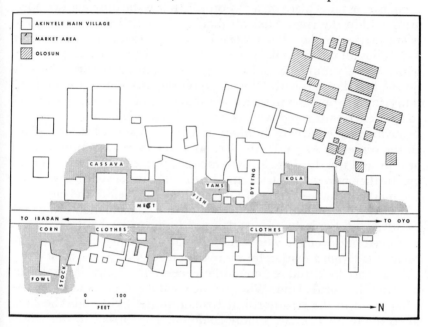

FIGURE 5

Olosun Village and Market (Yoruba)

to are in fact the same as those referred to in this essay as the four-day and eight-day cycles. Markets may thus occur on Monday, Friday, Tuesday, Saturday—four-day markets; or on Monday, Tuesday of the following week, Wednesday of the following week—eight-day markets. This is, of course, a common phenomenon in West Africa and has been noted frequently outside Nigeria (Verger and Bastide 1958). It appears to be related to time factors operating prior to the adoption of the seven-day week towards the latter part of the nineteenth cen-

(4) A great many meanings have been attached to the word 'ring' in this context. As used here, a ring is formed by a complete and integrated sequence of markets operating over four-day or multiples of four-day periods.

tury as European control extended inland. According to Talbot, "the original week appears always to have been composed of four days . . . The subdivisions into weeks in all likelihood originated from the necessity of differentiating between the days on which the various markets were held" (Talbot 1926 : 869). As Fig. 4 indicates, eight rural markets are distinguished in the Akinyele ring, and all take place at eight-day or, in one case, at four-day intervals (Hodder 1959). With one exception, all occur on successive days in such a way that each market takes place on a day on which it is the only market operating within the ring. After all markets have had their turn, there is one marketless day. The process is then repeated in the same order 1–7. Thus all markets take place every eight days here except Ijaiye, which is every four days and so occurs simultaneously with Akinyele on the first day and with Olorisaoko on the fifth day of the period.[5] This ring also operates in such a way that the change from one market to the next occurs roughly diagonally. This phenomenon has not yet been observed elsewhere, but here at least the first market takes place in the center at Akinyele, the second at the extreme southern edge at Ojo, and the third at the extreme northern edge at Iware. There are further movements back and forth until the seventh day, when the market near the center at Onidundu occurs before the eighth or rest day. No satisfactory explanation of this phenomenon can as yet be advanced; but it does mean that the timing of marketing activities is evened out over the whole ring so that no hamlet or other settlement is far from a market for more than three days at the most.

There are local and regional differences in the cycles of rural market rings in Yorubaland. Whereas the eight-day cycle is more or less ubiquitous in the area north of Ibadan, in the Ekiti and Abeokuta areas the four-day cycle is more common; and further to the southeast the eight-day cycle again becomes usual. Any explanatory comment on these regional variations must be made with caution, but it does seem that the four-day cycle correlates with the smaller and less clearly defined rings. According to Talbot, the change from four-day to eight-day "weeks" took place "when the numbers of markets increased and surpassed that of the days" (Talbot 1926 : 869). On the other hand, there is some evidence today that wherever there is a close network of good roads, there is a tendency for the larger markets to be held more frequently—that is at four-day intervals—and for the smaller markets either to die out altogether or to become pre-market collecting centers known in some parts as *aroje*. The different cycles

(5) In a personal communication, P. C. Lloyd suggests that this may reflect the greater social and political influence of Ijaiye as the only "town" (in the sense of having an *Oba* and a clearly defined political hierarchy) in the Akinyele ring.

may also be related to the density and pattern of settlements. The Abeokuta area, for instance, with its dense rural population contained in hamlets, shows a four-day cycle (Mabogunje 1958 : 109–123); but where the density of rural population is lower the eight-day rural market appears to be adequate. It is, in fact, difficult to avoid the conclusion that although the eight-day week may have developed out of the four-day week as markets increased in number, nowadays the four-day cycle often develops out of the eight-day cycle as rural population density increases and accessibility improves with the building of roads. This conclusion is supported by several attempts to change from eight-day to four-day cycles in the Akinyele ring. Such an attempt was made recently at Ojo, but without success.

However the differences between the four-day and eight-day cycles are explained, there is no doubt that the integrated timing and pattern of markets in market rings is remarkably logical and convenient. It is also of great interest to the human geographer in that it involves what in sum constitutes large diurnal movements of people. Within any one ring, the majority of women attend more than one market within the ring and may in fact attend most of them. A woman living near Abeshe, roughly halfway between Akinyele and Arulogun, for instance, normally attends Akinyele, Iware, Olorisaoko, Arulogun and Onidundu markets; she thus walks up to nine miles to market, covers some fifty miles or more a week in travelling on foot to and from market, usually with a basket or calabash of goods on her head, and is occupied in travelling and trading or buying in the markets five out of every eight days. This is not unusual, and most women attend at least two markets in every eight-day period.

In the Akinyele ring some 5,000 people—equivalent to about 30% of the total population—move to and from rural markets in any one day. Over the whole of Yorubaland, at a conservative estimate, over half a million people move daily along paths and roads to and from rural markets. Streams of people converge on the market site in the morning, and after several hours brisk trading the site empties. In any one rural market the population is likely to increase from a handful of people on the evening preceding the market, to some 3,000–4,000 persons by midday on market day. At Akinyele, which has a permanent population of only 280, there is crowded into the market site around midday on market day up to 3,500 women. Other rural markets, as at Elekeru, have no permanent settlement at all, and so are quite empty on non-market days. The economic functions of each rural market, whether associated with a village or not, are almost exclusively confined to the one day in a four-day or eight-day period. There is very little trading on non-market days. Even if there is an associated village settlement nearby, it will be mostly deserted: most of the men being on their farms and many of the women being away at the market operating on that day or out buying and collecting goods ready for the next market day.

It will be readily inferred from the remarks already made, that women rather than men are concerned in rural marketing activities. Rarely will a rural market contain more than 5 percent men, though there is some seasonal variation in this respect; during the slack season in cocoa farming, for instance, or where there is stock to buy or sell, or when there is much heavy work in the packing of kola nuts or cassava flour, men are rather more in evidence. It has been suggested that this female predominance in rural marketing may date back to conditions of internal insecurity in which it was unsafe for men to move away from their farms, while women enjoyed relative immunity from attacks (Pedler 1955 : 139). On the other hand, night markets and the urban nightly markets are usually thronged with men. In the Oyo nightly market, for instance, the numbers of men and women are about equal, though it is again the women who do most of the trading, whereas the men appear to attend chiefly for social reasons.

This raises the whole question of the place of the woman in Yorubaland, without which the significance of the rural market as an important social and economic institution cannot by fully appreciated. Women in Yorubaland certainly enjoy very considerable economic independence and may be trading on their own account, often with money or goods borrowed from their husbands. To the Yoruba women, moreover, marketing, petty trading, or at least attending a market, is part of their way of life; and their rewards lie as much in the social life offered by the markets as in their cash profits. It is as true of the Yoruba women as of most West Africans that they "do not regard trade as an occupation . . . and would not refer to it as such" (Bauer 1954 : 11). Yet it is inaccurate to assume that Yoruba women are wholly dependent on the market for subsistence. In many cases their primary sources of subsistence do not come out of the market at all. Though the rural market here may not have the same social and political significance in tribal life as when both sexes are equally involved in marketing, the social and economic importance of the rural market in Yorubaland cannot be overemphasized. Local farm produce—either cash crops or food crops—are marketed at the local market, almost invariably by women. In a polygamous family, agricultural products destined for sale are carried home from the farms by the several wives, and the marketing of these products may be supervised by the senior wife. Yet most of the women who buy produce from the farmer before beginning their marketing activities are not in fact related to the farmer. Most farmers, at least in the Akinyele ring, believe that they will get better prices from unrelated women traders than by allowing their own wives to do the actual marketing of their produce. Apart from local foodstuffs, such as maize, cassava, yams, bananas, kola, and vegetables such as tomatoes, okra, *oyo,* and *amuno tutu,* women carry into markets locally made pots, calabashes, palm oil, palm wine, firewood and bundles of leaves in which to wrap food (Table 11). Although the various classes of products thus brought into the market from the immediate environs within the ring appear to come in quite haphazardly, in fact there is usually some kind of specialization in the various 'feeder' areas. Thus at Ijaiye, the following specializations were noted in December 1958:

Commodity	Feeder Village or Hamlet
Cassava flour and yams	Innini
	Ajaja
	Fayunwa
Pepper and fowls	Laleye
	Oretu
Baskets	Adetola
	Olowode
Palm Oil	Elekeru
Tomatoes	Ajibode
Maize	Idigba

Whereas some women buy such goods from the farmers and carry them into the market to sell wholesale, others will sell direct to the ultimate consumer. The variants, in fact, are almost infinite. In a few cases, articles have been seen to change hands as many as five times during the course of one day, and the profits made at each transaction have been thought to be quite negligible.

The large-scale movement of women to and from markets with local foodstuffs and cottage industrial products is at first sight wasteful in time and energy. In the Akinyele ring of something under 300 square miles, on seven out of eight days up to 5,000 women converge on the market operating on that day from farms and settlements in the area. The "large numbers selling in the markets and the small margin of profit with which most of them seem to be content, suggests that there is much underemployment of labor, a liking for trade as an activity among Yoruba women, and few other activities offering larger returns for the capital and labor commanded" (Galetti, Baldwin, Dina 1956 : 65). In rural markets the turnover is certainly very small and slow. On the other hand, the loads that can be carried by women headloading along bush paths for several miles are limited: a woman is generally thought to be capable of headloading 80 lbs. compared with 120 lbs. for a man, though in fact heavier loads are not uncommon. Consequently, the daily repetition of such movements is likely to be necessary if local produce is to be effectively distributed. Where headloading is still so widespread as it is in Yorubaland, the scale of individual marketing operations must remain severely restricted.

The rural market, however, has functions other than the collection and distribution of local produce. Many goods imported from other parts of Nigeria and from abroad are sold by women traders, many of whom are itinerant. In the Akinyele ring markets, goods such as cloth from Manchester are usually bought in Ibadan or Oyo by market women, most of whom live in Ibadan, who then come to the local rural markets to sell at a very small profit. These women, of whom there are a great number, normally visit several markets within the ring before returning to town to replenish their stocks. They are less in evidence in those markets which are not easily accessible by all-season motor roads—notably Elekeru and Arulogun in the Akinyele ring. Individually, again, the scale of trading is very small, a woman's total wares often being contained in one medium-sized suitcase. Once more, it is the constant repetition and large number of such operations that gives them such significance. Such traders from Ibadan and Oyo clearly serve an important function in bringing within reach of the rural dwellers such products as gari, melon seeds, beans, rice, fish, mats, sugar, salt, gunpowder, matches and stockfish, as well as cloth. Other traders who buy in the rural markets for resale in the towns take away such goods as fowls, sheep, goats, cassava, yams, plantains, tomatoes and peppers.

The urban influence on rural markets is particularly well shown in this area north of Ibadan, and the whole nature of this influence is often evident in the composition and proportion of different kinds of goods sold in any particular market (Table 11). Especially along the main road, the three markets at Ojo, Akinyele and Onidundu may not as yet be wholly urban in character, but they are nevertheless "such important centers of local trade that the economic life of the farming families seems to revolve more around purchase and sale than around farm production" (Galetti, Baldwin, Dina 1956 : xxvi). To varying extents this is also true of other markets in the area. And even at Elekeru, the most isolated and rural in appearance of the markets, as many as twelve lorries come from Ibadan each market day and bulk purchase cassava flour, tomatoes, and similar produce. The dependence of the urban centers on the rural markets is in fact greater and more direct than is at first apparent. Two main categories of movement to and from the urban centers may be distinguished as far as rural markets are concerned: first, the movement of first-level middlemen to the market to bring back bulk quantities of produce bought from the market women, some of whom may already have acted as intermediaries by buying tiny quantities before selling to the middlemen in rather larger quantities. The second category includes all those who come to the markets from the large towns to buy goods which are either unobtainable or are too expensive in town. The dependence of towns on the rural areas is also indicated by the perpetuation in many cases of the practice of levying dues in the form of such produce as plantains, beans, and yams, by the family in Ibadan which has this traditional right: in Ojo market such dues are levied by the Fijabi family from Ibadan. This levying of dues is payable as an acknowledgement of suzerainty and is not to be confused with the dues payable as rent for the holding of land.

In appearance, most rural markets have but few permanent shelters and lie in the open, taking shade normally from trees or from temporary shelters made from branches and palm leaves or grass thatch. In Ojo market there are some 115 market stalls of this type; each shelter takes an average of three market women so that there are in effect about 350 covered stalls. Several of the covered stalls are in fact cooked-food stalls, which do a brisk trade in fried yams, *eba, iyan,* and *eko* during marketing hours. Other stalls are entirely in the open, and may consist simply of one shallow basket of goods with the seller squatting behind.

Although it is true that there is some specialization of activities among market women by age, this is by no means so clear cut as is often supposed. In Akinyele rural market the following breakdown was found among women sellers in May, 1959:

Young women (under 25) . . Salt, mats, pepper, beans, calabashes, gourds, soup, corn

Women aged 25–55 . . . . Pounded yams, soups, trinkets, dried fish, mats, fish, fowls, eggs, pepper, plantains

Old women (over 55) . . . Cloths (imported), beans, buttons, exercise books, thread, corn, medicine, poultry.

The only general conclusion, drawn from observations in markets in the Akinyele ring, is that the older women deal with most of the imported goods, or with goods of high value in relation to bulk. According to a number of informants, certain commodities, notably cloth of various kinds, are taboo to the younger women in the Akinyele area.[6]

Within the markets there is normally some degree of area specialization by commodities. In Akinyele market this occurs very clearly (Fig. 5), though chiefly in certain commodities such as kola nuts, livestock, fowls, yams, meat, cassava flour, mats, clothes, and fish. The degree of areal specialization of this kind varies with the market and appears to be related to one or other of two factors: the degree of any particular crop dominance in the immediate neighborhood and the age of the market, the newest markets having the least area specialization. In most cases this areal specialization by commodities is laid down and perpetuated by market organizers, most of whom are men, and many disputes about the location of stalls or indeed about any other matters relating to the market, are settled by the *bale*[7] of the associated village. Such area specialization clearly facilitates the organization of bulk buying and selling as well as making price controls easier to enforce.

In the earlier years of the present century, most groups of commodities were organized in trade guilds, each of which had some kind of recognized head, herself often subject to a powerful head of all market women in the market. But this practice is lapsing in most markets in the Akinyele area: at Ojo, for instance, there has been no market woman head since 1946 and no evidence is to be found of trade guilds organized within the limits of the market there. This is not to say that trade guilds do not exist. But they have certainly become less rigid and affect rural markets within the Akinyele ring only in the sense that most visiting or itinerant traders are members of one guild or another organized from the large urban centers, notably Ibadan. Yet even the sellers of farm produce are usually specialists and have their own organisations which rule that all members shall trade in one commodity or group of commodities only; and that other traders shall be prevented from infringing the rules. Partly for this very reason, it is not common in the Akinyele ring for a woman to be selling all the produce of her husband's farm. In the prevailing conditions of an overabundance of sellers, competition is a strong feature of the marketing economy. Haggling is in fact the normal method of dealing.

(6) This confirmed in a personal communication from A. Mabogunje.
(7) Normally the head of a village.

Though the chief economic characteristic of the rural market is still dominantly the small-scale individual selling and buying of goods in very small amounts, there are three other features of increasing importance to be noted. The first is the provision of facilities for the machine milling of maize or cassava. The mill is usually a permanent building on the edge of the market site; and the milling of maize and cassava is carried out both for individual farmers and for bulk buyers prior to packing or bagging. The second feature of increasing importance is this bulk packing and selling of an increasing number of goods, though it is so far most striking in two commodities—kola nuts and cassava flour. Both operations are carried out almost exclusively by men: the kola packing by Hausa traders and the cassava flour bagging by Yoruba town traders. Thirdly, there is the provision of services of various kinds. At Akinyele, for instance, there are normally some five tailors working in the village, all of whom however complain of poor custom, which is hardly any better on market days because of an influx of some twenty five itinerant tailors. Similarly there is an influx of about eight itinerant carpenters on market day to compete with the one permanent local carpenter. Such itinerant craftsmen are a feature of the rural market and they "do the rounds" together with the itinerant traders already referred to. In all cases examined in the Ibadan-Oyo area, both the permanent and itinerant craftsmen claimed that they took no part at all in agricultural work. In servicing of this kind, as in marketing, underemployment is clearly an endemic feature. Ojo is not unusual in having a permanent population of only 260 including three carpenters, three blacksmiths, one goldsmith, five tailors, and three barbers—and this on non-market days.

Seasonal differences in the rural markets are perhaps most noticeable in the kind and origin of goods sold rather than in the number of people attending the markets. Local foodstuffs for sale have seasonal characteristics following the time of the yam and maize harvests and the production of palm oil. Moreover, there is usually a shortage of food from January to May and at Akinyele market, for instance, the source of "local" foodstuffs at that time is frequently as distant as Iseyin (for *elubo* and *esu*) and Ilorin. Yet as the peaks of the various agricultural activities do not easily coincide, the activity of the local markets is to some extent maintained throughout the year.

Nevertheless the size of markets is affected by a number of factors: by the occurrence of such festivals as *Ileya* and *Egungun;* and by the success or failure of food crops, which are very much dependent on the amount and timing of rainfall in any particular year. The better the harvests the larger and more vigorous the markets; in Yorubaland there is certainly no relationship between the size of markets and food shortages of the kind noted in Tiv country (L. and P. Bohannan 1953 : 53). The size of markets in Yorubaland is also affected by seasonal differences in prosperity dependent upon cocoa, undoubtedly the "most important single governor of seasonal differences" in prosperity. The kola-harvesting season is roughly simultaneous with the cocoa-harvesting season—October to November—and the marketing of cocoa follows with a lag of about six weeks. One of the main food-harvesting seasons also occurs then, so that "the income of the primary producers and of the intermediaries nearest to them in the market chain has a pronounced rise between September and February, and an equally pronounced fall between March and August," when farm operations are vigorous but only the early season crops (largely consumed by the producers) and palm kernels fetch any cash (Galetti, Baldwin, Dina 1956 : 37). This rhythm of agricultural activities, dependent as it is primarily upon rainfall distribution, affects a whole range of wider activities of work, production, earning and spending, which have their repercussions throughout the rural and urban economy in Yorubaland. It certainly affects the rhythm of prosperity in rural markets. At Akinyele in October 1958 the average peak attendance was 3,500 each market day: in May 1959 it was only 1,200.

The rural market in Yorubaland is an important institution in the social and economic landscape. It not only acts as a site for petty trading throughout the year, under conditions which require very little capital outlay. It is also a place where first-level middlemen can be contacted and is a vital link in the marketing chain. It has an important social function for the Yoruba women. Yet in spite of several common characteristics, in detail the rural markets often defy generalization. This is to some extent an expression of the intense individualism of the Yoruba market women, of the individually very small-scale nature of the trading, as well as of the various natural, social and economic environments in which these markets occur.

TABLE 11

Analysis of Sellers in Three Yoruba Markets

	Ojo 8-day	Elekuru 8-day	Oyo (Akesan) Nightly
Foodstuffs			
Yams, cassava, cocoyams	22	11	18
Yam flour, maize flour, *gari*, rice	20	15	2
Beans, maize	24	14	2
Peppers, melons, groundnuts	40	10	110
Green leaves, *okro*	14	4	1
Onions and garlic	11	5	1
Bananas, plantains (fresh and dried)	14	7	5

	Ojo 8-day	Elekuru 8-day	Oyo (Akesan) Nightly
Meat (fresh)	9	18	3
Salt, limestone	9	6	6
Palm Oil	37	9	1
Kola nut	148	22	5
Cooked foods	23	17	39
Shea butter	10	1	1
Poultry	13	21	45
Sheep and goats	1	3	38
Stockfish	16	3	2
Fruits (citrus)	3	–	8
Others	8	–	6
Total Foodstuffs	422	166	293
Non-Foodstuffs			
European cloth	38	13	76
Yoruba cloth	–	3	–
Raw cotton	9	4	5
Cotton yarn (local)	–	–	–
Yoruba slippers	3	–	–
Local tobacco	3	2	8
Local soap	13	6	–
Firewood	2	–	–
Calabashes	–	5	69
Baskets	8	1	–
Pots	7	–	14
Mats	1	–	14
Hoes and knives	2	–	–
Yoruba medicines and charms	11	5	27
European beads, pipes, cotton, cigarettes, biscuits, cycle parts, bowls and plates	28	15	90
Kerosene	6	1	9
Leaves for wrapping	10	–	–
Chewing sticks	–	–	15
Others	1	7	3
Total Non-Foodstuffs	142	62	330
Percentages			
Foodstuffs	75%	72%	47%
Non-foodstuffs	25%	28%	53%
Imported goods	17%	14%	31%

Note: the above figures apply to January 1960.

CHAPTER 5

Afikpo Markets: 1900-1960[1]

BY SIMON AND PHOEBE OTTENBERG

In the sixty years covered by this account the Afikpo Ibo have changed from a self-sufficient group of warriors and head-hunters living at a borderline subsistence level to a prospering community of farmers, fishermen, and traders, with economic ties with many parts of Nigeria and the outside world. The transition has been made from a close inward-looking people to a population including many outsiders; gerontocracy has been largely replaced by government by elected representatives; and from a group of farming villages the beginnings of an urban community have emerged.

Here we attempt to trace some aspects of this change in a description of the market system of Afikpo village-group. Following a brief discussion of the social and cultural setting, we describe the market at the beginning of the present century, trace its development up to 1952, when we first carried out field research at Afikpo, and then analyze it in detail as of 1960, in terms of how it is constituted and with reference to its relationship to the numerous markets surrounding Afikpo. Note is also taken of certain major economic activities which are peripheral to the marketing system or completely separate from it.

Afikpo is one of more than two hundred independent village-groups that comprise the Ibo-speaking peoples of southeastern Nigeria, whose total population is more than five million. Traditionally autonomous and relatively self-sufficient, these village-groups possess local markets, have a marked interdependence within local areas, and often take part in wider trade relations. Afikpo is one of sixteen village-groups forming Afikpo Division,[2] all but two of which are Ibo. Its population in 1953 was 26,305 (Nigeria 1953 : 25), with a density that we estimated to be slightly over four hundred persons per square mile. Located on the west bank of the Cross River in the

(1) The authors carried out fieldwork in Afikpo from December 1951 to February 1953 as Area Research Fellows of the Social Science Research Council of New York, with the aid of a grant-in-aid from the Program of African Studies, Northwestern University. Further investigation was conducted from September 1959 to May 1960. Mr. Ottenberg's research during the second period was made possible by a Research Grant of the National Science Foundation, Washington, D.C.

(2) When the term Afikpo is used alone it will be understood to refer to Afikpo village-group. Afikpo Division will be referred to by this designation.

Eastern Ibo area, it is in a transitional region between tropical forest and savanna (Forde and Jones 1950 : 51–56). In the villages nearest the river, many of the men are fishermen and may be on the river from January to July or August. The people of other villages are farmers, growing mainly root crops. The land is hilly, composed of a series of sandstone ridges separated by swampy valleys. The soil of the area is poor, and Afikpo has never been a productive agricultural region. This fact is important in terms of the type of market system that has developed there. Similarly, while forest products, particularly palm kernels, palm oil, and palm wine, are found in the area, they are not available in large commercial quantities and, for example, there is no power operated palm oil mill in the Afikpo region for the processing of oil and kernels, though such mills are common in some other areas of southern Nigeria.

The major root crops are yams, grown almost exclusively by men, and cassava and coco yams, which are women's crops (P. V. Ottenberg 1959 : 205–23). In addition, corn, another women's crop, and rice, grown by both sexes, are cultivated as well as other crops of lesser importance. The main farming season is from February, when clearing of the fields begins, until December, when the yams and most other crops have been harvested. Cassava, however, matures the year round. Cattle cannot be kept in the area long except for the tsetse-resistant dwarf cattle *(muturu)*, but these have been banned from Afikpo because they are a menace to the crops.

The social groupings are of a type characteristic among the Eastern Ibo. There are twenty-three Afikpo villages, each forming a separate compact living area with well-defined borders. The villages are composed of groups of compounds, based on residential patrilineal lineages clustered around squares which are the meeting places of the men's secret society of each village. These villages are grouped into five subdivisions of the village-group: Ozizza, Mkpoghoro, Ugwuago, Oha Isu, and Itim, each of which forms a geographic and social division of Afikpo and has its own tradition of origin. While two of the five subdivisions and several individual villages are larger and more influential than others, no one village or subdivision dominates the village-group, whose corporate activities are carried out chiefly by age groupings that draw their members from most of Afikpo. The traditional government of the village-group is based, as are the village governments, on an age-set organization without well-defined chiefs or heads.

Certain features of the social system, such as nonresidential matrilineal corporate groups that are the major landholding groups in Afikpo, and village secret societies and title societies, are of less importance to the market study than the age groupings and have been described elsewhere (S. Ottenberg 1957; P. V. Ottenberg 1958). Others will be discussed here in terms of their relevance to the market.

Afikpo is closely related historically and culturally to four neighboring Ibo village-groups, each of which has its own system of markets. These are Unwana, to the south; Edda, to the southwest; Amaseri, to the west; and Okpoha, to the northwest. It is with these four groups that much of the Afikpo's trade was carried out in the past and still is today. The non-Ibo groups of Agba, to the north, and Nkumuru, to the east, also possess markets, but until the last two decades Afikpo did not trade a great deal with them because of hostilities and mutual suspicion.

Five basic factors are important in the consideration of the Afikpo market system. The first is the system of time division into the four-day Ibo week, the days of which are *orie, aho, nkwo,* and *ɛkɛ.* There is no tradition of a daily market at Afikpo, and the main Afikpo market meets on *ɛkɛ,* while those of surrounding village-groups meet on other days of the Ibo week. The markets are all within walking distance of one another, so that one can go to a different market each day of the week. Afikpo farm on alternate days, *orie* and *nkwo,* and *ɛkɛ* and *aho* are nonfarm days. The whole idea of trade and exchange is geared to the four-day week as the basic unit of time.

Second, Afikpo market is part of a vast network of markets, large and small, found throughout southeastern Nigeria, usually within five to fifteen miles of one another. Traditionally, each Ibo village-group controlled at least one market within its area. Since there was no formal political superstructure, such as a state or kingdom, uniting these groups, the control of most Ibo, and even non-Ibo, markets in Eastern Nigeria has generally been highly localized. Through these markets, meeting on different days of the Ibo week, a great variety of goods and foodstuffs flow, frequently passing through the hands of middlemen before reaching their ultimate consumers. We believe that Afikpo market is typical of some of these and may serve as one type case of the Eastern Nigerian and Ibo market.

Third, within Afikpo Division, Afikpo is the most acculturated village-group, mainly because of the presence of the divisional administrative headquarters there. The form of the market and the nature of the economic exchanges found within the village-group are clearly related to this fact.

Fourth, the Afikpo women tend to take a larger part in economic production than the men, and they appear to work harder. Men are responsible for the growing of yams, for the collection of palm products, and, in the riverine villages, for fishing. Women grow all other crops except some newly introduced ones, such as rice, and they do virtually all the processing of food for home consumption and for sale, as well as making large numbers of pots. They are also the major carriers of heavy loads from the farms, to and from the markets, and as carriers for contractors and river traders. Men control the major ritual and ceremonial activities in Afikpo, and have more leisure than women. Formerly, however, because of endemic warfare between village-groups, the men were much occupied with fighting and preparations for warfare.

Finally, women have long taken an active part in marketing activities at Afikpo. They willingly carry heavy loads for many miles to market, and work long hours making pots and processing palm oil, cassava, or rice to earn a few pennies. If they do not dominate the economic and social aspects of market life, they have a major share in them. As an influential Afikpo man said when asked why women had a spirit shrine in the market place: "Why shouldn't they? They take the market to be their village square and they can do anything there."

1900

The earliest market Afikpo remember is that which existed about 1900, two years before a British military expedition "opened up" Afikpo and established an administrative headquarters that has remained until the present. The main Afikpo market, *ahia ɛkɛ ukwu* (market—day of Ibo week—big), met at a place between and central to the major Afikpo villages. A few years before it had been moved to this location from about a mile away as a result of a dispute between the Mkpoghoro subdivision, whose villages were nearest this earlier market, and the rest of the village-group. The dispute arose over a perennial claim of the Mkpoghoro villages, particularly the largest, Ndibe, to be the "rulers" of Afikpo, a claim discounted by a great many of the Afikpo but maintained to this day by the people of Mkpoghoro. In the memory of the Afikpo this dispute is but one of a series that have arisen between these villages (especially Ndibe) and the rest of the village-group over issues such as the ownership of palm groves, the right to regulate the time of yam planting and harvesting in the village-group, and, more recently, the right to appoint a traditional chief to represent Afikpo in the Eastern House of Chiefs.

At the time the market was moved, the Mkpoghoro villages had been trying to dominate it, frequently charging tolls, seizing traders' goods, and otherwise attempting to exert their influence. The rest of the Afikpo, in removing the market about a mile further away from Ndibe, hoped to prevent further interference with trade. For a time the Mkpoghoro villages attempted to maintain their own market outside Ndibe, but it failed, and gradually persons from these villages began to use the major market again. Thus the market, like other institutions of Afikpo, was involved in intervillage rivalries within the village-group.

In its new site the market was considered the corporate property of the village-group, and the land on which it stood was regarded as belonging to all Afikpo, including the Mkpoghoro villages. The market was a visible symbol of the village-group, a people sharing a common culture and dialect, and considering themselves distinct from, though related to, the neighboring Ibo groups to the north, west, and south.

The market met on *ɛkɛ*, a day when traditionally no one in Afikpo went to farm, except perhaps in the early morning to collect food to sell at market. Elders who remember the market at that time have said that it was much smaller than the market of 1952, which was in turn considerably smaller than that of 1960. The variety of goods sold was also less, and the distance goods traveled to market was, in general, shorter than in 1952. Most of the food was locally grown and was sold unprocessed. Yams, coco yams, *edo* (a vine-borne vegetable resembling the potato), and palm oil were major food products. Cassava and rice, later so important to the Afikpo economy, were not grown at Afikpo then, nor were maize, coconuts, and other foods that subsequently became important. Intertribal rivalries on the Cross River kept Afikpo fishermen close to their home area, so that while dried fish was available in the market it was not available in large quantities. Soap, either native or imported, was not known in Afikpo at this time, washing being done by soaking and rubbing. Pottery was produced in large quantity by Afikpo women and sold by them in the market, and mats, made by young boys and men, were also sold there. Men of certain Afikpo patrilineages living in different villages were blacksmiths, selling knives, machetes and hoe blades at the market or at their place of work.

Certain additional products were obtained by direct or indirect trade from nearby Ibo village-groups, for example, pink chalk used for body marking and rope for fishing nets from Edda, to the southwest, and native salt from Okposi, in the northwest. While the products from Edda were exchanged directly, the Okposi salt was traded through Amaseri and Okpoha village-groups, which lie between Okposi and Afikpo. Other goods such as iron, gunpowder, and European liquor were traded up the Cross River from the coastal areas through several tribes to Afikpo.

Certain aspects of trade in Afikpo were dominated by a group of Ibo traders, the Aro, who came or whose ancestors came originally from Aro Chuku, about forty miles to the south. These men were active in trade and colonization in many parts of Ibo country (S. Ottenberg 1958), and they were the first real commercial agents at Afikpo. Here they lived scattered about the various villages and made frequent trips to their homeland, taking Afikpo as clients to consult their famous oracle, *Ibini okpabe* (the "Long Juju") to find solutions for various misfortunes and disputes, or as laborers to carry their wares to and from Aro Chuku at previously determined wages. The Aro had long dominated the slave trade in this part of Nigeria, and they traded slaves throughout much of eastern Ibo country. Despite the prevalence of raiding and warfare, they were relatively free to travel wherever they wished because they were greatly feared and respected. In Afikpo, slaves were not sold in the market but in the houses of the Aro. They could be selected by the buyer in Afikpo or could be procured on order from other parts of Ibo country. Afikpo occasionally also sold to the Aro some of their own people, particularly younger sons and daughters and social misfits, as well as outsiders captured in warfare or petty fighting. Afikpo usually exchanged slaves and sometimes other goods with Aro traders living in their own villages. The Aro also recruited mercenaries for villages and village-groups who desired to fight others, and they were known as peace-makers between various Ibo groups. They were, on the whole, wealthy and feared, and in their position of dominance they did not themselves farm or make war. Though they did not totally dominate Afikpo trade or politics, they were very influential.

In addition, the Aro were the most important traders in a number of other products which they frequently sold at *eke* market. These included European cloth, gunpowder, guns and iron, rope, tobacco, and snuff, traded from the coastal area of Nigeria; native cloth from the Nkalagu area about forty miles northwest of Afikpo; and some native iron and iron products from the Nkwerre region, an Ibo area to the west of Afikpo that is famous for its blacksmiths. It was through the Aro that the Afikpo first obtained European goods, even before they had even seen a European. Although the Aro trade dealt with products from the coast, these were traded mainly by land, rather than up the Cross River. Afikpo was one of their minor trading centers, linking the large Uburu market to the northwest with Aro Chuku to the south.

At the turn of the century most of the trade in Afikpo market was by barter. If a person wished to buy some palm oil he brought an article, perhaps a yam, to exchange for the oil. Bargaining was an

integral part of the exchange process, as it is today. Money existed
in the form of brass and copper rods about three feet long, but these
represented relatively large denominations, so that they were used
mainly in the purchase of expensive items, particularly slaves. The
rods were carried on the head, bent double and wrapped in native
cloth in order to conceal the extent of the owner's wealth. Cowries
and manillas, important forms of currency in other sections of eastern
Nigeria, were never used as money at Afikpo. The rods were not produced in Nigeria but came from European traders along the coast,
and the Aro were their major distributors in the Afikpo area. A brass
rod *(okpogho loghologho)* is said to have been worth three shillings
at the time of European occupation, and a copper one *(mkpola)*, six-
pence. These rods were used for gifts and for payments in funerals,
titles, and other ceremonies, as well as for trade. A man who possessed
a few pounds' worth of brass rods was considered wealthy. However,
the basic pattern of Afikpo economic life was corporate ownership of
property by lineages, clans, and residential groups; sharing of foodstuffs and other goods without trade or the use of money was common.
Title societies, for example, were based mainly on the distribution
of large quantities of foodstuffs at ceremonial feasts.

Despite the presence of Aro traders, *ɛkɛ* market was relatively
isolated as compared with later years. Afikpo women traded pots and
some food to the neighboring Ibo markets at Unwana, Edda, and
Okpoha village-groups, which met on *aho,* two days after *ɛkɛ.* On
orie, the day following *ɛkɛ,* some women traded at Amaseri, another
Ibo village-group to the west of Afikpo, but only when Afikpo and
Amaseri were not engaged in one of their frequent boundary disputes. Traders, particularly women, came from Unwana, Edda,
Okpoha, and Amaseri to *ɛkɛ* market to purchase pots, mats, and
sometimes dried fish and other foodstuffs, and to sell chalk and other
products. But Afikpo men and women rarely went beyond these
neighboring markets, and with the exception of the Aro and Cross
River trade, goods from farther away reached Afikpo only after being
traded through these neighboring village-groups. Because of endemic
warfare between Afikpo and non-Ibo village-groups to the east of the
Cross River, trade between them was rare.

Much of this inter-village-group trade was carried on by women,
who would walk to the market in groups, fearing seizure if they
traveled alone. When arriving at market the traders of each group
tended to sit clustered together to sell their wares, so that spatially
the market was divided into groups of persons from the various
village-groups with a separate section for Aro traders, in contrast to
ɛkɛ market today, which is arranged mainly in terms of the type

of commodity for sale. The paths to the markets were narrow and flanked by tall vegetation, often hidden in gullies that had been cut through the soft sandstone by water and constant use, and people moved along them quickly and silently. At times some villages near the paths leading to εkε and other markets claimed the right to charge a toll for each passing trader. Only the Aro, and traders escorted by them, travelled to the large and more distant markets of Uburu and εkε moha to the northwest and north, respectively. Children and infants were rarely taken to market, but were left home in the care of family members or friends. Afikpo believed (and still do to a certain extent) that it was dangerous for children to be brought to market, although it is no longer unusual to see them there. They feared seizure by Aro slavers, and some held to the idea that the market was harmful for children. Similarly, young women were not active in market activities. There was thus a certain restrictive air about trading and market activity at this time.

Within Afikpo village-group, trade and movement were much freer. In addition to the main market, small markets met on *aho* at two fairly central Afikpo villages, Amachara and Ugwuago,[3] and two other similar markets met on *nkwo,* the following day, in more peripheral Afikpo areas, Ozizza in the northeast, and Anohia in the south. These four markets were smaller than the main market and were used almost exclusively by women, who sold small quantities of yams, coco yams, palm oil, leaves, fruits, and other foods for the immediate use of persons living in adjacent villages. The goods for sale came mainly from the farms rather than being obtained in the main Afikpo market for resale. Therefore there was little direct association with εkε market or with the markets of other village-groups. Most of the trade was by barter, and rods were rarely used. Aro traders did not attend these small markets. As far as is known, such markets had no formal means of social control. Disputes were apparently settled by women who happened to be present, particularly the elder women.

The main Afikpo market possessed a system of social control that was part of the larger pattern of authority in Afikpo. At the market there were three shelters where sat the elders' age grades of Afikpo. The senior grade, *oni ekara* (no English equivalent) were the venerated elders of the village-group, perhaps numbering five to ten persons, distinguished by their red stocking caps and the leather bags they carried over their shoulders. As a rule too old and too weak to govern, they played an important ritual role in Afikpo but had no

(3) There is evidence that at some time before 1900 two other local *aho* markets were found in the central Afikpo village area.

part in the control of the market.[4] The next senior age grade, the
ekpe uke esa (society-grade-seven), consisted of six age sets (not seven
as the name indicates) and formed the major legislative and judicial
body of the village-group. They met in the market in their shelter on
ɛkɛ only, passed laws concerning Afikpo customs, and tried cases and
disputes brought to them for settlement. They were the highest
secular court at Afikpo. They also had another meeting place where
they met on nonmarket days in conjunction with the other two
Afikpo grades. The noise and lack of space in the market made it
difficult for all three grades of Afikpo village-group to consult
together at the main market over important issues. The *esa's* shelter
there was sometimes also used for meetings of the elders of Afikpo
with those of neighboring village-groups who were trying to settle
a dispute or to arrange some common action. But these meetings were
frequently carried out outside of the market, so that it would be
incorrect to say that the market was the focal point for the settlement
of inter-village-group disputes or problems; rather, it was the elders
themselves, wherever they met.

The youngest Afikpo age grade, the *ekpe uke isi* (society-grade-
six), also consisting of six age sets (roughly middle-aged to elderly
men), had their own shelter as well. They acted as the police of
Afikpo, reporting disputes to the *ekpe uke esa,* and stopping fights
and other disturbances throughout the village-group. In addition
they acted as the market police. If a dispute arose there they would
attempt to settle it. However, if it was serious they would take it to
the *ekpe uke esa* court, where the case would be tried then and there.
Howover, Aro were too much feared to be brought to the court as a
rule, so that a dispute between an Aro and a non-Aro at the market
was generally settled on the spot by the Aro in his favor. Aside from
these activities there was little regulation of the market, though in
order to prevent fighting there was a strict rule against carrying
machetes or large knives in the market. While traders generally sat
with others of their village-groups, there was no strict regulation as
to where they should remain, and there apparently were no price
controls. The traditional market possessed sanctions against mis-
conduct but otherwise was essentially unregulated. The market, however, was clearly a center of government, and a central forum where
political affairs could be discussed.

ɛkɛ market also, of course, served certain social functions. It was
a center where news and gossip were freely passed about. It was a

(4) However, they owned a large rest house along a major Afikpo path where they
would sit on *nkwo* and insist on a small gift ("dash") from all passers-by, including
traders.

likely place to meet another person when it was difficult or less convenient to meet him at home. This was particularly so since many adult Afikpo went to the market sometime on *ɛkɛ*. The market also was a place of ceremonials: persons performing titles or funeral ceremonies and their friends and relatives, and groups carrying out certain rituals, paraded and danced to announce what they were doing. Again, a person who had sworn an oath of innocence at a shrine and had survived a year without dying or becoming seriously ill (the penalty for swearing falsely) had the right to parade through the market shouting and singing to celebrate his freedom from the bond of swearing.

The Afikpo markets had apparently existed for a considerable period before European contact. It is desirable before turning to a discussion of Afikpo markets at a later time to discuss why markets existed there at all at the turn of the century. One answer might simply be that markets existed in southeastern Nigeria and that the idea of the market diffused to Afikpo from neighboring areas. While this, of course, seems likely, other conditions must have existed at Afikpo before markets could develop. This question is difficult to answer except in general terms, and all that we can do here is to list some of the conditions that appear to be related to the market.

1. The high density of population in this area means that personal face-to-face contact of large numbers of persons within ready walking distance of one another was possible and clearly did occur despite military and political considerations.

2. The division of Afikpo into two major food producing groups, fishermen and farmers, necessitated some system of exchange between them. Other occupations, such as the production of palm products, while not usually full-time occupations, also needed regular outlets for exchange.

3. Some differences in productive capacities existed between Afikpo and neighboring village-groups. Clay for pots seems to be better and more abundant at Afikpo than in surrounding areas; palm products, including palm wine, and chalk are more abundant at Edda; and salt is available at Okposi. While the relative presence or absence of these items in a village-group did not always explain the exclusive pre-occupation of certain village-groups with certain products (after all, Afikpo could mine some chalk and Edda produce sufficient clay to make some pots), it does help to explain the need for some system of exchange.

4. Even among producers of the same basic goods, such as yam farmers, there are seasonal variations in production, personal differences in productive skills, differing needs for yams for ceremonial

purposes that may make a producer of one product sell surpluses of this product at one time and buy the same product at another.

We do not claim that these four factors were the specific cause of the development of Afikpo markets, but they are in some way related to it.

We can therefore characterize the Afikpo market system as of 1900 as small in scale and based mainly on locally produced goods. Afikpo possessed a relatively self-sufficient economy that was augmented somewhat by trade, but trade was distinctly a secondary activity. It was a system based essentially on barter, with only a small range of goods for trade, and a system where larger amounts of foodstuffs were exchanged in ceremonial and ritual events. The political and military situation prevented the development of wide-scale trade and contact except for a limited few. The market was controlled by the elders, the traditional rulers of Afikpo, with Aro traders dominating certain specialized aspects of the trade. The markets of neighboring Ibo village-groups were apparently similar in these characteristics, though differing somewhat in size and in the products exchanged. It is against this background of the traditional market that we must view the developments following British conquest.

1900–1952

The conquest of Afikpo in 1902 led to the gradual pacification of the area. The government administrative center came more and more to control the affairs of people of Afikpo village-group, as well as of the other village-groups that made up Afikpo Division. Nevertheless, the period from the time of British conquest to 1952, when we first carried out research at Afikpo, was one in which traditional social controls still dominated the market and in which the greatest changes were in the economic aspects of market activity. During this period *ɛkɛ* market, though remaining in the same location and meeting on the same day of the Ibo week, increased considerably in size and changed from a largely traditional to a partially commercialized market. By commercialization we mean a considerable emphasis on the profit motive in trade and in increase in the importance of full-time professional traders in the market. In 1900, by contrast, most trade was more casual and limited, and the profit motive does not appear to have been as important as the desire to obtain required goods through simple exchange for more or less immediate use.

This commercialization was related to the increased diversification of goods for sale. Although the slave trade no longer existed, and the sale of native gin, having been declared illegal by the government, had been relegated to the houses and compounds of certain producers and traders, most of the traditional commodities were still available in 1952. In addition, a large number of new products that had appeared as a result of culture contact were present for sale. "Article" sellers offered schoolbooks, stationery supplies, hardware, patent medicines, cosmetics, and soap. Imported shoes and cotton cloth made in Europe and Japan for the West African trade were available. The cultivation of certain new crops, namely cassava and maize, had been firmly established at Afikpo, and women dominated their production and trade. This increased the volume of women's trade and did much to free them of their former economic dependence on men (P. V. Ottenberg 1959). Moreover, the introduction of these crops put an end to the famine period during June and July, when yams from the previous year's harvest had been eaten or had spoiled and the harvest of new yams had not yet begun. By 1952 cattle were being brought to Afikpo from the north, one animal being slaughtered each market day. The pottery industry had expanded, and many Afikpo pots were shipped down the Cross River to the Calabar area by canoe. In addition to new foods and products, service industries, namely bicycle repairing, tailoring, and mending, had become a feature of the market, and many engaged in these occupations worked at home or in their own shops on nonmarket days.

The increased diversity of goods and the introduction of new products and services can be related to the developing economy of Nigeria during the first half of the twentieth century, when major trading cities which were developing, such as Aba, Port Harcourt, Onitsha, and Calabar, became the focus of the European import and export trade in Eastern Nigeria. These were the centers from which came the impetus for much of the growing trade in non-Nigerian goods in the thousands of markets in this part of Nigeria. The linkage of Afikpo to these large urban markets was facilitated by the building of many bicycle paths and the improvement of existing footpaths. At Afikpo the first half of the present century saw the disappearance of many of the fears and restrictions concerning travel, the opening up of transportation routes, and the adoption of the bicycle as the chief means of long-distance transport. In addition there was an expansion of the Cross River canoe trade following the cessation of intertribal hostilities on the river. While most of the major roads in the Afikpo area had been built by the mid-1930's, even as late as 1952 there was little motor transport to Afikpo, and most trade goods came by bicycle or canoe, or for shorter distances by head-load.

The four small local markets in Afikpo, meeting either on *aho* or *nkwo* day, seem to have changed little during this period, though new crops such as cassava and corn were added to the commodities for sale. A new small market, near the government station along a path leading from the farms to one of the larger Afikpo villages, had appeared by 1952. Meeting for only a few hours on *aho,* the market dealt exclusively in cassava freshly brought from the farms by the women who had grown it. The history of the development of this market is obscure. It seemed to serve some *gari* (cassava meal) processors in the neighboring villages, as well as non-Afikpo living at or near the government station.

The cessation of hostilities between Afikpo and non-Ibo groups across the river led to the development of some trade between them, though there was still much suspicion and fear. Trade between Afikpo and the neighboring village-groups of Okpoha, Edda, and Unwana—and Amaseri when not disputing with Afikpo—increased during this period; Afikpo traders went further afield to the markets of more distant village-groups to buy and sell, and traders from these markets began to appear at Afikpo.

Afikpo men took to trading long distances on the Cross River. Some traders exported pottery to Calabar, while others went north along the river to buy yams, also to sell at Calabar. Afikpo returning from this coastal area generally brought European dried stockfish and other kinds of local dried fish purchased in the Calabar area to sell at Afikpo. A European factory on the Cross River, established shortly after British conquest, became a collection point for palm oil and kernels for much of Afikpo Division, from where they were shipped by boat to Calabar for export. However, Afikpo village-group contributed little to this trade, as it was not a rich palm tree area. Aro traders were active in long-distance trading from Afikpo but they no longer dominated this trade.

Other Afikpo traders brought European goods by land from Aba, Port Harcourt, and Onitsha, but traded few products from Afikpo to these cities. The expansion of Afikpo trade outside the area of its villages was facilitated during the period under discussion by the migration of Afikpo men, often as clerks and laborers, to all the major cities in the Eastern Region. Afikpo traders generally could visit and rely on the help of Afikpo wherever they went to urban centers for trade. Some of these resettled Afikpo became traders in the cities to which they had migrated.

Furthermore, outside traders, mainly Ibo, seeing possibilities of lucrative trade in "articles," cloth, bicycle parts, iron products, and other commodities, settled at Afikpo, particularly in a stranger's quarter called Number Two, developing near the government station. There they often had shops, which were open daily, except on *εkε,* when they would take some of their goods to sell at the market. This was the first indication of a trend toward the development of a daily market. Other traders, both outsiders and Afikpo, began trading in cloth, "articles," and other goods at Afikpo market on *εkε,* Amaseri market on *orie,* either Okpoha or Edda (or occasionally Unwana) market on *aho,* and sometimes Abba Omege market (north of Okpoha), or Aka Eze market (west of Amaseri) on *nkwe,* and then returning to Afikpo on *εkε* to begin the cycle again. They moved from market to market, carrying their heavy loads packed in boxes or cartons on the backs of their bicycles. Not all of these traders lived at Afikpo, some staying at Amaseri or elsewhere in the circuit.

The Afikpo blacksmiths lineages had given up their profession by 1952 and Ezza blacksmiths, from a large Ibo village-group about thirty miles north of Afikpo, came at the beginning of each farming season to reside in various Afikpo villages where they made and repaired hoes, machetes and other iron tools. The Ezza, who were famous Ibo yam farmers, also provided hired farm labor, the Afikpo yam planting season coming at a somewhat later time than their own. In addition, by 1952, palm wine tappers from Okposi, about twenty miles northwest of Afikpo, a high quality palm wine area, had moved into different Afikpo villages, rented trees or whole groves, and were enjoying an important share of the Afikpo palm wine trade, selling both in the villages and in *εkε* market. Taking into account all the above-mentioned classes of traders, it is fair to say that by 1952 we find the beginnings of heterogeneous groups of full-time professional traders.

The majority of the sellers in the market, however, were casual traders who earned their living chiefly by other means. Farmers brought their surplus yams to market; mat makers came to sell the products of their craft; carpenters sold doors, windows, or furniture they had made in their shops on other days of the week. There were no woman full-time traders such as have long been found in urban Ibo areas. While a few women bought such products as dried prawns, rice, or dried peppers in quantity and sold them by the cigarette tinful, most lacked sufficient capital to do so. Although a great many women sold in the market, they traded on a very modest scale, usually selling surplus farm products, pots of their own manufacture, or food such as fermented cassava or *gari* that they had processed themselves. With the exception of a small European-acculturated element, few young women sold in the market, the women traders being primarily middle-aged or elderly. The place of the young women was thought to be in the home and the farm, away from the distractions and temptations of the market place.

A further economic factor that must be mentioned is the virtual disappearance of the barter system of exchange and the relegation of the use of rods as money exclusively to ritual and ceremonial occasions. These changes were the result of the introduction of British West African currency, which was everywhere in use. The availability of small monetary units such as the halfpenny, and the penny (and earlier the *anini*, worth one-tenth of a penny) facilitated petty trade in a manner that had been impossible with rods. Bargaining, however, was still the standard method of reaching an agreement on price, though certain European goods had come to attain fairly set prices. There were no formal price controls. While in times of unusual scarcity the sellers of a given product might agree informally on a minimum price, there was no means of enforcing the agreement. A marked seasonal fluctuation in prices was evident. The prices of root crops such as yams and coco yams were highest in the late rainy season during the few months before their harvest. Although cassava could be harvested at any time of the year, the increased scarcity of other root crops raised its price and also that of *gari* at this time of year. The prices of some products were relatively stable for most of the year but were markedly lower following the harvest. For example, groundnuts were cheapest from September to December; rice, from November to February. The prices of palm oil and of various types of dried fish were highest at the end of the rains and early in the dry season. In the case of the latter, the increased demand during the festival season, November to January, was responsible for the rise in prices. There seemed to be no buying of products during a period of plenty and holding them until they were scarce in order to obtain a higher price.

From 1900 to 1952 standards of wealth as well as prices had risen considerably. Certainly, a person who had appeared wealthy in 1900 with £3 worth of rods would no longer be considered so with £3 worth of currency in 1952, and by this latter date a person who owned £15 was only a moderately wealthy person. While much property was still corporately owned by traditional groups such as lineages and clans, individual ownership of wealth was increasing. There was less of a tendency for a wealthy individual to distribute his wealth among his kin than formerly. Title societies now collected and distributed currency, the feasting and food-distribution aspects of their rituals having decreased in importance. In traditional social activities, currency was more and more being used as a substitute for food, rods, and other items, so that it was common for a man to say at a ceremony, "Here is your chicken, here is your goat," while giving 3/6 and £1, respectively.

An examination of the Afikpo authority structure in 1952 shows that during the preceding half-century the elders had retained much of their influence. They maintained control of the market, settled disputes arising there, and continued to carry out their police and judicial activities. The traditional regulations against the carrying of machetes or knives had now been augmented by one forbidding the riding of bicycles within the market. The elders' controls of Afikpo traders included restrictions on Afikpo women's trading at two nearby markets; by 1952 the elders had forbidden women to go to nearby Amaseri market, where there had reportedly been sexual contacts between Afikpo women traders and Amaseri men, and from trading at Usumutong market, on the other side of the Cross River, where an Afikpo woman had been severely beaten during a dispute. But the position of the elders' age grades had become weaker as a result of the institution by the British of a system of Warrant Chiefs between the time of conquest and the 1930's, in which a number of influential elders were appointed as "chiefs" of Afikpo, with the right to hear and settle certain kinds of disputes. In the 1930's this system was replaced by a Native Authority Council, and later a Native Authority Court as well, each having representatives from the major villages of Afikpo village-group. While the Coucil had the right to effect certain changes in the market, it had not passed any major market legislation by 1952. The Native Authority Court, however, had sometimes exercised the right to try cases arising in the market and trade disputes in general. While litigation of these kinds were generally taken to the elders in the market-place in the first instance (that is, to what was by then an illegal court in government's view), if any of the disputants were not satisfied with the elders' decision they could still take the case to the Native Authority Court, which met about half a mile from the market, frequently on the same day as the market[5]. Although the Native Authority Court members were middle-aged or elderly men who usually did not wish to go against the rulings of the traditional elder's group, the Court decisions were nevertheless subject to review by the District Office. The mere presence of such a court in addition to the "illegal" nature of the traditional elders' court, represented steps toward removal of market controls from the hands of the traditional rulers, a trend which continued from 1952 to 1960.

By 1952 there was a Native Authority Sanitary Inspector who was in charge of the inspection of cattle and other animals slaughtered

(5) By 1952 there was also a Divisional Magistrate's Court following English judicial procedures. However, most disputes concerning the market or trade were not of a serious enough nature to be taken to this court.

at the market and of sanitary conditions in general. Actually, he exerted little in the way of sanitary controls at this time, but his presence marked the introduction of bureaucratic control of the market which later increased greatly. In 1952 the District Office at Afikpo and the Afikpo village-group Native Authority Council were already making plans for the reorganization of the market through the extension of the market site, the building of permanent stalls for which rent would be charged, the orderly arrangement of individuals selling different products in clearly demarcated sections of the market, and the improvement of market conditions. The market was considered by the District Office and by some Afikpo to be dirty, unorganized, and difficult to control. By 1952 these plans had reached the stage where a section of the proposed enlarged market was being cleared by communal labor of the villages near the market under the direction of the Native Authority Council, but the work did not progress rapidly since many Afikpo elders suspected that the Council intended to take over full control of the market and did not encourage the work.

The market continued its social functions of 1900 in relatively unchanged form. It still served as a center for news and gossip, a place to meet others, and to pass through while performing certain ceremonies. Because women now went more freely to the market than previously, it meant that it was more of a gathering place for female friends and relatives than ever before.

If we were to characterize *eke* market in 1952 we could say that social and economic controls of the market were still minimal and still largely in the hands of the traditional rulers, trade and marketing activities had expanded and become diversified, and professional traders, with the bicyle as the basic means of transportation, had appeared. Outsiders had come to take an increasing part in the Afikpo trade, and Afikpo traders had begun to travel to other parts of eastern Nigeria. The size of the market had increased, and a money economy had come to replace a barter system of trade. The market was thus partially commercialized, though still controlled by traditional groupings and still serving mainly local needs.

1960

While the Afikpo market could be said to have undergone a gradual growth and expansion from 1900 to 1952, its development between the latter date and 1960 would be more accurately described as mushrooming. In addition to a striking change in the volume of trade, there were important qualitative changes: the degree of commercialization increased greatly, social and economic controls over the market became more bureaucratic, and it changed from an essentially local institution to a transshipment center for goods intended for other parts of eastern Nigeria. Furthermore, other types of exchange had developed outside of the market place.

While trends in the direction of these changes were discernible by 1952, the speed with which they occurred was unprecedented. Some of them can be attributed to the economic prosperity of Nigeria as a whole during these years and to marked improvement in transportation, but others are related to developments within Afikpo. Among the former are several factors. The first is the increased buying power of individuals. A second is the widening and paving of major roads to the west and north of Afikpo and the building of a bridge across the Asu River ten miles north of Afikpo, where formerly a small ferry provided limited service and was often out of operation during the rainy season. Third, lorry service in and out of Afikpo increased greatly, and lorries began to replace bicycles as a means of transporting goods. While in 1952 the only regular service was the lorry which made a round trip to the railway station at Afikpo Road, forty miles to the west, on Mondays, Wednesdays, and Fridays, by 1960 there were several lorries a day to Afikpo Road and Okigwe to the west, to Aba in the south, and to Abakaliki, forty miles to the north, a provincial headquarters and transfer point for travel to Enugu and the Cameroons. Also a daily bus provided service to Onitsha, on the Niger, a major link between eastern and western Nigeria. These improvements were part of a general economic development and expansion that facilitated the growth of trade rather than resulting from the pressures of business interests. Work on the roads was government sponsored, and the increase in transport services came as a consequence both of prosperity and the feasibility of travel.

Changes having to do with developments in Afikpo were the building of three residential secondary schools in the community and the establishment of the Afikpo District Council. The students and District Council employees formed a consumer population with semi-urbanized tastes and demands that in turn affected market trade. For example, in February, 1960, there were more than 650 students boarding at schools at Afikpo, whose food supplies mainly came from the Afikpo market. Most of these students were not from Afikpo. Also, the rapid development of primary schools at Afikpo since 1952, coupled with that of secondary schools, brought many new teachers into the area. Afikpo had become an educational center.

It is difficult to assess the actual increase in the volume of trade in εkε market between 1952 and 1960 since no records have been kept

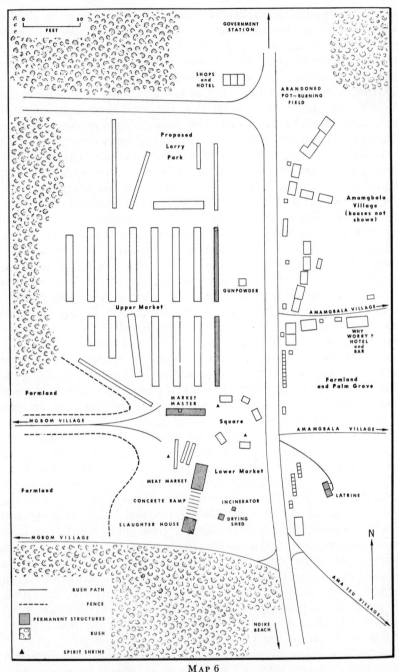

MAP 6

SKETCH MAP OF ɛkɛ MARKET, 1960

of the amounts of goods exchanged or money involved. An impressionistic idea can be gained, however, by the comparison of amounts of space devoted to the sale of particular commodities during the two years. In a map of the market in 1952, the space devoted to European cloth and "articles" was the equivalent of perhaps a dozen stalls for each type of products. According to the Market Master's records of stall rentals for the month of January 1960, the number of rent-paying cloth sellers was 73 and that of "article" sellers was 80. Because formerly dried fish was not sold in stalls but out in the open market, it is difficult to make comparisons for this product, but there was obviously a great increase in its sales. While the number of sellers was probably not over 30 in comparable months of 1952, the number of rent-paying stall holders selling dried fish in January 1960, was 144, and in addition there were quite a number of traders selling these fish outside stalls. Although there was never more than one cow or bull slaughtered for beef each market day in 1952, by 1960 the usual number was three or even four.

Another factor in the increase in trade was that in 1960 the market began earlier and closed later in the day than in 1952. Whereas the bulk of the selling had formerly been between ten or eleven in the morning and four in the afternoon, the heavy trade was now extended for an hour or more at each end of the day.

In εκε market the most readily apparent changes were the physical ones. Located on the west side of the north-south road from the government station to Ndibe Beach, on the Cross River, it became more easily accessible by automobile and bicycle with the building of a paved motor road connecting the north end of the market directly with the main road to the west. Whereas formerly most people came to market by bush path on foot or bicycle, many now came along the road, a great number on bicycles, many by lorry, and a few in their own automobiles.

While the market covered an area of about 2.7 acres in 1952, in 1960 it covered about 5.5 acres within the market proper, and also spread eastward across the road where a number of shops and services were located in sheds or private houses. The simple comparison of areas is misleading, however; whereas the old market was an unplanned sprawling affair with a large proportion of the wares simply spread out on the ground, the newer part of the market was much more compact, with goods and dealers closely packed into row upon row of stalls.

The layout in 1960 was actually a compromise between the old rural market, in a grove of trees with its maze of crooked paths and a few tiny bamboo and thatch shelters for protection from sun and rain, and the prototype of the urban market, in a cleared and leveled area with long, straight ranks of concrete and permanent-roofed stalls. Though "progress" was everywhere in sight, there was still much of the casualness and disorder of a bush market, and in the newly added section the setting up of orderly rows of concrete stalls had only begun, the stalls being far outnumered by bamboo and thatch structures designated as temporary. In the older part of the market a new slaughterhouse, meat market, drying shed, and incinerator had been built of concrete with permanent roofs, but all around these buildings casual traders sat on the ground with their wares for sale.

What might still be called the heart of the market was the small square opening onto the north-south road at the main entrance to the market and flanked on two sides by the traditional thatch-roofed shelters of the three elders' age grades of Afikpo, virtually only part of the market that was unchanged. Here the elders still sat on market day and friend greeted friend. The surroundings were vastly different, however. Formerly at the north end of the market, the square was now toward the south end, since the market had spread northward with the construction of the new stalls as well as expanding considerably to the west. While the elders were still treated with deference and listened to as men of wisdom, market business matters were referred to the Market Master, an employee of the Afikpo District Council, who sat in his office in one of the ranks of concrete stalls that extended back from the square.

Several phases of the proposed market reorganization had already been carried out although the conversion was by no means complete. *ɛkɛ* market was now formally under the control of the District Council, established in 1955, which had gradually assumed responsibility for it, following a plan drafted by the District Engineer in that year. After the building of the first permanent stalls in a newly cleared area north of the old market, the Council attempted to move traders in some commodities to this new site late in 1956, meeting strong resistance on the part of Afikpo. Although this had largely been accomplished by 1960, it was not without difficulty, and the market was still far from the model envisioned by the planners.

In 1960 the area surrounding the market, on palm forest and bush, was becoming a neighborhood of small shops and taverns (designated by the term "hotel and bar" though few provided sleeping accommodations) as more and more people built alongside the road opposite the market in the hope of profiting from the rapid commercial growth of Afikpo. To the east of the market, where several villages came quite close to the road that bordered it, the space between them had been filled with a small but crowded settlement of houses that included several taverns and stores and the sheds of a number of workmen. While not under the control of the market, this settlement was in fact a part of it. To the north of the market, along the road to the west, one hotel and two shops opened during the early months of 1960.

For purposes of description, the market proper can be divided into two principal sections: the lower market, including the square, which corresponded quite closely to the market of 1952 except for a small section east of the road which was now devoted to shops, and the upper market, or part extending north and west from the square, almost all of which had been built after 1955. In 1960 the upper market was nearly twice the size of the lower. As has been mentioned, except for the slaughterhouse, meat market, drying shed, and incinerator, the lower market was much the same as it had been for many years, with a considerable number of trees still standing and the land still following its natural contours. Here so-called casual traders (as opposed to those who rented stalls) sold pots, vegetable produce, rope and mats, poultry, and prepared foods such as fermented cassava. The new meat market carried on its flourishing trade surrounded and, to a certain extent ignored, by the more traditionally oriented traders. Behind it were three crooked lines of tiny stalls jammed close together. Four and a half feet high at most, they consisted simply of a series of bamboo uprights supporting thatch roofs, there being no partitions between the individual sections other than the poles that supported the roofs. In these traders sat on the ground, selling chickens, ducks, and eggs in two of the rows, and small pots made for sacrifices in the one furthest back from the meat market. These stalls were not rented, but used by casual traders, and the District Council had made plans to tear them down.

In the lower market also, the traditional spirit shrines were found. The middle elders' age grade, *ekpe uke esa,* had a shrine, *Ibini okpabe,* outside their shelter, which was linked with the "Long Juju" oracle of Aro Chuku. While it was for the general health and welfare of this grade, it was also believed to encourage people to come to the market and to help keep peace there ("to keep the market cool," as the elders put it). Sacrifices were not made at it regularly but only occasionally—for example, after there had been considerable trouble in the market, such as disputes or fighting, and usually only after the grade leaders had consulted a diviner who indicated that the spirit of the shrine was calling for a sacrifice.

The senior elders' grade, *oni ekara,* had a similar shrine outside their market shelter, but it was primarily for the grade members' welfare, rather than for the market. The junior elders' grade had no shrine at all. All of this is in keeping with the three grades' position within the village-group. The senior grade members were old, beyond the age when they had much authority, and largely concerned with keeping alive. The middle grade was the political arm of Afikpo and it is thus proper that they should have a shrine relating to control of the market. The junior grade members were not ritual or political experts, but served largely in a police capacity. Therefore there was little need for them to have a shrine at the market.

A third shrine *oma ahia* (soul-market), was the property of the old women of Afikpo. It had been moved from the former market site when ɛkɛ market was established shortly before 1900. Like similar shrines in the markets of neighboring village-groups, *oma ahia* was thought essential to women's success in selling, and, at least, many of the old women felt that without its help their trade would be doomed to failure, though the younger women were less concerned with the shrine. The immediate area of the shrine was taboo to men, and any man who passed too close to it was fined a few pence by the old woman who kept watch over it on market day and who would save the money for one of their periodic sacrifices to the spirit.

During the reorganization of the market, the building of the meat market on the site of the shrine necessitated its removal to a position several yards to the west. The old women were greatly offended at this, and a number of them subsequently refused to move to the upper market as the planners wished them to, for fear that if they did, *oma ahia* would no longer help them.

While the market square was not primarily a trading area, several commodities were still sold there in 1960. At the north edge toward the back of the square, native cloth, used for loincloths and wrappers, was displayed on the ground and on bamboo racks. Mats were laid out for sale on the ground in front of the *ekpe uke esa* shelter. In addition to the three shelters for the elders' age grades there were two sheds, one for the sale of bush meat such as antelope or cutting-grass (cane rat), either fresh or dried, and the other for yam baskets made of sticks lashed together with fiber. At one end of this shed large wooden mortars and pestles for pounding yams were also sold. Along the road at the north and south ends of the square, women sat in clusters selling palm oil, roasted groundnuts, oranges, and paw-paws to persons entering and leaving the market. In keeping with the traditional orientation of the square and those who sat there on market day, the products sold there were all produced locally or nearby and were not associated with the European way of life.

In the upper market, north and east of the square, there were twenty-two ranks of stalls, fifteen of them double lines with two rows of stalls back to back, and seven single. Of the total, three (two single and one double) were permanent concrete structures with asbestos roofs and the rest were placed in accordance with a long-range plan of market development. Except for a few that did not follow the plan, the ranks were 125 feet in length, with a distance of 25 feet between them. Most of them extended north-south, more or less parallel with one another, in two main sections extending westward from two ranks of permanent stalls about 75 feet from the north-south road.

At the south end of the upper market was a double rank of permanent stalls extending westward from the middle of the square for some 80 feet. Here, on the north side, the Market Master had his office and a number of cloth sellers were located. The south side was completely empty, a sort of no man's land between the old market and the new. A few used it as a resting place, and some parked their bicycles there, but for purposes of trade it did not seem to be recognized. Behind this rank a single row of tiny bamboo and thatch stalls extended for 150 feet diagonally to the northwest, following the course of a former bush path that had been replaced by the east-west road.

At the north end of the upper market, five ranks of temporary stalls had been set up more or less at random around a central clearing designated as a lorry park, though it was not used as such until late April 1960. Until then the space was used by casual traders selling produce and salt, and the lorries parked at the extreme northeast corner of the market.

Like the arrangement of stalls in the upper market, the products sold in them reflected, to a great extent, the rapid culture change of the 1950's. Here there was a predominance of products and services that were either European in origin or associated with a more urban way of life and a higher standard of living than those of the lower market. Of these the most conspicuous were imported European cloth, "articles," dried fish,[6] rice (a new food for Afikpo), and food and beverage service.

Though a number of the stalls in the upper market were not rented at the time of the study, it was crowded indeed, especially toward the back of the market, with a number of traders such as sellers of dried fish, kerosene, and palm wine setting themselves up in the spaces between the ends of ranks. Also, some of the rows of stalls seemed to have overflowed, with lines of rice sellers, for example, sitting outside on the ground, facing the stalls, and the prospective buyers picking their way between them. Undoubtedly this was partly seasonal, since this was the time of post-harvest ceremonials when these

[6] Dried fish had long been used by Afikpo, but formerly in much smaller quantities.

products were in great demand, and they were in plentiful supply during the dry season, but it also seemed to be symptomatic of the transitional state of the market in which many of the traders still resented being asked to pay stall rentals and claimed the right to sell where and as they pleased.

Except for the 75-foot-wide strip of land along the north-south road, the upper market had all been cleared and work on leveling the ground had begun, though there were still several low places that flooded during the rains. In addition to the casual traders sitting on the ground in the proposed lorry park, there were also several lines of sellers seated on either side of footpaths leading into various parts of the market, principally from the northeast corner where the lorries parked. The most notable of these was the *gari* line, actually two double rows of over one hundred women seated close together along a forking pathway behind great basins heaped high with *gari*. In season there was also quite a long double line of women selling oranges, as well as a shorter one selling leaves for soup.

In the wide grassy strip along the road, where quite a number of palm trees still remained, the market was also visibly spreading. Immediately to the north of the square, where several paths criss-crossed the land between one rank of permanent stalls and the road, sellers of used clothes (which became available in profusion in the autumn of 1959) hung their wares on lines strung between the scattered palm trees or placed them on temporary racks they had made by attaching crossbars to bamboo poles stuck in the ground. Between the next rank of stalls further north and the road, a tiny bamboo and thatch shed, which had suddenly appeared between one market day and the next in December 1959, was devoted to the sale of gunpowder, in great demand for the shooting of Dane guns in ceremonials, and carbide, used in headlamps by night hunters in the bush. Further north, livestock sellers tethered sheep and goats where they could graze in the shade of the palms. Thirty feet to the east of the above-mentioned traders, middlemen stationed themselves at intervals along the roadside as buyers of palm oil and kernels for resale in city markets or to European companies for export.

The casualness of some of these arrangements was only temporary, however. During the first few months of 1960, a new row of temporary stalls was built onto the back of the two single ranks of permanent stalls nearest the road, and the second-hand clothing sellers were moved into them. The Market Master expressed his disapproval of the place chosen by the livestock sellers, since in the plan a special section had been reserved for them in the back of the market, and in February he presaged their ultimate removal by ordering the poultry sellers to move from the lower market to a new location toward the rear of the upper market. Despite the fact that he expected resistance from them they did comply, though not without grumbling. It appeared that the parkway the planners had envisioned bordering the market might yet become a reality.

In the settlement of shops just east of the market, there was some duplication of commodities sold in the market proper, and also some additional services. In a series of small sheds along the road carpenters, blacksmiths, bicycle repairmen, and a barber plied their trade. Some of the houses served both as residences and places of business. A few were used also as warehouses for the storage of such products as groundnuts, dried beans, gasoline, and kerosene.

With the growing congestion of the area, commercial activities were spreading along the path leading to the nearest village. Several buildings were under construction, and a series of carpenters' sheds led to the more imposing Why Worry Hotel and Bar. On the other side of the road, just south of the market, a good-sized house built originally as a private residence had been rented, one room to a palm kernel buyer for a major European company and another as a hotel and bar where palm wine was sold. Beyond them, the building of other houses had begun.

While the main access to the market was by roads from the north, south, and west, a number of bush paths extended to the east, southeast, and southwest. The area directly to the west of the market place was mostly bush, with a small section of farmland near the southwest corner. Here, however, two houses under construction foretokened its complete encirclement.

Despite the sense of disorder and lack of planning that a non-African might register on first visiting *eke* market, there were often logical connections in the juxtapositions of various products and reasons for their locations. The wholesalers of dried fish, for example, sold their wares in the close vicinity of the hotels at the back of the upper market, when the buyers, many of whom had come great distances by bicycle, could refresh themselves before the long journey home. Sellers of the popular snacks, roasted groundnuts, pawpaws, and oranges—the most popular Nigerian thirst-quencher—stationed themselves at the front of the square and along bush paths leading into the market. Like a bakery shop in a commuters' railway station, the *gari* line bordered the main path leading to where the lorries were parked, an ideal place for outgoing passengers to pick up the main ingredient of a quick meal on the way home. In the lower market, what seemed on market day to be a confused welter of paths (along which the casual traders lined their wares according to type) was in reality not so. The paths followed the drainage contours of the ground, which rise gradually from the road to the back of the market, so that the sellers sat on slightly raised platforms where customers could inspect their products as they moved among them, comparing those of the different sellers and choosing the ones they preferred.

Although the analogy is perhaps strained, it is no more possible to describe a Nigerian market in terms of only one of the senses than it would be to convey to a foreigner the impression of rush hour in the New York subway by telling merely what it looked like. One can begin, and at quite a distance, with the sound. As the reader is so often told in ethnographic works on West Africa, one hears from the distance of up to a mile the muted roar of thousands of voices, which steadily increases in volume as one approaches the market. As he enters, this roar is punctuated by calls of greeting, sudden vociferous outbursts of quarreling, infants' cries, and the honking of lorries and clang of bicycle bells. The smell of stockfish is combined with the pungent aromas of palm oil and kerosene. The sun—or the rain—beats down. Squashed oranges sucked dry of their juice lie scattered in the thick dust or in the slippery red mud. The brilliant colors of the African trade cloths, the garish array of plastics that has invaded West Africa, and vegetable foods, oranges, bananas, chili peppers contrast with the uniform dullness of bale after bale of dried fish, mounds of groundnuts, endless rows of yams, and basins of rice and beans.

Somehow, though, it is on the next day that one receives the most powerful impression of the market. The people and the goods are gone, and the stalls look strangely dead and decrepit. But the smells linger, the animals are back again, and the clean-up man is patiently sweeping up the orange peels to take them to the drying shed and thence to the incinerator.

Market Trade and Activities.

By 1960 there had been a marked change in the trade in ɛkɛ market. The number of professional male traders had greatly increased, and women, though still not usually trading full time, were buying and selling on a much larger scale than formerly. Probably the advent of the professional market woman would await the development of the daily market, since women's family and household responsibilities precluded their moving about constantly as in the case of many men traders.

In addition, there were many more middlemen, both buying and selling in Afikpo, than in 1952. A number of men brought dried fish upriver by canoe from Itu and Calabar areas and also by lorry from

Aba and Port Harcourt to sell to young men for resale in the outlying markets of Afikpo Division. Some men bought salt from European companies in Calabar and sold it to Afikpo women, who packaged it and sold it in *eke* market. Others brought products from te north, often down the Cross River (for example, dried beans and groundnuts), which they sold to women retailers in Afikpo. Some bought yams in quantity either from Aka Eze to the west or from Abakaliki and other areas to the north. These yams, larger than those grown in Afikpo, were in great demand there. Men and some women bought unmilled rice in the Afikpo area and steamed it preparatory to milling, though the milling and retailing were done by women.

Although most of the middlemen in Afikpo market were there in the capacity of sellers, there were some buyers of locally-produced palm oil and kernels and of *gari* made in Afikpo for resale at Abakaliki, where this food was in great demand but where few knew how to prepare it.

There were still many nonprofessional sellers who brought commodities to market in small amounts, though these were proportionately fewer than before. A distinctive class of traders that seemed to be emerging was what might be called semi-professional women traders, who devoted most of their productive efforts to the buying and processing of commodities for sale in the market rather than to farming, as had formerly been the case. While there had been a few such women in the market in 1952, there were many more in 1960 and they were on the whole younger than their predecessors.

Actually, the categories of traders had changed less than their relative proportions. While there had been a few full-time men traders and a small number of semi-professional women traders in 1952, there were now many of both types; and, as the emphasis of the market shifted more toward Western and urban tastes, the casual sellers had become less important in the total market picture than before. This is not to say that their number had decreased, however, for on a busy market day they filled up all the lower market and a considerable part of the upper as well. If they had been moved to the section intended for them by the planners in the back of the upper market, it would have been found to be much too small. In the eyes of the District Council, with its emphasis on the market as a money-making enterprise for the community, they played a relatively minor role in trade yet they were still an important social and economic force in Afikpo.

There were distinct patterns of specialization both in market producing and selling. Division of activities according to sex, though less strict than before, was still marked. Most productive activities were still in the hands of women. The most important of these were pot-making, the steaming of rice and taking it to be milled, the processing of palm oil and kernels, and the preparation of fermented cassava, *gari,* cooked foods, roasted groundnuts, and salt (bought in 90-pound sacks and repacked in small raffia containers for resale). Of these, the production of pots and *gari* were the most important, and the processing of rice was becoming more popular. Pot-making, greatly respected by Afikpo tradition, was practiced mostly by middle-aged and elderly women. While some younger women made pots, many felt that the amount of work involved in making them was disproportionate to the profits obtained, and they had gone into more lucrative activities.

A number of women also processed rice and sold it in the market. This, however, required a greater capital outlay as well as considerable skill in steaming it before milling in order to obtain good quality rice. For a woman with little money but with the necessary physical stamina to carry loads of cassava long distances, *gari* production was potentially profitable activity. For example, the *gari* made from three shillings' worth of cassava, with the work of processing and the addition of a small amount of palm oil, would fetch six or seven shillings at *εkε* market. Here Afikpo women were in a favorable position. *Gari* was in great demand in eastern Nigeria, but since it had only recently been introduced in many places, relatively few people knew how to make it. The knowledge had probably been brought earlier to Afikpo than to surrounding areas because as an administrative center it had had more contact with the outside.

Men's processing industries were butchering, bicycle repairing, blacksmithing, carpentry, and tailoring. With the exception of the butchers, who worked also at other markets, most of these men had shops where they worked each day, either across the road from the market or in another part of Afikpo. Some carpenters brought their products to market, and a few tailors set up shop in a market stall on *εkε,* taking orders for work to be done in their shops. In addition, a few men and a considerable number of women brought their hand-operated portable sewing machines to market and provided mending service on market day.

There was also considerable regional specialization in *εkε* market in 1960. For commodities and services from outside Afikpo, this followed traditional patterns and showed little change from 1952. Tappers from Okposi supplied palm wine for the market, though the native salt from this area had been largely replaced by European salt. Blacksmiths and iron products still came from Ezza and chalk and rope from Edda.

As formerly, the women of different villages and subgroupings of Afikpo villages specialized in making various kinds of pots, some producing water pots, others, pots for eating, cooking, bathing, and so on. In *εkε* market these women grouped themselves according to the type of pots they were selling, and hence according to the part of Afikpo they came from. This appeared to follow the custom of having the sellers of a commodity in one location rather than the older practice of the people from one community's staying close together in the market, since the sellers of others commodities seemed to pay no attention to place of residence in seating themselves.

As in production, there were distinctive patterns of sexual division in the selling of different products. Several generalizations can be made. The sale of products requiring the greatest amount of capital, and hence most imported goods, was in the hands of men. Types of goods that required the seller's traveling considerable distances to obtain them were also sold by men. Here, of course, it is impossible to separate the factors of freedom of mobility and the cost of travel and transporting goods to market, but it is safe to say that women were both less mobile and poorer than men. The legendary figure of the wealthy Ibo woman trader who supported her husband and sent her sons to a university abroad was not to be found in Afikpo.

Craft products were sold by persons the same sex as the maker though not always by the maker himself. Men sold mats they had made themselves or had bought in Ezza country to the north, where mat making was a specialty. Women from Edda sold rope of their own making, or Afikpo women sold rope they had obtained from Edda for resale. Women sold cooked food, both in the hotels where the buyers could sit inside and eat it, and in the form of bean cakes, various types of breads, and roasted groundnuts sold by casual traders for snacks.

Except for yams, meat, and stockfish, most food was sold by women though some men sold certain foods in quantity that were retailed only by women. This pattern corresponds with the traditional division of responsibility for the food supply in Afikpo: men provided yams, with occasional meat or dried fish, while women supplied all other foods.

Here a note should be made concerning the three categories of dried fish sold in *εkε* market. First, stockfish imported from Europe was sold exclusively by the men. Second, two types of Nigerian dried fish, *bonga* (a river fish from eight inches to a foot long, sold impaled on sticks), and *enya oca* (eye-white—a river fish three to five inches long, sold on wooden racks shaped like snowshoes) were sold principally by men but also by women. These fish are here designated by the term large dried fish to distinguish them from a third category, small dried fish (including both minnows and tiny prawns, known locally as crayfish), sold exclusively by women. (In the Market Master's register of stall rentals, only two of these categories were recognized: "stockfish," including our first two categories and "crayfish," our third category, so some confusion in enumerating the fish sellers was unavoidable.)

A number of products were sold by both men and women. These generally fall into the categories of foods—usually from outside Afikpo—obtained in quantity and sold retail (for example, certain dried fish, raw groundnuts, and dried peppers) or of livestock (sheep, goats, and poultry) brought to market by their owners.

One distinctive category of products—cigarettes, matches, sugar, and soap—was sold exclusively by boys. Young boys also walked about the market calling "Ci-ga-rette!" and selling cigarettes singly. The products sold by men, women, and boys, are shown in Tables 12 and 13.

TABLE 12

Products Sold in Upper Market

By Men	By Women	By Men and Women	By Boys
Cloth	Small dried fish	Large dried fish	Cigarettes
"Articles"	Rice	Palm wine	Matches
Stockfish	Egusi[b]	Groundnuts by the	Soap
Used clothing	Tobacco and crystal	boxful[e]	Sugar
Native cloth	salt[c]	Dried beans[f]	
Native ironware[a]	Chew sticks[d] and	Used cloth and	
Native medicine	fiber sponges	paper sacks	
Gunpowder and	Cooked food (service)	Kola nuts	
carbide	Bread	Dried peppers	
Empty tins and	Onions	Sheep and goats	
bottles	Coconuts	Kerosene	
	Garnishes for soup		
	Leaves for soup		
	Gari		
	Salt		
	Fruits		
	Roasted groundnuts		
	Tomatoes and green		
	vegetables		

(a) Also sold in blacksmith shops across the road. (b) Melon seed used in thickening soup. (c) For making snuff. (d) For cleaning teeth. (e) About one cubic foot in capacity. (f) One man only.

Sometimes a woman was seen selling "articles," yams, or stockfish, but on inquiry it turned out that she was selling for her husband, who was temporarily absent. From time to time a young boy or girl was seen selling for his or her mother while she shopped for herself in the market. Though boys sold on their own behalf, girls did not. According to Afikpo tradition girls did not go to market at all before marriage, and though they sometimes went there with their mothers the idea of their staying there alone was still unthinkable. In cases where girls did sell for their mothers, the mothers turned out to be "strangers" from Number Two, the government workers' quarters, or one of the schools.

TABLE 13

Products Sold in Lower Market

By Men	By Women	By Men and Women
Beef	Pots	Poultry[a]
Bush meat	Unpeeled cassava	
Yams	Fermented cassava	
Mats	Coco yams	
Native cloth	Palm oil (retail)	
Yam baskets	Eggs	
Yam mortars and pestles	Native chalk	
	Rope	
	Cooked food (snacks)	
	Roasted groundnuts	
	Tomatoes and green vegetables	
	Dried peppers	
	Fruits	

(a) Moved to upper market in February 1960.

Another basis for specialization in selling was that of the degree of acculturation of the trader. This was true in 1952, when the cloth and "article" sellers particularly had had more experience of the world outside Afikpo than sellers of traditional products, and women who had been to school or had lived in cities for considerable periods restricted their selling to products such as kerosene and cooked foods. In 1960 the continuation of this pattern was shown in the Market Master's register of stall rentals, and it was especially marked in the case of women selling bread, onions, pap, and other prepared foods (relatively new in Afikpo), used paper and cloth sacks, and a variety of soup ingredients. In January, fifteen of the twenty-two stall holders selling these products were listed as coming from one of the small neighborhoods of shops growing up in Afikpo, government workers' quarters, or the various schools in the neighborhood, while only seven lived in Afikpo villages. Most of these sellers were Christians and did not come to market when ɛkɛ fell on a Sunday. In fact, in contrast to 1952, the market tended to be noticeably smaller on Sundays than on week days.

Because of the fluidity and lack of ordering among the casual traders in the lower market it was difficult to discern patterns of regional specialization in selling other than those of products originating outside Afikpo. However, in the upper market, certain such tendencies could be seen. Among the stall holders in January 1960, the cloth sellers were about evenly divided between Afikpo, Amaseri, and Edda village-groups, with 25, 21, and 22, respectively. Amaseri and Edda markets are the two largest within ten miles of ɛkɛ market, and most of the cloth sellers commuted from one to the other, as mentioned above. Actually some of these men came from cities such as Aba and Onitsha, both major textile centers, and the addresses given in the register were their local residences rather than their homes. Of the "article" sellers, on the other hand, 62 were listed as living in Afikpo, while only 18 came from other village-groups; of the stockfish sellers, 48 came from Afikpo and 17 from outside. In the case of the other sellers holding stalls in the upper market, virtually all were from Afikpo. Of the menders, listed under the category of "seamstress" in the register, 31 were from Afikpo, 5 were from Edda, and 1 from Amaseri.

Another factor that appears in the records of sellers' place of residence is that almost all women stall holders were from Afikpo rather than outside. This is consistent with the pattern of women's more limited mobility and wealth than men's. This was not true of the lower market, however, where many women came from other village-groups. Those renting stalls in the upper market represented the emerging class of semi-professional traders,[7] almost all of whom were from Afikpo, which was considerably more acculturated than surrounding village-groups. Many of these women had reached the state of economic security where they did not have to walk ten or fifteen miles to get a product cheaply that they could sell for more at Afikpo, and some, considering themselves "a little bit civilized," would have felt that to do so was beneath their dignity. Among the sellers in the lower market, the Edda women who sold rope and native chalk, for example, regularly walked twelve to fifteen miles each ɛkɛ they came to Afikpo. Here, in contrast to men's trade, the correlation was between distance and lack of money.

Within Afikpo certain villages emerged as leaders in market trade. Here again, records were available only concerning the stall holders of the upper market. The largest number of traders was from the village closest to the market, Amamgbala, from which there were 74 out of a total of 539 rent-paying stall holders in January, 1960. The

(7) This is not to say that all women classed in this category rented stalls, however, for some commodities in which they dealt were not sold in stalls.

next largest number from one village, 55, was from Ukpa. This village is about a mile from the market, but being the nearest village to the government station and also bordering on the strangers' quarter, Number Two, its people were more acculturated than most of the rest of the Afikpo, and they had had a long tradition of trading in *eke* market. The village with the third largest number of stall holders was Ndibe, one of the largest Afikpo villages, with 38. Ndibe people are very active in river trade, and of the 38 sellers 20 dealt in dried fish. Ama Izu, quite close to the market, had 36, while Ngodo, a little further away, had 33. All these villages with the exception of Ngodo were fairly large for Afikpo. There were 33 stall holders from Number Two, several of whom also had shops there that they operated on the other days of the week.

There were a few instances of domination by one village in the trade in a particular commodity, but this was not a general pattern. These seemed to be associated either with specialization in production within one village or the closeness of the village to the market. Villages that were far from the market were poorly represented, at least among the stall-holders. From the farthest outlying subgrouping of Afikpo villages, Ozizza, only one trader had a stall in the upper market.

There was a wide range in the amount of capital a trader needed to set himself up as a seller in *eke* market, depending on the product sold and the scale of his trade. A boy selling cigarettes, matches, sugar, and soap might have started with 2s. or 3s., with which he purchased a package of cigarettes, a box of safety matches, and a bar of laundry soap. If he was successful and found that he liked trading, he might, as he matured, have forsaken this "trade for little ones" and begun to sell other products. With 15s. he might have bought a four-gallon tin of kerosene to sell by the beer bottleful, or with 10s. or £1 he might have bought a few cuts of beef from the owner of an animal slaughtered at the market and tried his hand as a meat seller. If he had £3 he might have bought twenty stockfish, or if he had £10 or £11, a whole bale, at *eke* market to sell singly or cut in pieces. If his trade prospered he might, when he had amassed £40 or £50, have traveled to Port Harcourt or Aba, where a bale of stockfish cost £9 or £9 10s.

Trade in "articles" represented considerable progress along the road to success for a self-made trader, or might be the starting point for a man who had been given financial help by a kinsman or friend. A man with £10 could buy a modest stock of singlets, towels, scarfs, and so on, or he could lay in a stock of small items like buttons and thread, inexpensive costume jewelry, three-penny exercise books and shilling ball-point pens. If he were successful he could expand his trade into a miniature haberdashery or variety store with an inventory worth £100 or more.

There was in market trade, as in other aspects of Ibo life, a strong desire for upward mobility. Among men traders, for many the ultimate goal was to be a cloth seller, for this represented the greatest income, and hence security and prestige. Once he had amassed the amount of capital necessary to buy a stock of cloth, the great demand for new styles and patterns of prints, plus the effects of the climate and local laundry methods on clothing, assured his success if he was a skillful buyer. It was the cloth seller who sat in his permanent stall in rainy weather while his less fortunate colleagues scrambled to cover their stock beneath the leaky thatch, and it was he who often refused to bargain with a prospective buyer.

The number of traders in *eke* market varied at different seasons of the year, probably being greatest in December and January, a season of ceremonials and feasting when there is little farming done and many people are home in Afikpo on leave from their jobs elsewhere. According to our enumeration, made in mid-December 1959, 588 out of a total of 647 stalls in the upper market[8] were occupied. The number of stalls devoted to different products and services is shown in Table 14.[9] The actual number of sellers of some products was considerably higher than these figures indicate since several products were also sold outside stalls.

In a count made between 11:30 A.M. and 1:30 P.M. on an *eke* early in February 1960, there were 2,010 persons selling in the upper market and 1,280 in the lower, giving a total of 3,290. This is a rough count at best, and it must also be taken into account that some sellers leave before noon and others do not come until midafternoon, since trade is usually brisk from around nine in the morning to four or later in the afternoon.

In 1960 the traditional ceremonial and social functions of *eke* market continued much as before. An important addition, however, was the hotels, serving cooked food and palm wine. While both types of product had formerly been available, cooked food was sold in the form of snacks to be eaten while standing or walking about the

(8) According to the Market Master's records, there was a total of 654. The difference can probably be accounted for by variation in size of some of the stalls which are not divided by partitions, and by the observer's interpretation of whether some of the stalls had collapsed or were still standing.

(9) There are a number of discrepancies between these figures and those of the market register for stall rentals in the following month. Two factors here are that the volume of trade in December is usually greater than that in January. and that there is considerable illegal use of stalls without payment of rent.

market, and palm wine was taken out of the market before it was consumed. The new hotels, where restaurant and bar service was available, had added a new social dimension to the market, and drinking at the hotels was becoming a popular pastime for Afikpo men.

TABLE 14

Occupation of Stalls in Upper Market—December 1959

Product	Stalls
European cloth	67
"Articles"	102
New clothing[a]	26
Stockfish	64
Large dried fish (retail)	42
Small dried fish (retail)	53
Rice by cigarette tinful	30
Egusi	24
Bread and soup ingredients	23
Dried beans	20
Groundnuts by boxful	14
Tobacco and crystal salt	22
Kola nuts	10
Soap, sugar, cigarettes, matches	14
Native ironware	3[b]
Native medicines	2
Native cloth	1[c]
Cooked food (in hotels)	30
Palm wine (in hotels)	16[d]
Tailoring and mending	25
	588

([a]) Included under "articles" by Market Master. ([b]) Three blacksmith shops across the road also sold ironware. ([c]) Plus two other casual sellers in square. ([d]) A number of hotels across the road from the market also sold palm wine.

Market Controls.

The period between 1952 and 1960 saw a radical change in the authority controls over the Afikpo market. In 1953 the Afikpo District Office established the Afikpo Divisional Council, composed of elected representatives of the village-groups in the division, including Afikpo village-group. This council was formed in preparation for the full introduction of local government in Afikpo Division and was the first real deliberative body on a divisional basis. It did not, however, replace the local Native Authority village-group councils, and it had little money to spend and little real authority. In 1955 it was replaced by the Afikpo District Council, a true local government body representing the various village groups in Afikpo Division) (except Edda, which formed its own district council), with the power to

levy taxes and spend considerable sums of money. Similar developments were also occurring at this time through all of southeastern
Nigeria as part of a general plan of local government development
preparatory to the granting of national independence. The Council,
composed of elected representatives, was under the general manager-
ship of a Secretary and a Treasurer, who were civil service appointees,
and of a small group of more or less permanent office workers, road
laborers, and other workers. It held at least one general meeting each
month. Council committees were created, composed of Councillors
and staff members, namely Roads and Works, Health and Medical,
Education and Library, Finance and Staff, and General Purposes.
These also met at least once a month, and actually performed much
of the basic work of the Council. The powers of the District Office
were reduced, becoming largely supervisory, and the village-group
councils became Local Councils under the local government scheme,
but with few new powers.

Between 1955 and 1960 the Council gradually took over control
of *Eke* market and greatly altered its organization. We can only outline briefly the steps that occurred. In 1955 the District Engineer,
at the suggestion of the District Office, drafted a map for the proposed
reorganization of the market and for the placement of lines of market
stalls. In 1955 and 1956, sixty-eight cement stalls were built in a new
section of the market, directly north of the existing market, and a
meat market was partially completed (finished by 1959). In 1956 the
Council passed a market bylaw that was approved by the Eastern
Regional Government in the same year. This gave the Council
authority to take over any market in Afikpo Division, to charge rental
fees for temporary and permanent stalls, to set aside certain areas for
marketing various different commodities, to maintain order and
sanitary control in the market, to take persons to court who committed offenses in the market, and to appoint a Market Master. *eke*
market was placed under Council jurisdiction at this time.

At the end of 1956 and the beginning of 1957 there was an attempt
by the Council, particularly its Secretary, to move the market into
the newly cleared area just north of the old market, where the new
stalls had been erected, leaving the elders' shelters where they were,
and to clear the old market area of the many casual traders who were
displaying their wares on the ground. Stalls of bamboo and thatch
that some traders had erected in the old market area in rather haphazard fashion were destroyed. There was also an attempt to force
traders in certain goods, particularly cloth, to rent the permanent
stalls at the fee prescribed in the bylaws (five shillings a month) and
to get others to build temporary stalls in carefully planned rows in

the new area, for which they were to pay a rent of two shillings a month. The traders objected strenuously to these measures, as did the elders, who resented the disarrangement of the traditional market and claimed that the women's shrine *oma ahia,* in the old market, had been needlessly burned in the cleanup. Police action was taken to maintain order. Petitions were presented to government officials by the traders and the elders, and the Council Secretary was brought to court in a civil action. At about this time some of the more influential market traders formed a permanent organization, the Afikpo Traders' Union, to protect their interests.

By the end of 1958, however, the dispute had simmered down, part of the market had been moved, many of the permanent cement stalls were being occupied (mainly by cloth traders), and temporary stalls were being built by other traders. By this time, also, an incinerator had been constructed on the old market site to burn market refuse. Four laborers and a Market Master had been appointed by the Council, and soon afterward an *ɛkɛ* Market Subcommittee of the Council's General Purposes Committee was formed which included four Councillors, a member of the village-group council at Afikpo, and a member of the Afikpo Traders' Union. Between 1958 and 1960 the Council also passed a bylaw for eating houses, a hawker's bylaw, and a bakery bylaw, all of which had potential influence on the market and on trade at Afikpo, though by the early part of 1960 none of these were being rigorously enforced.

It is worth while to discuss the actual functioning of the market in terms of these changes as of the early months of 1960. In January of that year there were, according to the Market Master's records, 68 permanent stalls renting at five shillings a month, and 586 temporary stalls of bamboo and thatch, renting at two shillings a month, of which 40 permanent stalls and 499 temporary stalls were actually rented. Nearly one-fifth of the total number of traders in the market were thus formally renting stalls. In addition, cattle owners who killed their animals at the market slaughterhouse (as they were required to do) paid a fee of five shillings per animal. The income from these fees, which was paid to the District Council Treasury and was not specifically allocated for market improvement, varied between £30 in June and July and a peak of about £60 during November and December. The desire of some Council members in pressing for the development of the market was clearly to increase the revenue of the Council, rather than coming from any immediate concern with market development.

The Market Master used as his office a permanent stall in the central part of the market. Here he sat on market days, collecting fees, and he and his four laborers checked the stalls to see that they were properly occupied. While a single stall was supposed to be for one trader, there was in fact much sharing and subletting of stalls, which was difficult to control. The Market Master had the power to force persons who were not renting stalls to sell their products in a certain section of the market devoted to casual traders. He had definite ideas of what goods should be sold where and occasionally moved sellers of one type of commodity to a less crowded area and replaced them with others. He could and did take persons whom he found violating market regulations to the Afikpo village-group court. For example, he could take those to court who sold in the wrong part of the market and refused to move, and persons who were fighting, riding bicycles in the market, or otherwise causing trouble. The court was usually in session on market day in the nearby courthouse, and it was a simple matter for him to call for court messengers and to take the offenders to the court for trial then and there. The Market Master was reluctant to prosecute if he could avoid doing so, preferring to use discussion and persuasion to settle the matter. Nevertheless, almost every market day brought one or two court cases. While he had the authority to take cases to the Magistrate's Court, he preferred not to since there the fines, even for minor offenses, were much higher than those of the village-group court.

On other days of the working week the Market Master saw that the market was cleaned by the laborers, and helped guide the construction of new temporary stalls. At the beginning of 1960 the Council had no money to build permanent stalls, and was in any case unable to rent all those it had already, particularly in one line that was built in a lowland that flooded badly during the rains. Traders who wanted to rent temporary stalls applied to him for permission to build them, and he indicated what line they should construct them in. If a trader who built a stall later quit the market, the next renter had to pay him something for the cost of building. In fact, it happened that (particularly during the early days of the construction of the temporary stalls) a few persons actually built a great many stalls at the market and then sold them to renters who subsequently took them over. While this was contrary to the original market policy, the desire to open the new market was so great that it was permitted, and a few men made considerable profits out of stall construction.

From time to time the Market Master attended meetings of the ɛkɛ Market Subcommittee, and of the General Purposes Committee, and he provided the latter with a monthly report of money collected, stalls rented, and the general condition of the market.

There were two other Council workers whose duties were directly related to the market. The Health Overseer, formerly the Native Authority Sanitary Inspector, was responsible for checking the condition of the meat and organs of cattle slaughtered at the market, as well as the condition of the nearby latrines. The Land Settlement Officer was in charge of surveying market boundaries, laying out new lines of stalls, planning the motor park, and looking after other matters relating to the physical layout of the market. In addition, a Government Veterinary Officer had recently begun to check the hides of cattle killed at market, and was trying to encourage the development of a small local hides industry. These three officials, of course, had numerous other duties not connected with the market or trading.

It was, however, the Land Settlement Officer and the Market Master who were most directly concerned with the development of the market, though the ɛkɛ Market Subcommittee played a role in discussing and evaluating their plans, which eventually had to be approved by the General Purposes Committee of the Council and by the Council itself. Actually, these two officials held the initiative in directing market development. The Roads and Works Committee was involved in any construction undertaken at the market (other than that of temporary stalls), the Health Overseer reported on the health conditions of the market to the Medical and Health Committee, and the Finance and Staff Committee was responsible for any financial aspect of the market. There was thus a complicated organization of committees and personnel connected with the market and market planning, truly a bureaucracy tending toward rational-legal authority, as Weber might put it, with fairly well defined role specifications and divisions of duties.

The committees and the officials associated with the market, as well as some of the traders, had a strong sense of planning for changes in the market. Their models were the large daily markets at Aba, Onitsha, Enugu, and other major urban centers. Their desire was for greater order and control of the market. It was their goal eventually to put all the traders in rented stalls, so that there would be virtually no casual traders and regular fees would then be paid to the Council in large amounts. The daily market, meeting every day except Sunday, had also become a goal. Teachers employed at the schools in the area often complained about this lack of a daily market, and headmasters and principals said that it was hard to attract qualified persons without this facility. The Land Settlement Officer and the Market Master were preparing to have the two small *aho* markets at Ugwuago and Amachara villages closed down and the sellers removed to the main market site to augment the number and activity of traders already selling at ɛkɛ market on *aho*. This would create a good-sized market every other day at Afikpo, a start toward a daily market. It was, of course, not only the concept of a daily market that was involved, but also of that of a large centralized market serving the whole community. The market planners were preparing to build a motor park for the lorries, of which more and more came to the market, and to charge parking fees, and they hoped eventually to charge casual traders a fee for the right to sell outside the stalls in the market. Eating places at the market were also to be regularly inspected and licensed. These planners hoped to inculcate cleanliness and prevent overcrowding, two features ignored in the traditional conception of the market. Two other large markets in Afikpo Division, Uburu and Aka Eze, were now also under the authority of the Council, and had their own market masters. They were, however, not so fully developed as Afikpo, perhaps because they were farther from the administrative headquarters of the division.

The Afikpo Traders' Union, although not a government body, played an advisory role in market matters. Formed originally in protest against actions taken by the District Council without consulting the traders, it called to the attention of the *εkε* Market Subcommittee and the Market Master problems it wished to have discussed or acted on. Its effective membership, of less than thirty traders, was composed of both Afikpo and non-Afikpo Ibo, mainly sellers of "articles," cloth, groundnuts, and dried fish. Many of its members cycled from market to market on different days, as previously described, and this task, which had seemed so adventurous in the early days of the bicycle at Afikpo, was now considered simply arduous. The traders wanted a daily market so they could remain at home and sell every day. They also wanted permanent well-constructed stalls at low-rental fees, improved sanitation, and the right to a strong voice in market planning. They were too small in numbers to represent the Afikpo traders as a whole, but they took as their model the influential market traders' association in the larger cities of eastern Nigeria.

Although there was a small branch of the Nigerian Motor Workers' Union in Afikpo, it did not yet regulate passenger loading at the market (or anywhere at Afikpo) as other branches did in other sections of Nigeria. Finally, there was a Developed Area Association (formerly called the Number Two Strangers' Union), whose members were drawn mainly from the Number Two area, which included traders, contractors and other businessmen. The Association acted not only to represent its members' interests, all of whom were nonindigeneous to Afikpo, but as a protective organization in the case of any dispute or court case involving a member, as a group to settle quarrels among its members without reference to outside courts (mainly over payments for goods between members), and as a union to insure that the Number Two area received adequate representation in the political organizations at Afikpo. The Association was not directly concerned with market matters. The Afikpo Traders' Union, the Nigerian Motor Workers' Union, and the Developed Area Association, all of which were in the early stages of development, represented trading and business interests which were growing at Afikpo, and such organizations were sure to play a stronger role in market activity and economic planning at Afikpo in the future.

Finally, what remained of the traditional role of the elders in the Afikpo market? The age grades still met there, and their shelters were formally incorporated in the market plan. Members of the middle age grade, *ekpe uke esa,* still held court there and still passed regulations limiting the right of Afikpo to trade at other markets, though these were not now so easy to enforce as before. They now tried cases arising from disputes at the market only rarely. The junior elders' grade carried out little policing in the market, the Market Master and his laborers having taken over this duty. In reality, while the elders met in the market, they had virtually lost their controls of former times. The truth was that bureaucracy had taken over from tradition without much of a struggle, that planning had replaced a laissez-faire attitude, and that it was likely that the controls of the Council over the market would grow more and more effective as time passed. Such was also occurring at many other markets in eastern Nigeria, especially in the more urbanized centers, but also in rural areas, such as Afikpo, which were in the early stages of urbanization. In fact, the daily market with a fair percentage of professional traders can be taken as one index of the degree of urbanization and of the substitution of cosmopolitan for traditional values.

Other Afikpo Markets.

Another aspect of the growth of *eke* market was the establishment there of a small market on *aho,* two days after *eke.* Meeting in a section of the upper market place, it was only informally supervised by the Market Master. The small *aho* markets at Ugwuago and Amachara still met, but were smaller than formerly since quite a number of sellers now went to the main market on that day. In the first months of 1960 the Market Master, with his goal of a daily market approved by the District Council, was planning to close these markets in order to bolster the *aho* trade at *eke* market, but he had not yet done so. Many of the food sellers, as well as a few article sellers, now sold at *Eke* market on *aho* as well as on the main market day. While there were no cattle slaughtered for the small market and there were fewer sellers, the products sold were similar to those that were available on *ɛkɛ*.

A growing trend in 1960 was that of small daily markets in several of the outlying villages near the Cross River. Formerly meeting on only one day of the four-day week, they now consisted mainly of women selling such products as yams, soup ingredients, and prepared foods such as fermented cassava, *gari,* and various snacks. Two of these met during the early evening, when they served last-minute demands for meal preparation, and a third met in the daytime but extended into the evening. In 1960 the food tastes of the Afikpo included a considerably greater variety of ingredients than formerly, including a number of prepared foods not formerly sold in markets, and the people seemed to be oriented toward the quick satisfaction of their demands rather than thinking of most products as being available only on the main market day.

For Afikpo village-group the trend seemed to be toward expansion of trade and greater centralization of market activities in the villages close to *ɛkɛ* market, with a movement toward the development of a daily market. At the same time new demands had arisen that were not satisfied by the central market. In the outlying villages small daily markets were developing to serve specific local needs, and in several parts of Afikpo small neighborhoods of shops and various services were rapidly growing.

Markets Outside Afikpo.
Between 1952 and 1960 there were definite shifts in the relative positions of the more important markets within thirty miles of Afikpo. While most of them increased in size, the growth was by far the most striking at Afikpo. The market at Uburu, about twenty-five miles to the northwest, which met at eight-day intervals with a large two-day market every twenty-four days, diminished considerably in importance. Once a major slave market controlled by Aro traders, it had been located in the center of the town where the slaves could be conveniently hidden, but it was now in a grassland area along the road outside the town. It consisted of orderly rows of permanent stalls and was under the control of the Afikpo District Council, the days of Aro domination being long past. It was still a center for the exchange of horses and cattle, used for second funeral ceremonies, and carried on an active trade in commodities common to this part of Nigeria, but it had lost its position as focal point for much of the trade of the area. Its location away from the main motor roads and its relative inaccessi-

bility during the rainy season seemed to have given other markets an advantage over it in the volume of trade.

The market at Aka Eze, about twenty miles west of Afikpo on the main motor road to the Afikpo Road railway station and Okigwe, while still a major trade center, had grown proportionately much less than *ɛkɛ* market. Here a qualitative difference between the two markets was much more marked than in 1952. Located in a fertile agricultural area, Aka Eze was a producers' market, supplying large quantities of locally produced yams, rice, maize, and groundnuts to the cities of Umuahia, Aba, and Port Harcourt to the south. This presented a strong contrast to the increasing emphasis at *ɛkɛ* market on the transshipment of goods and the supplying of a nonindigenous population with foodstuffs and other products. While in 1952 the Aka Eze market had looked like a very large *ɛkɛ* market, by 1960 they were of much the same size but served quite different functions.

In the central markets of the village-groups surrounding Afikpo, there had also been changes. The dispute between Afikpo and Amaseri, five miles to the west, had been settled, and the elders once more permitted Afikpo to trade there. During the ban on trade with Amaseri many Afikpo had gone to Abba Omege market, fourteen miles to the north by road (or eight miles by a difficult footpath), which met on the same day, *orie*. With the re-establishment of peaceful relations a great many Afikpo started to go again to Amaseri market, which they could reach easily by the main motor road.[10] The Afikpo going to Amaseri were mostly women, buying rice and cassava. A few sold pots or dried fish at Amaseri, but most went primarily to buy.

Abba Omege market, already affected by the removal of much of the Afikpo trade, sustained further losses in the late 1950's, when the Igbo, a non-Ibo people a few miles to the east, as the result of a dispute established their own market three miles east of Abba Omege, meeting also on *orie*. This became a very popular market, with a strong emphasis on the selling of rice, reducing Abba Omege market, so to speak, to a shadow of its former self.

Of the markets of other nearby village-groups, Edda market was somewhat increased in size and had a number of well-built permanent stalls, promoted by the establishment of a separate district council for Edda in the mid-1950's. Others such as Unwana, Okpoha, and Okposi were little changed.

(10) In a count taken between the hours of 7:00 A.M. and 7.00 P.M. on an *orie* in mid-January 1960, we enumerated 772 traders going from Afikpo to Amaseri either on foot or bicycle, and 615 returning. In addition, many went also by lorry, for frequent service between the two village-groups was provided throughout the day.

We see therefore that quite different types of markets existed in the area. Afikpo market formed a transshipment center which also served a growing stranger population, Aka Eze market was a heavy food exporting center with a variety of foodstuffs, Igbo market a one-crop export market, and Uburu a large bush market that was formerly a link in the Aro system of trade, which had not grown in importance in recent years. There were also, of course, the large urban markets of Abakaliki, Aba, and Port Harcourt, with which Afikpo market had contacts. Perspective on the nature of the Afikpo market is gained when we realize that it is only one kind of market in a rather complex typology.

It is also important to note that in 1960 Afikpo women traveled to at least ten other markets[11] on non-*εke* days in search of two food-stuffs which they brought back for processing and resale, generally at Afikpo but sometimes also at the markets where they had obtained them in the first place. These were unprocessed rice and raw cassava, from which, respectively, processed rice was produced at the three Afikpo rice mills and *gari* made by hand processing. The particular markets surrounding Afikpo the women traveled to depended to a large extent on which was nearest to the particular section of the village-group in which they lived, and on the physical strength of the individual women. This search by Afikpo women in the surrounding markets for the raw foodstuffs upon which so much of their economic life depended was a major characteristic of Afikpo trade.

Extra-Market Exchange.

If there were on one hand a tendency toward the development of a larger and larger central market, there had also come into being a considerable number of exchange activities which did not touch the market at all, or did so only in a peripheral fashion. Extra-market exchanges existed previous to 1960, such as slave-trading in pre-conquest days, and the selling of blacksmiths' iron goods, some pre-pared foods, and palm wine in the villages (as well as in the market) in past times, a practice that has continued to this date. In addition, of course, many traditional ceremonial feasts involved the distribution of foodstuffs, later replaced by money, so that there had clearly been some extra-market exchange. It is clear, though, that by 1960 the economic needs and wants of Afikpo had increased so greatly and become so diversified that the markets, as then constituted, were incapable of serving as a basis for all exchange activities. Rather, we find that important exchanges and transactions were also occurring

(11) These include Usumutong, Ediba, Ebom, Ogada, Unwana, Owutu Edda (the main Edda market), Osu Edda, Amaseri, Okpoha, and Abba Omege.

outside the markets. Some of these had already developed by 1952, but others were of more recent origin.

There are various reasons for these extra-market activities. The most striking has been the development, mainly in the 1940's and 1950's, of the many small shops crowded for the distance of an eighth of a mile along the road from the government station in the strangers' quarters, Number Two.[12] This was an area in or near which lived government workers, traders, craftsmen, contractors, and others. It existed along the northern borders of the Afikpo village of Ukpa and had none of the attributes of a typical Afikpo village.

The villagers of Ukpa received considerable rent for some of the stalls and buildings along the road. It was a narrow, crooked roadway where the shops were open daily and in the evening there was much drinking and merriment. A count conducted in February 1960 indicated that there were seventy-five shops, sheds, or hotels[13] in Number Two, and about sixty casual sellers displaying their wares at the ends of the shopping area or in front of some of the shops. The range of shops and services offered can be indicated by the following listing: there were ten selling articles, ten carpenter shops (though the carpenters were often away building houses or doing other construction work), nine shops for tailors, two for seamstresses, ten hotels, seven bicycle repair shops, four shops for barbers, three for photographers, three for tinsmiths, two for watch repairmen, three for shoe repairmen and one shoe store, three places to purchase gasoline and oil, one bookshop, a distributor for a major Nigerian newspaper and magazine, a photographic supply shop, a radio and battery store, a wine and beer store, a mattress and pillow maker's shop, a rice mill, and the shop of an agent for a major Nigerian tobacco company. Among the casual sellers were five who sold used clothes, ten palm-wine sellers (the number varies according to the time of day), a number of persons selling firewood, thirty-four persons, mostly women, selling processed and unprocessed food, and a perfume seller from northern Nigeria. In addition on *nkwo*, the day before the main Afikpo market, when beef was scarce, Hausa traders killed a cow at the concrete slaughter slab at Number Two and sold the meat in front of a prominent trader's store. There were also a number of prostitutes living and working at Number Two and in the nearby village of Ukpa. Several contractors had their homes and offices in these two communities.

(12) Both the name Number Two and that of the area called Number One, to be discussed below, were originally names given to areas that were primarily residential quarters for government workers.

(13) These were usually buildings of three or four rooms where palm wine, beer, and prepared food might be obtained, and sometimes a bed or a room rented for the night.

Most of the shops were closed on Sundays and many also on *eke*, when the traders were found selling or offering their services at the market.

Such is typical of the crowded semi-slum areas of Lagos, Aba, Onitsha, and almost any Nigerian city. Unregulated and unplanned except for some of the government workers' residences at the north end of Number Two, it had grown to serve very real needs, not only of the stranger population but also of the Afikpo. Some of the traders there were strangers, mainly Ibo from other regions of Nigeria, but there were also Afikpo who traded and lived there, sometimes also maintaining a residence in their home village.

A smaller and less crowded section of twenty-one stores, mainly shops for selling articles, for tailors and for carpenters, but also a bookshop and a photographer's studio, had grown up within the past five years about three miles away from Number Two near the Roman Catholic Mission hospital and school headquarters at Afikpo. Here persons associated with these establishments had built houses or lived on the mission grounds. The area, called New Site, was several miles from the nearest Afikpo village and market; there was room there for expansion, and a great deal of house and shop building was going on in 1960.

In the late 1950's a third small shopping center, called Number One,[14] had developed near a housing area for government workers about a mile from Number Two. Here one found a John Holt's store, which was a small branch of a European company which also sold building materials and had a palm kernel collection depot associated with it, an employment agency for recruiting workers for Fernando Po, a motor repair shop, three carpenters' workshops, a small printing press, a hotel, three tailors' shops, and a drinks and tinned food store. In addition, a number of private houses were found here. A fourth shopping center, along the road opposite the main Afikpo market, has already been discussed. In addition, in or near the major Afikpo villages were stores or stands selling palm wine which were gathering places, particularly for young men in the evenings, and small article shops, bicycle repair sheds, tailors' shops, and sometimes private houses where prostitutes lived and worked. Such places tended to be nuclear Number Twos.

At most of the schools tiny markets had sprung up, meeting from mid-morning until around noon on Monday through Friday. At these markets a few women sold penny snacks of cooked food and roasted groundnuts to the teachers and pupils during recess periods and often to passers-by as well. The Nigerian school day, running from eight

(14) It was also called P. W. D. Camp, after the residential quarters of Public Works Department workers which were also located there.

in the morning until 1 : 30 P.M. or later, provided a ready market for such traders. Similar markets were found near the Magistrate's Court and the Afikpo District Council hall on days when these bodies were in session.

The development of these major and minor shopping centers served new tastes and needs to some extent. Though virtually everything offered at these centers could be obtained at the market, it was frequently more convenient to obtain the desired goods without having to wait for market day. Much of the goods in the shops came from Port Harcourt, Aba, and Onitsha, and the traders made trips to these cities to purchase supplies when necessary.

Clearly related to these developments was the great activity in housebuilding which had been going on for five or six years. Until the late 1940's building a mud or cement block house with a metal roof was something a man did only after he had performed the second funeral ceremonies for his parents and had taken the major Afikpo titles. By 1960 housebuilding was, in effect, an important title, taking precedence over many others. This was partly because, when built, all or part of the house could be rented (rentals in Afikpo were by the room), and because the cement block, metal-roofed house with wooden doors and shutters had become a symbol of wealth and prestige. These houses often took years to build because the owners lacked funds to complete them. Though some were built by contractors, or partially constructed with their aid, many were built largely by their owners. A number of Afikpo men employed women to collect sand, particularly at the main Afikpo beach on the Cross River, Ndibe Beach, to sell to building contractors or to individuals who were building houses. These women were usually paid by the head-load, and this had become a substantial source of income for some. In addition, carpenters in Afikpo spent a good deal of time working on these houses or making furniture for them, so that the building of a modern-style house might involve a number of persons working for wages or on contract over a considerable period of time.

While some of the new-style houses were being built in the rather crowded compounds, there was a tendency to erect them just outside the villages and along the roads in Afikpo, where there was more room. It was the custom in Afikpo that anyone could build a house on land outside the village or on farmland regardless of which group owned the land, provided the builder first went through the formality of notifying the owners. While this had not been strictly adhered to with reference to housing at Number Two and the borders of *eke* market, where the value of land was high, it had been elsewhere. As a result the villages, formerly separated by short stretches of farm or forest land, were beginning to be joined by rows of houses between them. With the growing number of these houses and of shops, Afikpo was becoming a single urbanized community in which the physical identities of the villages were beginning to disappear.

There were a number of commodities, namely firewood and timber, palm kernels, rice, yams, pottery, illicit liquor, and bread, which were important in trade in Afikpo and of which some or all were bought and sold outside the markets. Every morning at a very early hour, men and women from Amaseri village-group to the west of Afikpo brought large headloads of firewood to Afikpo for sale, at from one to three shillings a bundle. Some of this wood was sold on contract to the secondary schools for their kitchens, while some sellers had arrangements with government workers or other individuals living near the government station. Wood was not sold at the Afikpo markets, perhaps because there was enough in the farms for the everyday needs of the people, because wood was simply not something that Afikpo considered they should spend money on, and because the greatest demand for wood was from the strangers' quarters and the government station and school areas, which were all some distance from the market. There was insufficient wood to be found in Afikpo to supply the needs of all those who wished to buy it, and though some Afikpo did collect wood for sale, Amaseri appeared to have greater supplies. The firewood trade appeared to be lucrative for those who were willing to carry the wood in head-loads for the five or more miles from the Amaseri area or who were enterprising enough to hire others to do it for them.

There was also a representative of a European timber company living on the outskirts of Afikpo, whose company owned six lorries and hired others, which carried *obechi* and other timber to Ndibe Beach, where it was lashed together and floated downstream to Calabar for export. These logs, however, were mainly brought though Afikpo from about June to November, when the water level of the river was high enough to float them. This local branch of the company, which had existed at Afikpo for several years, employed more than fifty persons, some of whom were Afikpo, but the logs themselves came from other areas of the division than Afikpo village-group and also from Abakaliki Division. Afikpo village-group has no suitable trees.

Afikpo men and women took baskets, or sometimes sacks, of palm kernels to the John Holt's agent at the Number One shopping center, or to their agent at the edge of the main market, both of whom were there to receive kernels every day but Sunday. In both cases the kernels were sifted and bought at prices set by the company, and packed in bags for shipment to export centers. From these two depots they moved to the John Holt's factory on the Cross River and were shipped by boat to Calabar. Afikpo, as we have indicated, is not a major palm produce area, but some Afikpo, particularly women, went to market across the river or to the southeast or northwest and purchased kernels to sell at these two depots. Other persons from these surrounding village-groups came to Afikpo to sell their kernels, sometimes moving as many as fifteen or twenty bags by lorry. Kernels and palm oil were also sold in small amounts at the Afikpo markets, mainly for home consumption. There were six hand-operated palm oil presses within the village-group which produced small quantities of oil and prepared kernels mainly for local consumption, though some kernels were sold to John Holt's. The presses were owned by Afikpo who had obtained them either through the former Afikpo Native Authority Council as part of a development scheme or purchased them elsewhere, and they were a lucrative source of income for their owners. Much oil for local consumption was also prepared by traditional pressing techniques in the Afikpo villages.

We have already mentioned the role of the three Afikpo rice mills in the preparation of rice for sale in the market. The development of this trade and the appearance of the mills occurred after 1952. Much of the rice, which came mainly from neighboring village-groups, was sold right at the mills after millings to traders who took it to major cities in eastern Nigeria, particularly Port Harcourt, Aba, and Onitsha, where it was much in demand. However, some rice owners preferred to sell their milled rice in smaller quantities at the market, feeling that they could secure a higher income for their supply in the long run. The rice traders who exported from Afikpo were mainly Afikpo themselves, as were the mill owners. This was a new and growing export trade, rice being a popular urban food. The mills required considerable capital to start, since their machinery is expensive,[15] but they brought considerable returns after a time.

Afikpo brought yams by lorry from two rich yam producing areas, Aka Eze about twenty miles to the west, and from the Abakaliki area thirty or more miles to the north, to Ndibe Beach, from where they were taken by canoe to the Calabar area for sale, mainly by Afikpo. Here they brought very good prices. Some of these yams were purchased by Afikpo in these two areas, but some Afikpo had taken to growing yams on rented land in these regions and thus traded in a product that they had grown themselves. The yams of Afikpo were considered, in general, to be too poor for the Calabar trade.

Many Afikpo women, instead of selling their pots in the market, sold them to Afikpo traders who took them downstream to Calabar,

(15) One mill, about a year old, was sold in 1960 for £400.

or gave them to a brother or other relative who was a river trader to sell there. During the dry season many canoes went from the Afikpo area laden with pots. The advantages of the river trade over selling at the market were mainly higher prices and a more guaranteed income. Some traders bought certain women's output for the entire year.

Along with the dried fish brought from Calabar to the Afikpo area by canoe, the trade in which has already been discussed above, a considerable quantity of smuggled Spanish liquor from Fernando Po, particularly brandy and gin, came up the river to Afikpo. These did not find their way into the market, as traders were afraid to sell them publicly, but they could be bought in almost every Afikpo village. Afikpo sold these beverages to nearby village-groups, and traders from these neighboring areas came to Afikpo. It was impossible to estimate the extent of this trade, but it seemed to be regular and profitable. There was also a steady trade in native gin, produced and sold in almost every Afikpo village.

Finally, most of the bread sold in Afikpo came from bakeries in Abakaliki and Enugu, and one Abakaliki bread firm had a local outlet shop at Afikpo. Bread had become very popular there during the 1950's, particularly among the nonfarming population. Some of it was sold to traders who took it to the market or sold it in shops at Number Two or at one of the other small shopping areas, but bread peddlers with wooden carts also travelled about Afikpo, particularly in the area of the strangers' quarters and schools.

The extra-market place economic activities discussed above do not contradict the conclusion that Afikpo village-group was by and large a non-productive area which also was a transshipment center. Timber, yams from Aka Eze and Abakaliki, and much of the rice and palm kernels, originated outside Afikpo and ultimately left the area. Of the items discussed here, only pottery was produced in large quantities at Afikpo, most of it for export.

The sale or passage of all these goods outside the markets, and the presence of more shops at Afikpo, indicate that some trade was not dependent on the Afikpo markets and, that while ɛkɛ market was growing in size and importance, a lively commerce was also developing outside it and more or less independent of it. In the diversity of goods and services that were available for purchase, sale, or transshipment through Afikpo, some were not well suited to a large main market, even if it were to meet daily, and some fitted local needs better if located near the purchaser or consumer. The main market could satisfy many economic wants in Afikpo, but by no means all of them.

CONCLUSIONS

Between 1900 and 1960 the main Afikpo market changed from a small local market with some external trade with neighboring markets and with longer trade links provided by the Aro to a much larger market serving as a transshipment center for certain products and as a supply center for the growing nonindigenous population. Money replaced barter, and the small number of professional Aro traders was supplemented by a much larger contingent of non-Aro traders from outside Afikpo who dealt largely in imported or nontraditional products. Though the canoe remained as a means of transportation of goods, the use of head-loads was to some extent replaced by the bicycle and then partially by the lorry. The trade routes expanded, and Afikpo became linked to the urban trading centers of eastern Nigeria. There was an increasing emphasis on the profit motive in trade and on the selling of processed foodstuffs and goods rather than raw materials and unprocessed foods. The mild controls over ɛkɛ market exercised by the elders and the Aro gave way to the more stringent measures of the bureaucratic District Council, which had as its aims not only the improvement of the market but also the collection of revenue from it for other uses.

During this same period nonmarket economic activities increased greatly, so that while ɛkɛ market remained the focal point of Afikpo trade, significant economic activities occurred in the shopping centers and other areas outside it. It seemed likely that this trend would continue.

Certain features which characterized Afikpo trade in 1900 remained relatively unchanged in 1960; for example, bargaining as a basic exchange technique, the importance of women in trade activities, and the role of the market as a social center. Again, the trade in Afikpo has always been dominated by Ibo; there has never been a question of another ethnic group's seriously competing in Afikpo economic activities. However, despite these and other regularities, the essence of Afikpo economic life since 1900 has been growth and change, closely related to the general social and political development of the area and of Nigeria as a whole.

CHAPTER 6

The Bulu Response to European Economy

BY GEORGE R. HORNER

THE PRE-WHITE BULU

History.

The Bulu, now numbering 100,000 people, live in the tropical rainforests of southeastern Cameroon on a hilly plateau 1,200 feet above sea level, between $2^1/2$ degrees to 3 degrees north and $10^1/2$ and 12 degrees east.

The Bulu came into the forests at the end of the Fang invasion about one hundred years ago. They migrated from the east to escape Arab slave raiders, moving westward and seaward toward a source of European trade goods. The Bulu moved in joint family groups, remaining in one area only long enough to replenish their food supply, then once more migrating in the pattern of shifting cultivators. Today, older Bulu remember moving at least three times during their lives: childhood, youth, then settling down since 1930.

The traditional Bulu of pre-1860 came within about fifteen miles of their ocean goal only to find their final destination effectively blocked by the Mabea, a powerful coastal tribe. The Mabea, like other coastal tribes of the period, so controlled the coast and the trade monopoly that, not only did they prevent interior tribes from reaching the coast and trading with the Europeans, but they also prevented white traders from traveling to the interior tribes. Their monopolies were broken soon after the economic-political treaties with Germany were signed by the coastal chiefs in 1884–85.

BULU SOCIETY

Social Organization.

Fifty autonomous non-segmentary lineages *(ayong)* collectively formed the "Bulu." They were not socially unified, thus making it difficult to call the Bulu a tribe. They had in common only general cultural elements, such as origin, customs and languages. There was no sense of larger unity, so that any individual Bulu would not have the ties of kinship and safety in a lineage-village not his own, as among relatives. Neither were there political, religious, social or economic links which might give a sense of tribal unity to the Bulu. The lineage, synonymous with three English words, "village," "family," and "lineage," was the Bulu center of unity, loyalty, and all duties and obligations. The lineage-village was composed of either a father and his sons, their wives and children, or a man, his brothers, their wives and children in whom (the father in one case, the brother in the second) loyalty was centered.

The structure of the lineage-village was non-hierarchical and with the exception of the "richman", *nkukum*, socially egalitarian. This is reflected in the kinship terminology system of the Bulu, in which classificatory terms are used with differences based only upon generation, role and sex, but with no rank content implied in them. Each Bulu of the same lineage addressed every other villager with one of the five following intimate family kinship terms: father, mother, sister, brother and/or child. The term "father" was addressed to one's own father and to all other men of one's father's generation. All the other terms were applied in the same way. Affinal relatives had the same terms applied to them. Behavior between two individuals was determined by the given kin label. For example, a Bulu acted toward all women labelled "mother" as toward his or her biological mother, with the same reciprocal behavior based upon understood duties and obligations due one in that classificatory kin group.

So strong was this sense of lineage-village loyalty, lacking ties even with neighboring villages, that the traditional Bulu lineages were constantly raiding and feuding. A lineage-village broke up either when it became too large, or at the death of the father, at which time the younger brothers would leave the village to found their own.

Though the Bulu lacked a political head of their village, the oldest male was the social head, sometimes the richest man, *nkukum*. Respect and obedience were due him on that basis. The Bulu social system, fragmentary in structure, probably prevented the formation of markets or a system of formal interlineage exchange, at least in this early period.

Political Organization.

This egalitarian structure is observed in the Bulu political organization. There was no one with political authority, a chief over all the Bulu, neither was there a political head over each lineage-village. Rather, political power and responsibility were assumed by the male heads of each household who as a group became a Council of Elders, *benya boto*. As a body politic, the Council had political power and made political decisions affecting the lineage-village. One of its duties was the allocation of jointly owned land for kitchen-gardens to each family head.

Decisions at the Council meetings were made by voting *(tili)*. Each household head had one vote. Although the social head, *nkukum,* could try to influence votes, he had no greater power than anyone else; he too, had only one vote when the Council met.

All of the Bulu recognized, and tried to attain, the same cultural wealth and prestige goals. Each man wanted to be a "true man," *(nya mot),* to have many wives, children, sheep, goats, ivories, spears; in short, more "things" *(biom)* and "wealth," *(akum)* than anyone else. Lineage solidarity and autonomy were so rigid that economic surplus could not be exchanged with a neighboring lineage unless these barriers were in some way removed. Not long before the coming of the first white man, lineages, through the offices of the Councils of Elders, entered into a series of agreements or alliances *(avuso)* to permit both social and economic exchange.

Such alliances would provide:

1. that arbitration rather than blood feuds would be the basis for settling future interlineage injuries. Compensation would be in goods, not in blood.

2. that peace would be assured through interlineage marriages. Such marriage would symbolize the contractural basis of the alliance and, in a patrilocal system of marriage, the girl would be a "willing hostage" as a wife. This would also provide kin in the other lineage.

3. that trade friendships *(ngba)* would be similarly established between any two male members of these lineages, providing an additional way of distributing both goods and services.

By the year 1892, when the first remembered white man, American missionary A. Good, visited the Bulu, most of Bululand was crisscrossed by a network of alliances. (There remain to this day, however, many neighboring lineages who, in various covert ways, continue their traditional feuds). In many instances one lineage would form an alliance with two or more neighboring lineages, thereby ensuring greater opportunities to exchange goods and services and a chance to enhance their social prestige over a wider area.

Such marriage and trade links strengthened Bulu society. It did not unify all of the Bulu; lineages continued to splinter and new ones to form, but those which were united provided a means by which goods were exchanged.

Economic Organization: Production and Distribution.

The traditional Bulu were horticulturists following the typical African slash-and-burn technique with a division of work by sex in a subsistence economy. The women cultivated kitchen gardens; the men, hunted, built the dwellings, were the iron smiths, etc.

The family produced the following commodities for consumption and distribution: (a) Domestic plant foods; (b) Animals and meat; (c) Manufactured goods.

a) Domestic plant foods. Garden plots were allocated to each family head by the Council of Elders. If such land was not cultivated in one year, it was redistributed by the Council. Land could be used by the same family so long as the village remained in the area. However, the family did not own the land; it could not be bought or sold, rented or inherited. Garden plots varied in size, depending upon the number in a family, a single plot, 50 yards square, would be the maximum size a mature woman could cultivate alone and produce sufficient food for a family of four for half a year.

On such plots were grown *macabo,* a tuberous plant the Bulu claimed to have brought with them on their migration; plantain *(ekon),* taro *(atu)* and, since 1880, peanuts *(owondo),* American Indian corn *(fen),* seeds of a cucumber-like plant *(ngon),* and cassava, both the bitter and sweet varieties *(mbong).*

Surplus from gardens was not exchanged *per se.* Hospitality obligations required that each family produce and store sufficient surplus to feed marriage and funeral guests for a period of ten days (three and four times a year) as well as trade-friends. A trade-friend would remain as long as three months and sufficient food would have to be produced to feed him and his family. Such visits were reciprocated.

b) Animals and meat. Living in the tsetse fly area, the Bulu were not cattle keepers. Dogs, sheep and goats were their only traditional domestic animals. The sheep and goats were produced for exchange and to give their owners prestige.

Although the sheep and goats were of Portuguese origin, they are thought of as "traditional" animals by the Bulu of today. They were rarely used for food, although they were occasionally ceremonially eaten. As surplus, they were exchanged for more "wealth," either directly between trade-friends or as bridewealth. These were socially the most important commodities for exchange, but not the most numerous. To the Bulu, sheep and goats were the most conspicuous and measurable commodities.

Animal products such as ivory were not exchanged among the traditional Bulu. Ivory became a trade good only after white contact and then only for a period of about thirty years, until cocoa was grown in sufficient quantities for export.

Family obligations determined the distribution of meat, both wild and domestic, considered then as today an important and scarce commodity. Specific cuts of meat were invariably given to the same socially defined individual: hunter, his helper, father, mother (unless the meat was taboo to her), brother(s), grandparents and a choice portion sent to the special friend. "The whole which is divisible is the Soo (an antelope)" *("mimbiae be soo")* is the principle underlying the distribution of meat. This principle is so deeply imbedded in Bulu economy that cash earned today must be divided following the formula of the division of the antelope.

Live animals alone were distributed between lineages; meat was distributed within the socially defined family, including the intimate friend.

c) Manufactured goods. The exchange of manufactured goods was limited only by the variety of objects produced, rather than the quantity produced. Clay cooking pots, wooden dishes, raffia mats and objects of iron almost exhaust the variety of objects produced for both family use and exchange. Of these the iron objects, cutlasses, spears, lances, hoes and four-inch pieces of iron (100 to a bundle) produced only for bridewealth were most valued. As many as 6,000 spears might be required in the traditional bridewealth settlement. Exchange between trade-friends would require an even greater production of these commodities, so that the total production of iron products must have been very high in any one year. Unfortunately, the early Bulu kept no records of this output.

Exchanges through trade-friends were established as a part of the *avuso* alliances between lineages. Although bridewealth was a means for the distribution of surplus, through the continuous movement of sheep, goats and girls, there was also a more specific exchange, called in Bulu a gift exchange *(bia koan meyeng)* including an exchange of services between established trade-friends of two lineages. In this type of exchange one friend would bring a variety of commodities to the village of the other and give them to him, who would accept or reject them according to his judgment. The visiting friend would plan to stay a month or two during which time his wife would help his friend's wife in the garden, while he would hunt, gamble or help build a new house for his friend. The following year a return visit would be made completing the cycle. In this way a network of exchange crisscrossed lineage boundaries enabling a wider distribution of goods and services.

A second form of exchange was between two rich men, *nkukum*. The purpose of this exchange was to establish one's prestige over a wider area, more than one lineage, through a gift exchange not unlike the "potlatch" of the Kwakiutl Indians of the American Northwest coast. In the Bulu form, one rich man would invite another to his village. The guest would bring his family, including brothers, with him. With all of the village inhabitants present and in the open court where all could see, he would give the visiting friend everything movable in sight: ivory, slaves, goats, spears, iron hoes, etc. These, too, would be examined, accepted or rejected, and then carried to the home village. Later the process would be repeated, the other rich man playing host to the first. He would not only have to meet the value of the gifts presented to him but would have to give twice the number—either in value or numbers. His brothers of the village would help him, expecting "return" for their outlays at a later date. This continued until one of the rich men could not meet the gifts. He and his village would become impoverished, enslaved to work off the debt owed the successful rich man. The one who succeeded in this gift giving competition would be an *nkukuma*, a rich, rich man, a man with great prestige and influence.

When the first white traders came into the Bulu area, it was comparatively easy for the Bulu to understand and to adopt the white concept of exchange since it followed their own. One must have a white trade-friend today and in simple face-to-face exchange, give what he wants in return for European commodities. This concept remains latent today often to the embarrassment of an unsuspecting white man who becomes party to a "contract" he is not aware of, such as did the author.

Summarizing, traditional distribution of surplus was: a) between members of a joint family, b) as a result of alliances and marriages, c) an exchange of goods and services between recognized trade-friends and d) a gift-exchange competition between rich men for social status and respect.

WHITE PERIOD, 1860–1946

Some Factors in Modernization.

By 1894 the Bulu were middlemen holding a trade monopoly between the Germans on the seacoast and the still further interior tribes. At this time the Germans had no real administrative control over the Bulu due to the length of time it then took to travel comparatively short distances, as between Douala, the capital of the Kamerun, and Bululand. Between 1899 and 1900, the Bulu lost their trade monopoly as a result of losing a "war" to the Germans. This defeat brought the Bulu under the direct administrative control of the colonial government. Modernization was begun at this time with specific policies directed to change Bulu economy. Parenthetically it should also be noted that by 1894 the American Presbyterian mission was first established among the Bulu with the goal of changing the Bulu way of life. Schools and churches were started. Practical trades such as carpentry, masonry, cobbling were encouraged and ideas of thriftiness, saving of time, etc., were inculcated in accordance with the Protestant ethic.

Between 1900 and 1913, the German administration introduced legislation which provided the basis for change: (1) *Pax Germanica;* (2) establishment of administrative and trade centers; (3) road building and enforced moving of all Bulu villages onto these roads; (4) introduction and required use of cash in 1907; (5) establishment of schools and required elementary education for all children; (6) introduction of cocoa as a potential cash-income crop in 1913.

1) *Pax Germanica.* German peace put an end to the overt lineage feuds, thus removing one obstacle to the socio-economic unification of the area. In eliminating the need for a warrior group it created a potential labor force. Peace also allowed travel without fear of attack, enabling movement of both individuals and goods within the area, thus providing the setting for the modern Bulu economy.

2) *Establishment of Administrative Centers.* Administrative/commercial centers were established in Lolodorf, Ebolowa'a and Sangmélima, providing centers for political control and encouraging local trade. Markets and market places were opened in each of the centers. The "factories" of the German firm C. Woermann, which controlled all trade in the Kamerun, exchanged salt, cloth, fishhooks, blankets, guns, gunpowder, pots and liquor for ivory, palm kernels and rubber. Both liquor and guns were later banned in the colony.

3) *Road Building.* Following the "Bulu war," roads were built. All Bulu villages were forcibly moved and relocated on these roads, thereby permitting administrative control. The Germans appointed to each lineage-village a "chief" *(éveteman,* derived from English *"a white man")* who would represent the administration in village affairs. Each village was obliged to keep the road adjacent to it in good repair. The individual labor involved was in lieu of a head-tax. (At this time the Germans conscripted Bulu labor for the building of the Douala-Yaounde railroad, although its route did not cross Bulu territory.)

4) *The Introduction of Cash.* In 1907 money was introduced and required in the payment for all goods, salaries and other services. The barter system had become too unmanageable for economic efficiency. Lacking a standard set of values, it was virtually impossible to convert Bulu trade objects into German money accurately in a computation of costs, profit and loss, etc.

5) *Elementary schools.* Elementary schools, although introduced and run by the missions, were required by the German administration. They equipped young male Bulu with the fundamentals of

arithmetic, reading and writing necessary to the modern economy. They also created clerks, teachers, pastors, catechists, hospital assistants, carpenters and civil servants. By the time French began to administer the Kamerun at the end of the First World War, there existed the beginnings of an educated group.

6) *The introduction of cocoa.* Perhaps the most important single factor in the modernization of Bulu society was the introduction of cocoa in 1913. Up to this time comparatively few Bulu had a cash income. A few were employed in various capacities by white men, some exchanged palm-kernels, rubber or ivory for trade goods. In proportion to the number of Bulu, only a few had a cash income from these sources. Cocoa, on the other hand, could be produced by anyone who would plant it and give it minimal care. Whereas formerly a few might become rich, cocoa insured a relatively large income to *all* who planted it. By the end of the 1920's a majority of the Bulu men[1] were *planteurs* each with his own cocoa plantation.

Cocoa not only became the basis for a cash income but, in time, provided the Bulu with an export crop for the world market. Cocoa was the factor which made all of the foregoing factors meaningful, each supporting and reinforcing the other, in the process of modernizing Bulu economy.

POST WORLD-WAR II, 1946–1960

Socio-economic changes.

This modern period in Bulu history is marked by crucial political events at both ends: the founding of the Fourth French Republic in 1946; following the Brassaville conference, when the Cameroun emerged as an "associated territory" rather than a "colony," and the beginning of an independent state in 1960, when it became an autonomous Republic within the Communaute.

During this time, the factors described above brought about specific socio-economic changes in Bulu society. Four relevant changes have been selected here: (1) a cash income (2) the sedentary or fixed villages (3) the emergence of new roles and (4) changes in the organization of Bulu society as related to bridewealth and marriage.

1) *A cash income.* In 1956 all of the Bulu had a cash income from one or more of the following sources: (a) wages or salary, (b) bridewealth, (c) agricultural activities, (d) handicrafts, (e) gifts or "dash", (f) cocoa, and (g) other. The total cash income of the Bulu area was estimated as 21 million CFA francs (Binet 1956 : 57), indicated in Table 15.

---

[1] It should be mentioned that cocoa cultivation became the chore of the male in spite of the fact that, in the traditional society, women were the horticulturists.

Although all of the figures in Table 15 are estimates, it will be noted for our purpose (a) that the Bulu had a cash income, and (b) that the major source of that income was from cocoa production—70 per cent of the total. A more detailed treatment of cash income from cocoa and bridewealth appears later in the paper.

TABLE 15

Cash Income in the Bulu Area (1956)

a. Salaries of all types	1,545,080 francs	7.5% of total
b. Bridewealth	1,950,000	9.5%
c. Other agricultural products	476,654	2.0%
d. Handicrafts	480,000	2.5%
e. Gifts or "dash"	800,000	3.5%
f. Cocoa	15,673,481	70.0%
g. Other	900,000	4.4%

Cash income reached its peak during the Korean war when, for example, one week in October 1951, Bulu cocoa growers received on the Ebolowian market an all-time high of 210 CFA francs for one kilo of cocoa, as compared with about 90 francs before the war and 107 plus francs in 1958–59.

In a survey of 480 Bulu-Fang families living in the Cameroun-Gaboon border, the 1951 estimated gross income from cocoa alone showed the following (Alexandre and Binet 1958 : 32): Some Bulu *planteurs* have grossed as high as 1,000,000 francs in one year.

All of Bulu life seems to have become centered around the cash income derived from cocoa: bridewealth, house construction, purchase of bicycles, sewing machines, payment of taxes, the settlement of debts. As one Bulu expressed the point: "only fools do not grow cocoa." Everyone grew cocoa no matter what other sources of income he had; clerks, teachers, pastors, *fonctionaires,* and "boys" had cocoa gardens in their home villages.

TABLE 16

Estimated Cash Income in Cocoa (1951)

28 Families with a gross yearly income	3,720 CFA francs
113 Families with a gross yearly income	10,000 CFA francs
217 Families with a gross yearly income	29,600 CFA francs
87 Families with a gross yearly income	71,500 CFA francs
36 Families with a gross yearly income	152,000 CFA francs
5 Families with a gross yearly income	440,000 CFA francs

In approximately forty years, millions of cocoa trees had been planted in the Bulu area, the center of cocoa production in the

Cameroun, with an average of 2,000 trees per man (Binet 1956 : 61). Cocoa production, most of it again from the Bulu area, rose from 0 in 1913 to a forecast of 67,000 tons in 1958 (U.S.D.A., F.A.S. 1959 : 9).

By 1951 individual incomes, based upon the above figures varied from roughly 3,000 CFA francs to more than 400,000 CFA francs with about 45 per cent of the Bulu population having an average income of 30,000 CFA francs (Binet 1957 : 131–141).

2) *Sedentary or fixed villages.* By 1930 the traditional shifting cultivators were becoming a settled people largely due to the requirements of cocoa cultivation. This should not be viewed only in the sense of location of the village but that the people, too, have remained village oriented. Unlike other parts of Africa, there is no labor migration from the bush villages to the political/commercial or urban centers. Comparatively few men leave their natal villages for work; none plans to remain away permanently. The few who leave as *fonctionaires,* clerks, teachers or unskilled laborers return each year to care for their cocoa plot during their vacations and all look forward toward spending the years of their "retirement" in their natal villages where they will be considered as a "true Bulu" *(nya moto),* a rich man *(nkukum),* a member of the Council of Elders, directing village affairs *(nda mot).*

Another effect of cocoa on village life is observed in the new rights related to land and cocoa gardens. With the introduction of cocoa, land continues to be allocated by the Council of Elders to each male household head, with slight modifications of the traditional pattern: (a) the amount of land allocated, (b) the rule of cultivator of the cocoa garden, and (c) the idea of ownership.

a) More and usually the best land is allocated to the household heads for greater cocoa production, sometimes at the expense of land for kitchen gardens.

b) There has been a shift in work roles. Cocoa plantations are cultivated by the male family head although the women of the family are expected to help as a "labor force", a change in role requisites.

c) A man owns his trees and their produce, but not the ground in which they are rooted. The trees may be inherited, either by the oldest son, or by some specific individual at the death of an owner. The trees cannot be sold. Women may not own, inherit, or in any way control the cocoa trees.

3) *The emergence of new roles.* There was no social hierarchy in pre-white Bulu society except for the role of the rich man *(nkukum).* As noted above, it was egalitarian. New roles are emerging in the modern Bulu society. There has been a trend to classify these roles vertically in an hierarchical classification according to the

following variables: (a) cash income, (b) education, and (c) religion (Binet 1957 : 137).

a) *On the basis of cash income.* On the basis of cash income, Binet has constructed a hierarchical structure. Those Bulu with an income of more than 100,000 CFA francs belong to the emerging "rural elite." They are the chiefs (85 per cent of whom are also *planteurs*) and civil servants, or *fonctionaires.* The middle-class group have an income of 30,000 CFA francs. Forty-five per cent of the Bulu are in this group. (They are exclusively *planteurs.*) The remainder of "lower class," with under 15,000 CFA francs. (These are young *planteurs,* those just beginning.)

b) *On the basis of education.* Binet also constructs another hierarchical structure, on the basis of ability to use French as the only variable, and notes that 72.4 per cent of the Bulu are literate in French, 9 per cent of the Bulu are both speakers and writers only in Bulu, while only 10 per cent can speak but not write either in French or Bulu.

It should be noted that even French-speaking Bulu are literate in their mother tongue and that the chiefs, who have the highest income, are the least literate in French. According to Binet, 75 per cent of those elected to the political post of municipal representatives are not literate in French but are literate in Bulu. It is somewhat confusing to observe the emergence of what seems to be three separate elite groups: (a) on the basis of income (b) on the basis of the use of French and (c) on the basis of elected representatives.

New roles are emerging on the basis of professions, a result of education: "Professional class" including teachers, pastors, nurses, mid-wives, dentists, lawyers, etc.; and "non-professionals"—artisans and unskilled laborers in such roles as *planteurs,* bus drivers, "boys," laborers, etc. Of these new roles 85 per cent are planteurs (Binet 1957 : 135) who also command the greatest income, and the elected representatives, who are the elite.

c) *On the basis of religion.* The Bulu have the following religious preferences (Binet 1957 : 139–140):

TABLE 17

Religious preferences in the Bulu Area

Protestant (Presbyterian)	52 %
Roman Catholic (White Fathers)	34 %
Adventists (USA)	1 %
Jehova's Witnesses (Watchtower)	1 %
Pagan	4.5%
Unknown	7.5%

A majority of the Bulu are Protestant which reflects the sixty-five years the American Presbyterians have worked among them. Binet (1957 : 140) adds that "the Protestants are the richest, and have the greatest influence in the presentation of democratic ideas to the Bulu population." Such a classification would result in a Protestant, *planteur* elite group.

On the basis of Binet's study there is not one clear, well-defined emerging elite group but different elite groups based upon cash income, political elections, education or lack of it, and religion.

4) *Changes in the Bulu social organization as related to bride-wealth and marriage.* Cocoa helped introduce cash into the traditional Bulu bride-price system. (a) As cash incomes increased bride-price in money increased, as did the other items required in the bridewealth exchange. (b) This, in part, resulted in changes in the marriage form.

The earliest bridewealth was recorded by Tessman (1913 II : 260)[2] in the Fang-Bulu area of Gabon-Cameroon. It included 6,000 spears, 500 lances, 10 sheep/goats, 20 bundles of iron, and various other objects, but required no money.

A dowry recorded in the 1920's included 110 cutlasses, 10 sheep/goats, 20 bundles of iron and an unspecified sum of money. It was not until the 1930's that specific amounts of money were required as bridewealth. A dowry reported in 1935 required, in addition to the usual number of sheep/goats, etc., 2,000 francs. Cutlasses, spears, lances or bundles of iron were no longer required by this time.

Consistently, more cash was required by the Bulu from the 1940's to the present; sheep/goats and other commodities were still included. Cash requirements were:

TABLE 18

Cash Requirements for Bridewealth in the Bulu Area

1942	5,000	CFA francs
1945	10,000	CFA francs
1947	25,000	CFA francs
1950–55	50,000	CFA francs
1956–60	50,000 to 100,000	CFA francs

Other objects included dresses, a bicycle, sewing machine, shoes, etc. One girl asked that the shoes she had requested from her fiancé remain in their unopened package to show the Paris postmark.

Although cocoa prices have declined since their high during the

(2) Pangwe is the German, for the French Pahouin, for the Spanish Pamues, for the English word Fang. Today, French writers are inclined to use Pahouin to include: Fang, Bulu, Ntum and other groups, generally.

Korean war, the amount of cocoa produced has increased with no reduction of income for the *planteurs.*

Balandier made a study of the possible connections between bride-wealth and cash income derived from cocoa. He shows a correlated slow rise in both cocoa income and bridewealth between 1938 and 1950. In 1947 there was a very sharp increase in bridewealth with a parallel increase of cocoa income. This period coincides with the end of World War II and the local transportation problem. (During the war no cocoa was transported from interior points due to lack of both gasoline and automobiles.) (Balandier 1952 : 45; 1955 : 176)

Cocoa and cash income seem also to have had effects on Bulu marriage. Of these the following are worth noting here: (a) the increase of polygyny, (b) the increase of common-law marriages, and (c) the postponment of marriage from the traditional marrying age of thirteen for girls and eighteen for boys to eighteen and later for most girls and past twenty-five for boys.

Before these can be adequately discussed an explanatory word about modern marriage must be given. Traditional marriage was considered in part "heathenish" and in part "wife-buying" by the missionaries. A Christian African must marry in Christian fashion. This is true of both Roman Catholic and Protestant Christians. (This became, in fact, two different marriage forms from the Bulu point of view.) The French administration recognized only one legal marriage and that was the Civil marriage. (This became a third European marriage form.) The Bulu who might still want the traditional ceremony might be "married" in that way, but he would have had to be married also by the Church and then by the Government. A traditionally oriented Bulu had to go through three marriage ceremonies; a non-traditionally oriented Bulu, but Christian, had to engage in two ceremonies while an educated, non-Christian, nontraditional Bulu was married only by the civil ceremony, or by none at all.

(a) The older Bulu male generally is a traditionalist. Having grown cocoa for a long period, he has had time to enlarge his plantations, and he tends to recruit his labor force through the simple expedient of taking a second and third wife. Polygyny, however, is recognized by neither the Church nor the State, only by Bulu society. The girls such a man marries are ordinarily sisters, so in fact this is a revival of soral polygyny which was common in the pre-white period. Only a wealthy cocoa grower can afford these wives considering that the bride-price "cost" is 50,000 to 100,000 CFA francs. By refering again to Binet's study, one notes that by 1956, of Bulu men, 36 per cent between the ages of forty and forty-five were polygynous (Binet 1956 : 45).

(b) In marrying younger girls the older man competes with the young men, and wins. Young men cannot afford a bride-price of the above sum even if there were available girls. If a girl is available and can agree to a nontraditional, nonchurch marriage, she would probably be willing to be a common-law wife, locally called a "bush marriage."

(c) In a study of thirty-eight villages, Binet shows that 39 per cent of young men under twenty-five years but over twenty were not married, and 25 per cent of the group at twenty-five to thirty years of age had yet to marry (Binet 1956 : 32). This postponement of marriage can be considered to result from increase in commodities, cash, and the bride-price, again a by-product of cocoa.

Summary.

The receipt and payment of bridewealth have been permeated by the use of cash, which in turn is related to the increased dependence on cash cropping. The traditional marriage system has changed in a number of ways: (a) attempts to discontinue it entirely, in favor of various western forms of marriage; (b) by forcing Bulu youth to remain single until a sufficient number of commodities, including cash, may be collected to permit the still preferred traditional marriage as a preface to the western forms, or (c) to repudiate all forms of marriage and enter into a common-law residence, now a socially recognized form of marriage.

The continued use of commodities along with cash indicates the persistence of traditional bridewealth concepts. Traditional marriage is still preferred to the western forms. The western marriage forms have brought about a change in the system of marriage rather than the organization of marriage and its relationship to the social structure. Structurally, as a contract symbolized by the union of two individuals fulfilling the old political lineage alliance, the *avuso,* marriage has not basically changed even though various western forms are in use.

THE MODERNIZATION OF BULU ECONOMY

The changes described in previous sections will be interpreted here as they relate to the kind of changes taking place in the present Bulu society and culture. For a clearer picture of the kind of change, two lines of investigation will be presented: change relative to Bulu culture and social structure, and change relative to a shift in Bulu economy, from a subsistence to a market economy.

George R. Horner

Change Relative to Bulu Culture and Social Structure.

It is often assumed that the introduction of western traits to a non-western culture *ipso facto* causes some kind of cultural and social disorganization, which may eventually lead to the disintegration of a culture. Such a culture may either disappear or survive in a new or different form. Results of cultural and social shock have given rise to concepts phrased in terms as "acculturation" and "transculturation," with further implication that this is an inevitable process in a normal order of events. It is further assumed that the culturally stronger traits will always replace, or structurally change, the weaker, local traits. The stronger trait is usually considered as "western" and the weaker, those traits of a local culture. There is evidence that this kind of cultural impact has occurred in the past, as among certain American Indian societies, and continues today among certain African societies.

Neither of these concepts, it seems to me, is applicable in explaining the kind of change among the Bulu. As has been described above, change has been taking place among the Bulu, from white contact alone, for at least sixty-five years; either despite, or because of, this contact the Bulu seem more culturally intact and socially unified than in their pre-white period. Western (and other) traits have readily been both adopted and adapted into Bulu culture—a process of *accommodation* and modernization rather than *westernization,* which both acculturation and transculturation imply. The point, then, is that traditional culture has persisted while, at the same time, undergoing superficial or external change. The traditional goals, concepts and system of values (the internal "core" of Bulu culture) have "sorted" introduced traits, keeping and changing those which were culturally relevant, and discarding those traditional traits which were no longer useful in a modern context. Persistence is a phenomena to which more attention should be given in any study of a changing society.

To illustrate further what is meant by persistence, a summary will be given of the four crucial changes in Bulu society. The changes include: (1) a cash income, (2) the sedentary or fixed village, (3) the emergence of new roles, and (4) changes in Bulu society relating to bridewealth and marriage.

1) *A cash income.* The traditional Bulu have consistently treated commodities (things, *biom*) in at least two ways: (a) as surplus, to be divided among kin and trade friends and (b) as a means to achieve the culturally recognized and expressed goal of social prestige. The modern Bulu conceptualize cash as a commodity. A few examples are the following:

(a) The traditional importance of obligations to one's family, the role of kinship, remains a major force among the Bulu. Cash earned in any way is divided according to the traditional principle found in the "division of the antelope" where specific shares were given to socially designated individuals; a specific sum to one's wife; the cash equivalent of fifty pounds of cocoa (the amount varies) to village "brothers;" the same amount to the special friend; the same to oneself and unspecified amounts to other members of one's village who are in need.

Binet effectively established the point that the Bulu earn cash incomes and that these incomes are an important factor in modern Bulu life. He was too hasty in drawing conclusions, based upon this empirical data alone, without taking into account cultural factors as the basis for a new societal hierarchy. The traditional rule of kinship obligations, observered in the division of surplus, reinforces the traditional concept of an egalitarian society since the cash, instead of being kept by one person, must be divided among one's socially defined kin, according to a built-in system of social sharing.

The traditional cultural concepts persist in treating cash as a commodity and distributing this commodity as a surplus following the customary procedure, based upon the socially-defined principle of equality.

(b) A cultural goal among the traditional Bulu was to accumulate things *(biom)* in order to have wealth *(akum)* for social prestige and status. This goal is ceremonially expressed at the birth of every male child: "you will have riches, sheep, goats, wives, children and villages will be yours;" it is verbally expressed nightly, around the family fire in the folktales (Horner 1950) which constantly remind a boy of his life's goal.

Traditional wealth was acquired by exchange, gambling or inheritance. Today cash has become the modern means of achieving the traditional goal of wealth. It is a western trait which has fit neatly into the traditional way of life; achieving it, a man can be a true man *(nya mot)* and possibly a rich man *(nkukum)*.

Binet has shown that of those Bulu having an income of over 100,000 CFA francs, 85 per cent are traditional "chiefs" (rich men). This is not evidence, as Binet suggests, for an emerging, new, rural elite based upon income. Rather, it seems to me, this follows the understood traditional pattern of one lineage-village rich man (incidently, none of the chiefs of whom Binet writes has any political power even within their villages, which suggests their traditional idea of rich man). This same group of "chiefs," according to Binet, are the least literate in French; 75 per cent of them are not able to read or write in that language, while all are able to read and write in their own language.

2) *Sedentary or fixed villages.* The German administration forced the Bulu to establish their villages along the newly-built roads; cocoa forced the Bulu to give up their seminomadic life for a sedentary one.

Two Bulu villages lost their "native" characteristics to become large westernized towns, Ebolowa'a and Sangmélima. Both are commercial and administrative centers, the former a mission center as well. Both towns have paved roads, electricity, running water, western buildings and sections where non-Bulu Africans live as members of the administration.

Such towns are in sharp contrast to the typical roadside Bulu villages, which follow the traditional patterns of construction. Even here the traditional ties are not broken with "home" village.

The lineage-village remains the center of the life of each Bulu. Kinship and lineage systems have remained unchanged. Political alliances with other lineages remain in force both for exchange and marriage. Since 1953 there has emerged a more distinct sense of Bulu political unity, largely through the efforts of Mvondo David who visited each lineage village of the Bulu and united them "for greater social benefits among 'brothers' ", in a political association, which in turn is a part of a political party, the *Action National.* This gives each village a sense of unity with other villages which it never had had before and gave birth to the expression "la race Bulu."

Such external change has not influenced the local village in its internal structure but has reinforced the concept of Bulu society, even beyond that which was possible in the traditional period.

The Council of Elders continue to control all of the village land despite the size of the individual plantations, and the amount under cultivation by each *planteur.*

Although there has been a shift in work roles, the men being the chief cocoa cultivators, this change is a superficial one, since basically the economic provisioning remains a male responsibility. Had the women controlled, owned, and (as owner) cultivated the cocoa trees, this would have brought about an internal change which would have had an impact on all of Bulu society, perhaps to the point of disorganization. This was prevented by the male, in the role of provider, assuming the work role as cultivator. The traditional pattern is further observed in that a man may will his trees (not the land) to any male individual, never to a female.

3) *The emergence of new roles.* Internal changes in Bulu social organization, changes in terminology, might be an expected result of

the introduction of the new occupational roles as a part of a new social orientation. Binet, as quoted above, for example, has attempted to construct a new role-centered hierarchical social system based upon factors of cash income, education and religion, which would imply internal changes in the Bulu social structure.

Binet's picture of a hierarchy is confusing, due mostly to his methodological framework rather than his data. To him, new roles are equated almost *ipso facto* to a new social order. It is confusing because his data leads to three and possibly four hierarchical systems, with a different elite group at each apex. He is in error because his methodology was limited to observable factors alone. He should have included such unempirical cultural factors as "goals" and "values" and the relationship of new social roles to them.

With the inclusion of such culture factors, there does not seem to be a new social structure, a new hierarchy. His so-called new elite behave very much in a traditional way. They still use the same classificatory kinship terms of, e.g., "brothers," suggesting the continuity of an egalitarian society; all males still have only one vote in the meeting of the Council of Elders; there is one village rich man, although others are achieving the status of "true men, *benya bot*," none have more political power than any other within the village. The new roles are only external changes of organization, new ways of achieving traditional wealth goals, new and faster means of achieving prestige and status. The Bulu have accommodated western roles into their traditional culture and social structures.

4) *Changes in the Bulu social organization as related to bride-wealth and marriage.* In the history of Bulu bridewealth, indicated elsewhere in this paper, the Bulu use commodities and exchange them as a part of their bridewealth system in marriage. Over the years certain commodities have been dropped while cash, considered as a commodity, has not only taken their places but has increased in use. This is a change in the traditional system.

An increasing bride-price and the competition for young girls by older men (who can meet the high bride-price) has made the traditional marriage difficult to achieve for most Bulu young men. Marriage age is postponed or common-law mates result. In addition, government legislation and church rule has forcibly changed the traditional marriage form with the view of completely replacing it. Still, 80 per cent of the Bulu preface western marriage practices—a church marriage and civil ceremony—by the traditional form. No one can predict how long this will continue. It does show the strength of the traditional form and its persistence despite legislation which is trying forcibly to change it.

5) *Changes relative to a shift in Bulu economy: from subsistence to a market economy*. The distribution of surplus among the traditional Bulu was based upon kinship and inter-lineage ties. Only a few commodities were distributed. Cocoa enlarged the Bulu's economic horizons. They are now a part of the world market. Does this also imply that the economy of the modern Bulu can also be divided into two sectors, a subsistence and a market? Since the subsistence sector has been described, some market aspects of Bulu economy will be considered here.

In investigating the possibility of a market sector in present Bulu economy, three questions, one analyst says, need to be considered: "(a) the extent to which the resources of land and labor of the indigenous agricultural economies have become commercialized; (b) the ways in which money earning activities have been combined with the subsistence activities in the process of the enlargement of the exchange economy, and (c) the relation of this process to the economic development of the territory as a whole" (United Nations 1954 : 3).

(a) Under this first section, the author states that the extent to which resources of land and labor is used to produce marketable items is useful as an indicator of "commercialization," or of a market economy. If more land and labor is used to produce export or cash crops than subsistence crops, such an economy is said to be in the process of change from a subsistence economy to a market economy.

Although we lack specific statistics relative to the Bulu, one notes for the Cameroon as a whole that 80 per cent of productive acreage is used for subsistence crops while only 20 per cent is used for market economy crops (U.S.D.A. 1959 : 64). This is probably equally true among the Bulu whose only export and cash crop is cocoa.

There is no hired labor force. The traditional Bulu family produced its own cocoa. It sells it to the buyer. There are no individually or corporately-owned plantations with a hired labor force to run them. As was pointed out elsewhere, the male head of a biological family cultivates his own garden, with only wives and daughters recruited as a labor force. Cocoa, although a cash crop, has neither commercialized the use of land nor the labor force.

(b) Of all of the money earning activities of the Bulu, listed elsewhere in this paper, the selling of cocoa is the most important. Seventy per cent of the Bulu (and Cameroonian) cash income is from cocoa. It is important then as a factor in possible change from a subsistence to market economy. Analytically, certain requisites must be met. A very relevant one in a market economy is the relation of "profits as a guide to production" (Karp 1960). Subsistence economies, by contrast, do not produce foods in response to market forces on a profit or loss basis. In the production of cocoa by the Bulu, no payment of money is required either in the use of land or the hiring of labor. These are not explicit costs either in production or the pricing of cocoa.

The government sets the local cocoa price according to the world market, not local production costs. The Bulu produce cocoa in about the same way they produce subsistence crops. There is no evidence for dependence upon a market economy, although cocoa is sold in the market, and hence considerable cash is handled. Bulu economy nevertheless remains primarily in the subsistence sector.

CONCLUSIONS

The pre-white Bulu distributed their surplus in a culturally defined exchange system which, in turn, was based upon a close relationship between wealth goals and social prestige. The modern Bulu, in their response to European economy, have not changed their basic cultural goals. What has changed is the means to this cultural end. The Bulu have only modernized their traditional way of life by appropriating European economic institutions as *the means* to achieve traditional goals faster. It is a new means to a traditional end. Cash will allow a Bulu to have more "things" *(biom)* and through these, a man is measured as a true man *(nya mot)*.

One Bulu expressed the kind of change all Bulu are experiencing in this way: "custom and practice are not so easily changed as garments, as these are in the 'blood'."

CHAPTER 7

Trade and Markets Among the Kuba

BY JAN VANSINA[1]

KUBA ECONOMY

The Kuba dwell in the country between the rivers Kasai and Sankuru in the Kasai province of the formerly Belgian Congo. The name Kuba is given by their southern neighbors to the kingdom formed by an amalgam of eighteen tribes, numbering about 70,000 people. These tribes do not all partake in a single culture, although the majority of them is culturally akin to the leading group, the Bushong. But all these peoples were a part of the kingdom and participated in a single system of economic distribution.

The Kuba are mainly agriculturalists, although hunting and fishing still are important in their economy. The main crops grown are corn, manioc, beans, groundnuts and *voandzeia*. Secondary crops are sugar cane, tobacco, pineapple, pawpaws, etc. Four kinds of palm are used, one of which, the raphia palm, is very important. It yields wine, materials for weaving, and building materials; even the grubs which live on its stem are eaten. The forest and the savanna supply the people with all kinds of raw material: bamboo, timber, firewood, grasses, medicinal herbs, etc., as well as insects, grubs, caterpillars, ants, molluscs and the like, which are regular additions to the meals.

Fishing and hunting are communal operations requiring considerable equipment, nets, weirs, traps, dugouts, artifical ponds, dams, dikes. Game and fish are plentiful. Other communal operations are the melting of iron ore and the making of salt from plants in the marshes. The country is rich and the people exploit most of its possibilities. In comparing them with their neighbors, the Lele, one is struck by the difference in effectiveness of exploitation of the natural resources.

Labor is valued in this society. The people work hard. A study of the daily occupations of a number of people shows that about three quarters of their time is given to work; indeed, almost one-third of it is given to production of goods that are not necessary for subsistence

(1) The fieldwork on which this account is based was carried out under the auspices of the *Institut pour la Recherche Scientifique en Afrique Centrale* (I.R.S.A.C.) in 1953–54 and 1956.

but used in trade (see Table 20). This means that the Kuba have a tradition of production beyond subsistence needs as part of their cultural values. Wealth is a powerful means of acquiring prestige, and prestige is the basic value of society. Wealth is displayed in order to give prestige; it has to be shown in rich clothing, furniture and hospitality. This has led to a material culture of a richness and a diversity which is not found in the surrounding cultures. Table 21 shows the inventory of two houses, one of an ordinary man and one of a high dignitary. It will be seen that both of them have sufficient equipment to be comfortable, but that the dignitary is richer in clothing and ornaments. Display of wealth, of course, furthers even more the production of all kinds of goods.

In such circumstances specialization of crafts is well developed. The main specialists are political and religious officials, woodcarvers, smiths, hunters, fishermen, tailors, potters and jewelers. But within each craft there tends to be further specialization. One sees wood-carvers making bowls for pipes and others making the stems. The specialization in crafts is paralleled by a regional specialization which is due both to the somewath different physical environments of different tribes and also to the different cultural traditions. Table 21 shows the specific outputs, exports, and imports of each area.

Production in Kuba economy is, then, characterized by a great diversity of products, by a tradition of production beyond subsistence needs, by a specialization of crafts and by a diversification of regional production. Such characteristics also make for patterns of economic distribution that are extensively developed.

ECONOMIC TRANSACTIONS

Both internal marketing and external trade are typical features of Kuba culture. Economic exchanges and movements of goods can be carried out by barter, by socially obligatory payments, by sale outside a market, and by sale in a market.

Barter. Barter can be carried out between people of the same village. It is, however, very rare; even between husband and wife or parents and children, many transactions are carried out by money transaction. The only case of barter discovered in the course of field work was one in which eggs were bartered for salt in a market.

Socially obligatory payments. A certain amount of goods changes hands without any payment. These are not gifts in the usual sense, but rather payments of a socially obligatory character. At funerals the patrilateral families and the friends of the deceased (mainly his age-mates) make gifts of objects in red camwood *(mboong itool)* to the

brother or the nephew of the deceased, who is his matrilineal successor. These objects can only change hands or be destroyed by succession. At marriage a bride-price is paid by the father of the groom
to the parents of the bride. Formerly these goods were not exclusively
used for marriage payments, but were typically those which are most
common in the markets, as well as cowrie shell money. But this
payment was small, and the real "bride-price" consisted in labor
performed by the groom for his mother-in-law.[2] But actually the
custom of working for the mother-in-law has fallen into disuse and
the bridge-price has risen to some Fr. 600 or Fr. 700.

More direct payments had to be made in the payment of tribute and
in the type of marriage known as *ngady*, both of which have fallen
into disuse. It was possible to marry a woman, not as a full wife but
rather as a concubine *(ngady)*, which meant that the offspring of this
woman did not belong to the clan of the mother, as is usual, but to
the father's clan. The bridewealth in such an arrangement was very
high as it involved transfer of the children from one clan to the other.
The motives for such a marriage were, on the side of the groom, a
desire to repopulate his nearly-extinct clan section; on the side of
the clan section of the bride, the motive was a desperate financial condition. Clan sections could be repopulated either by the purchase
of female slaves or by *ngady* marriage, which shows that the transaction had an economic aspect.

The following case gives a good illustration to the situations under
which *ngady* marriages occur:

A tailor working for a high dignitary at the capital stole a cloth *(mapel)*
and four bars of red camwood. Discovered and condemned to refund the
value of the stolen objects, he proposed to the dignitary to give him one of
his daughters as a *ngady*. The transaction was accepted before witnesses.
The woman bore six children which were considered as members of their
father's clan. After that, the woman was raised to the status of a full wife
(mwaamsh) as a reward for her fertility.

In another case, a clan section was unable to pay a heavy fine in court.
They gave a daughter of a slave family, which they owned, as a *ngady* to a
depopulated clan section who provided them with the means of paying
the fine.

---

(2) In indigenous Kuba society, people worked for one another in the following additional situations: (1) working bees, mainly in housebuilding and agriculture, for which
only food and drink were provided; (2) communal work for the lineage (digging fish
ponds and fishing in them) and the village (hunting, clearing paths); (3) tribute in labor-
chiefs could summon people to build storehouses, fences, etc., at capitals; other villages
were charged with providing capitals with food, wood and water; still others had the
duty of clearing fields for chiefs or kings and their matrilineal kinsmen.

Tribute among Kuba is divided into two sorts: a "tribute of sovereignty" which comprises skins, teeth, horns, meat, feathers of so-called "noble animals." They are generally of small value with the exception of elephant tusks. They were given to the chief or the king to show the political allegiance of the giver. The second kind of tribute was intended to give disbursable wealth to chiefs and kings, so that they could entertain a large retinue and make gifts to their officials. It consisted of products which are the normal export wares of the community which pays them: the Ngyeen will give cloth, the Cwa meat, the Pyaang knives, etc. Tribute was paid once a year to special dignitaries, then brought to the chiefs who kept part of the levy for themselves, and finally taken to the king. The amounts to be paid varied from year to year but were important. The produce supplied the means to run a government, which benefited everbody in maintaining law and order.[3]

Sale outside the market. Another form of economic transaction was the direct sale of products without going through the market. It often happened, and happens, that local specialist smiths or woodcarvers will provide their wares directly to the customer who orders them. One smith I saw had orders placed for several months ahead. Actually other forms of sale outside of the market have become prominent. Products traded long distances are sold in shops, and many shopping centers have arisen near the villages. Other produce, such as cash crops, are sold directly to the stores of the exporters. A cooperative of woodcarvers buys the produce of its members and sells it in its own shop. Other people sell along the streets of the railway centers or organize to send one of their number to far-off places like Katanga to sell by hawking. This modern practice contrasts sharply with the former practice of transacting most produce exchanges in market places.

THE MARKET SYSTEM

From remote times there has existed in this area both interregional and international trade carried on through a regular market complex. It is difficult to tell how markets arose. We know that they have existed at least since the end of the seventeenth century. The existence of markets depended in the first place on the existence of a political structure which could guarantee the security of the traders and the maintenance of peace in the markets themselves. This is corroborated by the absence of markets among the Lele where there is no political organization able to guarantee market security and peace.

(3) The second type of tribute is a classic example of what Polanyi has called "redistribution." Eds.

Similarly, despite many attempts, no market has survived among the
Lulua because at one time or another the market peace was disturbed and traders looted. In the second place, markets were important only in strategic places along the trade routes on the borders
of areas with different products. Regional specialization is tied very
closely to the location of the main markets. Table 22 shows the most
important markets for the Bushong. It will be seen that all these
markets are near the borders with the exception of *Nsheng*, the
capital of the kingdom, and a few secondary markets clustered around
the capital. Another point concerning location of markets is that
they were formerly never held in a village but on a cleared open spot
on a hill between villages. A neighboring village was in charge of
the practical organization of the market; but, in order to give confidence to customers from other villages or regions, the market was
always held in a safe neutral spot.

It is possible to divide the Kuba markets into local and interregional ones. The latter may be truly international or not. The market
of Yeek, for instance, was used only by Bushong and Kel traders,
whilst the market of Ibaanc invalued Lulua, Luba, Pende, Ovim-
bundu and several Kuba tribes trading with each other. But the
products exchanged on these interregional markets were practically
the same. They found their way from the main markets to the
small centers and from there to the local markets. But, although
the same range of goods was sold on every market, every place had
its special reputation, which depended on its position on the main
trade routes. At Ibaanc, for instance, ivory was exchanged for cowries,
copper, salt, and slaves. The ivory came from the Sankuru, where it
was bought at Kin aNcwey by the Bushong. The other products in
the market of Ibaanc came from the Lulua area (slaves) Katanga
(copper and salt) and Loanda (cowries). Table 21 gives the exports
and imports of every tribe, the location of markets and the tribes
which meet there. From a comparison of the two it is possible to
assess the peculiarities of every market in the Kuba area.

The Kuba divide markets in two groups according to the commodities for sale in them: the *imboom* or general market and the
mwaak or market for sale of food in small quantities. There is only
one market of the second type and it is located at the capital. The
citizens of *Nsheng* never produced their own food and needed a
market to buy their food. Nowadays they till fields but the *mwaak*
continues to exist. Details of the articles sold on the *mwaak* are given
in Table 23. As nearly everything can be bought or sold on the *imboom*, no detailed chart is given. Table 24 lists only a number of
metal objects which appear regularly in such *imboom*. Thus it gives

a general idea of the diversity of articles which can be found there; for each of the items listed—carved objects, cloth, basketry, pottery, foodstuffs, etc.—a similar range of related items is available.

There does not seem to have existed a special class of merchants in Kuba culture. The producers brought their products directly to the buyers at the market. They still do so now, especially at the *mwaak* where one sees people selling only a few handfuls of corn they can spare.

Some people formerly joined in caravans of Kuba producers, who went together to foreign markets in the Luba area. But it seems that most of the traders carried out their business more with a spirit of occasional speculation than with the idea of making a professional career from it. Everbody at one time or another could become a trader, and it seems that everybody turned away from trading after some particular aim had been achieved. An illustration of this is the following story; "When the Kuba saw that their clan sections were depopulated, they went to the Shoowa and sold chickens at ten cowries apiece. With the money thus acquired, they set out for the Ndengese where they bought tusks which they offered for sale in the markets in the south to buy slaves with them. For a big tusk they could obtain twenty slaves, for a small one ten slaves. The woman slaves would bear children and the clan section would grow. If, however, not enough money could be obtained by the sale of the chickens, one could associate one's self with another person and buy the tusk together. The slaves obtained would then be divided between the associates. One could start also by selling pottery instead of chickens."

This lack of specialization explains why there is no division according to sex among traders. Products made by women are sold by them; although women might sell products made by their husbands, one often sees men trading themselves.

Professional middlemen between producers and consumers therefore do not exist among the Kuba. But in large markets there seem to have existed some people who specialized in acting as witnesses for important transactions and also as brokers, telling customers where they could find what they wanted to buy. These brokers received a small fee from the sellers. But even here one can hardly speak of true specialists.

Formerly the markets were attended by as many as a thousand people, which meant that an internal organization was needed to keep law and order in the market places. Such was the duty of the market chief, who was oppointed by a political chief. He saw to it that no armed persons were allowed on the market place, and that the dealers in similar products were grouped together. His policemen repressed any uproar, and settled on the spot any dispute about transactions.

The general rules enforced in all markets were that no weapons were allowed in the market place, that there were fixed places assigned for the sale of every type of commodity, that there was a duty to be paid by the traders to the market chief, that every important transaction had to be carried out before witnesses, that the politica' chief could forbid or activate the sale of particular commodities (such as tusks), that for some products a first choice in buying (at fixed, maximum price) had to be reserved to certain dignitaries (the first shrimps of the season were offered to the *muudy* official), and finally that the political chief could fix maximum and minimum prices in time of crisis. Generally this last measure was only taken when customers boycotted the market.

In many regions of the Kuba area, the male customers were members of an initiation association, the *nkaan*.[4] Complaints about prices were lodged within the *nkaan* and a boycott was decreed. Another general rule was that the main markets were held only on rest days. The Kuba week counts three days of which *nkil* is a day of rest. On *nkil* it is forbidden to work in the forest, because it is said that the spirits and the deceased roam about. They want also to make their purchases on the markets, and that is why markets must be held on that day. Smaller markets were held on the two other days of the week so that any trader could attend three markets in the same area.

The market organization does not seem to have been very elaborate, but it was sufficient for its purpose. Nowadays regular police supervise the market places, but the chiefs have kept their control of the prices although they have lost the power of forbidding sale or having a right of first choice. This last right seems to have been very restricted, even in former times. The market chief does not exist any more, so differences are not settled on the spot, but are brought to the ordinary courts, which of course hampers a speedy settling of disputes. Actually all international trade is carried out through stores, and the markets have declined seriously. But the internal trade still goes on. The demands for local products decrease but slowly, and the needs for foreign wares rise continually but not rapidly, so that the replacement of the market purchases by those at stores is not rapid. However, this trend continually weakens the markets. But the moment of their death has not come yet. The Kuba still feel a need for Bushong masks, Pyaang knives, Ngyeen mats and the like.

(4) For further information on the *nkaan*, see Vansina 1955 : 138–153.

MONEY

Until twenty years ago the cowrie shell was the main money of the Kuba, and to some extent it is still now functioning as such. The cowries were imported into Africa by the Portuguese and found their way to the interior by the trade routes from Loanda to the Pende, the Lulua and the Kuba, and from San Salvador in the lower Congo to the Stanleypool and through the Kwango to the Kuba.

The cowries have a number of characteristics which made them very handy as a currency. They are light, the supply was big enough to permit its use as a means of exchange and small enough to warrant a high value as a rare product; the unit was small enough to be useful in the purchase of the most commonly bought commodities; the standard of the shells is sufficiently set to avoid complications from abnormally beautiful, big, small or ugly shells; and finally cowries can be used as ornaments. When large quantities of cowries were needed, the Kuba used the *mabiim,* which are small pieces of woven raffia cloth onto which 320 cowries and a circle of beads in two colors are stitched. The value of a *mabiim* is slightly superior to that of the cowries which are stitched onto it.

Other monies have been competing with the cowrie as currency. The first of these is the standard square of raffia cloth, which seems to have been the first currency and to have been ousted by the cowrie. Ten lengths of cloth made into a dress and adorned with embroidery constitute the *mapel* and the *mapel* still constitutes a unit of value, and to some extent a unit of standard for very large values. From 1900 onwards the copper croisette of Katanga were imported in sufficient quantities. They were the main currency in the countries to the south of the Kuba area in addition to the cowrie. But by about 1925 they had become so numerous that they depreciated in value. Finally some beads and especially the *amandrilha,* white and green beads, were used as means of payments at the end of the nineteenth century. They also lost their significance with devaluation following too large an importation. Only the cowrie survived, although it is now superseded by the Congolese franc.

Might one say that the cowrie is real money? If one assumes that money must have two essential properties, being a standard of value and a unit of real exchange, there is no doubt that cowries were money. Everything was calculated in cowries and most of the exchanges were made in cowries. But it was only one of several currencies in use and therefore it could be argued that it was only money in the limited sense that it was *a* unit but not *the* unit of exchange. The fact that cowries are used as ornaments as well as in their monetary function cannot be invoked to say that they are not money. Money is commonly used for jewelry or ornamentation. The case of gold or silver or even metal coins can be cited. On the other hand, the behavior of the cowrie in relation to the Congolese franc and the fluctuation of the cowrie over the last seventy years shows that it reacts like modern all-purpose currency.

The extent of devaluation of the cowrie over the last seventy years cannot be assessed exactly, but some light is thrown on it by the following data:

TABLE 19

Depreciation of the Cowrie

Cost in Cowries	Around 1850	1885	1907	1953
1 chicken	10 c.	25 c.	300–500 c.	400 c.
Bridewealth	30 c.	500–1000 c.	3000 c.	30,000–35,000 c.
Female slave	1000 c.			

The value of the cowrie in 1953 was 10 cowries to the Congolese franc. But in the case of the payment for bride-price, the 30,000 cowries were equivalent not to 3000 but only to 700 francs. The franc is thus valued at about 43 cowries for bride-price, since the franc is given cultural preference to cowries in this payment.

Table 19 shows enough to indicate that cowrie prices rose at least tenfold between pre-European times and the installation of the first European factories (1890–1905). Moroni, a trader, stated in 1904 that after a huge import of cowries, this article had been superseded as a means of payment in the east of the country by the copper cross. In 1907, Torday, the first anthropologist in the area, stated that the value of the cowrie had decreased a hundredfold in fifty years' time. One may surmise that the most rapid depreciation took place between 1880 (when the first European arrived in the country) and 1905. As early as 1893 a trader, de Macar, stated that although the currency in use on the markets of Ibaanc and Kaba was still the cowrie, this unit was so small that for most of the transactions the unit actually used was one of 10,000 cowries. At that time, then, the inflation was already nearly complete, as this note shows. But after 1905, the inflation was stopped. Table 19 shows only a slight increase in the price of chicken between 1907 and 1953. Of course, some products or services have become more expensive as the case of bridewealth indicates, but a commonly used article, such as the chicken, gives a clear idea of the progression.

The question to be asked then is: what measures were taken by the Kuba to stop cowrie deprecation? Although I have no proof of the exact procedure, it seems to have been the following one. As more and more cowries flowed in the country and inflation was at its worst, it was decided to eliminate some cowries and to retain as money only pieces of a certain size, shape, and color, with the result that a reduction in the quantity to be used as money was attained. This factor explains how it comes about that a kilogram of cowries is sold for Fr. 70 by the importers today and that the cowrie has still a value of Fr. 0.10. Buying a kilogram of cowries is a speculation. One may find far more than this value in francs of "good" cowries or one may find less than the value. The importers do not seem to realize the new requirements about size, shape, and color and go on selling mixed lots. The people use the "bad" cowries nowadays for decoration and so it happens that no cowries are ever refused by them, and that the importers do not realize the change in value. The procedure to maintain the currency is, of course, of such a nature that one can assimilate it with the introduction of a new type of money.

The other factor which makes us conclude that cowries are money is that their value relative to the Congolese franc changes as any other currency would. For instance, in 1935 a chicken was worth 400 cowries or 5 francs, while in 1953 a chicken has a value of 50 fr. but the same 400 cowries. The cowrie holds its own and the value of the Congolese franc has been diminishing with the general increase in the cost of living. Unfortunately there are too few recorded instances to give a more accurate idea of the price fluctuations in terms of both currencies during the years since 1925. Actually for most transactions entailing European goods (e.g. bride-price), payment in francs is preferred; but when local products are exchanged cowries are still as good as francs. As a matter of interest, one can see that both currencies are limited to certain types of goods, but that the franc is ousting slowly the elder of the two.

PRICES

The most important characteristic of prices in Kuba markets is that they behave in exactly the same way as prices do in European markets. The price is set by the relation of supply and demand. When shrimps first appear on the market, they fetch a high price. Later on, the price falls. A second consideration with regard to price is the value of the raw material used, both in specific value and in bulk. Large baskets are more expensive than small ones and copper objects are more expensive than iron ones. This, of course, is again a consideration of relative scarcity. A third consideration is the amount of work needed to obtain either raw materials or to fashion the goods. Melting iron ore is a process which involves combined labor of many men. It has been abandoned now because it cannot compete with the price of raw imported iron. Weaving a square of cloth takes more time than cutting the reeds used for basketry and so forth. But this correspondence between price and work is affected by another factor as is shown in Table 24. The prices in this Table do not correspond closely to time outlay. The reason is that certain objects are considered of primary necessity and others are luxuries. As luxury objects are sold more seldom than ordinary objects, they fetch higher prices. A classical instance is the prices for sale of a *velours du Kassi* cloth and an *ikaangl* mat. Both take the same time to produce, both use the same raw materials or similar ones, but the cloth is sold at Fr. 300 and the mat at Fr. 700. This anomaly is explained by the different demands for each: cloths are commonly sold to tourists. Mats are seldom sold, but are used on the floors of the huts as carpets and also to make coffins.

This brings us to the question of the influence of prestige on price. Objects which are luxuries have high prestige; possessing them is an indication of wealth. It may be that they are sold at very high prices not only because they are sold rarely, but also because people are prepared to pay for prestige. As both factors go together, it is difficult to ascertain this. Both the ability to preserve or store a product and its freshness at the time of sale also influence its price. In the case of food, it makes small difference whether groundnuts are sold fresh, dried or roasted, but fresh maize is more expensive than dried maize, and the prices of fish reflect even more the exact state of freshness of the fish. Similarly, new goods fetch higher prices than used ones with the effect that old carvings are far less expensive than the new imitations also sold.

The influences of all these factors affect prices in exactly the same way as they would in European markets. This applies also to the so-called prestige factor which is no more conspicuous here than in Western prices for such commodities as perfumes, cars, furs and the like.

The incentive of trade is, of course, to acquire material income. This can be done by selling cash crops at the stores or goods without commercial value for Europeans in the markets. In the latter case, they can be sold in the *imboom* when the quantities are not too small, or when the commodities are not food, or in the *mwaak* for small quantities of food. Marketing income can also be acquired by buying large quantities of some product and selling them at retail prices. Nowadays this procedure has become very common. In the *mwaak* one sees cigarettes sold by the piece, palmwine by the glass, small fish piece by piece, when the traders have bought these products by packets, jars and baskets. That the retail trade can yield give handsome profits to the traders is borne out by Table 25.

One trader sold a stock of bean leaves worth Fr. 14 for Fr. 17, another made Fr. 27 of his Fr. 20 stock of white ants, etc.

It has not been possible to study the prices in the *imboom* more closely, but some data have been gathered for *mwaak* and are set out in Tables 23, 25, 26 and 27. From these it will be seen that the total value of the stocks on sale every day in this market is not very high. Table 23 shows conclusively that the *mwaak* deals with a retail trade. The goods are sold in the smallest possible quantities, with the expected result that there are many buyers for most of the products, as Table 27 tells when one knows that in the *mwaak* there are seldom more than a hundred customers a day. To encourage sales, a small increase is given to persons buying more than the minimum quantity. In some cases, as for palm oil, the increase is one sixth of the quantity sold. The increase will be rather larger for members of one's family or for a neighbor than for a foreigner as it would also be in Western markets. But it will never be so big that the trader would lose on it. A last characteristic, which is common also to market places, is that there is much haggling; but one soon finds out that the basic commodities have common prices. A small case of cigarettes has a value of Fr. 5 in the stores. In the market there will be much haggling, but it will be sold at exactly the same price.

To show its special function as a food market, the different Tables describing the *mwaak* list the produce sold, and Table 27 gives the relative frequency of the goods sold. It will be seen that there is a definite preference for food which is a relish or for snacks. Roasted groundnuts, sugar cane, etc., are snacks; bananas, palm oil are relishes. This is to be explained by the fact that nowadays most of the people grow their staple food themselves and that the function of *mwaak* as a provider of every type of food has been therefore narrowed.

CONCLUSION

Economic activity amongst the Kuba flourishes because there is relatively high production, a tradition of specialization and hard labor, and regional specialization. It is well developed in the first place because of the existence of an adequate political structure, which brought different cultures into contact, which guaranteed security for traders and which organized and controlled a market complex. Although it is not yet possible to say if it were relative abundance that gave rise to political structure or if it was the contrary, the historical facts known imply that probably political evolution preceded the flourishing economy, which would explain the vast differences between Kuba and Lele economy.

The marketing process itself is characterized by a conspicuous absence of any obstructive regulations. The currency used and the price systems resemble those in Western markets. The only transactions which radically differ from typical transactions in a modern market economy are those without payment, as in the case of the *ngady* marriage. But all in all one gains the impression that the market spheres of Kuba economy closely resemble our own.

There is, however, one important difference: the market occupies a relatively minor position in Kuba economy and certainly in Kuba culture. It is not the basis of social organization or of all production, as is the case in modern Western society. Relatively little subsistence goods or labor go into the market; should the market place cease to exist, Kuba culture would be greatly changed, but the basis of society and subsistence would not have been removed.

TABLE 20

Bushong Labor—Workhours of Fifteen People in a Compound—Nsheng Spring 1954

People	Number of Days	Work-hours	Average per Day	Hours Devoted to Producing for Market or Trade
Girl	10	77.35′	7.45′	42
Woman	11	92.55′	8.26′	21.55′
Woman	12	90.45′	7.33′	18.50′
Woman with two babies	12	71.45′	5.59′	29.55′
Girl	10	82.30′	8.19′	21.05′
Woman (all)	13	92.50′	7.08′	47.
Tailor	8	46.40′	5.40′	31.50′
Woman	8	57.30′	7.11′	28.45′
Woman	14	116.20′	8.18′	20.25′
Young girl	13	94.30′	7.16′	16.20′
Woman	7	63.50′	9.07′	10.20′
Woman	15	127.	8.28′	34.05′
Old man	13	86.40′	6.40′	64.25′
Woodcarver	11	90.25′	8.13′	84.20′
Chief of the compound (smith)	11	80.30′	7.19′	36.10′
15 persons	168	1.271.45′	7.34′	507.25′

$\dfrac{507}{1271}$ = slightly less than $1/_3$ of total work hours.

Observations (1) The average time of observation was about ten hours/day. Three quarters of this time was given to work. (2) Not included as work: social gatherings, care for children, meals, washing, dressing, etc. (3) All labor was not observable. It was difficult at times to know what happened inside the houses, e.g. during a rain. The results are therefore minimum results. (4) Three more men were not included in the sample as they were traveling for most of the days. (5) Included as labor for trade: manufacture of cloth, *mabiim* and the sale of products in the market. (6) The hours of production for trade are also a minimum. But attention is drawn to the fact that the study was done in the capital where the marketing possibilities are higher than elsewhere.

TABLE 21

Inventory of Houses

A. *An Ordinary Home*
1. Mortar for spices
2. Hearth
3. Small oil container (here gourd)
4. Stones for the hearth
5. Granary on loft
6. Winnowing basket
7. Firewood
8. Gourd containers for corn
9. Charcoal
10. Oil lamp in wood
11. Oil container in wood
12. Bench
13. Big groundnut container in basketry
14. Bag for clothing
15. Another container for oil in wood
16. Torches of raffia thread
17. 18. Different parts of a loom
19. A gourd with flour (maize)
20. A gourd with water
21. Pot for dough
22. Pot for relish
23. Pot for meat or fish
24. Bed and matcovering
25. Bag for *mapel*
26. Bag for *velours du Kasai*
27. Basket type *Kweemy*
28. *Velours du Kasai*
29. Wooden box
30. Bicycle
31. Gun
32. Pot for enema
33. Toaster (potsherd)
34. Ladle
35. Bedcurtains
36. Door (Venitian)
37. Wooden box
38. Basket for work in the fields *nkaangl*
39. Rags for cleaning
40. Leaves for covering the pot with dough
41. Broom for outside
42. Broom for inside
43. Tobacco pipe in bamboo
44. Sieve
45. Pestle for spices
46. Awl
47. Straw cloths
48. Groundnuts
49. Maize

50. Knife *(machete)*
51. Knife *ikul* for parade
52. Lemons
53. To the cleaner
54. Ropes in raffia
55. Big mat *ikaangl*
56. Fresh manioc
57. Granary for maize
58. Gourd with palm wine
59. Main house
60. Kitchen

B. *The House of Cikl, an Important Dignitary*
1. Door in wood
2. Granary on loft
3. Bench
4. Pot with dough
5. Pot for relish
6. Pot for meat or fish
7. Hearth
8. Charcoal
9. Firewood
10. Fresh and dried manioc
11. Dried maize
12. Parrot's feather (badge of his rank)
13. Hat
14. Four hatpins
15. Bracelets for arms and legs with pearls
16. Hat of office *lapuum*
17. Belt in leopardskin
18. Iron staff of office
19. Special basket of office
20. Iron parrot's feather holder
21. Decorated hat
22. Seat of office
23. Two big mats
24. *Mapel* for festivities
25. Bag for women's garments
26. Bag for women's garments
27. Kerosene lamp
28. Knife *ikul* for parade
29. Pipe in wood
30. Charms for the spirit of Mikomiycol
31. Bed with ornamented mat
32. Tobacco
33. Gourd for water
34. Gourd for palm wine
35. Bows for wearing as badge of office

Inventory of Houses (continued)

36. Five *mapel* with different decorations
37. Trough for pounding vegetables
38. Hoes
39. *Machetes*
40. Oil container in wood
41. Mortar for oil
42. Stones for the hearth
43. Ladle
44. Oil container in wood
45. Oil container for oil lamp in wood
46. Plate for dough
47. Plate for meat and fish
48. Spices
49. Ordinary *mapel*
50. Raw cloth
51. Prepared cloths
52. Tipoye (litter)
53. Ornaments for belt
54. Goats skin
55. Torchs of raffia threads
56. Torchs of raffia threads in white black and yellow colors
57. Broom for outside
58. Broom for inside
59. Large belt in barkcloth
60. Equipment for enema
61. Adze of office
62. Large mat type *ishyaash*
63. Feathers of bird *moot ambyeenc (booboo)* (badges of office)
64. Feathers of bird *nkidy* (badges of office)
65. Special hat of office *(ngyeengdy)*
66. Pot for ablutions
67. Toaster (pottery sherd)
68. Special hat with *nyeny* feathers (badge of office)
69. Different charms
70. Fly-whisk of office
71. *Mabiim*
72. Special *mabiim* for funerals
73. Cowries
74. Ax
75. Pot for enema
76. Goats skin used as a seat in certain councils
77. House
78. Kitchen

TABLE 22

Regional Specialization and Trade

Tribe A. Regional Specialization	Products Local	Export	Import
Bushong	Maize, manioc, beans, groundnuts, palm trees, iron	All kinds of carvings, masks, belts, hats, embroidered cloth, *mabiim*, razors, knives *ikul, mapel* women's dresses	Pottery, salt, camwood (Sankuru), cloth (raw), meat, fish, ivory, cowries, copper, slaves
Shoowa	Manioc, fishing, products of the forest, palm trees	Meat, fish, skins, ivory, embroidered cloth, pottery, camwood (Sankuru), camwood (Ding)	Salt, Bushong products, iron, cowries, copper, slaves
Kel	Manioc, fishing, beans, groundnuts, palm trees	Fish	As Shoowa. In addition: dugouts, drums, Ding cloth, Lele cloth, camwood (Ding).

Regional Specialization and Trade (continued)

Tribe A. Regional Specialization	Products Local	Export	Import
Bulaang	Manioc, palm trees	Mats, raw cloth, meat	As Shoowa In addition: pottery, ivory, Bushong products
Pyaang	Iron, manioc	Knives *ikul*, swords *iloon*, mats, meat, raw cloth, salt	Camwood (Sankuru), cowries, copper, slaves, ivory
Kete and Coofa	Millet, manioc, some iron, salt from marshes	As Pyaang but more salt and less iron	As Pyaang
Ngyeen	Manioc, palm trees, wood for carving, in one region iron	Raw cloth, special mats, *ikul* knives	Bushong products, cowries, copper
Ngongo and river dwellers of the Sankuru	Fishing, products of the forest, clay, palm trees, wood for carving	Pottery, camwood (Sankuru), fish, meat, ivory, skins, raw cloth	Slaves, ivory, as Shoowa, without Bushong products
Cwa	Products of the forest. Wood for carving	Ivory, meat, skins, mats	As Ngongo

Origin B. External Trade	Export	Import	Origin
		Colobusskins	Songye
East	Ivory	Slaves	Lulua
South, South-East	Camwood (Sankuru)	Cowries	Loanda
	Fish	Salt	Katanga
	Meat	Copper	Katanga
	Mats	Pottery	Lulua, Pende
	Finished cloth	Amulets, charms	Lulua
West	Copper	Special cloth	Ding, Lele
	Bushong products	Special camwood	Ding
		Dugouts	Ding
		Drums	Lele
		Pottery	Pende
		Carvings	Pende, Lele
North	Cowries	Ivory	Ndengese
	Bushong products	Camwood (Sankuru)	Songo Meno
	Copper	Special pottery	Ndengese
		Iron spearheads	Nkucu, Ndengese

Observations (1) Export, import means exported from the Kuba area, imported from elsewhere in the Kuba area. (2) Cultural differences affect trade by affecting demand through different preference scales. Interesting too is the fact that the Bushong import much raw material and sell finished products.

TABLE 23

Products and Prices on the Market Mwaak

Product	Unit	Price per Unit
A. August 1954		
Oil	Small milk can	Fr. 0.5
Imported salt	Handful	Fr. 0.5
Local salt	Parcel	Fr. 1
Groundnuts roasted	Handful	Fr. 0.5
Idem not roasted	Handful	Fr. 0.5
Manioc	Three small roots or two big ones	Fr. 1
Maize	Five ears	Fr. 1
Beans	Handful	Fr. 0.5
Voandzeia roasted	Handful	Fr. 0.5
Idem not roasted	Handful	Fr. 0.5
Spices	Five big fruits or handful of small ones	
Banana bread	One loaf	Fr. 0.5
Manioc bread	One loaf	Fr. 0.5
Bananas	Two big ones or three small ones	Fr. 0.5
Plantains	One big fruit	Fr. 1.50
	One small fruit	Fr. 1
Calabashes	Each	from Fr. 0.5 to Fr. 7 according to size and shape
Pineapple	Each	from Fr. 0.5 to Fr. 5 according to size
Pounded pineapple	One slice	Fr. 0.5
Eggplant	Seven to nine big ones	Fr. 1
	Ten to eleven small ones	Fr. 0.5
Manioc leaves	Bunch	Fr. 0.5
Leaves of beans	Bunch	Fr. 0.5
Mushrooms	Handful	Fr. 0.5–1
Roasted groundnuts	Ball the size of a mandarine	Fr. 0.5
Sweat potatoes roasted or not	One big and one small or three small ones	Fr. 0.5
Sugar cane	One stick	Fr. 0.5–2 according to size
Mabol (fruit)	Two pieces	Fr. 0.5
Yams	One big and one small root	Fr. 0.5
Cake (*mukat*)	Two pieces	Fr. 0.5
Cake *(Mukall)*	Each	Fr. 5
Cut manioc	Five small parcels or one big parcel	Fr. 5
Cut yams	One parcel	Fr. 0.5
White ants	Handful	Fr. 1
Black ants	Milk can	Fr. 1
Palm wine	Glass	Fr. 1

Products and Prices on the Market Mwaak *(continued)*

Product	Unit	Price per Unit
A. August 1954		
Eggs	Each	Fr. 1
Raffia cloth (softened)	Standard size	Fr. 16
Raffia cloth (raw)	Standard size	Fr. 15
Ladles	Each	Fr. 4–5
Mushrooms *(boo)*	Bunch	Fr. 1
Prawns *(mingosh)*	Handful	Fr. 5 *mabiim* or Fr. 5 according to freshness
Caterpillars fresh or dried:		
Mishiing, minaang, ket, mabolbol, mipakl	Ten pieces / Ten pieces	Fr. 1 / Fr. 1
Mangwoonc	Twenty pieces	Fr. 1
Myaaloom	Ten pieces	Fr. 1 if soft
Misheky, mingol	Forty pieces	Fr. 1 if big
	15–20 pieces	Fr. 1 if very big
Moot ambul	7 pieces	Fr. 1
Mamongy	3 pieces	Fr. 1
Mipyepyem	20–25 pieces	Fr. 1
Other *(mimamaan, misheky) Kwookwook, mikokody, mimbembengy, kalaal, Mikuung)*	Handful	Fr. 1
Cooking pot	Each	Fr. 5–25 according to size
Broom for inside	Each	Fr. 1
Tobacco	Parcel	Fr. 1
	Handful	Fr. 0.5
Cockroach	Ten pieces	Fr. 1
Chicken	One	Fr. 30–60 according to size and sex
B. June 1956		
Palm wine	Glass	Fr. 1
	Calabash	Fr. 5
	Jar	Fr. 60
Oil	Small milk can	Fr. 1
Ananas	Slice	Fr. 5
Sugar cane	Stick	Fr. 0.5–1.5 according to size
Rice	Cup	Fr. 2.5
Cake	Piece	Fr. 1
Small fish, *shyengy*	Piece	Fr. 5
Elephant meat	Balls	Fr. 10
Oil	Cooking pot	Fr. 15 + one *mabiim*
Chicken	One	Fr. 40–60 according to size and sex
Raffia cloth (raw)	Four lengths	Fr. 48

(2) One dollar is equivalent to Fr. 50.

Products and Prices on the Market MWAAK *(continued)*

Product	Unit	Price per Unit
A. AUGUST 1954		
Mapel cloth	Eight lengths	Fr. 800 (1)
Sleeping mat	A piece	Fr. 10
Awl	A piece	Fr. 5
Cooking pot	A piece	Fr. 15

TABLE 24

Production and Value of Smithing

Product	Price	Days Required for Fabrication	Approximate Price/Day
Needles:			
Ndwoong dish	Fr. 1	Part of a day	–
Ndwoong ndyeeng	Fr. 2	Part of a day	–
Ndwoong laket	Fr. 5	Part of a day	–
Ndwoong imbaang	Fr. 100	Five days	Fr. 20
Ndwoong maloom	Fr. 100	Five days	Fr. 20
Ndwoong ishal	Fr. 30	?	?
Ndwoong ikwa miking	Fr. 50	Five days	Fr. 10
Ndwoong shakeep	Fr. 100	Five days	Fr. 20
Knifes for parade:			
Ikul inkody	Fr. 100	Four days	Fr. 25
Ikul imbaang	Fr. 50	Five days	Fr. 10
Ikul ikal	Fr. 150	Four days	Fr. 37.5
Ikul isham	Fr. 20	One day	Fr. 20
Ikul ibwiin	?	One day	?
Razor blade	Fr. 5	Part of a day	–
Arrowhead	Fr. 10	Part of a day	–
Spearhead	Fr. 50	Three days	Fr. 17
Axes:			
Ikyeng imba	Fr. 50	One day	Fr. 50
Ikyeng ilyeem	Fr. 50	Two days	Fr. 25
Ngyeem	Fr. 60	One day	Fr. 60
Hoe	Fr. 25	One day	Fr. 25
Instrument for drawning wine *(pal)*	Fr. 40	One day	Fr. 40
Sword	Fr. 100	One day	Fr. 100
Knifes of office:			
Mbombaam	–	Two days	–
Ngopdy tepyen	Fr. 100	Three days	Fr. 33
Ngopdy bushong	Fr. 100	Three days	Fr. 33
Footrings	Fr. 300	Four days	Fr. 75
Adze	Fr. 20	One day	Fr. 20
Anvil	Fr. 3.000	–	–
Hammer	Fr. 800	One day	Fr. 800

(1) A normal *mapel* will have ten lengths or more when stitched and ready for wear.

Production and Value of Smithing (continued)

Product	Price	Days Required for Fabrication	Approximate Price/Day
Other goods:			
Ishal	Fr. 3.000	?	?
Nshoong	Fr. 10	Part of a day	–
Mbyesh	Fr. 5	Part of a day	–
Kosh	–	Part of a day	–
Itwok	–	Part of a day	–
Ngwoom mupok	–	Part of a day	–
Bells *(ngwoong)*	Fr. 100	One day	Fr. 100
Bell of office *(mwaangl)*	Fr. 100	Two days	Fr. 50
Double gong	–	Three days	–

TABLE 25

Sample of Dealings on the Market MWAAK

Date	Products	Number of Customers	Sold	Value of Stock	Stock Left
27.4.56	Manioc bread	3	Fr. 13	Fr. 50	–
3.5.56	Elephant meat	4	Fr. 110	–	–
18.5.56	Sugar cane	5	Fr. 8	Fr. 10	–
	Small fish	8	Fr. 130	Fr. 300	yes
	Fresh groundnuts	3	Fr. 5.5	Fr. 5	–
	Yams	3	Fr. 3	Fr. 6	–
	Imported salt	4	13 eggs (1)	–	–
	Beans	3	Fr. 10	Fr. 20	–
	Leaves of beans	3	Fr. 9.5	Fr. 10	–
	Wine per glass	4	Fr. 22	–	–
23.5.56	Eggplant	6	Fr. 21	–	no
	Manioc leaves	11	Fr. 38	–	no
	Leaves of beans	5	Fr. 17	Fr. 14	no
	Small fish	4	Fr. 55	Fr. 600	yes
	Palm oil	10	Fr. 47	–	–
	Manioc	6	Fr. 24	–	–
25.5.56	Ananas	4	Fr. 20	–	–
	Bananas	2	Fr. 10	–	–
	Bananas	4	Fr. 15	Fr. 13	–
	Maize	3	Fr. 8	–	–
	Manioc bread	1	Fr. 5	–	yes
	Sugar cane	4	Fr. 5	–	–
1.6.56	Rice	2	Fr. 7	Fr. 30	yes
	Yams	5	Fr. 6.50	Fr. 7.50	–
	Manioc leaves	7	Fr. 19	Fr. 19	–
	Leaves of beans	6	Fr. 16	Fr. 20	yes
5.6.56	Beans	8	Fr. 14	Fr. 14	–
	White ants	9	Fr. 27	Fr. 20	–

(1) Direct barter of salt for eggs. (2) Last column – : unknown, yes: stock left, no: no stock left.

TABLE 26

Frequency of Products Sold on MWAAK

Products	Times Sold	Prices per Unit
Roasted groundnuts	85	Fr. 0.5
Bananas	48	Fr. 0.5–1.5
Sugar cane	44	Fr. 0.5–2
Palm oil	33	Fr. 1
Gourds	25	Fr. 0.5–7
Manioc and banana bread	21	Fr. 0.5
Caterpillars *(misheky)*	20	Fr. 1
Manioc	19	Fr. 0.5–1
Manioc leaves	16	Fr. 0.5
Dried groundnuts	16	Fr. 0.5
Imported salt	16	Fr. 0.5
Beans	14	Fr. 0.5
Leaves of beans	12	Fr. 0.5
Tobacco	10	Fr. 0.5–1
Ananas	9	Fr. 0.5–5
Eggplants	8	Fr. 0.5–1
Yams	7	Fr. 0.5
Voandzeia	3	Fr. 0.5
Mbok (fish)	3	?
Local salt	2	Fr. 1
Caterpillars *(mimbembengy)*	2	Fr. 0.5
Spices	2	Fr. 0.5
Prawns	2	Fr. 5–5 + one *mabiim*
Palm wine	1	Fr. 1
Caterpillars *(mamony)*	1	Fr. 0.5
Mushrooms	1	Fr. 1

Observation: The quantity sold each time is not known.

TABLE 27

Value of Goods Offered for Sale on the Market MWAAK

Date	Number of Articles	Value
27.4.56	39	Fr. 221 incomplete
4.5.56	45	–
11.5.56	22	–
18.5.56	22	Fr. 847.5
23.5.56	28	Fr. 932
25.5.56	15	Fr. 630.5
1.6.56	22	Fr. 1.919.5
6.6.56	20	Fr. 516
8.6.56	13	Fr. 928
13.6.56	18	Fr. 553.5

Observations: The listing of articles and the value of the stocks was intended to be complete, but in fact some articles escaped notice or were noted without the value of the stock. The total values expressed here are therefore less than the real total value of what was offered on the market. They probably represent about $3/4$ of this real total value. To understand the figures it must be remembered that the market is visited daily by a hundred customers.

CHAPTER 8

Lele Economy Compared with the Bushong

A STUDY OF ECONOMIC BACKWARDNESS

BY MARY DOUGLAS

The Lele[1] and the Bushong[2] are separated only by the Kasai River. The two tribes recognize a common origin, their houses, clothes and crafts are similar in style, their languages are closely related.[3] Yet the Lele are poor, while the Bushong are rich. The Lele produce only for subsistence, sharing their goods, or distributing them among themselves as gifts and fees. The Bushong have long been used to producing for exchange, and their native economy was noted for its use of money and its specialists and markets. Everything that the Lele have or can do, the Bushong have more and can do better. They produce more, live better, and populate their region more densely.

The first question is whether there are significant differences in the physical environment of the two peoples. Both live in the lat. 5 Degrees, in the area of forest park merging into savannah, which borders the south of the Congo rain forest. They both have a heavy annual rainfall of 1400 to 1600 mm. (40 to 60 inches) per annum. The mean annual temperature is about 78°F. (25°C.). As we should expect from their proximity, the climatic conditions are much the same for both tribes.

Nonetheless, a curious discrepancy appears in their respective assessments of their climate. The Bushong, like the local Europeans, welcome the dry season of mid-May to mid-August as a cold season, whereas the Lele regard it as dangerously hot. The Bushong in the

(1) The Lele are a tribe, inhabiting the west border of the Bakuba Empire. They are divided into three chiefdoms, of which only the most westerly has been studied. The Chief of the eastern Lele, at Perominenge, apes Kuba fashions in his little capital; the men wear basketry hats held on with metal pins, the chief has some of the dress and paraphernalia of the Nyimi. How much deeper this resemblance goes, it is impossible to say, since conditions at the time of field work were not favorable for study of this chiefdom. Everything that is said here concerning the Lele refers to the western Lele, whose chief, when visits were made in 1949–50 and 1953, was Norbert Pero Mihondo. The field work was carried out under the generous auspices of the International African Institute, and of the *Institut de Recherche Scientifique en Afrique Centrale.*

(2) The Bushong are the ruling tribe of the Kuba Kindom. They were studied in 1953–56 by Dr. Vansina, to whom I am deeply indebted for his collaboration and for supplying unpublished information for this paper.

(3) According to the Lexico-statistical survey conducted by Dr. Vansina, there is an 80 per cent similarity between the two languages.

north tend to have a dry season ten days shorter (Bultot 1954) than most of the Lele, (see figure 7), and the Lele soils retain less moisture, and the vegetation is thinner, so that the impression of drought is more severe, but otherwise there seems no objectively measurable difference in the climate to account for their attitudes.

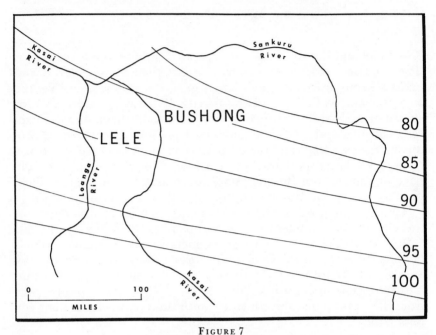

FIGURE 7
Average Length of Dry Season Expressed in Days
(From: F. Buitot - "Saisons et Périodes Sèches et Pluvieuses
au Congo Belge." Bruxelles, 1954)

There are certainly important differences in the soil, drainage and vegetation. The Lele are distinctly less fortunate. Their soils belong to the most easterly extension of the Kwango plateau system, and to some extent share in the sterility characteristic of that region. On that plateau, the soils are too poor to support anything but a steppe-like vegetation in spite of the ample rainfall. The soils consist of sands, poor in assimilable minerals of any kind, lacking altogether in ferro-magnates or heavy minerals, and so permeable that they are incapable of benefiting from the heavy rainfall[4] (see figure 8). On the Bushong side of the Kasai River the soil is altogether richer, and mineral deposits, particularly of iron ore, occur. Whereas Lele country is

(4) We are very grateful to M. L. Cahen, Director of the *Musée du Congo Belge,* Tervuren, for guidance on the physical environment of the two tribes.

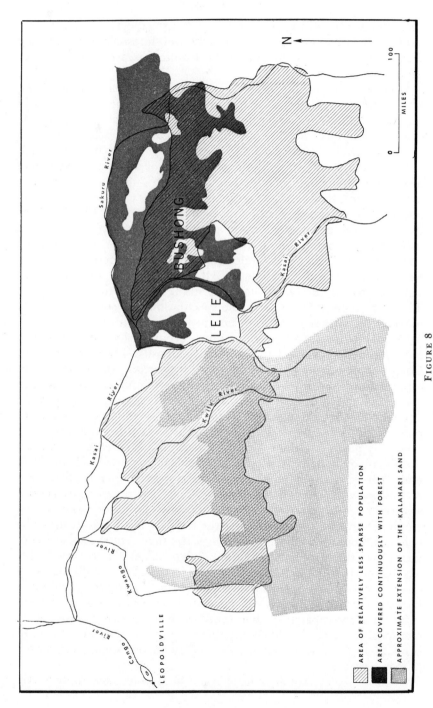

FIGURE 8

(From: N. Nicolai & J. Jacques – "La transformation du paysage Congolais par Chemin de Fer" 1954 p. 112)
Population Density and Forest Cover (Lele and Bushong)

AREA OF RELATIVELY LESS SPARSE POPULATION

AREA COVERED CONTINUOUSLY WITH FOREST

APPROXIMATE EXTENSION OF THE KALAHARI SAND

characterized by rolling grasslands with forest galleries along the river banks, Bushong country is relatively well-forested, although the sketch map tends to exaggerate the forested area on their side of the Kasai.

With such important differences in their basic natural resources, we are not surprised that Lele country is poorer and more sparsely populated. But how much poverty and how low a density can be attributed to the environmental factor? Can we leave the matter here?

There is no certain method of estimating the extent to which environment itself limits the development of an area. The Pende of Gungu, immediate neighbors of the Lele, inhabit an area even poorer in soils than the Lele area, and as poor as those worked by the notoriously wretched Suku of Kahemba and Feshi. The Lele are poor, but the Suku are known as a miserable, dispirited people, incapable of exploiting to the full such resources as their poor environment offers. The Pende are famous as energetic cultivators, well-nourished and industrious. All three peoples grow different staple crops; the Pende, millet; the Suku, manioc; the Lele, maize. There is obviously no end to the speculation one could indulge as to what the potentialities of the environment might be.

Congo geographers have been much occupied by the question of the relation between soil and population density. The whole Belgian Congo is an area of very low density. Fifty per cent of its surface has a population of less than 2.4 to the square kilometer (roughly 6 to square mile) (Gourou 1955 : 4). It is generally agreed (Gourou 1955 cites Cohen; Nicolai 1952 : 247) that there is a rough correlation of poor sandy soils with low densities, insofar as the small stretch of relatively more populous country occurs in a favored gap between the Kwango "kalahari" plateau and sands to the north. However, it is also agreed that soil poverty in itself is not an adequate explanation of the pockets of extra low density which occur, especially on the second and fifth parallels of South latitude. Professor Gourou says emphatically and repeatedly that the sterility of the soils cannot be held to account for all the densities of less than 2 to the square kilo-meter (5 to the square mile) in the Belgian Congo (Gourou 1955 : 52, 57, 109; Nicolai 1952). In Northern Rhodesia we have an illuminating case. The Ndembu live at an average density of 6 to the square mile, in many areas at a density of only 3, but according to a careful cal-culation of the capacity of their land, worked according to their own methods, the area should be capable of supporting a population of from 17 to 38 to the square mile, (6.8 to 15 per square kilometer) (Turner 1957).

In short, we cannot assume, as some have done, that there is any universal tendency to maximize food production (Harris 1959), or that the food resources of a region are the only factor limiting its population.

For the Lele and the Bushong the relative densities are as follows. The territory of Mweka, where the Bushong live, has an average density of 4–5 to the square kilometer (11 to the square mile). The BCK railway running through the area has attracted an immigrant population of Luba. If we abstract the railway zone from our figures, we find that the Bushong proper live at a density of (Gourou 1955 : 109) only 3 or 4 to the square kilometer, (7–10 to the square mile). The Lele[5] inhabit Basongo territory, where the average density is from 2 to 4 to the square kilometer (5–7 to the square mile), but since the Lele account for only half the population (among recent immigrants of foreign tribesmen to work in the Brabanta oil concession, refinery and port, and among Cokwe hunters), we can suppose that until recently Lele themselves used to live at a mere 1.7 to the square kilometer (4 to the square mile).

When the geographers agree that poverty of soil is not a sufficient explanation for the degree of poverty prevailing in similar areas, we are justified in looking for a sociological explanation to supplement the effect of environmental factors. For one thing, it is obvious that the demographic factor works two ways. Low density is partly the result of inferior technology, applied to inferior resources, but it may also inhibit development by hampering enterprises which need large-scale collaboration.

If we now consider technology, we find many suggestive differences. In certain processes marked superiority would be likely to increase output. Others are proof of a higher standard of living. Surveying these, we find that in hunting, fishing and housebuilding, the Bushong worker uses more specialized materials and equipment than the Lele, and in cultivation he spends more energy and time.

Take hunting first, since the Lele are passionately interested in it and pride themselves on their skill (Douglas 1954). In the eyes of their neighbors, it seems that they are notorious as inefficient hunters, particularly because they do not use nets, and only rarely make pit traps.

Hunting is the only occupation in which large numbers of Lele men regularly combine. They reckon that fifteen to twenty men and

(5) According to P. Gourou, 1951, the average density of the population of all tribes for the Basongo-Port Francqui region, in which the Lele now account for only half, is 3 to 4 to the square kilometer. This agrees with calculations based on the total number of Lele in that area, about 26,000, and the extent of their territory, about 63 by 110 miles, which give a Lele density of roughly 4 to the square mile, or 1.7 to the sq. km.

ten dogs are necessary for a good hunt. Using nets, the Bushong need a team of only ten men, and can hope to do well with five. In short, the Bushong hunter uses better capital equipment, and his hours of hunting are more productive.

Why should the Lele not have nets? The materials are present in the forest on both sides of the river, and the Lele know what nets are. Making a net is presumably a long task. In view of the local deforestation and the resulting paucity of game, it may be a case in which costly capital equipment is simply not worthwhile. Bushong nets are made by their women. Perhaps the rest of the answer lies in the different division of labor between men and women in each tribe, and the larger proportion of the total agricultural work which Lele leave to their women. Whatever the reason, we note that the absence of nets is consistent with a general Lele tendency not to invest time and labor in long-term equipment.

The same applies to pit-traps. Lele know how to make these, and frequently talk about them. The task requires a stay in the forest of several days and nights, or regular early dawn journeys and late returns. The traps are hard work to dig with only a blunt matchet for spade, and once set, they need to be watched. In practice few men ever trouble to make them. I suspect that the reason in this case is again that the amount of game caught by pit-traps tends to be disappointing in relation to the effort of making them, and that the Lele have felt discouraged when using a technique which is more productive in the thicker forests on the other side of the river.

Lest it be thought that the Lele neglect capital-intensive aids because hunting is a sport, a pleasure, and a religious activity, let me deny any parallel with English fox-hunting. The Lele would have applauded the French Brigadier of fiction who used his sabre to slay the fox. Their eager purchase of firearms whenever they can get the money and the license shows that their culture does not restrict them to inferior techniques when these do not require long-term collaboration and effort.

In fishing the Lele are also inferior. Their country is well watered by streams and rivers, and bounded on two sides by the great Kasai, and on the west by the swift-flowing Loange. Along the banks of the Kasai are fishing villages, whose men dot the river with elaborate traps and fishing platforms. These fishermen are mostly Dinga, or Bushong, and not often Lele. In one northern village, near the Kasai, Lele women used to go every two days to the nearest Dinga village where, lacking claims of kinship, they obtained fish by bartering manioc. Compared with the Bushong the Lele as a whole are not good at fishing, nor at canoe making. There is no need to describe in detail the diversity and elaborate character of Bushong fishing equipment, but it is worth noting that in some types of fishing, using several canoes trailing nets, the team may consist of twenty men or more. These skills may be a legacy from their distant past, since the Bushong claim to have entered their territory in canoes along the Kasai river, while the Lele claim to have travelled overland (Vansina 1956) and to have found the river banks already occupied by Dinga fishing villages.

If the Lele were originally landsmen, and the Bushong originally fishermen, this might account for more than the latter's present technical superiority in fishing. For primitive fisherman are necessarily more heavily equipped than are primitive hunters and cultivators. The need for fishing tackle, nets, lines, hooks, traps, curing platforms, and for watercraft as well as for weirs and dams makes quite a different balance in the allocation of time between consumer's and producers' goods. If they started in this area with the typical balance of a fishing economy, this may have meant an initial advantage for the Bushong in the form of a habit of working for postponed consumption.

Be that as it may, Lele mostly leave fishing to their women. Their simple method is to block a slow-moving stream, so as to turn the nearest valley into a marsh. In this they make mud banks and ponds, where they set traps for fish scarcely bigger than minnows. A morning's work draining out such a pond and catching the fish floundering in the mud yields a bare pint or so of fish. In the dry season they make a two-day expedition to the Lumbundji, where they spread a saponaceous vegetable poison over the low waters, and pull out the suffocated fish by hand, or in baskets.

As to housing, Lele and Bushong huts look much alike. They are low rectangular huts, roofed with palm thatch. The walls are covered with rows of split bamboos or palm ribs, lashed onto layers of palm-leaf, on a frame of strong saplings. Deceptive in appearance, Lele huts when new look much sturdier than those of the Bushong, but in practice they last less well: the Lele hut is more roughly and quickly made. A well-built one will last about six years without repair, and, as they are capable of being renewed piecemeal, by the substitution of new walls or roof thatch, they are not replaced until the whole village is moved to a new site, and the owner decides that he has neglected his hut so long that it will not stand removal. A hut in good condition is transported to a new site, with from six to eight men carrying the roof, and four at a time carrying the walls.

Bushong huts are also transportable. They are made with slightly different materials. For the roof thatch, they use the leaves of the raffia palm, as do the Lele. For the walls, they use the reputedly more waterproof leaves of a dwarf palm growing in the marshes. Over this, instead of palm ribs split in half, they sew narrow strips of bamboo, where available. Lele consider bamboo to be a tougher wood than palm, but it is rare in their region. The narrow strips are held in place by stitching in pleasing geometric patterns (Nicolai & Jacques 1954 : 272ff). A rich Bushong man, who can command labor, can build a hut that will last much longer than the ordinary man's hut, up to fifteen years without major repairs. The palace of the Nyimi at Mushenge, which was still in good condition in 1956, had been originally built in 1920.

The Bushong use an ingenious technique of ventilation, a movable flap between the roof and the walls, which lets out smoke. It is impossible to say whether they do this because their building is too solid to let the smoke filter through the walls, or whether they are more fastidious and painstaking about their comfort than the Lele, whose huts do certainly retain some of the smoke of their fires.

Within the hut, the furnishings illustrate the difference in material wealth, for the Bushong have a much greater refinement of domestic goods. They sit on stools, lay their heads on carved neck rests (often necessary to accommodate an elaborate hair style). They eat from basketry plates, with iron or wooden spoons. They have a bigger range of specialized basketry or wooden containers for food, clothing, cosmetics. A man who has more than one hat needs a hat box and a place for his metal hat pins. Lele do not make fibre hats, and only a few men in a village may possess a skin hat. The beautiful Bushong caskets for cosmetics are prized objects in many European museums. When a Lele woman has prepared some cosmetic from camwood, she uses it at once, and there is rarely enough left over for it to be worth storing in a special container. Only a young mother who, being cared for by her own mother after her delivery, has nothing else to do but grind camwood for herself and the baby, stores the prepared ointment in a little hanging basket hooked into the wall, enough for a few days.

Dr. Vansina was impressed with the high protein content of the Bushong diet, with the large quantities of fish and meat they ate, and the variety in their food. The Lele give an impression of always being hungry, always dreaming of meat, often going to bed fasting because their stomach revolts at the idea of a vegetable supper. They talk a lot about hunger, and *ihiobe,* an untranslatable word for meat-lessness and fishlessness. The Bushong cultivate a wider range of crops and also grow citrus fruits, pineapples, pawpaws, mangoes, sugar cane and bananas, which are either rare or completely absent in the Lele economy.

In short, the Bushong seem to be better sheltered, better fed, better supplied with goods, and with containers for storing what they do not immediately need. This is what we mean by saying that the Bushong are richer than the Lele. As to village-crafts, such as carving and smithing, the best of the Lele products can compete in quality with Bushong manufacture, but they are much scarcer. The Lele are more used to eating and drinking out of folded green leaves than from the basket plates and carved beakers common among the Bushong. Their medical instruments, too, are simpler. If, instead of cutting down a gourd top, they carve a wooden enema funnel for a baby, they make it as fine and thin as they can, but do not adorn it with the elaborate pattern found on some Bushong examples.

Before considering agriculture, we should mention the method of storing grain, for this is a rough index of output. Both Lele and Bushong houses are built with an internal grain store, suspended from the roof or supported on posts over the hearth. Here grain and even fish and meat can be preserved from the ravages of damp and of insects by the smoke of the fire. Most Lele women have no other grain store. Bushong women find this too small and use external granaries, built like little huts, raised a few feet above ground. These granaries, of which there may be one or two in a Lele village, are particularly characteristic of the southern Bushong villages, while in the north the huts which are built in the fields for a man to sleep in during the period of heaviest agricultural work are used as temporary granaries. The Lele are not in the habit of sleeping in their fields, except to shoot wild pig while the grain is ripening. This may be another indication that they do less agricultural work than the Bushong.

When we examine the techniques of cultivation, we find many contrasts. The Bushong plant five crops in succession in a system of rotation that covers two years. They grow yams, sweet potatoes, manioc, beans, and gather two and sometimes three maize harvests a year. The Lele practice no rotation and reap only one annual maize harvest. If we examine the two agricultural cycles, we see that the Bushong work continuously all the year, and that the Lele have one burst of activity, lasting about six weeks, in the height of the dry season.

Here is the probable explanation of their dread of the dry season. There is, in fact, surprisingly little range in the average monthly temperatures through the year. For the coldest month, July, it is only 2°C. less than the hottest month, January (Vandenplas 1947 : 33–38). Nonetheless, the Europeans and the Bushong welcome the period from mid-May to mid-August as the "cold season", probably because they enjoy the cooler nights and the freedom from humidity. But the

Lele, enduring the sun beating on them from a cloudless sky while they are trying to do enough agricultural work for the whole year, suffer more from the dust and impurities in the atmosphere and from the greatly increased insolation. The relatively cooler nights may make them feel the day's heat even more intensely.

Apart from the differences in crops cultivated, we may note some differences in emphasis. Lele give hunting and weaving a high priority throughout the year, while the Bushong think of them as primarily dry-season activities. Traditionally, the Lele used to burn the grassland for big hunts (in which five or six villages combined for the day) at the end of the dry season, when the bulk of their agricultural work was done. If the first rains had already broken, so much the better for the prospects of the hunt, they said, as the animals would leave their forest watering places to eat the new shoots. As the end of the dry season is the time in which the firing could do the maximum damage to the vegetation, it has been forbidden by the administration, and if permission is given at all, the firing must be over by the beginning of July. The Bushong used to burn the grassland in mid-May or early June, at the beginning of the dry season, when the sap had not altogether died down in the grass.

The cycle of work described for the Lele is largely what the old men describe as their traditional practice. It was modified by the agricultural officers of the Belgian Congo. Lele are encouraged to sow maize twice, for harvesting in November, and in April. Manioc is now mainly grown in the grassland, instead of in the forest clearings. There are some changes in the plants cultivated. Voandzeia has been replaced by groundnuts, some hill rice is sown, and beans in some parts. These are largely treated as cash crops by the Lele, who sell them to the Europeans to earn money for tax. The other occupation which competes for their time is cutting oil-palm fruits to sell to the *Huileries du Congo Belge,* whose lorries collect weekly from the villages. Lele complain that they are now made to work harder than before, to clear more land, keep it hoed, grow more crops. They never complain that cutting oil-palm fruits interferes with their agricultural program, only that the total of extra work interferes with their hunting.

This is not the place for a detailed study of Bushong agriculture. It is enough to have shown that it is more energetically pursued and is more productive. One or two details of women's work are useful indications of a different attitude to time, work and food. Lele like to eat twice a day: in the morning at about 11 o'clock or midday, and in the evening. They complain that their wives are lazy, and only too often the morning meal consists of cold scraps from the previous night; they compare themselves unfavorably with Cokwe, who are reputed to have more industrious wives. In practice the Lele women seem to be very hard-working, but it is possible that the absence of labor-saving devices may make their timetable more arduous.

TABLE 28

Annual Cycle of Work

	Bushong		Lele
Dry Season			
Mid-May	Harvest beans, maize II, yams. Clear forest	Hunt, weave draw wine	Clear forest for maize
	Burn grassland for hunt		
June	Hunt, fish, weave, repair huts	,, ,,	
Mid-July to Aug. 15th	Burn forest clearings, gather bananas and pineapple. Plant hemp	,, ,,	Women fish in low waters
	Hunt, fish, plant sugar cane and bananas		Burn forest clearings
	Send tribute to capitalperiod of plenty		Sow maize
Wet Season			
Mid-August	Lift ground nuts	,, ,,	Fire grassland for hunting
Sept.	Sow ground nut. Sow Maize I	,, ,,	Sow voandzeia, plant manioc, bananas,
	Collect termites		
Oct.		,, ,,	peppers; sugar cane, pineapples
Nov.		,, ,,	(occasional) and raffia palms in
Mid-Dec.		,, ,,	forest clearings, with maize
Little Dry Season			
Mid-Dec.	Sow maize II; sow voandzeia	,, ,,	Green maize can be plucked
Jan.	Sow tobacco, sow maize II	,, ,,	Maize harvest
Wet Season			
Feb.	Lift ground nuts, sow beans, collect termites and grubs	,, ,,	Lift voandzeia
	Reap maize I (Main crop)		
March	Reap maize I. Sow tobacco, beans, yams, manioc	,, ,,	
April to Mid-May	Gather beans, sow voandzeia and tobacco	,, ,,	

For example, one of their daily chores is to fetch water from the stream. At the same time, they carry down a heavy pile of manioc roots to soak for a few days before carrying them back to the village.

Bushong women, on the other hand, are equipped with wooden troughs, filled with rain water from the roofs, so that they can soak their manioc in the village, without the labor of transporting it back and forth. Bushong women also cultivate mushrooms indoors for occasional relish, while Lele women rely on chance gathering.

Bushong women find time to do the famous raffia embroidery, perhaps because their menfolk help them more in the fields. Lele men admiring the Bushong *Velours,* were amazed to learn that women could ever be clever enough to use needle and thread, still less make this eleborate stitching. The Bushong culinary tradition is more varied than that of the Lele. This rough comparison suggests that Lele women are less skilled and industrious than Bushong women, but it is probable that a time-and-motion study of women's and men's work in the two economies would show that Lele men leave a relatively heavier burden of agricultural work to their women, for reasons which we shall show later.

Another difference between Bushong and Lele techniques is in the exploitation of palms for wine. Lele use only the raffia palm for wine. Their method of drawing it kills the tree; in the process of tapping, they cut out the whole of the crown of the palm just at the time of its first flowering. During the few years before the palm has matured to this point, they take the young yellow fronds for weaving, and after drawing the sap for wine, the stump is stripped and left to rot down. Lele have no use for a tree which has once been allowed to flower, except for fuel and building purposes. The life of a palm, used in this way, is rarely more than five years, although there seems to be some range in the different times at which individual palms mature.

The Bushong also use this method on raffia palms, but they have learnt to tap oil palms by making an incision at the base of the large inflorescene, a technique which does not kill the tree. Presumably this technique could be adapted to raffia palms, since the Yakö of Cross River, Nigeria use it (Forde 1937). But neither Lele nor Bushong attempt to preserve the raffia palm in this way, and Lele do not draw any wine from oil palms, althought these grow plentifully in the north of their territory. According to Lele traditions oil palms were very scarce in their country until relatively recently, and this may account for their not exploiting it for wine. But here again, consistently with other tendencies in their economy, their techniques are directed to short-term results, and do not fully use their resources.

To balance this picture of Lele inefficiency, we should mention the weaving of raffia, for here, at least, they are recognized as the better craftsmen. Their raffia cloth is of closer texture than Bushong cloth, because they use finer strands of raffia, produced by combing in three stages, whereas the Bushong only comb once. Incidentally, the fine Lele cloth is not suitable for velours embroidery.

Lele take pride in producing cloth of a regular and fine weave, and they refuse inferior cloth if it is proffered for payment. A length of woven raffia is their normal standard of value for counting debts and dues of all kinds. How little it has even now become a medium of exchange has been described elsewhere (Douglas 1958). Raffia cloth is not the medium of exchange for the Bushong, who freely used cowries, copper units, and beads before they adopted Congolese francs as an additional currency. Raffia cloth is the principal export for the Lele, whereby they obtain knives, arrowheads and camwood. This may explain why unadorned raffia cloth holds a more important place in the admittedly simpler economy of the Lele than its equivalent in the diversified economy of the Bushong.

If we ask now why one tribe is rich and the other poor, the review of technology would seem to suggest that the Lele are poorer not only because their soil is less fertile, but because they work less at the production of goods. They do not build up producer's capital, such as nets, canoes, traps and granaries. Nor do they work so long at cultivation, and their houses wear out quicker. Their reduced effort is itself partly a consequence of their poorer environment. It is probable that their soil could not be worked by the intensive methods of Bushong agriculture without starting a degenerative cycle. Hunting nets and pit-traps are less worthwhile in an area poor in forest and game. But certain other features of their economy cannot be fully explained as adaptations to the environment.

When Lele timetables of work are compared with those of the Bushong, we see no heavy schedules which suggest that there would be any shortage of labor. Yet, their economy is characterized paradoxically by an apparent shortage of hands, which confronts anyone who seeks collaborators. When a sick man wants to send a message, or needs help to clear his fields, or to repair his hut, or to draw palm wine for him, he will often be hard put to find anyone whose services he can command. *"Kwa itangu bo—No time,"* is a common reply to requests for help. His fields may lie uncleared, or his palm trees run to seed for lack of hands. This reflects the weakness of the authority structure in Lele society, and does not imply that every able-bodied man is fully employed from dawn to dusk.

Some anthropologists write as if the poorer the environment and the less efficient the techniques for exploiting it, the more the population is forced to work hard to maintain itself in existence; more productive techniques produce a surplus which enables a part of the population to be supported as a "leisure class."[6] It is not necessary to expose the fallacies of this approach, but it is worth pointing out that, poor as they are, the Lele are less fully employed than the Bushong. They do less work.

"Work," of course, is here used in a narrow sense, relevant to a comparison of material wealth. Warfare, raiding, ambushing, all planning of offensive and defensive actions, as also abductions, seductions, and reclaiming of women, making and rebutting of sorcery charges, negotiations for fines and compensations and for credit—all these absorbingly interesting and doubtless satisfying activities of Lele social life must, for this purpose of measuring comparative prosperity, be counted as alternatives to productive work. Whether we call them forms of preferred idleness, or leisure activities, or "non-productive work," no hidden judgment of value is implied. The distinction between productive work and other activities is merely used here as rough index of material output.

If we wish to understand why the Lele work less, we need to consider whether any social factors inhibit them from exploiting their resources to the utmost. We should be prepared to find in a backward economy (no less than in our own economy) instances of decisions influenced by short-term desires which, once taken, may block the realization of long-term interests.

First, we must assess in a very general way, the attitudes shown by the Lele towards the inconveniences and rewards of work.

For the Bushong, work is the means to wealth, and wealth the means to status. They strongly emphasize the value of individual effort and achievement, and they are also prepared to collaborate in numbers over a sustained period when this in necessary to raise output. Nothing in Lele culture corresponds to the Bushong striving for riches. The Bushong talk constantly and dream about wealth, while proverbs about it being the steppingstone to high status are often on their lips. Riches, prestige, and influence at court are explicitly associated together (Vansina 1954).

On the other hand, Lele behave as if they expect the most satisfying roles of middle and old age to fall into the individual's lap in the ripeness of time, only provided that he is a real man—that is, normally virile. He will eventually marry several wives, beget children, and so enter the Begetter's cult. His infant daughters will be asked in marriage by suitors bearing gifts and ready to work for him. Later, when his cult membership is bringing in a revenue of raffia

(6) For the most widely read statement of this view, see Herskovits 1952 (Part V, The Economic Surplus) and for a list of reputed subscribers to this view, see Harris 1959.

cloth from fees of new initiates, his newborn daughter's daughters can be promised in marriage to junior clansmen, who will strengthen his following in the village. His wives will look after him in his declining years. He will have stores of raffia cloths to lend or give, but he will possess this wealth because, in the natural course of events, he reached the proper status for his age. He would not be able to achieve this status through wealth.

The emphasis on seniority means that, among the Lele, work and competitiveness are not geared to their longings for prestige. Among the Bushong, largely through the mechanism of markets, through money, and through elective political office, the reverse is true. It also means that Lele society holds out its best rewards in middle life and after. Those who have reached this period of privilege have an interest in maintaining the *status quo*.

All over the world it is common for the privileged sections of a community to adopt protective policies, even against their own more long-term interests. We find traces of this attitude among old Lele men. They tend to speak and behave as if they held, collectively, a position to be defended against the encroachments of the young men. Examples of this attitude have been published elsewhere (Douglas 1959). Briefly, secrets of ritual and healing are jealously guarded, and even knowledge of the debts and marriage negotiations of their own clans are deliberately withheld from the young men, as a technique for retarding their adulthood. The old are realistic enough to know that they are dependent ultimately on the brawn and muscle of the young men, and this thought is regularly brought up in disputes, when they are pressing defense of their privileges too far: "What would happen to us, if we chased away the young men? Who would hunt with us, and carry home the game? Who would carry the European's luggage?" The young men play on this, and threaten to leave the village until eventually the dispute is settled. Although it does not directly affect the levels of production that we have been discussing, this atmosphere of jealousy between men's age-groups certainly inhibits collaboration and should probably not be underestimated in its long-term effects.

Lele also believe in restricting competition. At the beginning of the century, the Lele chief NgomaNvula tried to protect the native textile industry by threatening death for anyone who wore European cloth (Simpson 1911 : 310). If a Lele man is asked why women do not weave or sew, he instantly replies: "If a woman could sew her own clothes, she might refuse to cook for the men. What could we give them instead of clothes to keep them happy?" This gives a false picture of the male contribution to the domestic economy, but it is reminiscent of some modern arguments against "equal pay" for both sexes.

Within the local section of a clan, restrictions on entry into the the skilled professions are deliberately enforced. A young boy is not allowed to take up a craft practiced by a senior clansman, unless the latter agrees to retire. In the same clan, in the same village, two men rarely specialize in the same skill. If a man is a good drummer, or carver, or smith, and he sees an aptitude for the same craft in his son or nephew, he may teach the boy all he knows and work with him until he thinks the apprenticeship complete. Then, ceremonially, he hands over his own position, with his tools, and retires in favour of the younger man. This ideal is frequently practiced. The accompanying convention, that a boy must not compete with his elder kinsman, is also strong enough to stop many a would-be specialist from developing his skill. Lele openly prefer reduced output. Their specialist craftsmen are few and far between because they are expected to make matters unpleasant for rivals competing for their business. Consequently the Lele as a whole are poorer in metal or wooden objects for their own use, or for export.

Lastly, it seems that Lele old men have never been able to rely on their junior clansmen for regular assistance in the fields. As a junior work-mate, a son-in-law is more reliable than a fellow-clansman. This is so for reasons connected with the pattern of residence and the weak definition of authority within the clan (Douglas 1957). An unmarried youth has no granary of his own to fill. Work which he does to help his maternal uncles, father, or father's brothers, is counted in his favor, but he can easily use the claims of one to refuse those of another, and escape with a minimum of toil. Boys would be boys, until their middle thirties. They led the good life, of weaving, drinking, and following the manly sports of hunting and warfare, without continuous agricultural responsibilities.

The key institution in which the old men see their interests as divorced from those of the young men is polygyny. Under the old system, since the young girls were pre-empted by the older men, the age of marriage was early for girls (eleven or twelve), and late for men (in their thirties). It would be superfical to suppose that these arrangements were solely for the sexual gratification of the old men. One should see them as part of the whole economic system, and particularly as one of the parts which provide social security of the old.

The division of labor between the sexes leaves the very old men with little they can do. An old woman, by contrast, can earn her keep with many useful services. But old men use their rights over women to secure necessary services, both from women and from men.

Through polygyny, the principles of male dominance and of seniority are maintained to the end. To borrow an analogy from another sphere, we could almost say that the Lele have opted for an ambitious old-age pensions scheme at the price of their general standards of living. We shall see that the whole community pays for the security in old age which polygyny represents.

In the kingdom of ends peculiar to the Lele, various institutions seem to receive their justification because they are consistent with polygyny of the old men and delayed marriage of the young. The latter were reconciled to their bachelorhood, partly by the life of sport and ease, and partly by the institution of wife-sharing by age-sets. They were encouraged to turn their attention away from the young wives in their own villages by the related custom of abducting girls from rival villages (Douglas 1951). Intervillage feuding therefore appears to be an essential part of the total scheme, which furthermore commits the Lele to small-scale political life. The diversion of young men's energies to raiding and abducting from rival villages was a major cause of the low levels of production, for its effects were cumulative. The raiding gave rise to such insecurity that at some times half the able-bodied males were engaged in giving armed escort to the others. Men said that in the old days a man did not go to the forest to draw palm wine alone, but his age-mate escorted him and stood with his back to the tree, bowstring taut, watching for ambush.

Coming from Bushong country in 1907, Torday was amazed at the fortified condition of Lele villages:

"Here, too, we found enclosures, but instead of the leaf walls which are considered sufficient among the Bushongo, the separations were palisades formed by solid stakes driven into the ground. Such a wall surrounded the whole village, and the single entrance was so arranged that no more than one person was able to enter at one time." (Torday 1925 : 231)

Simpson also remarked that Lele men, asked to carry his baggage from their own village to the next, armed as if going into strange country. Such insecurity is obviously inimical to trade.

We have started with polygyny as the primary value to which other habits have been adjusted, because the Lele themselves talk as if all relations between men are defined by rights to women.

The point is the more effective since the Bushong are monogamous. We know well that polygyny elsewhere does not give rise to this particular accumulation of effects. Are there any features peculiar to Lele polygyny? One is the proportion of polygynous old men, indicated by the high rate of bachelorhood. Another is in the solutions they have adopted for the problems of late marriage. In some societies with extensive polygyny, the institutions which exist for the sexual satisfaction of the young men[7] are either wholly peaceful, or directed to warfare with other tribes and not to hostilities between villages. Thirdly, where the chain of command is more sharply defined (as in patrilineal systems, or in matrilineal societies in which offices are elective or carry recognizable political responsibilities, as among the Bushong), then polygyny of older men is less likely to be accompanied by attitudes of suspicion and hostility between men's age-groups.

Having started our analysis with polygyny and the high rate of bachelorhood, tracing the various interactions, we find the Lele economy constantly pegged down to the same level of production. Something like a negative feedback appears in the relations of old to young men: the more the old men reserve the girls for themselves, the more the young men are resentful and evasive; the more the young men are refractory, the more the old men insist on their prerogatives. They pick on the most unsatisfactory of the young men, refuse to allot him a wife, refuse him cult membership; the others note his punishment, and either come to heel or move off to another village. There cannot be an indefinite worsening in their relations because, inevitably, the old men die. Then the young men inherit their widows, and, now not so young, see themselves in sight of polygynous status, to be defended by solidarity of the old.

So we find the Lele, as a result of innumerable personal choices about matters of immediate concern, committed to all the insecurity of feuding villages, and to the frustrations of small-scale political life and ineffective economy.

If we prefer to start our analysis at the other end, not with polygyny but with scale of political organization, we come to the same results. For whatever reason, the Bushong developed a well organized political system (Vansina 1957), embracing 70,000 people. Authority is decentralized from the Nyimi, or paramount chief, to minor chiefs, and from these to canton heads, and from these to village heads. Judicial, legislative, and administrative powers are delegated down these channels, with decisions concerning war and peace held at the center by the Nyimi. Political office is elective or by appointment. Appropriate policing powers are attached to leaders at each point in the hierarchy. Leaders are checked by variously constituted councils, whom they must consult. The Nyimi maintains his own army to quell rebellions. Tribute of grain, salt, dried foods, and money is brought into the capitals, and redistributed to loyal subjects and officials. The chiefly courts provide well-rewarded markets for craftsmen's wares so that regional specialities are salable far from their sources. Even before the advent of Europeans there was a food-market at

(7) For example, Tiv "sister-marriage" of the "manyatta" of the Masai.

Musenge, the Nyimi's capital. No doubt the Kasai River, protecting them from the long arm of the Bushong Empire, is partly responsible for the Lele's never having been drawn, willy-nilly, into its orbit, and accepting its values.

The Lele village, which is their largest autonomous unit, is not so big as the smallest political unit in the Bushong system. (The Lele villages average a population of 190, and the Bushong villages 210.) True, there are Lele chiefs, who claim relationship with Bushong chiefs. Each village is, indeed, found within a chiefdom—that is, an area over which a member of the chiefly clan claims suzerainty. But in practice his rights are found to be ritual and social. Each village is completely independent. The chief has no judicial or military authority. He claims tribute, but here we have no busy palace scene in which tribute payers flock in and are lavishly fed by the special catering system which chiefly polygyny so often represents.

When a chief visited a village, he was given raffia cloths, as many as could be spared. Then the villagers asked what woman he would give them in return. He named one of his daughters, and they settled a day to fetch her. The girl became the communal wife of one of the age-sets, the whole village regarding itself as her legal husband and as son-in-law to the chief. Son-in-lawship expressed their relation to him until the day that he claimed the girl's first daughter in marriage. Then the relation became reversed, the chief being son-in-law to the village. The raffia gifts and women which went back and forth between the chief and village were not essentially different from those which linked independent villages to one another in peaceful exchange. None of this interfered with the autonomy of the village.

The simple factor of scale alone has various repercussions. There is no ladder of status up which a man may honorably climb to satisfy his competitive ambitions. There is no series of offices for which age and experience qualify a man, so that in his physical decline he can enjoy respect and influence and material rewards. The Bushong lay great emphasis on individual effort and achievement, but the Lele try to damp it down. They avoid overt roles of leadership and fear the jealousy which individual success arouses. Their truncated status system turns the Lele village in on itself, to brood on quarrels and sorcery accusations, or turns it, in hostility, against other villages, so promoting the general feeling of insecurity. The latter makes markets impossible, and renders pointless ambition to produce above home needs. The old, in such an economy, unable to save, or to acquire dignity in their declining years by occupying high political office, bolster their position by claiming the marriageable women, and building up a system of rewards reserved for those who begat in

wedlock. And so we are back again to polygyny and prolonged bachelorhood.

This picture has been partly based on deductions about what Lele
society must have been like twenty years before fieldwork was begun.
Before 1930 they could still resort to ordeals, enslave, raid and coun-
terraid, abduct women, and pursue blood-vengeance with barbed
arrows. They still needed to fortify their villages against attacks. By
1949 the scene had changed. The young men had broken out of their
restaining social environment—by becoming Christians. They enjoyed
protection, from mission and government, from reprisals by pagans.
They could marry young Christian girls who, similarly, were able to
escape their expected lot as junior wives of elderly polygynists. Raiding was ended, age-sets were nearly finished. Old men had less authority even than before. The young Christian tended to seek employment with Europeans to escape the reproaches and suspicions
which their abstention from pagan rituals engendered.[8]

It would be interesting to compare their performance as workers
in the new and freer context. One might expect that, away from the
influence of their old culture, Lele performance might equal or sur-
pass that of Bushong. Unfortunately the framework for such a comparison is lacking. Neither tribe has a high reputation for industry
with its respective employers, compared with immigrant Cokwe,
Luba and Pende workers. This may simply be because the best repu-
tations are earned by tribes which have longest been accustomed to
wage-labor.

One is tempted to predict that, in so far as it is due to social factors,
Lele are likely to change their name for idleness and lack of stamina
before long. In 1949-50 they were not forthcoming in numbers for
plantation labor or for cutting oil-palm nuts. By 1954, when a scatter-
ing of small shops through the territory had put trade goods within
their reach, they had become eager to earn money. The restrictive
influence of the old social system was already weaker.

We may now look again at the demographic factor, and distinguish
some effects on it of the economy and the political system. It is obvious that in different types of economy, the active male contribution
may have different time spans according to the nature of the work.
If there were a modern community whose bread-winners were international skating champions, footballers, or miners at the coal-face,
their period of active work would be briefer than in economies based
on less physically exacting tasks. A primitive economy is, by definition, one based on a rudimentary technology, and the more rudimentary, the more the work consists of purely individual physical

(8) This process has been described in Douglas 1959 b.

effort. Moreover, the simpler the economy, the smaller the scope for managerial roles and ancillary sedentary work. The result, then, is that the period of full, active contribution to the economy is shorter.[9]

If we compare Lele and Bushong economies on these lines, we see that the "age of retirement" is likely to be earlier for the Lele. The typical Bushong man is able, long after he has passed his physical prime, to make a useful contribution to production, either by using his experience to direct the collaboration of others or in various administrative roles which are important in maintaining the security and order necessary for prosperity. The Lele economy, on the other hand,

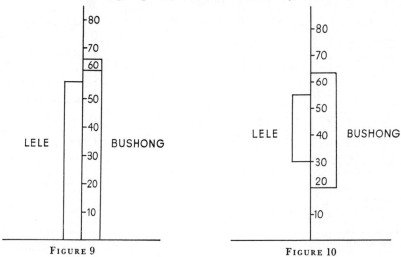

FIGURE 9
Age of Retirement from Work

FIGURE 10
*Period of Full Work, Showing Age of Entry
into Full Agricultural Responsibility*

with its emphasis on individual work, gives less weight to experience and finds less productive work for the older man to do. We can only guess at the differences, but it is worth presenting the idea visually, as in Figure 9.

Furthermore, at the other end of the life span, the same trend is increased because of the late entry into agricultural work of Lele men. The young Lele is not fully employed in agriculture until he is at least thirty and married, the Bushong man when he is twenty.

Figure 10 illustrates the idea that the active labor force in the Lele economy, as a proportion of the total population, is on both scores smaller than it is with the Bushong. The total output of the economy has to be shared among a larger population of dependants.

The comparison of the two economies has shown up something

(9) This approach was suggested by Linton 1940.

like the effects of "backwash" described by Professor Myrdal (1957). First we see that in the environment there are initial disadvantages which limit development. Secondly, we find that in the social organi-

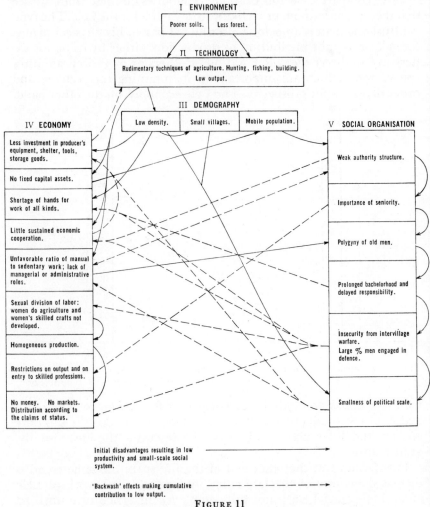

FIGURE 11
Lele Economy and Social Organization

zation itself there are further inhibiting effects which are cumulative, and which work one on another and back again on the economy, technology and population, to intensify the initial disadvantages. We have tried to present the interaction of these tendencies in a simplified form in Figure 11.

"Nothing succeeds like success." Somehow, sometime, the Bushong took decisions which produced a favorable turn in their fortunes and set off interactions which resulted in their political hegemony and their wealth. The Lele missed the benefits of this civilization because of their location on the other side of the Kasai River, their poorer soils, their history. The decisions they took amounted to an accommodation of their life to a lower political and economic level. Their technology was inferior, so their efforts were backed with less efficient equipment, and their economy was less productive. Their old social system barred many of the chances which might have favored economic growth.

Anthropologists sometimes tend to discuss the adoption or rejection of new techniques in terms of a cultural mystique, as if dealing with irreducible principles, of which no analysis is feasible.[10] The Lele may be taken as a case in point. Their preference for their own inferior techniques, in spite of awareness of better methods used across the river, depend on certain institutions, and these again on their history and environment. Through economic analysis we can break down the effect of choices, each made reasonably enough in its own restricted context. By following up the interactions of these choices, one upon another, we can see how the highly idiosyncratic mold of Lele culture is related to a certain low level of production.

(10) See Benedict (1956 : 187): "Among primitive peoples, this lack of interest in 'progress' has been proverbial ... Every primitive tribe has its own cultural arrangements which ensure its survival ... They may be culturally uninterested in labor-saving devices. Often the value they put on time is extremely low, and 'wisdom' is far more valued than efficiency. Our cultural system and theirs are oriented around different ideals."

THE WESTERN SUDAN

CHAPTER 9

Trade and Markets Among the Mossi People

BY ELLIOTT P. SKINNER

The Mossi represent the dominant population of the Voltaic Republic, numbering about 1,600,000 out of some 3,200,000 inhabitants. They represent the unique example of a group which has preserved its ethnic identity and political autonomy through all the vicissitudes of Sudanic history until it was conquered by the French in 1896. Tradition records that the people who became the Mossi left the Dagomba region in present-day Ghana during the eleventh century and moved into the bend of the Niger River, carving out three large kingdoms and smaller principalities in the process. At the head of these still extant kingdoms are rulers *(Moro Nabas)* who formerly held feudal-like control over the provinces, districts and villages which comprise their domains. The villages, with their patri-local, polygynous, extended family households, formed the basic Mossi settlement pattern. A complex hierarchical administrative apparatus carried the power of the Mossi rulers into the smallest villages, and funneled taxes and tribute back to them. This structure still exists, but of course it has been modified by the French.

The Mossi were and are still divided into stratified royal, noble and commoner patrilineages. Characteristic of this lineage system is a process by which royal sub-lineages descend serially until they merge with the mass of commoner lineages. Below the lineages there once were large non-Mossi groups of serfs and slaves, but these people have now been grouped into lineages and have become Mossicized.

The topography of Mossi country is typical of the Sudanic grasslands. It is an immense plain, some 1,500 feet above sea level and broken only by three low mountain ranges and numerous small hills. The annual total rainfall is between 30 and 40 inches, and falls almost entirely as heavy showers or thundershowers during the period from June to September. So narrow is the margin of rainfall for successful crop cultivation that any variation in the cycle results in low crop yields and a difficult "hungry period" the following year before the new crops are harvested. The Mossi do not practice irrigation, and would have trouble doing so because the three Volta Rivers which drain their territory serve as drainage chiefly during the rainy season. Only the Black Volta has water all year round; the

Red and White Voltas are merely a series of small stagnant pools during the dry season. In some low-lying areas around the main water courses, trapped water provides the moisture for dank riverine vegetation.

The soils of Mossi country are mainly ferruginous with red argils and pure silicates of aluminum predominating in the northern region. The soils in the south are thin, sandy, and formed from the decomposition of crystalline rocks and sandstones. During the dry season the Mossi landscape appears too sterile to produce plant life, but with the first drops of rain the entire country soon becomes covered with the grasses and shrubs which are characteristic of this Sudanese region. The uncultivated but valuable trees of this area include the Baobab *(Adansonia digitata)*, the locust bean *(Parkia biglobosa)*, the shea-butter *(Butyrospermum parkii)*, the tamarind *(Tamarindus indica)* and the kapok *(Bombax costatum)*. The plants which the Mossi cultivate include varieties of cereals, roots and legumes. Sorghums *(Sorghum vulgare)* and millets *(Pennisetum typhoides)* are their staples, with maize *(Zea mays)* filling the role of a secondary but rather useful crop because its growing cycle is shorter than that of other important crops and it breaks the "hungry period." Maize would be a more important crop to the Mossi if it could grow on soil less fertile than what is normally available around the Mossi compound—the area where it brings the greatest yield. Peanuts, onions, rice, beans, okra, peas and sweet potatoes are other food crops. Tobacco is grown for local consumption, but the crops which have the greatest export value are cotton and indigo, used for making cloth and dyeing it.

The wild fauna of the country does not provide a major part of the food needs of the Mossi people. The several species of deer and antelope, monkeys, rabbits and wild pig are hunted and used for food. But the elephants and lions which are also found in the country are sources of great distress to the people because the former decimate the growing crops and the latter attack and kill the grazing animals.

The Mossi rear two main types of cattle: a zebu-like one in the northern regions and a small dwarf variety in the south. These animals are kept primarily for their milk and for export, and are seldom killed for meat until they are very old. The animals which provide the Mossi with meat are goats, sheep, chickens and guinea fowls. Pig-raising is not widespread and seems to be declining in importance with the increasing observance of Islamic food taboos, even among people who are still pagan. Fish forms only a minor part of the Mossi diet and is obtained mainly from traders rather than from local activities. The Mossi also rear donkeys and horses for which they have long been famous. The former are sometimes ridden but are used primarily as beasts of burden. Horses were and are still important for military and ceremonial purposes and for external trade to other areas.

The Mossi have never excelled in metalworking. The people in the northern part of the country have worked indigenous ores since aboriginal times. Those in the south get iron mainly from traders and caravans. The other metals which the Mossi smiths manufacture into tools and ornaments are also obtained from traders.

TRADE IN HISTORICAL TIMES

The geographic position of Mossi country has much to do with its being an important trade and market center. The country itself has always produced grain, cotton and livestock for export. And for several centuries caravans have passed through this region carrying Sudanese and Saharan products to the forest zones to the south, and carrying forest products back to the arid north. The beginning of this trade is lost in the dim past, but it safe to say that it developed shortly after or along with the founding of Timbuktu about 1100 A.D. The Mossi themselves were not definitely linked to this important *entrepot* until they raided it in 1328, but we can assume that they had been trading there for some time before that event took place. Similarly, we have no record of when the Mossi began trading with the forest zones, but we can also assume that this trade began around the same period or even before.

Our first evidence of Mossi trade and commerce comes from Europeans who were themselves interested in conducting their own trading activities with the peoples in the Bend of the Niger. Bowditch, an Englishman who had journeyed to Ashanti to sign a treaty facilitating the reopening of a profitable trade with the coast, wangled the first important piece of information about the Mossi from his reluctant hosts:

Five journies from Yngwa is Mosee, a more warlike but less visited kingdom: it consists of many states, but the superior monarch is named Billa, and the capital Kookoopella. I place it to the N.W. because its merchants pass by Yngwa; they do not cross the Karhalla [White Volta] nor any river which is not fordable. (Bowditch 1819 : 180)

This information is not strictly correct since Koupela was not the capital of any of the Mossi kingdoms, but Bowditch's informant had probably heard of Koupela because it was the largest political entity near the large caravan center at Pouitenga.

Dupuis, who replaced Bowditch in Kumasi in 1817, obtained surprisingly good data on trade relations between the Ashanti and the
Mossi, considering the reluctance of the middlemen traders to furnish
any help in this matter. He discovered that Ashanti traders

> ... sometimes travel as far as Aughoa, the Magho, and to the east of
> Kasogho. Aughoa is distant from Coomassie twenty-five journies by the
> Salgha and Yandy Roads, which would give a distance of three hundred
> that vegetable substance ... by the name of Shea butter. (Dupuis 1824 :
> App. cvii)[1]

The Hausa merchants and caravaneers knew a great deal about the
Mossi and their resources, but it was only with great difficulty that
Clapperton persuaded Sultan Mohammed Bello of Sokoto to give
him the following information:

> The country of Mouchier or Mouchi is situated to the west of Ghurma.
> It is vast and possesses a gold mine, rivers, forests and mountains. It is
> inhabited by tribes of the Sudan who possess many fast horses, and large
> donkeys. Their king is called Wagadougou; their asses are sent down to
> the Gondja to carry the drums of the army. (Clapperton 1829 : 323)

It is obvious that either Clapperton or his informant confused the
capital of the Mossi with their king, and included parts of Ghana in
their territory. Nevertheless, one does get an indication of the importance of livestock in Mossi trading.

The great bulk of the trade between the Mossi and their neighbors
to the north and to the south was done through the medium of
caravans which crisscrossed their territory. The first person to signal
the existence of these caravans was Barth (1859 : III, 646–648) who,
although he did not enter Mossi country during his extensive travels
in the Sudan from 1849 to 1855, reported the existence of several
caravan routes which traversed the Mossi from the desert to the
forest. The first route he described proceeded from "Kirotashi, a town
on the east side of the Niger, one day south of Say, to Woghodogho."
Ten days out of Kirotashi caravans usually reached Tengkodogo, and
on the thirteenth day they arrived at Koupela which according to

---

(1) The Aughoa referred to here is really "Wagha," the term often used by the Mossi
when talking about their capital, Waghadougou. Magho is really "Mogho" the name
of Mossi country itself, and Kasoagho is the name of a province of Wagadougou commanded by a minister of the Moro Naba, the Kasoagho Naba. Dupuis' report on the
actual distance between Kumasis and Waghadougou is almost the same mileage as that
of today. Koelle (1854 : 6) received a report from a slave liberated in Sierra Leone in
1854 that the great Mossi trading center "Kupeala is four days from Wardugu, the
Mossi capital, whither the king of Asante often sends presents; and one month from
Salak (Salaga), an Asante town, where they bring their cola-nuts."

Barth was "a well-frequented market place of Mosi, and of greater importance than all the other towns of Mosi; the governor's name is Nabere Gager. The inhabitants are celebrated archers." Barth states that by the fifteenth day, or two days later, the caravans usually arrived at Wagadougou, but he tells us in a note that:

Other people, in going slowly from Kulfela to Woghodogho, spend eight days on the road, sleeping the first night in Pashipanga, the second in Tangay, the third in Zorogo, the next in a place ruled by a man called Mane Bogonje, the fifth in another village called Tangay, and reach Woghodogho on the eighth. (Marc 1909 : 27)[2]

Finally, he reports that another spur of this caravan route ran from Tengkodogo to Sansanne Mangho, in what is now Togoland. This journey took five days.

The second caravan route described by Barth ran from Djibo, the capital of the province of Gilgohi or Jilgodi (about 60 miles south from Montdoro, 55 miles West-Southwest from Aribinda and 35 miles South-Southwest from Tinie) by way of Kaya, to Mane and finally to Wagadougou. A caravan leaving Djibo entered Kelbo, the first village of the territory of Mossi on the eighth day, but according to Barth the "border district in general is regarded as very unsafe." On the fourteenth day the caravan entered Kaya;

... an important place where several roads meet. And from Kaya the route went to Wagadougou by way of Boussouma, Mane and Yako. It took a caravan ten days to traverse it.[3]

The third major caravan route that Barth described lay entirely within Mossi country. It ran from Mane to "Yadega" (probably Wahigouya, the capital of the kingdom of Yatenga) by way of Yako, and it took a caravan eight days to travel it. The fourth caravan route lay between Mane and a place called Kong by way of Tema, Yako, La and other places. On the tenth day a caravan reached Kong;

... a large place, according to my informant, inhabited by Bambara. It can scarcely be identical with the well-known Kong, if the itinerary be correct; but nevertheless it may be the case.

The first day after the caravan left Kong to return to Mane, it

(2) Barth received fairly accurate information about the caravan routes, and Marc was impressed with his data. Nevertheless, Marc finds it impossible to believe that caravans took two days to travel the twenty-five miles between Tengkodogo and Koupela, and only two more days to travel the ninety odd miles from Koupela to Wagadougou. Barth obviously erred here, but the timetable he gives for those persons "going slowly" from Koupela to Wagadougou appears to be quite correct.

(3) It is highly unlikely that a caravan going to Wagadougou from Kaya would have gone through Mane and Yako unless the caravaneers were interested in tapping the resources of these two western towns before heading straight south to their destination.

stopped at "Fura, a large market place." On the fourth day it stopped at Dullugu (probably present-day Doulougou), and on the fifth day at "Dakay [or Rakay] a place belonging to the territory of Mosi." Finally, on the thirteenth day it arrived at Mane.[4] The last caravan route that Barth reported ran from:

> Kaye to Belussa [Boulsa], and thence to Belanga [Bilanga] ... From Belussa a person on horseback reaches Belanga comfortably the second day, the great station between these two towns being Alitinga, still belonging to Mosi, and an important place, inhabited by Mosi and Hausa traders; but common native travellers generally halt twice between Belanga and Alitinga, in Nyennyega and Koburi [Kouri], and once between Alitinga and Belanga, in a Gurma village called Yamba.

The goods which these caravans carried appear to have varied a great deal. Barth met a Mossi caravan at Dori, southeast of Timbuktu, and reported that to this market:

> The people of Mosi bring chiefly their fine donkeys, which are greatly sought after; and a numerous body of people of the Sheikh A'hmedu, of Hamda-Allahi, had left a few days before with a number of asses which they had brought here. Besides asses, the people of Mosi supply this market with gabaga [cotton strips] or tari, as the Arabs near Timbuktu call them, cotton being extremely cheap in their country, so that in the great market place of that country, especially in Kulfela [Koupela, but really at Pouitenga a few miles away] an indigo-colored shirt is not worth more than from 700 to 800 [cowry] shells ... Besides salt, cotton strips, dyed cloth, Kola nuts, corn, and asses, some copper manufactured chiefly into large drinking vessels is also brought into the market by the people of Mosi. However, I do not think they manufacture the copper vessels themselves, but bring them from Asanti. (Barth 1859 : III, 203–4)

Adolphe Krause, a German who was actually the first European to enter Mossi country, went through Wagadougou with a load of kola nuts destined for Timbuktu. He joined the caravan at Salaga on July 7, 1885, stopped at the Bere market in Mossi country during August, and then proceeded to their capital where he remained until October 26 before resuming his northward journey (Krause 1887–8).

Felix Dubois, who visited Timbuktu in 1895, gives us some information on the actual products which the Mossi traded there. He reported that the Mossi came to the market organized into caravans of oxen, donkeys and porters, and brought such commodities as livestock, millet, rice, manioc, peanuts, honey, kola nuts, peppers, dried onions, tobacco, dried fish, soap, iron, antimony, lead, cotton bands, straw hats, mats, jars, pots and calabashes. These goods the Mossi

---

(4) Barth's skill as a reporter is evident here. He is quite correct in disbelieving that the caravans could have reached Kong on the tenth day. Marc. 1909, agrees with Barth.

traded for such articles as needles, mirrors, beads, coral and amber, tea, coffee, fezes, tailored robes, and most important of all, salt (Dubois 1899 : 292–304). Presumably, by the time Dubois reported on this trade, the Mossi had stopped trading slaves and eunuchs into this region, because we know from other sources that these people were sold through Timbuktu as far north as Algeria and Constantinople.[5]

The caravans which brought desert and northern goods into Mossi country collected grain, cotton cloth, livestock and slaves to be sold in the forest areas. Captain Lonsdale, an Englishman who visited Salaga in 1881 and gave a good description of its markets and traders, includes among the latter

... the Mossi with his cattle, sheep and slaves—these latter, generally Gurunsi, are not exposed for sale in the street or market, but can be seen where the owner resides. (Lonsdale 1882)

The extent to which the Mossi people themselves participated in all aspects of the caravan trade which crossed their country is far from clear. Barth, Lonsdale and Dubois all report that the Mossi were members of the caravans both in the forest zone and in Timbuktu, and my own informants agree with these reports. In contrast, however, both Marc and Tauxier believe that the Mossi were seldom the actual caravaneers. Marc declares that the Yarse

... are the most numerous group devoting itself to commerce in the region which we occupy. This is equally true of the Hausa, but probably only over the last years. Moors come sometimes from Dori as far as Wagadougou. One seldom meets Mande-Dioulas. As for the pure Mossi, it was only a short while ago that they themselves began to follow the caravans. (Marc 1909 : 170–71)

Similarly, Tauxier states that

... it is not the Mossi who do this [caravan] trading but the Yarse we know so well, and the Hausa settled in Mossi territory. Mossi trade, therefore, is not really Mossi, or at least it was not in the past. If it has now begun to be to some extent, it is thanks to the French settlement in the territory. (Tauxier 1912 : 538)

In the face of the early reports by Barth and others, how does one resolve the contradiction apparent in Tauxier's comments? These early travelers might have mistaken the Yarse for Mossi since these

(5) Marc, 1909 : 170–171. "We met in Mossi country two natives who, when children, had been seized [as slaves] and led through Timbuktu as far as Algeria ... The commerce in slaves was doubled among the Mossi by commerce in eunuchs. Mossi country was one of those rare countries where people knew how to make them, and the Moro Nabas exported with great profit as far as Constantinople those whom they had had mutilated."

people have become Mossicized in language and culture, but it is
doubtful whether they would have taken the Hausa for Mossi. The
true Mossi may have played a minor role in the caravan trade, but I
am certain that they took part in it and that they did so before the
French conquest of their country.

There is little doubt that the Mossi traded with the caravans that
passed *through* their country. Crozat, who visited Moro Naba Wobogo
six years before the conquest, reported that the king

> ... appeared to have had some business relations with white merchants
> who came up to Salaga every dry season. He sent horses to them in ex-
> change for silver. He claims that he had no reasons to be pleased with
> their integrity and that the silver which they sent to him contained plenty
> of copper. It happens also that traders may come as far as Wagadougou,
> bringing merchandise of German origin. There was one of them on hand
> during my stay at Wagadougou. I was told that he was an important mara-
> bout, a shereef, perhaps an Arab or a Moor, for I was assured that he was
> very light in color. As was repeated to me several times, his relations with
> the king were limited to the solemn greetings on Fridays. He has never
> entered the royal hut in spite of being an important marabout. He was at
> Wagadougou for about three and one-half months, but he was compelled
> to return to the coast since the merchandise which he had brought was
> exhausted. He spoke no Mossi. (Crozat 1891)

The caravans which passed through Mossi country were well organized but seemed to have lacked the regularity which was characteristic
of the trans-Sahara ones. Those caravans coming from the north were
apparently more regular since they had to await the coming of the
great trans-Sahara caravans, which brought them salt and other
valuable merchandise. Those coming from Salaga and points south
traveled at all times of the year, a fact which is corroborated by the
voyage of Krauss, who arrived at the Bere market during August and
the height of the Mossi planting season. This was a period of scarcity
or "hungry period" as Krauss himself observed, and it is doubtful
whether the Mossi had much to trade at this time. Nevertheless,
caravaneers always found some trade goods at the larger Mossi market
centers all through the year, even if only cloth and cotton bands.

The main season for external trade in Mossi country came after the
harvest. In the words of Marc, who served there shortly after the
conquest:

> Towards the end of the rainy season, in September or October, the
> Yarse begin to assemble the livestock in order to leave for the south. In
> certain large commercial centers like Kaya, Pouitenga, Dakay, one finds
> around this period the owners of livestock: Mossi chiefs, Fulani or rich
> natives, who are ready to sell their animals. People also assemble sheep of

the Mossi variety, which are very puny. The larger variety of long-haired Macina sheep are seldom exported. Once the livestock has been assembled, the chief of the caravan would also provide himself with cotton bands. This native fabric has often been described; it is commonly used on the caravan routes to pay for the food of the travellers. (Marc 1909 : 172)

Most of the caravans through Mossi country traveled as much as fifteen or twenty miles a day. They left at the first sign of dawn, traveled steadily until the heat became too intense, and then stopped to rest. They resumed their march when the sun was midway between the zenith and the horizon, and then stopped at some village or stream for the night. This schedule was followed on the next day if the caravan was far from a market center, but in the vicinity of a large market the caravan might remain stationary as many as six days while its merchants traded for more livestock or merchandise. This being the case, it is difficult to gauge how long it took the caravans to make the journey from Salaga in Ghana to Timbuktu. Our best data come from an analysis of Krauss' itinerary. He left Salaga with a caravan on July 7, 1885, heading north through Walwale, and arrived in Bere, a distance of some 250 miles (today's road mileage) towards the end of August. Famine delayed the caravan at Bere for some time, and he did not complete the 50 miles or so to Wagadougou until September 24. He remained in the Mossi capital until October 26, some thirty-two days, before his caravan headed north again through Tema, Yatenga and Bandiagara. Krauss does not tell us when he reached Douentza, some 400 miles northwest of Wagadougou, or how long he remained there, but on December 7, a few days after he had left Douenzta on the last 200- or 250-mile leg of his voyage to Timbuktu, the Moro Naba ordered him to return to Wagadougou. It is possible that it took Krauss' caravan some thirty-five odd days to make the trip from Wagadougou to Douentza. His return to Wagadougou took him only about thirty days, since he arrived there on January 7, 1886. He apparently had to wait some fifteen days there for a caravan going south, because he did not leave the Mossi capital until January 22, 1886 (Krause 1887–88). Judging from this itinerary, it probably took caravans between five and six months to travel from the forest zones to the desert, a distance of about a thousand miles at the most. This averages about six or seven miles a day, with the normal stops for rest and marketing, instead of the fifteen or twenty miles a day which the average caravan covered when it was on the road.

The caravans did not encounter many dangers or difficulties during their voyage. When the caravaneers had friends along the way they stopped at their friends' homes for the night, and when they camped in uninhabited places men were posted to protect the goods and livestock against marauding beasts and thieves. All caravaneers had to pay a tax to the local chiefs to cross their borders or to stop in their markets to trade. Binger reported that the caravans which passed through the market center of Wagadougou had to give the Moro Naba a share of their merchandise, aside from the presents which they gave to him. He also reported that the horse traders from the Yatenga, in the north of Mossi country, and the Hausa caravaneers, were sometimes forced to sell part of their wares to the Moro Naba at one-hundredth the purchase price (Binger 1892 : II, 292–300). Not all the caravaneers submitted to extortion, however, and at one period many of them traded with Mane instead of passing through Wagadougou where the tariffs were too high. On the other hand, the Mossi chiefs did not tolerate any trespassing on their territories by caravans that did not pay taxes. Those who tried to avoid doing so were subjected to attack by the mounted nobles *(nakomce)* on behalf of the district chiefs. Wise caravan leaders not only paid their taxes but established close relationships with the chiefs in order to receive adequate protection from some nobles who illegally attacked and looted the caravans.

It is impossible to know the actual volume of caravan trade which passed through Mossi country, but we can get a fairly good idea of it by examining the customs reports on goods crossing the border between Mossi country and the northern territories of the Gold Coast in the few years just following European conquest.[6] For 1901 and 1903 the official figures were:

TABLE 28A

Mossi Trade (1901–3)

Year	Horses	Cattle	Sheep and Goats	Loaded Donkeys	Bales of Cotton Cloth
1901	126	3,111	18,181	2,095	236
1903	196	6,624	30,892	4,294	369

Lucien Marc, who had the opportunity to check the volume of this trade for 1904 and 1905, guessed that about 16,000 cattle and 75,000 sheep and goats passed through the customs post in Mossi country. Furthermore, he believed that since

... the Mossi also supply in part the markets of Togoland and the market at Bondoukou [Ivory Coast], one can estimate at least an annual export of 20,000 cattle and 100,000 sheep or goats. The import of kola nuts is at least 500 tons. (Marc 1909 : 178)

(6) Great Britain Parliamentary Papers: Cd. 788–27, no. 357, Northern territories of Gold Coast, report of 1901 in Acc. and Papers, vol. LXIV 1902. Cd. 2238–6, no. 429, N.Ts of Gold Coast, report of 1903 in Acc. and Papers, 1904, and 1905, vol. LI.

It is clear that the volume of this trade could not have been enlarged since the French conquest which, as we know, had disrupted Mossi society. Therefore our conclusion must be that it must have existed prior to the coming of the Europeans.

The caravaneers used cowries and cloth as trade currency and in some cases even bartered one type of commodity for another. Cowries appear to have been the chief currency used and came close to being used for all purposes. Evidence for the use of cloth as currency comes from Barth and Marc. Barth met a trader who had

> ... a good quantity of the gabaga, or cotton strips, of Mosi with him, which form the staple currency in the whole tract of country from Libta to Timbuktu, ten Dr'a being reckoned equal to one hundred shells. (Barth 1859 : III, 198)

The big rolls of cotton cloth which Marc saw being loaded by Mossi caravaneers were said by them to serve the purpose of buying food ("They are for eating") in regions where cloth was the necessary currency (Marc 1909 : 172 f.n.). The traders apparently resorted to barter whenever and wherever they could or when their currency was in short supply. This appears to have been the case when Binger visited the Mossi in 1888. Cowries were then in short supply and the people were using slaves, valued at 50,000 to 65,000 cowries apiece, to obtain goods. Horses could be bought for as many as two or four slaves apiece. Traders apparently kept the cowry equivalence in mind when using other commodities to barter with, but we cannot be sure of this since Binger himself, and not the traders, may have been conscious of the equivalence (Binger 1892 : II, 498).

The prices which the traders paid and received for their goods differed greatly from place to place, according to the season of the year and over a span of several years. The earliest price data are given by Barth for the 1850's:

> As regards Selga [Salaga], the district to which the Hausa traders go for their supply of this article, three points are considered essential to the business of the Kola trade; first, that the people of Mosi bring their asses; secondly, that the Tonawa, or natives of Asanti, bring the nut in sufficient quantities; and thirdly, that the state of the road is such as not to prevent the Hausa people from arriving. If one of these conditions is wanting, the trade is not flourishing. The price of the asses rises with the cheapness of the guro [kola nut]. The average price of an ass in the market of Selga is 15,000 [cowry] Shell: While in Hausa the general price does not exceed 5,000. But the fataki, or native traders, take only as many asses with them from Hausa as are necessary for transporting their luggage, as the toll, or

fitto, levied upon each ass by the petty chiefs on the road is very consider-able. From 5,000 to 6,000 guro, or kola nuts, constitute an assload.

Selga, the market place for this important article, being, it appears, a most miserable town, where even water is very scarce and can only be purchased at an exorbitant price, the merchants always manage to make their stay here as short as possible, awaiting the proper season in Yendi, a town said to be as large as Timbuktu, or in Kulfela, the great market place of Mosi; and they are especially obliged to wait in case they arrive at the beginning of the rainy season, there being no kola nuts before the latter part of the Kharif. The price of this nut in Timbuktu varies from 20 to 100 shells each, and it always constitutes a luxury; so that, even on great festivals, alms consisting of this article are distributed by the rich people of the town. (Barth 1859 : II, 364)

The other data we have on prices paid for goods come from the period between 1890 and 1910, at which time French francs had been introduced. At this time the official value of one franc was 1,000 cowries. Around 1904, a trader paid about 50 francs or 50,000 cowries for a head of cattle in Mossi country and sold it for about double the price at Salaga. With the proceeds of this transaction he bought kola nuts at the rate of one franc or 100 cowries per hundred. Thus with the sale of one cow a trader could obtain 10,000 kolas, these being valued at about 500 francs or 500,000 cowries in Mossi country and at 20 or 200 cowries each at Sarfere and Timbuktu (Marc 1909 : 173–4). At Timbuktu about this same period, 1895, traders could buy salt at about 30 francs for a slab weighing between 60 and 100 pounds and sell it for 45 francs at Sarafere, for 60 francs at Djenne, for between 70 and 80 francs at San, and "thus progressively more until they reached Mossi country" (Dubois 1899 : 276). In 1910, Mossi traders bought cattle for about 40 to 100 francs, horses for about 90 francs, donkeys for 25 francs, and so on, and sold these animals in Salaga for three times the prices. There they bought kolas at 2 Fr. 50 per thousand, and sold them at 20 per thousand at Leo on the Mossi border, 35 francs per thousand at Wagadougou, 50 francs at Wahi-gouya, 60 francs at Saravere, and 100 francs per thousand at Tim-buktu. Here these traders bought bars of salt weighing about 75 pounds for between 10 and 12 francs a piece, and sold them for between 40 to 60 francs at Wahigouya, and for from 80 to 100 francs a piece at Dedougou and points as far down as Wagadougou (Tauxier 1917 : 221).

Not all the profit from this trade went into the pockets of the traders. We have the report of Binger that the chiefs, besides com-mandering the goods at less than one-hundredth their purchase price, received taxes on each caravan which passed through their

territory. This report is substantiated by Barth. Marc adds that the
caravaneers had

> , . . . a considerable amount of incidental expenses. Ten thousand kolas
> called for two asses or four porters for whom it was necessary to provide
> food during close to two months. Formerly there had been a certain
> number of local exactions to pay each time that the caravans crossed a new
> country. Now there are taxes on the caravans in the Gold Coast and also
> in French territory. It is also necessary to pay for ferryman who transports
> the livestock across the Volta [River]. There are risks, and occasionally
> cattle, fatigued by the trip, arrive in such bad shape that they are sold
> more cheaply than they had cost. Finally, the realization of profits is often
> difficult, the kola market being, in the commercial centers of the Mossi,
> subject to considerable fluctuations at the time when the caravans return.
> (Marc 1909 : 174)[7]

Sometimes the caravaneers made extensive use of middlemen and
did not realize all the profits. Marc, who was stationed at the customs
post at Leo on the Mossi border with the Gold Coast, wrote:

> The livestock is bought upon arrival by interpreter-brokers, middle-
> men between the butchers and the meat merchants, to whom the cara-
> vaneers are practically forced to resort. These men buy all the kola nuts
> brought by the forest natives, and control the market prices . . . These
> interpreter-brokers apparently speculate on livestock in a most curious
> way. They have scouts who go out to meet the caravans, sometimes two
> days' march to the north. These scouts attempt to alarm the travellers with
> tendentious remarks, until they are willing to cede their herds at a low
> price. Some times, at the height of the business season—that is, in January
> and February—the livestock prices may fluctuate by one hundred per cent
> within a few weeks. The Mande-Dioula vie in eloquence, the Yarse and
> Mossi in politeness, the Hausa in friendliness. In reality, there is here, an
> embryonic trading center, a veritable stock exchange, using extensively
> indigenous methods. ((Marc 1909 : 173)

According to most reports, all the larger market centers of Mossi
country were like this.

Caravan centers, like all the lesser market centers in Mossi country,
provided merchants not only with trading opportunities but also
with occasions for conviviality after hectic days of travel. At Dakay,
south of Wagadougou, livestock traders found musicians, singers,
and the most beautiful dancers in the country. And according to Marc,
during the whole caravan season the market was abundantly furnished
with beer (Marc 1909 : 175). But if the Mossi enjoyed themselves at

---

(7) Tauxier (1912 : 539) states that each porter was paid 35 francs for the thirty-five
days of travels or at the rate of one franc per day. In addition a caravaneer spent about
300 cowries a day on food for each of his bearers.

their own commercial centers, they acted quite differently outside their country. Dubois reports that at Timbuktu, "the great town of pleasure" with the freest morals in the Sudan, the merchants from Bamako, Djenne, Sansanding and Touat spent a great deal of money in pleasure and in gifts to the beautiful women, but the "Mossi did not waste their money and left as soon as they had finished their affairs" (Dubois 1899 : 292–300).

The days of the caravans are now over in Mossi country, even though large groups of traders carry on the traditional commerce in livestock, cotton, kola nuts, some dried fish, and salt. As soon as the French conquered th country they formulated plants to control the caravans. One of the earliest reports, for June 1899, reads:

> The country is calm and direct administration was established at Kou-pela, Mane, Yake ... The Mossi trade is mainly with the English colony of the Gold Coast. It consists mainly of livestock, very plentiful in Mossi country, which is exchanged for merchandise from England; copper and material goods ... Our task will be to discover the materials of the north-ern Ivory Coast which could be exchanged for cattle, and when this information is forthcoming we should be able to direct the caravans quite easily to the Ivory Coast. At the same time the English will see their pro-visions of cattle and sheep diminish. They will flood us less with their cotton cloth, with their glass beads, and with their kola nuts. In their place, the products of French manufacture can arrive to us through the Ivory Coast after being exchanged for the products of our colony there.[8]

These plans did not succeed. The Mossi still export a great deal of their products towards the forest zones of Ghana, including their "numerous laborers" which, according to Beauminy writing in 1919, were "the principal riches actually utilizable in Mossi country". (Beauminy 1919 : 71–78). The migrants themselves are, in a sense, the greatest traders in contemporary Mossi society.

PRESENT-DAY TRADE

There is a constant flow of goods between Mossi country and the Ivory Coast and Ghana. Much of the trade to the former region is in the hands of the large commercial companies and as such is beyond the purview of this paper. What is of interest here is the trade which is conducted by the ordinary people. A great deal of this trade is highly unorganized and the result of one or two men, or as many as five men, joining together to trade goods to and from Ghana and the Ivory Coast. The types of goods sent down to these two areas are the

(8) Unpublished document in the archives of *Institut Français d'Afrique Noire,* Wagadougou, Voltaic Republic.

same as those traded in pre-European times. For example, my notes for March 22, 1956, record that five young men were transporting 50-kilogram sacks of onions on their bicycles for trade in Ghana. On March 23, the next day, I wrote the following: "This appears to be the season of increased trade and the donkey trains are passing to and from Wagadougou and the Yatenga to Po (a town on the Ghana-Voltaic Republic border) and Bolgatenga in northern Ghana. Very often the donkeys carry nothing down, and at other times they are loaded with beans, millet, cotton bands, onions, peanuts and other vegetable produce. On the return trip they are laden with kola nuts going northward. This afternoon I counted twenty-eight asses coming from Ghana and going towards Wagadougou. Eighteen of them were laden with kolas, and ten were carrying long pieces of scrap iron which I was told, were to be converted into hoes for use during the coming planting season."

There is also a steady trade in livestock between Mossi country and the southern lands but the height of this trade occurs just prior to Ramadan. Beginning from one month to one week before this important Moslem feast day, the roads of Mossi country are clogged with thousands of sheep and goats being driven south for the use of religious households in Ghana and the Ivory Coast. Cattle are also shipped during this period, but not in the same volume since they are most often used collectively by Moslem families too poor to have their own sheep or goat.

The total volume of trade between Mossi country and Ghana and the Ivory Coasts is difficult to ascertain since despite the existence of Customs Posts a great deal of contraband trading takes place. My notes for December 12, 1955, read *"Contraband":* Two customs men came into the village to complain to the district chief about the behavior of Naba, one of his village chiefs. This is what happened: About two days ago, two agents saw in the forests the tracks of some thirty-five asses (heavily laden as can be seen by the depth of the tracks) and the marks of a bicycle with new tires. The agents followed the tracks all day and rested during the night. Yesterday they had to interrupt their search when the bicycle of one of the agents broke down, and when they resumed the search later in the day they came across five asses laden with kola nuts inside the compound of a man in Naba's village. Since they were forbidden by law to go into the man's compound and seize the animals, they went to the village chief in an attempt to have him tell the man to put the animals outside so that they could be seized. This the village chief refused to do, stating that it was not his affair, and adding that the agents should have seized the animals in the forest. The agents, now helpless, came and complained to the district chief. Unfortunately for them the district chief was absent, but his assistants did send out a call for the village chief. However, the chief refused to appear, saying that he would only do so when the district chief returned. The last thing I saw was the agents leaving the district chief's compound still unsatisfied with the whole affair." The sequel to this comes from my notes for December 26, 1955. "I inquired about the aftermath of the contraband case and was told that the whole affair is being referred to the courts at Abidjan. If the village chief is found guilty, he will have to pay a fine of 10,000 francs for the first ass and 3,000 francs for each subsequent ass, or in lieu of this go to jail. Informant said that since the village chief is a poor man, he would probably go to jail."

In spite of the contraband, the actual volume of trade appears to be considerable. The production, trade and export of goods largely produced by the Mossi people in 1954 are set forth in Table 29.

TABLE 29
Production, Trade and Export of the Mossi (1954)

Product	Amount	Export	Destination
Almonds	35,000 tons	3,602	France and African countries
Peanuts	50,000 tons	3,031	France and African countries
Cattle	1,560,000 tons	101,000	Ghana, Togo and Ivory Coast
Sheep and Goats	2,115,000 tons	238,255	Ghana, Togo and Ivory Coast

These figures do not include the numerous items that drift over the frontiers of Ghana and the Ivory Coast with the thousands of migrants who go to these places each year. While the actual number of such migrants is difficult to ascertain, Pierre Dufour believes that it is "about 150,000 men per year, of whom 100,000 go to the Gold Coast and 50,000 to the Ivory Coast". (Dufour 1956 : 3). And since almost every one of these migrants takes with him some trade item such as a chicken or two, a small sheep or goat, a small sack of cereal or other vegetable produce or a few bands of cotton to defray part of his transportation costs, the amount of goods actually exported is considerable. These statistics rarely enter into the account of goods exported from Mossi country, since custom officers do not usually tax migrants for small items, and do not make any record of them. Of course, when the migrants carry large loads, these are recorded and the migrants must pay export taxes.

Greater attention is paid to the goods which those migrants who work in Ghana (but not in the Ivory Coast) bring back with them after one season or after several years of work, since the government of the Voltaic Republic derives a great deal of its tax revenue from duties on these goods.

The migrants bring back all types of goods with them. According to Dufour: "Money as such is not brought back in very large proportion because manufactured products of the English colony (Gold Coast) cost less. Consequently, each year there is a great introduction of bicycles, sewing machines, fabrics". (Dufour 1956 : 140). One might add to this list kerosene lamps, zinc buckets, all types of wearing apparel, and all manner of household goods. An inventory of the common trunk of two returning migrants revealed the following merchandise: two kerosene lamps, two bottles of kerosene, two burnoose of black serge trimmed with pink silk, one white burnoose, two blue shirts, two khaki shorts, two tubes of Thermogene (a medicated rub), eight women's headkerchiefs, two Moslem fezes, two hand mirrors, two jars of Vaseline petroleum jelly, two pairs of sandals, one black scarf, packs of camphor balls, and one bottle of perfume. These goods represent the migrant's work over one season, from October to the following April, in the cacao fields of Ghana. Other migrants return with more, but few return with less. The actual value of these goods has been estimated by Dufour at about one billion francs C.F.A. per year. The custom duties which the migrants pay amount to more than 150 million francs C.F.A. annually—the sum they actually paid into the treasury of the Haute Volta in 1953 (Rouch 1956 : 139 ff.).

The migrants distribute to their relatives a good part of the goods they bring back, but a large proportion gets into the hands of other people either through the market or through more direct channels. Here is an example taken from my notes of March 24, 1956: "*Trading in bicycles:* Moussa gave Souliman a cow and an old bicycle for a new bicycle which Souliman had bought for 5,000 francs from a passing migraunt. Souliman was trying to sell this same cycle for 6,250 francs, thus trying to make a profit of 1,250 francs just two or three days after he had bought it . . . Souliman slaughtered the cow which he received from Moussa and sold the beef to the local *restaurateur* at an additional profit. Souliman appears to be a sharp individual. He recently bought another bicycle for 5,000 francs from a migrant and resold it for 7,500 francs." This type of trading is not unusual, but the most typical articles resold by migrants in the local markets are lamps, worn shirts, shoes and other articles of clothing.

The growth of migration among Mossi men has led to a new type of commercial activity in the country. This is the selling of cooked food by the women to passing migrants. These women and young girls prepare food such as chicken, rice, millet balls, millet flour water and fried cakes which they bring to the principal thoroughfares to sell. Many of them arrive at the central village areas as early as four o'clock in the morning to sell food to those migrants who have slept under the trees or in the deserted market place and who are going on towards Ghana or to Wagadougou. At about 8:00 or 9:00 A.M. the majority of the food-sellers leave for home, but some of them remain around all day to sell to those migrants who pass by in the few trucks which can travel during the heat of the day. The food sellers then return at about 5:00 P.M. because from this time until about 1:00 A.M. most of the trucks bearing migrants stop for water and to allow their passengers to eat and rest. The amount of money these women gross varies from day to day depending upon the amount of traffic and the time of year. During the off-season from June to October, when most of the migrants are home planting, a woman may make as little as ten francs per day. In contrast, at the beginning of the dry season when the young men are migrating in droves, the women may make as much as 100 francs a day, even though twenty or thirty women line the road at trucking centers. Many women welcome this opportunity to earn money because by so doing they are free to buy in the local markets the things they need.

MARKET

The Mossi have always conducted most of their commercial activities in market places even though some extra-market trading continually takes place. These markets were and are still divided into two main types: (1) those specializing in external trading, such as Pouitenga, Dakay, Kaya, Mane, Yako, La, Beloussa, Tema, Wagadougou; and (2) those specializing in internal commerce such as the markets in the villages and district centers. Of course, there is an overlap between the two types of markets in the sense that some people from the villages go to the larger markets to dispose of their commodities and, in turn, buy goods which they bring back for resale on the local level. Similarly, in former days some caravaneers visited the local markets to buy commodities and in the process disposed of their goods. However, the main pattern is for local commodities to filter into the large market centers through local markets, and for goods from these centers to filter back down to the local markets. The more goods and traders available, the more numerous and successful the markets are.

The Mossi do not appear to have any legends about the origin of markets in their country. When asked how and why markets first arose, they say that markets developed simply because people wanted to exchange goods with each other, or because the chiefs wanted markets in their own villages so that their people need not go to other districts. When one asks the Mossi directly, "What is a market?"

the response to this question is: "A market is a place where people meet to buy and sell. People travel from one market place to another market place, and on the way they stop and see their friends in other villages. In the market one often meets and drinks with one's friends. People also go to distant markets to find things which they do not grow themselves or which cannot be found in their own markets."

Lending support to the Mossi contention that markets are places where one goes to buy and sell is the fact that most important markets in their country are found at the intersections of well-traveled routes. These intersections are often the places where chiefs have their capitals or compounds and this leads to the further idea that there is a connection between chiefs and markets, if only because the power of the chiefs makes markets possible. This does not mean, however, that the market is a purely physical entity which can only exist under the aegis of a chief, or that it is a purely economic institution. First of all, some markets, especially the smaller ones, are moved periodically without too much difficulty. Secondly, and of great importance, is the fact that whenever and wherever there is a large gathering of Mossi there is a "market." Indeed one can say that Mossi seldom come together in large numbers without coming to a market, or without creating one. It appears that the Mossi cannot interact with one another in any circumstance without also exchanging goods of some kind. For example, when a pagan chief holds the annual festival to his ancestors, the people who attend form a market in the vicinity of his compound. In those districts where the chiefs have become Christians and celebrate their birthdays rather than the traditional ancestors' rites, the people go to pay them homage and also "make a market." Similarly, whenever there is a funeral of an important chief, the people from the surrounding villages or even districts bring commodities to his hamlet and hold a market during the ceremony. On Christmas day, 1955, the people of Manga district "moved their market" about 500 yards to the Catholic Mission grounds where the Christians were celebrating their holiday. And after celebrating the prayers of Ramadan, the Moslems and their pagan townsmen repair to the markets to spend the rest of the day.

Most Mossi markets are inaugurated with religious ceremonies except those which develop by accretion—that is, by more and more persons coming voluntarily to trade. When a chief orders that a market be created or when a market is moved from one place to another place for any reason, the chief is the person who gives the order for the ceremony to be performed. First of all he speaks to his Raga Naba (market chief), usually a non-Mossi slave, about the need for the market or the desirability of changing its location. This man then consults a *teng-*

sobu (earth priest) who must be also a *barga* (soothsayer) to find out where in a certain area it would be most propitious to locate the new market. After the *tengsoba* has ascertained the number and nature of the *tengkouga* (earth deities, plural of *Tengkougri*) in the designated spot, he tells the *Raga Naba* what type of sacrifice would be appropriate. A few days later the *Raga Naba*, his young assistant and the *tengsoba* take *zom kom* (milletflour), *dam* (sorghum beer), and a chicken (or goat) of the designated color, and go to the new market place. Here they pick out the stone or three which is the abode of the spirit or spirits, if there are several of them, and prepare to make the offering. The *Raga Naba* takes the millet water and pours some on the ground saying: "Good God, take this water, drink it, and take this other water (here he pours the beer), and give it to all the *tengkouga* in the villages so that the market will aways be good and there will be no fighting in the market!" Then the *Raga Naba* takes the sacrificial animal, and in the case of a chicken pulls off the neck feathers and cuts its throat, saying: "Good God, take this chicken and heed all the prayers of the people of this market!" He releases the chicken and waits to see whether it will fall on its back, thereby indicating whether the petition has been accepted. Of course, if it has not been accepted, a new site is chosen. If the sacrifice has been accepted, then the *Raga Naba* gives the chicken to his young helper to be cleaned and roasted. He then prays to the *tengkouga* who live in the market place and begs them to help with the market. When the boy brings back the dissected chicken, the *Raga Naba* cuts the liver into two parts; one for God and the other for the local *tengkouga*. He then says, "Now that God and the *Tengkouga* have eaten, they should drink," and forthwith pours out the remainder of the millet water. The *Raga Naba* then distributes the remainder of the roasted chicken among those present saying, *"Winnam dege* (God has accepted the sacrifice)." Only after this ceremony is completed can the market be opened.[9]

All Mossi markets, except those which specialize in one type of trading, have the same basic physical structure even though they vary in size from one-eighth of an acre to as much as four or five acres. We do not know the size of some of the traditional markets such as Pouitenga, La, Yako, Dakay, Belousa, Mane, and Tema, but we have Crozat's report that "The market at Wagadougou, which is found at Kounkounbissi, the royal residence ... is large" (Crozat 1891 : 4848). Since the market at Wagadougou was smaller than some of the other important ones, we may assume that some of the markets must have been quite large. At the same time, the physical appurtenances of Mossi markets are not elaborate, or were not so until today. In the

(9) See Zahan (1954 : 371) and Mangin (1921 : 53).

larger markets there were and are solid stalls which are built and tenanted by merchants. In the small district and village markets, these stalls are built out of millet stalks which offer little but protection against the noonday sun on market days. Men build these structures for their womenfolk and for themselves. Some of the shelters which are not used for trading serve as galleries where the young blades look out and comment on the passing scene. Others are used as meeting places by adult men who sit and discuss all sorts of affairs. Still others are used by the older men, who gather there to arrange marriages between their several families, wait for gifts from younger men who seek wives, or spend a great deal of time reminiscing about their youthful adventures. Those persons who do not have such shelters sit in the sun or use grass lean-tos as protection from the sun.

Except in the large towns, Mossi markets are held between the hours of 10:00 A.M. and 4:00 P.M. every fourth day. In the larger towns there are daily markets, but these remained unimportant until today when they serve a growing urban population. The capital city of Wagadougou now even has an "evening" market which opens about 4:00 P.M. and closes at about 9:00 P.M. In addition, numerous daily markets have sprung up in many of its wards. The three-day markets are, however, the traditional type, and they are still the most numerous through the country. By "three-day market" I mean that a market is held one day, not held over the two following days, and then held again on the next day. These markets also have a 21-day cycle from one *Ragakasanga* or *Rag'kasanga* ("larger market") on a Friday to another *Rag'kasanga* on a Friday three weeks later, a total of seven markets between the two important ones. The people give no adequate explanation for the observance of the three-day cycle or the 21-day cycle. One man did suggest that it took the women three days to prepare beer and this was why markets could not be held more often, but even he did not speculate about the 21-day cycle.[10] This same man did point out, however, that the cycle made little difference to persons who really liked to go to market, since it was possible for

(10) Zahan (1954 : 373) apparently found one of the few Mossi informants with a mystical bent; he reports that the seven three-day cycles of markets in the 21-day cycle have the following significance for the Yatenga people: "The first of these numbers explains the cycle of the person (7 symbolizes the complete person: male [to which the Mossi assign the number 3] and female [to which they assign the number 4], the second that of the creation." He believes that each market starts a new cycle, a beginning and an end: "the seventh market signifies the most perfect equilibrium: the one which exists between the universe, mankind, and the divinity." In a footnote he suggests that this sybolism is not too different among the Dogon, who are "ideologically and geographically close to the Mossi." Peter Hammond, who worked in Yatenga, could not find this kind of symbolism.

such individuals to find a market everyday in one neighboring district or another.

Every Mossi market not only has its own schedule but is also part of a cycle of markets in the sense that its main customers can and do regularly attend two other markets on the two nonmarket days without missing their "own" market. Table 30 takes the district market at Nobere as the home market and lists the markets which Nobere's people can attend and the reasons they themselves give for going there.

TABLE 30

Markets near Nobere

	Distance Away	Reasons for Going
First Day:		
Nobere		Home Market
Manga	12 kilometers	Good Pottery
Vooko	15 kilometers	Butter and Millet
Twese	20 kilometers	Millet and Sorghum
Binde	35 kilometers	Good Pottery and Mats "Very far and people do not go there very often"
Second Day:		
Basgana	10 kilometers	Good Pottery
Sakouliga	15 kilometers	"To Have Fun"
Giba	10 kilometers	"To Have Fun"
Third Day:		
Nobili	27 kilometers	"Good Millet"
Pinse	6 kilometers	"Small Market; to have fun"
Parougre	10 kilometers	"Good Millet and Pottery"

Nobere people scarcely ever go to Manga because the market there conflicts with their own and its one unique product, pottery, can be bought at Basgana on a day when there is no market at Nobere. A person is likely to go do Vooko when he wishes to buy butter and millet at cheaper prices than he can obtain in his own market. But he scarcely visits the Binde market unless he is there visiting a friend or relative. Nobere people think nothing of going to Giba or to Pinse to show off their clothes or to have fun at those markets. If any commodity is cheap there they take advantage of the prices, but in general they believe that they can obtain better and cheaper products at their own market.

It is now possible to find a great variety of products at Mossi markets, and the larger the market the more varied its merchandise. Apparently this was not always so. Crozart (1891 : 4848), who visited the country just before it was conquered, reported that in the market at Wagadougou, he found "millet, rice, millet beer, butchered meat, small cutlery, morocco-leather goods, basketwork and jewelry items, all of local manufacture and in great abundance. Local cloth is also very abundant. However, there are scarcely any imported objects salt, kola nuts, copper rings and extremely rare European fabrics. The salt always comes from the north. During my stay at Wagadougou I saw the arrival of a convoy of five or six small-sized mules loaded with this merchandise." Crozat felt that the Wagadougou market with its mainly local products was inferior to the markets at Woroudoy and Bobo-Dioulasso which he found less crowded, but which were, in his words, "true *entrepots* of imported merchandise."

Tauxier gives us a better picture of the goods found in the markets of Mossi country before the Europeans arrived. His reports list few imported products except salt and kola nuts. The preponderance of goods sold were such local foodstuffs as maize, manioc, peppers, tomatoes, squash, karite or shea butter, locust-bean balls, locust-bean flour, rice and a local variety of potatoes. Other foodstuffs included were honey, beer, butchered meat, chickens, and guinea fowls. Tobacco both for chewing and smoking was also available, and so was hemp for making rope. Raw cotton, cotton thread, cloth and tailored cotton garments were also present, and so was indigo for dyeing the cotton materials. Other goods included hides, sandals, pouches, amulets, iron items such as axes, hoes, knives, scythes, locks, clubs and spearpoints, bracelets and anklets made of copper by the lost-wax process, baskets, mats and hats made out of local grasses, pottery, pipes and wooden stools (Tauxier 1912 : 466 ff.). By 1914 Mangin could add little to this list of local products, sold in the markets, but added such foreign items as "matches, glass trinkets, handkerchiefs, basins, dishes, perfumes, and even firecrackers" (Mangin 1921 : 53).

The markets of contemporary Mossi society contain all of the articles found in pre-European times and those seen there by Mangin in 1914. In the larger markets one now can find such additional items as bicycles, razor blades, plastic raincoats and other plastic products, and the latest "rock 'n roll" records from the United States. The goods found in the smaller district and village markets tend to be of the traditional variety. But even here it is possible to buy refined cane sugar, matches, plastic necklaces, shoe polish, nail polish, toilet water, glass beads, costume jewelry, chinaware, and glass and enamel containers. In some of the smaller markets it is even possible to buy wheat bread made of imported flour, and bottled beer and soda water. The more different types of goods entering the larger markets, the richer the variety found in the smaller markets, since local merchants are quick to take advantage of the prestige value of any new produce and introduce it into the rural areas. The only barrier to this type of commercial activity is the relative poverty of the rural people.

Cowries used to be chief medium of exchange in Mossi markets until the Europeans arrived. In addition the people bartered specific goods for other products. The prices of goods in these markets fluctuated from time to time. Prices were highest during the planting season when most goods were scarce, and lowest during the harvest periods, but we have little precise information about the prices of goods in the traditional markets. Even Barth's information is too sketchy to deal with. Our first reliable data come from Tauxier, whose writings cover the first decade (1896-1906) of the conquest. Using the then official rate of one franc equals 1,000 cowries, the prices of a few representative products were: horses, 40 to 100 francs (40,000 to 100,000 cowries); cattle, 30 to 40 francs (30,000 to 40,000 cowries); chickens, 250 cowries; guinea fowls, 250 to 300 cowries; hides, 3,000 cowries; pottery jars, 300 cowries; cotton trousers, 200 cowries; baskets, 1,500 cowries; and locust-bean balls, 100 cowries (Tauxier 1912 : 466 ff.).

Mangin, whose work covers the period from about 1910 to 1913, when the value of the franc was lowered to one franc equals 700 to 800 cowries, lists the approximate prices for the following goods; "Millet, 0.02 franc a kilogram; rice, 0.10 franc a kilogram; *fabirama,* 0.05 franc a kilogram; shea butter, 0.50 franc a kilogram; milk butter, 1.50 francs a kilogram; peanuts, 0.07 franc a kilogram; peanut oil, 0.50 franc a liter; one jar of ordinary millet beer, containing about six to eight liters, 0.20 franc; one jar of strong millet beer *(tose),* containing about six to eight liters, 0.40 franc; hydromel *(bese),* 0.15 franc a liter; chicken, 0.40 franc; average goat, 3 to 4 francs; large goat, 8 to 10 francs; average sheep, 3.50 francs for a ram, 4 francs, for an ewe; large sheep, 8 to 10 francs; donkey, 25 to 30 francs; horse, 150 francs; small cow (no hump), 50 francs; zebu cow, 70 francs; goat skin, 0.30 franc; cow skin, 1 franc; salt bars, from 1.50 to 2 francs a kilogram; kola nuts, from 0.03 to 0.10 franc apiece; one hoe, about 0.60 franc; cloth: strip of white cloth, 0.05 franc, about 0.60 franc a cubit; white blanket, 2 francs; indigo-dyed blanket, 3 francs; striped blanket, 4 francs; medium-sized shirt, 2.50 francs" (Mangin 1921 : 53). In dealing with these prices, a number of things should be kept in mind: first of all, these prices fluctuated very much during the year; secondly they varied from region to region within the country; and thirdly, although these prices are given in francs during this period, it was still possible to use cowries to buy a large number of the products.

Enormous changes have taken place in the Mossi economic and exchange systems over the decades following the studies of Tauxier and Mangin. Even before, but certainly after World War I, the French pressure on the Mossi to pay taxes in francs finally resulted in the adoption of this currency as the medium of exchange in most markets.[11] The one-franc piece and coins of smaller denominations were those most often used because they were ideally suited to the petty trading that took place in the markets. The franc even became the standard of value in the larger markets, but one receives only 3 local francs for a five-franc note C.F.A. or seven francs for a ten-franc note C.F.A. These changes in value seem to occur by common concensus, since it is impossible to discover who it was that changed the exchange rate. A further fact is that many Europeans remain unaware of these changes since they seldom go to the local markets themselves. When they do go and insist upon the official exchange rate, the "unofficial" market chief appears and takes over the situation, giving the *nansara* ("conqueror" or "master," the way in which every European is regarded) what he wishes.

While the equivalence between the cowrie, the old brass franc, and the franc C.F.A. works splendidly when products are sold in small quantities, I found the system difficult to understand when more expensive goods are traded. For example, when one buys meat, an expensive item, the butcher accepts either the official francs or the local currency and gives change in both. The difficulty here is that since the butcher uses no scales, one is never sure about the price or about the system of value the butcher is using. The most that can be done if one does not receive as much meat as expected is to haggle with the butcher until he adds more. However, this haggling leaves unresolved the problem of the value of one's official money in terms of the unofficial money, and the product which it is intended to buy. One is thus left with the *impression* that there must be an internal consistency to the exchange system, or barring this, that the local people accept the system as it is as a matter of expediency. On the other hand, the vendors of products with fixed prices such as matches, cigarettes and the like appear to make differential profits when they

(11) Mangin (1921 : 61–62) reports that the Mossi had great difficulty obtaining the five-franc piece which they needed to pay their taxes because the "Europeans who live in Mossi country, including all the riflemen and provincial guards do not put into circulation a quarter of the five-franc pieces which are required each year from the natives. At first the Mossi were taken by surprise and had to give 10 or even 15,000 cowries to obtain this famous coin, this *greegree* which was to free them from all difficulties with the white man. And yet at the official rate of exchange this coin is worth 5,000 cowries. Nowadays it is very difficult to find a native willing to give this much for one of the coins. The usual exchange rate varies from 3,500 to 4,000 cowries: the French currency has been depreciated. This must mean that the natives find elsewhere –through trading– this indispensable coin. They know that the tax must be paid every year, and instead of waiting till the last minute, as soon as they have accumulated the necessary cowries they secure the five-franc pieces from those who have fetched them from far away. The coins flow into the country, and the rate of exchange goes down."

use one type of currency rather than another. For example, a petty trader often buys a package of European cigarettes for 20 francs C.F.A. in the Wagadougou market for retail in the local markets. Here he sells some individual cigarettes at the price of two for 5 francs C.F.A., some at two for 3 old-fashioned francs (making a total of about 21 francs C.F.A.). The vendors are fully aware of this profit differential, but make no attempt to insist on one currency over the other. Furthermore, they appeared indifferent when I suggested that I planned to take advantage of the price differential which I suspected in the two systems. It appears that they believe it would be a waste of time to try to obtain the profit differential.

Barter as a form of exchange had just about disappeared from the larger markets in Mossi country, but it exists alongside the use of currency in the local markets, especially in connection with foodstuffs and other vegetable commodities. People tend to resort to barter when they wish to exchange a specific product for another. Thus, a woman who normally sells rice for currency sometimes will suddenly refuse to accept money and insist on exchanging the rice for cotton or peanuts. The bartering then takes the form of a half-calabash of rice for a half-calabash of either peanuts or cotton, depending upon which products are desired. This equivalence seems always to be maintained regardless of the currency value of rice, cotton, or peanuts at the market on the day in question. For example, a woman who was looking for persons with whom she could exchange peanuts for rice and she refused to sell peanuts to me. I asked why she would not sell the peanuts and then take the money and buy rice with it. She said that if she did so, she would suffer a dual loss: first, in selling the peanuts, each valued at 100 cowries (one-half franc of unofficial currency) for 5 francs. I counted the nuts, which amounted to about 120, and then asked for the customary *lenga* (bonus) and received 36 more peanuts worth 1.5 franc. On the next market day I observed that peanuts were not being sold but only bartered for cotton which was being sold. I decided to test the system. I bought 2 old-fashioned francs' worth of cotton at 100 cowries a ball, and took them over to the woman bartering peanuts for cotton. She accepted the balls of cotton, measured them in a calabash, and then gave me the same volume of peanuts in exchange. I counted the nuts and discovered that I had received some 200 nuts for only 2 francs. When I discussed this experiment with some of the people, they admitted knowing about this practice and said that they did this at times. I then suggested that it would be possible to manipulate the system to one's advantage, but was again greeted with a show of indifference by most of my auditors. One man eventually said that I would lose because prices changed. I remain ignorant of what the real facts are, but still suspect that it may be possible to speculate on the system.

Barter is very specific in Mossi markets in the sense that not every product can be bartered against every other product. Some days rice would be bartered for cotton, and on other days only for peanuts and vice versa. It is not possible either to exchange vegetable produce for livestock, even though livestock may be exchanged for livestock. Sometimes people take chickens or guinea hens to market to exchange for goats or sheep, and often these animals are exchanged for young cattle. What is not at all clear, however, is whether or not the people see the value of the things exchanged in terms of currency value, or in terms of some value which has no reference to the European currency system. The ordinary people in the markets, like ordinary people everywhere, are not concerned with these problems as long as they believe that they are conducting their commercial activities with equity and are deriving satisfaction from them.

The most significant feature of all the Mossi markets is the segregation of certain merchants into certain areas. The makers and sellers of one product are found only in one part of the market, and anyone wishing to buy or sell these products must go to the place where they are traded. The other type of segregation is by reference to the trader's place of origin. For example, a woman who sells beer would be found in the section of the market where beer is sold, but she would be found sitting with her back towards the village or facing toward the direction from which she came. There are often some variations on this pattern. For example, if there are a large number of traders with one type of product, they will form a large open circle in which each person will sit with his or her back towards the point of origin. Inside of this circle, and separated by a few feet, would be another circle of people selling another product with their faces toward the general direction from which they came. Sitting with their backs to the people of this circle would be other people forming another circle and selling one type of product. These people would have their backs towards the region from which they came. When the group of persons selling one type of product is very small, they may form a small circle in a corner of the market with their backs towards their points of origin. All of these patterns often exist simultaneously in Mossi markets, but it is obvious that two basic configurations prevail. One configuration is in terms of goods, and facilitates trading. The other configuration is a social one and facilitates the social interaction which is an integral part of the Mossi market. This seating pattern makes it easier to find one's friends, to converse and drink with them, to find someone through whom to send messages to specific villages, to find the help needed in the event of a fight, and finally to find an escape route by which one can leave in the event of trouble.

The vendors in the larger markets of Mossi country include Yoruba, Hausa and other ethnic groups, many of whose members were born in Mossi country and have never visited the land of their fathers. The lives of these people are usually centered around the markets; where the markets are held every day, many of the men, women and children of these foreign groups spend almost all of their lives at the markets. In marked contrast to the Mossi, they usually sell products of foreign provenience, whether African or European, and seldom deal in the local products. These vendors are tolerated by the Mossi and are valued for their commerce, but are always regarded as outsiders. And as outsiders the markets do not belong to them, but only to the Mossi. Even so, the Mossi do not really like the larger markets. True, one can buy all kinds of wonderful goods on the large markets, but to the Mossi, a market is more than a place where one goes to buy and sell, even though everyone who goes there tries to do some of both.

There is a marked division of labor among the vendors in a Mossi market—a division which can be seen at its best on the local markets. Here only the women sell cooked food, beer, millet, rice, peanuts, shea-butter, tobacco, and all of the other locally grown vegetables and vegetable products, except cotton which may also be sold by a man. In contrast, women do not sell such local products as cotton cloth, hemp, jewelry, iron implements and leather goods, which are the province of the men. Only men may butcher and sell animals and meat in the market. And they alone control the commerce in foreign food articles such as salt and dried fish. Both men and women sell the valuable imported kola nut, but only men sell goods of European manufacture such as cigarettes, matches, sugar, mirrors and so on. Small girls sell calabashes of water to everyone, and small boys wander through the market selling single cigarettes, bundles of a few matches, single lumps of sugar, chickens and guinea fowls, and skewers of roasted meat.

There is little competition about someone else having "stolen" a customer. The reason for this is mainly that every person in the market is a potential customer of everyone else. Normally, a buyer simply moves from seller to seller sampling the goods if that is possible (some unscrupulous men can even get drunk in the process of "sampling" beer) and trying to get the best bargain. No seller would think of running after a customer, and customers seldom, if ever, move away from a vendor in the hope that he would be called back to be sold the article at a lower price. The result is that the pace of commerce in a Mossi market is somewhat relaxed, but the lack of intense competition prevents a great deal of hositility and quarreling among the market people.

The amount of small trading which takes place in a Mossi market is fantastic, so much so that one gains the impression that some people trade simply for the sake of trading. Everyone tries to get money so that he or she can buy some desired object, but it is impossible for one to obtain a clear idea of what kind of profit, if any, people make from their commerce. In fact, the idea of a profit does not seem to be important when people are selling their own products. Most people only think about profit when they buy things to resell—whether these things are of African or European manufacture. This, incidentally, is one of the reasons why the prices of foodstuffs are about 10 per cent lower in the country districts than at Wagadougou, and concommitently, why imported products are 10 to 20 per cent higher in the rural districts than at Wagadougou where they are bought. When a woman takes such products as cotton, beans or millet to market, she may gross about 100 francs in the course of the day. But out of this she may give a few francs to her husband to buy kola nuts, a few francs to her daughter to buy a plastic necklace, and spend the rest for a cotton skirt, a piece of meat and condiments for her sauces. Men whose wives do not bring many goods to market must usually give them about 100 francs to spend on the various products the family needs. There are no official restrictions on the kinds of goods which may or may not be sold in the Mossi markets. In pre-European times slaves and eunuchs were the common stock-in-trade of the major markets and of some of the smaller ones as well. The only active supervision that existed and still exists concerns the butchering of meat. Every person who sells meat in the market must exhibit the skin of the butchered animal in a public place so that there will be no question as to the ownership of the animal. If the meat in question is the remains of a cow killed and half-eaten by a lion, then the village or district chief must be notified before the meat enters the market. The person in charge of this task used to be, and often still is, a man called the Kos Naba, a kind of sales chief. He also formerly doubled as a tax collector for the rulers and chiefs. Another official, the Raga Naba, where he still exists, is more concerned with protecting the lives and property of the people who trade at the markets, but he also supervises the sale of some commodities there and formerly also collected taxes for his superior.

In pre-European times, every important Mossi prince and district chief had the counterpart of a Kos Naba and Raga Naba, to collect taxes in their markets. The French abolished both of these offices when they took over the country, because they looked upon them as purely exploitative rather than regulatory agents. But like so many other Mossi political institutions which the French have "abolished," the Kos Naga and Raga Naba persist in many of the districts, and perhaps even in such large centers as Wagadougou. These officials persist because one of the basic assumptions of the Mossi is that everything must have a "chief." They believe that even the animals in the bush have chiefs, and if men, too, did not have chiefs then social life would be chaos. Thus, in the rural areas many or most district chiefs have retained their market officials even though the roles of these officials have become highly attenuated and so secretive that their existence is often denied.

Taxes collected at the market places played an important part in supporting the traditional political hierarchy of the Mossi people. The Kos Naba collected 250 cowries in taxes for every beef cattle slaughtered at the market and took their humps and gave them to a palace official called the Nemdo Naba (meat chief) for distribution in the royal household. He also collected 250 cowries on every cow sold there, but did not usually tax goats and sheep. In lieu of this he occasionally took a head or two of these animals from each herd that passed through the market and sent them to the palace kitchens. Donkeys were also taxed at the rate of 200 cowries per head sold in the market. Horses sold to the nobility were not taxed, but those exported were taxed about 300 cowries.

The Raga Naba collected the taxes on other commodities sold at market. Cotton weavers paid him taxes according to the size of their bolts of cloth, and cotton producers paid as much as 20 cowries on especially large sales of their raw produce. The tailors and dyers paid no fixed tax on their wares, but were asked to send clothing to the palace. Every donkey- or ox-load of salt which entered the market place was assessed a tax of 300 cowries. The smiths were not taxed in cowries, but had to supply the wives of the Moro Naba with hoes and the palace personnel with arrowheads, spearpoints and iron clubs. The jewelers also sent bracelets as presents to the ruler. There were no fixed taxes on cereals, vegetables and cooked food sold at market, but each day the Raga Naba, accompanied by several pages or retainers carrying baskets, went from vendor to vendor taking several calabash-fuls of their produce for use in the palace. In addition, the vendors of cooked food had to feed the young grooms of the Moro Naba who were not regularly fed by the palace household. The beer sellers, too, while they were not assessed taxes, contributed a good percentage of their beverage to palace and market personnel who demanded the customary "taste" with greater frequency and freedom than did ordinary buyers. But the most valuable tax collected by the Raga Naba was on the sale of slaves, whose buyers paid a tax of 1,000 cowries per head.

There is some evidence, mainly from Europeans, that the Mossi occasionally may have found the market taxes prohibitive. Binger reports that during his visit to the Mossi in 1888, the high taxes exacted by the Moro Naba were "one of the causes which placed Wagadougou in second place [as a market town] and which made Mane the commercial capital of Mossi country" (Binger 1892 : 467). Binger, himself, was caught in the institutionalized gift system and wrote sarcastically: "The day of the market [at Wagadougou] the receipts are good. People bring every-thing to the palace including millet as well as hoes or peanuts, and everything is accepted. *All this giving is left to the generosity of the customers . . .*" (Binger 1892 : 465) (his italics). Even so, one cannot be sure that the Mossi felt the same way about paying taxes to their rulers as Binger felt. There is, incidentally, always an air of mutual recriminations among the Mossi and their rulers about the level of reciprocation between them. The people admit that the chiefs are indispensable; yet they complain that they are greedy—they "eat" too much. The chiefs insist that it is difficult to rule a territory and complain that the people are ungrateful.

SOCIAL AND RITUAL ASPECTS OF THE MARKETPLACE

Although the offices of Kos Naba and Raga Naba have been abolished officially, these officials still exist in many Mossi districts, and even when they do not exist, some men acting in their stead appropriate commodities in the markets for the chiefs. Furthermore, the *nakomce* (plural of *nabiga*—chief's child) or nobles still wander about the market places taking handfuls of kola nuts, peanuts and everything they need without the people becoming angry or complaining to the French about it. Once when I visited a market in the company of a *nabiga,* the local Raga Naba came up to where we were buying meat and indicated to the butcher that one of his customers was a *nabiga* and that he should treat him accordingly. It is not because of ignorance that the market people continue to grant these privileges to the nobles and the chiefs, but rather because they believe that only the market officials, and not the Europeans, can take care of the markets.

One of the most important tasks of the Raga Naba (or in the absence of this official, the Kos Naba) is to propitiate the *tengkouga* in the market place, or supervise the sacrifices which the *tengsobas* make to them. The task of the market spirits is believed to be so difficult—

due to the bickering, quarreling and even fighting they have to prevent by cooling the tempers of the market people—that they become quite angry. When the spirits are not satisfied, they fail in their tasks and real trouble breaks out in the market, disrupting the trading; and if they are not pacified they may even cause the death of the market officials.[12]

In the days before the market officials were banned, these sacrifices were performed regularly. At that time the Raga Naba simply asked the Kos Naba to seize the appropriate animal in the market to perform the rite. The problem today is that since the French have abolished the office of Raga Naba, and in some districts have prevented the chief from even naming one secretly, the markets in the latter localities are considered "dangerous markets." Once a market acquires such a reputation, people do not like to visit it because they fear that they would get into fights or quarrels. Not only this, but it is believed that if a market has been without a Raga Naba for a long time, the *tengkouga* there become so angry for being neglected that they kill the first chief appointed to it. This was the reality or belief behind a series of misadventures of which I was the victim.

I had spent an entire day in a market, and on returning home could not find my pen. The next morning I sent an assistant to the chief telling him about the loss and asking him to have an announcement made in the market on the next market day that I would pay a handsome reward to whomever should find and deliver the pen. The chief sent back a reply saying that since there was no Raga Naba, he would have the Kos Naba acquaint the people with my loss. On the day of the market, I waited until midday, when most of the people had arrived, and then went to see whether the Kos Naba had any news of the pen. I checked with several of my friends to see whether they had heard about the pen and discovered, to my chagrin, that no announcement had been made about it. I went and told the Kos Naba that the people were not hearing about the pen and suggested that one way to do so would be to have the Binderes (drummers and griots) circulate through the market announcing the loss. The Kos Naba refused to do this, and when I enlisted the aid of the chief's secretary, he, too, said that it could not be done because there was no Raga Naba. I had some notes on the institution of the Raga Naba, but as I did not know everything about it, I was, therefore, frankly puzzled

---

(12) Zahan (1954 : 371) states that "the place where all kinds of merchandise accumulate and where strangers come is a place charged with forces. In time, these forces build up to such a point within the precincts of the market that some purifications are necessary to liberate them. To omit making them would expose the participants to excitements leading to brawls and compromising the place of the transactions."

and a bit peeved at not being able to put my idea into practice. I next sought the advice and consolation of an elder noble who listened quite calmly and then said: "The customs of these kafirs (heathens) are foolish." Being a Moslem, my friend was very often critical of the pagans, and could be relied upon to explain why their customs were "foolish." He said that in former days the Raga Naba would have climbed a tree and announced to the crowd any message from the district chief. Moreover, he was the custodian of all lost articles and restored them to their owners. The Moslem said that my request could not be granted because there was no Raga Naba, and that probably there would never be another. When the French first banned the institution, the local chief dismissed the Raga Naba. With the passage of years, however, the market became so dangerous that the chief tried to appoint another ex-serf to the job. This man soon died, and his successor died shortly after being appointed. Since that time the chief has made no attempt to name a new market chief.

With this new knowledge I called my aide and inquired from him whether this information was true and if so, why did he not tell me the true state of affairs. His reply was that he did not wish to say that the market was bad because the local people believed that they had solved the problem of the lack of a Raga Naba. When the last Raga Naba died, the chief decided not to name a new one, but in order to placate the market *tengkouga,* he ordered his *tengsoba* to make sacrifices to it. It was believed that these sacrifices would be acceptable as long as the officiant did not bear the title of Raga Naba. The other functions of the Raga Naba, such as collecting goods for the chief and preserving peace in the market, were taken over by the Kos Naba and another servant of the chief. However, the Kos Naba had to be careful lest he overstep his authority in such a way as would acquaint the *tengkouga* with the real situation. In my case, the chief was acting by trying to get the Kos Naba to acquaint the people with my loss in as inconspicuous a manner as possible. The consensus was that the Kos Naba would have risked his life had he made any kind of announcement to the market people, because the *tengkouga* would have thought that he was the new Raga Naba, and if not contented with the people would have killed him. Under these circumstances, I withdrew my request. I discovered later that my pen was not lost but had been in the hut all the time.

Those chiefs who have succeeded in retaining their market officials even secretly have been able to maintain their control over public behavior there. The Mossi are fairly law-abiding despite the persistence among them of a warrior tradition. Every man who goes to market, or anywhere for that matter, usually carries a baton over his shoulder; but when he arrives in the market, he calmly places his weapon on top of one of the sheds before he makes his rounds. The women do not carry any weapons to market except their "words" but even these are not often used because of the desire to avoid hostility— which the Mossi do not like to have disrupt one of their major institutions.

The rural market is the center of Mossi social life, and friends as well as enemies meet within its confines. What Mangin wrote some forty years ago is still true: "Every self-respecting Mossi—man or woman, child or elder—must go to market at least once in a while, were it only to look . . . and to be looked at, if he can put on some handsome clothes" (Mangin 1921 : 53). Except for the Moslems who are now experimenting with a form of Purdah, there are few persons who do not go to market. The absence of someone from the market for more than two consecutive occasions is a sure sign of illness, travel, or family crisis. As one man said to me, "I must go to market, and when I get there I look for three persons: my girl friend, my debtor and my enemy. If I do now know whether any of them are at the market I am ill at ease. And when I go to the market and do not see them all, the market is not good."

The lively character of the Mossi market will be discussed later, but throughout this kaleidoscope of activities certain consistencies can be discerned. For example, one notices many different kinds of greetings and salutations in the market place, but each one of them correctly indicates the exact relation or relationship between the persons involved. Young girls on passing each other on one of their innumerable circuits of the market bend their knees slightly and place both of their cupped hands on their own breasts. Only then will they stop and exchange news. At the end of the conversa. 'on they repeat the same greeting and continue their rounds. Both girls and women greet casual male acquaintances in the same way, but invariably kneel if the male stops and talks to them. Women sometime kneel when speaking to each other, but always do so when addressing any male relative of a respected category, who may then send them on errands such as buying tobacco from the vendors. A man who meets a female benefactor, such as a woman who has given medicine to one of his children, invariably kneels down before her. She may do the same thing out of respect for his male status. However, when a man meets either his mother-in-law or his father's sister, he is the one to kneel down in order to greet her. Two men who are equals normally shake hands, but if not, the junior in status or in age kneels down before his elder or superior. Sometimes a high status man will prevent his greeter from kneeling by raising him. When greeting a lower status benefactor, a man will get down and greet him from a kneeling position. It is because of this elaborate system of greeting, with the many opportunities thus provided for one person to slight another, that many important persons never go to the market. As a rule, the failure of any one person to give the required greeting to another when they meet in the market place is always an indication of strained relations between them.

The persons from whom an individual may buy goods, and the kinds of goods which may be purchased by one individual from another, are governed by convention and social relationships. A person may not buy anything from a relative except European goods. A man cannot buy any but cooked food in the market place, and often he asks a female relative or a passing female to buy it for him. To do the contrary is held to be unmanly and indicative of a bad character. A woman will not buy cotton cloth but will send a man to buy it for her. She would hate to have people believe that she has no male relative to weave it for her, or what is more likely, that she is too lazy to spin the cotton thread which would then be woven for her. A woman may purchase any type of commodity from other women, but she must be careful not to patronize men who are known to be libertines or with whom she is suspected of having an affair. She must also be careful about running errands for men, since people know that men often use this device to establish amorous relationships with women. Men also use this device to give presents, or to arrange secret meetings with them. If any man sees a female relative involved in any of these misadventures, he chases her away and more than likely curses the man, if he does not fight him. In any event, he warns the man to leave the woman alone.

The market is one of the few places where men and women can initiate relationships not sanctioned by their relatives. Under normal conditions marriages are arranged between unrelated individuals through the lineage members who establish "friendly" relationships. Two friends might ask their lineage heads for women to exchange as wives or the "friend" who has received more gifts from the other will give over a wife. Because the older men most often have goods and women at their disposal, they are usually the ones who receive wives. The result is that most young men have no wives, and until they inherit wives from lineage members, are continually seeking to establish intimate relations with women whom they meet on the market place. The technique which a young man employs to gain the favors of a woman he sees at market is highly stereotyped. First of all, he must ascertain that the woman in question is not a member of his maximal lineage or married to a member of his own lineage. A responsible man even refrains from making overtures to a woman whose husband's female relatives may be married to a member of his own lineage. He fears that a wronged husband may have the wives of his lineage brothers recalled, thus causing dissension within and between the two lineages. If none of these complications are present, a man seeks out a person who knows the woman and sends a message declaring his intentions. If the response is favorable, the man then buys four large kola nuts (four being the number for a woman), wraps them together with 44 francs, and send them to his lady. This procedure may be followed on subsequent market days without the two parties ever coming into direct contact with each other. Finally, however, a rendezvous is arranged, and on the pretense of leaving the market to visit a relative for several days, the woman goes instead to her lover's village.

These casual affairs started at the market sometimes become quite serious, and if for any reason they are sanctioned by the relatives of either the man or the woman, they often lead to the breakup of a marriage. And since the market is the place where disputants of any sort most likely come into contact, it is here that fights over "stolen" wives break out.

This pattern of extramarial relationships centering around the market place is so common among the Mossi that the younger men, and even some of the older ones, are disappointed with the "market" when their mistresses do not appear. Mossi men who sit under the shelters around the market place can usually give an inquirer not only the name of a woman, the name and village of her husband and father, but also the name and village of her paramour. Characteristically enough, they are always "ignorant" of the escapades of their own female relatives or of the wives of their lineage members. The only time when men act as though their relatives might be involved in extramarital affairs is when for some purpose or another a man has to recall a wife or daughter who has gone to visit a relative in another village or district. Regardless of how pressing the problem may be, a man will seldom go directly to his father-in-law's house to recall the woman. He goes to the market nearest to his in-laws' village, and seeks his wife there. If he does not find her or any of her relatives, he goes to the part of the market in which people from her village sell their products and sends a message to her family that he will come for her the next day, or that he would like her to come home.

A market place is also one of the best places to look for news of a runaway wife, or of any stranger in an area. The Mossi say that women have footprints like an elephant in that they can be found quite easily, but that the footprints are always clearest in the market.

What this really means is that the market is the main communication center of Mossi society and news of happenings in the region can be heard there. If a person is in an area one can be sure that the people in the market will know about him, or that he will sooner or later visit the market.

The young men who have returned from work in the cacao fields or towns of Ghana and the Ivory Coast add a great deal of color and excitement to the rural markets of contemporary Mossi country. During the time these young men spend away, they give a great deal of thought and planning to the show they hope to put on when they make the grand tour *(mane do)* of their district's market place. The best day for this is the day of the "great market" and regardles of what day many migrants return to their homes, they wait for that Friday before they show themselves publicly.

On the morning of that day, the typical migrant dresses in his best clothes, lends the remainder of his wardrobe to relatives, and together they go to pay homage to the chief during the morning ceremony *(Wend pous yan)*. The migrant offers the chief such presents as a small amount of money, an article of clothing or kola nuts, and replies to the chief's questions about the health and welfare of all Mossi in the area whence the migrant came, the whereabouts of "lost" migrants, the nature of the work the migrants were doing, and so on. As soon as the young man receives the chief's permission to leave, he goes to the market where he is quickly surrounded by *griots* who accompany him in periodic circumambulations of the market place, drumming and singing praises in honor of his ancestry. The migrant is also greeted warmly by his many friends to whom he then gives presents of money, beer and kola nuts. He acknowledges the general praise for having brought goods and clothing for his relatives and takes pride in seeing these relatives dressed in the cloths and clothing he has brought them. If young and unmarried, the migrant also seeks to take advantage of his new-found importance to make the first overtures to available young women or to renew his relationship with former paramours. Towards evening before going home, he rewards the *griots* with money and bear. Many a migrant attempts to prolong this feeling of grandeur by visiting other markets and by dressing up on subsequent grand market days, but after a few weeks he is re-incorporated into the ordinary market routine, and has to make room for the other newly-arrived migrants.

The market is also the place where important rites marking the changing social status of individuals are carried out. Under normal circumstances, the ceremonies attending the birth of a Mossi child are performed at home. When a woman has a number of stillbirths or

loses her children when they are still babies, however, it is believed
than these children were embodiments of the same *kinkirsi* (spirits)
who must be tricked into remaining on earth when it returns, and
the market place is chosen as the site for this trickery. As soon as such
a woman gives birth to a child, and old woman places it in a basket
and on the next market day takes it to the market place. Her intention
is to "sell" the child in the hope that it would not die if owned by
someone other than its mother. The old woman walks around the
market place shouting: "I have something to sell!" Invariably a man
will walk up to her, and after ascertaining the contents of the basket,
offer to buy it. The price varies with the fortune of the man, but
traditionally the amount paid has been 500 cowries or their equivalent. The man takes the child for a few minutes and then returns
it to its vendor, telling her in a loud voice so that the kinkirsi will
hear: "I would like you to give this child to 'X' (the child's mother)
to be reared for me and I will pay for its upbringing and will come
for the child in a few years. He then gives the child the name *Yamba*
(slave), or *Yemdaogo* (male slave) if male and *Yempoko* (female slave)
if a girl. The old woman then returns the child to its mother, relating
what has passed in the market and indicating who the "owner" of her
child is. The "owner" of the child may not even see the child again,
and naturally does not take this ownership seriously. In many cases
the money with which he bought the child was given to him by the
child's father.

The market also plays an important part in the circumcision and
incision ceremonies of Mossi boys and girls. For about two to three
months after the actual operations the young children, especially the
boys are secluded in the circumcision lodges or compounds and have
almost no contact with the village population. Their re-introduction
to society always takes place on the great market day. The parents of
the children buy new clothing for them this occasion, and on the
appointed day the boys or girls parade together in the market and are
offered gifts by the market people. Later in the day, they are dismissed
and individually feted by their relatives.

Owing to the relatively unceremonious nature of Mossi marriages,
the market does not play a role in Mossi weddings. However, the
same thing cannot be said about the last important *rite de passage,*
especially the funeral of a chief, or important elder. Prior to the intervention of the French, and to a lesser extent even today, the announcement of the death of an important ruler was seen as the breakdown of law and order and was ritually dramatized by a popular raid
on the markets throughout the territories (Skinner : ms). During the
interregnum the vendors are subject to constant raids by members of

the noble class, whose actions embody the ideology that the exercise of sovereignty is a corporate right which reverts to all of them when the head ruler dies. Much of this raiding is symbolic and does not interrupt market activities.

Many of the ceremonies connected with the funeral of chiefs and respected deceased elders take place in the market. Sometime between the interment of the dead person, the *keema,* and the first burial ceremonies, the sister-in-law *(dakia)* of the dead man in her role as joking relative—a role she plays until the funeral ceremonies are completed—impersonates him in the market place. On the day chosen for this rite the *dakia* dresses in the clothes of the *keema* and goes to market. While there, she acts as she observed her brother-in-law to have acted in the past: she circles the market and buys goods; she buys beer from his favorite beer seller and drinks with his friends; and for a moment, at least, she sits with his old cronies in their favorite haunts and takes part in their discussions. She may even be serenaded by *griots* who sing praises in honor of "her" ancestors, and she rewards them before leaving the market place that evening.

The market is the scene of an important ritual during the final funeral ceremonies, which are held about one year after a man was buried. On the morning of this ceremony the female relatives of the *keema,* led by his eldest daughter and his *dakia,* appear in the market and go from stall to stall buying all the things the deceased used in his lifetime. These include meat, *zumbala* (locust bean balls), cotton, tobacco, salt, kola nuts, peppers, *kumba* (a tomato), cakes, cooked millet-mush balls, potatoes, etc. When they have gathered all of these things, they retire to a spot near the market where they lay out all the foodstuff in baskets. In the meantime, the drummers play the royal airs, if the dead man was a chief, or ordinary rhythms if he was a commoner. Then the *keema's* eldest daughter places a basket on her head and, accompanied by four men, leads a procession of drummers and of the other women, also with their baskets, around the market. While this procession is circling the market three times in honor of the deceased, the *dakia,* carrying a very old basket containing the stalest food she could find, weaves back and forth through the marching throng making a nuisance of herself. After the third round the marchers return to their assembly point whence the eldest daughter and some of the older women now rush into the market, stealing merchandise from the stalls and placing it in their baskets. This assault is often so quickly done that it is fairly successful. The raiders then join the other mourners at the assembly point, where with bowed heads they listen respectfully while the chief drummer recites the genealogy of the *keema* and tells him that the people from the surrounding villages and districts were present to honor him. This being completed, the *griots* are paid, everyone rises and shouts *Ne Wardo* (the salutation at funerals), and that part of the funeral ceremony during which a man takes leave of the market community is concluded. Now his relatives, descendants and friends all return to the market, whose sights and sounds make it an integral part of the life cycle of the Mossi—the one institution of their society in which almost everyone participates actively.

Preparation for a market day, especially the tri-weekly Friday market or *Raga kasanga,* usually begins on Thursday. This day is characterized by a great deal of activity: preparing the commodities which are to be sold the next day, washing body and clothes, and combing hair. The women who prepare the beer and fried foods work late into the night preparing their wares, and a visit to the homes of the *griots* finds them preparing their drums. The little boys who go to the roadside to chant Moslem prayers to the passers-by, and the little girls who sell water to these strangers redouble their efforts until late on Thursday night to get enough money to buy presents in the market the next day. Finally, when it is quite late and the beer-making fires are out, everyone retires until the morning of the market.

At 7:00 A.M. on Friday the market is deserted except for a leper who sweeps out the stalls of the sellers in return for bits of food or presents of money. Looking at the empty stalls, one has a certain amount of difficulty imagining that this spot will be crowded with human beings five hours hence. But one is also conscious of the fact that even at this early hour scores of persons have already left their homes in distant villages and are on their way to market loaded with produce and with high hopes for the day. About 9:00 A.M. the first women arrive, balancing net-covered bundles on their heads, and take their positions in the various sections of the market with either face or back pointing to the direction from which they came. By 9:30 A.M. the butchers have arrived with their bleating sheep and goats and an aged cow. The first beer sellers have also arrived and are giving "sips" to men before they settle down to sustained drinking.

The pace of the market quickens about 10:30, and in the distance the first tap of the Bindere's drum resounds. All of a sudden, the market seems to have become a giant magnet, drawing long lines of people towards it along every path and from every direction. Women dressed in brightly colored print cloths and dresses, with babies straddling their backs and the inevitable bundles on their head, saunter into their places. Young children run ahead of their mothers or stumble behind them. Those vendors of European products who customarily transport their goods in boxes on bicycles arrive in the market and set up their small tables to display all types of goods from trinkets to single lumps of sugar. And the more numerous young men, who have no goods but have money in their pockets, go to the leaf-covered sheds, place their weapons on top of them, and take seats from which to view the passing parade. Imperceptibly, the hum in the market increases as people find their places and greet one another with *Ne Raga*, the market greeting, until by 11:30 A.M. the whole market reverberates with sounds of drumming, cries of vendors, and the shrill voice of water hawkers and juvenile vendors. Now the market is in full swing.

From midday until about 3:30 P.M., the Mossi market is a sea of humanity—talking, laughing, arranging rendezvous, quarreling, selling, buying, parading, and (where youngsters are concerned) often crying for want of money to buy a desired object. The return of migrants lends additional color and excitement to the market as these young people walk about in their new clothes, encouraging the drummers to sing louder praises, the maidens to feel jealous of the clothes of the migrants' female relatives, the former migrants to reminisce about the days when they too had bright new clothes, and the young boys to dream of going off one day to obtain the things they need.

Men, noting that their female relatives are spending too much time looking over the wares of a vendor of European products or of the kola-nut seller, wander over ostensibly to help in the purchase but really to prevent love affairs. The failure to observe such a precaution may be the cause of the shouting a man hears in the distance, and off he hurries to see whether a lineage brother or a friend may need his aid. He may either get into the battle himself, or aid the Raga Naba and the other elders to chase the battlers out of the market place, or to take them to the chief. This may indeed restore some peace and good fellowship to the market.

Elders, now more interested in beer than in other pleasures, pass the heat of the market day under the beer sellers' shed. From time to time one of them may be interrupted by a young man bringing him three kola nuts, one or two of which are immediately broken and given to friends. However, when an oldster, whether a drinking pagan or a Moslem teetaler, sees or overhears a young man buying four kolas, he may frown or smile in the knowledge that mischief is afoot. Loud-voiced predictions of the consequences of evil-doing may suddenly disturb the merrymakers as American missionaries speaking in perfect More (the language of the Mossi) appear and harangue the market people. Then, as suddenly, the *Americadamba* depart in their large cars, and the curious pagans, amused Catholics or hostile Moslems who had gathered to hear the gospel return to their "evil" and "non-evil" ways. A little later the young men who possess bicycles may be seen suddenly hurrying to avoid the other *nansara,* this time, the French official, who comes into the market to apprehend those individuals who have not bought a bicycle license. All the *nansara* know that the market is the best place to find a Mossi.

Towards 3:00 P.M. the matrons in the market, having sold most of their own goods and bought those which they need, make the last rounds to see whether there are any bargains to be had. In their rounds the women may be badgered by sons, daughters and other relatives, but seldom by husbands, for extra francs to buy kolas or tobacco to bridge them over the two non-market days. Or the women themselves may seek out their male relatives to buy kola or goods, from the stranger who is making the rounds of the local markets. By this time of day the market place is emptying—at first this happens so imperceptibly that one does not notice it. However, by 4:00 P.M. a mass exodus begins as women collect their little children, hitch their babies on their backs, place baskets on their head and set out in the direction of their own villages or to the villages of relatives where they plan to spend time. By this hour also the Bendere are drunk, and for an extra calabash of beer are willing to recount genealogies for which, if sober, they would demand a sheep or goat.

Evening finds the market deserted except for scavenging dogs which hunt the scraps of food dropped by the now departed human beings. The market place finally falls silent, until late at night passing migrants retire there to sleep. These persons leave the market place at dawn to buy food from the women whose hawking cries herald another day of roadside commerce. The women use the profit from this trade to buy goods on the following market days.

CHAPTER 10

Social and Economic Factors Affecting Markets in Guro Land

BY CLAUDE MEILLASSOUX[1]

The Guro number approximately 100,000 people, the great majority of whom live inside the limits of the administrative district called *Cercle de Bouaflé* in Ivory Coast. Our observations were limited to the Guro living inside this district.[2]

The Guro country is roughly divided into two ecological areas: on the southwestern side of the Marahoue River, an affluent of the Bandama, lies the tropical forest. As we proceed towards the northeast, the forest thins out and savannah gradually replaces the forest. But up to the northern limits, large patches of forest or forest galleries remain: it is what is commonly called the savannah-forest.

A fraction of the Guro people occupy the tropical forest country in the southwestern part of Guro country. The density is comparatively low[3]: in Sinfra Subdivision clusters of villages (or "tribes") are separated from each other by wide unoccupied stretches of forest. A greater population is settled in the northeastern section of savannah-forest. There the density is higher and the villages are spread more uniformly[4]. The high density of this area contrasts with the southern forest land also with the savannah-country to the north.

The occupation of the country by the Guro is probably 250 to 300 years old. They stem, according to Delafosse, from the Mande-Fu stock, and seem to be related to western populations such as the Dan, the Guere, the Kru, and in the west and southwest, the Bete. On their progress eastward, they met the matrilineal Baule on the Bandama River. The northern neighbors of the Guro are of the Malinke group, commonly called *Vaa*[5] by northern Guro while they have no

(1) This paper is based on research carried out in Ivory Coast in 1958 under the auspices of *l'École Pratique des Hautes Études* (VIe Section Centre d'Études Africaines) Paris, and with the supplementary aid of a scholarship from *l'École Française d'Afrique* (Dakar).

(2) The *Cercle de Bouaflé* is divided into three Subdivisions: Zuenoula to the North, Bouaflé in the center and Sinfra to the South.

(3) In Sinfra Subdivision, the average density of the Guro population varies from 4.8 to 7.5 to the square km. In Bouflé, from 4.1 to 7.1.

(4) Density in Zuenoula Subdivision averages 21.1. Some Guro *cantons* reach 40 to the square kilometer.

(5) They are today commonly called Dioula, a generic term associated with traders and applied to any individual of Guinean or Sudanese origin, peddling or trading in the southern part of Ivory Coast.

indigenous name among the southern Guro. To the south the Guro are bounded by the Gagou, a population with whom they have various similarities, according to Tauxier's work (Tauxier 1924).

Money-cropping has become the main economic activity of present-day Guro. Their agricultural vocation is a new one, having actually started around 1950 with the development of coffee growing and the end of forced labor. In the indigenous system, the main male activity was hunting; many cultural or social features were linked to this activity. They practice shifting agriculture, the bulk of work depending on the woman. Men do only the bush-clearing and miscellaneous tasks. Cattle breeding has completely disappeared since the extermination of the stock during the French conquest. In any case it was not very important and limited to a trypanosomiasis-resistant dwarf-cattle of southern origin. Milk or dairy products were not consumed. Cattle were, for the most part, used as matrimonial compensation, at funeral occasions and for sacrifices.

The Guro people are patrilineal and patrilocal. The main social and economic unit is the lineage *(Goniwoo)* counting from 25 to 200 individuals.[6] The head of the lineage is the *Goniwoozan.* Two to six lineages may live together in a village. In some cases, they derive from a putative common ancestor, but more often the different *Goniwoo* populating a village come from various parts of the country.

The *Goniwoo* is roughly an exogamic unit (though exogamic rules do not always coincide exactly with it). Marriage is sanctioned by a matrimonial compensation paid by the groom or his family to the bride's guardian. This compensation guarantees the paternity of the husband on all children born of the woman for whom it is given. Polygamy and divorce are frequent.

Inheritance of titles, duties and of some prestige goods goes from the elder brother to the next one in such a way that family control remains in the hands of the elders.

The Guro have no boys' or girls' initiation. Knowledge is transmitted in casual ways, through story-telling or mere imitation.

Remote from the Sudanese area where kingdoms rose and fell, off the main slave-hunting area, and commanding large available space, the Guro enjoyed comparative security and peace. The low density and the absence of outer threats did not contribute to the constitution of a centralized power. Actually, the Guro have no word for "chief." Inside the village, the pre-eminent position was acknowledged in

---

(6) Some of the large *Goniwoo* are divided into sub-lineages averaging around 50 people. The notion of *Goniwoo* is itself not everywhere precise in the mind of the Guro. They were probably driven to give it a more concrete meaning under administrative pressure and for tax purposes.

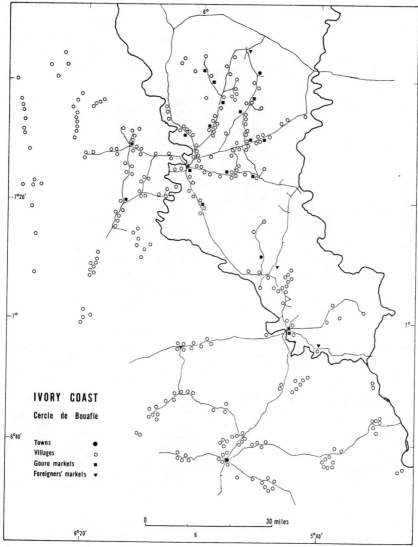

FIGURE 12
Towns, Villages, Foreigners' Markets and Guro Markets

favor of an elder, or wiser or "richer" *Goniwoozan* who was consulted
on various litigious affairs. But he had, of course, no power to enforce
his ruling which had to be backed up by social consensus. Occasionally, this peacemaker could be the head of the warriors and the earth
master. But in many cases, the various elements of communal power
were shared among several individuals: the peacemaker, the earth

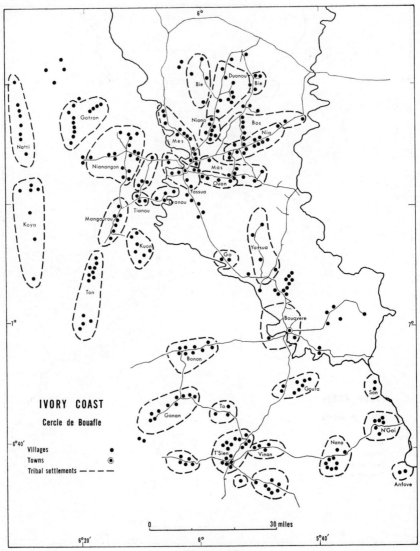

FIGURE 13
Tribal Settlements of the Guro

master, the wizard, the warrior, etc. Furthermore, the pre-eminency might shift from one family to the other, due to various circumstances among which the variation in the number of people controlled by each *Goniwoozan*.

The same political pattern developed among several villages, either of common descent or linked together by a formal alliance. Such groups of villages would be known under a collective name. Though the word "tribe" or any equivalent was unknown to the Guro, this is what the administrators call them today. These villages were usually allied in war, and settled their conflict through conciliation or through "brother-war," differentiated from war against alien groups.

Furthermore, a "tribe" might develop a formal alliance with another "tribe," which meant again that conflicts occurring between individuals or families or villages of opposite groups would be settled through judiciary process. But it did not imply military alliance.

Between unallied groups of villages, the normal process of solving conflicts was war. War occurred exclusively in connection with women (elopements, murders). But women were respected during these wars, since their destruction would have been self-defeating. It meant that they could freely travel during these periods of insecurity and continue the trading activities of which they were active agents.

MARKET DISTRIBUTION AND TRADE IN PRE-COLONIAL TIMES

Forest vs. Savannah-Forest.

The map showing traditional markets in the Guro country, reveals a striking difference between the southern part, where markets were nonexistant, and the northern area, where they were extremely numerous.[7]

This distribution coincides both with an ecological feature—savannah-forest vs. forest—and with the density variations of the population. This market distribution suggests two hypotheses. Either the savannah-forest milieu creates a need for exchange between complementary areas or a high density of population promotes a greater trading activity.

Substantiating evidence for these hypotheses is not conclusive. In this transitional ecological area, patches of forest can be found up to the northern part of the Guro country, while savannah area exists down to the southwestern limits. Hence no sector of the population is excluded from either savannah or forest resources. Villages are frequently established at a place where savannah and forest join, and the people exploit both environments.

Soil types and physical features are fairly uniform all through the country. Hence, the need for complementary exchanges between neighboring groups does not seem to have been imperative. Actually, the total absence of markets in the southern area shows that, on staple

(7) I was given the names and locations of thirty-one marketplaces existing before colonial times in the area now known as Zuenoula Sub-Division.

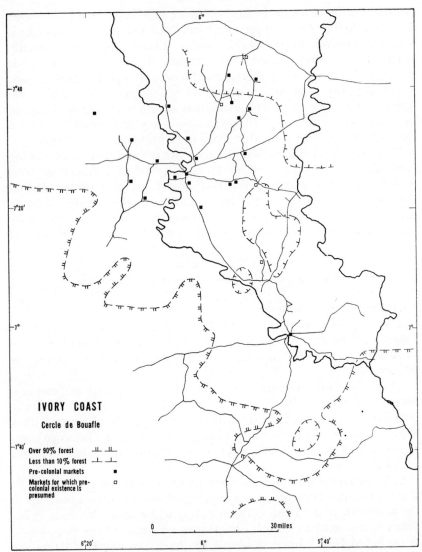

IVORY COAST

Cercle de Bouafle

Over 90% forest

Less than 10% forest

Pre-colonial markets ■

Markets for which pre-
colonial existence is
presumed □

0　　　　　　　30 miles

FIGURE 14
Relation of Markets to Forests

food and local resources at least, each group could live self-sufficiently.

If, on the other hand, high density involves greater trading activity, it remains to explain the higher density of the savannah-forest area. Any superiority of this milieu sufficient to lead to three or four times the density found in the forest is not patent.

Traditional agriculture undergoes only minor variations from one end of the country to the other. Crops are the same all over: essentially rice, yams and bananas with emphasis on rice in the forest and yams in the savannah. Rice is more appreciated but yams are said to have a better yield in the forest and the forest is the natural environment for bananas (plaintains). Clearing the ground offers greater difficulties in the forest than in the savannah, but the effort is repaid by greater yield.

Due to the distribution of savannah and forest all over the country, game was to be found equally abundant everywhere and hunting was equally good. In the forest, it was said that villages were often founded near good hunting grounds. The northern part, opened towards the sudan country, did not offer greater security or protection against possible invasion. Forest, on the contrary, was an efficient barrier against the cavalry of the northern conquerors.

A greater density, then, might have occurred from an unachieved historical migration towards the forest. But, here again, the facts do not support the assumption: the main stream of migration, according to village traditions, was moving from the southwest to the northeast, that is, from the forest area to the savannah.

A population density map of the Ivory Coast shows clearly that this area of savannah forest is an island of density: 20 per square kilometer against 5 to 10 in both the southern forest and in the more northern savannah. No modern circumstances explain this higher density left over from the pre-colonial period. It shows, therefore, the exceptional quality of this area both in relation to the savannah and to the forest and it must be explained in relation to both.[8]

Therefore, if it is true that higher density promotes greater trading activity we must also consider the reverse proposition that great trading activity entails a higher density. In order to support this assumption, we must enlarge our field of observation and consider the Guro country in the network of exchanges of pre-colonial western Africa.

Staple vs. Prestige Goods.

It it well-known that the countries of the Sudan were supplied with kola nuts by the forest peoples. It is not so often emphasized that forest population (this is, at least, the case of the Guro) completely lacked iron ore, while iron was essential for all kinds of economic activities: weapons for hunting or agricultural implements.[9]

(8) If we observe today a rather feeble reverse move towards the forest, it is due to a better cover for coffee growing. But this concerns only small families, and people of the savannah do not show any intention to follow *en masse*.

(9) Even if we admit that primitively the Guro could do without iron—though we

The consumption of kola by the Sudanese peoples was quite high, enough to induce sustained external trade. The exchange of iron for kola became the basis for all further exchanges between the two complementary areas: the Sudanese savannah and the tropical forest.

Local informants claim that the Vaa (or Dioula) also used to buy food such as yams, rice and cassava. In exchange, they brought soap, relishes, trinkets and medicine. They also paid for food with iron, in the form of iron rods *of standard size,* called *sombe* by the Dioula and *bro* by the Guro.[10]

During the Samory war, trade of foodstuff became a real necessity for the Almamy's armies. Though some villages fled on his approach, the country was not pillaged. On the contrary, trade took place and captives were exchanged to the Guro at the rate of one slave for a single basket of cassava or for half the quantity of *sombe* previously paid.

The opportunity of converting foodstuffs into *sombe* or even into slaves,[11] induced the opening of many markets. In several instances it is reported that markets were created by a rich man (or, occasionally, a rich woman) who had yams, chicken or kola in great quantity to sell to the passing Dioula traders.

To this traditional African stream of exchange, oriented north-south, another one, induced from the European pre-colonial trade, was added. The bulk of European products, though also coming in small quantities from the Sudanese area, reached Guro country through the Baule.[12] The most important of these goods were guns

found no record of such a situation—from the time when iron was introduced, it set a standard of culture which once known could hardly be given up.

(10) One could collect "prices" of food in rods, such as 4 rods for a chicken or one rod for some quantity of rice. It is almost impossible, however, to get any information of the *extent* of the use of rods on the subsistence level. But several economic and social data can be taken into consideration: the iron rods, a convenient aliquote and durable item, undoubtedly pervaded the local trade in market places, but since their use on the subsistence level was a way to break into the prestige sphere of exchange, it was also resisted by the conservative elements in Guro society. On the other hand, only large quantities of *sombe* were considered prestigious (I was told that some rich men owned as much as several granaries of *sombe*). Hence, to the extent that sombe could be earned through trade of subsistence goods or other non-prestige items by commoners, their hoarding value may have overshadowed their use for purchasing. Therefore, the iron rods did not have the same "quality" once inside Guro society, where they tended to be preserved as prestige goods, as they had between the Guro and their northern neighbors where they played the role of a currency.

(11) The exchange of slaves for food was a very exceptional one for the Guro, and was linked with war emergency.

(12) The Fage historical map No. 29 shows clearly the main points of impact of the European trade. The closest trading ports were in Assinie (1705) and then in Grand Lahu (1787). Local information confirms that European goods came from these directions. (Fage, 1958).

and powder. They were carried by successive exchanges towards the savannah country. Hence the Guro were in a privileged situation, producing a commodity—kolas—highly demanded by the savannah people and being on the route of goods coming from two outside sources.

To this, let us add that cattle and traditional craft goods were exchanged with the Bete and the Gagou to the south.

Now the question occurs as to why trading points developed on the Vaa border and not near the Baule country. The factors in such an explanation are many. The kola trade remained basic, since it was the source of iron. Kola is consumed in vast quantities by the Sudanese peoples, and is of comparatively small value in relation to its weight. It also requires careful packing and handling. Thus a large number of people were interested in the handling and transportation of large quantities of kolas. Though the Guro were not commercially minded, in the modern sense of the expression (see below), it was a fairly important activity.

In exchange of kola, the Sudanese offered mostly *sombe*. With *sombe* an item of great convenience and usefulness was introduced into the Guro country. It could be used not only as a raw material for ironsmithing but also as a medium of exchange. The active agents of the kola trade, the Dioula people, did not go far down into the country but plied their trading activity for the most part in the savannah forest area. Therefore, several favorable conditions for marketing activity co-existed in this area: a contact area between two complementary regions; exchange of staple products; existence of a medium of exchange; the presence of active trading agents.

But as we go south, the trading process thins out and takes another form. It is generally reported by all the Guro that women from northern Guro tribes came in great numbers to the forest-villages to collect the kola "from door-to-door." They offered in exchange either *sombe* or local products such as woven goods. Hence the exchange of kola in terms of *sombe* was less favorable in the southern area. Twenty packs of *sombe* were received for a basket of kola (100 units) from the Dioula. Among middle populations (Bouavere, Gonan, W. Yasua, Bonon) the price was five to ten packs for a basket. To the Bete, the traders gave five packs of *sombe*. Among Southwestern tribes of forest peoples, reported terms were between two and five packs, never as much as ten. Consequently, the quantity of *sombe* in the southern area was comparatively smaller, the *sombe* being retained in the areas further north. Thus, they were bound to be restricted to ironsmithing or matrimonial compensation in the south. Few of them were available for monetary purposes, therefore local trade.

Trade with the Baule was of a different sort. Baule people do not use kola nuts and do not produce iron. The goods exchanged were "prestige goods;" guns, powder, tusks, slaves, golden objects. They did not need handling or conditioning. Terms of these exchanges were often fixed by custom. Each party used to offer not a single commodity but several, among which *sombe* were only (and not always) one of the many components.

Baule traders did not penetrate far into Guro country, but conversely it is reported that pre-eminent Guro often sent over men of their own into Baule country to fetch the precious weapons.

Given the nature of the products exchanged, the comparative lack of a convenient medium of exchange, and the absence of penetration by active trading agents, there were hardly any economic inducements for market trading on the Baule border.

Aliens vs. Allies.

The contention is that exchange and trade explain, partly, the differential distribution of markets in Guro country, and further, the differential density of population. This contention can also be supported by an analysis of the socio-economic behavior of the Guro people in relation to their neigbors and among themselves.

Karl Polanyi has shown brilliantly how external trade in ancient and primitive society does not take the same form as in our modern capitalistic world, of market-organized industrialism, and how in many substantive economies the social status of the trading parties is of great relevance to the exchange process. His analysis appears to be entirely confirmed in the Guro country.

Even today, it is frequent that, when asked about the "price" of a product or a service, the seller sets different rates according to the status of the buyer. To members of one's family, it is gift. From fellow-villagers, a token gift is expected in reciprocity and food during the period of work. To members of other villages, it depends on matrimonial alliances or friendship. To alien Guro a bargaining rate is offered and to alien people a still higher "price," unless prestige or hospitality requires it to be a gift. Conversely, we were told that it was proper for a rich and prominent man to pay highly for some goods as guns or slaves, etc., in order to exhibit his wealth both to his fellow-villagers and to the foreigners. Roughly it can be said that the "price" went higher as social bonds dwindled and that between parties of comparable status it varied according to the nature of the goods involved in the transactions (prestige or subsistence goods).

Exchanges as they took place among the Guro are, we think, a good example of the variation in the dominant concern governing socio-economic relationships. In the northern part of the country, the Guro face an alien population. Guro people scarcely penetrated the country of the Dioula, whom they feared. Occasionally Dioula men married Guro women, but the reverse was very exceptional and the matrimonial exchanges did not have the same character of reciprocity as among Guro. Social bonds were thus not strengthened through matrimony. Few personal links were likely to develop and affect the rates of exchange to any degree. Official records from the colonial army mention violent clashes (not war) between Dioula travelling traders and Guro due to swindling and fraud. In these conditions, we may assume that trade between Guro and Dioula was dominated more by considerations of material gain than by the quest of social or political alliances and that they did not in general temper their economic relationships by social considerations.

If we turn towards Guro-Baule trade relationships, we find quite a different picture. The intermediary area between the Baule and the Guro is populated by several groups of Baule origin, but assimilated to Guro culture. They claim their homeland to be the Baule, admit they were formerly matrilineal, still speak the Baule language concurrently with Guro, and claim to be either kinsmen or affines of the Baule people on the other side of the Bandama River. They maintain social contacts with the Baule and travel frequently among them.

These marginal tribes were the natural intermediaries between the Guro of the hinterland and the Baule. Toward affines or kinsmen, i.e., towards Baule or Guro people, their trading behavior was greatly affected by social considerations, as it was by the nature of the exchanged goods (guns, powder, woven cloth, cattle, *sombe* — used as matrimonial compensation) which involved prestige, and not subsistence. Frequently, according to informants from this area, the terms of trade with the Baule were exactly repeated with the next Guro tribe, leaving absolutely no profit for the intermediary.[13] All-in-all, trade was not what we would call in modern terms "a profitable business." It was, rather, that goods moved between people of preeminent status, on customary terms, until they reached the upper part of the country, whereupon they were traded at terms of exchange which profited the upper Guro.

A brief description of these variations from the Vaa to the Baule illustrates this process. As we have seen it above, kola was exchanged for *sombe* to the Vaa and for cloth to the lower-Guro. Such was not the object of trade with the Baule.

[13] S. F. Nadel (1947 : 76) notes that "rifles—the most valuable single property in the Nuba hills—are invariably exchanged for their original value (in spite of the fact that they are more and more difficult to obtain)."

Guro from the north recall the existence of slave markets in the
Vaa country where slaves could be procured for kola or *sombe* or,
later, during the Samony war, for food. But Guro from the Bouaflé
area say that slaves were not marketed but exchanged "from man to
man"[14] for high valued products offered in batches: guns, powder,
tusks, cloth and sometimes cattle. The same type of exchange took
place with the Baule.

Cattle were rarely obtained from the Dioula who bred the humped
variety which is not resistant to tripanosomiasis. But when they were,
they were bartered for kola or *sombe*. Among Guro they were also
exchanged for powder and cloth; with the Bete or the Baule, mainly
for cloth. Guns came mostly from the Baule, for cloth and livestock,
sometimes *sombe;* they were exchanged with the Dioula for slaves or
sombe.

Tusks were high prestige goods, offered "from man to man" as
gifts mostly for slaves among Guro and Baule, but rarely to the Vaa.
Gold was imported from the Baule, but as jewels or plated objects
(headgear of sceptres) for personal use, not for re-exportation.[15]

In short, we can say that staple and subsistence goods were the
basic elements of trade with the foreign Vaa to whom they could be
offered against some prestige goods, while prestige goods were traded
with the allied Baule to the near exclusion of staple or subsistence
goods. Among the Guro themselves, a process of conversion from one
type of goods to the other took place along with substitution of imported goods for domestic goods.

The various sets of trading conditions, the difference of products,
of partners found on the Vaa border and on the Baule border, and
the greater opportunity of conversion of staples into prestige goods
near the Vaa country, strongly contributed to the creation of markets
and to the fixation of a larger population in the northern area.

The Market as a Political and Social Institution.

Undoubtedly, these markets became a convenience for the Guro.
It was easier for women to go to market and trade their excess
products than to collect all necessary products in the bush or in the

(14) This phrase, which I did not fully appreciate while I was in the field, is a translation of *"d'homme à homme"*, used by the Guro in French to distinguish this form
from both market exchange and door-to-door trading. The phrase *"entre camarades"*
was used in a similar context.

(15) The Guro did not stand as intermediaries for, or providers of, some basic
products of the African trade, such as gold and ivory. They were on the contrary gold
buyers; ivory was mostly reserved to the Baule. As for salt, they imported some, but
apparently not in large quantities since they could make vegetable-salt.

fields. The use of *sombe* among themselves, even in the exchange of subsistence goods, was a further incentive to market trading.

But purely economic factors—i.e., quest for material gain—account less for the development of markets and subsistence trade among the Guro people than do political and social considerations. The founder of a market was usually a pre-eminent and rich individual, a *"Fua"* who sought social recognition. The opening of a market was the occasion of a celebration: cattle were killed and people from the neighboring villages were invited to share the meat. It was usual to give the market the name of its founder.

By opening a market a man acquired not only social recognition of his wealth, but also a jurisdictional area, since conflicts occurring on the market-ground, distinct from the village grounds, were within his competence. He even had police, a rare instrument of power in these societies, by appointing men to maintain order in the market. Furthermore, he stood in the position of an eventual peacemaker in conflicts happening between villages or tribes attending his market.

Markets were not only an instrument of political status, they were also places for social gathering, entertainment, dances and various social activities. We have been the witness of a persistent custom which testifies to the social role of market places. In Zanzra, an important traditional market, villages in turn send their women dressed with their best outfits. They go round the market place in a procession, carrying on their heads some of their richest clothes, then sit on chairs set apart for them and offer themselves for the admiration of the crowd. Suitors, friends, parents come and offer them kola nuts and money. After they have completely changed their dress for an extra outfit picked up from their load, they return as they came.

"Young men who wished to get married were attracted to the markets," say the old men. This striving for matrimony often took a violent form, and many a woman eloped or was carried off on these occasions. Sometimes this caused wars and eventually the disappearance of the market.

Since markets were generally places of violence and fights, they were always located outside the village. Fines were inflicted in case of fight or insults, and as we have said before, there were men responsible for maintaining peace. It is recalled that sometimes markets were established because a child or a woman had been beaten up in another one. Palm wine drinking was not always allowed.

In spite of this "explosiveness," several markets together created a social network. As seems frequent in Africa, the days of the week are called by the names of the surrounding markets held on successive days.[16] People from any village will find themselves in a network of seven markets that they can attend in turn.

In Zanzra for instance, before the colonial rule, the days of the week corresponded to seven markets attended in turn by people of about seventy villages from three different "tribes." Today's matrimonial exchanges cover very much the same area. On the other hand, exhibitions of women in Zanzra were restricted to fewer villages all belonging to one tribe.

As we see, markets were occasions for tightening social bonds either inside a more integrated unit, as in this women's display, or towards distant groups belonging to the same market "calendar." The overlapping of "calendar areas" created a chain of social relationships so that no group was self-enclosed.

Through them, the Guro people came to know itself *de proche en proche*. Markets were the occasion of extensive social mixing, trading was the opportunity to scout further areas. It might have been the dawn of a "Guro" consciousness on which R.D.A. propaganda could build in 1947 a campaign for the administrative unity of Guroland.

THE IMPACT OF COLONIAL TRADE

Dioula trade vs. Colonial Trade

With the colonial period, several factors occurred which affected trade and markets in Guro-land. Even before the actual occupation of the country by the French, the impact of colonial economy was felt.

As early as 1904, it was reported that Dioula were killed by Guro from the southern forest where they had come to collect latex. In 1906, similar facts were reported: Dioula who had come to fetch ivory and latex in the forest were accused of extortion and robbery by the local people. Violent clashes occurred. Furthermore, they brought with them an epidemic of smallpox.

The French army intervened to close Guro country to the Dioula traders. As this point, an interesting event occurred: the French army reported that the Guro demanded of the French the re-opening of their country to Dioula trade. To achieve this end, they went so far as to accept the drastic conditions set by the French army, conditions putting their country under colonial rule. It is interesting to note that Guro country was conquered through a "commercial blockade" (in the very words of the administrative reports), and it testifies to the importance of the traditional trade in this area. After five to six years of fighting, during which the *Pax Gallica* was not readily accepted by

(16) In the South, where there are no markets, days are called by ordinal numbers. The Guro have a seven-day week.

the Guro, the kola trade with the savannah was resumed. The Dioula followed the French columns and penetrated the whole country.

It seems that the military administration was greatly concerned with the protection of the Guro people against the exacting Dioula. Indeed, the Dioula traders were competitors of European commerce. Several restrictive measures were taken against them. Their settlements were limited to areas near the military stations in order, it was said, to prevent possible friction with local people. "Native markets" were created in the *chef lieux* by the administration to compete with markets controlled by Dioula people. Guro were compelled to carry palm kernels and rice to Dimbokro to be sold to European traders. Sales of kola were taxed. Last but not least, the new power attempted to impose its own currency in place of the *sombe*.

In spite of these measures, European trade was slack. In 1914, thirteen European trading posts are reported in the Guro *Cercle*. In 1915, they closed up. They were not sufficiently integrated to the local economy to resist the impact of World War I. It was not until 1921 that nine of them reopened, only to close a few months later.

In 1922 the Dioula were reported to be the only trading agents in the area. They exchanged salt and cattle for kola and cloth. The *sombe* were still used among the Guro. French money found no use save in payment of tax. Indeed, the money income of the natives was hardly more than they needed for tax payment. In 1920, it was even less, for in 1919 the Government stopped buying the palm kernels ordered by the Defense Department. Since 1918, latex prices had gone down and collecting had stopped. In 1924, when the silver coins were removed from circulation and replaced by paper money, the *sombe* showed up again in the markets "with the Dioula's encouragement." Zanzra, a local market where they were widely used, grew greatly to the detriment of Zuenoula's administrative one. During all this period, the old pattern of trade with the same products, the same agents, the same medium of exchange tended to persist alongside the colonial economy.

The opening of motor-roads in 1924 and the use of trucks brought a decisive advantage to colonial trade. European or Syrian shops opened again, and for good. European goods penetrated in larger quantity. French money, though made of paper, found an outlet and the *sombe* disappeared gradually. In 1924, for the first time kola was carried by truck. The same year, the Dioula were given freedom to operate. Their natural move was to integrate themselves to the new pattern of trade. This integration was completed when coffee and cocoa became the main money crops. They became the traveling coffee buyers.

Dioula trading relations with the Guro compared to the pre-colonial period are apparently the same: in addition to kola—of which they largely control the trade today—they buy coffee and cocoa. They even improved their position with regard to their geographical extension. But they no longer control the currency. They are only the intermediaries at the first level in the coffee buying process. Actually they often act as agents for the Lebanese traders or the European concerns from which they get advance payment. Even in the bush they undergo growing competition from the Lebanese and from the government cooperatives who send their trucks to the remotest villages. In the towns, trade belongs to Lebanese and European shops, and in the major cities, to the large trading companies. They are no longer the sole controlling agents of trade in Guro country.

Market and Trade Today.

The general pattern of market location and frequency of distribution has hardly changed since pre-colonial times. The major events in this connection were the creation of administrative markets in Sinfra, head-town of the southern subdivision, and in Bouaflé the *chef lieu* of the *Cercle*.[17]

In the Bouaflé Subdivision, a few minor markets were created under alien impulsion: in Sehizra, near a Dioula settlement and in the Mossi villages. Bouaflé market, the major one, affects the near totality of the Bouaflé subdivision, or approximately 15,000 people.

In Sinfra, there is a single market for the whole subdivision— that is for 14,000 people. Of course the frequency of attendance of distant groups is lower. Price of transportation prevents numerous trips to the town: purchasing and administrative errands are usually combined.

Given this very loose network of markets in the forest area, it will be more informative to study the modern market structure in the Zuenoula Subdivision where marketing is still the most intensive.

We found eighteen market-places in the Subdivision, which gives an average of one market for approximately 3,300 inhabitants.

The Pattern of Market-Trading and its Personnel in Zuenoula Area.

The modern pattern of distribution is a complex one and varies with the different kinds of products considered.

---

(17) It is reported that a market existed in Bouaflé (which means "fish market") before colonial times and that it disappeared during a war between the Bouavéré and the Goura. Unfortunately I have not been able to gather much information on this market.

Manufactured goods of European make originate from trading centers located outside Guro country. Bouaké and Daloa are the two main centers commanding the Zuenoula area, where the goods are bought to be resold on the minor markets.

Native products, such as palm oil, tobacco, peanuts, and corn; imported foodstuff such as rice, salt, dried fish, and sugar; and various "luxuries" such as bread and kerosene are bought in major markets, Zuenoula or Trafesso[18], by intermediaries and resold in the minor ones. Sometimes they go through another market of middle importance before reaching a minor one. As for local subsistence goods, they come from neighboring villages and are not sold through intermediaries.

According to the extent of the network of each product, various trading agents will be involved. Trading of printed cloth, fabrics and miscellaneous manufactured goods is controlled almost exclusively by Dioula men. In 1958, the forty-one retailers registered in the Zuenoula Subdivision, were Dioula. They are often residents of towns where a major market is held, Zuenoula or Trafesso. They buy their goods from wholesalers in the trading centers mentioned above and carry them through public transportation to the various markets held on successive days.

Palm oil, salt and rice are bought mostly by Dioula women or sometimes men, also resident in the major towns, and carried to the minor markets where they are retailed. But an increasing number of Guro women are engaging in this profitable business—essentially women living in villages closer to the major markets. Women selling such commercialized products cluster together in the market: all palm oil merchants sitting in a circle, all rice merchants sitting in a row, etc. This makes it possible to distinguish at a glance the imported foodstuffs from the native ones. Local subsistence goods, products of domestic crops or gathering, are sold by Guro women exclusively. Women of the same village sit together independently of what they sell; several wives of the same man may even sit next to each other. They sell either a single commodity such as rice, or bananas, yams, peanuts, corn, palm oil of their own making; or several products at the same time, usually dried cassava, relish, kola-nuts, mushrooms and dried caterpillars. Dried fish is sold both by registered merchants (Niger people from Mopti, or Dioula) and by Guro women who offer fish bought in Abidjan on the occasion of a visit to kin.

---

(18) Trafesso is situated outside the administrative limit of Zuenoula subdivision and on the edge of the Guro country. Guro from Trafesso still call the town Traafla and claim that it was a Guro village before the Dioula came in such numbers that the town is now officially considered as Dioula with a Dioula name.

The settlement of Dioula in the country has transformed the craft-product trade. Most agricultural implements, except the bush knives of European making, are made by Dioula smiths and traded occasionally in the markets. It seems, however, that iron goods are often purchased on commission as are some other craft-products such as mortars, also made today by Dioula men.

Mat and winnower making is the near monopoly of Guro men. Such products are made in the villages by young men who carry them sometimes to very distant markets, depending on the price expected. Bouaflé seems to be a center of such products and prices increase as one moves away from Bouaflé market.

Pots are still made in a few villages by the women and brought occasionally to the markets. But large pots come from the savannah through middlemen.

In major markets we find, in addition, foreigners from further afield: Hausa traders and their medicine and trinkets; Fulani herdsmen and their cattle; Anango selling odd manufactured goods; craftsmen from British Africa selling sandals of their own making. Services are numerous: hairdressers (men and women), photographers from British Africa, "cafés", prepared food, etc. Baule women, wives of administrative agents employed in the town, specialize in processed food such as cassava-semolina or fritters. As a minor market grows in importance, people to perform these services will move to it.

The reason for the pervasive marketing activity in Zuenoula area is twofold. On the one hand, markets provide a better distribution of utility goods among a population of greater density. On the other hand, they have become a permanent trait of political and social life. This permanency is expressed in the persistence of social activities taking place on market days, as described above. Attendance of a market still coincides very much with the tribal area.

Politically, the market remains a platform of prestige for the family who controls it. While village chiefs have been installed under administrative pressure, market chiefs, who are very often distinct personalities, still represent a traditional authority. The control of some markets is still at stake between rival families.

Today however, marketing express a new economic reality. There have been drastic changes in the nature of the marketed commodities. *Sombe* exist only as relics; kola is the object of large scale trading by Dioula wholesalers, who directly collect and transport the product by trucks to the savannah towns; staple foods in great quantities are collected by trucks in the villages to supply larger cities. The new pattern of marketing is now organized around European products instead of the traditional kola-iron exchanges.

The installation and longevity of a market place today are subject to such considerations as the pattern of distribution, its location inside a general network of markets, its calendar in relation to neighboring markets. A market pattern is also affected by modern phenomena such as the settlement of Dioula traders in certain towns. Not enough evidence has yet been brought to light to isolate the social elements proper from economic and geographical factors.

In modern markets two types of exchange exist side by side and overlap. Subsistence goods remain mostly the province of women, but if imported they also fall into men's trading activities. If the sale of local foodstuffs is reserved to Guro women, Dioula women permeate it eventually through profit-trading. Craft goods provision has shifted partly from natives to foreigners and at the same time from a "subsistence exchange" to a market-exchange process.

It remains true, however, that market trading is limited; such market exchange still excludes prestige goods. Cattle or bridal cloth are not sold in the market; they are transacted at a socially higler level and according to traditional rules. Men still weave cloth for matrimonial purposes or as gifts.[19] Money itself has not yet completely pervaded and transformed the sphere of matrimonial exchange; there is still a strong tendency to demand bridewealth to be made up of a special variety of goods.[20]

Even money acquires a new quality when it reaches a certain amount, say beyond 10,000 f C.F.A. Its possession becomes a new indication of prestige. That "quality" of "money" does not change hands in the markets, since no single transaction ever entails such an amount.

CONCLUSION

Our observations in the Guro country lead to a few remarks on the complex role played by markets as social and political institutions in a substantive economy:

In such an economy, local needs of exchange for foodstuffs or craft products do not seem sufficient to promote marketing activities. Gifts, reciprocity, redistributive processes can take care of the circulation of these products. Markets are primarily induced by external exchanges of complementary products with an alien population. When such a situation occurs, the markets tend to be localized at the contact

---

[19] However, this custom is nearly completely lost in villages surrounding Bouaflé.

[20] This is of course a devaluing process. Through legal administrative divorce procedure, bridewealth is converted into money and the new groom can refund its totality in money or marketable goods.

area between complementary zones. Hence, they can help to indicate the limits of substantive economic areas.

With marketing, new opportunities to convert prestige goods into socially less valued goods will appear. In the process, social relationships and consequently social structures may be in danger of being altered. This is a real danger when an all-purpose money is introduced into the economy. However, we observe that a great deal of resistance is opposed to such a devaluing process: market trade tends to be firmly restricted to the lowest sphere of exchange.

Alongside this socially disintegrative potential, markets also possess integrating virtues. They contribute to the formation of overlapping political areas, reaching beyond the traditional social and political units and able to cope with the more intensive conflictual situation brought about by a more dense and diversified population. In so doing they may delay the emergence of a centralized power of equal integrating force.

Investigations along these lines may open interesting vistas.

CHAPTER 11

Exchange and Marketing Among the Hausa

BY M. G. SMITH

THE HAUSA, THEIR HABITAT AND HISTORY

The Hausa are a mixed Negroid people, several million strong, most of whom live in northern Nigeria between latitudes $10^1/_2°$ and $13^1/_2°$ North, and longitudes 4° and 10° East. The term Hausa isolates a linguistic and cultural population of mixed origins which is organized in several states. Hausa are Muhammedans of this area whose native tongue is Hausa. These Muhammedans share a common religion and patterns of social, economic and political organization. Their organization is explicitly hierarchic, the primary groupings being large states, most of which formerly belonged to the Fulani Empire of Sokoto; secondary groupings are major subdivisions of these states, which were formerly fiefs, but are now known as districts; and these are themselves subdivided into a number of village-areas, each under its own chief and having as components a number of wards and hamlets. The capital of each Hausa state is a large walled town of considerable age, and this is the economic, political and cultural center of the kingdom. Official titles are basic to the political system, and relations between commoners and their rulers are regulated by rank. Among officials also, seniority by rank regulates relations. Thus village chiefs are subordinate to the district-chief; and all senior officials are directly subordinate to the emir. This autocratic hierarchy formerly had at its apex the Sultan of Sokoto, the Sarkin Musulmi or Commander of the Faithful. As simplified and systematized by the British, it has proven its value as an instrument of native administration.

The Hausa population consists mainly of two ethnic groups, the Fulani, and the Habe or original Hausa. Fulani conquered the Hausa states in 1804–10, during a Holy War or *jihad* declared by their leader, Shehu dan Fodio, the founder of the dynasty of the Sultans of Sokoto. The Shehu's *jihad* aimed at the purification of Islam in Hausaland and ended in the overthrow of the Hausa states. Some Hausa rulers who escaped from the Fulani established themselves elsewhere and continued to fight until the British under Lugard occupied northern Nigeria at the start of this century. The Hausa had already practiced a form of Islam for centuries before the *Jihad* of 1804; but it was probably impure. After the conquest, Fulani established themselves as the ruling class of these states, and proceeded to expand their empire into areas such as Adamawa or Nupe which lay outside the boundary of Hausaland. The Fulani term for their subjects, Habe, was applied to free Hausa, to non-Hausa, and to slaves indiscriminately. However, as time passed, those Fulani who had established themselves as rulers of the conquered states came to share a greater cultural community with the populations over whom they ruled than with their nomad cousins, the pastoral Fulani. Settled Fulani now speak Nupe at Bida and Hausa at Zaria as their native tongues, while their pastoral cousins, many of whom are still pagan, do not. Thus, the settled Fulani of Hausaland now belong to the general Hausa population together with their Habe subjects, and both groups are distinguished from others with which they are linked by descent but which either practice paganism or differ in language and culture.

The influence of habitat on Hausa culture and economy is historical as well as immediate. Hausaland falls fully within the savannah and orchard bush country of the north Sudanic climatic zone. Rainfall is low, averaging 35 to 40 inches per annum for most of this region, and confined to the period between May and September. The rainy season *(damina)* is followed by the harvest *(kaka)*, which lasts from October to December and gives way to the cold dry season of the harmattan known as *rani,* itself followed by *bazara,* the period of intense drought and heat which heralds the rains. This regular seasonal cycle governs the annual round of Hausa activities. In its influence on farm and forest, it also affects their content.

The basic Hausa pursuit is farming, and their food staples are grains, such as sorghum, millets, maize and upland or marsh rice. In addition they cultivate a number of roots—sweet potatoes, cassava, and where conditions permit, coco-yams or yams. Other standard food crops include cow-peas, chili and other peppers, okra, onions, squash, bambara nuts and sugar cane. The typical field combines two or more of these crops interplanted, onions, sugar cane, tobacco and rice which are the principal marsh-crops being generally planted as pure stands. Besides these food crops Hausa traditionally cultivate groundnuts and cotton, indigo, and gourds of various sorts. Nowadays their main export crops are groundnuts and cotton; indigo, sugar cane, onions, grains or tobacco are marketed within Nigeria or adjoining French territory.

From the surrounding orchard bush, the Hausa extract sheanuts, locust-bean, silk-cotton, raffia, damson, gutta-percha, baobab, dates, deleb palm, timber and a variety of herbs and grasses which are used for food, tanning, dyeing, building, oil and ink, thatch, mat-making and basketry. They also grow certain fruit trees, such as mangoes, paw-paw and limes, and gather some honey, fish and wild game. Until 1900, they mined and smelted iron and tin for their own use. They also extracted potash and some salt in certain areas. Clay is available for pottery, and the local laterite is used for building compound or city walls. In addition, the Hausa savannas support large herds of Fulani cattle which provide the meat and dairy supplies Hausa need but do not themselves produce, together with much-valued manure for their farms. The Hausa themselves show little interest in cattle or camels, but rear goats, sheep, poultry, and asses. They hold the horse in special esteem for its own sake as well as its value in war.

Regional and seasonal differences in the quantities of many of the products which Hausa use regularly make for temporary local shortages and surpluses alike, and so emphasize the importance of distributive trade. The traditional centers of this distributive system were the state capitals, its main organ was the market, and its arteries were the trade-routes along which the *fatake* (long-distance traders) moved in caravans. Nowadays, the railway and motor road have established a new distributive geography, which European banks and firms, telephones, telegraph, advertisement and corporations of various types both service and complicate. The Hausa economy now has many strong links with markets in Europe and in southern Nigeria. Before this century its closest relations were with the neighboring peoples of the Sahara and western Sudan, who have been the channels through which Islam and other Eastern elements found their way to Hausaland.

Hausa history is a story of immigration and conquest. Lying in the open savannas of the western Sudan, for centuries this country has attracted traveler and invader alike. The traditional Hausa myth of origin refers to an immigration from Bornu which introduced new cultural elements and replaced the indigenous ritual chiefs by more effective rulers. From these immigrants, the seven Hausa states of Kano, Rano, Katsina, Zaria, Biram, Gobir, and Daura trace their common descent. However, these states were mutually independent and frequently fought one another. For centuries they were tributary to the large Kanuri Empire of Bornu whose center lay near Lake Chad; and at various periods some of the western Hausa kingdoms were overrun by armies from Songhai near Timbuktu, and from Kebbi near Sokoto. The Jukun, whose capital lay at Wukari on the Benue, also overran Kano and Zaria in the seventeenth and eighteenth centuries. The Fulani entered Hausa territory from the west centuries before they became its masters. The Tuareg and desert climate between them set the northern limits of Hausa settlement; and the Tuareg with their camel teams were the great carriers of the desert trade, bringing salt, horses, metals and luxury goods to be exchanged for slaves, cotton, leather, and grain. Merchants, many of whom were Arabs, found this trade with the populous Hausa capitals attractive for its profits and for the supplies of desert necessities which it provided. The Hausa chiefs sought to protect these trade routes by patrols from fortified towns sited at stageposts, ten to fifteen miles apart. Markets sprang up at these rural centers linked with the capitals by this long distance trade, which was busiest during the long dry season. With the merchants and invaders came the missionaries of Islam, bringing new ideas, techniques, articles, languages, religions, laws and social institutions. The country had no natural frontiers and served this movement like a highway. Tied to their farms and villages by their social and economic organization, Hausa depended on more mobile peoples to bring the meat and salt which they needed, and learned to welcome immigrants, especially Muslims.

Islam reached Hausa in the fourteenth and fifteenth centuries, coming from the northwest. At first it spread peacefully and somewhat erratically, the chiefs adopting it in some states, the commoners in others. For some time the home of Hausa Islam lay in Katsina, one of the main southern termini of the desert trade; but the Arab and Tuareg merchants whose movements reflected the fortunes of trade carried Islam wherever they settled, and the economic rise of Kano duly attracted them there. *The Kano Chronicle,* which is the fullest history of any Hausa state available, gives a useful and substantially accurate record of these developments which, with allowances for local differences, is broadly true of Hausaland (Palmer 1908).

The *Chronicle* starts with an account of the ritual chieftainship of the Hausa-speaking pagans of Kano before Bagauda conquered it.

> The greatest of the chiefs of the country was Mazauda, the grandfather of the chief of the blind. Gijigiji was the blacksmith; Bugazau was the brewer, Hanburki doctored every sickness; Danbuntunia, the watchman of the town at night, was the progenitor of the Kurmawa. Tsoron Maje was the Chief of the Youths, and Jandodo was chief of the drummers. Besides these there was Maguji who begot the Maguzawa [pagan Hausa], and was the miner and smelter among them. Again there was Asanni, the forefather of the minstrels and chief of the drummers. Bakonyaki was the archer. Awar, grandfather of the Awrawa, worked salt of Awar. He was the Sarkin Ruwa [Chief of the Water] of the whole country. In all there were eleven of these pagan chiefs, and each was the head of a large clan. They were the original stock of Kano. (Palmer 1908 : 65)

Thus, the Hausa conceive the political association of hereditary occupational groups under titled heads having defined roles as the origin of their society. The senior chief was priest of the god, Tchunburburai, who was their common protector and oracle. The myth lists mining, smelting, archery, music, brewing, medicine and salt-working as indigenous Hausa crafts, thus suggesting that weaving, dying, leatherwork and other current specialties were developed or acquired subsequently. For our purpose, it is important to note that the social organization outlined by this myth entails some system by which these occupationally-differentiated clans regularly exchanged their special products peacefully. Another system of ceremonial transfers for ritual and kinship occasions is also implied by this account. Thus, whether these exchanges involved gifts, labor, barter, or currency, the Hausa myth of origin itself assumes some form of internal exchange and occupational specialization; and to the best of my knowledge there is no Hausa myth dealing with the origin of market institutions *per se,* although certain spirits *(bori)* such as Inna (the Mother) show active interest in markets.

The Kano Chronicle simply records that "It was Dagaci who made the market at Karabka" (Palmer 1908 : 75) in Kano city during the reign of Abdulahi Burja, 1438–52, several decades after Islam had been introduced. Dagaci was an immigrant noble from Bornu; and it is not clear whether his was the first market at Kano or merely a new one. The details of commercial history given in the *Chronicle* are indeed prosaic; but together with the record of new elements and activities, they present a useful picture of parallel economic and political growth.

Work began on the walls of Kano city before 1134 A.D. Tribute was collected and shields were in use before the end of that century, and early in the thirteenth century, the ruler "collected a land tax of one-eighth of the crop from all husbandmen." (Palmer 1908 : 67) Then followed a hundred years of struggle between the people and their rulers who traced descent from an Eastern immigrant. By 1370, the king had adopted Islam and obtained Muslim aid in this conflict. Chain mail, cotton armor and iron helmets were in use by 1410, and muskets from Bornu and eunuchs and kolas from Zaria were introduced by 1440. Camels became available by 1450, when the market at Karabka was built, Fulani missionaries came soon after, and by 1500, the "Tuareg came to Gobir (that is, Adar) and salt became common in Hausaland ... Merchants from Gwanja (Zaberma) began coming to Katsina; Beriberi came in large numbers and a colony of Arabs arrived." (Palmer 1908 : 11) At this time , too, the great Kano ruler, Muhammad Rumfa, rebuilt and extended the city walls. He also established another market at Kurmi in Kano city which still flourishes.

Thus, the growth of important city markets is clearly linked with the spread of foreign contacts, initially east to Bornu, then north and westwards to the desert. At this time, cloth, salt, and metal goods such as arrowheads or knives served as currency, along with slaves and horses for large values. These items passed in tax and tribute as well as trade. "In Sharefa's time, cowries first came to Hausaland," (Palmer 1908 : 90) that is, between 1703 and 1731, soon to be followed by silver coins known as thalers which were manufactured in Europe for export to the Sahara and western Sudan. Thalers and cowries then formed a common currency.

At first the Kano rulers seem to have left its markets in peace, but early in the eighteenth century, Muhammad Sharefa began to collect taxes there, and in the next reign, "the market was nearly killed, the Arabs left the town and went to Katsina, and most of the poorer people . . . fled to the country." (Palmer 1908 : 90) Kano's commercial decline brought Katsina prosperity, but the long wars, first between Katsina and Gobir, and then between the Fulani state of Katsina and the Habe state of Maradi, caused the Arab merchants to move back to Kano, and when Dr. Barth visited the country in 1851 he found Katsina ruined and Kano more prosperous than ever (Barth 1857 : I, 278–80, 296).

The record indicates that exchange by gift and barter among occupationally-specialized clans preceded markets, and that the markets emerged with the large-scale caravan traffic before the development of a uniform currency such as the cowrie. When cowries and thalers became available, the trading area expanded, and with the establishment of the Fulani Empire, it expanded further still. Under the Fulani system of tribute, large surpluses of slaves, horses, cloth and other Hausa products accumulated annually at Sokoto; and in the view of Major Burdon, the first British Resident at Sokoto, the two main markets of Hausaland in the last century were Kano, the great commercial *entrepot* of Central Negroland (Barth 1857 : I, 296) and Jega where the Sokoto surpluses were put up for sale. Burdon remarks first on "The slave trade, for which Jega, a neutral market open to Kebbawa, Maradawa and Fulani, had been the centre, not only for this province (Sokoto), but also for Nupe, Lagos, Borgu and French territory . . . The importance of this market is I believe little less than that of Kano. It is the meeting place of caravans from Kano to Gambaga and south to Lagos. The market is full of Accra and Yoruba traders, and it collects and distributes all the commerce of Adara, Asben, Kebbi and Zamfara. The main roads leading to it are from Yelwa and Illo on the south, from Yelu on the West, and from

Bakura on the East. There is no through caravan route to the North, the routes there being merely lines of distribution."[1] Like Jega, the Kano market in the last century was also a center of slave trade, and Barth estimated its annual turnover of slaves at 5,000 in his attempt to calculate its yearly trade (Barth 1857 : I, 300–309).

COMMUNITIES AND THEIR MARKETS

This general background provides the context within which Hausa communities live and practice various types of exchange. These local units reveal in simplified miniature the effects which history and environment together have had on Hausa culture and society as a whole. For with economic expansion and prosperity came an increase in occupational diversity, and although male occupations have tended to remain hereditary, their original status equivalence has given way to hierarchic rankings which broadly correspond with social and economic position. During the last century craftsmen were organized in units under local craft leaders, who received official recognition and were responsible for collecting tax or organizing such services or supplies as the chief required. To a lesser extent, these senior craftsmen were also responsible for controlling the quality and price of the goods marketed locally. An occupational structure reminiscent of guilds resulted, and, if membership were hereditary, apprenticeship began in childhood. Brokers, commission agents and *fatake* learned their occupation *(sana'a)* likewise, but were less bound by hereditary rules. Joking relations, *zumunta* (quasi-kinship), bondfriendship and periodic craft rituals may be survivals of pre-Islamic social customs. Many other ancient principles still persist within the systems of exchange, as we shall see.

Hausa communities are easy to identify. Each rural community has its own chief, priest *(imam)*, mosque, Beiram prayer-ground, titles, boundary, and market place where markets are held at set times. Subdivisions of these communities lack separate chiefs, prayer-grounds and markets, and may lack fixed boundaries also. Traditionally, the center of a rural community was a walled town, at which the chief, *imam,* and market were found. Even today, when population or other changes lead the authorities to establish a new village and village-chief, one of his first tasks is to promote the development of a regular market at his headquarters. If this fails and another settlement in his area has a viable market, the chief will go to live there. Likewise, when the capital of an old village area declines and the

(1) Major J. A. Burdon, Report No. 8, 1903. File 129/1903, Sokoto Series, National Archives Kaduna, paras 72, 87. Unpublished.

market dies, the chief will select a new headquarters where the market is likely to flourish. I can recall no Hausa community having an officially recognized chief which lacked a market at its center, even if it meets but once a week.

The Hausa market *(kasuwa)* is an officially recognized and controlled gathering which meets at a particular place on fixed days and has a fixed organization and form. In these respects the *kasuwa* differs sharply from small *ad hoc* groups of petty traders and peddlers who collect at their leisure under shade trees or by building sites in the village during the afternoons. These informal groups of vendors are known as *yara,* and lack official recognition or control. *Yara* only serve retail trade, and offer little scope to commission agents or craftsmen who wish to market their products.

To establish a new market, the first step is to bring the local *yara* together at least once weekly in some open space at which crude sheds can be erected. This weekly meeting should be called on a day when there is no market meeting nearby. If it attracts attendance from other communities, the village-chief will then be urged to set up the market officially. For this he needs approval from his immediate superior, nowadays, the District Head, and formerly, the fief-holder. In this negotiation, the proximity of nearby markets and the days on which they meet are carefully considered, and the village chiefs concerned may be consulted to secure their support and to arrange that they should encourage their people to visit the new market. If this actually lies at the District Headquarters or capital of the fief, the senior official is popularly credited with responsibility and initiative for the new market, although the village-chief is directly in charge.

As the new market begins its life, and the layout of sheds indicates permanence, its attendance may fluctuate, and its future be in doubt. Its development requires organization, just as its failure invites ritual action. As representatives of Islam, neither the village-chief nor his superior can properly do more than call on Allah to prosper the new market and the local Muslim community. This is done through the local mallams or clerics whose sanctity *(baraka)* give their prayers special power. They may instruct the chief to distribute alms or to take certain other actions required by Allah, such as Islamic sacrifice. These Muslim rites are usually supplemented by others, which the local devotees of the ancient Hausa cult of spirit-possession *(bori)* carry out independently to propitiate those spirits *(iskoki, s. iska)* especially Inna, whose support is essential for success. The aim of these *bori* rituals is to settle one or more benevolent spirits on or near the market site (See Mary Smith 1954 : 218–221). For fear of alienating the people whose support is also essential to the market's success, the chiefs who represent Islam officially dare not obstruct these pagan rites. Moreover, the gathering of *bori* adepts from far and near ensures favorable publicity for the new market. Bori rituals may also be held when the village moves to a new site, or when the market changes its site within the village. Such changes of site have been mainly due to European activities.

Official organization of the market takes the form of appointing supervisors, who vary in title and function from village to village and from period to period. There is generally a Magajin Kasuwa in charge of the market and directly responsible to the village chief, a Sarkin Pawa or head of the butchers, a Sarkin Awo or Korama who is a woman in charge of all who sell grain by measure in the market, a Sarkin Makera who supervises blacksmiths, and usually a Sarkin Dillalai in charge of the local brokers and commission agents. If the market lies on a roadway with frequent traffic, there will also be a Sarkin Tasha in charge of the "station" where this transport is concentrated. In the last century, the Sarkin Zango, in charge of the caravans had a similar role. These market officers are rarely given official stipends, but do not find their duties unrewarding.

These official appointments indicate the oldest and most important marketing interests among the Hausa, namely, meat, grain, cloth, and metal goods. Vendors who sell salt or kola nuts have no appointed heads; but the Magajiya, chief of the local prostitutes (the main devotees of *bori*), has an important informal voice in market affairs. The Sarkin Pawa is also especially important, since no Hausa market is complete without an ample supply of fresh meat for sale; and beef, the preferred form of meat, is only available from Fulani nomads. The Sarkin Pawa is always responsible for the market meat supplies, and in many areas he was put in charge of the market as a whole, responsible to the local chief, whom he supplied with free meat and with certain traditional levies from market vendors. The Sarkin Pawa also controls the rotation of killings among butchers, and nowadays supervises the removal of the hide as well. Slaughtering follows Muhammadan convention, and is the work of another market official with some Islamic knowledge, the Sarkin Yanka. The chief drummer, Sarkin Makada, is employed to drum messages detailing the next days' kill on the eve of the market, and does so on the large talking drum, formerly used in war. The Sarkin Pawa spends much of his time negotiating the purchase of cattle, which the nomad Fulani are very loath to sell, especially on credit. Since meat marketing involves both large cash outlays and risk of loss due to spoilage, the Sarkin Pawa also organizes cooperation among local butchers to sell supplies quickly. In some Hausa emirates, the Sarkin Pawa was also empowered to appoint the Korama or Sarkin Awo in charge of the grain-sellers, receiving a gift of grain from her each market day.

The chief of the grain sellers was responsible for maintenance of fair measures and prices. Until 1900, Hausa grain was not sold by constant measures and even today in certain areas near the French border, grain is still sold in the old way. The purchaser says how much grain he wishes to buy, and the vendor pours out threshed grain to this value, bargaining over their differing estimates. Nowadays this method has given way to the use of standard measures such as the *mudu,* a metal bowl of standard capacity, the weight of which varies with the contents.

The control exercised by the Sarkin Dillalai over market brokers was rather less well-defined; but he was called on by the local chief to value articles or to track down local thefts. In the last century commission agents were more highly specialized than at present, some dealing with slaves only, others with horses and camels, while others dealt with cloth or objects of small value. Nowadays, the main articles sold on commission are cloth, meat, threshed grain and kola nuts; but *talla* (retailing of kolas or kerosene and the like on commission) is mainly left to young folk, who learn their market skills in childhood. Commission agents and brokers are the Hausa market specialists who have the most detailed and extensive knowledge of market prices and conditions. They sell articles to which reserve prices may or may not attach, keeping a commission of roughly 10 per cent, or all in excess of the reserve price. In the larger towns they have recently taken interest in the sale of second-hand vehicles, and sometimes arrange loans for purchasers, thereby receiving another commission. Their devotion to marketing provides a valuable service for occasional sellers and purchasers alike.

Besides the market offices mentioned above, which are still in general use, there were certain others which have now lapsed. Thus in nineteenth century Katsina, the Sarkin Tafarki was charged with collection of caravan tolls. In Kano and Sokoto, caravans were not officially subject to toll. In Sokoto, the official directly in charge of market was the Lomu, and the judge who settled market disputes was the Muhutasibi. Many minor officials, including some royal slaves, also collected periodic levies (*al'ada,* customs) in the city markets of Daura, Katsina, and other capitals, and these levies were subject to varying degrees of abuse. Their incidence affected the relative success of rival markets, and in an earlier day these customs evoked the wrath of Shehu dan Fodio who forbade them.[2]

(2) *Shehu Usman dan Fodio,* unpublished, c. 1812. *Bayan wilayati alhalil Islami wa bayana wilayati alhalil kufuri.*

The layout of a Hausa market is deceptively simple. It seems an orderly arrangement of vendors grouped by commodities: butchers remain together, as do grain-sellers, haberdashers, pot-sellers, blacksmiths, leatherworkers, machine tailors, sellers of processed foods, woodworkers and the like. Though those who sell kolas and cloth also occupy special places, many hawk their wares around the market. The throng is in continuous movement, as individuals exchange information and opinions. Traditionally, chiefs announced their general orders or important decisions in the market by special town criers, and it was also the scene of official executions. Nowadays village chiefs may visit the market in order to collect tax, and to discharge other business; otherwise they do not attend.

Nomad Fulani men stay to one side in a group, waiting to be approached by local men who want the herds to manure their farms. The Fulani herdswomen who sell milk and butter form another distinct group. Nowadays some politicians try to use markets for speech-making, but emirate administrations oppose this. As the largest recurrent form of meeting, markets are the most important communication channels among the Hausa, except in large towns where radio and newspapers are now widespread. Accordingly, Hausa rulers take a political as well as an economic interest in markets. To the peasants, markets are legitimate occasions for courtship, entertainment, and relaxation, as well as trade. The market brings together the men of neighboring communities under conditions which minimize the ceremonial of status. Native authorities may use these gatherings for communication. Young men attend for the maidens' dance with which the market concludes. Strangers and mallams find the market an occasion for making useful contacts or strengthening those already established; and, in the larger towns, the market provides an important source of employment for migrant laborers and porters.

In the last century, the principal markets lay along trade routes. As new roads and railway have redrawn the communications map, many old market-towns have died out, and many new market-towns have sprung up. Gusau, Funtua, Ceranci and Kare are among these new towns. The Anglo-French international boundary has also stimulated the development of new towns and markets near it, as, for instance, at Jibiya in Katsina. Large Hausa markets are especially sensitive to changes in trade routes. In the last century, key towns on these routes were fortified and garrisoned, and caravans were protected by officials in return for tolls. Nowadays such arrangements are unnecessary, and population increase has woven closer relations between markets in neighboring rural communities.

Market days rotate so that every day a market meets in one or other of a group of adjacent communities. When market days clash, the larger market stifles the weaker by taking its trade; and for this reason care is taken to reduce these clashes as far as possible, especially since the *'yan-kasuwa* (traders) and *dillalai* of each community attend neighboring markets also. Such linkages serve to stabilize price levels in neighboring markets, and to redistribute supplies among them; but the further one moves from any center, the more variable are price and supply.

Communities which have weekly or bi-weekly markets differ from those in which the market meets every day; and it is useful to regard this as a criterion differentiating village and town (Smith 1955 : 143 ff.). Markets which meet daily have a composition, turnover, volume, complexity, and range of commodities which differ in kind as well as degree from those which meet only once or twice a week. The daily market acts as the major distributive center for the surrounding country, and exercises corresponding influence on dependent rural markets; but these daily markets are themselves dependent in greater or less degree on others which are larger and further away. The capital of an emirate is usually the site of a primary market, and is itself linked with other units at Lagos, Ibadan, or Port Harcourt, which are in direct contact with the world market. The emirate capitals and these larger commercial centers have several daily markets each, and often, a regular night market as well. They also contain the local headquarters of large-scale traders, including expatriate firms; and they normally lie at the center of the local communication and transport systems. In short, as an index of rural-urban difference, Hausa market organization distinguishes the large townships from the rural villages. It also serves to distinguish smaller towns which have a single daily market and which exhibit rural and urban features simultaneously.

CUSTOMARY EXCHANGE

Though markets provide the main organizational mechanism for exchange among Hausa, they are by no means the only one; moreover, markets are influenced in various ways by other patterns of exchange. I shall therefore describe the exchanges which occur outside of markets, and shall try to indicate their relative volume, before proceeding to examine Hausa market economics directly.

Hausa combine their dependence on subsistence agriculture with production for exchange. The domestic unit, based on polygynous marriage and agnation, subsists on its own farm produce, and depends on its own exchange production for the money with which to purchase the goods and services it needs. Since wives are restricted to compounds, men shoulder the main burden of farmwork, and they are also responsible for providing the household supplies, which they do, either individually or in association with close agnates. Women have marginal subsistence commitments, and produce mainly for exchange; their specialties are food-processing, weaving, spinning, rearing small stock, and various forms of petty local trade. Men grow cash crops, trade, and pursue a variety of crafts which include services, such as praise-singing or barber-doctoring, or such activities as smithing, dyeing, or weaving. Young men in economic difficulties may attach themselves to influential persons as menial clients, and are rewarded with accommodation, clothing, food, a farm, and, in due course, a wife. In rural areas, wage-labor *(kodago)* is still rare, although increasing, perhaps due to the prevalence and advantages of menial clientage. In the towns, a higher ratio of young men depend on *ad hoc* wage-labor for their cash incomes (Smith 1955 : 155, 175–7, 223–4). Such persons are generally wifeless immigrants. Among Hausa peasants, the purpose of production is the subsistence of the domestic family; and the division of labor within this unit broadly defines the form such production will take; likewise, subsistence of the domestic family defines the minimum acceptable levels of production. Thus, only those men who lack domestic families or cannot otherwise maintain them engage in wage-labor or menial clientage. The kinship structure, which is so closely related to Hausa economic organization, is also expressed in nonmarket spheres of customary exchange.

Hausa practice gift-exchanges in set kinship contexts such as childbirth, naming, circumcision, marriage and death, and in others which establish special social relations such as bond-friendship or clientage.[3] Islam provides another frame for transfers and exchange at fixed festivals, such as Id-el-Fitr, Id-el-Kabir, or on the tenth day of Muharram. Islamic practice also enjoins distributions of grain at the end of the Fast, and the transfer of grain-tithes *(zakka)* at harvests. Religious alms are distributed in expiation or propitiation. The Islamic emphasis on charity is perhaps most clearly expressed among Hausa in the institution of Koranic schools, in which both teacher and pupils depend for their subsistence largely on alms from neighbors. *Sadaka* (alms) is also institutionalized as a form of marriage, the bride being given to her husband without any return in honor of the Prophet.

We have here a complex of exchanges which derive from religion and kinship, and which are explicitly noncommercial. The exchanges

(3) For examples see Mary Smith, 1954 : 31–3, 191–206.

which normally precede and accompany marriage are also of a customary rather than a commercial kind. Taken together, these customary transfers form a separate system and express certain interdependent values, especially those of religion, kinship, and community. These values are not insulated from Hausa commerce. Kinship and religion provide frames of reference in which customary and commercial exchanges are both consistent and complementary. So too with the political system, which itself involves another set of transfers. Some political transfers, such as tribute or tax, are obligatory and enforceable. Others, such as gifts *(gaisuwa)*, express relations of patronage and dependence inherent in Hausa political organization. In other contexts, such as the Sallah festivals or accession to office, gifts are transferred ceremonially to declare or to strengthen solidarity.

Political, religious, and kinship exchanges usually have ceremonial features, and their volume is difficult to quantify. My study of Zaria rural economy in 1950 showed that, of the cash expenditures of ninety households, Sallah expenses represented 4.1 per cent, gifts to or on behalf of women 4.25 per cent, other cash gifts 2.25 per cent, and tax, which was then quite low, 2.6 per cent. Of the average annual cash income of these households, gifts received was 2.9 per cent. Of their average annual kind incomes only, gifts accounted for 6.4 per cent; but of the average kind outgoings of £2.31[4] per household per annum, the *zakka* (grain tithe) had an average value of £1.34, and other ceremonial outlays, chiefly for kinship events, averaged £0.96 per annum. The tendency is for these proportions to increase together with income. Thus one District-Head, budgeted as CB, reported a gross income of £624, but paid a total of £13.55 in tax for himself and his retainers, gave £31 in cash to various people, another £20.2 to praise-singers and drummers, and spent £82 on kinship ceremonials, most of it on his marriage. Excluding his Sallah donations and all other gifts he may have made, the outlays listed above are almost one-fourth of gross reported income, that is, approximately twice as high as the average ratio among his subjects.

To exclude these noncommercial transfers from a discussion of Hausa exchange would do violence to the Hausa system, and could seriously mislead its analysis. This Hausa exchange system consists of two sectors, the commercial and the customary. The latter surrounds and sanctions the former, and also serves to modify the effect of strictly commercial activities on Hausa society by redistributing portions of income in channels provided by the key Hausa institutions of marriage, family and kinship, religion, government, bond-

(4) Cash values are given in decimals of sterling pounds here for the convenience of reader and writer alike.

friendship and clientage. Both the customary and the commercial exchanges assume reciprocity and involve goods or services; but customary transactions differ from market exchange in that they are induced by social obligations rather than the pursuit of material self-gain, they do not usually specify the equivalent return or period of delivery, and also in that they often transfer material for non-material goods such as political patronage, expiation, or kinship solidarity.

This system of customary exchange colors Hausa attitudes to wealth and its pursuit. As income increases so do an individual's social obligations within this customary exchange system. Only by giving can he discharge his social role with honor. Thus the richer or more prominent an individual, the greater his absolute and relative outlay on these institutional transactions. In this way, customary exchange marks wealth and its pursuit as legitimate at the same time that it demonstrates status and affirms prestige. The generosity of wealthy men evokes admiration for wealth and emulation in its pursuit. It also leads Hausa to set high value on the freedom to pursue wealth, within limits set by Islam on the one hand and by customary norms on the other. Thus Hausa admire industry and commercial skill for the wealth and status they bring and for the generosity and display by which this wealth and status is demonstrated. The prominent man has many dependents and makes generous outlays, and his means of obtaining his income is socially legitimized thereby. Misers have small hope of fortune among the Hausa since they violate these norms and suffer isolation, ridicule, and ostracism in consequence. The Hausa praise-singers *(maroka)* are institutionalized spokesmen of these social values (Smith 1957). The Islamic emphasis on charity among Muslims supports these attitudes, and provides religious outlets and sanctions.

The pressure of these demands on Hausa traders stimulates them to increased exertion. No margin of profit is too great or too small for their notice; no type of exchange is unsuitable providing it gives a good return and is not forbidden by Islam. With this ethic the Hausa are indefatigable traders, having a special flair for bargaining. They are willing to take high risks for the chance of commensurate profit. This description is less applicable to rural traders than to urban traders and *fatake,* since rural demand has a fairly fixed structure, the units and values of which are quite well-known. It is thus the urban merchant who exemplifies Hausa economic values most fully, especially the general trader. Such men have many contacts with firms, with officials, and with various rural communities. They must also be wealthy to engage in general trade; and this wealth is expressed as well by the number of their dependents, as by the generosity which they display. In short, the rich man has to pursue wealth single-mindedly and to display it freely.

The social solidarity which these customary exchanges promote is not all unproductive materially (Smith 1957b). Gifts are indirect investments in social relations of varying function and form. Some of these relations, such as kinship, provide the matrix within which subsistence production is carried out cooperatively; but exchanges between bond-friends, or between client and patron may also under-lie economic cooperation, and Islamic norms provide the basis for the maintenance of the Koran schools. Among women, institutional-ized gift-giving is essential for discharge of their relatively heavy periodic ceremonial obligations. And among both sexes, these obli-gations belong to differing levels of Hausa society and cultural history.

COMMERCIAL EXCHANGE OUTSIDE MARKETS

Hausa commercial transactions are not confined to markets. Im-portant towns have European canteens, Hausa *fatake* trade *en route*, Fulani women hawk milk and butter through the villages daily, and young girls peddle processed foods and other small articles between compounds. Craftsmen ply their craft and transact business at their work place between market days; sylvan produce is brought in for sale daily; and vendors retail kolas, soap, perfume, kerosene, matches and the like at set places most of the time. As their daily diaries show, Hausa business hours are their waking hours; and in rural areas, the volume of commercial exchange which takes place on the days be-tween markets bears comparison with that which takes place on market days.

Some crafsmen, such as builders or well-diggers, can scarcely sell their services in a market place. Others, such as barbers, clerics, or dyers, can conveniently sell theirs outside it. Purdah wives may not attend market, but spin, weave, or process oil and foodstuffs at home, retailing these through junior kin or through commission agents. Special conditions apply to those transactions which take place be-tween markets. The article or service and its price must be fairly standard for vendor and purchaser alike. Normally it is also a local product, or an import in such regular demand as to assure continuous supplies. Salt, cigarettes, and kolas are examples of such imports. The great bulk of the local exchange which takes place between markets involves goods and services produced by local craftsmen or by women who alone trade in processed foods.

In large towns, this informal marketing has less significance, since the market meets daily and attracts most of this internal trade. In the towns also trade is more important than in the country, both because urban households acquire less of their necessities from their own subsistence production, and because average incomes tend to be higher. Thus incomes from market exchange outstrip craft incomes in Hausa towns, in rural areas they are more nearly equal. As we have seen, internal exchange may have begun among the Hausa with the transfer of special craft skills and products among hereditary occupational groups. The context of these transfers was the local community; and even today, local units rely for their basic requirements on the skills of their craftsmen and restrict their demands to traditional forms. In the towns, this traditional demand structure and economy is more exposed to new influences.

European stores and depots are the largest trading ventures located at Hausa towns. Shops operated by Europeans or Syrians are called canteens, and many Hausa merchants now have their own canteens also. The Hausa demand for such foreign products as cloth, salt, bicycles, pressure lamps, iron beds, pots, basins, etc., is large and increasing. These articles are imported in bulk by expatriate firms of which the largest is the United Africa Company. To reduce their overheads and maximize adaptability, the UAC and other expatriate firms concentrate on the lucrative wholesale trade while leaving retail business in the hands of Syrian or native traders. By setting their prices slightly above those of the native traders, the firms protect their chief customers, the Syrian and native traders, but also put these in competition with one another. Syrian traders use their canteens as a base, but do not confine their trading thereto.

The important Southern traders in Hausaland are mainly Yoruba women, few of whom run canteens. The Yoruba women are well thought of by European traders, and tend to confine their activities to selling. In 1950, some of the Yoruba women trading in Zaria city and its environs had an average monthly turnover of £2000, and as credit-risks they had few Hausa rivals.

Hausa merchants, very few of whom are Fulani, usually take their goods on credit from expatriate firms. Interest on the loan may be added to the cost of stock; the total is repayable at a certain date in cash or kind. Firms which deal in export staples such as hides and skins, shea-nuts or gutta-percha, may accept repayments in these articles, purchasing them at prevailing rates; but the Hausa trader must repay his advance to receive further credit from the firm. To reduce the burden of interest cost the Hausa trader is tempted to purchase local produce for export with which to repay his debt in kind; such a procedure allows him to get a double return from the money and thus to reduce the interest burden. To this end, he may allocate so many bags of salt, rolls of cloth, etc., on credit to his customers and agents, requiring hides and skins, or shea-nuts in repayment. His agents then dispose of their stock in rural markets, where they also purchase the products with which to repay the advance. In this way, credit is basic to Hausa wholesale trading. Moreover, the larger the quantities involved, the lower the profit ratio. The highest profit margins attach to petty retail trade.

The Hausa merchant, seeking rapid purchase and sale, is also tempted to do business in commodities such as grain which are important in local trade but not dealt in by the firms. If he is in debt to the firms, the Hausa merchant who buys these local items may be unable to repay when the loan is due. A delicate balance must thus be maintained between the export-import trade and the Nigerian market exchanges, if these are to be successfully combined.

The merchant who decides to invest in grain crops seeks to buy these in the field as futures at knockdown rates before the harvest, and to hoard and sell dear at high prices during the following hungry season, May to August. For this end, grain, skins or locust-bean bought in Hausa enclaves among pagans may be marketed in Kano, Sokoto or Zinder six months later. Conversely, cloth or natron produced in Kano may be sold in pagan markets several hundred miles away. Hausa rulers whose subjects face prospects of famine may prohibit removal of foodstuffs from their emirates; but the larger local merchants have trading bases or contacts in two or more emirates, and can therefore move in supplies. Even administrative boundaries, such as the Anglo-French one, offer little obstruction to this regional trade.

Standing crops sold as futures include cash crops such as cotton, groundnuts and tobacco, as well as subsistence cereals. Farmers in need of ready cash for tax, marriage or court expenses, etc., may have no real alternative but to sell their crop futures. Payment may be made in cash or kind, but in either case the farmer obtains about half the harvest value of the crop, and has no further cultivation responsibilities. When peasants are economically hard-pressed, this traffic may give rise to alarm, and for the past twenty-five years the government of northern Nigeria has tried in various ways to reduce futures transactions. Tax-collection has been delayed. Statutory marketing boards have been established to control the major exports, cotton and groundnuts; and the unfluctuating prices offered for these have to some extent reduced the peasants' incentive to sell their futures. More recently, Government sponsored cooperatives advance loans to rural folk; but it seems likely that some of this money may be used to purchase crop futures also. Not so long ago, native officials charged with annual purchase of grain in bulk for emirate hospitals, prisons and schools, enjoyed excellent opportunities for enriching themselves and for helping merchants in this trade. Their position vis-a-vis the local cooperative societies nowadays may be somewhat similar; and in certain tobacco-farming districts, local chiefs have used the early collection of tax as a means of acquiring futures. Since the Hausa merchants and officials are the main links between the rural markets in which the peasants trade, and the larger city markets which handle the intra-Nigerian and overseas commerce, and since neither of these markets is ever static for long, the Hausa peasants are subject to changing economic pressures mediated by officials and traders. The greater rewards to be derived from trade in local staples and futures tempt Syrian merchants as well as Hausa to invest therein, although this may hold up repayment of outstanding loans.

One route by which Hausa traders acquire wealth and prominence is through this trade in local staples. From small beginnings with grain, the crop-trader with sufficient cash, credit or fortune, may extend his business to cash crops, which may be sold direct to the firms in bulk, or may be bought with money supplied by them, the trader acting either as an agent or a principal. In either case the step forward to general trade in European and other Hausa products is short and simple, providing that the firms advance goods on credit. The competition between these expatriate companies encourages each to support reliable local traders whose business seems likely to expand. The scale and variety of the trader's sales volume largely determines whether he remains in the country or moves to some town, where European canteens, railway and good roads are available. His over-involvement in the purchase of local staples, farms, or houses may lead the firms to withdraw their support when his debts are overdue.

The other route by which Hausa become general traders is *fatauci,* the long-distance trading expeditions which Hausa learned from Arabs and Tuareg, and on which their fortunes formerly depended. Hausa *fatake* begin as assistants of principals who are their kin or patrons, and they gradually acquire sufficient knowledge of routes and markets to engage in this trade on their own account, with such capital as they have. Nowadays the principal *fatauci* traffic is with southern Nigeria, Hausa moving cattle, groundnuts, cotton, locust-bean, Hausa cloth and other products southward, and returning with kolas, ginger, Yoruba cloth and such European manufactures as are cheaper at southern markets. This trade is pursued by road, rail, or on foot, and has several southern foci, such as Lagos, Ibadan, Ogbomosho, Enugu, or Aba. The successful long-distance trader eventually establishes sufficient business to be able to retain an agent at the southern market, while he himself remains mainly at his northern headquarters, purchasing stocks to be sent south, and pursuing trade in local staples. Some Yoruba banks provide short-term loans at high interest to cover some transport charges in this traffic. The successful Hausa trader is also likely to purchase his own lorries, and to run his own transport service near his base. His imports such as kolas are distributed to regular customers on part credit. His clients scout Fulani cattle-camps for beasts to send south. Their principal may then start to trade in European products in order to reduce his dependence on the *fatauci* traffic; alternatively he may invest in Hausa staples such as groundnuts and grain; or he may combine both activities. The number and scatter of the merchant's agents increase with the volume and variety of his trade, and so does his dependence on their integrity and skill. This dependence influences merchants to favor certain categories of close kin as their agents, since certain kinship relations carry mutual affection and trust *(amana)*.

We can now give a partial answer to the common question, why is it so rare for trading organizations to survive the deaths of their founders among the Hausa. Firstly, as we have seen, the merchant is expected to spend freely in contexts of religious, social, kinship and political obligations. Secondly his trade fortune depends on credit opportunities, on good relations with expatriate firms, and on a stable group of reliable clients. Thirdly, under Muslim law, his estate is subdivided on inheritance. Only the very large trader, such as Alhassan dan Tata of Kano, is likely to leave sufficient wealth to allow his trading unit to survive the division of his estate; Alhassan was further fortunate in having several sons whose interests in the inheritance made them reliable agents. His uniqueness lay in the application of bookkeeping and other organizational techniques learned in the Gold Coast to the large and complex trading establishment he built up at Kano from small beginnings. Hausa use of Arabic scripts complicates these routine functions. Only in the past twenty years have Hausa traders found themselves facing new problems of organization and investment, and initially their response has tended to follow traditional lines of social exchange and religious donations. Until 1900, the rich merchant usually invested in slaves; nowadays, merchants have begun to pool resources and undertake new forms of production jointly, such as the groundnut processing at Kano. They have also organized local traders' associations which present their views to the native administrations.

The statutory marketing boards which now control the export of

Hausa groundnuts and cotton abroad have limited the trading opportunities of Hausa merchants and expatriate firms in these fields. These boards fix local prices for various grades of the crop whose export they monopolize, gazetting purchase points, and licensing buying agents. Among their buying agents are expatriate firms and Hausa merchants, who receive a commission for their services. The Marketing Boards were established after the great depression had dislocated Hausa economic development in the 1930's. They were designed to protect native farmers from further violent price fluctuations of the world market—first, by building up large cash reserves through the control of local crop prices, and second, by securing better prices through bulk sales abroad. Since their establishment the boards have built up large reserves for which there now seems to be little immediate need as price stabilizers. Some of these reserves have therefore been diverted to local developments, such as roads, which serve crop production and removal. The boards have proven their value, and also enjoy government approval as sources of loans for economic development. They are therefore likely to continue.

Tobacco is grown in northwestern Hausaland for sale to the British-American Tobacco Co., which processes and distributes it locally from various plants. Cultivation of American leaf tobacco by the Hausa is the result of this firm's enterprise; and the process is guided and supervised by their field staff. At current rates, tobacco offers the Hausa farmer a greater cash reward than any other crop. In the 1959 season, local prices were 1/8d. per lb. Grade A, 1/— Grade B, and 5d. Grade C; and at Shinkafi in Sokoto, the Company's agent reckoned that more than two-thirds of the leaf bought was Grade A, as against 5 per cent Grade C. Judging from these data, one can see how it is possible for Hausa to gross £50 or more per acre of tobacco, although £20 may be closer to the actual average. Even this low figure is probably twice as high as the average return per acre from cotton, groundnuts or sugar cane. However, it is true that of all crops grown by Hausa, tobacco is the most difficult; and it is all bought by the firm which has fostered its production. This arrangement is backed and supervised by the regional government whose agents attend the gazetted tobacco markets.

MARKET OPERATIONS

The data already presented describe the context of Hausa markets and the conditions which govern them. To examine the marketing process itself, I shall use data gathered in northern Zaria during 1949–50 and in 1959. These data are drawn from studies of markets and household budgets. Their details cannot be generalized, but the principles which underlie them probably hold with local and seasonal modifications throughout Hausaland. This generality reflects the prevailing uniformities of Hausa social and economic organization, which has its base in household economy and in production for subsistence, market exchange, and customary transactions. These conditions produce a repetitive pattern of activity in households, communities, market areas and emirates. Between them, the regional government and its marketing boards, the expatriate firms and large native traders integrate the rural Hausa economy with other regions of Nigeria and with overseas trade.

The first points to stress in analyzing Hausa market conditions are the differences due to season and situation. Table 31, which sets out quarterly returns for foodstuffs during the year 1958–59 at the markets of Sabon Gari, Zaria city, and Giwa (20 miles off, on the main road to Funtua and Sokoto), illustrates both points quite well. The figures were collected by the staff of the Zaria Agricultural Department, now a section of the Ministry of Natural Resources; they were kindly supplied to me by the Provincial Agricultural Officer.

The main Hausa harvest begins in late November when the guineacorn, rice and groundnuts are ready, and continues until late February by which time cotton, tobacco, late millet, cowpeas and sugar cane are harvested. A secondary harvest occurs in late July or August, when the early millet, maize, and some groundnuts come in. Some crops, such as cassava and sweet potatoes, remain underground until needed; others, such as onions, and tree crops such as baobab and locust-bean, are harvested at different seasons. The annual crop cycle involves simultaneous shortages and abundance of different crops; and the local supply situation changes ceaselessly. Prices follow these movements of supply. Thus, in the market returns for Giwa, the greatest price fluctuations are linked with seasonal differences in the supply of cowpeas, yams, okra, groundnut oil and millet, all local products; and with such community 'imports' as cattle and palm oil. The prices of local and food staples at the Zaria market are steadily higher than at Giwa, but the seasonal movement is less marked, due perhaps to the large stocks concentrated by merchants at the capital. Price differences in these two markets also show the influence of position in the distributive system. Giwa acquires its supplies of salt and palm oil from Zaria city, and in turn sells grains, groundnuts and other local crops to the city market. In both instances, lower prices prevail at the source market. Cattle prices are consistent with this interpretation. Zaria railhead is an important center for the "export" of cattle to southern markets, and attracts Fulani herdsmen. By con-

TABLE 31

Prices of Local Foodstuffs in the Markets of Sabon Gari, Zaria, and Giwa, 1958–9

		ZARIA				GIWA			
Commodities	Units	March 1958	May 1958	October 1958	February 1959	March 1958	May 1958	October 1958	February 1959
Guinea-corn (dawa)	1 bag	–	–	52/–	43/–	–	–	–	–
Guinea-corn	1 ton	£26	£22	–	–	–	–	–	–
Guinea-corn	1 mudu	7d.	6d.	7d.	6d.	5d.	5d.	6d.	5d.
Early millet (gero)	1 bag	–	–	42/–	50/–	–	–	–	–
Early millet (gero)	1 ton	£33	£37	–	–	–	–	–	–
Early millet (gero)	1 mudu	7d.	8d.	6d.	7d.	6d.	6d.	4½d.	6d.
Late millet (dauro)	1 mudu	7d.	8d.	6d.	6d.	–	6d.	4d.	6d.
Maize	1 mudu	6d.	7d.	6d.	6d.	4d.	4d.	4d.	4d.
Rice, unthreshed	1 mudu	7d.	6d.	6d.	7d.	–	–	6d.	6d.
Upland rice, Threshed	1 mudu	1/3d.	1/3d.	1/3d.	1/5d.	1/6d.	1/6d.	–	–
Rice, threshed	1 mudu	1/–	1/–	1/–	1/–	–	7d.	(unthr.)	6d.
Groundnuts, Threshed	1 mudu	10d.	10d.	9d.	–	8d.	8d.	8d.	8d.
Groundnuts, unthreshed	1 mudu	3d.	3d.	2d.	–	4d.	6d.	4d.	4d.
Coco yam	1 portion	–	–	3d.	6d.	2d.	2d.	2d.	2d.
Cassava	1 portion	6d.	6d.	6d.	–	2d.	2d.	2d.	2d.
Onions	1 portion	3d.	3d.	3d.	–	3d.	3d.	3d.	1d.
Cowpeas	1 mudu	9d.	9d.	–	8d.	8d.	8d.	10d.	7d.
Locust-bean (kalwa)	1 mudu	9d.	9d.	–	11d.	–	–	11d.	–
Country peppers	1 portion	1d.	1d.	1d.	–	1d.	1d.	1d.	1d.
Chili-peppers	1 mudu	6d.	4d.	6d.	8d.	–	–	–	–
Baobab	1 mudu	6d.	–	6d.	5d.	–	–	–	–
Baobab	1 portion	–	–	–	–	1d.	1d.	1d.	1d.
Okras	1 mudu	6d.	6d.	5d.	8d.	9d.	8d.	6d.	8d.
Groundnut oil	1 pt. bottle	2/–	2/–	2/3d.	2/3d.	2/–	2/3d.	1/3d.	2/–
Palm oil	1 pt. bottle	10d.	10d.	10d.	11d.	1/–	1/–	2/–	1/–
Salt	1 portion	10d.	1/–	1/–	1/–	1/3d.	1/3d.	1/3d.	1/3
Beef	1 portion	6d.	6d.	6d.	6d.	2/–	2/–	2/–	2/–
Chickens	1 bird	3/–	3/–	2/6d.	3/–	2/6 to 3/–	2/6d. to 3/6d.	2/6d. to 3/6	2/6 to 3/–
Cattle per head		£17/10	£13/10	£17/10	£15/10	£19 to £20	£15 to £18	£22 to £25	£18 to £20
Cotton	1 portion	6d.	6d.	6d.	6d.	1/–	1/–	–	1/–
Yams	1 portion	2/6d.	3/–	1/6d.	1/3d.	1/3d.	–	1/3d.	11d.
Sweet Potatoes	1 portion	6d.	6d.	3d.	3d.	2d.	2d.	2d.	2d.

Units. The *mudu* is the standard grain measure in Zaria province, a bowl the weight of which varies with the grain as well as with the vendor. The average weight of a *mudu* of guinea-corn is here set at 2.5 lbs., that of early millet at 2 lbs. A bag of grain contains 100 *mudu*. The portion is a heap of approximately constant size per crop and per market. Prices may thus remain constant while the size of the heap changes, and heaps of the same crop at differing markets may have differing size and price.

trast, there are few Fulani nomads in nearby Giwa, and cattle prices are higher there. Without overestimating the accuracy of these market data, it is clear that geographical conditions of position and season influence Hausa market prices as functions of supply. This implies a fairly fixed and general demand structure among the Hausa; and, with due allowance for rural-urban and class differences, Hausa market demands are based on a traditional scale of wants and values which is stable and uniform.

TABLE 32

Goods on Sale in Community E on 7 and 10 August 1950, by Commodity-Groups

Commodity-Groups	7 August 1950		10 August 1950	
	Volume	Value	Volume	Value
Grain crops	966 lbs.	£ 6.15.11d.	688 lbs.	£ 4. 8. 6 d.
Stew ingredients (cefane)	348 lbs.	£ 6. 3.11d.	212 lbs.	£ 2.18. 5½d.
Palm oil and salt	29½ gals. 13 bags.	£ 18. 7. 0d.	30 gals.	£ 10.10. 0 d.
Cassava and yams	1099 lbs.	£ 4. 3. 2d.	1030 lbs.	£ 4. 8. 0 d.
Cotton, groundnuts	219½ lbs.	£ 4. 7. 5d.	454½ lbs.	£ 5. 3. 9 d.
Sugar cane, Hausa tobacco	222 lbs.	£ 1.16. 6d.	431½ lbs.	£ 1.12.10½d.
Total Foodstuffs		£ 41.13.11d.		£ 29. 1. 7 d.
Wood	72 lbs.	?	170 lbs.	?
Bulls slaughtered	2	£ 19. 0. 0d.	3	£ 27.15. 0 d.
Small stock slaughtered	2	£ 1. 1. 0d.	2	£ 1. 2. 0 d.
Total meat		£ 20. 1. 0d.		£ 28.17. 0 d.
European cloth, rolls	113	£136.12. 0d.	146	£192.15. 0 d.
Hausa cloth	91 blankets, 35 yds, fine-weave	£ 42. 7. 0d.	115 blankets 48 yds. fine,	£ 53.13. 0 d.
Ready-made clothing		£152. 2. 0d.		£183.13. 0 d.
Total Cloth goods		£331. 1. 0d.		£430. 1. 0 d.
Total value		£392.15.11d.		£487.19. 7 d.

Table 31 omits Hausa craft products and most European manufactures; but together these commodities provide much of the goods on sale in local markets. In 1950, I tried to make censuses of all articles brought into certain markets of rural Zaria, and summarize some results in Table 32. To make these two censuses, I cordoned off one market on two consecutive meetings with the assistance of the village chief, and weighed or counted all items brought thereto between 9 A.M. and noon, when people come to market, valuing these items at their current local price. The details of this census have already been published, (Smith 1955 : 247). Table 32 gives quantities and values by commodity groups.

This census omits those vendors who lived in the village where the market met, and who thus escaped my cordon on the roads. It also omits such specialists as magicians whose pharmacopeia it was not useful to quantify, and others such as the *'yan-koli'* (haberdashers) whose stocks of antimony, perfume, ginger, aphrodisiacs, beads, bracelets, needles, colored thread, black pepper, potash and mirrors simply defeated me. Omission of Hausa metal goods, leatherwork, or mats and pottery may either be due to evasion of the cordon or to the residence of these craftsmen in the village which was the capital of a unit numbering about 6,000 souls.

The two weekly markets of Community E are distinguished as big and little. The big market met on August 7, 1950, the little on August 10. My record shows that the articles brought in for sale on August 10 exceeded those brought in on August 7, by almost £100 worth; but that this excess was almost entirely due to the greater value of cloth-goods brought into market on August 10. Excluding cloth, the earlier market attracted a slightly larger volume of goods from outside the village, including almost twice as much foodstuffs, other than meat. Perhaps the Hausa classification of markets as big or little may rest on the relative quantity of foodstuffs they regularly attract.

In October 1949, I tried to study the volume sold in certain markets in northern Zaria with the assistance of the Provincial Agricultural

TABLE 33

Commodities Marketed at L, A, and Y on Selected Market-Days in October 1949

Commodity groups	Community L Volume	Value	Community A Volume	Value	Community Y Volume	Value
Grain crops	660 lbs.	£ 5.19. 9d.	216 lbs.	£ 1.19. 0d.	2673 lbs.	£ 23.19. 7d
Stew ingredients	More than 718 lbs.	£ 12. 6. 9d.	176 lbs.	£ 3.19. 0d.	490 lbs.	£ 8. 0. 5d
Palm oil, salt	30 bottles, 7 bags	£ 8. 6. 0d.	9 bottles	£ –.12. 3d.	57 bottles	£ 2.17. 0d
All root crops	780 lbs.	£ 2. 9. 0d.	152 lbs.	£ 8. 0. 0d.	5740 lbs.	£ 22. 0. 6d
Groundnuts, cotton	860 lbs.	£ 5. 0. 4d.	365 lbs.	£ 4.19. 2d.	3280 lbs.	£ 30. 6. 8d
Groundnut oil, bottles	100	£ 6.13. 4d.	26	£ 1.14. 8d.	23	£ 1.11. 6d
Sugar cane	8100 lbs.	£ 18. 0. 0d.	1890 lbs.	£ 4. 6. 6d.	1800 lbs.	£ 4. 0. 0d
Tobacco products Hausa cigarettes		£ 3.12. 0d.				
Total		£ 62. 7. 2d.		£ 18. 6. 4d.		£ 93. 4. 8d
Firewood. Loads	10	£ –.15. 0d.	—	—	45	£ 1.11. 6d
Bulls, slaughtered	5	£ 45. 0. 0d.	1.	£ 9.15. 0d.	1	£ 9.10. 0d
Sheep, sold live	1	£ –.12. 0d.	1.	£ –.12. 0d.	7	£ 4.11. 0d
Goats, sold live	6	£ 3. 6. 0d.	1.	£ –.11. 0d.	—	—
Wood & Stock total		£ 48.18. 0d.		£ 10.18. 0d.		£ 14. 1. 0d
Cloth, European	3 rolls	£ 3. 7. 0d.	—	—	15 rolls	£ 16.10. 0d
Cloth, Hausa	—	—	—	—	10 blankets	£ 6. 0. 0d
Grand Total		£113.19. 4d.		£ 29. 4. 4d.		£125.17. 2d

Department, then under Mr. M. G. Gibbon. Mr. Gibbon seconded three of his keenest Hausa assistants and their staff for the project. They were instructed to survey the amount of each commodity brought to market by vendors, and also the amounts which remained with the vendors when they were ready to leave. The difference is assumed to represent sales or other forms of transfer, and was valued at current prices in the market concerned. The details of this study are available elsewhere (Smith 1955 : 246); Table 33 gives a summary of the volumes and values exchange along lines similar to Table 32.

Before proceeding, let us enter a caveat. These market data vary in their accuracy and completeness. They are indeed the best I could do or arrange in order to study market economics in rural Zaria; but they are perhaps as informative about the difficulties of market surveys as about their composition and volumes.

The Hausa market is a busy milling throng which it is difficult to count and classify, and virtually impossible for the student to arrest or to interview individually. To study Hausa markets we must therefore observe, count, and classify as fully and precisely as we may, converting quantities into values at current prices, and indicating the sources of error explicitly. With these important qualifications, the data presented here are useful.

The compositions and levels of the volume of market goods presented in Table 33 reflect differing market situations. The three markets are more than fifty miles apart, lying in northern Zaria. L stands in the large, densely peopled area adjoining Kano province. A is Giwa, a District Headquarters and a new town with a new market in a sparsely-peopled area. Y is a commercial center on the railway and motor road between Jos and Zaria. In 1949 it contained branches of certain European firms, together with several large Hausa and southern traders, and served as the commercial center for a populous district which included large numbers of agricultural pagans. The market at Y met daily; at L and A, it met twice weekly on set days. A sample economic survey of Y which I made in 1950 indicates that it is more fully urban than rural (Smith 1955 : 147–56; 222–5). Incomes there were much above the rural levels, especially those derived from trade in local goods, such as kolas, guinea-corn, groundnuts, cowpeas, natron, locust-bean, peppers, timber, and sugar cane, which was grown and processed locally. Southern Nigerians dominated trade in European cloth and products. Most of the local products sold at Y may have been "exported" elsewhere, whereas most of those sold at L and A probably served local needs. Since the market meets daily at Y, the local demand for meat is met by a regular daily slaughtering. At L, where the population is dense and the market meets bi-weekly, several beasts are despatched each market day. At A, with its smaller population and market attendance, this meat demand is much less.

Of the estimated gross sales at L and A, 55 per cent and 63 per cent respectively involve foodstuffs and farm produce, excluding meat; and of these sales, the greater portions are local farm-produce. At Y, these commodities represent 75 per cent of market sales, less than one-twentieth of this being of "foreign" origin. At L and A, wood and meat together represent 43 per cent and 36 per cent of market turnover; at Y they account for only 11.2 per cent. At A, cloth sales are either unrecorded or negligible; at L, they form less than 3 per cent of total market sales, at Y, they are 17.8 per cent. These differing turnover compositions underline the functional distinction between rural and urban markets to which I have already referred.

The difficulties which beset a census of market attendance or turnover increase with market size. A census of attendance in the larger Hausa markets would require careful planning and a fairly large team. Later, I shall present the results of two attendance surveys made in the small Giwa market; but first, I wish to assess the significance of market exchanges in the Hausa economy. For this purpose, we can use other approaches and bodies of data.

In 1948, Mr. F. J. Pedler, then District Manager of the United Africa Company at Zaria, estimated the annual per capita net income of Hausa at the capital on the basis of commercial and administrative information available to him (Pedler 1948). Pedler's estimate ignored subsistence incomes and concentrated on the overseas rather than the internal trade; nonetheless, his per capita cash income average was remarkably close to that which I obtained by different methods and data (Smith 1952). Their correspondence suggests that these two estimates may be reasonably accurate, but since my study included kind as well as cash income and expenditure, I shall use it in the present discussion.

This survey comprehended budgets from ninety households in eight rural Hausa communities of Zaria. These households contained 100 taxpayers and a total of 605 persons, of whom 204 were married women. The average annual income of these taxpayers was estimated at £54.5, of which cash income was £26.77 or 46 per cent, and the remainder was income in kind. With my wife's help, I estimated an average annual cash income of £5.16 per married woman, or £10.33 per average household.

Annual trade and craft outputs of these sample taxpayers averaged £43.8 and £16.84, respectively, the comparative costs being £28.4 and £6.64, and the difference representing incomes in cash or kind retained by these producers together with losses borne by them. The average annual cash income per taxpayer from the sale of sylvan produce and labor was £0.71 and £0.74, respectively; from trade and craft it was £7.12 and £8.22; and from the sale of crops and livestock it was £6.14 and £1.58. Together, craft, trade, and farming brought in an annual average of £22 per taxpayer, or 83 per cent of average cash income. Average cash incomes from trade and craft totalled £15.94, or £0.53 less than the £16.47 which represented the total of average cash incomes from sale of farm produce, in which women have little share, and the annual earning of household wives. Of the £6.14 received by the average taxpayer from crop sales, £4.67 came from cash crops, such as cotton, groundnuts and tobacco, and £0.911 from sugar cane and rice, which were also "exported" from these communities. The exchange activities of married women are almost wholly confined to the villages in which they live; and their husband's incomes from craft and trade were also earned and spent locally. By far the greater part of the net increment in the annual cash income of these rural communities derives from the sale of their farm produce for "export" to other markets. Such sales account for 23 per cent of community income and, with loans or concealed debts such as the sale of crop futures, this probably balances all the net expenditures on "imported" commodities and on tax. My sample taxpayer averages for loans received and for sales of futures were £0.77 and £0.27, respectively, which with crop sales totals £7.18. As against this, average cash income from trade was £7.12 per taxpayer, and average annual cash outlay on "exports" such as tax (£0.7), clothes (£3.25), personal expenses (£1.56), and stimulants, such as kolas, snuff or cigarettes (£1.93), had a total of £7.44.

These figures form equations which are approximate rather than exact. Some of these "export" expenditures may have remained in the villages. Likewise some of the cash income from crop sales may have been purely local. Nonetheless, the equations are useful and revealing. By far the greater part of cash income from farming derives from community "exports;" and by far the greater part of the "export" expenditures listed above does represent a net outward flow from the community. In short, the figures allow us to distinguish broadly between the internal exchange system of these communities and their external trade relations. By this token, women's activities and local craft production belong to the internal exchange system, together with sales of livestock, sylvan produce, labor and processed foodstuffs. External exchanges involve sale of local produce or cash crops in return for money with which to pay for needed "imports." That portion of average community income received from external sales and used to acquire goods from outside the community totaled 13 per

TABLE 34

Composition of Giwa Market on 30 December 1949, and on 23 April 1959

	Vendors			Vendors	
Commodity	1949	1959	Commodity	1949	1959
k	64 women[a]	25 women	Tamarind	—	2 men
et potatoes, cooked	8 men	3 men	*Fura*[b]	57 women	23 women
ust-bean cakes	23 women	17 women	Cocoyam, cooked	5 men	—
:as	5 men, 4 women	8 men	Baobab leaf	19 men	7 men
intry peppers	3 men	3 women, 5 men	Chili-peppers	15 men	5 men
l cotton	5 men	3 men	Sugar cane	38 men	5 men
therworkers	4 men	5 men	Hausa rope	4 men	5 men
th-sellers, ndependent	6 men		Thread-spindles	2 men	7 men
isa blankets on ommission	16 men	15 men	Pots	2 men	4 men
men's cloths n commission	12 men		Ablution pots	3 men	
chers	12 men	8 men	*Allewa*[c]	2 men	4 men
undnut oil	7 women, 9 men	23 women, 12 men	Hausa thread	39 men	30 men
wing tobacco	17 men	4 men	Groundnut cake	14 men, 10 women	15 women
irettes	12 men	8 men	Onions	3 men	13 men
d-mats (*asabari*)	9 men	9 men	Kolas (independent)	9 men	13 men[d]
a brown-sugar	10 men	17 men	Kolas (on commission)	21 men	27 men
eb palm-fruit	9 men, 3 women	—	Mats	7 men	11 men
ked cassava	4 men	15 men, 3 women	Barbers	16 men	??
ava, uncooked	—	5 women	Haberdashery (*koli*)	9 men	9 men
iden mortars	2 men	—	Perfume	12 men	—
iatoes	3 men	9 men	*Kosai* (beancakes)	17 women	25 women
us	3 men	5 men	*Goji* (squash)	3 men	5 men
traders	—	7 men	Baskets	3 men	—
is	—	1 man	Machine tailors	3 men	7 men
na (grain-cakes)	—	22 women	Grainsellers	?	9 men
ey	—	7 men	Palm oil	—	10 men (3 Ibo)
irated calabashes	—	3 men	Basins, plates	—	5 men
sa brooms	—	5 men	Mangoes	—	11 men, 5 girls
king water	—	7 men	Small Hausa hoes	—	4 men
-handles, woodwork	—	3 men	Cooked groundnuts	—	13 women
			Dusa (grain-chaff)	—	25 men
			Fowls, eggs	—	2 men

(a) All were nomad Fulani women. (b) *Fura*, spiced balls of flour-paste, eaten as the midday snack. (c) *Allewa*, a sweetmeat made of honey, rice, and the black damson. (d) Kolas, independent: in 1959, these were seated at tables and also sold soap, perfume, and some cigarettes. Hence perfume-sellers are not registered separately in 1959.

cent. A further 46 per cent of the community incomes was acquired by the producers without entering into any form of exchange, that is to say, it was subsistence income in kind; and of the remaining 41 per cent of the community incomes which were locally derived and exchanged, approximately one-fourth, or 10 per cent of gross annual income, was transferred in the system of customary exchanges already described.[5] Thus, 31 per cent of their incomes was derived through commercial exchanges within these communities. Allowing for differences of season and locality, these proportions probably hold for most Hausa village economies today also. The differences between Hausa rural and urban conditions already mentioned render it unlikely that these ratios describe the economy of the towns.

To determine how far this rural economy is currently changing, we need to know such things as the composition and amounts of income and output, the ratios of income derived from subsistence, from local marketing, and from external trade; and data which indicate occupational categories. Lacking these data, I can only offer indirect evidence from Giwa. There I had carried out a census of market vendors in December 1949, which I was able to repeat in April 1959. When compared, these attendance surveys reveal certain differences over and above seasonal changes or the departure of nomad Fulani from the area. The Giwa market prices for 1958–59 already quoted also differ from those of 1948–49 in detail rather than substance.

On the market-day studied in 1949, two bulls were slaughtered at Giwa and two goats and three sheep were on sale alive. Three bicycles were available for hire also. On April 23, 1959, one bull and several goats were slaughtered, and six goats were on sale alive. On this occasion more than 120 bicycles were counted, and of these five were put up for sale. On that day there were fifteen large Hausa baskets of threshed guinea-corn, thirteen of early millet *(gero),* and ten of locust-bean flour *(kalwa)* available for sale by measure. These baskets were the large Hausa containers holding 100 *mudu* each. The five men then selling chillies each had a smaller basket with a capacity of 15 to 20 *mudu*. The seven Ibo traders then in the market sat at tables which displayed cotton vests, powder, canvas shoes, vaseline, bicycle parts, torches, and other European products.

Before analyzing or comparing these surveys, let us note their deficiencies. First, they contain errors of recording or reporting, of which the omission of grain sellers in the earlier survey and of barbers in the latter are the most obvious. Second, they deal only with market-vendors and not with total market attendance. Third, their differing seasonal incidence complicates comparison by introducing the factor

(5) For the details on which this analysis is based, see Smith 1955 : 175–219.

of seasonal variations. Bearing these qualifications in mind, we can still learn something from their comparison.

In December 1949, the Giwa market contained 363 male vendors, and 185 females, of whom 64 were nomad Fulani women selling milk and butter. To this total of 548 vendors, we can add 45 maidens, dressed for the dance which traditionally follows the market, and 70 youths whose only interest seemed to be in the girls. This gives a minimum attendance of 663 for that market day; and of the 548 vendors, 464 were Hausa, mainly drawn from Giwa and its environs. My occupational census of these settlements in 1949 yielded a total of 292 adult males and 421 adult women, exclusive of native officials and their families, who rarely attend the market.[6] Of these 292 men, 37 derived their total incomes from farming, and only 8 derived no part of their income therefrom. It is therefore likely that the majority of the 255 local men who had some craft or trade specialism were among the 363 male vendors in the market on the day of my survey. By contrast, even if all 121 Hausa women then selling in the market were drawn from the area of my occupational census, they would represent only 3/10ths of its adult female population. The remainder would be wives who had not yet reached the menopause, and who were thus bound by purdah in varying degrees.

On April 23, 1959, the market contained 534 vendors, 378 of these being male, and 156 female. Of these female vendors, 25 were nomad Fulani, and 131 were Hausa women—that is only 10 more than in 1949. Although the 1959 total of vendors is 14 less than in 1949, it includes an increase of 15 male Hausa vendors also, and owes its reduction almost entirely to the withdrawal of certain nomad Fulani from the environs of Giwa. In short, it seems likely that the small increase in the number of male and female Hausa selling in the latter market may represent local population growth and some expansion in the market itself rather than any major change in its composition or its relation to the local population whose occupational distribution I studied earlier.

In the 1949 market study, the vendors were classified by commodities into forty-five groups; in 1959, they fell into fifty-four commodity groups. Five commodities on sale in the earlier market are absent from the latter. Of these, three (namely, cocoyams, deleb palm fruit and baskets), are direct seasonal changes, while a fourth (perfume) is no longer sold as a separate retail line. The 1959 survey lists sixteen trade-lines absent from the earlier study, exclusive of grain sellers, which is an obvious recording error. Of these sixteen new trade-lines, mangoes, tamarind, honey, *waina*, yams, hoes and

(6) For details, Smith 1955 : 242–44.

hoe-handles are seasonal, the first five reflecting the cycle of crop supplies, while the two latter anticipate resumption of farming. The sale of cooked groundnuts by women recorded in April 1959 may indicate another seasonal variation or may be a switch of effort by some who found their previous activities unrewarding. It is also likely that the basket sellers of December 1949 include some of those who sold brooms in April 1959, since these two specialties are closely related, and the grasses are too dry for basketry in April. Likewise, the woodworkers selling hoe-handles in the April market may be the same men as sold mortars and pestles in December 1949, this change being seasonal also.

Omitting these cyclical variations, and such movements of vendors from one trade line to another as may also reflect seasonal factors, the commodity composition of the later market differs from the earlier in certain particulars. The 1959 study shows new or increased availability of palm oil, poultry, European metal basins and plates, bicycles, spare parts, torches, shoes, cotton vests and sewing machines, and changes in the distribution of cloth and perfume. Moreover there is a new Ibo trading element and new trade-lines such as grain-chaff and drinking water. These differences seem to represent certain changes in the demand structure of the Giwa population since 1949; but notably, they add to the traditional demand pattern which still keeps the market composition and commodity structure very similar to that of 1949.

Allowing for seasonal influences and for possible errors of recording, the difference in the numbers who sold the same commodity in these two markets might be due to several factors, separately or in combination—for example, migration, generation replacement, or to individual adjustments to market opportunities and risks. Such adjustments are simpler for men than for women, and for traders than for craftsmen. Of the sixty-three trade-lines listed in both surveys, only seven are exclusive to women and only five including grain-selling, are open to both sexes equally. Men dominate the market in the range of their interests as well as in numbers; and it is they who adopt and introduce new commodity-lines. Most of the craft goods are sold in these markets by their producers; and most of the market purchases are made by men who attend as vendors. The Hausa peasant goes to market with something for sale in order that he may get the money with which to purchase his needs. The vendor and the purchaser in the Hausa rural market is the same person; and since Hausa men are charged with the provision of household needs in cash as well as kind, their role is central for the market structure and for the domestic economy alike.

In Table 33, the gross sales of the Giwa market on a certain market-day of October 1949 were estimated at £29. 4. 4d. This estimate may be combined with the census of vendors in this market on 30 December 1949 to give a very approximate idea of the average sale per vendor at Giwa at that time. For this purpose, we may omit the sixteen barbers present in December, since they sold services rather than commodities; and we may also assume that the meeting studied in December had a sale twice as great as that estimated in October. This would mean that the 532 commodity vendors sold a total volume of goods worth approximately £60 on December 30, 1949. Their per capita sale would thus be about £0.11 each, of which perhaps 7d or 8d might represent income.

Naturally, this figure for the average sales per vendor is an imprecise estimate and is also open to severe criticisms for the method by which it has been derived. Without in the least underestimating these deficiencies, we can still use it to indicate a problem and to suggest its probable answer. The very low average sales and therefore income from marketing which had just been estimated raises the question why Hausa attend market so regularly and in such numbers, or rather, how can they afford to do so. For instance, our average market-day return of 8d. per vendor is far less attractive than the local rate of 1/6 d. per day for wage-labor which prevailed in 1949. Yet few men at Giwa undertook *kodago* (wage-labor) in between market days, preferring to work at their farms or crafts, while few would willingly miss the market.

Stated in this way, the problem admits of only one possible answer. Hausa, especially men, attend market regularly despite its low average return because under present conditions they cannot do otherwise. To obtain the cash with which to pay for goods and services they can neither produce themselves nor easily do without, they have to sell their own products or services and are therefore obliged to visit the market for the dual purpose of selling and buying. Their wives remain in purdah and have few responsibilities to the household economy. Given the Hausa occupational structure and traditional scale of values and wants, the men's dual participation in markets is inevitable and continuous. Of the 292 men living in Giwa and its environs in 1949, only 12 per cent depended solely on farming for their livelihood. Another 58 per cent practiced some other subsidiary occupation, whether craft, trade, or wage-labor, the latter being pursued by 20 men. A further 23 per cent had two subsidiary occupations each, and 7 per cent had three or more each. Of the 421 women who lived in this area, 142 or 34 per cent had one occupation only, 60 per cent had two each, and the remaining 6 per cent had three or more each. The economy of Hausa villages assumes and rests on this pattern of occupational diversity. Of the average income per taxpayer in my 1949–50 budget sample, £26.77 or 46 per cent was cash, £23.32 or 43 per cent was consumed by the producers without entering into any form of exchange, and £5.83 or 11 per cent took the form of goods transacted in customary exchange. The budgets describe a population which produces for home consumption and for market exchange almost equally, the goods and services sold by individuals providing them with the cash to purchase those which they buy. Hence the relatively large number of vendors and trade-lines in the Giwa market despite its low gross sales volume and low profit average.

The social function of Hausa markets is to satisfy this need for commercial exchange within communities which are occupationally diverse in their structure and which depend on production for both subsistence and exchange. The volume and the variety of items exchanged commercially far exceeds those which are transferred as gifts in the ceremonial and customary contexts, which serve religious or social ends since the commercial exchange supplies one-half of the material needs of the average Hausa household.

Excluding farmers who sell their cash-crops in special markets known as *floti* (plots) under government supervision, and those traders who range between several markets, the vendors in a rural Hausa market are mainly part-time specialists who spend their receipts from sales in the markets at which they trade. The traditional demand structure which influences these spending patterns is illustrated by my 1949–50 budget sample. Of the gross annual cash expenditure of the men in this sample, 12.2 per cent went on clothes, 5.9 per cent and 5.0 per cent on household and personal expenses respectively, 7.9 per cent on stimulants such as kolas or cigarettes, and 48.6 per cent on foodstuffs, processed or other. Clearly, the greater a man's involvement in trade or craft production, the less time can he devote to his farm, and the greater is his dependence on the market for the income with which to maintain his household. Since Hausa occupations are for the most part hereditary, their communities tend to have a stationary occupational composition and a conservative economy. In this rural economy, we can distinguish four sectors or levels of organization; first, the domestic subsistence sector; second, the system of customary exchange; third, the internal commercial system; and finally, the system of external exchange in which the community is involved.

We have seen that a balance obtains between the first sector and the two commercial ones; and outward and inward transfers also tend

to balance within each of the three latter sectors. Thus gifts made
and received tend to balance; and so do purchases and sales at both
the household and community levels; but the internal and external
commercial exchanges have to be taken together if the balance of
community "imports" and "exports" is to appear. As mentioned
above, this equation depends mainly on the value of crops exported
for its size. These crop exports are roughly equivalent in value to the
net outward payments for local imports; and in the communities
which I studied in 1949–50, the value of these external transfers was
13 per cent of annual income, as against 31 per cent derived from the
intra-community exchange system.

CONCLUSION

Among the Hausa, economic transactions are complex and varied. In
their customary forms they express values drawn from kinship,
religion, and political organization which themselves reflect differing
stages of Hausa culture history, and differ in their forms, functions,
and sanctions. Households are the basic economic units in Hausa
communities; they produce for exchange and for subsistence. The
commercial exchange system which balances their requirements
against their surpluses will simultaneously balance the community's
income and expenditure accounts. At this level, we find that rather
more than two-thirds of the values of these commercial exchanges are
purely local in character, the remainder being external. We have also
seen that for the most part craft production serves a local market in
rural Hausa communities. The Hausa community, like the household, but rather more so, provides itself with most of the goods and
services on which its subsistence depends; and the difference in the
subsistence ratios of households on the one hand and of communities
on the other is mainly made up by the value of local exchange. This
local exchange includes commercial and customary transfers together,
but the former has three times the value of the latter. In rural areas,
the market, which is the Hausa commercial institution *par excellence,*
is primarily concerned to facilitate and regulate this intra-community
commercial exchange, while other agencies such as *fatauci,* large
merchant traders, or *floti,* the export-crop selling points set up and
supervised by government, handle the external traffic. Excluding
floti, this was also the way in which exchange was organized and
conducted by Hausa before the British arrived; and the system owes
its impressive continuity to the diversity of subsistence and exchange
production on which Hausa economy is based. Since such integration
persists. households continue to supply services and goods to each

other within local communities, the character and techniques for production of these goods tend to remain fixed, and the market continues to satisfy primary functions of internal exchange. The account of Hausa habitat and history with which we began indicates the antiquity of this pattern and the factors which have contributed to its development and stability.

CHAPTER 12

Trade and Markets in the Economy of the Nomadic Fulani of Niger (Bororo)

BY MARGUERITE DUPIRE

The pastoral, nomadic Fulani, called Bororo,[1] who roam the territory of Niger, are neither traders nor have they themselves founded markets. Their economy does not allow them to be self-sufficient, and they are obliged to call upon the resources of the settled population in order to supply their basic subsistence needs. This is why, in all the areas where these cattle people live, one finds socio-economic symbioses between these two types of society; the nomads seem to have been more greatly influenced culturally than have the settled people.

It would nevertheless be unjust to underestimate the part which these pastoralists play in the trade, domestic and foreign, of the region in which they live. This role can be elucidated only by considering their economy in connection with the traditional trade habits of the settled population and with the general economic system of the territory.

Compared to the remarkably elaborate material cultures of some great pastoral or hunting societies—Maures, Tuareg, Lap, or Eskimo—that of the Bororo appears singularly poor. Not only are the objects in use of small account, they are almost never made by Fulani techniques. The Bororo themselves work only a minimal portion of the raw material furnished by their herds. They know neither how to tan hides, how to work bone and horn, nor to dig wells. The women make butter but not cheese from the milk of their goats. All their technical knowledge directly concerns tending their herds of zebus. This extreme specialization makes them dependent on the craftman-

[1] The ethnological fieldwork on which this chapter is based was done in 1951 among the Wodaabe tribe in Tahoua and Tanout (in Niger central and Niger oriental). The economic data gathered were few, general, and primarily of sociological interest. No quantitative economic study has yet been undertaken among the nomadic Fulani. It would, indeed, have been an extremely delicate matter to undertake. Nevertheless, the Veterinary Service of Niger has in the last years made every effort to control more systematically the various factors involved in pastoral economy. In addition, as part of the problem of labor migration, a study of cattle trade routes is being made in A.O.F. under the direction of J. Rouch. General information on animal husbandry in West and Central Africa can be found on six maps by M. F. Bonnet-Dupeyron (1945). I should like to thank Prof. G. Balandier for his kindness in reading and criticizing this manuscript.

ship of their neighbors—Hausa, Bellah, Tuareg—and on European imports. Hausa weavers, tailors, smiths, calabash engravers and tanners adapt their articles, with their well-known commercial opportunism, to the taste of their Bororo clientele.

At no period within their cycle of transhumance are the *Wodaabe* completely cut off from trade. In the dry season they frequent the markets and villages on the edges of the sedentary zone whither they move. In the wet season, when they go on transhumance to the ponds and pastures of the North, they are visited by the marabouts, healers, traders and smiths who sometimes stay several days in their camps to carry out work to order. They also meet with caravans and nomadic Tuareg or Bellah with whom they do business.

THE MAIN TRAITS OF BORORO ECONOMY

Goods and Income and Their Utilization; Economic Choices.

The wealth that *Wodaabe* produce consists essentially in dairy products and livestock. Utilization of this wealth corresponds to a fixed idea held in the society about a proper economic balance. Dairy products are either consumed or exchanged for grain. They belong to the women, whose pin money comes from selling the surplus above the amount used, from which they ordinarily buy clothes and ornaments or which they accumulate in the form of small livestock.

Indeed, the sheep and goats which, among the western *Wodaabe* are more often the property of women than of men, form "a small reserve granary," readily turned into money, which allows one at any time to procure consumption goods or other items of relatively high cost. Cattle, the property par excellence of men, are not considered consumers' goods, but rather the means of production (heifers, cows, bulls) or as a final reserve (steers) for the important expenditures of household or of ceremonial obligation. Only secondarily does the latter have any consumption value—when the meat of animals sacrificed at ceremonies is eaten by all those present. The Bororo do not kill cattle to feed themselves.

Other sources of income have only a secondary place in their economy: repairing calabashes or hiring out one's services to pound grain for the sedentary people; manuring the fields of others by means of one's herds. In general, the *Wodaabe* do not care for subordinate employment. When a young man becomes a herdsman for a stranger, it is because he is too poor to be his own master. The very few *Wodaabe* who have taken to grain farming do so only by necessity: they sow a few *ares* near a Hausa village at the edge of the sedentary nomadic zone and hasten to rejoin their herds which are in wet season pasture with the members of their camps. The amount they harvest from their small fields—if the latter have not been flooded, devastated by birds or trampled by livestock in their absence—constitutes only enough grain for a few months at the maximum.

The *Wodaabe* have probably never calculated the total yearly income from their herds nor that part of it which they could dispose of while maintaining a necessary margin of safety. One of their essential preoccupations is not to cut into their property, and the reasons they give for so doing, far from being mystical, are fundamentally practical. Although they are sentimentally attached to their livestock, they live off them physically, socially and morally and if their attitude towards them were not realistic they would long since have disappeared from the map of Africa. One is often struck by the opportunism and realism of these nomads. Moreover, the most important of their marriage customs (preferential marriage with the father's brother's daughter and the levirate) are founded on a basically economic motivation: the retention of beasts within the lineage. Livestock is destined for certain social usages. First of all, it is set aside for direct heirs, the sons, who, from the time of their birth, gradually receive in pre-inheritance their share of the paternal herd. Animal sacrifices are necessary for the official legalization of name-giving and for the marriage of each child, while another part of the herd is confided to wives, either as pseudo-dowry *(sadaki)*[2] or as milch cows. The master of the herd cares for livestock over which the members of the polygamous family have certain rights of usage or of unalienable ownership during their minority. In view of these multiple obligations one can understand how the portion actually belonging to the master of the herd diminishes as he grows old and as his sons set up for themselves.

Such property is thus oriented towards the future, and the Bororo have the unpleasant reputation of being extremely miserly. But is one really dealing with avarice under present conditions of pastoral life? In order to judge the matter it would be necessary to know the actual, realizable income from a Bororo herd and any possible risk of loss ocurring during the normal growth of the herd. We still have only approximate data on such matters. For this purpose it would be necessary to take into account an important number of transactions which still escape quantification: exchange loans, consumption, sacrifice. What one can say is that all expenditure above that for day-to-day consumption always seems very heavy to Bororo, par-

---

(2) No French or English word is suitable for the translation of the Bororo *sadaki;* furthermore it differs from the *sadaki* of the Koran, which is a dowry given by the husband to his wife.

ticularly tax, as weighed against their slender revenue, since their cattle are not traditionally meant to be sold.

Nevertheless their viewpoint does not appear to experienced verterinarians entirely bereft of good sense. Thus L. M. Feunteun, Veterinary Inspector for A.O.F. writes:

Mention has often been made of the conservative turn of mind of herders which leads them to keep in their herds a ridiculously large number of cattle and to sell their animals only in case of absolute necessity. This fact is generally considered deplorable. Outside of certain faults in breeding, related to the lack of selection, and of an overlong retention within the herd of sterile females or steers, we do not think this conservative turn of mind of the herdsman particularly open to criticism. It is thanks to this that it has been possible to reconstitute the herds after the periodically great losses brought by rinderpest. The herdsman keeps his old beasts because they are resistant to contagious diseases and constitute the safest element of his herd, the firm base of his possessions and the means of increasing them. This yearly retention is troublesome in the areas overpopulated with cattle; in other areas, and they constitute the great majority of instances, it is a factor important to economic and social progress. (Feunteun 1955 : 143)

It is a fact that the capital in livestock in Niger is not very productive. For the two administrative *cercles* of Zinder and Maradi, the revenue from transactions in cattle (meat, hide, export) was estimated by the veterinary services in 1957 to involve 24 to 30 per cent of the actual number of cattle.[3] Furthermore not all these cattle are in the hands of the nomads, for in this region cattle represent the accumulated wealth of ultimate value.[4]

The Bororo herds are rather small: that of an adult family head varies, on the average, between 10 and 50 head in the region of Tahoua. It is a sign of wealth to own 100 head.[5] The contribution of the nomads to the income of the territory is reduced by the fact that they show themselves as uninterested in the sale of their cattle for

(3) Report on livestock conditions in the economy of Niger, given advance announcement in a letter of 24/1/1957.

(4) Cattle are a mode of investment even among the sedentary people. Such behavior persists even when the type of economy changes. For example, the immigrant Dioulas of the Sudan, who have become cocoa and coffee farmers in the Côte d'Ivoire, invest a part of their income in plantations, another part in herds, while the indigenous farmers are attracted by other forms of investment. The subject has been considered for East Africa (Trouwborst 1956).

(5) The census of 1950, the figures of which should probably be increased by 20 to 25 per cent, gives for the subdivision of Tahoua 0.02 camels, 0.05 donkeys, 3.6 sheep and goats, 5.14 head of cattle per person. The figures are higher in the subdivision of Tanout (East Niger), where the pastoralists are in general richer: 0.04 camels, 0.06 donkeys, 7.2 sheep and goats, and 7.9 head of cattle per person.

butcher's meat as they are in the sale of hides. Therefore, in the region of Maradi where one finds a species of goat renowned for the quality of its hide, it is the settled people who have taken to raising them. On an average they possess one sheep for every eight goats, while the nomads have two sheep for one goat.

In what degree could this income, considered so slight from the viewpoint of a western type economy, be increased without jeopardizing the margin of safety? No study of pastoralism has attempted to answer this question. The Bororo constantly emphasize the dangers which menace the life of their herds: drought, exhaustion of pastures, epizootics, destruction by lightning or wild animals, and theft. One can find *Wodaabe* who, as a result of epizootics, have been forced to start building up new herds from scratch. It was in order to avoid this kind of insecurity that after the drought of 1950, a small number of them began to raise grain so that they would not need to exchange their cattle for grain.

The composition of the herds, both among the nomadic and the settled peoples, seems to be directly associated with milk production. An enquiry conducted in 1954 in the subdivisions of Maradi, Dakoro and Tessaoua (Robinet in Larrat 1955) covering 318 Bororo herds chosen at random, showed the following proportions: cows 45.50 per cent, heifers 16.85 per cent, calves and yearlings 26 per cent, bulls 8.08 per cent, steers 3.57 per cent. A very small number of sterile cows was discovered (1.3 per cent); the herdsmen very quickly rid themselves of barren animals. These figures show a characteristic orientation of the herd towards dairy production, there being a very small reserve to be used for other purposes (bulls and steers, 11.65 per cent; the percentage of old cows is very difficult to estimate). It is in this sense that one can consider the *Wodaabe* management of their herds as rational, for their species of cattle—the domesticated *zebu Bororoji*—is adapted to sub-Sahara climatic conditions but not as suitable for meat production. The pastoralists select good milch cows for breeding and demand this high quality in the ancestry of stud bulls. Moreover, they practice cross breeding, especially with *Azawak zebu* cows, whose dairy superiority over the *Bororoji* type is well known to them.

One of the differences that is often stressed between primitive and industrial economies is that of choice in the disposition of goods. "Such choices," Goodfellow writes of the pastoral Bantu, "are so limited that the difference in degree can be considered as a difference in kind" (Goodfellow 1939). Even though such choices are associated with different scales of values, they are no less real in the one case than in the other. Given their socio-economic value preferences,

the pastoral Fulani go about such choices, either in the accumulation
of goods or in the mode of their disposal, in such a way as to obtain
a maximum of satisfaction. The balance among the three elements
of pastoral economy—farming, sheep and cattle—implies important
choices, at the level of the group as well as on that of the individual.
In Niger the connections among these modes of production would
seem very diverse among the sedentary, semi-nomadic and nomadic
Fulani groups. But these types of economy are not frozen in time;
they evolve and are constantly modified by various factors, above all
ecological ones. The *Uda'en* Fulani for example, after having lost a
part of their cattle in Nigeria, settled and specialized in raising sheep.
Those segments among them who emigrated to Niger, where the
herds of sheep used to be transhumant, have again become nomadic.
They have not given up sheep herding, but their cattle prosper thanks
to the quality of the pasture, and cattle are gradually regaining their
value among them. Among the *Wodaabe* tribe there are observable
differences between one lineage and another. The *Njiapto'en* who
have few cattle, farm a bit. The *Godienko'en,* who have grown wealthy
and are tempted by luxury expenditure, own a greater number of
saddle animals, goats and sheep. The *Jijiru,* who also are interested in
sheep herding, have a tendency to neglect cattle raising; their herds
for the most part are made up of cattle tended for sedentary people.
   At the individual level, decisions are preceded by weighing the
advantages and disadvantages of each alternative, which sometime
raises internal conflicts. The greater part of the *Njiapto'en,* who have
decided to cultivate a few meager fields at the beginning of the wet
season, complain bitterly of having been forced by poverty "to scratch
the earth" in order to feed their families. This dissatisfaction is most
pronounced in the case of a household head who does not have a
shepherd to lead his herds in their transhumant movements. Out of
his deep concern, he asks himself if the nourishment to be derived
from a few sheaves of grain is equivalent to the loss that his stock,
deprived of the first rich, moist pasturage, will undergo. Those
Wodaabe who acquire a stock of sheep have brought themselves to
follow the example of the women (who are still the main owners of
such stock), having realized that it constitutes a source of exchange
value more readily realizable than cattle for current expenses.
Changes in production lines, then, are constantly undertaken, induced by ecological, economic or social motives.
   The organization of labor within the economic unit equally allows
for diversity. Shall full brothers continue to move and work together
after the death of their father? Who is to be the head of herds and
homestead of the joint-family? Is the recently married son, who as

yet has no one to work for him, to set himself up independently, separate from his father and younger brothers who could remain the shepherds of his flock? Should he take with him one of the latter to play this role until he himself has sons old enough to perform it? In almost every case of common residence (father and married sons, brothers, brothers and parallel cousins, consanguines or others) it can be established that economic considerations were paramount. This mode of residence is found together with that of the polygynous household: the latter accounts for from 26 to 61 per cent depending on the segment. It seems not to be merely the effect of cultural conservatism but rather a voluntarily chosen arrangement. The co-residents, who very rarely hold their livestock in common, benefit from many advantages: reduction in labor, exchange of services, assistance to the physically or mentally weak. It is rare that a family which is balanced in persons and economy would not rather be divided into households, for independence is today the ideal. In all these cases the solutions adopted are fitted to particular circumstances and correspond to problems of the organization of labor and to the social and economic exigencies of daily life. Among the forms of cooperative residence, that of brothers is the most frequent—30 per cent of the total number of cases—although it corresponds to no social imperative.

When it is a matter of sacrificing beasts for a marriage or name-giving ceremony, at first sight the traditional etiquette hides the possibilities of variation. There is a set formula for a first marriage: the slaughter of three head of cattle, the presentation of a cow, a heifer and a young bull to the fiancée's family. But, in order to understand that in the eyes of the Bororo cows are not regarded as interchangeable units, one must have witnessed the careful deliberation of the head of a family in trying to decide which animal to slaughter, and heard the long palavers of the fiancée's aunts on the value of the animals presented to them. The qualitative value of an animal is just as important as its quantitative value. The choice operative in the case of the head of family "obliged" to sacrifice a beast would appear in essence as a compromise between his desire for social prestige, which urges him to offer a fine animal, and his own economic interests. Common sense is not excluded from these sacrifices and collective feasts, and there is a scale of importance against which to measure one's self-deprivation: the naming of the first born and the final marriage sacrifice demands gifts of a higher quality (three year old bulls) than those for other ceremonies; one would not dishonor oneself by killing an old, sterile cow. Knowing how to choose wisely, and to weigh what is to be given against what is to be kept, belong to the list of an individual's qualities vaunted in songs.

Nevertheless ultimately these conscious choices come to quite specific results because they are motivated by a culturally determined scale of values and of satisfactions. A *Bodaado* does without a shelter because he would have to sell a head of cattle to get a hide tent from the Bellah, and then use a jack ox to carry it. His need for comforts is reduced to the minimum because it is subordinated to the welfare of the flocks. From this point of view, the Bororo mentality is quite different from that of the Tuareg. Although the economic yield of Fulani animal husbandry in the region of Agades would seem to be the equivalent of that of the Tuareg Kel Fardei, the latter, having more needs to be satisfied, market their stock on a far greater scale. The economic goal of the Bororo is not to raise their material standards but to accumulate livestock. The way in which a rich man lives is scarcely different from that of a poor man: he drinks a little bit more tea, smokes, owns sumptuous camel harness, his hospitality is more generous, he acquires an entourage of clients, praise-singers, and Muslim holy men; and when he has bought an old camp bed he uses it as an item of prestige. His satisfactions reach far beyond those of the less affluent when he silently contemplates the evening, his flocks back within the kraal, having assumed one of those meditative poses that express the pleasure of possession.

The circulation of goods and services within and without the group.
   The circulation of goods takes place through a large number of intermediary operations. Within the group, one uses no money: one gives, one exchanges, one inherits, one lends, and one participates in ceremonial obligations of a reciprocal nature.

   Those who have primary rights to the "gifts" of a father are his descendants. But some goods excape this transmission and enter a system of reciprocal relationships between groups of kinsmen; they are given up without any ideas of material interest or immediate repayment. Without compensation one gladly lends a sturdy bull or some milk cows to a friend or kinsman in temporary difficulties, so that he can feed his family. A woman often gives milk to a sister-in-law within her camp, to her mother or to kinsmen—more rarely to one of her co-wives, for they (granted the system of allotment of milch cows by the husband) are often jealous of each other. The herd master may give up some of his beasts to his relatives, to Bororo or foreign friends. Such gifts, which are in any case of only slight importance, cannot be made to the detriment of children or the rights of heirs. Such gifts are also socially oriented: a Bodaado consents to give an animal to a friend without any notion of recompense, but he never thinks of making one of his wives a non-customary gift of cattle—wife's and husband's goods remain quite clearly separate during the marriage. Finally, the liberty granted an individual in the disposal of his goods is denied him after his death, and the making of wills unknown.

Reciprocity appears in those ceremonies in which one slaughters cattle. Actually the flesh of the animals slaughtered by every family head at the birth or marriage of his children is eaten by all the members of the segment who are assembled during the wet season at a meeting called *worso*. These obligatory sacrifices not only sanction social relationships but also permit the equitable and reciprocal division of animal meat.

The elaborate forms of exchange of services are less numerous, but they are basic. There is first the matter of adoption, which is the temporary assignment of the labor of the child by the real parents to the adoptive parents. This arrangement allows households which are childless or made up only of old or physically handicapped persons to be self-sufficient.

The second form of loan concerns livestock: it is called *nanga na'i* (literally: take the cows) and deserves detailed analysis, for its extensive usage is one of the traits which differentiates the true nomads from the sedentary Fulani. In fact it is, next to inheritance from relatives, the most efficacious way of acquiring a herd. When a boy reaches the age of five or six, his father busily tries to find "lenders" among his paternal or maternal relatives or among his friends. Neither the ties of kinship nor those of friendship exclude a rigorous regulation of *nanga na'i*, and the observation of the agreement as a matter of honor to the two parties involved. The lender grants a heifer, most often a three year old, until she has thrice dropped a calf, according to a pre-established agreement. This increase belongs to the borrower, who will thereafter lead the heifer back to the camp of his benefactor.

This is not a matter of a promise which can be revoked, but of a firm commitment, the slightest details of the execution of which have been prescribed by custom. The lender who wants, for whatsoever reason, to take back his heifer before the expiration of the contract is obliged to give to his borrower the number of calves that she has not yet dropped. If the cow has remained sterile five or six years, she is returned to her owner who, as an excuse for not having realized his promise, generally makes his friend a gift of a yearling heifer or lends him another cow in order to fulfill his obligation. The borrower, without being held responsible for the death of the beast, ought (in case of its death) to bring its hide back to its owner as testimony of the accident. The owner returns half the hide to the borrower, or even all of it if the heifer has not yet given him the number of calves agreed on. To care for this trust as for his own is the first obligation of the recipient, but the lender's confidence in him is *de rigueur* and it would be out of place for him to ask for news of a heifer which he had given up in *nanga na'i*. The meetings which initiate and conclude the agreement take place in a friendly atmosphere. The host who receives the man to whom he has agreed to lend generally prepares a small feast of kuskus and sometimes even sacrifices an animal; then the host accompanies the borrower to his camp with the heifer. When the borrowed cow has produced sufficient offspring, the recipient brings the cow back in the presence of all the members of the camp and expresses his gratitude by placing in the corral of his benefactor some branches of *barkehi,* a talisman of luck and fertility. The death of one of the parties does not conclude the contract, which must be continued by their heirs.

The reciprocity of the agreement is not a legal obligation, but a moral duty to repay at a date not specifically fixed by custom. That is how a young man who as yet possesses only a few animals can demand *nanga na'i* from the descendants of those who received such a loan from his family, one or two generations before. There sedentary Fulani even consider *habba na'i* (to tie down cows) as a loan on credit which ought to be repaid as soon as possible in the form of *hokkorde,* when the lender asks for it. When a *habba na'i* cow has fulfilled the conditions of the initial agreement, she is returned to her owner with a heifer from the herd of the borrower which institutes an absolutely parallel obligation.

This service goes far beyond the limits of kinship and furnishes considerable assistance to herdsmen. Of the loans which assisted eight individuals, thirty came from friends and distant kinsmen, twenty from paternal relations and seven from maternal kinsmen. The amount of the loans received by each of these eight family heads during the course of their lives varied from two to eleven heifers (by an orphan) and as much as forteen (by an influential chief). In order to judge the importance of *nanga na'i* as a mode of acquisition of livestock in comparison with other means, one could cite the example of a segment chief who built up his herd beginning with thirteen cows, each of which bore young: four were given him as a gift by his father, he inherited three, he received four heifers as *nanga na'i* loan, and in addition he bought four steers. When I knew him his herd numbered 200 animals.

In Bororo opinion this institution provides security for the future: a helping hand for the beginning herdsman or a new start for the herdsman whose flock has been decimated by an epizootic. "Does one know what destiny brings?" they ask. What recourse could there be for the miser who never makes a loan or for the man whose father or grandfather had never offered any *nanga na'i?* This practice also facilitates the diffusion of the best stock, an attribute which makes of it a reciprocal loan of proven breeders, and especially lauded by Fulani.

The quality of the animal is important and the initiative to choose is left to the borrower. In order to express his choice the borrower does no more than make a special kind of notch in the ear of one of the young heifers which he has noticed in the herd of a kinsman or of a friend.

The social effects of *nanga na'i* are no less important: it reinforces the bonds of kinship and creates new relationships of reciprocity both within and without the tribe. Nothing is further from the spirit of this practice than the idea of lending at interest, for the creditor gets no immediate advantages and runs all the risks. This reciprocal loan, for a longer or shorter period, is a sort of draft on the future and seems to have the features of an exchange of services guaranteed by ties of kinship and friendship. It is perfectly adapted to the precarious conditions of pastoral life.

The extreme mobility of both consumer's and producer's goods is manifest at all levels of economic life. Such objects are converted, loaned, and given with an amazing facility. The same thing is true of livestock: *nanga na'i* contracts, loans of stock bulls or milch cows, exchange of animals, gifts, pre-inheritances—all permit a rapid circulation of goods which increase the total material wealth, and by passing through many hands benefits the whole society rather than a fortunate few. European travelers have so often accused these pastoralists of avarice because they have not put their own economic attitudes into a comparative perspective. The Bororo manages his livestock economically, for his stock is precious to him from three points of view: as a guarantee of the immediate material security for himself and his family, as insurance for the future of his children, and as a reservoir of gifts and exchanges, a supplemental form of security since reciprocity is an elemental rule. It is obvious that other reasons militate in favor of the hoarding of cattle but it is impossible to assign weights to essentially social motivations (obligations, prestige) compared to economic motivations. It has therefore seemed more useful to show how Bororo behavior reflects both determinant factors and by what means goods for immediate consumption and those for production circulate more or less rapidly, allowing their relatively egalitarian distribution within the group.

Outside the group, some intratribal forms of transactions persist in addition to new types of transactions and the use of money. By preference the Bororo resort to barter with outside people in order to obtain ordinary subsistence goods and basic necessities. Both linguistics and comparative history attest to the importance of this archaic form of external trade in Fulani society. To buy and to sell are derived from the same stem *(soodugo, sottugo)*, these two acts making up the parts of a single reciprocal operation, as in exchange *(wattutugo.)* The word *tyoggu* (or *choggu*) designates the contract for exchange of goods of the same value, in kind or in currency. The transaction is thus regarded as a reciprocal exchange of values.

The Fulani of Fouta-Jalon have even developed a complex system of reckoning exchange values, the standard unit of which—the *walare* —has multiples from two to thirty. These units are invariable; to them correspond variable quantities, according to the laws of supply and demand, of the items basic to the economy of the country (cotton, grain, cattle, sheep, goats, mats, chickens, slaves). The commodity equivalent of the unit of measure thus changes with prices. Measures of length, of capacity, of surface permit one to obtain a sufficiently precise estimation of goods which can thus be readily exchanged for each other, or divided in case of inheritance. In 1936 these terms were still used in Fouta-Jalon (Vieillard 1939 : 59, 111) and currency had been incorporated in the system of equivalents. Even though this latter is not known to the Bororo of the Niger, there are still traces of it in the local interpretation of the use of money. Exchange *(troc)* as practiced by the Bororo includes, together with products, services and money as intermediary links. It is also characterized by the multiplicity of operations, exchange going through two, three or four stages in order to end with the desired object. Thus a *Bodaado* woman will go repair calabashes among the sedentary Hausa for several weeks and be paid in millet. She will exchange or sell this grain for money, with which she will buy a cloth at market.

Fresh, or more often sour, milk and butter are the base of the system of exchange, and their primary use is for the acquisition of grain. The mound of butter *(taure)* exchanged for money or grain varies in quantity with the season and the scarcity of milk. The number of variations—on the order of one to four—corresponds to variations in the value of grain, but with delays. The millet and the dairy products which are exchanged thus both have a seasonal variation in quantity and during part of the year can be exchanged "measure for measure." The norms of these exchanges are more precise in the villages than in the bush where they result from the agreement of the parties, which often takes long to achieve and which depends on the value that each attributes to the object he wants.

Exchange, the classic form of trade for dairy products, is often also employed for cattle, even in the villages. In the region of Madaoua, the *Bi-koro'en* (one of the *Wodaabe* patrilineages) exchange a yearling for a woman's large cloth, a grown steer for six blue cloths and a gown, a yearling plus a sheep for a white gown, etc. No standard price seems to exist, but both parties know the trade value of the articles which they offer. During the wet season, when the Bororo are far from the markets and if they have need of anything which they neglected to buy before leaving the sedentary zone, they are forced to barter with the itinerant *dioulas* (independent traders) and the terms of such transactions are never in their favor.

From the strictly economic viewpoint, the barter system as practised is quite disadvantageous to the pastoralists. They generally suffer a loss thereby, except in the case of the exchange of dairy products, because it is difficult to apply a fine scale of values to indivisible articles (clothes, livestock) and the lack of commercial competition in the bush permits the *Dioula* to get very high prices from the customers on his route, making them pay dearly for transportation of the goods. Finally the successive operations, to which the pastoralists have recourse in order to obtain what they want, multiply their losses, while the time consumed in these transactions defies estimation. But for all these disadvantages the Bororo like this method, for it allows them to keep their livestock until the last extremity. The reduction of needs to their most limited expression is a primitive mode of economizing.

They use money only in those cases in which they cannot procure certain articles through barter or to satisfy certain obligations. They must have money for paying tax, for healers, for certain expensive jewelry and for at least a part of the salt for their animals, and for clothes and furnishings. It has already been noted that money was formerly used as an intermediate means of exchange. Coins have replaced cowries, but bear the same name *(tyede* or *chede)* as cowries, these latter thereafter being called "white shells" *(tyede daneje)* in order to distinguish them from western money. This word is also used to mean the "price" of an object. Money is still called *jamdi,* iron. *Jaudi* (plural of *nyaudiri,* sheep, ram) is an old term with a meaning deeply enmeshed in the whole culture; it means wealth, but to pronounce it brings bad luck.

Small change *(tyede)* is used as in the Fouta-Jalon system of reckoning, the five franc piece *(della)* being taken here as the unit. In the markets one buys small mounds of butter, condiments, grain, groundnuts, varying in quantity, for one, two or three della.[6] Money thus has

(6) We are obliged to Prof. P. F. Lacroix for the following remarks. The word *della* is probably a pidgin deformation of the word "dollar," introduced by Hausa traders,

a limited range of usage and in certain minor transactions it conserves the character of barter. Whichever method they employ, the terms of exchange are usually unfavorable to the Bororo for the reasons already mentioned, together with others which we shall analyze below.

Socio-Economic Relations.

The modes of remuneration used outside the group imply certain socio-economic relations and mostly concern shepherds and middlemen or *dillalai*. The Bororo do not pay their shepherds in money, as do the sedentary people, but in kind. Shepherds can thus accumulate in a few years their own herds, at least of sheep and become their own masters.

The relationships into which the Bororo enter with the *dillalai* cattle buyers form part af a complex system of sale and purchase by middleman that is widely spread throughout Hausa country (Forde and Scott 1945 : 133; M. G. Smith 1955 : 102, 143). Nevertheless, the form that these relations take in Bororo society is integrated with a socio-economic structure peculiar to the Fulani domain. The Fulani, as opposed for example to the Tuareg, seldom sell their animals directly to a private customer or to a trader; they turn to licensed middlemen. The *dillali,* who has no capital, brings together the seller and those who will buy most frequently at market but also in the bush. After he closes the deal, he receives only a small commission of 3 to 5 per cent. It sometimes happens that he cheats his client by telling him that the sale, at which the latter was not present, was at a price lower than was actually the case, keeping the difference for himself. These *dillalai* move about a great deal, accompanying their clients to different markets and, since they know the habits of their regular clientele, they succeed in satisfying both parties.

The role of a *dillali* is very important for it is adapted to a type of trade in which money is rare and trade risks quite considerable: it would be unjust to consider him as no more than a mere link in the trade sequence. By the fact that he pays for a license and that his profession is legally recognized, he guarantees the validity and the execution of the contract. This security is by no means negligible in a region where nomadic clients can disappear without having paid their debts or can try to get by with the sale of sick, imperfect or stolen

---

and its value is a souvenir of the time when a dollar was worth five francs. In those territories where there is French influence, the money units with a value of five francs have various names: *budi* (Fouta-Jalon and Volta), *sunkudi* (Bagirmi and North Adamawa). The system of sale which consists in making the quantity of merchandise vary is still applied by the hawkers of the region of Paris in selling their bunches of parsley and other herbs.

animals. Since the sale is generally on credit (the buyer at the conclusion of the bargain paying down only a third of the agreed price),
it is to "his *dillali*" that the Bororo seller turns if he has not recovered
his payment. At the frontier, it is the *dillali* who takes care of going
through customs and of changing money.

This economic role has social aspect, and the particular relationship which joins the Bororo with their *dillalai* takes the form of a
"social contract." Those to whom the Bororo of the Tahoua region
turn belong to the category *dillalai-mahautaa* or middlemen-butchers.
Normally they do not succeed in becoming independent traders
(dioula), as do certain middlemen of a superior category, who buy in
the dry and cold seasons at important markets in the interior in order
to resell in Nigeria. Some of these say they are the descendants of
captives who belonged to Fulani or Bororo families now in Niger.
This fact explains why in the Hausa language of the eastern sector,
the word *mahaucii* is synonymous with the word *baringe,* meaning a
slave living close to the village of his Fulani master. But if their
ancestors were of the butcher caste among the Fulani, today they do
not practice this profession and limit themselves to buying and selling.
They constitute one of the numerous branches reckoned among the
profession of butcher in Hausa society.

These *dillalai-mahautaa,* although they are today free, continue to
observe towards the descendants of their former masters certain of the
obligations under which their ancestors lay. The family butcher must
feed his master's horse when the latter passes through his village, and
the Fulani have kept the custom of having their butchers move with
them, as in the times when the latter lived in the master's village. In
family life, the settled Fulani rely on them for slaughtering and
cutting up the animals at their ceremonies and they pay them in food
and kola nuts. Among the Bororo, servile relations have become very
much lessened in content and have actually been assimilated into a
sort of joking relationship *(dendiraagal).*

Even within Bororo society this relationship is asymmetrical, the
brother's children playing the role of "masters" in relation to the
sister's children, called the "slaves." It was natural that this second
position be assigned to the *dillali-mahaucii,* who remains the inferior,
the subordinate. As cross-cousins they perform reciprocal services.
The *dillali* gives food and lodging to "his Bororo" when the latter
comes to do business in the village; the latter (the Bororo) receives
him in his camp, giving him, from time to time, the gift of a cow (in
the *dendiraagal* relationship the gifts given by the superior to the
inferior are always the greater). In addition, the *dillali-mahaucii* takes
orders for his Bororo clients and brings the goods they need to them

in the bush. Both of them indulge in verbal joking, and the "slave" is entitled, like the sister's son, to "rob" his "master" of a head of cattle to sell for his own profit: a simple simulacrum implying restoration under one form or another. No motive for disagreement, say the *dillalai-mahautaa,* can arise between them and "their Bororos." The sole difference of any account between this *dendiraagal* relationship and the relationship that holds between true cross-cousins is the scrupulously observed interdiction on marriage between these groups. This professional "guild" is the only one in Niger to benefit from this situation. In Fouta-Jalon this relationship existed in a parallel form between the sedentary Fulani and the traders whom they protected and whom they called "their *sarakolle."* (Vieillard 1939 : 23, 120). It is to them that the pastoral-agriculturalists turned to sell their cattle or their slaves.

This relationship is fitted into the ancient feudal structure of the Fulani states. Bonds of vassalage and of clientage in Fouta-Jalon tied families of the patron conquerors to the original holders of the land, to those who immigrated after the conquest, to scholars and marabout strangers, to certain specialist artisans (butchers and shoemakers) and to traders. Since even the sedentary Fulani have always avoided the activities of the artisan and the trader, they need middlemen. The particular place given traders is doubtless based upon the interest they have in common with their masters in the traditional element of Fulani economy—cattle. Their important role implies a mutual confidence in their relations with the pastoralists.

THE PLACE OF BORORO ECONOMY WITHIN THE REGIONAL ECONOMY

Trade Routes and Markets of Niger.

In this poor territory, one is struck by the number and importance of markets and of the traditional trade routes, the most important being those for cattle and salt. The reason is that historically this region was the transit zone between the Sahara and the farming lands of the south.

The Veterinary Service has registered 360 markets, more than half of which are situated in the central section, which is wealthiest in cattle. Their origins are not known, but according to the first Europeans who penetrated the interior of the country, the greater part of them existed before French occupation. One can make several classifications: markets held twice a week (extremely few) or weekly; principal and secondary (according to the number of animals brought in and the number butchered); urban (Maradi, Niamey, Tahoua) or bush; markets that are but slightly equipped or modern (the latter in the Maradi area, which is wealthy and produces groundnuts); markets for internal or primarily external trade and those where local buyers or strangers (generally in the Mainé area) dominate; seasonal markets or those which are active throughout almost all the year (Subdivision of Dakoro); markets specializing in the trade of cattle or sheep (Kellakam, in the Subdivision of Mainé-Soroa); markets dominated by the nomads, like that of Birni-Lallé in the region of Dakoro attended by many Tuareg and Buzu [or Bella] from Agadès, the Subdivisions of Madaoua, Tanout, and by the Fulani from Madaoua, Tahoua, Maradi and Nigeria; markets important for butchery or those oriented towards sale. This listing gives one an idea of the diversity of markets but does not explain the reasons for their importance and vitality.

One of the factors conditioning the development of markets is their location with regard to trade routes and the possibilities of export. The market of Diffa, in the region of Nguigmi, which is heavily attended by Fulani and Bororo—sometimes from a long distance away (Tanout, Sokoto)—owes its importance to its position on the border. Certain markets, especially on the border in the Maradi sector, are fundamentally assembly points for export cattle or transit points both for traders and for transhumant pastoralists. The crossing of transhumance routes and export routes often determines the situation of big markets (Dargué, N.W. region of the Maradi Subdivision). Those which are located at the convergence of many routes, coming from the areas rich in cattle and on the border, are heavily attended by both traders and smugglers.

In the same way that some markets die, like that of Myrriah following the installation of a military camp, others are born or grow with the creation of a new route: e.g., Dan Issa (Subdivision of Maradi) on the route from Maradi to Kano or Tabotaki, (see Map 16), the most important market in the subdivision of Madaoua (250 to 300 head of cattle at each of its weekly meetings during 1953). At the center of an area of rich pasturage, and situated on the salt-caravan route[7] running from Bilma through Marendet and Madaoua to Sokoto, Tabotaki is a veritable turntable, almost precisely at an equal distance from the market centers of Madaoua, Dakoro, Chadawanka and Tahoua. Since 1951 there has been an automobile road between Tabotaki and Madaoua. Traders coming here from Nigeria buy small and large livestock, and camels from Kell-gress or the south.

A glance at the map of the main currents of import and export from

(7) These caravans are usually called Azalais or Taghlemt.

the Sahara to the South[8] allows one to assess quite readily the importance of the great "relay-markets," most of them being located on the old Sahara caravan routes that brought salt and dates from Bilma and Fachi, Amadror (Hoggar), Teguidda-N'Tessoum, In-Salah and Taoudeni, and returned north grain and manufactured objects. Tahoua market is a good example,[9] being at the concourse of the salt routes coming from Taoudeni, Amadror/Teguidda-N'Tessoum, Bilma/Fachi and from the salt lands of Fogha (banks of the Niger). The caravan people from Taoudeni barter at Menaka and Tahoua a bar of salt for a donkey or eight to nine sheep and three or four bars for a camel or, again, some bulrush millet and cattle for export. These animals are then exchanged at Kano and at Sokoto, for pieces of cloth (Genevière 1950). Towards the south, Tahoua makes contact through Illela, the border market, with the Hausa countries and the great economic magnet of Kano. This remarkable situation explains how such a relay market has been a zone of attraction and influence, formerly more important than today, between the Sahara, the banks of the Niger, and Nigeria. The markets situated along the great caravan routes are generally the most ancient ones. Not all of them have kept the same importance, for these routes have been supplanted by others (competition of salt from Kaolack and Rosso by river and of salt imported from Europe). Some have become of secondary importance—like Tahoua which is but fourth in the Subdivision— while others have become notable in the border area where new resources have been developed (such as groundnuts in the region of Maradi). On the banks of the Niger, the other export route, are located several very large markets, such as Tillabery which drains cattle from Ansongo, bought by export traders.

If we consider only the trade movements having to do with cattle, we are equally struck by the importance of the traditional export routes. Most of them go to Nigeria or Ghana (from Tillabery), following valleys or trails.[10] On some of them livestock drawn from very large areas are brought together again. Thirty-two cattle export routes, together with numerous branches and relay point or collecting-point markets, can be counted in the territory. There are four in the western section;

(8) Cf. map. No. 58 de la Présidence du Conseil, "Le Sahara des nomades," in *L'economie pastorale saharienne*, Paris, 1951.

(9) Gabus 1955 : 33–40 for diagrams and maps of Tahoua market, of the flow of trade, of salt routes, of zones of attraction and influence. Map on p. 40: density of population in a zone of contact and markets.

(10) A large proportion of foreign trade in cattle is with Nigeria, which has a common boundary of 1,500 kilometers with Niger (85 per cent of exports in cattle, 92 per cent in sheep), then Ghana, Dahomey, Togo, Ivory Coast and Haute-Volta. There is also a cattle transit from the Sudan across Niger.

in Tahoua, eight; in Maradi, seven; in Zinder, nine; in Nguigmi, four. At Batiaka, on the Koroham-Kano trail, 13,000 head of cattle pass annually, while by the Gangara trail, which, with its three branches is the most important in the Maradi region, 17,000 head of cattle, 6,000 sheep skins and 200,000 goatskins annually arrive at Meadoua. Most of the cattle traders in Niger are engaged in export, as middlemen, or re-sellers, while the many who are engaged in subordinate positions function as collectors drovers, watchmen and shepherds (Larrat 1955 : Ch. VIII, § 4).

It is worth underlining the liveliness of these trade currents. In contrast to the salt-caravan routes, which have seen a decrease in traffic, the cattle routes remain in full activity and supply a livelihood to the population of Niger at all levels, far more from the rewards on the return from Nigeria than by the sale of things to be taken there. By means of their adaptation to local trade conditions and to demand from the wealthy regions of the South, the indigenous cattle routes have thus far succeeded in putting down all competition by other routes in the export of cattle to Nigeria. The French Administration did in fact try to open an export market in butcher's meat by air, from Niamey via Lagos. This enterprise came to nothing because it could not compete with the prices of the indigenous exporters of live cattle: the freight cost, out (meat) and in (clothes, perfumes, foreign goods), did not balance, the weight-value of the manufactured items being far higher than that of meat and their quick distribution being impossible in a area where secondary needs are still but slightly developed. It is therefore these traditional trade currents which prevent in Niger the establishment of new routes of export, while in those zones of production where such competition does not exist, an equivalent modernization has proven quite profitable (export of butcher's meat from Fort-Lamy, Abèchè, Ngaoundéré).

The professional organization of livestock trade is primarily in the hands of the Hausa. We have already seen the relations which unite them with the Bororo and we shall not consider the structure of Hausa trade, which is already the subject of another study (Smith intra; Forde and Scott 1945; Genevière 1950).

While raising and trading livestock remain traditional enterprises, the other wealth of the territory, groundnuts, is of European origin and its export poses difficult problems of transport out of the country, for the shortest route is by Nigerian ports.

Like other one-crop tropical countries, Niger is dependent upon exports. Transactions are at a maximum at the time of grain and groundnut harvests, and thereafter decrease progressively. This periodicity causes fluctuations in the cash holdings of the settled people, which influence the domestic demand for cattle and therefore the price. People spend this seasonal cash income in traditional ways, the most important outlay of which is capital investment in livestock. One can therefore state, in so far as we are dealing with domestic trade, that a significant portion of agricultural sales revenue is used to buy animals. The livestock market is thus dependent on the vagaries of agricultural production: rainfall, poorness or lateness of the harvest, and unprofitable sale. The development of the country and the industrialization of the region of Maradi are progressively modifying this picture and also increasing the demand for livestock as wealth.

The Bororo in Relation to the Trade of Niger.
   The Bororo not only supply part of the livestock for the domestic and foreign markets (they own 55 per cent of the cattle), but they also contribute the largest portion of the tax. The Fulani of Tanout, for example, who represent only one tenth of the population of the administrative subdivision pay one-fourth of the tax, for the sedentary people pay tax only on their cattle and for trade licenses, which are quite inexpensive. Although the commercialization of the nomads is to be considered as less than it could be, this quantitative aspect should not make us lose sight of the peculiar aspects of this contribution. It thus becomes a matter of analyzing how the Bororo take their place within the trade system of the region.
   What do markets mean to them? They are one of the main attractions in the dry season, and location of markets, as well as the location of pastures and of water, influences the successive sites of their camps. The Bororo suffer much less from lack of contact with the villages than from lack of contact with markets. Most of them go to market, at this season, once or twice a week. However, some of them have deliberately renounced this pleasure in order to move to pastures which are richer and less crowded: the *Bi-Nga'en* of **Ta**karatchwel go to market only two or three times a year in order to buy one or two bags of millet (bérets), some salt and some clothing. Barter in dairy products is of very slight importance among these small isolated groups; they consume the sour milk that they could sell only in villages too distant from their pasture areas. The *Wodaabe* completely stop going to market during the four months of wet season transhumance, but do not, however, cease bartering in the bush.
   The reasons which draw them to market are social quite as much as economic. If women necessarily go there to sell their dairy products, men, even when they have no business to transact, find there an occasion to meet friends and hear the latest news. It is at the market

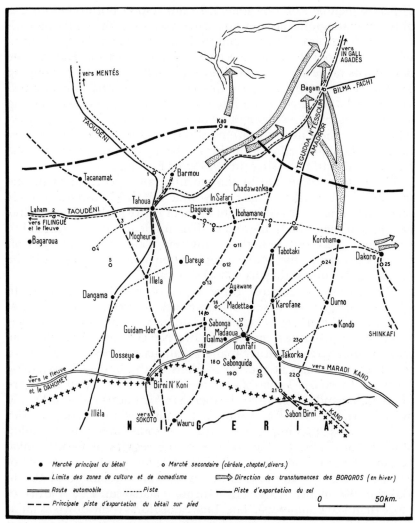

FIGURE 15
Markets and Trade Routes in Niger

that the segment chief finds his subordinates, between January and
March, in order to encourage them to sell their cattle and pay their
tax. It is there that a woman who wants to run away disappears. It is
there that all the youths and girls meet in order to dance the *Rume*
and *Yake* dances, when all those with business have already returned
to their own hearths. More important than being a contact with the
outside world, the market offers the possibility of the regrouping of

dispersed members of the segment. In this respect Bororo behavior is of additional significance, for one scarcely ever sees them mixing with other ethnic groups. They attend to their own affairs and hold themselves aloof from the noisy spectacles which attract the Hausa. The pastoralists move about in small groups, staff on shoulder, stopping to observe the points of cattle like connoisseurs, one foot propped against the other knee. Their attention is turned to note the training and gait of a camel just bought by one of them and ridden bareback. They prefer these demonstrations of skill to those of the Gobir wrestlers and show their admiration for the young man riding the bull he has not sold, without being thrown by its bucking.

The women come late in the morning and are grouped in one section of the market where they wait for their customers, their calabashes of milk placed in front of them between their knees. After having sold their goods, they go to their resident-*dillalai* to attend to household tasks and feed their children. Later every one sets off towards his camp, the young people often not returning until the following day unless they have flocks to watch.

The Bororo distinguish three types of markets, according to whether they go there to sell small livestock or cattle or only for social reasons. At all markets women find customers for their dairy products and the indispensable items of daily life. Nevertheless, they select the markets they attend. Rather than at Tahoua, the pastoralists prefer to sell their animals at the big markets of the bush—Chadawanka, Barmou, In-Safari, Tamaské—for the prices offered them there are often higher and millet often cheaper (a *taiki* of pearl millet is Fr. 450 at In-Safari, but Fr. 750 at Tahoua). The journeys they make in order to do business at an important market are sometimes quite considerable: Bororo come to Tabotaki from the regions of Chadawanka, Bagam, Dakoro, from 45 to 150 kilometers away. The *Bi-koro'en* of Madaoua come in numbers to the market of Koroham, and also to Dakoko, Karofane, Tabotaki, Ourno, Chadawanka (a radius of more than 120 kilometers). The Tuareg of Iforas come down as far as Barmou (Tahoua region) in order to buy bullrush millet there, as it is of an excellent quality and cheaper than at other markets. The markets most attended by the Bororo of the regions of Tahoua and Madaoua are situated at the edge of the sedentary-nomadic zone and are often crossed by one or several salt caravan trails and cattle trails (Chadawanka, Barmou, Takanamat, Tabotaki, Koroham, Ourno, Dakoro). They are also important relay points for exports to Nigeria. These are relatively close to their dry season areas, for at this time of the year they move their camps to sites not very far from the villages, the wells and the sumps dug in the river beds. The activity of these markets is influenced by the rhythm of pastoral life and decreases when the nomads leave the sedentary zone to move, in their cycle of transhumance, towards the valleys of the north.

The economic behavior of Bororo and Fulani seems, to foreigners, extremely irrational. Hausa never fail to mention this: "One must not," they say, "buy millet when the Fulani are buying it or build a house when they are building theirs." One could add to this pertinent aphorism: one must not sell animals when the Bororo are selling. It is not that they are unaware of local and seasonal variations in price. In fact, they often succeed in taking advantage of the former, but they do not do so for the latter, at least not for their transactions in livestock and for their most important purchases of grain. When it is time to pay tax, the head-owner himself sometimes moves to one of the close markets on the other side of the border, in order to get the greatest value from the sale of one of his animals. A woman will not hesitate to make a long journey of several weeks to buy cheaply a set of enamel plates to give to her married daughter. But the Fulani cannot adapt themselves to make the most of the seasonal variations in price.

The problem of supply and demand in the markets is embedded in an export-trade economy and conforms to principal needs which are all seasonal. The supply of cattle at the markets has three peaks: the first in March-April, the least important and the least general, when the pastoral peoples need money to pay tax; the second in July-August, when transhumants coming from Nigeria and semi-nomadic Fulani of Niger need money for paying the tax on pasture and to buy salt for their animals; also at this time those from the Bororo sell cattle who want to make purchases before their departure in the transhumance cycle; the third peak comes in December–January, on the return of the foreigners from their transhumance, and is the period for trade in agricultural produce.

The price of cattle also varies seasonally. It is at a maximum at the period of heightened agricultural trade: the important demand of the local farmers and of the *Dioulas* (independent traders) who have come from Nigeria in order to do business corresponds to the supply of the transhumants coming back down to the south with fattened cattle. A secondary rise in price occurs at the end of the wet season: some of the herds not having returned from transhumance, the cattle offered are few but in excellent condition and in demand by traders from Nigeria. The minimum price is found in May–June, at the end of the dry season: the depletion of cash has lowered the domestic demand and the bad state of the cattle the export demand.

The amount of rainfall in general influences prices and prolonged drought can induce sizable price drops. For example after the drought of 1949, traders bought steers at 1,500 francs which they resold in Nigeria at 5,000 francs, while after a rainy wet season, in February 1950, a cow was sold for 10,000 francs to a buyer from Nigeria. The density of population in a region and, consequently, a greater demand, raises prices: they are in general higher in the west (Niamey) than in the east (Zinder) and in the town markets than in the bush markets. Variations in the exchange rate for the shilling are equally reflected by variations in Niger. It is at the millet harvest that the exchange rate is the highest and at the moment of tax gathering that it is the lowest. Another factor in the fluctuation of the price of cattle is that in the price of groundnuts. In the region of Tanout the prices of cattle are extremely variable and depend on the harvest and on the price of groundnuts at Maradi. We have already seen the importance of Nigerian demand on the cycle of local price in Niger.

The price of millet and of salt, essential elements in the life of the nomad, vary in proportion to their scarcity. That of millet is at a minimum after the harvest and at a maximum just before the next harvest—variations on the order of one to four—while salt is less expensive at the return of the caravans which bring it back from the salt mines of the Sahara. In a general way, the prices of millet and cattle are inversely correlated, but slightly lagged in time, for when sales receipts for millet are high at harvest time, they are used in the subsequent month to purchase cattle, the price of which thereupon rises. At the period when millet is scarce and expensive, before the harvest in July and August, the price of cattle is almost at its minimum.

How is the commercial behaviour of the Bororo adapted to these seasonal variations which, although indeed influenced by many secondary factors, nevertheless remain predictable in their main outline? The Woodaabe sell their cattle primarily in March–April, in order to pay tax, when the price is already very low and their animals are particularly skinny. Some of them also trade in July before going off to wet season transhumance, in order to buy clothes and salt: the price at this period is only slightly higher. It is when they no longer have enough milk to exchange for millet that they buy millet—at the end of the dry season when the price of millet is already half way up the rising curve. We may say that this is very bad calculation, but it is not due to ignorance, for they are perfectly well aware that they get none of the benefit of the changes in price.

It is, in fact, actually impossible for them, for diverse ecological and cultural reasons, to behave more gainfully. They get rid of their cattle only in case of emergency; their motives for trade are as few as their needs. The reasons which attach them to their cattle are not only economic—we have already seen this in connection with the composition of the herds—but also cultural and moral. Ownership of cattle confers on a Bororo a social prestige which he can acquire in no other way and gives him psychic satisfactions in comparison to which the enjoyment of foreign goods or luxury articles remains qualitatively negligible. But why do they not sell ahead of time, in anticipation of the tax, when the prices offered are higher? To do so would be to run against the risks of saving in the form of money: theft, loss, not to mention the temptation of spending for other purposes. Also it is difficult for them to keep reserves of millet because of their nomadic life. Those who farm have no durable granaries; they consume their millet after the harvest and must purchase more when prices are very high. They save only in the form of livestock, but with a remarkable realism: their foundation of security is, as we have seen, formed by a core of animals which are quite old and which, having resisted epizootics, are likely to reconstitute the herd.

Not only do they fail to profit from seasonal variations in price without being in the least unaware of their failures, but the kind of cattle they offer for sale does not correspond qualitatively to the demand. The *Bororoji* zébu is not a good meat animal and breeding is practised with an eye to dairy qualities. What those who traffic in cattle require are fat, unmuscled slaughter beasts. To cap it all, the time at which they sell allows them to present for sale only animals which have suffered from drought and may well not survive the export voyage. For all these reasons the Bororo has not succeeded either in adapting himself to the seasonal price fluctuations of the region nor to an economy in which money income plays a role difficult to reconcile with the life of nomadic pastoralists. This lack of adaptation is as detrimental to the Bororo seller as is is to buyers.

CONCLUSION: ECONOMY AND SOCIAL STRUCTURE AND THE POSSIBILITIES OF CHANGE

This economy, so little adapted to the exigencies of the market, makes sense within the social structure. The quick and easy circulation of goods permits more or less egalitarian distribution of the resources of the group and the survival of its momentarily handicapped members. It also tends to result in the numerical maintenance of the group, for a *Bodaabo* without cattle disappears from the group in order to hire himself out to a stranger as shepherd. Flight remains the fundamental reaction to an economic or social situation which is revolting, degrading or shameful. That which provides power at all levels in this society is above all number: the future of a kinless child or of a segment chief without followers is inexorably constrained. To share resources is thus to cement tribal cohesion and promote in return, the well-being of each individual; in cyclical fashion, what the individual does for the group ends by rewarding the individual.

Certain social institutions, by which responsibilities are given into the hands of the most able, perform the same function of balance between productive forces and means of production. Custom does not allow the head of the family to save his cattle to provide for his old age: rather, he should give to his sons nearly all their part of the inheritance at the time that they marry and are themselves of age to manage their flocks. In the same way the segment chief almost always gives up his position to his successor when he becomes old. The choice even of the camp head of the extended-family is motivated in the same way: although the elder brother has a right to this position, in practice it is the most able among the elders on whom the collective responsibilities of the family group falls.

As these institutions make clear, the society in fact is but slightly stratified socially and economically, although the Bororo have a mania for hierarchy at all levels. The chief, who literally is only the leader of his segment, is not detached from it, and the tribe, which is composed of lineages linked by pseudo-genetic relations, has only a diffuse and acephalous political organization. There is very little difference between the way of life of the rich and the poor, and if wealth is considered a necessary attribute of chiefdom, it is because that position necessitates costly generosity to superiors and equals as well as to inferiors. Goods are thus shared out to the group. Economic rivalry nevertheless exists, but it is manifest much more at the level of the joint-family or the segment—all the intra-segment ceremonies and the inter-segment *gereol* are examples—than at the level of the individual.

However, goods circulate only within the group except for those which are used to obtain basic necessities of the kind which the Bororo do not know how to produce. Except the *nanga na'i* contract which, running beyond the range of kinship, might be compared to a kind of insurance system for the benefit of the herdsman, the cattle circuit is tightly closed: heritable goods do not leave the patrilineage any more than do the women and the livestock that they represent, for the extremely pronounced endogamy of this society makes of the traditional institution of arranged marriage a strange parody of matrimonial exchange.

The creation of mechanical deep wells in the Ferlo (Sénégal) is still too recent to evaluate their influence on the economic organization of the nomadic Fulani of this sector (Dupire 1957 : 19–24).

But the wells have already caused a shortening in the cycles of trans-humance and a consequent tendency to sedentarization. However, the old-fashioned ways of moving and watering cattle still bring on seasonal variations in the cycle of activity of the wells. In addition, their fear of settlement with all its dangers—exhausted pastures, contamination, conflicts with the sedentary peoples—is, perhaps, a healthy reflex on the part of the herders. The time that the nomadic Fulani of this region save by watering at mechanical wells is used to increase their gathering of gums, which bring them an appreciable secondary income. Here too, the herders who have become wealthy have scarcely modified their way of life and are content to established their prestige by making a pilgrimage to Mecca. One of the conse-quences of the creation of wells is psychological in nature. The Fulani, after being the repressed people they were, have begun to feel themselves the pivot of European interests; they are becoming more and more demanding of the administrative powers and aggres-sive towards the sedentary people, and their nationalism is de-veloping.

In Guinée, the Fula who have become sedentary have modified their pastoral ideas to such an extent that in this area the trade in livestock has reached disquieting proportions and wealth in livestock seems likely to disappear. The farmers who own herds tended by shepherds do not hesitate to sell heifers under two years old and other young animals scarcely fit for butchery; the sale of females is nearly equal to that of males.[11] The farmer-herdsmen here need cash, but 70 to 80 per cent of what comes onto the market is not sold. In order to satisfy their new needs, they are depleting their herds, an-other danger that abandoning the pastoral ideal brings in its train.

There is one sure thing to be said even on slight acquaintance with the needs of pastoral life in dry Savannah areas: the three basic elements—water, pasture, and sale of produce from the herd— cannot be dissociated. Any modernization that does not take all of them into account leads to ecological and economic disequilibrium. For example, the localization of creameries on one single route in the sector of Meiganga so rapidly caused the exhaustion of pastures that it became necessary to consider turning the nomads toward less fre-quented pastures by creating a new route equally well provided with creameries. The existence of deep wells also creates numerous difficul-ties. Excessive concentration of herds and camps provokes exhaustion of pastures around and about the wells and multiplies bush fires.

[11] Oral communication from Mr. R. Larrat who has studied the trade of livestock in Guinée. We want to thank him here for his kindness in giving us information from unpublished documents.

The growth of herds in quantity and quality cannot bring about permanent economic improvement if such development is not facilitated by a new infrastructure of routes. A mechanical failure can bring about genuine catastrophe: one must have seen thirsty herds at the end of the dry season, leaving a well that has been closed to rush another thirty kilometers, in order to understand that the best can be the enemy of the good. The necessity for vast and expensive planning often provokes pessimistic reflection on the part of specialists. It is not that the herdsmen cannot develop; rather it is that modernization of his economy in the dry Savannah region presents many difficult problems. It has even been claimed that neither wells nor the industrialization of dairying would be profitable enterprises in this area (Grosmaire 1957 and Larrat 1958).

Economic change should be sought only with prudence in order to avoid the outcome that the herdsman, tempted by the advantages of sedentary life, leaves those regions geographically given over to animal husbandry, wastes his livestock on tobacco, kola nuts, bicycles, and pilgrimages, and seeks his economic security in his little field and his millet granary. Thus one cannot reproach the true nomad for his resistance to change. According to the testimony of many veterinaries, it is in very many cases the reflection of a wise prudence, at least so long as he does not feel that his own security and that of his cattle, in an ungrateful region, have not been brought to a new economic equilibrium.

THE HORN OF AFRICA

CHAPTER 13

Lineage Continuity and Modern Commerce in Northern Somaliland[1]

BY I. M. LEWIS

LINEAGE, ECOLOGY AND HISTORICAL TRADE

There are few corporate activities and few collective interests among the northern Somali which are not dependent upon the segmentary lineage structure of their society. In this article I discuss some of the ways in which trade and lineage affiliation are entwined. I deal primarily with the British Protectorate which has a population of some 640,000 Somali[2], distributed among nine main patrilineal clans ranging in strength from 10,000 to 130,000 members each.[3] Although they have some association with specific territories, these are not strictly localized, and are genealogically grouped at a higher level of lineage segmentation into three clan families—the Isaaq, Dir, and Daarood[4]. At a lower level of agnatic grouping, clans are divided into a highly ramified system of patrilineages. In this system of genealogical cleavages which involves the whole of northern Somali society, the highest level of effective affiliation is that of the clan-family, but the largest group which acts as a corporate political entity is the clan.

(1) This paper is based on research carried out in the Somalilands between 1955 and 1957 under the auspices of the Colonial Social Science Research Council, London, whose generosity I acknowledge with gratitude. For criticism of earlier drafts of this paper I am grateful to Mr. J. G. S. Drysdale, Mr. Osman A. Hassan, and to Dr. J. van Velsen.

(2) The contiguous territories are French Somaliland (Somali population c. 28,000); Harar Province of Ethiopia (Somali population, c. 500,000); and Somalia (Somali population, between 1,250,000 and 2,000,000). The remarks made in this paper on the situation in the Protectorate are also generally applicable to French Somaliland and the northern province of Somalia.

(3) All northern Somali political units are lineages tracing descent through named generations from a common ancestor. I use the terms 'clan' and 'clan-family' to refer to the special social characteristics of these very large descent groups; genealogically they differ only in span from smaller lineage units.

(4) In central and southern Somalia there are three other clan-families—the Hawiye, Digil, and Rahanwiin—so that the Somali people as a whole are divided into six distinct clan-families, and, at a higher level of genealogical connection, the Digil and Rahanwiin are grouped together as 'Sab' and opposed to the other clan-families grouped together as 'Samaale.' But this primary division in the Somali nation has no significance in British Somaliland.

For the most part the country is barren and near desert in many places, and presents a generally harsh environment in which the majority of northern Somali (at least 80 per cent in the Protectorate) are pastoral nomads, moving over long distances with their herds of camels and flocks of sheep and goats.[5] Cattle are rare and most common in the few areas where sorghum is cultivated, mainly in the west of the Protectorate[6] and in the contiguous regions of Harar Province of Ethiopia.

Although local interests in wells, and in villages and townships, lead to some degree of attachment to locality, northern Somali lineages are not strongly localized; and the individual pastoralist ranges far and wide with his livestock in search of water and pasturage. At many seasons of the year and in many places, these are in short supply, and competition and strife over access to them is a regular feature of northern Somali life. Except at the level of the clan, where there is a more marked association with a particular territory, the members of a given lineage are usually widely deployed in the pastures. And except in time of war when they can only be maintained by force, prescriptive rights are not claimed to grazing which is regarded as the gift of God to mankind in general. Nevertheless, where they settle in temporary encampments, the nomadic hamlets, consisting of a few closely related nuclear families with their flocks,[7] and the camel-camps which contain the camels of a few close kin, tend to be grouped according to lineage affiliation. These lineage patterns of territorial distribution are particularly marked in time of war; but this does not mean that all the members of a lineage are ever found settled together in one area.

In this system of seasonal movement and of shifting agnatic attachment, for a man may act as a member of one lineage in one situation and of another larger or smaller lineage in another, the basic jural and political unit is the so-called *dia*-paying group. This is the primary unit of political allegiance and the primary focus of cor-

(5) The estimated stock population of the British Protectorate is: Camels, 1,200,000; sheep and goats, 4,000,000; and cattle 223,100. But little accuracy can be claimed for these figures since there has never been an accurate census of livestock.

(6) In this region some 140,000 acres are estimated to be under cultivation, but as yet the arable land is not registered. Individual holdings are rarely larger than an acre and produce about 800 lb. of sorghum grain and about twice that amount in weight of stover for feeding livestock.

(7) In a sample of fifty-eight hamlets, the median number of nuclear families was 2.6. Except in time of war, when for safety larger numbers of related families cluster together, hamlets rarely contain more than four nuclear families. Outside the extended family, the commonest pattern of hamlet structure is that containing men of the same dia-paying group grouped together with their families. All the members of a dia-paying group however are never found in the same hamlet, nor in the same settlement of hamlets.

porate interest in camels.[8] The group is a lineage or alliance of a few small lineages, tracing descent to a common ancestor through from four to eight generations. Its name, which has become standard administrative usage in the Protectorate, derives from the Arabic *diiya* (Somali, *mag*), meaning bloodwealth. For the dia-paying group is essentially a corporate agnatic unit whose members are united in joint responsibility towards outsiders, the most important aspect of their unity being in payment of blood-compensation. If one member of a dia-paying group is injured or killed by another group, or if his property is attacked, the injured group is pledged to collective vengeance, or, if reparation is made, to sharing compensation amongst all its male members. Conversely, if a man of a dia-paying group commits homicide or injury outside his group, all the other members are collectively responsible for his actions and jointly concerned in effecting reparation.

Dia-paying groups (of which there are some 360 in the Protectorate) act similarly in less serious issues, and the joint interests of their members are defined today by written treaties (sg. *heer*) which are lodged in District Offices. Since these treaties are recognized by the Administration as defining the primary political and jural status of the individual pastoralist, they are a source of law in the modern administrative system. The actual terms vary from group to group, with size, degree of internal segmentation (a general concomitant of size), wealth, and other factors. But in principle all northern Somali accept that a man's life is worth 100 camels and woman's half that number.[9]

Dia-paying groups with a strength varying between a few hundred and a few thousand males are not distinct territorial groups: and although stipended headmen, styled "Akils," have been appointed to most of the larger ones, there is no traditional office of leadership associated with them. In these respects they conform to the general characteristics of northern Somali lineages at all levels of division. Only at the level of the clan is there traditionally the office of clan-head, often styled "Sultan"[10]; and even this position, which carries little instituted authority, is not an essential feature since several strong clans have no clan-head to lead their elders. At all levels of lineage grouping, it is the latter who decide policy in the *ad hoc* assemblies at which all adult men have the right to speak. In this

[8] Camels are branded with a common dia-paying group brand while sheep and goats are usually branded individually.

[9] The rate varies locally, to some extent with stock-wealth, and within dia-paying groups is generally lowered. Between groups the amount of compensation payable may be increased according to the status of the person killed and the circumstances of the killing, and other factors.

[10] In Somali, Suldaan, Ugaas, Boqor, Garaad, etc.

connection it is important to stress that, despite its sharply defined
character, the dia-paying group is only one among many possible
levels of lineage solidarity. The contracts by which dia-paying groups
are constituted can be extended to embrace wider spheres of agnatic
relationship as occasion requires; and in general contract *(heer)* and
clanship *(tol)* are the two fundamental principles of corporate action,[11] not least in trade.

For centuries the northern Somali coast has been linked commercially with its Abyssinian hinterland, and with Arabia and the
East. From about the tenth century and probably earlier, Muslim
Arab and Persian settlers developed a string of commercial coastal
centers, in part probably a legacy from classical times, exporting
slaves and ivory from the Abyssinian hinterland, and locally produced
skins, hides, precious gums, ghee, and ostrich feathers. It was of course
from the export of myrrh and frankincense that the Somali coast was
most widely known in early times. But although Somaliland is still
the world's main source of these precious gums,[12] the export of hides
and skins and livestock on the hoof, chiefly to Aden, makes a far more
important contribution to northern Somali economy.[13]

The most important of these early northern coastal towns was
Zeila, part of the wider Muslim state of Ifaat, of which it was the
chief port, and with a mixed Arab, Danakil,[14] and Somali population.
From as early as the thirteenth century Muslim Ifaat and Christian
Abyssinia struggled for political control of the western part of the Horn
of Africa. In the second half of the sixteenth century, however, when
the Muslim threat to Ethiopia wat at last eliminated and Ifaat disinte-
grated, Zeila's prosperity declined. Yet the town still remained the
main gateway to the outside world for the caravan routes from the
hinterland; and in the early days of British colonization at the end of
the last century, recovered briefly something of its past prosperity.
This was soon lost, however, by the development of the French port of
Jibuti and the construction of the railway between Jibuti and the
Ethiopian capital. Zeila quickly ceased to be the chief port for the
hinterland and declined rapidly. Today the old city is little more
than an empty shell, a desolate place of crumbling and ruined mosques and tombs; and the ancient city population—the Reer Seyla—
with its distinctive culture, is broken and dispersed.

(11) For a fuller analysis of the interaction of these two principles in Somali political
structure see Lewis 1959 b.

(12) On the gum trade see Drake-Brockman 1912 : 239–61 and Lawrie 1954 : 26–30.

(13) The total value of domestic exports from the Protectorate in 1957 was £1,355,418,
to which livestock and skins contributed £1,275,571. Of the remaining amount £53,980
w is realized through the export of gums.

(14) A closely related Hamitic people living in French Somaliland and Eritrea.

Berbera, about which less is known from early times, but which is probably of similar antiquity, is now the main port of British Somaliland. Today the town has a population of some 30,000, mainly Somali of the local Habar Awal clan but with a smattering of Arabs, Indians, and Sudanese. As will presently be seen, Berbera is more typical of northern Somali trade centers than Zeila, for unlike the latter, the town has not produced a distinct city population separate in culture and character from the surrounding Somali.

Prior to the coming of steam vessels, these and the other smaller northern ports were open to foreign traffic only during the North-East Monsoon which blows from about October to March. It was and still is only at this time of year that dhows visit the northern coasts; the South-West Monsoon winds close the coast to traffic. In the past, caravans descended from the interior, from Harar[15] in the west and from the Ogaden to the south, to trade local produce for the goods brought by the Arabian and Indian traders from the Persian Gulf and from further afield. Thus travelers in the nineteenth century describe Berbera during the South-West Monsoon period as a poverty stricken collection of miserable huts with a population of some 8,000, but in the fair season as a prosperous center containing as many as 40,000 people; and this seasonal fluctuation is still evident today. When Burton witnessed this commerce, in 1855, the local produce brought to the ports was traded for coarse cotton cloth in pieces of seventy-five, sixty-six, sixty-two, and forty-eight yards; for black and indigo-dyed calicos in lengths of sixteen yards; for fillets for married women's hair; for iron and steel in small bars; for lead and zinc; beads of various sorts; and dates and rice. But money which is the chief medium of exchange today was also in use then, for Burton notes a preference for payment in dollars and rupees (Burton 1943 : 289).

The segmentary nature of Somali society with its many lineages often at war, and with no central authority to which common appeal could be made, had its repercussions in the organization of the caravan trade. To reach the coast in safety a caravan had to have protection on its journey among many different and often hostile clans. This was achieved by an institutionalized form of safe-conduct. The leader of the caravan of laden burden camels entered into a relationship of protection with those amongst whom he passed on his way

(15) Traditionally three caravans left from Harar to cross the Plains to Berbera each year. The earliest set out from the old city in the Abyssinian highlands in early January and carried coffee, ghee, gums, and other local produce to be exchanged for cottons, silks, shawls, and tobacco. Another left Harar in February, but the main one, bearing slaves and ivory and livestock, only reached the coast at the end of the season. The arrival of this last caravan in April 1855 is described in Burton, 1943 p. 228.

to the coast. A patron was selected for his probity, status, and above all in a society where force is all important, for the strength of his lineage. The position of protector is called *abbaan,* and the *abbaan*[16] is given gifts in return for his services. Having agreed to act in this capacity, the patron is responsible for the security of the caravan under his protection, for its goods and for the lives of those with it. Attacks on a protected caravan are attacks on the patron and his lineage whose honor and "name", as Somali put it, can only be upheld by prompt retaliatory action. It is the duty of the patron and his agnates to obtain reparation for any injuries inflicted on the caravan and to hand over the just amount of compensation to the injured lineage.

It is not to be imagined of course that all caravan protectors fulfilled their obligations with scrupulous honesty;[17] but here, quite apart from the danger of incurring the enmity of the caravan owner's lineage, a potent sanction was the bitter verses sometimes made by deceived caravan owners to vilify their protectors. These, if skillfully composed, might sweep through the country, and blacken a lineage's reputation.

Some idea of the complexities of the inter-relations set up through this patron-protege relationship may be gained by considering the position of the Dulbahante clan in the east of the British Protectorate. From the territory regularly grazed by this land-locked clan, two main routes led to Berbera. One lay through the village of Bohotle, to Burao, and then through Sheikh to Berbera, a total distance of some 300 miles. This route was traversed by caravans of sometimes as many as several hundred burden camels laden with precious gums, *ye'eb* nuts,[18] ostrich feathers, and ghee; and driving sheep and goats and camels and horses for sale in Berbera and for export. At Bohotle the caravans came under the protection of the Habar Tol Ja'lo clan; at Burao the Habar Yuunis assumed responsibility; at Sheikh the Habar Awal'Iise Muuse; and finally at Berbera itself, the Habar Awal Sa'ad Muuse. Another shorter route traversed the Sarar Plain, through which the Habar Tol Ja'lo conducted Dulbahante caravans as far as Berbera, where their patronage was exchanged for that of the Habar Awal. Thus in their access to the port of Berbera, the Dulbahante relied upon patronage relationships with the Habar Tol Ja'lo, Habar Yuunis, and Habar Awal, three clans with whom the Dulbahante marry and fight over access to grazing.

(16) This word may be derived from *ab* or *aabbe,* father, agnation, with the sense of one who stands *in loco parentis.*

(17) For comments on the unreliability and treachery of many caravan protectors, see Burton 1943 : 275-6; Ferrandi 1903 : 226-330.

(18) The fruit of Cordeauxia edulis, which is eaten.

Today, the caravan trade is largely in decline. Except on short journeys and in particularly difficult country, trucks have replaced burden camels in trade. And though clan and lineage fighting still regularly threatens the security of the traveler, the presence of a neutral overriding administration has diminished the need for the traditional trade patronage relationship. Thus Somali today observe that all, the weak as well as the strong, are under the common protection of the government which is the *abbaan* of all. In this context the proverb "the weak have found the European as protector" is often quoted. But the institution still persists in other spheres of trade which I mention presently.

EXTERNAL TRADE AND LOCAL MARKETING IN TOWNS

Today, the main exports of northern Somaliland are livestock, hides and skins, and gums and ghee. Within the country there is little regional diversification of production; except in the case of sorghum (consumed internally and not exported), which is grown in bulk as a cash crop[19] only in the relatively fertile areas of high rainfall (above 12 inches annually) in the west of the Protectorate and Harar Province of Ethiopia. The production of salt, however, is largely limited to the Zeila-Jibuti area (marine salt being the chief export of French Somaliland). Other less important regional specializations occur in the manufacture of fibre mats, the finer varieties of which are made from palm fronds on the eastern coasts; and the carving of stone censers which is limited to central Somalia. Another local product cultivated only in Ethiopia and thence distributed by truck in the west and center of northern Somaliland (and also exported by air to Aden) is the stimulant leaves of the *qaat* plant *(Catha edulis)*.[20] Most other local Somali products are common throughout the area.

The main imports today are foodstuffs and manufactured goods.[21] In the first category, sugar, tea, dates, rice, and millets are the chief commodities; and in the second white long cloth. These are carried, today mainly by truck, into the towns and villages of the interior

(19) No figures are available for the total production in the Protectorate. But since the total acreage is estimated to be about 140,000 acres, and the average acre yield about 800 lbs of grain, the total production is probably in the region of 50,000 tons. It is considered that a slight increase in the area cultivated would make the Protectorate self sufficient in grain.

(20) *Qaat* conserves its stimulant powers only when the leaf is fresh; and for this reason is not chewed in the east of the Protectorate which is too far distant from the center of production for the leaf to arrive in a fresh condition.

(21) In 1957 the values of these in British Somaliland were £1,240,957 and £1,031,402 respectively.

which are in turn collecting points for local produce for export through the ports.

With the exception of the farming villages in the west and of a few religious settlements (sg. *tariiqa*)[22] all northern Somali places of settlement are essentially trade centers. Here imported goods are sold by local merchants and a few expatriate Arabs and Indians, hides and skins and livestock purchased largely for eventual export, and a few local products sold for local consumption—milk, ghee, meat and, in the west, grain. The distribution of these market centers varies with the nature of the terrain and with the local economy. In the predominantly pastoral and sparsely populated[23] areas of the center and east of the British Protectorate, market centers are often as many as forty miles apart. But in the more densely populated sorghum growing areas of the west, especially in Hargeisa and Borama Districts, they are less widely spaced. Here grain to a large extent replaces livestock and animal produce as the mainstay of marketing.

These market centers vary in size, complexity, and permanence, according to local circumstances. Trade follows the pastoralists in their movements; and the most ephemeral and simplest of trade centers, sometimes boasting no more than a single shop housed in a rough branch and leaf shelter, spring up wherever people are concentrated for any length of time. Thus, especially in the dry seasons when milk, the staple diet of the pastoralist, is scarce, and when men turn to dates, rice and tea and sugar,[24] traders move out into the pastures to set up temporary shops. This is usually accomplished nowadays by truck, or in less accessible areas by a train of burden camels laden with imported provisions which are sold to the pastoralists for money, or exchanged for hides and skins. It is particularly at this time of year that sheep and goats are killed for meat, and their skins to some extent constitute a dry season currency[25] in the trade between merchant and nomad. They are certainly used as often as money at this time of year. Not all debts with traders, however, are discharged at once, and to a lesser extent young lambs and kids are often employed

(22) There are about a dozen such autonomous religious settlements, in some areas engaged in sorghum cultivation, in the Protectorate today. These belong to the various Muslim Orders which Somali follow. On this aspect of Somali Islam, see Lewis, 1955/56.

(23) The overall population density in the Protectorate is about 10 per square mile. No figures are available for the western regions.

(24) Somali tea (*shaah*) is a potent and sustaining beverage with the consistency of soup, made by brewing tea leaves, sugar, milk, and a little water. It is very highly sugared and nutritious. A man will often do a day's work on a mug of tea drunk in the early morning, waiting until the evening before eating rice or grain.

(25) In 1957 the local value of a sheepskin was between three and four shillings (East Africa).

by the pastoralists in the wet seasons to close outstanding debts carried forward from the preceding dry season. Thus, while money is widely employed in the trade of the interior, many commercial transactions are still conducted through the medium of livestock or hides and skins. And skins are a particularly desirable currency from the point of view of the merchant.

Small traders draw a draft or borrow money from a kinsman and use this initial capital to purchase skins. These are then dispatched from the interior by truck to a larger commercial center where they are purchased by a wholesale exporter. The latter loads the truck with such commodities as sugar, dates, tea, rice, and grain and a few items of hardware, razor blades, cigarettes, and cloth, etc., and returns these to the merchant in the interior who retails them at local prices. Much of the itinerant trader's takings are again in skins, and these are again sent back by truck to the town merchant. In this way small traders with little equipment beyond a pair of scales, follow the pastoral movements of their clansmen and often make quite substantial profits. Few know sufficient Arabic to keep accounts and the majority keep no written record of their transactions.

At regularly frequented seasonal waterholes and wells, permanent trade settlements of a few nomadic huts and mud-and-wattle stores grow up. These are the oases of northern Somaliland. The extent to which their prosperity and permanence depends upon the prevailing patterns of pastoral movements is seen in the frequency with which villages are abandoned and new centers established over the years. Here the principal cause of drift and migration is lack of water; and the ever-changing routes of the dust tracks which serve as roads are a constant witness to the transitory character of settlement in a predominantly nomadic society.

Apart from the ancient ports of the northern coast, few of the present towns with stone buildings are more than fifty years old, and all have developed from modest settlements of a few nomadic huts. The present policy of the Protectorate government is to declare as gazetted townships those larger settlements which have maintained fairly constant populations over the years. These then become subject to the provisions of the Township Ordinance (Cap. 84 of the Laws) and become centers of educational, social and economic and political advancement. Buildings have to conform to the requirements of the Town Planning Ordinance (Cap. 83 of the Laws), and the building sites for residential or commercial purposes are usually granted on a ninety-nine year lease. Schools are built partly from government funds, and partly by local subscription; police are provided; medical facilities; a community center equipped with a radio and some reading facilities; and eventually in the larger centers local government councils with fiscal authority are set up. The larger townships are also provided with a Kadi's and Subordinate Court, the first administering Islamic law in matters of personal status, and the second customary law and township rules. Subordinate Courts have very limited criminal jurisdiction and usually do not handle cases which concern lineages rather than individuals. In the main centers taxes are levied on industrial, and trading sites, and a form of octroi known locally as *zariba* dues is levied on livestock and grain brought to the center for trade.

A good example of a smaller gazetted township is the village of Sheikh in the hills south of Berbera. The population occupying mud-and-wattle and stone houses in the main part of the township numbered some 500 souls in 1955. The village which owes much of its commerce to the fact that Sheikh was formerly the headquarters in the Protectorate of the Education Department,[26] lies to the west of the main Burao-Berbera road, and the 120 permanent houses and shops built of stone or mud-and-wattle are arranged in six parallel lines, bisected by a main street, and intersected laterally by six smaller streets. The township has a small police station, a medical dispensary, a Kadi's Court, an elementary school, two mosques, and a branch office of the Somaliland National League and of the Somali Youth League.[27] There is a government meat market behind the town and also a small open market place where grain, charcoal, eggs, milk, and other local produce are sold. To the southwest of the main center lies a miserable collection of small nomadic huts (sg. *buul*)[28] mainly occupied by old women, mostly widows; when not living with their sons in the interior, they eke out a modest livelihood by selling wood and charcoal, water, and grain.

Sheikh lies within the spheres of interest of two clans, the Habar Awal and the Habar Yuunis, the first of which is numerically dominant. Some eighty-three householders and shopkeepers are Habar Awal or Habar Awal affiliated, and mainly of the Deereyahan lineage; the remaining thirty-seven are Habar Yuunis, mainly of the Muuse 'Abdalla lineage or members of other clans attached to them.[29] Some

(26) Close to the township are a vocational training school, an intermediate school, and a new secondary school. To the north-west lies the religious settlement (*tariiqa*) of Sheikh which I do not describe here.

(27) These are two of the main political parties in the Protectorate; both are nationalist movements.

(28) This is the typical hut of a widow, smaller than the nomadic hut (*aqal*) of a married couple.

(29) These included several Arab immigrants from the Hadramaut, local Somali of other clans, and *sab* bondsmen whom I discuss below.

twenty-four shops and eight "coffee-shops," where only tea is drunk,[30] are in the hands of the Habar Awal; and eleven shops and two coffee shops are in the control of the Habar Yuunis. The adjacent schools supply some employment and the majority of traders are general merchants, some of whom are also engaged in the export of hides and skins. There are several truck owners who hire vehicles for trade and other purposes, several shoemakers and blacksmiths, and a few tailors. But whatever local employment is followed, the majority of the inhabitants of the township also possess livestock in the interior in the charge of their clansmen. While most of these townsmen depend for their day-to-day livelihood on their urban occupation, their flocks of sheep and goats and herds of camels in the interior represent at once a source of capital and an earnest of their continued participation in the social and political life of their kin in the pastures. For as I shall presently show there are strong economic and political ties between town and rural society.

The largest towns of northern Somaliland today owe their size, prosperity, and permanence to their selection as District headquarters. In these administrative centers there is a greater diversification of trade and wider opportunities for employment in government service and in domestic service.[31] The export of livestock and of animal produce still remains, however, the mainstay of the economy, but except in the commercial port of Jibuti in French Somaliland, few local industries have yet developed to offer any substantial employment of labor, skilled or unskilled. All these towns remain essentially the focal points for the redistribution of imported goods and for the buying and selling of livestock and livestock produce. The main centers are Hargeisa, capital of the Protectorate with a population of about the same size as Berbera (i.e. *c.* 30,000); and Burao with a population only slightly less. The other District headquarters— Borama, Las Anod, and Erigavo—have populations of only a few thousand inhabitants each. The main foreign trading companies (Mitchell Cotts, Besse, etc.) have their head offices in Berbera and Hargeisa and these two towns are generally the main commercial centers of the Protectorate, Hargeisa having the largest expatriate European and Indian population.

But for Erigavo and Las Anod, all these towns now have elected local government councils and all enjoy similar social services which

---

(30) Before the introduction of tea from the East, coffee which is grown in Ethiopia, is said to have been widely favored in northern Somaliland. Today, however, tea is the universal beverage, although Somali invariably refer to their teashops as "coffee-shops."

(31) There are only a few hundred Europeans in the Protectorate, almost all of whom are expatriate government officials with their families.

are naturally most advanced in the larger towns, Hargeisa, Burao, and Berbera. The local broadcasting service, Radio Somali, is based in Hargeisa.

I have spoken of all these centers, irrespective of their size and commercial diversification, as markets since they owe their existence primarily to trade and to the exchange of goods and services. In Somaliland there are no markets outside of centers of settlement. All these trade centers consist of a core of stone and mud-and-wattle shops and coffees shops and, in the larger centers, of an open market place. Shops are concerned mainly with the sale of imported goods, while the open marketplace deals mainly with local produce and is dominated by women. Women bring in milk and ghee daily from the surrounding countryside and sell it in the market. They also sell woven bark containers, mats, rope and string, charcoal and grain, and some poultry, eggs, vegetables and fruit.[32] In the interests of public health, government meat markets where women sell mutton and goat's meat have been erected in most of the larger centers. The market place itself has no formal organization, and indeed spills over into a succession of stalls, where bread and meat pastries and other goods are sold, set up at convenient points along the streets within a town. The shops themselves also overflow into the streets, in as much as many of the general merchants have a tailor with a sewing machine sitting outside their premises.

The stalls where cooked foods and bread are sold are manned by men, who also serve at the counters inside shops, and work the sewing machines mainly engaged in shirt-making. The market place itself is usually devoid of formal stalls and most of the vendors squat on the ground, often on a mat, displaying their wares. Sometimes simple shelters are erected to shade the vendor and his customers from the heat of the sun. Finally, in another corner and usually some distance from the central shopping area there is the livestock market where stock are bought and sold for local use and for export.

There are no special market days; and little variation except in quantity and quality in the goods offered for sale on different days. But the supply of milk and meat is to some extent influenced by the seasons. Except on the Muslim Friday (which begins on Thursday evening and lasts until midday on Friday) when all trade and commerce stop,[33] the market resounds with the noise of trade and barter and the shops and coffee-shops are busy.

(32) The proceeds from the sale of livestock produce accrue to the family as a whole. Mats and other utensils made by women are sold to their own personal profit.

(33) For Somali, Friday is the day of repetition. A gift received on Friday is likely to indicate that more will be received; but a payment made on Friday is likely to mean that more will have to be expended.

Thus new trade settlements provide the primary source of livelihood of a relatively small class of entrepreneurs and merchants of whom the majority are now Somali but a few are still expatriate Indians and Arabs. Similarly widows domiciled in the towns manage to eke out a modest living by selling such local produce as mats, rope, poultry, eggs, fruit, vegetables, water, and charcoal. For the majority of the population, the pastoralists of the interior, they provide a market for surplus livestock and livestock produce, or for stock or stock produce which must be sold to gain cash. Except for gums, hides and skins, and much of the livestock sold, these products are all consumed locally, and the market is in this instance acting as a center for redistribution. The money thus obtained with that gained by women from the sale of women's manufactures and poultry, etc., is used to purchase rice and grain, tea, sugar, dates, clothes and other necessities, and a few luxuries, such as cigarettes and *qaat*. These transactions thus supply the pastoralist with what he now regards as essentials and additional foodstuffs which in the dry seasons especially help to alleviate his hard lot. With wages obtained from salaried employment they are also the means by which the pastoralist in the interior participates in the wider cash economy.

LINEAGE CONTINUITY IN URBAN ECONOMY

To understand the degree to which clanship[34] dominates trade in northern Somaliland, it is first necessary to consider the structural relation of the market center to the interior, of the urban to the rural community. Most modern towns of consequence are of recent formation. And in the economic, social, and political life of their inhabitants they represent an extension, or outgrowth, of the pastoral way of life. Jibuti with its unusual economic development is exceptional; and the only other northern Somali town which has evolved a distinct structure of its own—though for different reasons—is the ancient port of Zeila, now in ruins. The people of this city formed a separate political community with loyalties not so much to their lineages of origin as to their city of domicile. And even today, despite their reduced numbers, they are still recognized in the Protectorate legislation as a special category, a community distinct from, and independent of, Somali clanship.

With its much more recent origins Jibuti has not evolved a distinct town society; but its great heterogeneity and considerable industrial

---

(34) I use "clanship" here to refer to lineage solidarity at all levels of lineage segmentation.

development give it a character which is not shared by most northern Somali towns. Typically these have little civic identity. They are not independent fastnesses in a nomadic society; and their inhabitants have little sense of civic consciousness beyond that which depends upon lineage allegiance. This means that where a market center contains the inhabitants of a particular lineage its members are politically united as clansmen, but apart from this they have little sense of residential solidarity. In the larger centers occupied by people of several structurally remote lineages, or even clans, the community as a whole derives little sense of unity from its residential identity and is not an independent political unit.

Town and country are thus not polar extremes; but on the contrary closely associated. Indeed, one of the most significant aspects of modern urban developments in northern Somaliland is the structural continuity between urban and rural area. A pastoralist who goes to take up residence and employment in a town does not sever his economic and political ties with his pastoral kinsmen; nor does he adopt radically new social relationships in the urban community. This community is structured along the same lineage and contractual channels as the pastoral social system of which it is essentially a continuation. A man's lineage affiliation is as important in town life as in the pastures, in determining with whom he will associate and in what capacity. It is true, of course, that in proportion to the greater degree of lineage and clan diversification in towns, the range of genealogical connection recognized as socially significant is extended. Thus two men of the same clan, but of lineages which in the pastoral society are often opposed, see themselves as sharing common interests in opposition to townsmen of other clans. Thus in towns there is often a significant shift in the range of agnation which affects social intercourse, but social relations remain for the most part dependent upon the segmentary lineage structure of pastoral society.

It is thus not surprising that in towns people tend to preserve the same patterns of settlement which they adopt in the pastures. The desire to match lineage affiliation with area of residence—so that one's neigbors are also one's clansmen—is still strong. This is most evident in some of the smaller settlements where town planning has not upset lineage patterns of grouping. But, even in the larger centers, the tendency towards the assumption of residential patterns which conform to lineage ties is marked, particularly in the clusters of nomadic huts, occupied often mainly by only transitory settlers, which lie round the peripheries of large towns some distance from the more permanent core of stone and mud houses. For example, in Las Anod (the administrative headquarters of the Dulbahante clan in the east of the Protectorate), the area of the town composed of nomadic huts is divided into two distinct quarters along the lines of lineage cleavage. One sector is dominated by the Faarah Garaad segment and the other by the opposed Mahamuud Garaad, these being the two main segments of the clan, each divided into a hierarchy of smaller lineages.

And even in the permanent centers of towns where town-planning rules have prevented a complete congruence between area of settlement and lineage, when a lineage fight occurs, those concerned desert their houses and attempt to gather together in separate areas as far removed from their enemies as possible. Disputes between individuals readily take on a corporate character according to their structural distance in the lineage system in exactly the same way as in the interior. Indeed, many clan and lineage campaigns stem from town brawls between individuals of opposed lineages, and in the ensuing strife the center of conflict veers from town to rural area and back again as occasion offers. Pastoral lineage affairs are in any case often largely directed from the towns, where elders frequently live (at least during the dry seasons) and often own town property. Permanent townsmen equally have one foot with their clansmen in the pastures, and the economic links of clansmen are not severed because one lives in a town while another moves with the camels, in which both share common interests. The closest economic link between the two spheres arises when, as often happens, a group of brothers decide to form in effect a company sharing their profits, some going to work in the towns or in government service, while the others stay behind with their joint livestock.

At the same time, the pastoral dia-paying system is not replaced by some other organization in the towns. Merchants and others who live permanently in towns are still a party to the dia-paying contracts of their clansmen, and indeed the realms in which dia-paying solidarity operates are widened in modern conditions. Thus, although it was agreed some time ago in the Protectorate that fatal traffic accidents and other accidents in town life should not give cause for claims for blood-wealth other than on an individual basis, collective responsibility is often in fact recognized. Death in a motor accident often gives rise to negotiations between the dia-paying groups concerned and, if compensation is not paid, a feud may develop. In one case where a man was killed by a truck driven by a man of another clan, bloodwealth was claimed; but, when it had not been paid some months after the accident, the aggrieved lineage retaliated by murdering a clansman of the guilty driver. Such cases, however, are more usually settled amicably outside the courts.

All this indicates the continuing force of traditional lineage allegiances in urban life. And in keeping with this, commerce is very closely bound up with lineage politics. Wherever possible, business is brought to agnates. A man prefers to take his custom to the shop of a clansman where he can expect generous credit, whereas a stranger would expect him to pay cash. Thus, in towns, a merchant relies for his customers largely upon those of his clan or lineage who live nearby. And the organization of commerce follows the lineage structure. Each lineage in a market center regards certain shops as lying within its sphere of interest, and this applies equally to the coffee shops in which men spend so much of their time. In principle, every lineage of any size has at least one coffee shop, just as it has at least one member who is a general merchant or trader. Thus, in the township of Sheikh discussed above, the number of shops and coffee shops owned and patronized by the two locally dominant lineages is roughly in proportion to their numerical strengths. The coffee shop is of particular importance as an institution since it is the main center of gossip and often of lineage policy decision.

This division of commerce by lineage affiliation has further important repercussions. Lineages are constantly competing for the grant of trading licenses, just as they are continuously engaged in competition for appointments in government departments, in the police and administration, and indeed in all spheres. And here rivalry is as acute as it is in pastoral and now also party politics. It is typical of the lineage character of Somali trading interests that a peace settlement, reached at one stage in a long train of conflict between two clans contending for access to water and pasturage, should include a clause defining the trading rights of each in the disputed area. Monopolistic-like rights in trade concerning the economic prosperity of a lineage are an important consideration in politics in the interior as well as in towns.

Somali regard the extension of their corporate lineage interests into the spheres of trade and commerce as partly a natural continuation of the collective economic interests of agnates. More especially, this is considered necessary to safeguard the interests, economic as well as political, of the individual merchant. And quite apart from the fact that a man's prosperity is counted a direct gain to his clansmen, a trader expects the protection as well as the patronage of his dia-paying kinsmen as a matter of social right.

Foreign Merchants.

It will be evident that trade and commerce are based on the agnatic system, which is the foundation of collective interests in general among the northern Somali. It follows from this that the foreign trader has somehow to be fitted into this exclusive system. Is is here that the institution of trade patronage, which was mentioned earlier in connection with the caravan trade, is applied. The Indian and Arabian merchants, who once largely monopolized at least the export trade but of whom there are today only a few hundred in the Protectorate,[35] are brought into the Somali lineage structure, though not completely, by being attached as clients to Somali lineages.

Each foreign trader appoints a Somali *abbaan* to protect his general interests, preferably a man of high personal status and of a strong and respected lineage. The *abbaan*, who today is often paid a regular wage and sometimes receives a share in profits, acts as an agent, broker or general assistant. And in all Arabian and Indian stores Somali *abbaans* are to be seen often acting as little more than caretakers, or doorkeepers, responsible to their clients for maintaining order amongst Somali customers. They and their lineages are also entrusted with the general security of their client. The latter, however, is not required to contribute to, and does not share in, the financial and legal obligations of the Somali lineage to which he is attached. The client does not participate directly in payment of bloodwealth, and the remunerations which the *abbaan* receives are considered to exonerate the client from this responsibility.

The institution also operates in relation to those who practice the specialist (and in Somali eyes) degrading crafts of leatherworking, metalworking, pottery, and hair-cutting. These trades are despised by Somali and are followed by three groups of bondsmen, known collectively as *sab*, and traditionally attached to Somali lineages in a servile status. These are the Midgo (sg. Midgaan), traditionally hunters, leatherworkers, and barbers; the Tumaallo (sg. Tumaal), mainly blacksmiths; and the Yibro (sg. Yibir), who traditionally perform menial tasks and are above all feared as magicians. These *sab* bondsmen probably only number some 12,500 in the Protectorate and Somalia and thus form a very small proportion of the total population. Each of the three groups is divided into a number of small, nonlocalized, lineages segmented on the Somali pattern. Somali do not intermarry with *sab*, who marry among themselves, and traditionally *sab* individuals and families are attached to specific Somali patrons *(abbaans)* upon whom they are economically dependent, especially for bridewealth and blood-compensation.[36]

This is the traditional pattern of symbiosis between the numerically dominant and aristrocratic Somali pastoralists and their *sab*

---

(35) In French Somaliland, however, there is an Arab community some 6,000 strong.

(36) Traditionally *sab* have no voice in the councils of their patrons, but this discriminatory rule is disappearing today.

dependents who differ physically little if at all from their patrons (Goldsmith and Lewis 1958). Today, however, *sab* are increasingly finding work in the towns, and many have left their traditional protectors to seek urban employment. Thus most large centers contain small Midgaan and Tumaal communities, the former mainly employed as barbers, and the latter largely blacksmiths and motor mechanics, living in their own part of the town. Somali regard the *sab* quarter as the least desirable residential area. At the same time, with this partial emancipation which the development of townships and urban industry, however minimal, is fostering, there is a movement among the *sab* to set up their own independent dia-paying groups on an equal footing with Somali. So far, in the Protectorate no *sab* lineage has attained this status, although it has been achieved by some *sab* groups in northern Somalia.

Despite these indications of an increasing degree of autonomy, however, the traditional bonds of association between *sab* and Somali are reflected in urban patterns of commerce. For here, Somali tend to patronize those *sab* with whom their lineages have a traditional relation of protection. At the same time, when conflict flares up between rival Somali lineages in a town, there is a strong tendency for the local *sab* community to split up according to its traditional lines of allegiance. These are instances of the continuing importance of traditional lines of cleavage in modern Somali society, a topic to which I return presently.

WEALTH AND SOCIAL ORGANIZATION

I have stressed some of the consequences in trade and commerce of the economic identity of agnates, an identity which is strongest and most clearly seen in the structure of the dia-paying group. In the pastoral situation, apart from collective solidarity in effecting reparation, members of a dia-paying group help each other in time of want as much as in time of war and in general tasks, such as the watering of the camels which are part of the collective wealth of the group. Men borrow most frequently from clansmen, and the obligatory Muslim alms *(seko)*[37] are frequently distributed amongst poor agnates. These are indications of what clanship entails in sharing resources and profits. Here the ethic of reciprocity and of mutuality is paramount, and the rich trader is expected to assist his poorer kinsmen. Those who are absent on business, or in employment in a town or overseas, are expected to send regular remittances to their

_____

(37) An annual contribution to the poor from a man's current wealth.

clansmen in the interior.[38] These many kinship commitments increase with the individual's wealth.

The Somali for wealth is *hoolo,* which means primarily wealth in livestock. After horses, which are today rare, camels are the most prized possession, one of the familiar themes of poetry and song, and rivalry over them is a constant source of strife and loss of life. Ideally, it is in camels that bloodwealth and bridewealth are reckoned, and the exchange relation between a man's life and worldly goods is phrased in terms of camels. Today, however, money, with which Somali have a long familiarity,[39] is to some extent substituted for livestock in these transactions, the current value of bloodwealth in the Protectorate being 100 camels each valued at 45 Rs (i.e. 67 Shs. 50 cents East African). This is the standard (1958) valuation of bloodwealth.[40] According to the current market value of camels, however, a good young camel may fetch as much as 100 Rs, and fifty camels, whose market value is 90 Rs each (or twice the standard bloodwealth rate), can be paid in lieu of the 100 statutory beasts. Indeed, the quantity of camels required is now unimportant provided their total value is that of full bloodwealth. And money is frequently substituted today as part, or even the whole, of the statutory 100 camels.

Somali value money partly because they regard it as an independent form of wealth, and partly because it can be converted into more desirable kinds of wealth, such as livestock.

Most travelers who have recorded their impressions of Somali character have noted the acute commercial sense of the Somali, and have described the pastoralists as mercenary and avaricious. Somali

(38) As has been pointed out, there are few opportunities for local employment except in government service, and to a lesser extent in domestic service, and in trade. Labor migration hardly exists. A number of Somali, however, have always gone overseas, initially often as stokers on ships, and have formed small immigrant Somali communities in Europe such as those in Marseilles, Cardiff, and London. There is a Somali community of over 10,000 in Aden, and Somali traders in Kenya, Uganda, and Tanganyika. A very few Somali have even found work on the mines in South Africa. Many of these migrants return home after years abroad to invest their savings in larger herds of camels, and flocks of sheep and goats, and some go into business.

(39) Coins dating from the fifteenth century have been found in the ruined sites of early Muslim trade centers in northern Somaliland. See Curle, 1937.

(40) In other parts of Somaliland the value of bloodwealth varies and in the Protectorate itself the monetary value of a bloodwealth camel has increased considerably over the last 30 or 40 years. At one time the rate was 20Rs. It is important to note that these conventional evaluations refer only to blood compensation. There is no standard rate of bridewealth which in the Protectorate ranges between two or three and fifty camels or their equivalent in other currency—cattle, horses, money, rifles and arms, etc. A dowry of often as much as two thirds of the value of the bridewealth is paid in return to the husband by his wife's kin.

certainly seek to profit from financial transactions and would endorse the view that money talks, that wealth is power, and as such is highly desirable. Thus even in so egalitarian a society, it is proverbial that the rich elder commands ready support for his proposals while a poor man's words carry little weight. And Somali are very much alive to the exploitable resources of another. Some conception of their commercial attitudes may perhaps be gained from a conversation which I once overheard amongst typical pastoralists in the Protectorate. The merits of the French people were being discussed, and the view was put forward that since their currency was known to be so unstable they must be of little account as a nation.

But it would of course be quite wrong to imagine that Somali consider money to be capable of buying everything they value. Although riches, if wisely spent, bring renown and influence, pride, dignity, and "name" are in the end more important. A man, however poor, will readily reject a wage that he considers entirely disproportionate to his labors; he will withdraw from a transaction which has become repugnant to him with his dignity intact, if little the richer.

Above all, loyalty to one's kin is more important than the possession of wealth, even wealth of direct prestige value. And Somali are well aware of the conflict which frequently exists between the desire for personal gain and the responsibilities of clanship. Here the pastoralists quote the decision of one elder faced with this dilemma expressed in words which are now proverbial: "Between wealth and clanship, I chose clanship."[41] In a society where war and feud are still almost daily events, clanship in the last analysis is far more important than wealth. Ultimately a person's security depends upon the strength and goodwill of his clansmen, particularly of his dia-paying group, not on the amount of his worldly goods. Thus the ethics of clanship are more important than those of prestige founded on wealth; and honor, more precious than profit.

CONCLUSION

In this paper I have traced some of the effects in trade and commerce of the segmentary lineage structure of northern Somali society. I have argued that the economic and political continuity between the urban and rural society carries the bonds of agnatic solidarity into town life and commerce. It would, however, be contrary to the facts to maintain that the traditional pastoral social structure is exactly reproduced in town society. Today markets which are the traditional centers of

(41) *Tol iyo fardo, tol baan doortay. Fardo* is literally horses, prestige wealth *par excellence.*

pastoral politics are also the foci of social change in its widest sense. It is the new towns that most clearly show the effects of rudimentary industrial development, of modern economic and social progress, and of education. It is, moreover, primarily through the towns that the inspiration of African nationalism elsewhere and of modernism in general impinges on the traditional pastoral social system.

In response to these new influences and to recent constitutional developments in French and British Somaliland and in Somalia, and to what are regarded as the imperialist policies of Ethiopia, there is now in northern Somaliland a growing national awareness and a growing desire to replace clan by national patriotism. Today merchants who live permanently in towns show reluctance in continuing to meet their financial obligations towards their dia-paying kinsmen; and in the better policed and more orderly conditions of urban society they feel less need for the support of their dia-paying group. One economic correlate of this is a tendency to bank monetary profits rather than to convert them entirely into livestock wealth. Thus, there is an increasing desire on the part of the townsman to divest himself of those collective obligations which traditionally bind him to his clansmen. And new patterns of social relationships are developing where people are thrown together by occupation and residence. Equally there is a growing, if yet minimal, sense of class in place of clan not only among government officials and nationalist politicians but also between tradesmen. This new modernist movement which finds support and encouragement in the universalistic values of Islam has been sufficient to stimulate strong nationalist ideals and aspirations. But since the traditional economic and social order has not been radically changed, pastoral values persist. Commerce no less than modern party politics (Lewis 1958, 1959a) continues to bear the stamp of agnation.

CHAPTER 14

The Abyssinian Market Town

BY SIMON D. MESSING

INTRODUCTION

The purpose of this essay is to describe the marketing system of the Abyssinian economy and to analyze marketing in relation to other aspects of Abyssinian society. In order to reduce the problem to manageable proportions, field work was concentrated on the *Amhara* people, who are today the most "typical" representatives of Abyssinian culture. Also, they are politically dominant, having expanded the boundaries of their domain in the late nineteenth century to include most of what is now known as the Empire of Ethiopia.

Within the three Amhara provinces, an obvious caravan terminal suitable for concentrated study was the provincial town of Gondar. As Map No. 16 shows, caravans from the lowland meet the trails from the various high-plateau areas there; goods from the Sudan are exchanged for local products and goods from the Red Sea. Its position is enhanced by an Italian-built road.

At first sight, marketing in Gondar seems relatively simple when compared to the large, money-using West African markets. This first impression is strengthened when one has observed the near self-sufficiency of the predominantly agricultural economy of Abyssinia, the prevalent subsistence farming with a near absence of cash crops in most areas, the feudal-like land tenure that now constitutes what might more accurately be described as an uncertain "farm tenure." The larger markets are dominated by the basic cereals and pulses which, together with sheep and goats, form the basis of the Abyssinian diet. Vegetables, fruits and root crops, found in small quantities (if at all) on the northern plateau of Abyssinia, are found in the non-Abyssinian, conquered territories of southern Ethiopia. To the outside world, Ethiopia contributes economically only in modest ways: coffee harvested on plantations where little cultivation is done except weeding, so that the produce is more wild than planted; some civet musk; leopard skins and hides (often poorly tanned by modern standards); some cereals (if the cost of transportation is not prohibitive); and some gold from the southwestern desert lowlands of Ethiopia. Observation of Abyssinian personality suggests that the

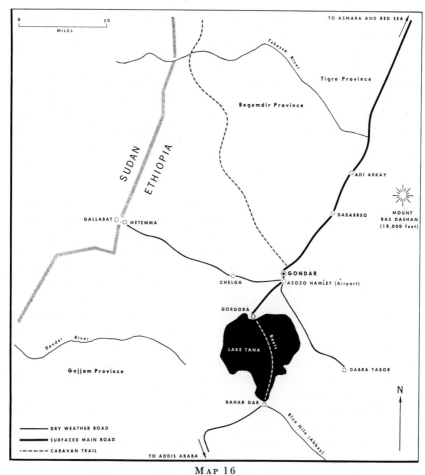

MAP 16

Main Caravan Trails and Roads Connecting Gondar Ethiopia

dominant Amhara, Coptic-Christian citizen is not primarily interested in trading except for hiring out to caravans as guide and helper
when in need of occasional funds.

But on further study, complexities emerge. There is relatively little
exchange of any kind outside the extended-family and rural hamlets
except for that taking place on daily and weekly markets. On certain
seasonal occasions, over 1,000 persons may gather in and about the
weekly market at Gondar. Money is used as both medium of exchange
and standard of value. The market is closely related to the division of
labor which is caste-like in its ethnic specialization of occupations,
such as smithing, pottery-making and tanning. The internal organi-

zation of the market is recognized by judicial and governmental authorities.

Absence of a highly mechanized, Western market economy does not mean the absence of complexities of a "substantive economy" (to use Karl Polanyi's term), nor does the fact that "money won't buy" the Amhara's pride in the public marketing operation. Psychological aspects of ethno-economics are involved in the fear of being shamed, which motivates the Amhara to forego an economically profitable transaction rather than face mockery of his peers that he could have done still better, and in the avoidance of any transaction that might involve the possibility of having to transport unsold goods back home again.

Finally, a large market such as Gondar has become sufficiently complex to attract middlemen. Though located in Coptic Christian territory, a number of Arab wholesalers, Ethiopian-Muslim retailers and even an Anglo-Indian trading company are established there and provide a link with world markets. During their brief occupation, the Italians built a surfaced road from the Red Sea coast to Gondar, a distance of about 400 miles. For the most part, the road followed a caravan trail that crossed both cold mountains 10,000 feet high and tropical river valleys. In Gondar they also built a sizable, modern bank building to take care of financial matters which they expected to increase in volume and complexity.

This essay deals largely with present conditions but also attempts to describe the main traits of Abyssinian marketing in their historical and organizational context.

THE ABYSSINIAN MARKET AND SOCIAL ORGANIZATION

The Market Town in Relation to the Traditional Division of Labor.
The economic basis for the growth of an Abyssinian town exists where caravan trails cross between residential kin-hamlets on "feudal" or church land, or when the daily market at which housewives buy the ingredients of their spiced sauce develops into a more complex "Saturday market" *(Qedamye gäbäya).*

Usually the market place is located on a little hill shaded by trees, and frequently not far from the little round parish church. In rural areas and even near towns, the church is little more than a well-built thatched hut, though in towns it may have solid walls, wooden doors and windows, and a corrugated iron roof. Caravans may camp over-night on the common pasture and assembly grounds below the hill, climbing it in daylight to reach the market.

Development beyond this point seems to depend on historical

events. A district chief or sub-governor may decide to establish a "palace" there, and his large court will draw retainers and office-seekers. A judge will be appointed to sit in the market. The pre-Italian Ethiopian government may have operated a telegraph station there, the Italians adding a hospital, a small power plant, municipal buildings, to which the post-Italian government may have added a modern elementary school.

If such a growing urban location has a history of some centuries, the fact that large-scale trading has long been conducted by Arabs and Muslim Ethiopians (taught by their co-religionists the desire to seg-regate such "infidels" and their "objectionable" practices of smoking tobacco and chewing the stimulating *qat* leaf) led to their residence in a Muslim ghetto located near the overnight camping ground below the hill of the Christian town. At best they were permitted to build modest homes on the slope up to the edge of the "Saturday market."

There, some of the Arab permanent stalls sell imported wares ranging from Egyptian tennis shoes, Czech razor blades and small, English Lux soap cakes to ready-made eyeglasses. Their teahouse, a respectable establishment for men only, features also sweet cakes and other snacks, and is a place where men of affairs of any faith can sit down to discuss business. It may be next door to the Abyssinian mead-house where many a peasant spends his crop money on honey-wine and flirtatious waitresses. Both establishments may be only a stone's throw from the "street of single girls," mostly divorcées living alone in corrugated iron shacks equipped with one European double bed each, and providing full hotel, restaurant and housewifely ser-vices to commercial travellers away from home.

Shortages of water and fuel have limited the growth of many Abyssinian towns. Ancient Abyssinian towns such as Aksum solved the water problem with huge stone cisterns. After cisterns ceased to be built, towns such as Gondar profited by their location just above two rivers. The introduction of the eucalyptus tree in the late nine-teenth century greatly helped to solve the fuel problem, and to a lesser degree the construction problem.

It is noteworthy that the term for town, *kätämä,* really means "permanent encampment." Once the economic requisites existed, most Abyssinian towns seem to have originated in connection with feudal social organization. The lord of the province *(ras)* might decide to dignify the place with his presence and order a large church to be built to serve the surrounding countryside. One of the priests would be appointed sacristan *(qes gobäz)* and/or chief *(aläqa)* over temporal aspects of church property. The installation of priests would be attractive to their nephews and other kinsmen whom the priests would

invite to settle in nearby rural hamlets and rent church land, thus
assuring food supplies and services to the church. In time, some of
the closest hamlet-parishes would be annexed by the town and become
urban parishes. A dozen chorister-scribes might attach themselves
to each of the various churches for a regular livelihood, as would
aged monks and widows-turned-nuns, as well as young boy deacons.
The widow-nuns do much of the baking and beerbrewing for the
church. The scribes and young priests operate the traditional church
school for boys, seated under the shade trees in the church yard next
to the Christian, unmarked graves.

The annexation of nearby hamlets and villages explains in part
the divergence of population figures. Gondar, with a permanent
population of at most 6,000, often claims a figure three times that
and more. Many "urbanites" own cows that graze on the river flood
plains below the truncated hill of the town, and send their sons down
daily to care for them. This common pasture and public assembly
ground long served as a military buffer against attack. For sneak raids
under guise of a caravan would be blunted by the time they climbed
the steep hill over its eroded and often slippery footpaths.

This same bottleneck also rendered the job of tax collecting easier
for the "chief of commerce" *(nägadras)* who could observe the movement of merchandise. Only the most important centers, including
Gondar, were given local rulers with the title *kantiba,* though most
had at least a city council. The chief of the feudal bodyguard on local
duty has in modern times become chief of police *(shälaqa).*

The historic event that brought about the founding of the town
of Gondar in the seventeenth century is connected with the name of
King Fasilidas, who reigned from 1632 to 1667. One of his first acts
was to expel all Portuguese from the country less than a century after
they had been welcomed as allies and protectors from Turkish mus-
keteers and Islamized Galla. Religious wars and rebellions had torn
the country after the Portuguese priests had converted Fasil's royal
predecessor to Roman Catholicism. However, the masons and other
skilled Abyssinian workmen trained by the Portuguese were still on
hand and Fasil employed them to build stone bridges, castles, palaces,
a stone bath and even a tomb for his favorite horse. These building
skills lasted for three generations before they were lost, and most of
the buildings still stand.

Fasil desired to leave his father's capital, Gorgora, located at the
northern shore of Lake Tana, the large lake from which the Blue
Nile emerges. In Abyssinia this is "lowland" although its elevation is
3,000 feet and it is subject to floods and malaria. He decided to build
his capital at Gondar, on the edge of the higher plateau, at an eleva-

tion of 5,000–6,000 feet. Here stands his castle, that of his prime minister, son and grandson, surrounded by the thatched huts of the populace and the Italian-built bungalows of the officials, clerks and teachers. Covered and walled "king's rows," now crumbling, led to the royal fig tree under which King Fasil and his immediate successors sat to judge appeals brought before them. A huge sycamore still graces the spot.

It is likely, therefore, that no Portuguese set foot in Gondar, which did not exist as a town during their ninety-year stay. The wine culture and oranges which they are believed to have introduced have long since disappeared. One of the daily spices, *capsicum Americani,* remains among the survivals. The power of Gondar itself and its function as a nation's capital faded away in the eighteenth century. After that it remained a provincial town, owing its urban continuance to the cotton sheeting trade from the Sudan, and its position as terminal for various items of commerce toward the coast. Some of the old aristocracy remain to this day, but have long since become impoverished. Emperor Theodore in the mid-nineteenth century called Gondar a city of "traders and thieves." In 1889 Gondar was sacked during the Mahdi *(därbush,* i.e. dervish) invasion from the Sudan, and the old urban stone houses have not been rebuilt. Most urbanites who have emerged from mud huts live in shacks of wood, hard-clay walls and corrugated iron roofs.

The Muslim ghetto was apparently added some time after the building of Gondar, as its name, *Addis Aläm* (lit., new world) indicates. Today it is the oldest remaining section of the town, apart from the restored Fasil palaces.

Since manual crafts in Abyssinian culture are relegated to low-class ethnic elements of the population, usually non-Coptic, many of these craftsmen have long since settled in rural hamlets of their own within walking distance of the "Saturday market" of Gondar. They provide the iron tools, sun umbrellas, tanned leatherwork and pottery without exposing themselves to the mockery, insults and occasional assaults at the hands of the Coptic Christian townspeople. Smithing is largely done by Falasha (Ethiopian Jewish) craftsmen whose women make pottery. The tanners are non-Amhara non-Copts and have what seems to be a pre-Biblical religion of worship under trees in secluded spots remote from inhabited hamlets.

Amhara and most other Abyssinians despise manual labor, and the more skilled it is, the more it is despised. At least that is the tradition which still dominates the overwhelming majority of the population. A rational basis for this attitude may possibly be found in their historical experience. Acquisition of special labor skills frequently led to enforced migration in the supply arms of feudal armies on campaign, and these armies had to be on the move lest the produce of the countryside around the camp be consumed entirely by the soldiery.

Obversely, the Amhara purchaser has more faith in the quality of a product made by the ethnic craftsman from a family that has specialized in the same product for generations. This discourages a poor Amhara who might be tempted, in modern times, to turn to this craft. In fact, the very suspicion in which the blacksmith is held as a likely sorcerer strengthens the faith in the quality of his plowpoint, axe, adze, sickle, and other tools.

The ethnic division of labor is one of the factors related to the need for middlemen. The Falashas, for example, as strict Saturday-Sabbath observers, have to employ Muslim middlemen to sell their iron tools on the big Saturday market at Gondar. This practice protects them from being exposed to insults such as *"kayla"* (lit., manual craftsman). Moreover, the Falashas are craftsmen and not adept at commerce. In the past they were often forced to accompany armies to make and repair weapons, such as spears, knives, and swords; despite their simple tools, they can recast every part of a rifle except the barrel. Some Falashas became so essential in the Abyssinian armies of conquest of the late nineteenth century that they were given the title *"bajirond"* (treasurer) and rewarded with land which was usually prohibited to Falashas. (Even today most Falashas do their subsistence farming on rented land.)

Income from smithcraft is not large when the labor involved is considered. A team of five men receives Eth. $1.50 (U.S. $0.60) for the labor of making a plowpoint when the customer brings the iron scrap, double that if he does not. If the customer comes to the hamlet of the smith, he must be fed free of charge while the job is in process. To cut a dull axe down to a sharp adze, the fee is Eth. $0.50. The requirement to feed the customer about equals the overage added by the middlemen at the Saturday market.

Falasha women who have worked on one large beer jar for two days prior to firing, without benefit of wheel or kiln, produce a remarkably symmetrical and comparatively sound pot for Eth. $0.50 to Eth. $1.00. The latter is more likely to be the price at the market where the middleman takes a large share.

Most carpentry is unspecialized and primitive, but such items as the wooden, skin-covered saddle *(korecha)* require craftsmanship. A well made one costs Eth. $25.00 but part of this price goes to the tanners for affixing the skin. A saddlemaker earns about Eth. $8.00 for his labor, but some are so proficient that they do nothing else as long as the demand lasts.

The consumption of leather articles among the Amhara is considerable. Most of these articles are made by the *Faqi* or tanners who prefer to be addressed as *arabännya*, which carries a connotation that they deal in imported (Arab) goods. They, too, were frequently forced to serve as ordnance men in the armies of conquest in the late nineteenth century, making rhinoceros-hide shields, scabbards, saddle-skins, etc. Today they more frequently make skin covers for food baskets in which commercial travelers carry sauce mixed with bread and other basic food staples. They can make parchment from goat skins, interlace bed frames with strips of oxhide, grain sacks, half sacks for carrying an infant, drumheads for church service, drinking horns, etc.

Silversmithing is done mostly by Muslims, either Arab or Ethiopian, in towns or some other big markets. The raw material used is frequently the old Maria Theresa Thaler, and often the smith is permitted to keep as much as two-thirds of the "raw material" as his fee. But middlemen more commonly deal in silver goods at the big markets than do craftsmen. Traders sit behind wooden chests filled with silver filigree earwax removers, crosses, rings, etc. Casting is by the *cire perdue* method. Goldsmithing was limited to the royal court and is not to be found at the markets.

Weaving the toga is largely the work of Ethiopian Muslims and Falashas, though poor Amhara who have left their families or have intermarried with persons of other ethnic groups are also found in this occupation. Homespun cotton thread is supplied by the Amhara housewife to the weaver, who may work on order (which is more common in Gondar), or else sell his product at the big market (the prevalent pattern in Addis Ababa). The texture ranges from the lightest muslin to the most coarse and tightest cloth, with or without embroidered and dyed borders. In Gondar, most weavers *(shamani)* carry their portable looms unless the demand is "in season," when they prefer to work at home. A cheap peasant toga costs Eth. $5.00 to Eth. $8.00 when no middleman is employed. The average experienced weaver can readily earn Eth. $200.00 per year, which gives him more cash income than any farmer or other craftsmen can earn readily. In social status, the occupation ranks above that of smiths, pottery-makers and tanners, and about even with that of musician.

The only "respectable" occupations Coptic Amhara engage in are farming, husbandry, warfare, government and the church. However, poor Amhara do not lose status by working for a wage *(damoz)* provided the work is unskilled or semiskilled, involves fewer manual than mental responsibilities, and does not imply a permanent taking of orders (unless the employer is a nobleman). To avoid shaming his family, the poor Amhara prefers to hire out in another province or at least another district. Present wages for unskilled labor are about Eth. $30.00 per month plus food, shelter, and perhaps sandals. The most common source of unskilled labor, particularly for manual work, can be found in towns among the liberated former slaves (mainly *Shanqalla* or *Barya* tribes) brought from Central Africa or the Nilotic regions, and their half-Amhara offspring.

Chamberlains *(agafari)*, formerly employed at the feudal courts, now serve at urban weddings as caterers, ushers, waiters. Women musicians *(azmari)* act also as singers, impromptu composers of lyrics, and dancers; accompanied by male musicians, they are employed at urban weddings and at big markets. An infrequent but honored occupation is that of painter *(seelsali)* of religious or royal themes, commissioned by well-to-do sponsors for a church. More common, and regarded as strictly commercial without status designation, is the occupation of woman tatooer *(täqwari)*. Her clients are women, and her main "seasons" occur after harvests and before the important holy days of "Feast of the True Cross," Christmas and Epiphany. These are also high "seasons" for the woman hairdresser, who braids the hair into 12–32 thin braids and charges Eth. $1.00 for a fine, two-hour job. Most of these services, particularly those of the women, take place very near the big "Saturday-market," or are arranged for at that location.

Wages rise appreciably as soon as modern education, even a few grades of elementary school, can be offered. The graduate of a rural church school receives credit for only two grades of modern elementary school. A graduate with eight grades of elementary school can obtain a job as teacher with the basic pay of Eth. $125.00 per month, or as municipal clerk with equal income. He earns about as much in one month as the average landowning peasant does in a year. Even after only five grades a young man can obtain a teaching job at a rural school at Eth. $50.00 a month. High school graduates quickly find much more highly paid jobs with the central or provincial government or with a foreign trading company. The demand for admission into elementary school is very great.

In provincial towns such as Gondar the gradually increasing number of teachers, clerks, medical "dressers," etc, who possess much of the ready cash, dominate certain phases of marketing in place of the "great men" and country squires who did so until recently.

Daily and Saturday Markets.

Both the daily and Saturday markets supply a place to buy and sell food, livestock and luxury goods. There is some duplication in the items for sale, but the distinctions are significant.

The daily market, whether it is the comparatively elaborate *"Arada"* in Gondar or one located at a rural crossroads, is primarily a "sauce market" at which the housewife purchases the many diverse ingredients that go into her daily stew. In rural areas there is a different daily market at a different spot every day in the work week, Monday through Friday. For example, in the district of *Seqelt* west of Gondar, the "daily market" meets only on Tuesday, near the hamlet of Maqwamiya, and is known in the district as the *"Tuesday market."* This arrangement permits both customers and suppliers to find some market on any day but Sunday. The attraction of the daily market for the supplier is that it provides a small but regular income in form of cash. Also, since the daily market is more socially intimate and ethnically homogeneous, the rustic peasant is less fearful of being shamed by a "city slicker" during trade and is not quite so fearful of having to carry goods home. He might even store them briefly at the nearby hamlet with friends or kinfolk.

The daily market features such items as butter—some fresh and sold on a leaf, some melted and sold in European bottles. Either form may be used for cooking or hair dressing. Red pepper of a variety of strengths; cereals, particularly *tyeff (Eragrostic abyssinica),* the small-grained field crop from which the daily flapjack-bread is made; and barley, used for beermaking, mule feeding, and as parched condiment—all are available in moderate quantities. So is the field pea and more commonly the small chick-pea, often sold still on the stalk, and beans. The variety of vegetables is limited, but they become important during the long Lenten season when even milk, butter, eggs, fish and all other animal products are taboo. Cabbage is considered emergency or "poor" food, one of the many crops grown by the peasant as a safety measure against crop failure, warfare rapacity, and locusts.

Oil seeds are abundant and varied. The commonest are *nug (Guizotia abyssinica),* an Abyssinian variety of Niger seed, and flax seed. They are eaten crushed, mixed with water as energy givers, or carried by travelers as "instant food" mixed with pepper, butter, onion, and smeared on bread. Oilcake is sometimes used as fodder, as is the stalk of the flaxseed (from which no fibers are made). Sometimes castorbeans are grown as shrub crops, most often by the tanners who use them as lubricants. Other shrub crops, not infrequently grown near the town in wind-protected ruins of stone houses, are myrtle which is boiled with butter to make pomade, hops *(Ziziphus mitis),* and *qat (Catha edulis)* for the Muslims.

Such a variety of spices, mainly domestic but some imported from as far as Yemen, are available to the housewife that every husband immediately recognizes his wife's individual sauces. Common field crops are fenugreek, ginger and *abusda,* which resembles Niger seed. Garden crops include rue, coriander, sweet basil, caraway seed, mustard seed, thyme, onion and garlic.

Imported spices which may find their way to the daily markets are commonly sold in five-cent lots (the same quantities of domestic products cost only two cents). Among them are cardamon, saffron, cumin, nutmeg, cinnamon, oregano and cloves.

Small livestock, such as chickens, sheep, goats, and donkeys, may be sold at the daily market for cash. So may firewood.

Large livestock, such as cows (which are featured in marriage contributions on a mutual basis, not as *lobola),* oxen for plowing, Sudanese *(Senar)* mules, and horses, are bought and sold only at the big Saturday markets, such as the old one in Gondar or the one on the Italian road at Qollarba in the Dembeya lowland. This latter "new" market will probably not last, since it is in the malaria belt just north of Lake Tana where epidemics are frequent in September-October just after the end of the rainy season, so the Gondar Saturday market can be considered as important as it was prior to the Italian occupation.

The Saturday market supplies a number of services and basic needs, as well as those luxuries that reach the Abyssinian market. Basic needs include salt (formerly traded in bars which served as small change money but now sold by weight in very coarse grains), raw cotton needed by every housewife for home spinning, coffee from Jimma in southern Ethiopia, and surplus farm produce, especially cereal staples. The cereals, sold by the sackful, include many sorghums *(durra),* some of which are used to stretch the daily bread made of *tyeff.* The commonest sorghum is *mashella* known as "kaffir corn" in other parts of Africa. Another is *zengada (Eleusina multiforma)* which peasants grow as crop insurance especially against birds, and *dagussa (Eleusina tocusso,* or *E. coracana)* which is used in beer making or to stretch *tyeff* at times of great poverty. Not to be confused linguistically is maize *(baher mashella,* lit. "sorghum from overseas," *Zea mays),* often grown as crop insurance with other grains, or on lower elevations in cotton fields to protect the cotton from cold and wind. Since the grain is larger than the others, it is well-liked in boiled form during lent. Wheat *(sende)* is a luxury grain grown on high elevations in small quantities. It is harvested late, and can be afforded mainly by the church (e.g. for the Eucharist), and by commercial travelers who have a solid, nearly unleavened bread baked from it.

It is of course the comparatively well-to-do customers—traders, the church, the feudal nobility and former warlords, plus, nowadays, the officials teachers and clerks—who create the demand for products other than the basic ones. The Saturday market therefore emphasizes goods that require long-distance transportation (though this includes salt, a basic need) and specialized craftsmanship.

Travelers are usually the only persons to buy the semi-processed foods, such as spiced butter paste, spiced pea paste, oil paste, or ready-baked bread sold by women, usually poor Amhara part-time bakers. This is not because of expense, which is five cents per bread, but because of the shame involved in eating food not prepared in a regular household. This does not apply, however, to the Arab teahouse and the innkeeper-prostitute whose services are regarded as more trust-worthy. A traveler may buy ready-made bread for his low-class caravan helpers, but most Amhara employees will insist on bread and sauce prepared in a household arrangement, be it ever so temporary.

Honey is a ready-cash item for many peasants who sell it at the Saturday market to the owners of the mead-houses. Fish is seasonal, and a number of peasants and even urbanites catch fish with nets in rivers below the towns during the three-month rainy season. The fish must be sold immediately since no method of preservation is employed.

Though most herb medicines are kept secret by Amhara empiricist healers, some are more or less widely known and found at the markets, especially the weekly markets. The best known is *kosso,* the rosewood (which provides a livelihood to poor Amhara collectors who bring the twigs, bark and flower in dry bundles) for use against tapeworm which is common. Jasmine is remedy for milder intestinal upsets. Wild honey is sold for any chest ailment, and rue against fever. Scrofu-la sufferers can buy *mäqmäqo (Rumex abyssinicus),* and those who need a stimulant can find Jimson weed *(Datura stramonium).*

Incense, mainly for the church and healing cult *(zar)* but occasion-ally also for noble homes, is also sold on the Saturday market. Most common is frankincense; then there is myrrh and sandalwood. Im-ported yellow sulphur *(kabre)* is used in the *zar* cult. A domestic incense known as *bukbuka* and leaves of a *wägärt* bush are used to fumigate a headache away.

Peasants supplying all these necessary and/or useful products un-fortunately have to sell at low prices.[1] For example, a quintal (100 kilos) of *tyeff* brings as little as Eth. $10.00 when there is no seasonal

(1) There is another major factor, in addition to the fear of feudal exploitation, that has inhibited the cultivator from producing beyond the subsistence level. Several years ago handbills were issued by the present imperial government, urging peasants to grow castor-beans and other cash crops, with the promise that ink and a number of other manufactured products would be made from them. When some did so, they found no market and returned to traditional farming.

demand at Gondar (though at Addis Ababa the price would be Eth. $30.00). *Nug* seed brings Eth. $30.00 per 100 kilos at Gondar, *gesho* (hops) as much as Eth. $1.00 per kilo so that some "urban farmers" grow it as a part-time cash crop.

Sale of livestock is an important cash income producer for the peasant. The Saturday market supplies the better sheep, including fat-tailed ones, cows that have stopped calving and giving milk, oxen too old for plowing—all for food. Gondar (unlike cities such as Harrar) has no abbatoir and there is no commercial butchering. Most commonly an old cow is purchased by a group of householders, who gather after church early Sunday morning, butcher the animal and immediately parcel it out. What is left is quickly "cleaned up" by the vultures or hyenas.

Livestock bring in little cash because of the distance from, and poor transportation to, world markets. The hides that are exported are merely sun-dried, salted, and book-folded. Even a good sheep brings so little revenue that the raw sheepskin can be resold for one-third the cost of the animal. Goats are so cheap that the herding is entrusted to children or halfwits who can do little else. There are many cattle diseases; besides cauterization scars, one frequently sees cows with large nicks cut out of the ears to "cure spirit diseases." In the dry season the drought often stops calves from growing and reduces milk supply, which the Italians estimated as averaging only 300 kilos per entire lactation period of an average cow. However, the domestic cattle are resistant to many diseases—some unidentified—that regularly kill imported cattle.

While cattle are valued as the main form of wealth, agriculture is the dominant concern. Cattle are not bred to produce good milkers, but to produce strong, well-humped oxen for the plow. Sometimes mineral salt is fed to steers to fatten them and to cows to make them produce more milk.

Ethiopian horses are small, wiry and enduring, but used largely in warfare, aristocratic games and the tournament on Epiphany. Ethiopian mules have the same qualities but are considered more intelligent, more trustworthy on steep mountain trails, and are therefore ridden for transportation far more frequently than horses even by "great men;" they also cost twice as much as horses. Owners who rent them out will not permit them to be taken to the lowlands where hot climate and diseases assail them. The large Senar mule, offspring of an Arab donkey and an Ethiopian mare, is double again in price, but is usually imported from the Sudan. A nobleman may own it, and commoner bridegrooms may rent one to take the bride home from the wedding.

The average Amhara peasant owns about five cows, which is not much when one considers that a respectable minimum to contribute to a daughter's dowry is three cows, even though they can be transferred in installments. Price of large livestock is quoted in Maria Theresa Thalers, though the cash at the market that actually changes hands consists of Ethiopian dollars at the rate of Eth. $1.50 (US $0.60) equalling 1 M.T. A good milker can bring 50 M.T., but an old cow ready for slaughter only 15 M.T. Oxen are not contributed in dowry, but a farmer needs a team of two for plowing. A strong ox is worth 40 M.T. but a farmer would hesitate to sell it except in exchange for two male calves. An old ox brings only 15 M.T.; its hide, if it is good, can be sold for up to 4 M.T.

Sheep at the Gondar market bring only Eth. $3.00–Eth. $6.00 depending on the season (the higher price at Easter). Since the skin can bring Eth. $1.50 the meat is so cheap that almost anyone can eat it frequently. The farmer keeps about a dozen for his own needs, guests, gifts and for petty cash. To keep more would rob his cattle of grass.

Chickens are small and scrawny, and bring as little as Eth. $0.50 or even Eth. $0.25. Therefore peasants do not usually bother to bring them to the Saturday market except just before Easter. The same is true of eggs, which are small and sell at 1 cent (Eth.). Both are common ingredients in the daily sauce.

Mules do not usually provide income unless the peasant rents them to caravans. The rate is Eth. $1.00 per day (double that to a foreigner). Relatives can borrow mules free of charge. Most peasants rarely own more than one mule, which is valued at 40 M.T. (Senar mules at 80 M.T.). Donkeys are much more frequently for sale at markets, but are very small and even a good donkey rarely brings more than 12–15 M.T., dropping below that when no caravans are about to leave.

In some regions as many as one fourth of the peasants earn income from honey, especially when there are many bees in the neighborhood and a Saturday market with a mead-house is nearby. Five skeps set in trees can contain (at most) 50 kilos honey total, for which Eth. $50.00 can be obtained at the market.

Thus an average freehold farmer could derive the ready cash revenue in one year from his sales at the market, as stated in Table 35.

When one considers that basic cash expenditures would include salt, raw cotton, one or several togas, some imported spices, coffee, and the cash education tax, the cash income is small indeed.

Moreover, the Saturday market and the fixed Arab stalls at the daily Arada market attract the peasant's cash because of the increased variety of goods, many of which once were luxuries but are becoming necessities. Kerosene for the little clay lamps was bought for the church and noblemen, but is becoming popular among peasants. Matches, now a government monopoly in Addis Ababa, have replaced all earlier methods of making fire. The glass decanters *(berelle)*, in which Turkish perfume was traded to noblewomen in the nineteenth century by Arabs, have now become as commonplace as beer and

TABLE 35

Cash Revenue of Average Freehold Farmer

2 old cows	Eth. $ 45.00
1 old ox	20.00
3 sheep	15.00
10 chickens	3.00
300 eggs	3.00
50 kilos honey	50.00
milk	5.00
	Eth. $141.000

honey-water cups among peasants, practical objects since the small opening can be sealed with the thumb and wax and dead bees float to the surface and can be flicked away easily.

Clothing requires more cash outlay than before. The knee length, narrow-sleeved cotton shirt for which the material alone costs Eth. $8.50 and the heavy cotton jodphurs *(surre)*, Eth. $5.50 for material, used to be the prerogative of noblemen. The tailoring fee is now Eth. $5.50. But though peasants on the farm content themselves with knee length breeches and coarse cotton togas, they wear "urban dress" when going to market or to church. In recent years khaki cloth from the Sudan has been made into shorts by tailors using foot-operated Singer sewing machines near the Saturday market; since they are "mass-produced," the shorts are somewhat cheaper, but they do not carry the honor of jodphurs, worn by peasants and rural nobles. The reason cotton cloth for shirts and jodphurs is so expensive is not only the distance of transportation but also the import duty, Eth. $9.00 per *taqa* (about 45 meters) of even low-quality material, when imported from the Sudan. Of course modern clerks, low-level teachers, minor officials and minor urban nobles wear the wide, loose European trousers and, frequently, khaki bush jackets. Suits and ties are afforded by higher officials, high school or Indian teachers, and upper nobility (though this garb is spreading downward to Addis Ababa).

The sun umbrella, once the prerogative of royalty, has become the ambition and property of the peasant housewife. Little porcelain cups from as far away as Hong Kong are treasured in huts even in remote hamlets and used to serve coffee to honored guests. The family bread-basket-table *(mässob)* has to be purchased by the peasant, but is relatively inexpensive since it is a domestic craft. The same is true of the wooden bed-frame *(alga)*.

The Italian roads and the big, overloaded "trente-quatro" trucks which still service the Saturday markets have brought and created a demand for goods such as single-edged razor blades, glass-bead necklaces (popular for scouring clay pots), sandals, Egyptian rubber sneakers, sewing needles, laundry soap, and many other items.

The hypodermic needle and its efficacy in quickly curing almost any disease has become widely popular. At the Saturday market one can usually find male "dressers" equipped with the needle, who will give an injection for a fee of Eth. $0.50. Penicillin can be bought for Eth. $2.50. Neither is exactly legal, and sometimes the government provides free dresser service and injections against spotted fever, typhus, etc. But there is a steady demand, and the trade goes on. Hospitals, however, are still feared; such fear is strengthened when serious cases arrive too late.

Amhara trading practices are motivated not so much by the desire to drive a good monetary bargain as by the desire to carry out the transaction without being mocked, especially by Coptic peers. Unlike Arabs, the Amhara are too proud and not so intent on economic "maximizing" as to resort to badgering a customer. Amhara basket-makers may refuse to admit that their wares on display are for sale, claiming they were previously ordered and are waiting to be picked up by the customer. Then, to avoid having to carry unsold goods home, they sell cheaply when the market begins to close at about 4 P.M., two hours before dusk. Hence the proverb advises the buyer:

"To church (go) early,
to market (go) late"

The seller may refuse to state a price and ask the buyer to make an offer. If the offer is reasonable and the purchaser is on the same socio-economic level so that no problem of "honor" is involved (which would require a foreigner to be charged at least double), the trans-action will be concluded promptly. If a social problem is involved, the seller has to guess how high he must increase the price *(waga asärrärä)* to avoid being mocked. This makes him uncomfortable and he tries to disconcert the customer with veiled insults. The customer can play the same game; when buying sheep for food he may remark, "I am not expecting a hyena for dinner," (i.e., the animal you are trying to sell me is so lean, sick and old that it is close to death and would soon be fit only for a hyena).

When two Amhara have concluded a major transaction, they touch each other's outstretched palms while standing very close and, in presence of witnesses, seal the bargain by swearing *"Haile Selassye yemut"* (lit., "May Haile Selassie die", i.e. if I break this agreement).

The Amhara broker *(mäden)* fulfills a social as well as an economic role (unlike the Muslim whose function is purely economic here). He knows all the "honor" complications. Frequently he acts as a labor broker. When livestock is sold, he guarantees that the animal is not stolen, and he must make good the loss if it has been. For this verbal bond he charges at little as one per cent payable in cash, plus a barley-beer repast. If business is slack, he may employ Amhara loiterers to gather around at the beginning of a likely transaction and contribute their wit, urging the buyer to close the deal.

Internal Organization of the Markets.

The daily markets, especially in rural areas, have little governmental supervision except for the village headman, who can arrest a thief to bring him before the *danya* or judge in the town.

The *danya* is traditionally both a civil and criminal judge; he also hears disputes which the unofficial "curbstone judges" have not been able to settle. He often sits at the Saturday market, under a shady tree, not far from the gibbet from which criminals (into the 1940's) were hanged in public. Next to him may sit the central government's collector of trade revenue and supervisor of trade practices. Traditionally he fixes, alters and supervises tolls on trails and river crossings, and keeps an eye on commercial travelers. The presence of market judges who would promptly punish breaches of the peace, levy fines, require restitution from thieves, etc., was an important factor in the growth of a town such as Gondar. This is especially true in view of the concern of the Amhara for justice and love of litigation. Muslims still have their own *Qadi*, who functions both as ecclesiastical and temporal judge in their disputes with one another.

The Saturday market may include a barbed wire fence around a shady tree, behind which government "dressers" give free injections particularly when epidemics threaten. Similarly, treasury clerks from Addis Ababa may set up tables and chairs to collect import and export duties (e.g., on incoming cotton sheeting, and on outgoing coffee).

Since Arab and other Muslim traders often cannot read and write Amharic and therefore need help with filling out government forms, Amhara schoolboys—usually boys in their teens, since most in provincial areas begin their studies late—find ready "piece work" at the Saturday market. They often do their work on the tables in the local teahouse. Since many Amhara have not yet accustomed themselves to deposit money in the State Bank, they often let Arab traders serve as personal bankers, frequently to their later sorrow.

Non-Economic Functions of the Market.

Commercial travellers would often protect their wives from the rigors of travel, especially before the Italian roads existed. Therefore, during their long absences, they would provide themselves with temporary wives *(damoz,* lit. salaried) who would cook, wash, care for and sleep with the traveler. This was a commercial transaction, usually renewed monthly before witnesses, but children conceived during the contract were considered legitimate heirs. Though less practiced now that long distances are covered by roads and big markets provide full "housekeeping" facilities, *damoz* wives can still be recruited from the poor Amhara or half-Shanqella women at a salary of Eth. $20.00 per month plus food, usually arranged at the Saturday market.

For lonely and bored housewives of the town, the market has many fascinating attractions. Even when they have no money, they like to attend. They amuse themselves and even profit by using their "nuisance value." Before returning home they loiter at the stall of the Arab or Ethiopian Muslim merchant, toying with the merchandise on display while he nervously watches for theft. Finally, he gives each of them a little gift known as *ayn mämäläsha* (turning the eye, i.e., greed, away). The young wives thereupon hop away in loud glee at having bested the shrewd Arab. The husbands do not like this very much since flirting at the market can easily lead to more serious consequences. Some women like to see their kinfolk more often than on official duty visits, and the market provides such opportunities. So they go even when no economic transaction is planned.

Provincial nobles, even those living in town, take pride in riding to market in the old style, on a tall mule, their servants beating out a path for them among pack donkeys and pedestrians. It would be beneath their dignity to do much purchasing themselves, but they may direct servants from horseback, and visit the local market official present, or merely put in an appearance to show the modern young officials from Addis Ababa the ways of conservative nobility and their contempt for motorcars.

Marketless Exchange.

Perhaps one reason for the importance of money marketing lies in the complex social system, with its ethnic division of labor and the noble-commoner class distinctions. Transactions between classes or ethnic groups are most often market transactions. Within many of the social groups or levels, however, patterns of economic cooperation, marketless exchange and mutual aid exist. Members of a religious sodality (mähabbär) who take communion together in apostolic imitation and drink beer together in the home ceremonial meeting, and who are usually of the same age and socio-economic level, frequently share in common purchases. The purchase of an old cow or ox for butchering after church on Sunday morning was already mentioned. Only persons who trust each other to parcel out the meat quickly and fairly could cooperate in this way, and beef would otherwise be too expensive for any of them. Such sharing arrangements are more common in town, for on the hamlet level numerous patterns of cooperation exist.

Two peasants may aid each other in clearing land, or sell each other's produce on the market in partnership. They may lend each other a team of oxen for plowing or threshing, in exchange for help with the harvest or the loan of a donkey or mule.

Mutual aid without money economics may take the form of "bees," especially when expenditure of energy at a given time and place is necessary. While no cash is paid at such aid in harvesting, threshing and winnowing, hut-building, roof-thatching, etc., a feast and return services are expected. Cooperative work on irrigation canals is called "bringing home the bread". Sometimes the degree of cooperation in rural hamlets astonishes urban Amhara. Yet the same hamlet may be on a strict cash basis with a nearby hamlet of another ethnic occupation, religion or class.

THE ABYSSINIAN MARKET TOWN IN THE ETHIOPIAN ECONOMY

Centralization and Modernization.

Ethiopia is an underdeveloped but not a poor country. There is no endemic starvation. In fact there is a potential surplus of grain, cattle, and the like available for export if processing industries and transportation can be developed. Meanwhile, agricultural extension experts and engineers are only beginning to arrive, and in small numbers. The Imperial Highway Authority barely manages to keep the roads open after each rainy season but cannot as yet keep them from deteriorating. Electricity at Gondar lasts only five hours each evening and urban electrification is very limited. Drinking water in the towns must be boiled. Professional men, particularly doctors, are nearly all foreigners. Middlemen in the main cities are largely Greeks and Armenians; in the provincial towns they are Arabs.

Before he could modernize his country, the present Emperor, who has governed longer than any other living monarch, had to centralize his power. This was a long, slow struggle, for during his regency the country was still divided by feudal armies. The first and only railroad to the capital of Addis Ababa was completed only in 1917. Until 1924 debtors could be seized bodily by the creditor. The first law against the slave trade was proclaimed the same year, and slavery was abolished only in 1942. Serfdom *(gabbar)* was officially abolished at the same time, but continues in the shape of sharecrop peonage and local custom. Expenditures for memorial feasts *(tazkar)* are still ruinous to many families despite the Emperor's example. He tried to soften the ethnic division of labor by forbidding the term of address to a common laborer, *"Gurage"* (a tribe near Addis Ababa), and replacing it with "coolie." His request to the Abyssinian Coptic clergy to "raise to Christianity" the many despised ethnic groups has not been complied with. Another example of the massive resistance of the conservative forces is the refusal of the old Abyssinian provinces, including the one in which Gondar is located, to have the land measured and registered.[2]

Addis Ababa is the center and focal point of change, which fans out from there by every means of communication. In towns like Gondar this takes the shape of young, modern-educated officials in every phase of municipal, provincial and national administration. Often they come from "lower" ethnic groups such as Galla (Oromo) or Amhara-Galla from the central province of Shoa. It will take time for their work to become cumulative.

Migration of Skilled Labor.

Skilled manual labor is traditionally regarded as a misfortune. As described earlier, it often led during feudal times to long-term military conscription. Hence the proverb:

> "From cleverness of hand, (you get) serfdom;
> from cleverness of mouth, (you become) boss!"

[2] The Abyssinians certainly are aware that the intent of the modernizing central government to create boundaries defined in terms of modern land "titles." This is particularly true in the proud, "aware," northern, Coptic provinces, where kinship groups and the Church own most of the fertile land. Rough border stones or natural landmarks indicate customary ownership, and different plots are cultivated or used as pasture from one year to the other. The great fear is that if the new officials of the central government ask too many searching questions, much of the frequently unused land would be declared "government land" and assigned to tithepaying squatters. Another fear is that the land would be more highly taxed. Both fears are justified by the experience in the southern provinces where such developments have taken place since 1942. Furthermore, there is an Abyssinian idea that size of land should not be separated from its fertility. The concept *"gasha"* embodies both aspects, the area varying with fertility. In 1942/43 the central government tried to overcome the problem by setting up a system for land tax based on the fertility of the gasha: Eth. $15.00 for *"lämm"* (fat, fertile), Eth. $10.00 for *"lämm tyeff"*, and Eth. $5.00 for marginal but still

However, the traditional attitude toward migration was negative. It meant living among strangers, possibly hostile ones. Before the twentieth century even an ambassadorship abroad was considered exile, hence punishment. The combination of these factors has discouraged labor migration of the sort found in some other parts of Africa.

The federation with Eritrea in 1952, has brought a number of skilled, young Eritreans into Ethiopian towns. In Gondar nearly all the hospital "dressers" are Eritreans. They also fill posts as pharmacists, teachers, specialized clerks, construction workers, mechanics, and the like. They are attracted to Ethiopia not merely by the job openings there, but are compelled by economic necessity to leave Eritrea since the sharp shrinking of the Eritrea economy in 1952, when the Italians closed their stores and factories and returned to Italy. Eritrea's loss was Ethiopia's gain in needed skills.

Money.

The Gondar branch of the State Bank of Ethiopia run by a young, modern-educated Amhara manager, a Sudanese bookkeeper, and the latter's assistant, serves the Arab and Indian wholesalers there almost exclusively and operates at a loss. The rest of the population prefers to bury its coins, and sometimes even modern paper money (which rots quickly and is lost in the rainy season).

The reason for that pattern is not specifically distrust of the State Bank of Ethiopia but rather distrust of any impersonal agency. Since taxes are still generally viewed as a sort of tribute to the feudal chief, a deposit of money is regarded as surrender.

This is particularly true of the Maria Theresa Thalers, the holding of which became illegal in 1945 when the State Bank began issuing its own currency and of the Ethiopian 50-cent coins issued at that time. The latter have been taken out of circulation by hoarding and burying to a greater degree even than the occasionally visible M. T. Thaler. The 25-cent silver coin and smaller ones are in common circulation, though in certain regions temporary fads develop and producers demand a certain coin in preference to others, whereupon that too is hoarded for a period.

Maria Theresa Thaler came into major circulation in Ethiopia, from the Red Sea Coast, only in the middle of the nineteenth century. It evidently filled a need for in the twentienth century more recently minted coins have been imported by the tens of millions. Maria

---

usable agricultural cereal land (*"tyeff"*). The solid opposition in the northern provinces succeeded, and these were permitted to remain unmeasured by default. Meanwhile the land tax at the old rate of 1927 applies to them, based merely on estimated holdings.

Theresa Thalers still play a major role in silversmithing because of high silver content, and they are the standard in big livestock sales, though the hoarded coin itself may not change hands. Silversmiths have no difficulty in obtaining their minted "raw material," at least in Gondar.

About the turn of the century Emperor Menelik ordered the minting of a silver coin named *temum*, sixteen to the M. T. Thaler. They are now used mainly as visible silver ornament. In value it was about equal to the Egyptian-Turkish *"gresh,"* the piastre coined in 1899, which is no longer used, although the term survives in the concept of "gratuity," monetary or otherwise, known as *"gursha"*.

Before the M. T. Thaler, it seems that the salt brick had some money uses. It increased in price with the distance from its point of origin; it finally became "small change" for the M. T. and Menelik's coins.

The Abyssinian Market Town in Relation to World Markets.

The Abyssinians are predominantly subsistence farmers who produce only incidentally for the market. Their economy is almost self-contained. The increase in its major export, coffee, is due largely to Italian-built roads and the increase in world prices of coffee since World War II. Both are external factors.

A market town such as Gondar, remote from the coffee districts (Jimma and Harar), has little to supply to distant areas of Ethiopia beyond cereals, oilseeds, beans and peas, skins, beeswax, honey, and as much livestock as can brave the road on the hoof. The decay of the roads, against which a losing battle is being fought, will probably make worse the national and international economic role of such towns. Transportation is therefore a major bottleneck.

At the same time the needs and aspirations of townspeople and nearby peasants are on the increase. The largest single import into Ethiopia is cotton sheeting with khaki close behind. The Abyssinian town today functions perhaps more significantly as a center for distribution of imports than for collection of exports.

Processing industries, even of food, are limited in Gondar. There are simple one-man flour mills and oil presses, both owned and operated by Italians. But at Gondar there is no timber mill, no soap factory, no brick factory. Some of these are found at Addis Ababa, but the direct road can be used only by caravans. Lightweight products manufactured in Ethiopia, such as matches (a government monopoly), do find their way to Gondar and the rural markets.

CONCLUSION

Trade is a low-status occupation among Abyssinians; large scale trade is therefore still relegated to Arabs or other Muslim minorities, to Greeks, Armenians and East Indians. However, going to market is a social event, involving concerns of "fear of shame" for men, and a release from drudgery for women. The main motivation for increased income through marketing is the steadily increasing desire to own imported goods available at the town's Saturday market.

A person from the dominant Amhara class may not shame his kinfolk by doing manual, especially skilled, labor. Hence there is very little labor migration except in great need. Strong kinship ties make it possible to subsist without great exertion but also require sharing with kinfolk. The ethnic division of labor in Abyssinia has been at the root of many of the transactions involving money, despite the simple economy of subsistence farming. Conquered tribes and available low-class ethnic groups could be entrusted with unavoidable skilled labor and remunerated in money. Feudal land tenure and a history of provincial warfare, with traditional long-term conscription of skilled workers, have discouraged the development of skills.

Since agriculture, including some husbandry, is the main economic activity or nearly all Abyssinians, they can best relate to world markets by modernizing such activities. Food processing and other secondary industries are greatly needed, but in turn can function only through maintenance and building of new roads.

Modernization of the limited market economy would presuppose a basic change in the attitude toward skilled labor, not merely an increase in the quantity and quality of production.

CHAPTER 15

The Konso Economy of Southern Ethiopia[1]

BY RICHARD KLUCKHOHN

INTRODUCTION

An attempt will be made here to present a description and partial analysis of some of the economic practices of southern Ethiopia. To present *the* economic practices of this area would be a task impossible both in terms of the present stage of research and in terms of the documentary space which would be required. It has been estimated by a research worker recently in the area that within the boundaries of Ethiopia there are more than eighty-five societies, each having distinct languages and cultural patterns. Focus here will be directed toward the *Konso,* an Eastern Cushitic-speaking people of the south-central region of Ethiopia. Some comparative remarks will also be made concerning other peoples within this broad area.

The selection of the Konso would appear to be fortunate in that they are representative of one of the oldest peoples in this region (i.e., the Cushites, and particularly those of the eastern branch). Indeed, Murdock believes that the Konso may well be a modern representative of an old, neolithic culture which he terms "megalithic Cushite," whose participants were widely spread in southern Ethiopia and in many parts of East Africa, and further that these peoples may well have been related to the founders of the mysterious Azanian trade center (Murdock 1959 : 196 ff.). In any case, the Konso are typical of most of the peoples of this area save the Galla tribes. Their most interesting feature is that they tend to elaborate on, or perhaps preserve, economic development to a greater extent than other peoples of the area.

The Konso in the central region number about forty thousand persons, though there are additional enclaves of Konso all over southern Ethiopia and northern Kenya. Those in the central region live primarily in forty-two major villages, though some are found in small hamlets and even isolated households. As noted, they speak a language of the eastern branch of the Cushitic family of the Afroasiatic stock

(1) The materials presented here represent part of those gathered as a part of a research project made possible by a grant from the National Institutes of Health, United States Public Health Service, to whom the author is deeply indebted and grateful.

(Greenberg 1955). Therefore, they are related linguistically to all other peoples of Ethiopia save those of the Macrosudanic group, located primarily on the western borders of Ethiopia. Their closest neighbors both in cultural similarity and physical proximity are the *Gauwata, Gidole, Gardulla, Burji, Busso,* and others (Cerulli 1956). The Konso are known in prior literature from the research of A. E. Jensen and his colleagues (Jensen 1936, 1942, 1954).

The Konso are pagan, though Ethiopian government statistics class a large number as Coptic Christians. Such classification, however, is based on the fact that some years ago there were coerced, mass conversions in which a large number of people had water and words poured over them, not understanding what the process meant. Islam has made no inroads at all in the Konso area. Native belief centers around one supreme deity *(pampelli* or *waka)* and a series of evil spirits *(oritta* and *ella).* The supreme deity is rather distant and unapproachable, but the spirits are everpresent and may cause harm unless propitiated through "priests" *(iswaita* and *sipilla).*

The social organization of the Konso is complex, and need not concern us except insofar as its effects can readily be discerned in the organization and provision of goods, services, and labor. At any point in time, the Konso male (and female to almost the same degree) belongs to a series of groups, each of which makes specific demands upon him. Most importantly, he is always at a certain stage within a complicated system of cyclical age-grades (Jensen *op. cit.*). There are six of these age-grades, not four as previously supposed, each of eighteen years' duration. One's position is always determined by that of one's father; an individual is always automatically two grades behind his father. Membership in any given age-grade gives the person a definite status and general role; in the first, the individual is regarded as being useless and devoted to pleasure; in the second he is a member of the mobile labor and military force; in the third he is a householder and father; in the fourth he may have judicial or governmental authority and is much respected; in the fifth and sixth he no longer commands any great power and his position is that of an elderly dependent.

Each individual also belongs to a friendship group composed of persons who went through initiation together, and this group remains constant throughout the members' progression though the age-grade system (Murdock 1959 : 202, calls this second group an age-set). One is also always in a certain age-class, based on chronological age. In addition, one belongs to a patrilineal kinship group, to a nuclear family, an extended family, to a village, possibly to a depressed caste (weavers and smiths), and one has certain obligations to a named groups of one's mother's relatives. The obligations imposed by membership in these groups apply to all Konso.

Political and judicial control are vested primarily in the members of the fourth age-grade *(Orshata)*, but some positions within this group are inherited and some chosen by the group itself. Enforcement of the judgments of these men rest on the second age-grade (the warrior grade, *Xella).* There was little integration of the Konso nation in prior times save in time of emergency, such as a major war when the people came together under the leadership of an overall religious leader *(apo jilla).* In normal times, however, there was much intervillage warfare, with two or three villages usually forming a mutual alliance for a period, and then usually breaking up and regrouping. Within the village or small group of villages, there are individuals of higher authority than others, but actually most major decisions are reached by more or less a consensus of the *Orshata* grade. The Konso have little regard for high individual or central authority.

Konso society has changed a good deal since its conquest by the Amharas in the early part of this century. Conquest was followed by the imposition of a centralized, Amhara authority, supposedly controlled by the Government in Addis Ababa, but actually by the policy decisions of the local Amhara governor, often but not always in consultation with his superiors, the provincial sub-governor and provincial governor. An Amhara court has been set up, and much Konso land has been acquired by the conquerors. Still, much of the old system has been deliberately preserved by the new rulers; we shall discuss this in more detail below, insofar as it relates to changes in the old economic system.

In the sphere of external relations, the Konso had few except trading contacts (see below). Their relations with their (Borana) Galla neighbors were primarily those of armed hostility. It is said that at one time there were treaties with the Gauwats, but treaties with others are not remembered. The Konso are cut off from most of their culturally similar neighbors by plains, inhabited by the warlike Galla. Indeed, except for trading relations through intermediaries, external contacts were slight enough as to be immaterial to the present study.

THE GEOGRAPHICAL SETTING

The Konso live at a position approximately 5° North by 37° East. They are just south (approx. 75 km.) of the last lake of the great southern chain of Ethiopia, namely Lake Chamo (Ruspoli), and up on the left (eastern) wall of the Rift Valley as it turns toward Lake

Rudolph. The country they inhabit is composed of an extensive series of high hills (average alt., approx. 1400 m.), surrounded on one side by mountains, by plains on the others. Of recent years, warfare having abated and raiding being only slight, more Konso have moved into the plains areas though a few have always lived on the fringe.

In general the country in these hills is very rocky; natural vegetation in limited to scrub brush, bush grass, and cactus. There are some trees, but they are few and many groves are feared as habitations of evil spirits. In addition to loose rocks and boulders, there are extensive cliff deposits of basalt and granite. Natural flora are little used by the Konso, save for several varieties of cactus, which are used for fences, and various types of brush used for housebuilding. Fauna within the area are utilized more fully, particularly the following: lion, leopard, civet cat, wildcat, dik-dik, rabbit, and various small animals of the antelope family. Larger gazelle and antelope are available after a day's walk, and are sought when travel is thought to be safe. The area also has snakes of several varieties, including the cobra, puff-adder, and python. Wild boar and many types of birds are present, but are not utilized by the Konso.

Water is scarce, a valuable resource. There are some streams which are full the year around, but they are often half a day's journey away. Very deep wells of the *Borana* pattern have been dug in most areas, but they are privately owned or owned by a specific group. The nearest large body of water is Lake Chamo, far enough away not to be accessible for ordinary use.

In a normal year, heavy rains come from the middle of February to the end of April, and there are light rains in September and October—light and heavy in this case referring to frequency rather than intensity as the rains are usually very intense. In other seasons of the year, occasional showers occur, but can hardly be counted upon. Annual rainfall amounts to about 40″ per annum. Temperature runs between a normal low of about 55°, slightly lower during the rains, and a high of about 90°. Generally, the humidity is low.

THE BASIS OF PRODUCTION[2]

Agricultural Produce.

Agricultural produce forms the core of the Konso economy, both for their own consumption and for marketing and trade. The basic

(2) In the interest of brevity, economic factors relating to religious observances will be omitted from this point. While there is a good deal of religious paraphenalia, it is not significant in the overall view. Also, while some sacrifices are made and the priests are paid for services rendered, these also have no great effect on the economic situation as a whole.

crop is sorghum, of which they distinguish eight separate types, each preferred for a different use. In addition, wheat, barley, maize and teff are grown, as well as gourd and squash vegetables, and a leafy vegetable similar to cabbage; potatoes were introduced at some unknown period.[3] Some lemons and a very few bananas are grown in the lowlands. Cotton and coffee are produced in volume. There are also additional products of specialized or restricted cultivation and use, primarily wild herbs and other plants transplanted for ritual use.

Agricultural Techniques.

The basic technique of land utilization is the terracing and contour plowing of the predominantly hilly country. Diversion dams are made and there is a form of definite irrigation practiced in the highlands, though permanent reservoirs are not built. Streams have diversion ditches made toward nearby land, but, as noted, streams are not readily accessible to most land. Terraces are built as high as several meters, all built up with retaining walls constructed of small stones set into a simple mortar. In some of the lowland areas, there is year-round irrigation with water taken from the larger rivers to be found in these areas. The land is tilled with plow, hoe, or digging stick, depending upon the width of the terrace or the amount of stones present. In prior times, the donkey was the draught animal, hitched to a wooden plow with a single, metal-sheathed blade. At present, mules and oxen are used more commonly, with the same plow. Both the hoe and digging stick are similarly sheathed or tipped with metal.

The fact that there are two good rainy seasons each year allows two crops per year of most of the above produce, excepting coffee, cotton and some of the root crops. Production yield is very high compared with other areas of southern Ethiopia; in most years production is well above the subsistence level.

The Means of Agricultural Production.

Land tenure, prior to the advent of the Amhara, was almost wholly on an individual basis. The father left most of his land to his eldest son, who traditionally lived with the father. If the father was moderately wealthy, he would apportion sufficient land to support a family to his other sons at the time of their marriages. Failing this inheritance, the other sons were obliged to seek out unused land within the areas assigned to their village or coalition of villages. A council of

(3) These are white potatoes, and represent an interesting anomaly in that they are not raised by other groups in the area, nor are they a part of the Amhara diet. Some informants claimed them to be old; some did not know.

the *Orshata* would view a request for such land, and would grant it in normal circumstances, i.e., if his need for land was based on marriage and both partners were of the proper age-grade. This was a formality in most cases, but not in all. The man making the request would then be taken to a place where land was available, and there he would set a brush fire at a time of his choosing. The area burned by the fire would then be his, in theory no matter how great or small. In practice, he would have been taken to a place where under favorable conditions he would be able to obtain only that amount of land considered "reasonable" by the elders, i.e., the fire would be stopped by some natural barrier or would have to be put out because it was about to infringe upon some land already apportioned. The place to which the young man is taken would normally be decided in council with a view toward his service to the community, his father's service and position and quite often the degree of petty intrigue and jealousy already set into motion by his age-mates, relatives, wife's family, etc. Land obtained by this means or that which was inherited was held absolute, or until the individual should be convicted of some crime and fined, banished, or executed.

Land can also be purchased, provided such a purchase passes again the council of the *Orshata* grade of the village concerned. Purchase might be effected in terms of money in its several forms, livestock, or other lands.

While land, one of the two basic resource ingredients of agricultural production, may be held in greater or lesser quantity, the second major resource, labor, is largely organized on the basis of enforced reciprocity and is distributed equally. The basic agricultural task, day-to-day care of the crops, is done by the landowner, his family, and possibly friends. Sowing and reaping, the more difficult and sporadic operations, are communal tasks, a custom called *fedeta*. According to one informant, "This man might be weak and have no family to help him in his work, but the other has no trouble at all with his land; this is why we have the *fedeta*." The working system for *fedata* is as follows: When a given district (village or group thereof) is ready to sow or reap, a group of elders *(Orshata)* assembles and they decide how and where to begin. When such are decided, all members of the second *(Xella)* age-grade, plus all other able-bodied men and girls, start work in the chosen place and continue until the whole area is finished. Married women are not expected to work on on any but their husband's land. The only obligation of the owner of land under work on a given day is to provide food and drink for the workers; when his land is finished, he stays with the group as it moves to other men's property.

Husbandry.

Save for the breeding of donkeys, animal husbandry never seems to have been very important among the Konso. Some sheep, goats, and cattle are bred, but primarily in the lowland, peripheral areas. This does not mean that animals are not important; many more animals than are bred are acquired as import goods. Donkeys, however, are bred domestically and are much in demand. Mules and horses are post-Amhara innovations and still relatively unimportant. The Konso do have one trait unique in the area: they largely stable their livestock and hand-feed rather than graze them. The reasons for their doing so are (1) the animals are a threat to the tilled fields, (2) extensive use is made of manure gathered, (3) it facilitates milking, an important activity, and (4) the *mashilla* (sorghum) stalks are easily gathered and carried to the beasts. In general, livestock are important economically but not in terms of their production.

Hunting and Gathering.

These activities are relatively unimportant in the Konso economy but both are done. Various animals are hunted for a combination of prestige, skin value, and protection—leopard, lion, civet cat, servel cat, and the like. A few antelopes are hunted for hides and meat, especially in the lowland areas. Gathering activity consists largely of seeking firewood, an important item almost exclusively gathered from unoccupied areas. Some herbs are gathered for medicinal purposes.

Animals, especially of the cat family, are often trapped. The traps are stone enclosures containing bait which close after the animal enters; occasionally pitfalls are used. Spears are used on mass hunts, and the spear or arrows with poison on small individual hunts. The sling, of jute fibre, is used on small game.

Industrial Produce.

Goods and artifacts crafted, erected, and otherwise fabricated, as opposed to those cultivated or raised, are made both for exchange and for self-use. From cotton comes raw, baled cotton, cotton yarn or thread, and cotton cloth of various types. From the latter are made blankets, clothing, and other utilitarian items. Cactus rope is made, and from that bags, pouches, slings, etc. From gourds come bowls and other containers, from wood bowls, trays, pillow-stools, looms, spear shafts, bows and arrows, ploughs, burial statues and a host of other items. From metals come knives, projectile points, hoe and digging stick blades, axe blades, ploughshares, etc. From wild animals come ornaments in bone and horn, hides for shields, rugs, and so forth. Domestic animal skins are prepared for clothing, rugs, blankets, door-covers, etc. The soil provides clay for cooking utensils, storage vessels, pipe bowls. There is also a jewelry and ornament industry utilizing metal in combination with beads, stones, glass, horn, quills, etc. This is but a partial list of the elements of material culture requiring handicraft and workmanship.

Industrial Means.

It is obvious that the material means of industrial production are largely available in the local environment, whether self-obtained or traded for. Certain items (beads, jewels, metals, etc.) come from external trade and will be discussed below.

Labor, on the other hand, is variously regulated. Labor for public construction (bachelor houses, town improvements, paths, walls, etc.) comes exclusively from the *Xella* age-grade of the village concerned. This is one of the primary functions of the group. The actual weaving of cotton (as opposed to the carding and spinning) is the exclusive enterprise of a depressed caste of weavers. These persons do weaving for the owners of the yarn or raw cotton, either on a straight fee or percentage basis. Some thereby acquire sufficient capital (usually livestock or movable goods) to purchase outright the raw material, in which case the sale of the final product is also undertaken by them. Much the same is applicable to the smiths, except that they work with an imported, raw material in the form of unworked iron and other metals (truck springs being the preferred item at the present time). The smiths work iron for a price, but prefer to obtain their own material and market their own product. The remainder of the goods listed are turned out by ordinary householders, in varying degrees of volume and craftmanship. Some become proficient enough to specialize almost completely in craft industry rather than in agriculture—though without stigma. In such cases, the change is based on the skill of the individual and his voluntary inclination rather than on caste status.

TRADE AND MARKETS

The network of Konso markets provides the major means for circulation of goods both internally and externally. Almost every village has an enclosed space outside the inner village wall, and usually within an outer wall. It may extend to a larger area just outside. These are the market places. By mutual agreement within village clusters, market times do not fall on the same day in two adjacent places, but most villages had a market day once a week or so. In the present time, much of the small village marketing has been absorbed into the very large markets held in the several Amhara administrative centers, but this is by no means uniformly the case.

In former times, on the morning of the market day people would arrive from many places, foreign traders often coming the night before. During the morning people set up their wares, gossip, and generally prepare for the afternoon's business. Also during this time petty complaints are taken up by the *pokwalla* (head man) and the judges selected from the ranks of the *Orshata*. The area is patrolled by members of the local *Xella* group, whose function it is to maintain order under the direction of other members of the *Orshata*. At the present time, however, these functions have been taken over by the Amharas, a court having replaced arbitration within the market place and uniformed police having replaced the *Xella;* moreover, a tax collector has been added to the scene.

Below we shall discuss some special aspects of market transactions before relating the market transactions to other aspects of the economy.

Foreign Traders and Goods.

As far as anyone knows, the traders working in the Konso area have always been Somalis. The author's oldest informant, a man generally accepted to be over one hundred years of age, states that except for a very occasional Borana Galla who had left his group for some reason, the traders have always been Somalis. Today this is still the case, though some of the Somalis now live permanently in the area and some have adopted trucks for transport. Still, most ply their way back and forth from the Konso country to the east and south by camel. Some merchants have but one camel (or donkey); others have strings of twenty or thirty. The area is attractive to traders because of brisk demands for their goods at both ends of the trip; such trade is attractive enough to induce one Somali recently to move into the Konso area after ten years in the United States, where he acquired a large amount of working capital for use in trade.

Salt and metals are the primary imports and presumably have been for at least several hundred years. Neither item is locally available and both are much needed. In addition, the traders bring trinkets, beads, needles, small manufactured items, soap, oils, etc. In recent times store clothes, small luxury items, buttons, fine thread, flashlights, kerosene, and others, have been added to the list.

Local Marketers and Goods.

Women have almost exclusive rights to set up market stalls, even when the products they handle were made by their husbands. The exceptions are the weavers, the smiths, and ordinary men who sell butchered meat (this is done just outside the usual market area and and is handled exclusively by men and boys). The male weavers and smiths usually sell, barter, or trade their own produce, though their wives may also do so. The women with goods to sell arrange themselves and their wares in the morning, in specified areas where similar goods are to be found, rather like the different counters in a western store. Preferred positions are those in the shade, but they are for the most part on a first-come, first-served basis.

During this time the men gather around the sides of the market place to drink beer, talk, and, for those with a large amount of grain to sell, to arrange for the sale or barter thereof—usually with a trader buying for export. Cotton and coffee are usually brought into the market place, unlike grain in volume, as the traders like to ascertain their quality directly. Other local goods on display include the total list given in the preceding section. We shall discuss below in more detail the items involved, in describing the direction which these take in the exchange.

Barter, Money, and Credit.

For the most part, barter was and remains the most common method of exchanging goods. All the marketers at one time or another inspect the other items on display and look especially for those which they themselves need. One person, selling primarily earthenware, may go over to another's stall where some tanned hides are displayed; if each is interested in the other's product, bargaining will ensue and an agreement may be reached. If one party is not interested, he or she will say so and the second will seek another similar stall. The foreign trader may also use this method. He comes up to where cotton, coffee, or other goods he requires are being displayed, and will then begin to tell what he has brought with him, hoping that the other may want to exchange, and again bargaining may begin.

Some form of money, however, has long been in use. In the very old days, iron in both raw and worked forms was used as money, with quite fixed values understood for certain weights, qualities, and types of tool. This was largely replaced in the middle of the nineteenth century by salt bars brought up from the coast. These in turn were replaced for the most part by the Maria Theresa dollar (Thaler) toward the beginning of this century. Money values are still counted in terms of these dollars, though at present the actual coinage is that of the Ethiopian government (whose dollar the Konso devalue to 90 cents in any form other than silver). Thus in a money transaction value will usually be reckoned in terms of the Maria Theresa (and sometimes still in salt bars) but payment will be in another form. Not long ago several material culture items had assigned to them specific values and could be used in payment. For instance the more or less standard type of knife was valued at two M. T. dollars, the common hoe blade at one dollar, the salt bar at one dollar, etc. It is probable that originally evaluation was made in the other way, i.e., the dollar and salt bar were valued in terms of the older equivalents of these metal tools. It does not appear, however, that other (non-metal) items were used as a medium of exhange in the strict sense.

In prior times, credit took the form of loans between Konso individuals who had some kind of tie through common membership in a close social group. Such transactions usually took place in the village, between men, and not in the market setting. This however has changed considerably, as we shall see below.

Prices.

It appears that in the main there has always existed a rough correspondence of supply and demand insofar as external trade is concerned. The Konso produced more and a better quality of those goods which the trader needed, primarily cotton and its products; the Konso are also more accessible. On the other hand, the Konso also need badly the goods brought by the trader. Furthermore, there are enough traders and Konso marketers, both without formal organization, that it would be hard for either side to fix prices artificially. If there were a definite advantage on either side, it probably fell to the Konso in prior times as they could prevent any individual trader from working in their area, if for instance he were judged to be dishonest. On the other hand, the trader bilked by a Konso had little recourse save to be wiser in the future. This has changed to some extent today in that the traders have banded together more recently and they also enjoy more favor from the local administration than do the Konso themselves.

In intra-Konso market transactions, generally accepted price ranges also existed and for the most part still do, subject of course to haggling. Any case of deliberate fraud could be brought up before the *Orshata* court, which had the power to impose fairly stringent penalties if it felt that deliberate criminal intent was involved. There was also freedom to appeal to that body against "unneighborly practices." Such a practice would be said to occur if a man (Konso) were to buy up large stocks of, say, salt when it was available, and then sell it at a much larger sum when it became scarce. Accumulation of wealth was highly regarded, but wealth must not be "misused" against co-members of one's village or other social group.

In general it may be said that prices seem to have stayed within a fairly narrow range. Supply and demand was the basic adjusting mechanism for prices, but great fluctuation did not occur because supply and demand of internal goods remains relatively constant through the year, and traders did not come for the most part at times when cotton, especially, was not available—usually during the rains when communication is difficult at best. To some extent there has been artificial price-setting by the Amhara in the last twenty years, but this has been confined in the main to Amhara-Konso relations, not to Konso-Konso. The only notable exception to this generalization is in the fact that in times of emergency, such as severe drought, the elders would step in and oversee the distribution of goods and their prices—nonetheless, this was rare enough that only a very few people can remember its happening.[4]

Directions of Flow of Goods and Services.

For pre-Amhara times, one can distinguish three primary channels

TABLE 36

Commodity Prices; a General Average for a Medium-Size Konso Village

Item	Price US $	Usual amount Available for Sale
Coffee	16/quintal	4– 5 quintals
Cotton in bales	6/bale, 25 kg.	10–12 bales
Cotton yarn	.30/half-kilo	40–50 packages
Blanket (large)	5	20–30
Blanket (small)	2.50	40 or more
Ceremonial cloth	4/each	5–10
Wooden bowls	.20–.60 each	15
4 gal. ceramic bowl	4	A few
Small pots	.40–.50	20 or more
Basic knife	1.20	20 or more
Spear points	.60 & up	?
Adze-axe blade	.60 & up	25 or more
Salt bar	.60	Rare today
4 oz. salt	.02	100 kg. or more
meat (butchered)	.25/kg.	3 beefs, 6 sheep or goat
Chickens	.30 each (live)	5–10
Eggs	.01–.02. each	Varies widely
Grains	.15/2 ltr.	Varies widely
Whole vegetables	.02-.05 each	Varies widely

(4) We have not given specific prices in the text, nor specific amounts, nor wages, as we do not regard them central to the argument. Table 36 includes a few of the specifics. The figures represent a general average for a medium village in the first couple of months after a harvest.

through which goods passed: (1) Konso to Konso, (2) Konso to external trader, and (3) trader to Konso. Few goods, as opposed to services, passed from the individual Konso to his community as a corporate entity, or vice versa. In the first category almost all goods, either made locally or imported, changed hands through one of the aforementioned media. There was less tendency to barter or sell imported goods than those locally made, but it did occur fairly often. From the Konso to the traders passed cotton, coffee, bulk agricultural products, and sometimes a few handicraft products. We have already seen the trader's stock, and all of this was of course for trade with the Konso.

Services, labor rendered outside of one's own family, were governed by four primary factors: (1) the *fedeta* reciprocity pattern for agriculture, (2) one's membership in an age-grade within a given community or group of communities in alliance, (3) membership in an age-set or friendship group, and (4) one's relationship to one's own kinship group and that of one's mother. We have outlined the *fedeta* customs above. In the second case, it should be made clear that the *Xella* age-grade constitutes a mobile working and fighting unit, subject to the directions of the community as expressed by the *Orshata* council in consultation with specific authorities within this age-grade. The individual's duties as a member of *Xella* take precedence over all other obligations. Thus, the *Xella* is a self-replacing unit, always available for any work necessary to the community as a whole or for mass recruitment for the *fedeta*. In the third case, an individual may be called upon for labor by a member of his age-set, and ought, but is not strictly bound, to respond to this request, provided age-grade obligations do not interfere. Lastly, an individual may be called upon for work by a member of his patrilineal kinship group, and such also applies for one's mother's kinship group, toward which more general deference and respect is required. In the first two cases, participation is formally enforced; in the latter two, enforcement is by social pressure. In all, reciprocity is an outstanding feature.

Labor was rarely hired as such, though the practice is not unknown. Still, it was infrequent that an individual could not find help from his relatives or age-set co-members. It was, however, not uncommon for a wealthy man to distribute gifts among poorer people whom he called to work for him under the ties of social obligation.

THE KONSO ECONOMIC SYSTEM

The Konso, like many societies, exhibit features of several differing systems of economic activity. The technological base of the economy is agricultural, but husbandry, craft industries, and hunting also contribute. The market plays a very important part in the locational and appropriational movement of material items, but most Konso produce primarily for their own consumption and could exist in the absence of the market. Prices are generally the result of supply and demand in a situation of a stable technological base, but the mechanism for artificial controls is available in case of emergency. The accumulation of wealth is encouraged, but its use against fellow members of the society restricted. The flow of goods is not under much direct control; the flow of labor is. Nonetheless, the Konso economic system is an integrated one and does not appear to have undergone much change in any recent time save what change has been forced upon it by a conquering group.

One way to characterize the Konso economic system is in terms of four types of control and the interactions set up by these controls. They are (1) the control of natural resources, (2) control over the allocation and distribution of material items (3) import-export controls, and (4) control of labor resources.

Natural resources are under mixed and partial control. Inheritance customs, following definitely set lines, form a major factor in the allocation of land resources, but it has been seen that individuals may acquire property by other means, i.e., "homesteading" or purchase. These may be regulated to a certain extent by the members of the *Orshata* grade of the district involved. The second major resource, water, may be acquired by individuals only if they obtain land near a natural source—next to impossible save through inheritance—or by industry and luck, i.e., digging on the land that one does have and hoping a productive well will result. Small amounts of resources are available to the general public in the form of wood, plants, and game to be gathered or hunted on untilled land. The degree to which an individual exploits the resources available to him is a matter of his own choice for the most part. Some restrictions are placed upon the two depressed castes, and the utilization of resources to the definite discomfiture of one's neighbors is not allowed.

Goods may be made, bought, sold, or otherwise allocated for the most part as the individual wishes, subject primarily to supply and demand. Still, there is not absolute freedom: cheating may be punished, antisocial use of economic activity is discouraged, and in an emergency tight controls might be applied.

The one area in which internal controls are removed completely is in the conduct of import-export commerce. Here it is an individual's own affair what he buys and sells, and for how much. Some controls however may be placed on the foreign trader, but it seems that there are none on the Konso save that he should not monopolize a part of the import-export trade to his neighbor's misfortune.

In contrast, labor resources are under fairly rigid control, the primary mechanisms of which are the *Orshata* council and the *fedeta* custom, itself under the review of the *Orshata* when necessary. The effect of these controls is to guarantee that labor will be available both for the community at large and for particular members—thus allowing a man of small family and small capital to acquire income commensurate with his control of agricultural resources or for a village to be maintained and expanded without the need to collect taxes in money or produce. Added to these controls are those of the reciprocal labor exchange between members of common age-sets or kinship groups.

The Konso system allows scope for individual industry and material development, but provides checks and balances to ensure that the less favored individual has reasonable opportunity for competition with those who are better off. There is opportunity for material increase, but only within the framework of the social controls and values of the society as a whole. The exceptions to this are the two depressed castes, for they are not on a socially equal basis, not allowed to hold much land, and are not as well protected by the community as a whole. Still, members of these groups may go far toward the accumulation of wealth or personal comforts, provided that in so doing they do not come into conflict with the community.

While labor is transacted outside of the market place, the exchange of goods remains almost wholly within it, although there are of course some private transactions. The market is also the center of the village week. It is very old in this area — not even the oldest informant ever heard of a time when the market was not of central importance to the village. Additional evidence of antiquity is provided by the fact that the Konso have no names for days—days are referred to in turn by referring to a market day in one of the villages of the immediate area. Furthermore, the market serves as the exclusive setting for the import-export sector of the Konso economy, traders appearing in set places on the basis of a fixed schedule. Nor are the markets small; on a good day in a medium-sized village, goods to the value of $1,000 may change hands.

Given the degree of craft specialization and the size of the local population within a market area, it is clear that the market is also an effective way of distributing local goods among the Konso themselves, as well as allowing the trader and customer wide choice. These markets also transact a large volume of goods. The author has noted close to one hundred bales of cotton, fifty quintals of coffee, and thirty-odd large sacks of grain for exchange or sale at one time. Konso-to-Konso products are not great in volume at any given stall, but their total amount is quite large as there may be a hundred marketers present.

It might be well to add here that a traditional definition of "surplus," such as that of Herskovits (1952 : 395), seems to apply in the Konso case. They raise considerably more agricultural produce than they actually use for their own consumption, particularly cotton, coffee, and grain. However, in agreement with Pearson (Polanyi, Arensberg, & Pearson 1957 : 320 ff.), such a surplus may be more apparent than real for several reasons. In the Konso case, a major proportion of this "surplus" is devoted to obtaining, through trade, items that are essential to the Konso economy, especially salt and metal; only a small part goes for "luxury" imports. Nor could these essential items be obtained easily in any other manner.

The Konso economic system may then be described as being focussed on a market in which local and external exchange occur on a relatively free basis. Economic regulation occurs in the allocation of labor and resources, particularly the former, rather than of material items. One of the major effects of this regulation is the protection of the right of the individual to an adequate livelihood, a stated value in the society, yet on the other hand such regulation does not interfere with the accumulation of material wealth to any great extent. Where dispute may occur, however, the interests of the community take precedence over those of the individual in all cases. The power of regulation is vested in one of the cyclical age-grades, and the power of enforcement in another. Indeed, while kinship plays a part in the allocation of natural resources, primary control of the economic activity is given to individuals only as a function of their having secured certain status-role positions which are dependent upon position within the age-grade system. Should the age-grade system break down, which it shows no signs of doing at present, it is certain that this would have a grave effect upon the economic system. This would not be true if the system of patrilineal kinskip groups broke down, nor would changes in family structure or religious structure have much effect upon the economy.

Finally, there is the question of the overall importance of the market to the Konso economy and to the very livelihood of the people; there is also the question of the relative importance of intra-Konso trade to external trade.

As we have seen, most individual Konso follow agricultural pursuits and for the most part can sustain the lives of their own family members adequately. Also, most families have members who are adept at some craft or another. Within any single village, there would be craftsmen of almost all types; there would also be villagers who had a fair amount of livestock. If marketing activity were suddenly denied to the Konso, it is probable that a readjustment could be made before long on partially a family basis and partially a village one. Families would tend to broaden their capabilities in both craft and food production; the village *Orshata* would also organize supplies and manpower to meet the new situation. Everywhere one would see the trends away from specialization, just as the opposite is true now and probably has been for a long time. It would not be easy to make the change, but it could be made; the general standard of living would go down due to the lack of a relatively efficient system of distribution of goods of all kinds and due to increased diversification of economic activity on the part of the contributing individuals. Some people who have specialized would be hard hit, but to the majority loss of the market would be a hardship not a calamity.

On the second point, it can be said that internal trade outweighs external in volume of traffic, but it is hard to weigh absolute importance of one over the other. Save through external trade the Konso have no means to acquire metal or salt, both much needed. It might be supposed that they could organize expeditions out of their area to acquire these items, but they have never in a long period of time gone out of their own area to acquire anything, and they would probably be ill-prepared to defend themselves in the open against the hostile tribes which surround them. Furthermore, they would have no market for their surplus cotton and coffee, and would have to effect an agricultural reorganization, and would in this case also have to lower their general standard of living. On the whole, then, it is the author's opinion that external trade is certainly of equal importance with internal.

RECENT CHANGES

While the Konso system may be said to be stable under all normal conditions, some changes have naturally resulted from their conquest by the Amhara. The most notable of these is that much of the best Konso land has been appropriated by the Amhara and apportioned out to the governor, members of his entourage, members of the new central court, etc. This land is still worked in much the same way as before and still worked by Konso farmers, but it is now worked on a share-cropping basis. It is estimated that some 15 per cent of the Konso lands have been appropriated in this manner, but this percentage represents about a third of the productive power of the total. The farmer on these lands now takes what he needs for his family's subsistence, and sells the remainder of the produce; he then may or may not be allowed to keep a percentage of the receipts of the sale. Where this pattern does not apply, taxes have been imposed both on land and on most types of produce. One now sees the tax collector, in the company of some police, walking among the stalls at market, levying so much on this, so much on that. Because of both of these innovations, money is in much more general use than was the case thirty or forty years ago when the Amhara first came to live in the area (there are approximately 250 of them today).

Another change is that a group of Somali traders have come into the Konso area to live, dwelling in the administrative center of the Amhara government, Pekwalli. Three of these traders have set up regular shops, at which a permanent supply of imported goods is available. Each of these three also has a large truck which is used to carry goods between the Konso and the towns of Mega and Moyale, near the Kenya border. All in all, the effect of these resident traders and their trucks has been to increase the amount of cotton, coffee, and grain grown for export. On the other hand, these traders have extended credit on a fairly large scale, and not a few Konso have allowed themselves to be put into a position of almost permanent indebtedness, thereby allowing the merchants to dictate prices to them. A further change has come about because these new residents, with their ready cash, provide another market—for foods, utensils, wage labor, etc. The result has been an increase in the production of teff and capsicum, and further development of husbandry in order to have animals to sell direct to the Coptic and Muslim butchers. On the other side, the Amharas in the area have not gone into trading *per se* with the Konso, save for opening a few wine shops. There is one Amhara trader, brother-in-law to the governor, but he is the exception; typically, the Amhara disdains trade in favor of securing a post in the local government or becoming a feudal landlord (or both).

In the main, however, the major aspects of the Konso economy remain the same, particularly in the markets some distance from the governmental center. Control is still exercised through the *Orshata* grade, though this group in some cases must take orders from the Amhara. Police have replaced the *Xella* in the market, but the *Xella* remains the mobile working force of the community. Much the same goods are on display in the market as before, and the majority of traders still come and go by camel; the majority of Konso still have personal land and work it in the old manner. It is safe then to say that the Konso economic system has perforce adapted itself to a new situation, but is not changed in any great manner from its prior form.

CONCLUSION

We have seen that the Konso economic system consists of several spheres, the market sphere being important for both internal and external transaction. The Konso are noteworthy for the amount of their external trade, for their advanced agricultural techniques, for the way in which they allow individual enterprise within the limits allowed by the more important value of community solidarity, and for the mechanisms of economic control, the focus of these on labor and resource and not goods, and the focus of these in the age-grade system rather than in kinship groups or absolute authority. A question remains as to what extent the Konso economy is unusual in this area.

That these economic forms are not borrowed from elsewhere in any recent time can be assured, not only from statements of informants and internal evidence, but also from external evidence. That the Konso have a higher elaboration of agricultural technique, of craft industry, and of marketing than any other group in the area is witnessed both by the author's experience and by the literature. Contact with the Amhara dates only from the beginning of this century, and there has been no other contact with large, developed societies. Still, there are so many common patterns, economic and otherwise, among the Cushites and some other people of the area that it leads one to conclude that Konso production and economic organization are of considerable antiquity in the area.

The arrival of the Galla would seem to have had several effects. One of these was the increase of external trade, in that the Galla make little in the way of agricultural produce, craft goods, or cloth. Today they absorb a large amount of the Konso exports, a state of affairs generally found of Galla groups in reference to other Cushite groups (e.g., the Arussi Galla and their relation to the Western Cushitic Sidamo). Initially, the Galla had a deleterious effect upon the agriculturalists, in that they preferred to take things by force rather than to trade valuable livestock for them. But this situation changed as resistance grew greater, and they have provided a needed source of additional livestock for primarily agricultural peoples.

We may say then, in conclusion, that the Konso case provides a picture of an economic system which probably dates back a long way in this area of Africa, and that it has features indicating either an elaboration upon an old, basic set of practices, or that these practices have merely been retained from a prior stage of high economic development among some early Cushitic groups. They share most economic customs in kind, if not degree, with much of southern Ethiopia, and their present system is probably more widely typical of the area several hundred years ago than it is today.

EAST AFRICA

EAST AFRICA

CHAPTER 16

The Evolution of Arusha Trade

BY P. H. GULLIVER

The Arusha live on the southwestern slopes of Mt. Meru (an extinct volcano, 14,979 feet altitude) and in the adjacent plains in the Northern Province of Tanganyika. They numbered 63,000 in 1957. Traditionally they had a mixed economy. Bananas and maize were the staple foods, augmented by legumes and finger millet. However, considerable attention was given to cattle, goats and sheep which provided some milk and meat and were socially and emotionally important in both sacred and mundane affairs.

An account of Arusha economics and trade can conveniently be divided into three historical phases: first, the traditional trade with the surrounding Masai pastoralists, established before Europeans arrived but going on after the German conquest of the country; second, the minimal development of new trade and trading relations with the territorial expansion of the Arusha; and third, the beginnings of a cash economy in the post-World War II-era in response to severe land shortage. Like all narrative procedures of this kind, positing stages is in part an arbitrary action especially if there are, as here, no specific, critical events which decisively mark them. Nevertheless, while recognizing that there has, of course, been a continuum, it is thought that description and analysis are clearer by this approach and that the three stages do in fact represent three rather different and successive phases of Arusha economic enterprise and trade.

ARUSHA AND THE MASAI (nineteenth century to *c.* 1920)

In pre-European times the life of the Arusha was intimately connected with the surrounding Masai people. The Masai comprise a group of autonomous "tribes" of common culture who were, and are, wholly pastoralists. They eschewed agriculture as degrading and also, at least in part, because much of their country was poorly suited to it in the context of a mobile, pastoral regime. In pre-European times the Masai occupied a vast area ranging some 200 miles north and south of the present Tanganyika-Kenya border. As well as being pastoralists they were notably successful in raiding their mainly Bantu-speaking neighbors, capturing cattle and also women and children. Except in the northwest of their extensive lands, the Masai were bounded by peoples of markedly different cultures, languages and economy. In an apparently haphazard way local Masai sometimes traded with their separate neighbors largely, or almost entirely perhaps, through the women of either side exchanging pastoral produce (milk, meat, hides and skins, and some small stock) for agricultural and forest produce (honey, gourds, tobacco)[1]. Institutionalized markets at fixed places do not seem to have existed except where trading centers were established by Swahili, Arab, and later, European caravans (e.g. at Ngong, Baringo, Taveta, etc.). There Masai obtained mainly foreign trade goods such as iron wire, beads and cloth. Ndorobo, who were not subject to Masai raiding, supplied the pastoralists with some honey and gourds.[2]

In one case however, and it may have been unique, an established market center did exist in this period where Masai traded regularly with the Arusha. The Arusha inhabited an agricultural "island" completely surrounded by Masailand. Unlike other agricultural neighbors of the Masai the Arusha were culturally closely akin to them and had been greatly dependent on Masai support and even protection for their establishment as an independent, persisting tribal group.

In this paper we are concerned only with the Arusha, but traditionally Arusha trade was with the Masai and only the Masai. It was a most important feature of social relations between the two peoples although perhaps not entirely typical of Masai relations with their other neighbors, because the Arusha were culturally more akin to the Masai than the others.

* * *

The Arusha tribe only came into existence at the beginning of the nineteenth century and probably not before the second quarter. Various small groups of Kwavi refugees and of people of mixed Kwavi-Bantu origins[3] came to settle on the southwestern edge of the

(1) See, e.g., Humphrey 1945 : 38 on the Nyeri Kikuyu.

(2) I am indebted to Alan H. Jacobs for information, in private correspondence, on Masai trade relations in the nineteenth century.

(3) The Kwavi and Masai are closely related peoples (e.g. mutally intelligible languages, the same sort of age-group system, etc.) but it is likely that the Kwavi differed from the Masai in that they originally practiced some agriculture as well as pastoralism. They were severely defeated and scattered by the Masai in Kenya in the early part of the nineteenth century. "Pure" remmants of this people live today in the southeastern borderlands of Masailand in East-Central Tanganyika and number less than 5,000 persons, but it is probable that the descendants of others are scattered among a number of modern tribes of northern Tanganyika and Kenya in addition to the Arusha.

virgin rain-forest of Mt. Meru. The time of the first settlements can
be roughly determined by reference to Masai age-group chronology
and Arusha genealogies. Either before settlement or very soon after,
the pioneers sought the approval and assistance of the ritual expert
(*olaiboni*) of the Kisongo tribe of the Masai who traditionally lived
near Monduli mountain about eighteen miles from the new settlement. The ritual leader had neither military nor political authority
but he had a tremendous ritual power and prestige and his acceptance of the Arusha helped to give safety from Masai marauding. It
quickly came to mean more, however, because the existing inhabitants
of the other (southeastern) slopes of Mt. Meru, the Meru people, attempted to prevent the consolidation of the new settlement and the
Arusha obtained some active, Masai military support in resisting Meru
attack.[4] There were quite good reasons for general Masai acceptance
and even support of the small pioneer community (possibly about
2,000 people at first) in the middle of their territory. The Arusha
had little or no domestic livestock then and so were scarcely profitable
subjects for raiding; but they were skillful and diligent farmers in
an exceptionally fertile and well-watered land, and they were able
to produce substantial amounts of tobacco, gourds and cereals as well
as honey from the mountain forests which the Masai wanted and for
which they were prepared to trade. The Arusha, with strong cultural
leanings to pastoralism, badly needed milk, meat and skins and also
any animals they could get. Additionally (probably because of their
Kwavi backgrounds) they were able to construct channels to take the
water of mountain springs and streams down to the arid plains for
Masai cattle, which were also able to graze safely in poor seasons in
the partly cleared forest areas on the mountain slopes. The Arusha
were useful to the Masai without competing with them or forming
any kind of immediate danger; furthermore the Arusha began with
a marked Masai-like culture and they rapidly developed a devotion
to all things Masai, attempting to imitate their Kisongo neighbors
in every way short of giving up agriculture. They accepted the authority of the Kisongo ritual leader; they adapted their age-group
system exactly to that of the Kisongo, merely accepting Masai timing
of events and phases; and they followed Masai values and ideas as
the apotheosis of what was good and proper. For the Masai, they
had the advantages of any other of their neighbors plus the additional
one that they were Masai-like in many fundamental ways—a kind
of "poor relatives" to be patronized and used.

Just on the outskirts of the original pioneer settlement of the

(4) Masai assistance seems to have been in the form of attack on the Meru in their
own country who were thus weakened and unable to beset the Arusha.

Arusha (slightly to the west of the modern town of Arusha and near the Engare Narok River) was established at Sanguwezi the market center for the agricultural-pastoral barter trade. On the Arusha side the market was loosely supervised by the age-group "spokesmen" (*ilaigwenak*) of the local territorial group immediately adjacent, Sombetin; but such supervision was slight, intruding only when particular difficulties arose rather than maintaining continuous management. Trade was purely an individual matter between the Masai who sought, say, honey or tobacco and the Arusha who desired perhaps milk or a goatskin. As was usual in this Masai context, trade was to a large extent carried out by Masai women who traditionally were not subject to the dangers of warfare and retaliation. To some extent Arusha women responded but never to the same degree, for the Arusha men were clearly concerned in the disposal of agricultural produce and were primarily the honey gatherers. Perhaps for this reason, but also because for a long time Arusha and Masai did not raid one another, Masai men seem to have attended the Arusha market more frequently and more numerously than other comparable, contemporary markets. Arusha too were keen to obtain livestock and this, of course, was a male concern. Old men relate today how their fathers organized honey-gathering expeditions in order to exchange the honey for goats and sheep. The Arusha also made cereal-banana beer and honey-wine available in the market, and this too was primarily an appeal to Masai men.

It is difficult now to obtain many details of the operation of the market; memories are inevitably colored by modern marketing practices. The market does, however, appear to have been held at regular times ("once a week," say many informants) and always at this one center; and indeed this must have been so. Otherwise it could scarcely have flourished as it undoubtedly did. Obviously Arusha men knew the day when they should have their stock of honey ready, and women knew the day on which their brew of beer should mature. Masai women walked from forty or more miles away, usually sleeping at the market place the night before the market was held. Taking into account the informality of the institution, there are reported no particular disruptions of the periodic meetings because people on either side failed to attend. The market was genuinely important, enabling either side to obtain much wanted produce. Despite their acknowledged superiority, the Masai seem to have made no attempt to coerce the Arusha in the sphere of trading relationships. Haggling is reported over comparative values, and values did vary according to conditions of supply in particular; but in all this there was an atmosphere of economic exchange rather than of one group exploiting the other.

It was a wholly peaceful institution. For the Arusha it gained a particular importance for it provided the main opportunity for personal contact with the Masai in the conscious efforts to learn and imitate all they could of Masai culture.

During this traditional period there is no indication that there was any significant amount of trade amongst Arusha themselves in their own country. There was no effective economic basis for such trade. A very few specialists such as expert stool-carvers, blacksmiths and women potters developed a small trade but this was strictly in addition to, and not an alternative to, cultivation of their fields. These specialists were compensated by conventional payments in raw foodstuffs, or occasionally in beer. Such payments seem to have been standardized over long periods for each item with the idea of a "fair" price for each. A person who wanted an item had to seek out someone who was both able and willing to make it for him, or who had it on hand, and there is not reported to have been much if any scope for bargaining.

Some trading with Masai did occur outside the market center, largely based on the affinal relationships resulting from the marriages of Arusha girls in Masailand. A Masai would come to visit his brother-in-law on the mountain, bringing a goat or two—especially during poor seasons in Masailand. The visitor might stay for a short period being entertained generously by his affinal host to whom a degree of prestige accrued among his neighbors. The Masai would return to his own country taking a supply of honey or produce with him, acquired from his host and other Arusha willing to trade. At these times too the visiting Masai was often seeking to obtain the services of an Arusha boy or youth for herding work in Masailand, for which a payment of a calf or two was conventional.

All this became established during the earlier period when the Arusha were relatively weak in numbers, wealth, military ability and morale. After a generation had passed, however, the Arusha condition began to change. On the fertile mountain slopes their agriculture prospered and the people lived well. Their Meru neighbors were eventually decisively defeated and many of them came to live on the Arusha side of the mountain either by capture in war or by voluntary migration to a haven from Masai raiding. The young tribe was also augmented by large numbers of Chagga refugees from the southern slopes of Kilimanjaro who fled to the thriving pioneer community as a result of internecine wars and the exactions of rapacious chiefs. The Arusha absorbed these immigrants willingly and without difficulty while retaining their Masai ethic and culture; they expanded their settlements up and along the mountain slopes. In their imitation of Masai culture they embraced Masai military ideas. They began to accumulate livestock sufficient to attract Masai raids and they began at last even to raid the Masai themselves. At this point, and just before the Germans arrived, the Masai were terribly stricken by the spreading rinderpest plague which decimated their herds of cattle and brought famine. Many of the indigent Kisongo Masai sought refuge and hospitality among the Arusha whose agricultural prosperity was only slightly affected. This not only boosted Arusha morale—that they could remain economically flourishing when the Masai were destitute—but it brought them into very close contact with the Masai who taught their tractable hosts more of Masai culture, including military techniques. Thus weakened by the disaster, the Masai were a relatively easy target for the emboldened Arusha warriors who raided out beyond their guests' homelands and also to the countries of the Chagga and Iraqw.

The traditional trade was dislocated. Neighboring Masai had nothing to trade but instead depended on willing Arusha charity. Arusha had less need of trade for now they were beginning to acquire livestock by succesful raiding. At this point (1898) the Germans arrived, conquered the Arusha and seized control of the region. Raiding stopped, and after a few years the Masai herds began to grow again. The Arusha received a sudden and unpleasant setback and even lost some of their own growing herds to the Germans as a result of their attempt to withstand alien invasion. Arusha-Masai trade seems to have begun again fairly soon and, as before, in response to advantages gained on either side. A small trickle of foreign trade goods began to be added to the traditional produce involved—e.g. cloth, beads, ironware—which was handled either by Arusha or, more commonly, by a few alien Africans such as Chagga, Somali or Swahili who took advantage of the already existing market facilities. In this renewal and slight extension the Germans apparently took no part.

About this time (the date is obscure) the market center was shifted from its traditional site to a place about nine miles due west which has come to be called *Olkambi loo kule,* or in Swahili, *Kambi ya maziwa* (literally, "the milk center") in reference to the staple of Masai trade. The reasons for this shift were several: the Europeans were establishing an alien town to the immediate east of the old market center and white farmers occupied land close to it on the west, so that neither Arusha nor Masai found it so convenient or so easily accessible. The Masai had, moreover, withdrawn in the face of Arusha raiding and German occupation and were now farther away from the former center; at the same time the Arusha were beginning to make use of the plains below the slopes of Mt. Meru. That is, the Arusha-Masai borderland had shifted westwards and the market center followed for it was a border institution. This meant, however, that the new center was relatively more distant from the main area of Arusha population and it began to be less convenient for Arusha purposes at that time—after two or more decades of white supremacy— when for other reasons the traditional trade was becoming less important.

ARUSHA EXPANSION AND THE NEW TRADE (*c.* 1920–40)

As we have seen, the Arusha expanded rapidly in both population and area occupied. The Germans, and later the British, limited the traditional geographical extension up the mountain slopes at the edge of the forest by imposing a forest reserve boundary at rather less than 6,000 feet altitude. Expansion round the mountain along the contour was fairly quickly limited also—to the east by existing Meru settlements, and to the west by the aridity of the country even high up the slopes. The only opportunity for expansion was below the mountain in the drier plains recently vacated by the Masai. Population pressure built up on the already inhabited mountain slopes as people refused to colonize the less fertile, arid, lower country; but gradually and inevitably colonization and permanent settlement developed at the considerably lower population density consistent with the poor environment. A different agricultural regime was required. It is too dry to grow bananas or millet, and the hotter, drier climate demands a different agricultural cycle so that the annual harvest of maize and beans occurs roughly six months after the main harvest on the mountain. With increasing congestion on the mountain, and with growing herds, it became useful to keep more and more cattle in the plains, partly in special camps but partly in the homesteads of the new settlers. In many cases the new settlers were in fact the wealthy cattle owners who had realized the possibilities of the ex-Masai plains. In brief, the economic production—produce, times of harvest, agricultural regimes, etc.—of the two geographical parts of the country were differentiated while standards remained essentially the same in both: and so there became established advantageous conditions for trade *within* the country. The people in the plains required bananas and beer[5], and they wished to take advantage of the mountain harvest which came when their own stocks were becoming depleted. The people of the mountain slopes desired the herding services of the plains people and wished to obtain extra animals, milk, meat and skins from them; they also wished to take

(5) Water shortage in the peripheral plains made beer brewing impossible.

avantage of the plains harvest to supplement their own stores as they
grew low, and it was profitable to dispose of surplus bananas and to
brew and sell beer.

A rather hesitant trade gradually developed, but it never achieved
much success—and it produced a good deal of trouble. The need and
ability for trade and exchange did not adequately coincide in time
for the two groups of Arusha. The people in the plains wanted foodstuffs mainly in May, June and July whereas the main harvest on the
mountain slopes is in February; bananas tend to be scarce in the
middle of the year which is the dry, cool season. At that time of the
year the people of the plains had little to offer in exchange; they had
no disposable food of course, and mountain demand for pastoral
produce is then at its lowest. There was almost no artificial standard
or store of value (i.e., money) to assist to overcome the difficulties,
for barter was still the only technique of exchange practiced. For
some time, however, trade did develop—because of the pressing need
for it in the plains, mainly—and it followed principally the lines of
agnatic kinship. Men and women in the plains looked to their kinsfolk for assistance in their times of need of foodstuffs in return for:
(a) agricultural and pastoral foods later in the year in the plains; (b)
a willingness to herd livestock of their mountain-dwelling kin; and
(c) goats and sheep. Goats and sheep were, in general, too large and
valuable as a regular medium of exchange and they were not too
plentiful in any case. The other items of trade were unsatisfactory
as they involved either a period of waiting or a service difficult to
evaluate. With no effective method of maintaining an account over
time and of reckoning values easily, neither *quid pro quo* was really
adequate. People fell back on the already existing ties of kinship,
both to gain agreement to assist by providing goods when needed and
to attempt to ensure that reasonable equity was maintained. The
Arusha kinship system was not able to bear this strain. In any case
the people more in need of an exchange mechanism and more
frequently in need—those living in the plains—tended to try manipulate kinship sentiments and obligations to their own personal advantage, and this was resented by the mountain dwellers. More importantly, however, the genealogically closer agnatic ties which were
invoked for these purposes were not such as could withstand the
heavy strain of recurrent material obligations. Arusha set great store
on the economic independence of a man with his own wife (or wives)
and children and his own fields and herds acquired by inheritance
or pioneering, and they did not wish merely on account of kinship
sentiment to relinquish this independence. Close agnatic ties (particularly between brothers and paternal cousins), significant because

of both jural and ritual necessities, tended to produce conflict in the economic sphere. As land became scarcer and the desire increased for still relatively scarce cattle, the outstanding rivals were brothers and cousins. Many of the colonists in the plains were the very men who had not been able to gain a share of the paternal land on the mountain slopes and they were likely to be potentially resentful; alternatively some of the colonists had managed to obtain a share of mountain inheritance and to this they clung while also holding fields in the plains so that their mountain kinsmen were likely to be resentful. Thus, there was not only a traditionally weak economic obligation involved in close kinship but such kinship was already strained by novel factors. More distant kinsfolk, affines and others were not prepared to do more than give casual assistance, nor could they in any way be coerced to do more.

Internal trade and exchange limped along in a growing atmosphere of disfavor on both sides. No specialist Arusha agencies arose to deal with the situation, but gradually outside intervention developed to meet the obvious needs; but no longer was it Masai trade, for the Masai had little to offer to relieve the new Arusha condition. The neighboring Meru people soon saw the advantage of trade with the Arusha lowlands, especially in bananas and millet and, at first, in barter by the women. The same practical difficulties arose for the Meru as had arisen for the mountain Arusha, and they arose too when alien traders (Chagga, Somali, Indians) attempted to participate not only with foodstuffs but also with manufactured goods such as cloth, ironware, utensils, tools, beads, etc. The Arusha became obliged to accept at least minimally the device of money in order to meet novel needs otherwise inadequately dealt with by indigenous techniques, as well as to gain the advantages of trade with the outside world which was not prepared to tolerate for long the practice of barter.

Between the traditional Arusha country on the lower slopes of Mt. Meru and the surrounding plains which were being colonized lay a belt mainly occupied by foreigners. In this belt were European and Asian farmers and, more importantly, a new town inhabited by alien peoples of all kinds who brought with them organized government, many new material goods, techniques, ideas and attitudes, and channels of communication with the outside world. The town of Arusha, in which virtually none of the Arusha people themselves lived, began to emerge in this period as an important center of government, communications and trade with no reference to, or consideration of, the interests or needs of the tribes-people around. Nevertheless, the Arusha people gradually became glad to take advantage of certain features of the foreign town to satisfy novel, minimal economic requirements. With an organized market in the town, the Arusha were able to become gradually accustomed to sell their routine produce to urban merchants for cash. This was advantageous to mountain-dweller and to plains-dweller alike and the alien market tended to replace both the unsatisfactory internal trade (mountain/plains) and much of the older trade with the Masai.

The Arusha-Masai trade did not entirely die out, for it retained advantages to both sides, although by now it was relatively more important to the pastoralists who, though they had less absolute need and desire for trade, had much less opportunity. It seems that the terms of trade went against the Masai because of this and because they were less able in this kind of activity, regarding it as little less than an unfortunate necessity. The Arusha-Masai border market was invaded by the Meru people with both agricultural and forest produce, and by others who perceived a small Masai demand for trade goods and who found it profitable to tap Arusha and Meru who attended. Barter still remained more important but nevertheless money now began to be used here.

It is important to note what happened in this period. The Arusha did not accept and participate wholeheartedly in a money-using market economy; they merely utilized the alien complex of economic institutions and agencies to meet the difficulties which had developed as the tribe expanded and as certain indispensable needs had arisen. The Arusha sold for cash a little of their traditional crops of maize and beans, and to a lesser extent some bananas, millet, chickens and eggs; but their need and demand for cash were strictly limited. Cash was required especially to satisfy established need for foodstuffs which at certain times of the year and in certain areas (particularly the plains settlements) were scarce. Because of novel exigencies (e.g., the need to pay taxes) and novel opportunities (the relative advantages of buying, for instance, hoes, pots or beads from urban markets) a new demand was also stimulated and thus a further need for cash. Fundamentally, however, the traditional economy and, more especially, traditional economic attitudes and aims remained essentially the same.

It should be noted that crops were not grown specifically for the market, nor were new crops grown which gave better returns there. What sales there were involved only a small proportion of the routine production obtained by traditional agricultural processes.

The traditional economy rested on the near autarky of each of the small, individual producing units—a domestic family group comprising a man and his wife or wives and unmarried children.[6] It is

(6) Adult sons gain economic autonomy a year or two after marriage.

true that there were some minor specialists but they were few and all of them practiced their skills in addition to, and not as a substitute for, the ordinary economic activities of other men. Each family, the head of which owned the land by right of inheritance or of original pioneering, was almost self-sufficient in producing its own food, shelter, clothing and utensils. There was some inter-family cooperation based on kinship and neighborliness, but the only major cooperative task concerned was house construction and there only building labor was involved. Each family-unit had roughly the same standard of living and, apart from the tiny number of specialists, none had anything which another had not and which therefore could become an item of exchange. In their favorable environment the Arusha could produce a small surplus with no difficulty to use in trade with the Masai in order to obtain pastoral produce not at that time available at home.

In almost all essentials, the traditional economy persisted after the Arusha had come to utilize the opportunities of the alien market and its cash economy. Incentives, aims of agricultural production and the standard of living remained virtually the same. There was, for example, no attempt to grow more crops in order to sell more and thus get more money and buy more goods in the market. Agricultural production remained at about the same level, as far as can be judged now. Land usage was not altered to suit the market nor were new crops cultivated specifically for sale. The ready supplies in the market did not stimulate the Arusha to demand more goods or new goods. Apart from a very little cloth, Arusha continued to make and wear their traditional clothing; similarly their housing, domestic apparatus and tools remained as they had been. Sales in the market provided only a small proportion of their income and impinged very little on the indigenous economy or on traditional social institutions. Exceedingly few men took up wage-labor although there were generally plenty of opportunities for it on the nearby farms and in the town. Old economic goals remained: to provide sufficient foodstuffs and to increase one's holding of livestock in order to be able to marry another wife, or enable one's son to marry, and so have more children and to enlarge the size and prestige of the family. This, according to Arusha evaluation, was the proper channel of endeavor. To some extent the alien market was used to assist in this endeavor: a man could sell produce, save the money and eventually buy the animals, and even buy them in government-organized stock markets. On the whole, however, this did not happen, for even here the Arusha did not take advantage of the possibilities offered to them. They preferred for a long time to acquire livestock from the Masai and other herd-owners such as the

Mbugwe and Iraqw by barter and individual effort. Old methods of obtaining Masai cattle continued—by the marriage of Arusha girls to Masai men, by sending Arusha boys to herd for the Masai, and by begging Masai affines and friends. In part they did not perceive the possibilities newly open to them and in part they were not willing to take them up and become too deeply involved in alien affairs; and so the Arusha acquired cattle, sheep and goats much more slowly than could easily have been the case despite the strong desire for them.

In notably favorable circumstances for economic enterprise and cultural and social change, the Arusha remained adamantly and consciously conservative. Such rejection of alien culture and institutions and an eminent satisfaction with established culture have frequently been noted for the Masai people of both Tanganyika and Kenya. For these seminomadic pastoralists, commonly far from alien contacts and with a mode of life and homeland scarcely susceptible to Western, urban-orientated practices and values, this is perhaps not quite as remarkable as sometimes is thought. The Arusha, however, present a more notable case because they were in particularly close geographical proximity to the outside world which, as demonstrated elsewhere in similar circumstances, had much to offer to good cultivators in a fertile land next to a ready market. Nevertheless, the Arusha remained firmly attached to traditional institutions and values which were of course, and significantly so, Masai institutions and values.

It has been noted already how the Arusha, beginning originally with what was probably a distinctly Masai-like culture and dependent on a degree of Masai support, strived to imitate the Masai and to bring the details of their social life into conformity with those of the Kisongo Masai in particular. They accepted Kisongo tutelage and leadership, they regarded the Masai as a superior people and the Masai culture as the ideal pattern of life. The relative success of the Arusha raiding and their acting as hosts to destitute Masai after the rinderpest epidemic did not affect their deep admiration for and persistent emulation of Masai ways; indeed the very success of Masai military methods and the close contact with the Masai refugees at that time served only to intensify Arusha admiration. Many if not all of the numerous peoples around the lengthy borders of Masailand had been deeply impressed by the outstanding Masai wealth, military success, self-assurance and virility to the point of at least some imitation; the Masai age-group system as the basis of a military organization was especially copied. Generally, however, these latter imitations remained somewhat artificial, inadequately articulated with the elements of the local culture, and they were more or less rapidly dropped as contact grew with Western culture in peaceful conditions. For the Arusha the story was different. Masai institutions and values were far closer to original Arusha culture than to the cultures of these other peoples and the heterogeneous elements of the rapidly expanding Arusha population found unity and common orientation in adherence to and emulation of the Masai. The success of the pioneer settlement on the southwestern slopes of Mt. Meru was, in Arusha minds, intimately bound up with the evolution of a Masai ethic in the community.

In the decades following the imposition of peace and alien rule the Arusha not only refused to shift their ideological attachment, but they used it as a symbol of opposition to, or at least contradistinction from, the foreigner of whatever origin and kind (i.e., not only the European). Unlike other neighbors and imitators of the Masai, however, the Arusha could not eschew Masai standards without rejecting the basis of their own culture and social system. Their values and attitudes, the directive source behind many of their institutions, their language and orientations alike were rooted outside their own society. Arusha acknowledged their inferior status and their reference to an external source of culture. They were attached to a people who not only did not wish to change nor to adopt alien ways, but who had the excellent oportunity to reject change because of the relative remoteness and poverty of their own country and who were, in fact, offered relatively little by Europeans or others which would make change clearly advantageous. There were, of course, also intrinsic to Masai culture certain features which made conservatism not merely easy but preferable.

While the Masai did not change, the Arusha, remaining tied to them, found it almost impossible to change without a decisive rejection of fundamental values. For a long time Masai-inspired values were more highly regarded than any novel, alien ones in virtually all significant matters. There was *some* change of ideas, of practical techniques and of social relationships; but it was an exceedingly slow hesitant process which contrasted sharply with the reactions of other agricultural peoples in similar circumstances. For example, the Chagga, on the southern slopes of Mt. Kilimanjaro some fifty miles to the east, accepted a degree of rationalization of political authority and landholding, new crops and cash-cropping, education and Christianity, new skills, new commodities, etc.: they did not merely accept them passively but worked most actively towards their achievement. All of these similarly available things the Arusha opposed. For example, after more than half a century of missionary (Lutheran) endeavor, probably no more than a fifth of the people had even nominal allegiance to Christianity. There was little demand for schools and some places remained empty in those which were nevertheless provided. Arusha men and women alike acquired a notoriety among all outsiders who met them by their appearance in the alien town dressed in traditional fashion.[7]

During this period very many of the older men occupying the conventional authority-leadership positions in the age-group and clan systems either had been strongly influenced by Masai refugees during the rinderpest epidemic or they were sons of Masai women married to Arusha during that critical period. They had a vigorous attachment to Masai culture and expressed it in their acknowledged roles in the society. At a time when, other things being equal, there might have been a gradual slackening of adherence to the Masai ethic and a greater acceptance of change, tribal leadership was predominantly against it. As mentioned already, some minimal change was necessary to meet the needs imposed by the colonization of the dry, peripheral plains and the slight demand for a few manufactured goods. Yet the Arusha refused to change their agricultural routines, to adopt new crops, to seek deliberately to earn money by farming, to buy a wider range of imported manufactures or to aim at an increased standard of living.

LAND SHORTAGE AND A CASH ECONOMY (*c.* 1940–60)

The dominant feature of the last fifteen to twenty years in the Arusha country has been the increasing land shortage as the population has expanded rapidly and all available land has been occupied. In 1957 the Arusha were living at an average density exceeding 1,000 people per square mile on the mountain slopes, with local intensities up to 1,500 people per square mile. In the plains, although the density was much lower (about 110 people per square mile), the situation was no less critical because of the far less favorable environment. Between 1948 and 1957 the population increased at an average rate of more than two per cent a year, and there is every indication that the rate has been much the same throughout this century. In the same period the overflow from the town and the alien-held estates and farms produced an increase in the settlement of other Africans in the Arusha country which has exacerbated the situation in some areas. In response to this developing phenomenon, the Arusha (as previously noted) ex-

(7) Most Europeans, other Africans and Asians refer to the Arusha as "Masai," although a true Masai is rarely seen in the town or its approach roads. Part of the popular story of Masai resistance to change is certainly based on experience of Arusha in the town and environs who are incorrectly thought to be Masai.

panded off the crowded mountain slopes onto the surrounding plains which had formerly been Masai territory. This movement first began in the early 1920's, gathered momentum in the 1930's and became a flood in the 1940's. By the early 1950's virtually all usable land in the plains had been settled and taken into use, to the point where much marginal land was under cultivation when climate and soils scarcely warranted it. Despite this expansion the density of population on the mountain slopes continued to rise, at first because many men preferred even a small piece of land on the fertile, well-watered mountain to a large area in the hot, semi-arid, less productive plains; but later on because available land in the plains grew scarcer until there was no longer any to be had. A statistically average holding of land on the mountain slopes was about four to six acres in 1957 (i.e., about a half to three quarters of an acre per person), but in fact some land was too infertile for use or was taken up by water courses, roads, buildings, etc., and a small minority of men had well above the average-sized amount of land. Probably over 1,500 families (i.e., more than 11,000 people) were dependent on no more than about one and a half acres of land each for their livelihood. Only a tiny minority of men earned money by wage labor because Arusha men eschewed the locally low wage rates open to their unskilled employment.

This condition, progressively intensifying, has had critical influence on the whole of the social life of the Arusha; but, insofar as this present account is concerned, it has been decisive in forcing the people to begin to abandon their conservative attachment to traditional institutions and values and to adopt new economic practices and attitudes. It has become impossible for the Arusha to persist with a fundamentally "traditional economy." Amounts of land now available have made this simple economy no longer workable, for it became impossible to grow enough maize, beans, bananas and millet and to graze sufficient cattle to produce milk and meat for the family-unit. People became increasingly compelled to specialize in their production, concentrating on one ore more intensively cultivated crops (coffee, onions, peas, beans, wheat) at least sufficiently enough to obtain the money required to buy food, as well as other goods, to meet otherwise unobtainable minimum needs. This meant a change in agricultural enterprise and also a much greater acceptance of a cash or market economy. As we have seen, participation in a market economy had been accepted earlier to a restricted extent to meet certain kinds of limited needs, but there had been no attempt to make use of the potentialities of the new economy or of the exceptionally fertile land occupied: basically the traditional economy and all the values and attitudes associated with that system had persisted. But during the 1950's it became increasingly recognized by the people—albeit reluctantly and hesitantly—that production for the market was inevitable.

Coffee became the principal cash crop and the principal item of trade for the Arusha because of its high sale price in the world market. Compared with other possible crops, it requires far less land for a given income. It did, however, involve certain novelties, such as regular watering and careful shading of seedlings, pruning the bushes, washing and husking the cherries, etc., and it did not fit in too easily with established cultivation regimes. For these reasons, and despite its profitableness, it has not been cultivated as readily as might have been expected once the concept of cash-cropping was accepted. Peas, beans or wheat fit in easily enough, requiring only an intensification of existing practices; onions are grown on the same plots as cereals and legumes and can generally be picked before the planting of those crops, thus giving two harvests from the one plot each year. Coffee is, however, perennial and other crops, except for some banana trees for shade, should not be grown on the same land. These initial disadvantages are being overcome as the shortage of land becomes more serious. Apart from the retention of a tiny amount (usually of inferior quality) of the coffee crop for home consumption the whole harvest is sold for cash at world market prices, and it is the conscious intent of the people to do this.

Coffee cultivation is limited to the mountain slopes, for it will not grow in the hotter and drier conditions of the peripheral lowlands. It was adopted first in the east where land shortage is most severe, the rainfall most dependable and the influence of the neighboring Meru people most marked. By 1960 coffee was almost the only cash crop in the east—indeed it was by far the major crop of any kind—and it had spread westwards across the mountain slopes. In general, however, the farther west one goes along the slopes the less suitable is the environment for coffee and the less intense is the shortage of land; thus going westwards coffee is increasingly combined for market sale with onions, beans, maize and finger millet, until on the western slopes little or no coffee is grown. It could be grown there, although perhaps less easily, and probably in due course it will be, as land shortage intensifies and as the people there come increasingly to desire to increase their cash incomes and thus their standards of living. In the far west, high up on the slopes, a number of Arusha cultivate peas for the market and a number are experimenting with pyrethrum. In the surrounding lowlands the only important crops are maize and beans which are grown both for food and for sale. Attempts have been made to grow wheat, but the climate is not favorable for this and most Arusha have given it up as a result of poor success. Some of the larger farmers are, with European settler encouragement, specializing in the production of seed beans.

Concurrently with these latest developments there has been the beginnings of a break by the Arusha with their Masai-orientated and dictated culture. The ideological and emotional association involving imitation of the Masai and an accepted inferiority has been attacked by novel assertions of Arusha superiority to the Masai—stigmatizing them as poor, ignorant "country cousins"[8]—and claims that the common culture was originated by the Arusha and merely imitated by the Masai. New versions of Arusha-Masai history have been put forward (not all of which are mutually consistent), attempting to substantiate these sorts of claims and attitudes. There is a feeling among the Arusha that the conceptualization of former relations should be such that there is some kind of reasonable continuity between the alleged past and the evident present in which they desire cultural and moral autonomy in adopting new economic ideas and practices and new social roles and values which are now seen to be essential. So intense was the dependence upon Masai precept and leadership that for a long time the Arusha were tied by their relatively unchanging superiors: it seems to be necessary to attempt to justify their independence now by claiming a former superiority over the Masai.

Through the 1950's there was considerable ambivalence in their attitude towards the Masai, and this was particularly marked in the years 1957–59 during which preparations were afoot leading up to one of the two major age-group promotion ceremonies of the Kisongo Masai, in which for well over a century the Arusha had participated as followers.[9] In 1959 the Arusha not only followed the Masai lead again at this ceremony, but they devoted themselves to crucial traditional roles and values which are essentially Masai in nature. This renewed dependence on the Masai was notably in contrast with Arusha assertions of traditional independence, even leadership, and also with their newly begun modern changes and acceptance of

(8) The Masai, say Arusha now, are ignorant folk who have more cattle than they know what to do with, and who are foolish enough to pay high prices for the poorest quality produce (e.g. tobacco, beer) or to overpay in bridewealth. Humorous stories circulate concerning Masai simple-mindedness and rusticity. In 1957 the Arusha derived inordinate pleasure from a minor administrative boundary change at the expense of the Masai. These are examples of Arusha attitudes in this period.

(9) *Olngesher*, the transfer of the age-group in the formal grade of senior warrior to the grade of elderhood, which occurred in June 1959. Struggles to determine which ritual expert, *olaiboni*, should officiate and the timing of the event were confined to the Kisongo Masai. The Arusha merely followed the eventual Masai decisions and plans, despite some grumblings and threats to demand participation.

change. Nevertheless, external forces, particularly increasing land shortage, are compelling change and are leading Arusha to some realization of the advantages to them beyond merely minimal adjustment to procrustean necessities.

The gradual acceptance of the need for at least a degree of specialized production for the market has meant not only an acceptance of the use of money indirectly to obtain goods and services previously produced within the individual family farming unit by its own members, but also it has tended to lead to a new demand for money to obtain more goods and services which had *not* previously been consumed or perhaps even thought of. That is to say, cash crop production has enabled the Arusha to gain a rather higher standard of living and it has begun to lead them actively and consciously to seek to raise it further even while basic land resources shrink relative to population. Forced by irresistible pressures to turn from their old economy the Arusha have begun to seek something more than family autarky, to seek more than an economic minimum. This had not happened earlier during the first period of settlement off the mountain slopes: then a cash economy had been accepted *only* in certain limited ways sufficiently merely to adjust the traditional economy to current, novel necessities but retaining it in essence (cf. pp. 440–41). By the late 1950's elements of the old economy remained, of course. Families still sought to grow as much of their own food supply as possible—doing so remained a moral as well as an economic ideal—cultivating more or less only sufficient cash crops to realize the cash income required to augment the family food supply and to purchase a little above the old demand for store goods. The economically profitable, complete specialization in cash crops was not accepted by the majority of Arusha by 1958; nevertheless, the notion of deliberate cash-cropping and the extended use of money was quite clearly established, while the expansion of demand for cash, for consumption goods, for services—that is, for a higher standard of living—was developing. There was no longer a relatively static economy; there was an articulate desire to raise living standards for reasons not connected with traditional values or environmental necessity.

The new cash economy is, of course, a market or exchange economy with money as its intermediary instrument. The Arusha have access to a number of rather different markets in this context, some of which are established and some of which are new, some internal and some external. The alien town of Arusha provides the chief market focus as the people take advantage of the existing facilities there. The town itself grew in the first half of the century in direct response to the largely European needs of the local settler-farmer community and government officials[10]. Its stores, services and communications have been oriented to this end and, as usual in East Africa, they have been provided to a large extent by immigrant Asians with alien (i.e., non-Arusha) Africans as mainly unskilled workers. Thus, the Arusha have had a ready-made market center available to serve their new needs, both in the disposal of their agricultural produce and in the provision of goods and services.

Asian merchants buy in bulk the people's crops of onions, peas, beans and maize. Neighbors commonly combine to meet the cost of hiring a truck (African or Asian owned) in which to transport their produce to the warehouse of the selected urban merchant. Some operators send their trucks round the country on pre-arranged days after the harvest times in order to pick up Arusha and their sacks of produce for established fares. A number of new motor tracks have been roughly cleared by the local government and by local neighborhood cooperation in order that trucks may penetrate roadless areas and pick up heavy loads. Produce prices are closely related to those operative in the Territory at large and also in adjacent Kenya, although many Arusha complain that the urban merchants seek to profit too greatly at the producers' expense. A small number of Arusha holding very large areas of land have become members of the European-organized Tanganyika Farmers Association, a cooperative society through which produce is sold and some goods are obtainable at less than retail cost.[11]

There is also some selling in small, retail quantities. Some Arusha, mainly women who live within a mile or so, attend the regularized open-air market in the town established by the town council where they are able to take advantage of the demand for foodstuffs by the increasing number of alien, urbanized Africans. Here are sold such foods as bananas, corn, beans, vegetables, eggs and hens as well as tobacco and firewood. Some Arusha meet the similar demand from European and Asian housewives by hawking vegetables, fruit, eggs and poultry from door to door in the residential areas of the town; and a few have begun to specialize in market gardening for this purpose. In both of these kinds of retail market the Arusha have to meet

---

(10) The town of Arusha contains the headquarters of the Northern Province of Tanganyika and of some minor government departments. It has been a rail head since 1929 and is a focus of communications for northern Tanganyika. It is also the main center for big game expeditions in the Territory.

(11) These men were mainly early settlers in the plains who have been able to retain and use their original, large claims to land there. Encouraged by Government officers and one or two European farmers, some of these men have taken up large-scale, mechanized cultivation of maize, beans and wheat. There are only about twenty of these modern Arusha farmers and a few other scattered holders of large farms, and it seems certain that their lands will be split up among their sons by inheritance in due course.

direct competition from local aliens and from external suppliers. The receipts from this sort of trading are generally thought of as petty cash in contrast to the main receipts from the bulk produce sales; nevertheless the total sales from such retailing must produce a significant addition to the cash income of many Arusha living near the town.

All Arusha coffee growers should be share-holding members of the Koimere Cooperative Society as African-produced coffee can only be legally sold through this organization.[12] Although some non-members sell their crops through a relative or friend who is a member, this is highly disapproved by officials who seek to maximize both the numbers of members and the revenue from share subscriptions. Such illegitimate sales of nonmember's crops are prevented in so far as they can be detected. In this policy the Society is encouraged by the Cooperative Development Department of the central government. The Society's office and store are situated in the town. Arusha growers may deliver their coffee there or to arranged collection points where it is picked up by the Society's truck. Growers receive an initial payment on delivery to the Society and a later, final payment according to the actual price fetched in the auction market at Moshi, the center of the Tanganyika coffee trade. The Society's managing board is elected annually by the shareholders, but to the majority of Arusha this is merely an agency through which they have to sell their coffee. There is small interest in, and even smaller understanding of, the nature of its operations which are not notably efficient; and it is generally conceived of as a specialist purchaser of this one cash crop.

In one particular market in the town, the Arusha are able both to buy and sell the same commodity: this is the government operated "goat market" which is held twice a week on the edge of the town. Goats and sheep are in great demand for the fulfillment of both social and ritual obligations, and at the same time they are easily bred. They have little intrinsic or emotional value to the Arusha, who regard them as a store of savings to be used or sold as needs require. They should legally only be sold in this market and a small fee is charged for the cost of market upkeep; although some sales undoubtedly do occur outside, at the edge of the market area and in the homes of individuals, the bulk of Arusha small stock trading is done in the market where men say they get the fairest prices without pressures

---

(12) Koimere is the Arusha-Masai name for Mt. Meru. Almost everywhere in Tanganyika the sale of bulk cash crops (coffee, rice, tobacco, cotton) has been organized through locally established and self-administered African cooperative societies. This policy aims not only at the reduction of the costs of disposal, but also at assisting a mainly illiterate, inexperienced peasantry.

from kinsmen and friends. The animals are sold by auction, and in addition to the Arusha themselves the market is attended by a few butchers and traders.

The "goat market" serves more than the obvious economic, exchange needs. It is the one market common to all Arusha, where they come together at set times; it is attractive to them all and is centrally located. Men go there to watch prices even when they may have no immediate intention of buying or selling. They go also to meet other Arusha from different parts of the country whom they might not otherwise see without a special journey. They go to exchange news and gossip, to receive a message or to find someone to take a message for them. They go to meet men with whom they can discuss important affairs or with whom they can make plans or arrangements. They go for the sheer pleasure of attending and participating.

Because of all this, the environs of the "goat market" have become the accepted place to buy and sell peculiarly Arusha commodities—spear heads, particular metal ornaments, Arusha bead work and woodwork, bush and forest herbs for medicinal and ritual purposes, red ochre, Masai-type sheath-knives and calf-leather sheaths, leather collars and bells for cattle, milk gourds, etc. Formerly, these commodities were not always easy to obtain for it was a matter of seeking out individuals who had the knowledge, interest and skill to make or gather the item in question. Now a little minor specialization is encouraged by the market opportunity and some men and women are able to augment their incomes.

These commodities are obtained only for cash payments. Prices do not fluctuate with supply and demand—unlike prices for goats—for, as in the traditional setting, it is thought that there is a "fair" and stable price for each kind of item. During the last decade the prices have all tended to rise slightly as a result of falling money values and of increasing circulation of money which have occurred in that period, but these prices have risen rather less than those of other commodities. On any particular market day, however, an accidental shortage of some item, or conversely a heavier demand than usual, does not affect prices. These imbalances between supply and demand are not uncommon, especially as the supply of some items is rather irregular, and prospective buyers may visit the market on two or more occasions in order to get the particular type of commodity they require.

This part of the "goat market" makes no attempt to compete with the larger, variegated market afforded by the rest of the town, nor on the whole does it compete with the local, internal markets described below. The "goat market" is the only kind of market which involves marked noneconomic functions and attractions (though of course all do to a minor extent) and it regularly brings together at one time and place more Arusha than any other market. An average attendance is of the order of several hundred men. Other marketing involves only individuals for the most part, who are engaged in satisfying their own economic needs at the time.

With a wide range of both types and qualities of shops and stores, the town is easily able to meet all Arusha requirements—both the common demand for clothing, foodstuffs, cigarettes, soap, tea, bread, beer, medicines, etc., and the limited demand for more European-type goods such as bicycles, crockery and household utensils, tools and implements, a wider variety and better quality of clothing, etc. Demand and incentive have not been restricted by deficiencies in supply in the way which has sometimes occurred in Africa; rather the reverse is true, for the very excellence of the already-existing market has served to stimulate demand and Arusha consumption standards. The stores most commonly used by Arusha are kept by Asians and alien Africans, but they are increasingly using, for example, the pharmacy or the agricultural supply store which are European-owned and operated and where Arusha-speaking employees are engaged particularly to serve Arusha customers.

The town, then, exists as an external phenomenon in respect to Arusha trade and exchange, and operated by forces and people neither controlled nor understood by the Arusha themselves. They merely dispose of their cash crops and their surplus crops for money, and with it they usually satisfy their customer needs from quite different merchants. Only the cooperative society is a purely Arusha association and even that is subject to general, territorial regulations and the even more distant world coffee market. Almost no Arusha feels obliged or attracted or even able to become an entrepreneur in this market complex beyond his own society.

There are, however, a number of small, local-market centers inside the Arusha country which are devoted mainly or entirely to the interests of the Arusha people. In some ten to fifteen localities small Arusha-owned stores operate, and in seven others such stores are augmented by one or more owned by an Asian, Somali or alien African (mainly Chagga). Most of these local centers have grown spontaneously as one or two men have tried their hand at retailing, perhaps investing the savings from military service or wage employment or the profits of coffee growing. Many of these stores are housed in ramshackle huts; many are unstable, operating erratically both in time and range of goods; many fail altogether. With a rising demand for consumer goods, however, many have become established in the

1950's with fairly regular hours and service. They specialize in the cash sale of small quantities of cigarettes, soap, kerosene, matches, beads, etc., and some foodstuffs. At each of these centers there is at least one butcher's shop to satisfy the demand for meat; such demand, traditionally large, has grown rapidly and is now expressed in cash terms. Individual butchers buy a steer or two at the government cattle market or on special trips in Masailand, and slaughter them one at a time as all the meat of the previous one has been sold. By local government by-law the butchers' shops must be brick-built and minimum hygienic standards are enforced with the effect that the number of these shops was reduced in the late 1950's. This is the most flourishing part of the internal market, for it scarcely (if at all) competes with the town market. The other local stores tend to suffer in comparison with the better organized stores in the nearby town, and Arusha retailers are often unable to obtain their stocks at such advantageous prices as their urban competitors and therefore cannot always offer low prices. Nevertheless their convenience for small, daily purchases in local neighborhoods gives them some advantage over the town.

In addition modern Arusha demand is met at a few of these local centers by the more or less regular sale of tea, white bread and bottled beer. Traditional beer is brewed and sold at a limited number of licensed "clubs" (s. *olkilabu*) which are owned and operated mainly by Arusha. These "clubs" serve both as places where men can meet and drink together, and as suppliers of the very large quantities of beer required for socio-ceremonial, ritual and judicial occasions[13]. They are open daily until the supply of beer runs out. There is no longer any home brewing whether for sale or not and therefore everyone is dependent on these "clubs." In the later 1950's the price of standard beer (i.e., brewed with the traditional ingredients) did not change from six shillings per four gallon can (*debe*). Occasionally less millet and more maize might be used and the price for such an inferior brew would be decreased by fifty cents or less per four gallons; but the larger "clubs", which desire to maintain a reputation and where supplies of ingredients are well organized, seldom resort to inferior brews for fear of losing customers. Beer is never sold except for immediate cash payment.

The traditional trade with the pastoral Masai continues at the center established after European conquest (cf. p. 436), but for the

---

(13) Beer must be supplied, for example, at the various stages leading up to marriage, at birth and mortuary ceremonies, in ancestor worship, at indigenous hearings of disputes and execution of judgments. As an indication of the quantities involved: a betrothed suitor must bring about 24 gallons on six to ten occasions to his father-in-law; the two parties to a dispute should provide 12–16 gallons each.

Arusha it is unimportant now. Masai women attend with their gourds
of milk, meat, skins, etc., and sometimes with a goat or sheep; they also
bring cash with them. Without doubt this market remains rather
important to the Masai as a convenient place where they can obtain
agricultural produce and, today, some store goods. Some Somali and
African stores have been established at the center to supply both local
Arusha in that part of the peripheral plains, and also Masai needs
for cloth, tobacco, ornaments and hardware. For most Arusha the
market center is too far away to be of value or interest compared with
the several alternative centers available. Masai no longer offer commodities required by the Arusha which are not more easily obtainable
elsewhere. Meat is locally obtained as described above; milk is more
readily available at the local, internal centers or at Asian dairies in the
town; small stock are more reliably and numerously available at the
town "goat market." Even to the Arusha who live fairly near the
Masai, trade is not very attractive, nor do they in the dry plains have
the tobacco, honey, gourds or beer which the Masai seek. Indeed the
Masai trade, though carried on at the same center, has largely been
taken up by the stores there and by outsiders (Meru, Chagga and other
Africans, and Somali) who come from the town and beyond on the
regular, weekly market day. The nearby Arusha are chiefly concerned
with the production and bulk sale of maize and beans. A small amount
of unorganized individual trading occurs also between itinerant
Arusha and the Masai in their own country, mainly in the purchase
of cattle and small stock for cash or barter goods, but Arusha have no
monopoly in this kind of business. Individual Masai still sometimes
visit Arusha affines or friends and bring a goat or two in order to
obtain gourds, honey and other produce. In all, however, Arusha-
Masai trade has become unimportant and is unlikely to grow less so.

CONCLUSION

In trading relationships the Arusha have moved away from a simple
dichotomy, involving the barter exchange of produce of farm and
forest for that of herds and flocks, to an increasingly complex and
variegated market economy involving the use of money, a variety of
alien peoples, Westernized production and trading practices, a world
market in at least one Arusha product and a wide range of commodities embracing the whole of these people's consumption. In this development they have been caught up in the Euro-Asian world as have
most other East African peoples by the second half of the twentieth
century. Their adoption of money as a standard, new production
techniques and new kinds of demand, their involvement in a complex

of new ideas and values and changed orientations is commonplace in Africa; and it is not easy to see how far the process may go and what will be the associated noneconomic concomitants. It is, of course, intimately bound up with several other similarly fundamental changes that are at work. The Arusha situation is, however, of some particular interest in that, despite the notably favorable conditions for economic development and trade in the modern world, there was for a long time a rejection of the possibility—not merely the passive refusal of rather difficult opportunities which has been evident in so many of the less fortunate regions of the continent, but an active rejection based primarily not on any economic grounds but on adherence to the external, cultural and moral imperatives of the pastoral Masai. The established market center of the alien town in their midst was merely utilized to maintain an approximate economic status quo under novel conditions of peace, expansion and colonization. Not until unavoidably compelled by the most acute land shortage—i.e., shortage of the fundamental source of livelihood—did the Arusha take advantage of what their own fertile country and the ready-made market had to offer.

It remains to make an assessment of the significance of market exchange to the Arusha people. A quantitative assessment is not possible because the figures are not available either for pre-European times or later. For pre-European times, however, it may be said that trade (which was wholly external) was not essential to the Arusha economy. Self-sufficient agriculture was the basis of their lives; production appears always to have been adequate and there was neither need, nor opportunity of augmenting it from the outside. With Masai-like orientations the desire for pastoral products was marked, but in fact the Arusha were fairly quickly able to develop their own herds and flocks with good pastures and ample water supplies and they learned to raid rather than trade for animals. Nevertheless the supplies of milk, meat, skins and even small stock in the Masai market were not insignificant. Even more valuable for the Arusha were the personal and cultural relations they were able to establish and maintain with the admired Masai through the contacts of the market. There was some feeling, too, of serving the Masai who had a keen desire for some of the items supplied by the Arusha.

In the second period of Arusha economic history, the significance of trade was almost wholly economic and was of particular importance to the newly settled colonizers of the peripheral plains. Trade with the Masai began to fall off as it became less advantageous and less convenient. But the new minimal trade with aliens had, consciously, little cultural quality to it. Economically, however, trade was much more significant than it had been because it became increasingly essential under the new conditions which were putting an intolerable strain on Arusha social relations, and on agnatic kinship in particular. The volume of trade rose very slightly, no more than was necessary to meet the stable needs of a growing population. Not until the third stage, commencing with a realization of the implications of land shortage, did marketing increase in either volume or general social importance. Exchange then became fundamental to the activities of all Arusha and it has involved, among other things, the final acceptance of a money economy. By 1960, whatever the orientations and aspirations of individuals, production for the market and cash purchases of all kinds of commodities are quite essential to the economy. That is, a livelihood of any kind is impossible without trade and without the town market through which it is mainly channeled. It is a foreign market devoid of indigenous origins; it creates not only a new flow of goods and a new kind of trade, but also creates new possibilities of further economic and noneconomic developments. This third stage of Arusha economic evolution will perhaps, in the long run, become something of a transitional phase between the traditional economy with its emphasis on subsistence and a more rationalized system of production and exchange in a different social system. In this third stage the Arusha remain somewhere between the two: by intention, they have by no means abandoned traditionalism—far from it, in fact—and yet they are turning away from it because of necessity, and increasingly by choice.

CHAPTER 17

Livestock Markets Among the Iraqw of Northern Tanganyika

BY E. H. WINTER

The Iraqw, who live in the highlands above the western escarpment of the Rift Valley in the Mbulu District of Tanganyika's Northern Province, are closely related on linguistic grounds to the Gorowa who also live in Mbulu District and the Alawa and Burungi of Kondoa-Irangi District to the south. More distant connections can be traced to the Mbugu of Lushoto District. Beyond this their affinities are a matter of dispute; some linguists, notably Greenberg, maintain that they are southern outliers of the Cushitic group while others deny this and consider the Iraqw cluster to be an independent language family.

The Iraqw are increasing in number at a very rapid rate. In 1948, when the first accurate census was carried out in Tanganyika, they numbered slightly more than 100,000. Only nine years later in 1957 when a second census was taken the population had increased to more than 130,000. There are grounds for believing that this rather remarkable rate of increase has been in operation for the last few decades.

In order to accommodate this expanding population and in order to exploit new grazing grounds, the Iraqw have pushed out from their homeland and have occupied an increasingly larger territory. Until the latter part of the nineteenth century it would appear that they were confined for the most part to the small area known as Kainam. Since then they have settled new land to the north, south and west. The major movements have been to the north and in particular to the south, westward expansion having been limited by the increasingly arid conditions and thick tsetse-infested bush encountered in that direction. The Iraqw have occupied all the country for some 50 miles north of Kainam up to the boundaries of the European-owned farms at the foot of Mt. Oldeani and the line formed by the edge of the forest covering the slopes of Ngorongoro crater. In the south they have penetrated new areas even farther afield. Many of them have entered the country of the Barabaig and a number of them have emigrated to the Gorowa country.

The history of the Iraqw is rather prosaic. In the pre-European period, they constituted a small, non-aggressive group dwelling in a favorable highland area, their chief fear being the ever present threat of a cattle raid by the warlike Masai, whose proximity, however, was at least partly responsible for sparing the Iraqw from contact with the slave trade. The Germans arrived in the area near the end of the nineteenth century, although a government officer was not stationed in the Iraqw country itself until the first decade of this century. During the first World War political control passed into the hands of the British. European administrators devised a hierarchical system of chieftanship culminating in a Paramount Chief for the political control of this previously acephalous society.

The Iraqw who live in dispersed homesteads as is common in East Africa, practice a mixed pastoral-agricultural economy. The principal subsistence crop is maize, except in those areas which are too dry for its successful cultivation; there it is replaced by millets and sorghum, more drought-resistant grains. Cattle, sheep, goats and donkeys are kept, cattle being valued mainly for their milk and the prestige which their ownership confers, while sheep and goats are important primarily as sources of meat. Donkeys, of which there are relatively few, are used exclusively as pack animals. While elsewhere in Tanganyika among people whose economies can be classified as pastoral-agricultural one may nevertheless find many homesteads without cattle, this is not the case among the Iraqw where every house has a herd, however small.

The part of northern Tanganyika in which the Iraqw live is a very complicated area in ethnic terms; in fact it is one of the most complex in all of Africa. To the east of the Iraqw are the Bantu-speaking Mbugwe. The Nilo-Hamitic-speaking Masai live to the north and to the east as well. In the south are the Barabaig whose language, while it is Nilo-Hamitic, is only distantly related to that of the Masai. To the west, in the Eyasi Depression, live a small number of Click-speaking Hadzapi. Out in the Rift Valley around the foot of Mt. Ufiome and in the high country to the south of it live the Gorowa who are very similar to the Iraqw in language and general way of life.

The complexity of the ethnic situation is matched by that of the topography. The area is characterized by sudden and violent contrasts as a result of the presence of the Rift Valley and of volcanic peaks such as Hanang, Ufiome and Oldeani. Iraqw-occupied Kainam and Mbugwe are only a few miles apart. Indeed, from many places in Kainam, which lies above the western escarpment of the Rift, one can see clearly the houses of the Mbugwe on the floor of the valley far below. Despite the proximity of the two areas, the fact that one is below the escarpment while the other is above it causes astonishing differences. Mbugwe suffers from intense heat, while Kainam is always cool and sometimes cold. Kainam receives a high rainfall and as a result is perpetually green, while Mbugwe is arid and for much of the year is almost totally devoid of vegetation. These variations are not confined to territories inhabited by different tribes. Within the Iraqw country itself one finds that the rainfall received by one locality may be twice as much as that received by another only four or five miles further west.

In aboriginal times, as well as today, the various ethnic groups inhabiting the region have exhibited great diversity in the fundamental nature of their economic modes of adaptation. Two groups, the Masai and the Barabaig, are purely pastoral, while the Hadzapi provide one of the very few examples of a hunting and gathering society to be found in East Africa. The Iraqw, Gorowa and Mbugwe all combine agriculture with herding. On the agricultural side of their economies one finds considerable variation from one group to another in terms of such things as the identity of the staple crop; the Mbugwe for instance have depended traditionally upon sorghum, while the Iraqw have concentrated upon maize. These differing subsistence patterns can be related to environmental differences but the relationships are by no means exact. It is true that the pastoral Masai and the hunting and gathering Hadzapi inhabit dry areas, while the Iraqw in their well-watered homeland of Kainam depended for the bulk of their food upon agriculture. On the other hand, the Mbugwe have long practiced agriculture under very disadvantageous conditions in country which is as dry as most parts of Masailand. Again, those Iraqw who have moved into new and drier areas have continued their traditional agricultural activities and many Iraqw are now cultivating fields in areas formerly used exclusively for grazing by the Barabaig. To put the matter briefly, the principal determinant in most areas is the cultural tradition of the people living there with environmental conditions exerting only a secondary influence. Thus, for example, if in a given locality one finds an Iraqw-speaking group of people, it is certain that they will be practicing agriculture while if one finds a group of Barabaig-speaking people in similar country, one will find them leading a purely pastoral existence.

Given the great environmental differences which were to be found within a relatively small region—a region unlike many parts of Africa where one can travel for great distances without observing any but the slightest variations in such things as the topography, rainfall and dominant types of vegetation—and given the circumstance that the various groups inhabiting the region did in fact have markedly different economies, it would seem that basic factors were present which would have led to the development of a large volume of trade and to the establishment of markets. Although a certain amount of external trade did take place, a large-scale system of inter-tribal exchange did not develop, and markets did not appear. Despite the differences between the various tribal economies, they did not become specialized parts of a larger interdependent regional economy. The Masai, for example, did not concentrate upon livestock management in order to obtain agricultural produce from their neighbors in return for cattle or small stock. Instead, they desired and managed to live exclusively upon the milk, meat and blood supplied by their herds. It was their neighbors' cattle, not their grain which they desired and these they attempted to obtain not by trade but by armed raids. Most of the trade which did take place in the past occurred not because people were attempting to take advantage of their particular positions in relation to the factors of production as in a market-oriented economy, but because people were short of food as the result of crop failure. In such an event the people living in an area where the crops had failed would seek out people in a more favored area in order to exchange livestock for grain. Even today, when the government has made itself responsible for the relief of famine areas, the Iraqw continue to stress the value of having livestock which can be exchanged for grain in time of need. Transactions of this sort always took place on an individual basis. An Mbugwe or an Iraqw in search of grain in the territory of the other group would seek out an individual with whom he had some previous contact or who had been recommended to him by a relative, neighbor or friend.

At the present time there is a considerable movement of grain within the confines of the Iraqw country as the result of the introduction of a cash economy and the occupation of new and climatically diversified areas. However, despite the fact that markets for livestock and agricultural produce to be exported from the area have been organized by the government, similar arrangements have not come into being to channel exchange among the Iraqw themselves. A major reason inhibiting the development of a system of internal markets is the concern of the Iraqw with ritual purity. If a man dies, for instance, his house becomes ritually impure. If other people were to use grain from his house they too would become ritually impure and as a result they would find themselves endangered by the supernatural world. Consequently, an Iraqw would never consider obtaining grain from someone in a market place when he was unaware of the ritual status of the seller's household.

Among the Iraqw the most important transactions have always been those involving cattle. Although they depend primarily upon their agricultural activities for their subsistence, they are far more interested in their livestock than they are in their crops. It has been mentioned that all homesteads have herds attached to them, but this is not because all householders own more or less equivalent numbers of livestock. Instead, this situation is due to the existence of certain arrangements by which stock are transferred from one person to another and which permit people who do not own cattle to acquire them or at least the use of them. Most transactions take the form of simple loans. A man without cattle can borrow a cow from a stock owner. In this case the borrower has the responsibility for the care of the cow, in return for which he receives the right to the use of its milk. The lender has the right to reclaim the cow at any time, or to transfer it to a third person. Should it die, the owner has the sole right to the meat and the hide, although, as is often the case, if the lender and the borrower live at a distance from one another, making it impractical for the owner to distribute the meat, the borrower may do so. The latter is obliged, though, to keep the hide and give it to the owner as soon as possible, if for no other reason than to prove that the cow did in fact die. This arrangement is thought to benefit both parties and not merely the poor man, for the owner of a number of cattle is loath to keep all of them in one place for fear that a sudden but localized catastrophe such as an epidemic or, in the past, a cattle raid might wipe out the entire herd. By lending cattle to others he is able to distribute his herd in a number of different places. Furthermore, a man who owns a large number of cattle is unable to keep all of them at his own homestead in any case. The Iraqw do not build kraals in which the cattle are kept at night in the fashion of the Masai or the Barabaig and many other East African peoples. Instead, one room in the house is set aside for their use and all of them are driven inside for the night. This of course sets an upper limit to the number of cattle which can be maintained at any particular homestead, and a man who has more than this number is obliged to commit some of them to the care of others.

A second type of loan permits a man without cattle to acquire the nucleus of a herd of his own or to expand a small but already existent herd. Under the terms of this arrangement a man borrows a cow from its owner. He takes it to his own homestead and waits until it produces a heifer which then becomes his property. Once the calf has been weaned, the cow and any bullocks to which it may have given birth are returned to the lender. Traditionally, the borrower paid the lender in grain or in small stock. Today the owner is usually paid in cash, 60 to 80 shillings being considered a fair price.

At the present time, while each household attempts to make itself self-sufficient in terms of its basic subsistence needs, the Iraqw are simultaneously involved in the modern cash economy of the territory. Such involvement is unavoidable because every adult, able-bodied man is required to pay a tax which amounts in most cases to 24 shillings a year. A more positive incentive for the acquisition of cash is provided by the fact that the use of cotton clothing is almost universal, with the exception of a few old women and very young children—although some younger women continue to wear the traditional skin garments while they are working about the house. Again, money is needed for such things as the odd hoe, trinkets, oil for a small lamp, beer, etc. As the desire for education spreads, the problem of obtaining money to pay the fees demanded by both mission and government schools becomes more acute.

This general state of affairs is, of course, not unique to the Iraqw; with the possible exception of a few hunters and gatherers, all Africans in Tanganyika are involved in a cash economy. Broadly speaking, there are three main methods by which Africans can obtain cash. They can go away to the European-owned estates or mines, or to the towns, and seek wage employment; they can grow a cash crop for export; or they can produce something for which there is a market within Tanganyika itself. Although in any given tribe one may find individuals who employ different methods for the acquisition of cash, one usually finds that a particular tribal group has made a characteristic type of adjustment to the situation.

In the nineteenth century the primary exports from what is now Tanganyika were ivory and the Africans themselves, as slaves. Today the modern sector of the economy is based primarily upon three export crops: sisal, which is grown entirely upon alien-owned estates; coffee, which is grown both by Europeans and by Africans; and cotton, which is grown exclusively by Africans. The growth of European estates devoted to the production of export crops, a process begun by the Germans and fostered by the British, has given rise to considerable employment opportunities for the African population because these estates depend for their operation primarily upon large numbers of relatively unskilled workers. Again, the expansion of government activities and services, a process which has been greatly accelerated in the postwar era, has brought into being a large number of wage-paying positions, as has the rise of the towns—themselves responses to the extension of the cultivation of cash crops—government activity and associated commercial and transport development. As a result, some 400,000 Africans are now employed.

The introduction of a cash economy and the growth and diversification of the economy of the territory based primarily upon the production of the key export crops has brought into being an internal demand for certain products of which that for beef is of particular importance in the present context. The estates are required by law to give their workers a certain amount of meat a week. Wage earners in the towns are in a position to buy beef, as are people such as the Chagga who live on the slopes of Kilimanjaro and who have become wealthy—by African standards—through the production of coffee.

The position of the Iraqw can be examined within this broad framework. Opportunities for employment are readily available to them. The northern frontier of the Iraqw country is formed by a row of European-owned estates at the foot of Mt. Oldeani. In addition, there are a number of other European estates situated within a few hours walk of many parts of the Iraqw country on the floor of the Rift Valley. Although a certain number of Iraqw work on the estates in the north where the country is high and the climate cool, they refuse to work on the estates at the foot of the escarpment because they dislike the heat which they encounter there and because they are afraid that they will become ill if they remain there for any length of time, a fear which is apparently not without foundation. Wage employment, then, plays a minor role in the modern cash economy of the Iraqw.

The Iraqw do not grow either coffee or cotton, the two most important cash crops grown for the export market by Africans. They do, however, cultivate white potatoes, onions and wheat, all of which have been introduced since the arrival of the Europeans. The Iraqw do not eat white potatoes or onions and they do not make flour from wheat. Instead, they sell all of the produce to the local Indian traders. Relatively small quantities of these crops are grown, the main reason being that each of them can be grown only in certain restricted areas. Cash cropping has developed on a substantial scale only in one area in the northernmost part of the Iraqw country. In this area, most of which has been occupied by the Iraqw only since the last war, conditions are suitable for the production of wheat, and large acreages have been devoted to its cultivation, some of the land being worked by tractor. The marketing of agricultural produce is supervised by the government. Produce can only be bought and sold at specified points; an Indian trader, for example, is forbidden to buy onions from an Iraqw in his field or at his house. At each of the few trading centers where there are a half dozen or more Asian-owned shops, one finds a small open-sided building where the merchants buy produce from the Iraqw after it has been weighed on a government-owned set of scales operated by an African employee of the Mbulu Native Authority. These buying points, which are in operation on a daily basis during the season when the local crops are being harvested, are seldom attended by more than a few dozen people, and they attract relatively little attention. The merchant, when he has a large enough amount on hand to warrant the trip, transports the produce by truck to the resale point, which is usually Arusha.

The present-day cash economy of the Iraqw rests upon the sale of livestock for consumption within Tanganyika, rather than upon wage employment or upon the sale of cash crops. In 1957 the Iraqw sold just under 15,000 head of cattle, 11,500 goats and more than 1,000 sheep. From these sales they received some $400,000, the great bulk of it, over $360,000, being paid for the cattle. The Iraqw have been fortunate in that during the last two decades there has been a tremendous upward trend in the prices which they have received for their stock. For example, the average price in U.S. dollars per head of cattle advanced from $3.64 in 1934 to $7.00 in 1944, to $11.06 in 1950, and to $24.69 in 1957. Despite the fact that the prices received have increased spectacularly, the amount received per person from the sale of livestock remains very low. With a total population of over 130,000, a sum of $400,000 averages only some $3.00 per person.[1]

The livestock markets, in addition to playing a much more important role in the local economy, are far more interesting and socially important affairs than are the produce markets. While livestock markets are held throughout the year, in any given area they occur at the most once a month—which gives them the status of special occasions. In addition. they are intrinsically much more exciting events. One sack of potatoes is much like another and a seller usually knows within close limits the amount of money which he will receive for it. With cattle, however, a number of variables are involved and a seller never knows, except within a very wide range, how much he may actually be offered for his beast. Furthermore, very large sums of money by local standards, often several hundred shillings, may be at stake when a single animal is sold. Thus the sale of an ox is a matter for much anxious speculation beforehand and a matter to be mulled over long afterwards. Thousands of people congregate at the livestock markets, many of whom have little or no direct interest in the market itself. At the markets of Mbulu and Dongobesh, for instance, it is common to find crowds of 5,000 or more people. These are almost the only occasions upon which really large groups of Iraqw are to be found together. Weddings or dances seldom attract more than 100 or 200 people. Catholic church services on the great holidays

(1) Only aggregate figures can be given. Iraqw are extremely secretive about their stock. A man's sons, wife, and brothers usually do not know what he actually owns. Because of the loan system, the number of cattle at the homestead means nothing As a result, the only reliable figure is the amount of cash received by the tribe as a whole

such as Christmas and Easter draw large numbers of people, but even these events cannot compare with the markets. The nucleus of the gathering consists of a fairly large number of men interested in the market itself. In addition to those who bring stock for sale, there are those who attend in order to see how the prices are running. If the prices seem favorable on the first day they may decide to return home and bring one of their animals to be sold on the second day. Additional attractions are provided by the goods which are on sale in the immediate vicinity of the auction ring. There are sellers of cloth and of sandals made from old automobile tires, men selling spears, purveyors of soft drinks, and men cooking bits of meat on skewers over open fires. In houses nearby, although not at the market itself, large quantities of beer brewed for the occasion are for sale.

In earlier days, buyers of livestock came to the Iraqw country as individuals and went from house to house looking for people who might be induced to sell one or more head of stock. The British government brought an end to this system by organizing a series of markets. The first step consisted of designating certain places as markets and then setting up a schedule of days on which markets would be held, so that potential buyers and sellers alike could plan their movements ahead of time. There are now six places at which markets are held. At the four most important places, a market is held every month. At the others, they are held every two or three months. The major markets are open for two or three days at a time. A circuit has been arranged for the convenience of the buyers, with the northern markets being held first and then the southern ones, after which markets are held in the Gorowa and Barabaig countries. The schedule is so arranged that it does not conflict with the markets in Masailand, many of which are attended by the same buyers who frequent the Iraqw markets. In recent years a number of structures have been built to facilitate the operation of the markets. All of them follow the same general plan. An auction ring is constructed which is enclosed by stone walls five or six feet high; adjacent to it are pens for holding the animals which are about to be put up for auction and for those which have been sold.

The markets are supervised by a European government official, a Livestock Marketing Officer, who is employed by the territorial Veterinary Department, and who is permanently stationed in Mbulu District. Assisting him is a small African staff employed by the Mbulu Native Treasury. The important members of this group are the market master, who is in direct charge of the marketing procedures, the auctioneer and his assistant, and the clerks who record the sales, make out receipts, make payments, etc.

Of the dozen to twenty buyers at a given market, about half a dozen are usually Somalis, the others being Africans from other parts of Tanganyika. Each buyer employs three or four men who drive the animals which have been purchased to the place where they are to be resold, usually Arusha. All of the buyers hold government licences for the purpose, an unlicensed man being unable to participate. At some of the markets, for instance the one at Dongobesh, Indian traders leave their shops for the day and take their goods and often a sewing machine as well to the grounds where they conduct business from within a roped-off enclosure. They do not, however, act as buyers, this being the one major form of trade in which they do not participate.

As has been mentioned, cattle being offered for sale are held in a pen adjacent to the auction ring. Five or six head are admitted to the ring at a time. The auctioneer then taps one of the animals with his stick and the bidding is open. The bidding proceeds at a rapid pace. As in many countries where one finds similar types of auctions with professional buyers in attendance, many of the bids are made by esoteric signals, such as winks or, in one case which I noted, by sticking out the tongue. It is thus very difficult for an outsider to follow the bidding in detail. When the final bid has been made, the seller is told the price and he can then either accept it or witdraw his beast. This provision has been made in order to protect the sellers from price-fixing on the part of the buyers as a group. In the case of any particular animal, although the auctioneer and the buyers all have very shrewd ideas of its eventual price, bidding is opened at a low figure and only reaches the final amount after a large number of bids. While this procedure is time-consuming, the buyers believe that it causes the owner to be more willing to accept the final price. Once the owner has agreed to the sale, the animal is branded with the mark of the buyer. Then the auctioneer touches another animal on its back and bidding begins again. This continues until all of the cattle in the ring have been auctioned off; then they are taken out of the ring and replaced by a new set of animals. Once a sale has been concluded, the seller is given a slip by a clerk who has recorded the amount of the final bid. The man then takes the paper to another clerk who makes payment on behalf of the particular buyer, all of the buyers having deposited sums with him for this purpose.

Cattle buying is a highly skilled occupation. The cattle are not weighed nor are they touched by the buyers; the buyers must evaluate them from their vantage points on the wall surrounding the ring. The state of the market in Arusha and elsewhere where resale may take place has of course to be kept in mind, but—more than this— the buyer must take into consideration the fact that an animal which he buys at an Iraqw market must be driven for several days, at least, in the course of which it is bound to lose a considerable amount of weight. If the animal shows any sign of illness there is the risk that it may die on the journey before it reaches Arusha.

Livestock sold by the Iraqw supplies part of the meat demanded by the populations of the two sizable towns, Arusha and Moshi, which have come into existence in recent decades, and the European estates around the two mountains, Meru and Kilimanjaro, as well as those in the great sisal area closer to the coast along the Tanga railway. In addition, a considerable amount of meat is consumed by the Chagga living on Mt. Kilimanjaro.

Another important aspect of the livestock markets is the role which they have played in the destocking program. It was apparent to government officials for some time that the Iraqw pastures were overstocked and that erosion was becoming a serious problem. The herds were increasing at a very rapid rate, due partially to the virtual elimination of Masai cattle raids but more importantly to the introduction of modern veterinary practices. Drugs were made available to the herdsmen which brought about the recovery of many animals which otherwise would have died. Of even greater significance were the measures taken to prevent epidemics; all cattle, for instance, were inoculated against rinderpest, a disease which in the past periodically decimated the herds here as well as elsewhere in East Africa.

After the last war, an ambitious program was drawn up in an attempt to solve the grave problems faced by the Iraqw. The scheme was supported by a grant of more than $250,000 from the Colonial Welfare and Development Fund. This program, which is still in operation although the original grant has long since been exhausted, has a number of features such as the introduction of improved agricultural practices and the opening of new pastures and new areas for settlement by the eradication of the tsetse fly and the development of water supplies. However, the important aspect of the plan in the present context has been the attempt to radically reduce by compulsory sales the number of livestock utilizing the pastures. This was a very daring proposal when it was first made since previous attempts elsewhere in East Africa to implement similar programs had ended in failure due to the resistance of the stock owners. Among the Iraqw, a long propaganda campaign resulted in the acceptance of the plan by a number of the most influential elders. The livestock attached to each house were counted and the householder was required to sell a given number. If he had cattle on loan, it was his responsibility to arrange matters with the owner. One source of anxiety to the planners was the possibility that putting large numbers of cattle on the market might depress the price level. Fortunately, the inauguration of the program coincided with a rising demand for meat resulting primarily from the high prices being received in other areas for the sale of the export crops. After an initial reduction in the size of the herds following the full implementation of the plan in 1950, the government has attempted to keep the numbers down by ordering sales when the number of livestock brought on the market voluntarily is considered insufficient to offset the natural rate of increase in the herds.

In conclusion, we have seen that the livestock markets are the main way in which the Iraqw are integrated into the modern cash economy of Tanganyika. European-introduced currency, political stability, and cash cropping have brought the Iraqw into economic interdependence with people in other parts of the territory. The markets provide a method by which the demand for meat on the part of those engaged in new specialized parts of the modern economy are met in part. Furthermore they have provided a mechanism by means of which the government has attempted to restore an equilibrium between the carrying capacities of the Iraqw pastures and the number of livestock actually using them.

CHAPTER 18

Economic Exchange in a Sonjo Village

BY ROBERT F. GRAY[1]

A Sonjo village comes very near to being economically self-sufficient in that nearly all material goods are produced within the community from natural resources belonging to the village. Thus, if a village with its own lands and resources were to be isolated from the outside world, under normal circumstances the basic economic life of the village would be little disturbed and no serious hardships would result. A few goods, it is true, are exchanged between different Sonjo villages; these consist mainly in the transfer of goats as brideprice. But since the first marriage of a Sonjo woman is nearly always within her own village, intervillage marriage is limited to women who have been divorced.

The Sonjo have no trade relations with other tribes except the neighboring Masai, and this trade is very restricted. It might be expected when an agricultural society and a pastoral society are found in juxtaposition that substantial trade relations would exist between them, with products of the soil being exchanged for livestock and dairy products. This, however, is not found in the case of the Sonjo and Masai. The only agricultural products which the Sonjo regularly trade with the Masai, and these on a small scale, are the elongated gourds used by the Masai (and also the Sonjo) as milk containers. These gourds are not raised at the Sonjo villages, but at temporary settlements or seasonal camps on the shore of Lake Natron. An individual who produces a crop of these gourds exchanges them for goats with other Sonjo and also Masai. The prevailing rate of exchange was eight gourds for one goat. The Masai also exchange goats for Sonjo women and children, though it is difficult to estimate the volume of this exchange. It is forbidden by the government, and such transactions are now carried out secretly. Sonjo smiths formerly obtained iron from Masai smiths in exchange for goats, but at present they use only imported trade wire or scrap iron. All this trade external to a village is so small that it can be neglected for the purposes of this paper, which will be concerned with the economics of the village itself.

(1) I acknowledge my debt to the Ford Foundation for a research grant making possible the field work upon which this paper is based. The grant was administered by the Institute of Current World Affairs.

Within the village, rights to resources and goods are allocated to individuals and family groups, and these small groups are the basic units of economic production and consumption. To a very large extent, the family units individually produce the goods that they consume. This segment of Sonjo economy can be termed the *subsistence economy*. If we think only in terms of material needs, the subsistence economy alone appears to be almost adequate for the existence of the society. There is to be sure a small group of people who produce specialized goods—specifically, ironware and pottery—which circulate in the village in exchange for ordinary subsistence goods. There is no market place in any Sonjo village at which this exchange takes place. All the ironware is made on special order and paid for with an agreed quantity of subsistence goods—usually field produce, since the smiths and potters do not cultivate. Pottery may also be made on special order, but a potter normally keeps a small store of standard utensils at her home to be supplied to purchasers as required. This exchange, however, accounts for only a small proportion of the total volume of goods exchanged between individuals in the villages. This larger volume of goods exchange, which does not seem to be essential for the satisfaction of immediate material needs, will constitute the central problem of the present study.

ENVIRONMENTAL AND HISTORICAL FACTORS

Two outstanding factors—one environmental and the other historical—have limited the cultural alternatives available to the Sonjo and have strongly influenced the forms taken by their social and economic institutions. The crucial environmental factor is climate, which is so arid that irrigation is necessary for the cultivation of crops. The crucial historical factor is the incursion of the Masai into Sonjo territory some two centuries ago, one of the few events in Sonjo history that can be definitely ascertained. These two factors must be considered briefly in their relation to the economic system.

From Lake Natron, which lies in the Rift Valley of northern Tanganyika, the land rises to the west in steep escarpments. Between these escarpments and the elevated Serengeti Plain to the southwest, the country is dissected and rough. This is the habitat of the Sonjo, whose settlements form an enclave of Bantu agriculturalists well in the interior of the territory of the pastoral Masai Tribe. Because of the low rainfall in the region, permanent agricultural settlements would not be possible except for the existence of a number of small valleys containing streams and springs which can be used for irrigation. The six villages of the Sonjo occupy these valleys, each village having its separate supply of irrigation water and being organized as an autonomous political unit. Two of the villages adjoin one another, while the others are separated by distances of four to sixteen miles. The total Sonjo population, according to the 1957 census, is about 4,500. The villages vary in size from about 120 to 300 houses, and the population is distributed among the villages in approximately the same proportion as the houses. All the villages are much alike in construction and economic organization, and with one exception they can be considered as identical for the purposes of this study. This exception is the village of Kura, which differs from the others in being situated on a large stream that provides more irrigation water than is needed in agriculture. However, the amount of land to which this water can be applied is sharply limited by high embankments. At all the other villages, water is scarce. Therefore the pattern of water control and land tenure found at the village of Kura differs in some respects from the others, and this village will be excluded from the following discussion.

The Sonjo were presumably living in their present general location when the Masai came down from the north and made contact with them. It is extremely improbable that they would have migrated into the region after the Masai were already there. We have no evidence as to their earlier mode of settlement, but at least since the arrival of the Masai the Sonjo have dwelt in villages which are fortified with encircling hedges of closely planted thorn trees. These hedges are no longer intact, because the danger of Masai raids was removed with the pacification of the country. The former importance of the fortifications is suggested by the fact that the remaining portions of the hedges are now treated as sacred groves; the village gates of sturdy timbers are still maintained, and they are regularly repaired as a ritual task at each initiation of a new age set.

The joint effect of their geographical environment and their warlike neighbors was to place the Sonjo in almost complete isolation from other Bantu tribes for a long period of time. A few culture traits were borrowed from the Masai, particularly in the field of military organization, but their social institutions developed in essential independence from external influences. Their agricultural practices and technology remain archaic to this day. According to Sonjo traditions, they originally kept cattle, but discontinued the practice for supernatural reasons. More likely they were plundered of their herds by the cattle-loving Masai. Goats and sheep, however, are still kept in quite large numbers and play an important role in the economic system.

ECONOMIC RESOURCES

The basic resources of Sonjoland are pastures and irrigable land, though certain products of the forests are also important economically. The available pasture land is normally ample for Sonjo needs. Occasionally in very dry years there are disagreements over the use of choice stretches of pasture which are located midway between two villages, but they are only mild quarrels. The people deny any history of armed conflicts between villages resulting from pasture disputes. The pastures attached to a village are treated as common grazing grounds and individuals are not given exclusive rights to any part of it. The principal economic product of the pastures is goats; a few sheep are also raised, but for most economic purposes they are not distinguished from goats. A goat owner divides his animals into two lots: the young goats and their mothers are kept at the homestead within the village, while the rest of the herd is sent to a goat camp which may be located as far as six miles from the village.

Goats play two separate roles in the economic system. Their use as exchange commodities will be discussed later. In the subsistence economy they are regarded as a source of consumable goods. The milk of female goats, and the butter made from it, are significant items in Sonjo diet, and goat flesh is the main source of meat. The skins of goats are used for garments and various kinds of equipment. The Sonjo have no basketry; instead, they make bags and containers of leather. Raw skins have little economic value. They are not normally traded outside the village even though they seem to be in plentiful supply. There is not much use that can be made of a skin until a good deal of labor has been expended on it in preparing a leather garment or utensil.

Two kinds of arable land are cultivated by the Sonjo. These are planted in opposite seasons of the year and cultivated by somewhat different techniques. Every family must have plots in both kinds of land for its subsistence. The most valued land, because it is more reliable in producing crops, is the alluvial valley bottom; this is cultivated during the dry season entirely by irrigation. The land sloping gently up from the valley bottom is cultivated during the rainy season and normally requires both rainfall and irrigation. Crops on this land fluctuate from year-to-year and occasionally fail, because in dry years both rainfall and irrigation water may be insufficient to bring the crop to maturity. The bottom land alone seems to produce enough food to prevent actual starvation, and the elders that I questioned could not recall a year of outright famine. Nevertheless, there is only a small margin of safety in the water supply even in a "normal" year, which the year of my visit was considered to be.

The irrigation water comes from two sources. The water flowing from the highlands in small streams is diverted into a system of canals and applied to the higher land as supplementary moisture during the rainy season. These streams diminish in flow during the dry season and may even dry up. The second water source is a series of springs flowing from the base of the escarpments bordering the valleys on one side. This source provides the basic water supply for dry-season irrigation. It is just barely sufficient for crops in dry years and is carefully conserved. The spring water is a scarce and essential resource, and the springs themselves are regarded as sacred. This water is distributed to individual users by means of a system of several different categories of irrigation rights which are obtained through payment of goods. As will be explained later, the system of water distribution results in a considerable amount of goods exchange in a Sonjo village.

The rainy season crops are sorghum, millet, pigeon peas, and several kinds of beans. The principal crop in the dry season is normally sweet potatoes, but if the preceding wet season crop has been small, a proportionately larger amount of sorghum is planted in the valley bottom to replenish stores of this staple food. Sweet potatoes are consumed soon after being dug up, but the harvesting season extends over a number of months. Grain crops are stored in the houses and used as needed. Harvested grain above subsistence needs, which is seldom very much, may be exchanged for other commodities.

Among the forest products utilized by the Sonjo, the most important are building materials, beehives, and honey. Timbers and withes for housebuilding are usually gathered by the individual who needs them, helped by his close relatives. Thatching grass is cut in a common village meadow reserved against grazing for that purpose. The houses themselves are always kept within the family group, and thus are not regarded as exchange commodities. Beehives, which are laboriously carved from lengths of thick hardwood logs, constitute the most valuable form of moveable property next to livestock. Some men possess as many as 60 beehives, while nearly everyone has at least 10. There is always some demand for extra beehives, and they represent a useful reserve of goods which can be mobilized and exchanged for other goods, usually goats, when the special need arises. The reason for the high regard for beehives is that honey is much desired. A little honey is eaten by children and women as a sweet, but its main use is in making a kind of mead, which is the only alcoholic drink made by the Sonjo. The quantity of honey available varies from year to year but is usually less than the amount desired, so that a lively exchange of honey for other commodities takes place.

Iron ore is the one essential resource entirely lacking in Sonjo territory. Iron has always been obtained from Masai smiths, usually in the form of broken swords and spears which are reworked by Sonjo smiths. Iron is used sparingly by the Sonjo—for making arrow points, axes, knives, and short swords, but not for cultivating implements. Deposits of pottery clay are conveniently located near the different villages. Pottery is used for little except cooking utensils. Storage bins for grain are of leather, and water is carried in gourds. Large round gourds for storing water, and also for making various household bowls, are raised locally. A different type of gourd, narrow and elongated, is preferred for carrying water up the steep paths from the streams to the villages. These gourds are raised at the marshy estuaries of streams flowing into Lake Natron by colonies of Sonjo who camp there temporarily for that purpose. Lake Natron is also the major source of salt, and during the dry season Sonjo men make expeditions to the lake to gather the crusted salt from the dry lake bed.

LABOR

When considered as a labor force for exploiting the natural resources, the people of a Sonjo village are divided into several groups with different functions. We can first dispose of the specialists—the smiths and potters—who are a relatively small group organized as an endogamous clan. They were formerly present at all villages, but are now located at only two villages. A sharp decrease in the demand for locally made ironware has been brought about in recent years by the availability of cheap imported knives and axes. The work of smiths is now almost limited to making arrow points and swords, and the work of making the latter is simplified because blank bars of steel, specially manufactured for this purpose in Germany for the Masai trade, are now readily available: the smiths have only to shape and sharpen the blades and haft them. The smiths and potters occupy a pariah position in Sonjo society. Not only marriage but any form of sexual intercourse with other Sonjo is strictly prohibited. They are not allowed to own or cultivate land, but are permitted to keep goats. They obtain vegetable food from ordinary Sonjo in exchange for their manufactured products.

The first labor division of the general population is on sexual lines. The women are the cultivators of the tribe and there is no formal subdivision within this group. Young girls accompany their mothers to the fields and gradually learn the art of tilling the soil as they grow to maturity. They continue in this back-breaking occupation all their lives until they become too old for it. The only agricultural implement is a digging stick made of very hard wood. During the busy season a husband is expected to resharpen his wife's digging stick daily, but the men take no part in the actual cultivation of the crops. Each woman is responsible for cultivating her own fields; she may carry out the whole cycle of seasonal operation alone or with the help of her daughters. Usually, however, a group of women band together for the hard work of digging up the ground for a new seed bed; they work together and move from field to field until all the work is finished.

From the viewpoint of the men, the control over the labor of a woman is a valuable economic asset. Female labor is one of the three essential components in the agricultural economy of a household, the other two being ownership of plots of land and rights to irrigation water. Since able-bodied women usually are married, the rights to their labor are vested in their husbands. The marriage system involves the payment of a brideprice, and in return for this payment a man obtains rights to his wife's labor along with other rights in her (Gray 1960).

The division of labor among males is based on age-grades, of which three are formally recognized by the Sonjo. An initiation of boys into the warrior age-grade takes place every seven years, the initiated boys being between the ages of about ten and sixteen. Up to that time the young boys are entrusted with the task of herding goats. Very young boys tend the small herds that are kept in the village, and thus learn the rudiments of this work. After the age six or seven, boys are usually sent out to the goat camps to take care of the pasture herds, and from then on spend most of their time in the field herding. The goat camps consist of sturdy structures designed to protect the goats against leopards and hyenas at night. There the herd boys lead a life that is so separated from the rest of the village that they may almost be said to possess a subculture of their own. The younger boys are taught goat lore and fieldcraft by the older ones, with only minimum supervision by adults. Food is normally brought to their camps once a day, but they are expected to supplement their diet through hunting and trapping birds and small animals. They are held responsible for the safety of the goats under their charge, and are punished for culpable neglect of duty or for gross misjudgment. This herding system serves two general functions for the society as a whole. It provides a labor force and reservoir of technical knowledge for exploiting the natural resources of one of the major economic products—goats. It also serves as a rigorous training school to prepare the herdboys for their future duties as warriors[2].

(2) These boys are actually integrated into the military system by being taught to

After his initiation, a boy serves as a warrior for 14 years, first in the grade of junior warrior and then as senior warrior. The warriors, although they were of vital importance for the survival of the tribe in the days of Masai raids, had almost no participation in exploitative activities. This situation remains virtually unchanged today as regards the subsistence economy. However, many of the warriors now leave the tribal territory and spend several years earning money at various occupations. Through this means, a certain amount of money now enters the villages. This money is mostly used in paying government taxes and purchasing a few items of imported goods. It will be disregarded here, for as yet only a small part of the exchange of goods in a Sonjo village involves money payments.

At the same time that a new group of boys is initiated as junior warriors, the men who had occupied the grade of senior warriors leave the warrior grade and become "elders," and thereafter there are no formal age-based distinctions in the lives of the men. The elders contribute relatively little physical labor to the village economy. The younger men of this group place beehives in trees and gather honey, and some of them spend considerable time hunting and trapping game. For the most part, the elders occupy themselves with operating the irrigation system. Several times a year they turn out as a body to clean and repair the main irrigation furrows. Each man is responsible for keeping the small ditches supplying his own plots in good repair, and of course he carries out the actual flooding of these plots with irrigation water. All this does not involve very much physical labor, but these men spend a tremendous amount of time discussing irrigation problems and making arrangements to obtain shares of irrigation water. The control and administration of the irrigation system is in the hands of a special council of elders, which will be discussed later. Apart from their special duties and prerogatives, however, council members perform the same tasks on their own fields as the other men of the village.

In summary, the Sonjo division of labor, except for smiths and potters, is based solely upon differences of sex and age. It is unrelated to economic classes or political positions. Every domestic group, regardless of its social position or status, at some time in its developmental cycle supplies recruits to each of the different divisions of the labor force.

understand and give the signals indicating the approach of enemies or other dangers. In the old days, the boys at outlying camps would sleep in trees at night to escape capture and give warning in case of a surprise Masai raid; they were trained to give signals by imitating bird or animal cries which were then relayed to the village, so that a company of warriors could come to the rescue. Nowadays it is safe for them to sleep inside the goat shelters, but they still employ signals to warn of attacks by wild animals.

PROPERTY

Generally speaking, property is privately owned among the Sonjo. The only important exception is the building plots upon which houses are built. These are owned communally by clans. Sonjo villages are divided into wards—four to six at different villages—and each ward belongs to a patrilineal, exogamous clan. The house sites within a ward are reserved for the exclusive use of the men of the clan together with their wives and children. The houses of close relatives are usually clustered in one part of a ward, but these individuals can only retain their rights to their plots so long as they actually occupy them. The clan leader, advised by the senior elders of the clan, may allot empty house sites to men who need them, and he adjudicates in any disputes arising over them. The Sonjo villages are all situated on rocky hillsides and they are compactly settled because of the necessity for all houses to be within the perimeter of the defensive palisade. The stony ground is poorly suited for housebuilding and most of the sites have been excavated and leveled at the cost of considerable work. Therefore they are regarded as valuable by the clan.

The other common forms of property are owned by individuals, though only by men, for women do not have ownership rights to property except for small personal possessions. Thus, a piece of property such as a field, a beehive, or a goat, at any given time can be traced in ownership to an individual. The property may be found in the actual possession and use of a son or even a grandson of the owner, but if a question arises concerning its sale or disposal, the proper owner must be dealt with. According to Sonjo law, a man has the ultimate ownership rights in his own property and in all property possessed by his patrilineal descendants for as long as he lives. When he dies, these rights are inherited by his heirs. There are customary rules concerning the rights which his descendants have with regard to possession and use of family property, and also the reciprocal obligation among family members. This need not concern us here, for in all economic transactions with other people of the village a lineage group is represented by the lineage head, who is the legal owner of all its property. It should be remembered that men of the warrior age-grades stand essentially outside the economic system of the village, and thus are not in position to exercise any property rights actively; neither do they have any traditional economic obligations. However, in cases where a warrior earns money in the outside world and then comes home, his father can take possession of this money and any other property the young man may have acquired.

LAND AND WATER

In speaking of land ownership among the Sonjo, I refer only to land which is normally irrigated; land without irrigation water is useless for agricultural purposes. But although land and water are thus reciprocally and intimately related, they are dealt with separately in the economic system. Plots of land, as we have seen, are individually owned and in most respects are treated in the same way as other forms of property. They can be transferred from owner to owner—but this transfer is subject to special restrictions. Owners sometimes wish to dispose of land because they are not able to utilize it or because they are in urgent need of goats. Other men may wish to acquire more land because of a growing family. The system of land ownership is flexible enough to adapt to these changing circumstances. But the transfer of land does not constitute an outright sale; it is more like a lease transaction. The original owner surrenders his rights to the use of the land in exchange for payment in goats, but retains the right to recover his land at any time upon refunding the payment. In effect, he sells the land but retains an option to buy it back for the same price whenever he wishes. This option is not inherited by his heirs, and when he dies the transfer becomes irrevocable; the new owner then has uncontested rights to the land. These rules seem to safeguard the interests of an owner who really needs all his land, but who is willing to give up part of it temporarily because of a more pressing need for goats, perhaps as brideprice for a son's wife. The idea of pledging land without surrendering its use is unknown among the Sonjo.

Irrigation water is distributed by means of a system which tends to stratify the population into three economic classes. The control of this water is in the hands of a hereditary council of elders—called *wenamiji*—comprised of 16 to 18 members at different villages. The *wenamiji* are organized as a corporate group and come together for formal meetings at frequent intervals—almost daily in seasons of water scarcity. They also perform administrative functions and act as a court of law: in fact they constitute the village government. The *wenamiji* make certain ritual sacrifices as a group, and they collaborate with the tribal priests in arranging community rituals. In turn, religious beliefs and myths provide sanctions for the powers and privileges of the *wenamiji* and add to the legitimacy of their authority. Their main duties, however, are in distributing and regulating irrigation water.

During the dry season while crops are growing, irrigation operations are carried out both day and night. The day is divided into four six-hour periods for purposes of dividing water. The fields require flooding about every two weeks. Each of the *wenamiji* is entitled to one six-hour period of water use during the irrigation cycle, which altogether accounts for fewer than half the total number of periods. The remaining periods are distributed to a class of men, called *wakiama* (sing., *mokiama*), who are required as individuals to pay substantial tribute in goats to the *wenamiji* as a group. After all the available irrigation periods have been distributed, it still leaves the majority of the men of the village with no irrigation rights. This class of men, for whom there is no special native name, may be called "clients." They must obtain their irrigation water by purchasing it from individuals of the other two classes—the *wenamiji* and the *wakiama*. A six-hour period is usually sufficient for irrigating two or three sets of fields; first the person with primary water rights who has been allotted that period waters his own fields; then for the rest of the period the water is used by a client, or perhaps several clients, who pay him for this privilege.

The *wenamiji* obviously derive considerable material returns from their control of irrigation water, but they are said merely to act as custodians of the water supply, which is spoken of as belonging to the whole village. The goats which are paid to them as water tax by the *wakiama* are all supposed to be used in communal sacrifices for the general spiritual benefit of the village, but much of this meat ends up in their own family pots. Some of these goats are turned over to the priests, again with the understanding that they will be offered to God on behalf of the whole village. As individuals, the *wenamiji* profit (as do the *wakiama*) from the sale of secondary water rights to clients. But despite their commanding position as a group in the economic and political systems of the village, not all *wenamiji* are wealthy men, and they are often surpassed by the *wakiama* in ownership of goats, which is the chief native measure of wealth. Since the position is strictly hereditary and is strongly supported by religious sanctions, the *wenamiji* have little need to reinforce their authority and prestige by achieving personal economic power.

The agreement between the *wenamiji* and a *mokiama* whereby the latter is granted primary irrigation rights in return for regular tribute in goats is made secretly—or perhaps confidentially, since all the *wenamiji* are privy to the agreement. Therefore, I found it impossible to make any accurate estimate of the amount of this tribute. It is large enough that only wealthy men are able to pay it, and if a *mokiama* is unable to meet his obligations he loses his privileged position and reverts to that of a client; an affluent client may then take his place as a *mokiama*. Thus the *wakiama* are an impermanent group with a changing membership. The members never organize themselves to act in concert, and the group has no corporate functions. A *mokiama* has greater security in his irrigation rights than a client and enjoys definite prestige from his position, but I cannot say whether he derives a net material return when the tribute which he pays for his primary irrigation rights is balanced against payments made to him by clients for secondary rights.

The clients, a class which includes the majority of the village men, obtain irrigation rights by paying an individual with primary rights an agreed amount of honey or its value equivalent in grain or some other commodity, a separate payment usually being made at each irrigation operation. The amount of the payment during my investigation was about one-third the amount of honey that could be exchanged for a goat. Informants estimate that about six floodings are required during an average season. Thus, an ordinary cultivator pays the equivalent of about two goats for his yearly irrigation water. Some men have plots scattered in different parts of the valley and for each irrigation they must obtain water from several different sources, paying a proportionate fraction of the total payment to each source.

A client is not necessarily attached permanently to any one *wenamiji* or *mokiama,* but may change from one to another. While a client must periodically obtain irrigation water without fail, a man possessing primary rights is anxious to dispose most advantageously of all the water to which he is entitled. Therefore a certain amount of bargaining takes place before the two men come to an agreement. The arrangements that are made, however, must conform to the overall plan of irrigation which the *wenamiji* as an official council have currently decided upon, and this plan changes from time to time. This imposes no great hardship on the more prosperous men, but the indigent members of the community may find it difficult to produce the payment when needed without seriously depleting the subsistence, resources of their families. These men often take the risk of "stealing" water; they flood their fields secretly at night by illegally diverting water from its legitimate destination. Water theft is a common offense to be brought before the *wenamiji* acting as the village court; it is punished with a fine of one goat. The explanation for this relatively lenient penalty seems to be that the whole community would be weakened if a man's crops were destroyed through lack of irrigation simply because he could not pay the fee. A breach of the law is partially condoned if it prevents the loss of a crop.

THE EXCHANGE SYSTEM

Most of the situations involving exchanges of property have already been discussed, or at least mentioned. The total volume of this exchange is quite considerable, though unfortunately very few quantitative data are available. Here I shall review the different kinds of exchanges in their more strictly economic aspects, and attempt to indicate how they are related to one another to form a system. I assume, as I do with respect to any social system, that this system of exchange is in equilibrium, so that the parts are not only related to one another but also that changes in one part of the system are reflected by changes in other parts.

Taking first for consideration the mechanisms—the approved forms of exchange—we find that these are relatively simple for the Sonjo. There are two basic sets of rules governing exchanges, one for land transfers and one for the exchange of other goods. The seller of a piece of land retains specific residual rights in the land, namely the right to buy back the land for its original price at any time during his lifetime. This particular transaction can be said to involve a principle of *recovery option*, which, as we have already noted, has a useful function in the actual situations in which land is exchanged: it preserves an owner's rights in a scarce and highly regarded form of property, while permitting him to sell it when he has pressing, though perhaps temporary, need for additional goats. This principle, however, does not apply in exchanges of other commodities. In these other transactions, when a seller delivers goods to a buyer he has no further claim on the goods; while the buyer must accept the goods without reservations—he receives no guarantee that they will be satisfactory. The exchange transaction in these cases is irrevocable and final.

At first sight this kind of transaction may appear to be "natural" or self-evident, but rules of exchange which are actually quite different in character have been reported from some East African societies, particularly those which raise livestock. I refer, of course, only to traditional economies, not to the segment of these economies that has been assimilated to a market-exchange economy. This statement can be illustrated with an example which seems to be characteristic of several East African societies. The Kikuyu exchange rules are described by Kenyatta as follows:

According to Kikuyu law and custom, if Mr. A bought something from Mr. B for which he paid him four sheep or goats, should any of the animals die before it had a kid, Mr. B had to return the carcass to Mr. A who would replace the dead animal. On the other hand, if Mr. B failed to fulfill the contract for which Mr. A had paid the four sheep, then Mr. A had the right to claim back the original number with their offspring and without paying any compensation to Mr. B for looking after the animals. (Kenyatta 1953 : 218)

The principle governing these Kikuyu rules of exchange can be called the principle of *stipulated guarantee*. Among the Gusii of Kenya this principle is applied more strictly, so that in any exchange of livestock the original owner is held responsible for the animals that he delivers and must replace them if they should die, even though the particular animals had subsequently changed hands in further exchange transactions (Mayer 1950). This principle is not recognized by the Sonjo. The ruling principle in their system is one of *quitclaim exchange:* no guarantee is given by either party in an exchange, and both parties relinquish any further claims to their goods after delivery. The Sonjo rules, which seem to be unusual in indigenous East African economies, impart to their exchange transactions a relatively impersonal character, since there are no residual obligations or rights between two men who exchange goods.

The different kinds of goods which are of any significance in Sonjo exchanges are so few in number that the economic characteristics of each kind can be considered separately without the necessity of grouping them in categories. One important food product is not really dealt with as an exchange item at all. This is meat, which is distributed more as a gift than an exchange commodity. The Sonjo, like many other African peoples, seldom slaughter livestock for food except on ritual or ceremonial occasions. On some occasions, such as wedding feasts, goats are slaughtered without any special ritual and are then consumed by a group of relatives and friends who are invited as guests. When a goat is slaughtered as a sacrifice, the owner keeps a share of the meat for his own family, gives certain parts of it to specified relatives, and divides the rest among the neighbors of his ward. There are no techniques for preserving and storing meat; it is always consumed immediately. A good proportion of the meat supply is provided by communal sacrifices carried out by the *wenamiji*. The carcasses are divided impartially and each *mwenamiji* distributes his share among the people of his ward. The *wenamiji*, and also the different warrior companies, occasionally have corporate feasts, and these men thus enjoy more meat than the other villagers. This attitude towards meat was extended by the Sonjo to their dealings with me. Thus when an individual (usually a *mwenamiji*) brought me meat it was always as a gift for which he refused payment, whereas in the case of all other kinds of food and also beer a definite payment of some kind was demanded.

Goat milk is not much exchanged for other goods because of the fact that infants and herd boys are given preference and consume most of the supply. The standard daily ration for herd boys is a bowl of porridge cooked with milk. This is cooked in the village and taken out to the goat camps every day. If a goat owner has young sons of his own, they normally herd his goats and stay at the pasture camps. But if he has no sons of this age group, his goats are herded by other boys of his ward whether or not they are closely related to him. Thus, within a ward the herding duties are carried out somewhat communally, and the rationing of the herd boys, especially with milk, is regarded as a joint responsibility of the ward. If any milk is left over it is consumed by adults, and this may sometimes be exchanged for other goods—usually sweet potatoes—but I lack information as to customary equivalences.

Sweet potatoes, which are raised under irrigation during the dry season, may be planted several times on the same plot in one season, and different plots are planted at different times. The object of this is to insure a supply of mature potatoes during most of the season. As sweet potatoes are not stored for more than a few days at a time, and each family plans its own planting schedule without regard for other people of the village, one family may be temporarily out of potatoes while their neighbors have plenty. In this situation the first family may obtain potatoes by borrowing them from their neighbors with a promise of repayment, or they may exchange grain or (rarely) milk for the potatoes. The amount of goods given for the potatoes depends upon the relative scarcity of the two products. Some people dig their potatoes before they are mature, both for their own consumption and to offer them for exchange. These small potatoes have special value, like early spring strawberries in our country. Other Sonjo women, however, condemn the practice as inefficient utilization, explaining that much bigger and better potatoes could be obtained with only a little more patience and work. My wife was thus severely scolded by her informant for buying some of these early potatoes at a rather high price.

Grain, ground to flour and cooked as porridge, is the staff of life for the Sonjo. It is eaten at least once almost every day, even during the sweet potato season. A certain amount of grain is exchanged for other goods, but this exchange is limited by the fact that everyone, except for the smiths and potters, raises about the same amount of grain and at the same time of year. Thus in a year of good crops, no ordinary family has need for much grain in addition to its own harvest. The Sonjo use grain only for food and never for beer making. This differentiates them from most African societies, which make their beer from cereals so that there is often a demand for grain in excess of food needs. The sorghum crop harvested shortly after my arrival was considered to be fairly abundant, and people were not worrying about running out of food before the next harvest. Thus the demand for grain was small, but people were not averse to accepting a reasonable amount of grain in exchanges and storing it as a food reserve. These transactions usually involved the exchange of grain for irrigation rights and sometimes for honey. A certain measure of grain (the exact size of which I did not determine) was regarded as equivalent to the standard jar of honey (about two gallons), and exchanges were based on these equivalences. Payments for irrigation water were usually evaluated in terms of honey—one-third of a jar was a common amount for this payment—and if it was agreed to make the payment in grain, the honey equivalent was calculated and paid. I have no record of any direct exchange of goats for grain during my visit; I doubt if anyone would have wanted to receive this amount of grain at one time as it would have exceeded foreseeable food needs for the year. The situation is quite different, I was told, in years of grain scarcity; goats are then readily exchanged for grain. It is thus possible over a period of years for a family that is poor in goats to increase its herd through energetic cultivation and skimping on consumption in order to take advantage of the increased demand for grain and the higher equivalence rates in bad years. This was stated to be a recognized way of starting a herd or rebuilding a depleted herd.

In addition to these exchanges of grain among ordinary Sonjo families, a certain amount of grain and other vegetable food is exchanged for pottery and ironware. This is the normal means of payment for these specialist goods, because the potters and smiths are strictly forbidden on ritual grounds to cultivate crops; therefore they depend for their supplies of vegetable food entirely upon the exchange of their manufactured items. The Sonjo use pots only for cooking and storing honey—calabashes and skin bags are used as containers for all other purposes—and iron is used sparingly for technical equipment. Therefore, the expenditure of an ordinary family for these goods is relatively small. The economically significant point is that a group of some 20 people obtains its subsistence in part through providing the products of its craftmanship to 4,500 Sonjo in exchange for vegetable produce. Thus, although the sum of these transactions is extremely important to the smiths and potters, they are minor items in the domestic budgets of individual Sonjo.

Honey is entirely different in its economic character from the food items just discussed. I estimate that the amount of honey offered for exchange considerably exceeds the amount consumed directly by the producer. The total supply fluctuates from year to year, and in any one year there may be great differences in the production of individuals, even though they have the same number of hives. Only a fraction of the hives produce honey; men are constantly changing the locations of their hives, hoping thus to attract bees to them. The individual honey production of four informants for the previous year varied from four to thirty jars, and they attributed this inequality entirely to chance. A small amount of honey is required by every family for ritual purposes, but most of it is consumed as beer for pleasure, and this use is optional. That is, an individual may deny himself this pleasure, if need be, in order to exchange his honey for goats, irrigation rights, or grain. There is said to be always a demand for honey in excess of the available supply. The main consumers are the owners of large numbers of goats. These men are willing to exchange their goats for honey in order to enjoy the pleasure and prestige of having liberal supplies of beer at their homes. A common way of building up a goat herd is to exchange honey for goats. To accomplish this, however, one requires, in addition to luck, hard work, frugality, and the possession of technical equipment in the form of beehives.

No Sonjo likes to dispose of his beehives if he can help it, because they are his means of producing the highly regarded honey. Nevertheless, hives are frequently exchanged for goats. They vary considerably in quality according to the quality of the wood from which they are made. A beehive made of proper hardwood is said to last a lifetime, while a soft-wood hive, though much easier to make, may rot out in two or three years. The exchange equivalence of a hive depends upon its quality and also its age. A good hive may be exchanged for several goats, while a poor hive will be exchanged for only a fraction of that amount. The decision to exchange hives for goats is only made when there is sudden and pressing need for a number of goats, as often happens, for instance when the deadline for paying a brideprice draws near. For the purpose of gradually increasing a herd of goats, it is considered advantageous to keep one's hives and exchange the honey that they produce for goats.

Land transfers are restricted in the special manner I have already explained, but in many ways transactions involving land are carried out like other exchanges. The exchange equivalence of a plot of land depends on its size, location, and quality of soil. Land is usually, perhaps always, exchanged for goats. I cannot say for sure whether beehives might be accepted as payment for land under certain circumstances. If this happened, it would certainly be necessary to define the exchange equivalence of the beehives in goats, for there is always the possibility that the exact amount will have to be refunded, and bee-hives vary in quality and deteriorate with age.

Turning now to goats, which occupy a crucial position in the ex-change system, we are confronted with the question of how to de-scribe them in economic terms. Do they have any of the essential characteristics of *money* or *currency*? Can they be properly termed a *medium of exchange*? The answers to these questions depend to some extent upon how the terms are defined. As economists ordi-narily use the terms, probably none of them could be correctly applied to Sonjo goats. However, it might be argued that the usual definitions should be broadened in anthropological use so that the terms could be applied to the economies of societies which lack anything closely resembling our money, particularly since no alternative terms have yet been established for dealing with these primitive systems on an abstract level. As this paper is not a comparative study, I shall not attempt to decide whether or not Sonjo goats should be described as a medium of exchange or some other economic term. Instead, I shall simply indicate some of the economic characteristics of the goats which are relevant to these questions.

In the first place, goats represent a basic subsistence resource, which is hardly a characteristic of money. But the consumable goods derived from goats—meat, milk, and skins—are dealt with economically in a rather different manner from other subsistence goods. They are allocated by an owner to a wider range of persons than his immediate family, and according to principles other than by exchange of equiva-lent goods. Although a goat owner receives the largest share of the subsistence products of his goats, this is not the only, or even the primary, benefit derived from possessing goats.

Goats provide the most common means of payment, and in suitable circumstances they can be exchanged for any other kind of goods. The only limitation in this use is the fact that a goat is indivisible and therefore cannot be exchanged for any goods that are less than a whole goat in equivalence. That is, a small amount of honey or grain cannot be exchanged for a fraction of a goat. Honey provides another common means of payment, but it is much more restricted than goats. In general, honey is exchanged for any goods the equivalence of which is one goat or less. To obtain goods exceeding one goat in equivalence, honey is first exchanged for goats, and the goats are then exchanged for the desired thing—for example, a piece of land or a wife. We might imagine an analogous situation in a money economy in which goods less than a dollar in value could be paid for in coins, while anything with a value greater than a dollar would have to be paid for with paper money.

Goats undoubtedly represent the most stable standard of value of all Sonjo goods, if only because the available supply fluctuates the least. The value, as defined by exchange equivalence, of almost any other goods can be measured in terms of goats. Honey also has some claim to represent a standard of value. Since the goat/honey ratio is constant at any one time, the value of other goods—even land and marriageable women—could be calculated in terms of honey. This would be an abstract calculation, however, which had no counterpart in actual exchange transactions. The goat/honey ratio changes with fluctuations in the supply of honey, and in response to this fluctuation the exchange equivalence of goats vis-à-vis other items is probably altered from time to time. However, the diachronic data necessary to demonstrate this are lacking.

The domestic economy and consumption habits of the Sonjo are such that only goats are normally accumulated in amounts which exceed current subsistence needs. Goats represent the only form of property which is stored to any great extent. The acquisition of goats is in some respects analogous to investment, particularly if we remember that goats are subject to natural increase through breeding. A few men in every village possess so many goats that the natural increment rate exceeds the owner's expenditure of goats in subsistence and exchange. This wealth tends to increase progressively until the estate is dispersed through inheritance or repeated brideprice payments. I do not think that wives can be considered as a form of stored or invested wealth among the Sonjo, because of the low incidence of polygyny.

Another feature characteristic of goats alone is their multiple transfer from owner to owner. Other goods are acquired through exchange for the purpose of immediate use, consumption, or enjoyment; if they are later exchanged again, this is because of exceptional circumstances and is not a planned procedure. Goats, because they are accumulated in the absence of immediate needs, are later exchanged when new needs arise, and thus they may change hands frequently. In this characteristic, Sonjo goats resemble money.

Finally, goats—as distinct from other forms of property—are naturally divided into discrete units which are more or less equivalent in value. Individual goats, of course, differ in quality according to the sex, age, size, and health of the animals, and for this reason they are not interchangeable in the way that, say, dollars are. In any transaction involving the actual transfer of goats, the two parties must come to an agreement as to the particular goats to be exchanged. But nevertheless I think there exists the implicit idea of an average or standard goat against which the value of other goods is measured.

Thus the value of goods, such as honey, which are relatively unvarying in quality is normally stated at any one time in terms of a standard goat. The equivalency rate during my field work was about two gallons of honey for a goat, though when honey was exchanged for actual goats this ratio might be altered if the particular goats were above or below the average in quality. In discussing land or brideprice transactions, people would cite the number of goats involved as if they were quoting a price in equivalent units of some currency.

The most outstanding event in the economics of a family is undoubtedly the payment of brideprice. This happens only a few times in the span of a normal family cycle, but those are often times of economic crisis for the family. The Sonjo practice polygyny, but only about 12 per cent of the married men have more than one wife, and only a handful have more than two. A father must provide at least half the brideprice for his sons' first wives—the rest he collects from close relatives—and for a second wife for himself he usually provides the entire sum. The principle of quitclaim exchange governs brideprice transactions, as it does all other exchanges except land sales. Thus, after a man has paid brideprice to the bride's father he has no further claim on those goats, even though the bride should die before the marriage is consummated. Conversely, the bride's father has no recourse if the goats paid to him should die or prove unsatisfactory in any way. I have discussed in some detail the whole question of Sonjo brideprice elsewhere, (Gray 1960) and therefore will not elaborate further here. Certainly the brideprice customs have an effect on the economy. The average brideprice during my visit was about 100 goats; a government livestock census revealed that an average owner possessed 54 goats. These figures give some indication of the effort required of a man of the lower or middle economic class in order to collect enough goats to obtain a wife for himself or a son without depleting the family herd below the level necessary for subsistence needs. Other items may then have to be liquidated by exchanging them for goats. Honey and beehives may be sold; if the family can spare a plot of land it may be leased at that time; a *mokiama* may have to surrender his privileged irrigation rights because he is no longer able to pay the required tribute in goats.

On the other side of the picture, men periodically acquire goats paid to them as brideprice for their daughters. In the community as a whole, the receipts from brideprice balance the payments, and the same would be true of individual families if every family was comprised of an equal number of sons and daughters. In actual fact, the sex ratio of offspring of individual men is often unequal. When there are more sons than daughters, the family must find the additional goats necessary to obtain wives, from other sources than the brideprice received for daughters. On the other hand, fathers with more daughters than sons tend to accumulate goats which they can exchange for subsistence or luxury goods, land or superior irrigation rights. All these transactions resulting from brideprice permeate the exchange system.

In cases of divorce and remarriage—not infrequent among the Sonjo—a new husband pays brideprice directly to the first husband, with the wife's family taking no part in the transaction. A woman's second marriage is almost always with a man of a different village—though a first marriage is normally in her own village—and so on these occasions goats are transferred from one village to another. Since there is little regular trade in commodities between villages, and since each village has its separate irrigation system, these brideprice transactions constitute the chief form of intervillage exchange.

The last element in the exchange system to be considered here is irrigation rights. This can be studied from two different economic viewpoints. On the one hand, the irrigation allotments resemble a taxation system, with payments for water rights funneling upwards to the *wenamiji*, who represent the legitimate village government. This accumulated wealth in goats is said to belong to the whole community, and most of the goats are sacrificed to the tribal god. As a secular byproduct of these religious benefits, a share of this wealth is redistributed in the form of meat from the slaughtered goats. This aspect of the irrigation system does not primarily concern us here, though it is strictly germane to a study of the political and religious systems of the society. There is another aspect of irrigation which directly affects the exchange system. The need for irrigation water arises continually throughout a man's life, and to fullfil this need most men periodically gather together enough goods to make the payments necessary for the use of water. These innumerable transactions, large and small, concerning water rights promote the frequent conversion of one form of goods into another. As a result, all the exchange system is affected by water-right transactions.

MONEY

Although very little money circulated in the Sonjo villages during my field work, it seems likely that the use of money will increase rapidly in the near future. Therefore, a brief statement of the situation as I found it may be useful in any future investigation of the economic development of the society.

A number of young men of the senior warrior grade leave the

tribal area for periods of one to three years to work at various occupations, and their earnings constitute almost the sole source of money for the tribe. A favorite occupation is trading in goats at Government-supervised livestock auctions. The goats are brought at various tribal auctions in northern Tanganyika and driven to Arusha to be sold at a profitable price. Some of the Sonjo work at this occupation in the employ of other African or Somali traders. However, whenever they can raise enough capital through working as wage laborers, the Sonjo prefer to operate independently in buying and selling goats. It is perhaps surprising that these men, with no tradition in their own culture of trading for profit, should choose this occupation on their first venture in the outside world. The Sonjo, however, are expert at judging and handling goats, and they seem to be the only people who dare drive goats across remote stretches of Masai territory. Armed with their bows and deadly poisoned arrows, they are quite fearless of Masai raiders.

Government officials have been unsuccesful in efforts to induce the Sonjo to sell their own goats, which were judged to be considerably in excess of the subsistence needs of the people. Several years ago it was planned to institute a periodic livestock auction in Sonjo territory. On the day appointed for the first auction, a staff of auctioneers and buyers traveled to Sonjoland, but the auction was a complete failure: no goats were offered for sale, and the idea was abandoned.

The chief money need of the Sonjo is for payment of the annual tax, which in 1955 was set at 10 shillings per adult male. The earnings brought home by the warriors are sufficient to pay this tax, but very little money is left over for other uses. The money is distributed among the different families largely through the selling and purchasing of goats within the tribe, though honey is also purchased with money on occasion. The young men are aware of the goat prices prevailing at livestock auctions, and these prices are demanded in intratribal transactions involving money.

Imported goods purchased with money include blankets for the elders, cloths for the warriors, and beads for the women. There are sharp differences among the villages in the extent to which the young men leave home to work for money. In the villages which are more backward in this respect only a few of the elders possess blankets, while at the two most advanced villages—the sites respectively of the Lutheran mission and the Government court house and school—nearly every elder possesses a blanket. A single shop, owned by a Sikh firm at Loliondo and run by an alien African storekeeper, is located near the court house. It stocks beads, cloths, and blankets of rather poor quality. The Sonjo buy most of their blankets at Loliondo, where they are of better quality. The local shop also sells sugar, which is sometimes purchased to mix with honey in the making of beer, a practice which the native connoisseurs condemn as producing inferior beer. Imported knives and axes are largely replacing the locally made items. The digging stick, however, has not yet given way to the imported iron hoe.

Money is never used for paying brideprice or leasing land. It is seldom if ever used in transactions concerning rights to irrigation water, though I am not aware of any strict rule that would make this impossible.

CONCLUSION

One general conclusion to be drawn from this study is that the major characteristics of the internal exchange system are essentially unrelated to the subsistence economy. If this is true, the Sonjo do not conform to the pattern of economic determination and evolution sometimes suggested as a general theory, for example in the writings of Gordon Childe. His interpretation stresses improved techniques of production as the basic factor in economic differentiation. Thus when production exceeds basic subsistence needs, surpluses accumulate and part of the population not required for subsistence productions is freed for the production of specialized goods and services. The various groups of specialized producers then interact economically as domestic units to create a market exchange system and a highly differentiated economy. Specialization of production does exist among the Sonjo, but on such a small scale that it constitutes only a minor element in the exchange system. The major incentives for exchanging goods and producing beyond subsistence needs seem to stem from outside the need for subsistence goods. These major inducements in the production and exchange systems are land acquisition, brideprice payments, and transactions concerning water rights.

It seems possible to conceive of a society with the same basic ecological adaptation as the Sonjo, but lacking those specific features which have created the Sonjo exchange systems. Land tenure, instead of being based on individual ownership, might be on some kind of communal basis, as is often found in Africa, with clans, for instance, controlling blocks of arable land and distributing it for use to members according to their needs. Such a system would not necessitate any exchange transactions between individuals. If our own form of marriage were followed, with wives choosing to work as voluntary partners of their husbands—or if marriage were based on the actual exchange of daughters and sisters—there would be none of the brideprice transactions which are such important events in the Sonjo exchange system. Finally, the distribution of irrigation water might conceivably be controlled by some communal or democratic system which did not require any payments or property exchanges by individual water users.

This hypothetical society should be able to exploit the natural resources with the same techniques as the Sonjo use; the patterns of production and consumption would be basically alike. However, the exchange of goods—limited to movements of subsistence goods and the circulation of a small amount of specialist goods—would be on a much lower level than we find among the Sonjo. Our hypothetical society would necessarily have a different social structure, for the specific features that it lacked are integral elements in the Sonjo social structure. This seems to suggest that an exchange system may develop with, and be a function of, the differentiation of social structure as well as the mode of production.

CHAPTER 19

Land Use, Labor, and the Growth of Market Economy in Kipsigis Country

BY ROBERT A. MANNERS[1]

Formerly, wealth could only take the form of more wives, more sheep, more beer. Now there are innumerable ways of spending money delightfully: on European food, clothing and furniture, in cinemas, on gramaphones, sewing machines, cigarettes. (Leys 1924 : 245)

We have been informed by competent authorities that even among the Masai . . . this prejudice [against the sale of cattle] is breaking down under the influence of the desire to acquire the products of other countries. The influence of trade and shopping centers is sometimes underrated. (Ormsby-Gore 1925 : 157)

INTRODUCTION

The Kipsigis belong to the so-called Nilo-Hamitic cluster of East African tribes which includes, among others, the Nandi, Masai, Marakwet, Keiyo, Tugen and West Suk. Their Reserve lies within Nyanza Province in the southwestern corner of Kenya Colony. The westernmost portion of the Reserve's 1001 square miles is barely 12 miles from the Gulf of Kavirondo, the eastern arm of Lake Victoria. Most of the Reserve lies at an elevation of between 5000 and 7000 feet, and the entire area is included within 1° south of the equator. The Kipsigis are bounded to the north and northeast by lands alienated to European settlement. On the southwest is another area of European-occupied farms, a segment of which intrudes into the Reserve itself, almost cutting off the southern portion from the rest of Kipsigis territory. Remaining contiguous areas are occupied by the

(1) The research on which this paper is based was sponsored by a grant from the University of Illinois Project on Cultural Regularities, Ford Foundation, under the supervision of Professor Julian H. Steward. I received additional assistance from Rubin Foundation funds, Brandeis University. Among the many to whom I am indebted for valuable assistance in the collection of data while I was in the field, I wish to acknowledge a special debt of gratitude to the following: Frederick arap Soi, Inspector of Kipsigis Markets; A. T. Matson of Kabianga whose scholarly researches in the government archives at Entebbe, Uganda, uncovered the materials which he so generously made available to me; Cyril Barwell, District Agricultural Officer, Kericho District; Peter Walters, former District Commissioner, Kericho and presently Provincial Commissioner, Northern Province; Richard arap Koech, guide and companion in the field. Thanks are due also to Professor Elizabeth Colson of Brandeis University for her critical reading of the first draft of the manuscript and for many valuable suggestions.

Gusii and the Luo on the west and the Masai to the south and southeast.

When the Europeans first arrived in the country of the Kipsigis around the turn of the present century they found no markets, no formal patterns of internal trade, and only a desultory and limited external barter with the peoples of some adjacent tribes. The Kipsigis were a people who depended for their livelihood primarily upon their herds and flocks, their small household patches of *wimbi* (eleusine or finger millet) and a few cultivated garden vegetables. Their diet of milk, millet, blood, garden vegetables and occasional meat from one of their animals was irregularly supplemented by honey, wild vegetables, and game.

Because supplies of iron ore were not easily available in their territory, and the produce of their own smiths was allegedly inadequate in quantity and inferior in quality,[2] the Kipsigis obtained many of their spears, knives, and other iron objects from adjacent tribes (particularly Nandi and Gusii) in exchange for grain, goats, sheep, or honey. In times of extreme shortage or famine the Kipsigis traded their children with the Gusii for grain. However, most Kipsigis transactions of goods and services were not with other peoples, but were informal and intratribal. Sometimes such exchange involved the barter of several goats or sheep for a heifer or a young bull. Experts in thatching often exchanged their labor for beer as did the members of a *kokwet*[3] who had assisted in the preparation of a field or in harvesting of the millet crop. Kipsigis smiths and potters were usually paid for their products with beer, grain, or small animals. The *kimanagen,* an institutionalized form of cattle-lending within the tribe, was widespread and of considerable importance.

Broad inequalities in the ownership of cattle seem always to have prevailed, and these might have proved socially disruptive had there been no intratribal compensating mechanism such as the *kimanagen* which usually insured that men who owned few or no cattle of their own might acquire animals on indefinite loan from more prosperous friends, kinsmen, or agemates.[4]

(2) An unsigned letter in the Foreign Office Correspondence files at Entebbe, Uganda, dated August 3, 1905, states that the Kipsigis "cannot forge [their] own weapons." The letter adds that they capture them or buy them from the Nandi or Masai smiths. The Kipsigis report that they did make their own weapons long ago but had abandoned the practice almost completely by the time the Europeans arrived.

(3) A largely autonomous social segment occupying a particular locality, generally a group of anywhere from 20 to 100 monogamous or polygynous households.

(4) Cf. Gulliver 1955 : 196 ff. for a discussion of stock-association, a form of cattle exchange among the Jie and the Turkana which is sometimes compared with that of the Kipsigis but differs from it in important respects; also Krapf for a description of the

While the exchange practices just mentioned served a number of useful functions for the Kipsigis—not the least of which was that of redressing internal imbalance in wealth and skills—their existence did not in any sense imply the kind of structured or regular exchange involved in societies with more formal internal marketing arrangements such as those found in parts of West Africa. In a way, the goods and services exchanged among the pre-contact Kipsigis represent a few of the many kinds of intra and inter-tribal patterns that prevail among some of the most ostensibly "self-sufficient" peoples. Silent barter, gift-giving, the kula ring, potlatching, and other devices belong in this category too, and seem sometimes to be of greater social than economic importance.

In a lucid analysis of "Internal Market System as Mechanisms of Social Articulation," Mintz (1959) has stated that "the presence of markets defines nonself-sufficiency." I would, of course, agree that the presence of markets *reveals* a condition of nonself-sufficiency. If that is all that Mintz really meant to express, the objection that follows must evaporate. However, I am somewhat uneasy over the phrase as it stands, for it implies that markets and nonself-sufficiency are *indissoluble* and that markets are not so much a *possible* consequence of nonself-sufficiency but *the only possible* response. Self-sufficiency, or its absence, is far too complex a concept for such categorical treatment. The presence of many "things" other than markets, as I have suggested above, may define or reveal the nonself-sufficiency of a particular group, culture, or society. This is not a mere cavil. Since all transactional devices are by definition associated with some kind of interdependency, no single one can be said to "define" the status of nonself-sufficiency. Neither markets, barter, trade, nor other systems of exchange do, in fact, define nonself-sufficiency so much as their existence reveals some of the various mechanisms by which culturally defined nonself-sufficiency is compensated or rectified.

Moreover, since self-sufficiency must clearly involve isolation—voluntary or not—from other human groups, we are forced to invoke the image of the primitive isolate, the hypothetical social unit which exists completely for and by itself, as the pure example of such self-sufficiency. Any pattern of trade, or exchange of goods or services, which links a group with other groups refutes isolation and demonstrates the essential absence of self-sufficiency. If Lesser is right when he tells us (1959 : 11) that "it is certainly time to discard the notion of primitive isolation, and to accept the fact that society at any level of primitivity or complexity is characterized by external relations to

practice of cattle-lending among the Xosa as protection against theft, war, etc., cited in Thurnwald 1932 : 83.

other societies as well as by internal structural relations," we shall
have to accept the idea that nonself-sufficiency is a constant of human
culture, that it varies from group to group only in degree and in the
form in which it reveals itself, and that markets (or the kula ring, or
silent barter) are only one among the many possible manifestations of
nonself-sufficiency. But markets themselves, as Mintz clearly demonstrates in his discussion, do indeed serve special functions of "social
articulation." They do so in ways which are profoundly different in
form and consequences from such other transactional devices as silent
barter, the giveaway, and so on. It is with one of these articulating
functions in particular that I shall deal in the discussion of marketing
in Kipsigis country that follows.

CREATING A LABOR MARKET

The emergence and growth of markets among a people who had
never known them before contact with Western industrial society is
at once a manifestation of that contact and a virtually indispensable
agent of its intensification. Kenya was occupied and developed by the
British with the aim, among others, of making a profit from minerals
and other raw materials (not so good in Kenya's case), by the sale of
home-manufactured commodities (a process which could only follow
the conversion of the potential consumer from pure subsistence
activities to those involving the acquisition of cash), and by the production of export commodities for sale in a world market. The two
latter activities turned out to be the more appropriate for Kenya.
Circumstances—largely of climate, soil fertility, assumed labor potential, and the forms of aboriginal culture—determined that the
exports from Kenya would be agricultural and that they would be
produced on European-owned and run plantations rather than on
small, native, peasant properties. In any case, if export commodities
were to be produced they would require indigenous labor. And if the
laborers are technically free or unforced they must either have incentives or the absence of alternative modes of material survival
available before they will turn to the work that creates or makes
possible the production of items for market sale.

By the time they arrived in Kenya the British had acquired long
experience in the techniques of colonial administration and had
developed a variety of devices to entice the free laborer into a wage
and market economy. The harsher devices were finally abandoned
for several reasons: because the resentments they produced locally
threatened to defeat their purpose; because pressures exerted by the
Colonial Office in Great Britain eventually proved irresistible; be-

cause the regulations were difficult to administer; and because they became in time unnecessary. Such open and disguised labor levies as the Registration Ordinance, the Masters and Servants Ordinance, and Compulsory Labour Regulations are cases in point. In effect, the kind of legislation represented by these and other statutes was a crude rejoinder to the reluctance of many of Kenya's Africans, particularly the wealthier tribes, to work for wages (Dilley 1937 : 213–238).

Slavery was, for all practical purposes, dead, having been destroyed largely through the efforts of the British themselves. The few weak efforts to revive it failed. A middle way which would secure labor in the amounts, in the places and for the time it was needed was the solution required. Hence legislation against desertion, or legislation requiring stated amounts of *corvée* labor, or legislation sanctioning essentially one-sided contracts or specifying relations of employer to worker was invoked. But ultimately even these measures proved inadequate, and several less blatant and less harsh devices were found to be more effective in satisfying the growing demands of the white settlers for labor.

Two of these devices are familiar, indirect, and ostensibly more fair than coercive legislation, threats, or slavery. They are the hut and/or poll tax, and the creation of native Reserves. The tax must almost always be paid in cash which can be earned either by the market sale of produce or by selling one's labor for wages.

Sir Percy Girouard, Governor of the then-Protectorate of Kenya, remarked in 1913 that:

We consider that the only natural and automatic method of securing a constant labour supply is to ensure that there shall be competition among labourers for hire and not among employers for labourers; such competition can be brought about only by a rise in the cost of living for the native, and this rise can be produced only by an increase in the tax. (East African Standard, Feb. 8, 1913)

Creation of Reserves accompanied by the alienation of large areas of land to white settlers may ultimately limit an expanding agrarian population largely to the cultivation of inadequate quantities of subsistence commodities, hence forcing work for wages upon them if they are to meet tax obligations and satisfy new wants. However, should the Africans manage to grow saleable commodities in excess of their subsistence requirements they would be inclined to withdraw from wage labor. In these circumstances the plantations could find themselves faced with a labor shortage. Colonel John Ainsworth remarked that

Planters and others [are likely to oppose the development of cash crop production by Africans in Kenya] on the grounds that if natives are employed on their own plantations, they will be reluctant to take on service as indentured labourers. (Ormsby-Gore 1925 : 168)

In Kenya, the fear that an independent African peasantry might emerge to threaten estate and plantation dominance of cash crop production is an old one. From time to time restrictions, crop limitations, and other controls have been applied by the administration, and these have had the effect of discouraging the emergence of a large and prosperous native peasantry.

The Government found the people in occupation of as much land as they could use, and endeavored, not to increase their security from disturbance, but to turn peasants into wage-earners. (Leys 1924 : 187)[5]

Linfield emphasizes the difficulties posed by the prosperity of certain cattle-keeping tribes when he says:

Native tribes which are self-sufficing through cattle-owning are anathema to the contact theory of development. Such tribes are averse from sending out their young men to work as laborers, and find money to pay their taxes by the sale of surplus stock. (In Ormsby-Gore 1925 : 188)

The third element which has increased the supply of wage labor is the introduction or expansion of shops and other internal trading facilities. The manufactured products of Western industrial civilization excite new wants which can only be satisfied by acquiring money. In a plantation-based economy the acquisition of that money is almost certain to mean wage labor. The place where these new wants may be satisfied is the stall or the wagon of the trader, the shop, and the market place.

To increase the wants of Africans was the universally approved object to be pursued ... the real reason the authorities tried to persuade the Africans to want money and what money can buy was not that trade goods would do them any appreciable good. The object aimed at was to induce Africans to become wage-earners. (Leys 1924 : 185; cf Ormsby-Gore 1925 : 173)

Thus, if the imposition of taxes together with a shrunken land base seemed unlikely to generate a large labor force at low wage rates, it might be hoped that an efficient internal marketing system would help to deal with the problem. In order to avoid the complications of

(5) Leys here uses the term peasant to include any independent producer, whether he converts part of his produce to cash or not. This is one sense in which Firth (1951 : 87, 102) also uses the term. My own use of the term is perhaps more conventional and closer to that offered by Kroeber (1948 : 284), for I prefer to limit it to those rural people who devote at least part of their product to sale for cash. Redfield (1956 : 35–66) also has an extended discussion of peasantry as "part-society."

target work (one manifestation of which often shows up in under-developed areas as the backward-bending supply curve of labor) ever-expanding rather than limited incentives to cash accumulation had to be supplied. New material wants were stimulated by a continual increase in the amount and variety of consumer commodities that were offered for purchase—in short, by the growth of markets and marketing. In many respects the growth of markets in Kenya is comparable to that of the trading-posts of the New World. In the latter case, however, the object seems clearly to have been the encouragement of a peasant-type production of cash commodities for the external market as well as an increase in the sale of metropolis-manufactured items; while the markets in Kenya have encouraged the expansion of wage labor.[6]

MAIZE GROWING AND EARLY PEASANT CULTIVATION

When the first British settlers entered what is now the Kericho District in 1906–07 they took over, either on long lease, by outright purchase, or by a combination of both, estates averaging about 5000 acres each. Kipsigis in varying numbers lived on all of these lands. In some cases they chose to leave and take up residence in unalienated areas nearby; in others they were forced to evacuate; but in the majority of cases the Kipsigis were encouraged to remain as "legal squatters" (in later years more euphemistically termed "resident labourers"). In return for the privilege of remaining where they were, grazing their stock, and planting their small plots of millet and vegetables, the adult males of each household were generally required to perform a minimum of about 70 days paid labor a year for their new landlords.

They used this wage income and money realized from the sale of animals to pay the hut (later poll) tax. Cash surpluses were commonly used to purchase cattle. But even before wage labor and the arrival of the settlers, itinerant travelers began to stimulate an interest in cash with their stocks of blankets, beads, cloth, trinkets, salt, knives, axes, iron pots, and other items. The first reference to this trade which I have been able to discover in documentary sources occurs in a letter from Johnston to Hill, dated March 3, 1901.[7] In this letter Johnston refers to a meeting he has held with Nandi and Lumbwa (Kipsigis) chiefs at Ft. Ternan. The Kipsigis assured him "that their country is

(6) Cf. Leacock 1954 and Murphy and Steward 1956 for evidence of the role of the trading post in binding a peasant group of producers to the products of Western industrial society.

(7) Foreign Office Correspondence in the archives at Entebbe, Uganda.

open to trade. Numbers of Indians and Swahilis are going there to buy sheep and sell them again to the Railway . . . I have also allowed a trader named Boyce to enter Sotik country [southern Kipsigis area] under conditions."

The response of the Kipsigis to this earliest trade is alleged to have been enthusiastic. In the same files a letter from Lt. Wortham, dated just two months after Johnston's, reports that the "chiefs near Ft. Ternan are friendly and bring produce for sale. [They are] beginning to appreciate the value of money and the railway. They want situations as servants to Europeans." Two months after this, on July 16, 1901, the same writer tells us that the "Lumbwa [are] selling large quantities of grain to troops."

With the establishment of shops in Lumbwa, Kericho, Bomet, and Litein, the exchange was intensified. All of these early shops were owned and run by Asians or Europeans, for it was not until 1925–26 that the first Kipsigis-owned shop was set up at Chemosit. Itinerant Kipsigis traders were apparently non-existent or nearly so during the first 10 to 15 years of contact.

As early as 1907 the then-District Commissioner, Partington, began a strong campaign to encourage the Kipsigis to plant maize. He was concerned primarily with having an adequate supply of maize to provide for the needs of a growing and agriculturally non-productive administrative, military, and police force. The Nandi Wars had just been concluded and their effect on the production and sale of grain (chiefly millet and sorghum) in the area had been so harmful that the administration was forced to consider every means of providing a secure source of their anticipated basic grain requirements. It was Partington's apparent intention to get the Kipsigis to shift to the heavier-yielding maize, not in the hope of converting them into a tribe of successful peasant cultivators with maize as their cash crop, but to insure a handy supply of food for the growing township and estate requirements.[8] The need for Kipsigis labor at this time was apparently not so pressing as the need for their produce. In any case, Partington knew that the growth and development of the District required dependable sources of staple foods. Any cash that the Kipsigis might acquire by engaging in maize production would certainly take them to the shops and trading centers. Clearly, the administration wanted the Kipsigis to grow food for sale, and there was some apparent willingness on their part to comply. In a letter from Assistant Deputy Commissioner Hobley to Eliot, dated May 20, 1902, he reports that a board set up to consider Kericho as a site for a civil station re-

(8) Cf. Lord Lugard, 1929 : 397–398 for reference to the Kenya settlers' reluctance to see the native involved in the production of cash-export commodities.

commends it favorably for many reasons including the fact that "there is a considerable population of Lumbwa people within touch of the site, and when the harvest is reaped the station should be easily able to obtain its food supplies on the spot.[9]

Partington's efforts to convert the Kipsigis to maize growing was, however, opposed by the *laibon,* a group of sorcerers or witch-doctors who came to the Kipsigis from the Masai via the Nandi some time after 1875. They were all members of a single clan, Talai, and had used their assumed supernatural powers to achieve a strong measure of control and considerable prestige within the tribe by the time the Europeans arrived. For their continued opposition to the Europeans, their "disruptive" activities, and their role in the conduct of organized stock theft, the administration finally rounded them up and shipped them to Gwassi outside the reserve in 1935–36.

In 1907, however, the *laibon* exercised great power among the Kipsigis. Their opposition to Partington's plan appears to have derived on the one hand from a fear that they might lose their power to the Europeans and, on the other, from their real or pretended suspicion that land planted to maize would be appropriated at harvest time by the Europeans. Nevertheless, and despite the initial resistance of some Kipsigis and the efforts of the *laibon,* it was only a matter of five or six years before increasing numbers of Kipsigis took to cultivation of the dual-purpose—cash and subsistence—crop. Itinerant Asian traders, and others who soon settled down at Litein, Bomet, and Kisenoi in the native land unit as well as in Kericho and Lumbwa on the periphery, had been buying sheep, skins, and hides from the Kipsigis. And they were very much interested in the purchase of Kipsigis maize.

By the time the first World War had begun there was a growing market for maize throughout the highland areas of Kenya, for large numbers of Africans had withdrawn from subsistence activities in the native areas and were now working on the farms and estates of the Europeans. These workers had to be fed, and the food had to be supplied in part from enlarged production encouraged in the native areas. The local demand for foodstuffs received fresh impetus in the period after the first World War when the big tea estates with their exceptionally high labor requirements went into operation. Although the first $1^1/_2$ acres of tea had been planted in Kericho in 1912, it was not until 1924 that the first small processing factory was erected in the District. However, within six years, or by 1930, there were approximately 8000 regular and 3000 casual laborers working on the estates that border the Kipsigis Reserve. In that year, adult males

(9) Foreign Office Correspondence. Entebbe archives.

were earning 14 shillings per 30-day work period, and juveniles[10]—who do virtually all of the plucking—were getting 8–10 shillings. It is estimated that the expenditures of the tea companies in wages, transport, and food amounted to about £200,000 in 1930.

Although many Kipsigis were producing small quantities of maize for sale before the end of the first World War, they continued to use only the hoe for soil preparation and cultivation until 1921 when arap Bargochat of Belgut became the first Kipsigis to buy and use a plow. The hoe had been adequate for the cultivation of plots large enough to provide family subsistence and a small surplus. But if one really wished to acquire a sizeable cash income the plow became a virtual necessity. By 1930 there were 266 plows in use in Belgut location alone, 124 in Buret, and 10 in Sotik. There were 73 Kipsigis-owned water mills for the grinding of maize into flour, although the first Kipsigis-owned water mill had been erected on the Nyangoris River near Tenwek Falls only nine years before, in 1921.

While the data in the District Commissioner's files are rather spotty for the period between 1920–30, they reveal an unmistakable trend towards the expansion of maize cultivation and its market sale by the Kipsigis. The report for 1920 notes that "owing to the plentiful supply of maize very low prices were obtainable, not more than 1 rupee per load being paid to the natives." In the towns and trading centers alone, 20,119 loads are recorded as having been sold. Other sales are unrecorded. The 1923 report states: "A large amount of maize was sold to Indians and Europeans." In 1925: "The area under maize has increased enormously in the last few years." In 1927: "The maize acreage planted in Belgut ... considerably more than ever before." In 1928 the report notes an "encouraging increase in acreage under maize. Ploughs are on the increase and some natives ... are paying a European to use his tractor for breaking land in the Reserve." Sometimes the interest in maize suggests to the writer of the report that the Kipsigis may be "growing themselves out" of the labor market. In 1930: "The fact that comparatively few Lumbwa (Kipsigis) were employed on the Tea Estates is a good indication that the tribe as a whole was not hard hit financially."

In the District Commissioner's Report for 1929 it is estimated that the average number of laborers employed on the 176,260 acres of European-owned or leased land on any one day is 11,998, of whom 5738 are men, 1383 women, and 4877 children. A few of the estates grow their own maize with which to feed their labor, but the approximately 2500 European acres under that crop are devoted only in part to rations for the resident laborer. Much of it is sold in the Kenya

(10) A juvenile is defined as a "child or young person" and child is defined as "a

market at prices higher than those available to Kipsigis producers,[11] to satisfy demands from other parts of the colony; and the Kipsigis are in this manner encouraged to expand their own cultivation for what appears to them a dependable and growing market. As long as the Luo and Gusii and other tribes continued to flock to their farms in a generally adequate stream, the venture of the Kipsigis into considerable cash-cropping with a concomitantly threatened decline in their wage-laboring activities could not have provoked excessive anxiety on the part of the settlers. Moreover, the Kipsigis worker tended to be looked upon as inferior to the Gusii or the Luo or the Kikuyu. In any case, the "bad" years for labor, that is, those in which the settlers reckoned the supply less than adequate, appear to have been few. In 1924, for example, the District Commissioner's report notes that: "There has been a great shortage of labor, resident and non-resident, on many farms." But the situation is not mentioned again during the decade, so we may assume that 1924 is an unusual year in the period 1920–30.

It should be noted, however, that the Kipsigis were not completely outside the labor market by any means, for Kipsigis emigration for work in parts of the White Highlands not immediately adjacent to their Reserve reached an estimated peak during the decade of between 2500–3000. Non-resident labor on farms *near* the Reserve, however, was, as in other parts of Africa, another matter; for in 1925 we are told that "The Lumbwa casual laborer prefers to go to work well away from the Reserve." *Resident* Kipsigis labor on adjacent farms and estates remained high. At its peak during this decade, the number of Kipsigis families "squatting" on farms surrounding the Reserve seems to have reached around 2500–3000 out of an estimated total of 15,000 families. The 1926 report says that farms "with [ample] grazing lands" have no shortage of resident labor. In 1927 "no shortages" are reported. By 1928 "There is no talk of labour shortage; there is a superabundance of labour and Resident Natives are being contracted for a period of three years." It may be added parenthetically that many of the Kipsigis squatters were working for as little as six shillings cash for 30 days of work during the twenties and early thirties because

person, male or female, who has not attained the age of sixteen." *The Labour Laws of Kenya*, pp. 88–89. In practice, however, and since ages are not always known—or are "overlooked"—the large tea companies have worked out a policy for labelling juveniles according to stature. If a juvenile job applicant can walk under a stick which is set at 4 feet 10 inches above the ground, he is not to be employed. If he must lower his head or bend down to get under the stick, he is considered an employable juvenile.

(11) The difference in price is accounted for by grading and absence of weevils in European-grown grain and latterly by the provisions and activities of the Nyanza Province Marketing Board, a monopsony which pays a fixed price to African growers.

they were eager to have the additional compensation of grazing land for their animals.[12]

THE EXPANSION OF LOCAL MARKETING
AND THE EARLY USE OF THE PLOW

District records on early trade and markets are non-existent. As far as my information goes, the archival materials in Entebbe contain only scattered references to early trade. Therefore, except for occasional references in later reports, I must here be guided largely by the memory of elderly informants, Kipsigis and European, who have told me that the first traders were Asian, Swahili, and European—that the two former were usually itinerant, and that the first regular shops appeared with the establishment of the town of Kericho in 1906. Lumbwa, which is just a few miles outside the Reserve proper had several shops a few years before that, since Lumbwa is directly on the railroad.[13]

In the period between 1906 and the end of the first World War, other markets were set up in Sotik, Ft. Ternan, Longisa, Kapsamonget, and eight other sites "gazetted for the purpose." Some of these had few shops, and the shops in others were barely functioning.

With the coming of the British East Africa Disabled Officers Corp (BEADOC) settlers immediately after the first World War, and with the consequent rapid expansion of estate cultivation, first of flax and later—when the market for that commodity had collapsed— of tea, there was an enormously expanded demand for labor. In the case of tea, this expansion required a resident labor force, for at these latitudes tea is harvested all year round, each plant being plucked every 10 to 15 days. The estates aimed at a settled work force which could be augmented by varying amounts of casual labor from the adjacent Kipsigis Reserve. As this laboring force grew, the demand for maize (and meat) with which to ration it increased and the Kipsigis responded with an increased sale of animals and an expanded production of maize.

The plow began to replace the hoe. From arap Bargochut's single plow in 1921, the figure rose to 65 in 1927, 123 in 1928, 249 in 1929 and 400 in 1930. Water-powered mills for grinding the maize into flour increased from the original Kipsigis-owned mill in 1921 to 8 in

(12) The District Commissioner's report for 1931 notes that grazing rights "make a grown man accept less than a 'kitchen toto's' wage."

(13) Woodward 1902 reports in that year that trade near the railway in North Lumbwa is increasing slowly. He says ivory and produce are being exchanged for cattle, trade goods, cloth, beads, etc.

1923, 47 in 1928, and 73 in 1930.[14] Indigenous patterns of land tenure were still prevalent in 1930, but these tended to inhibit maximum effective utilization of the plow. The maize plots were generally the same size, or slightly larger than the traditional millet plots, only a few Kipsigis expanding cultivation to two or three acres.

Meanwhile, the number of *active* shops on the Reserve and in the towns seems to have grown. Although the District data on these are sparse and sometimes contradictory, it is clear that the volume of local trade and the variety and amount of goods offered for sale increased sharply in the decade 1920–30. Kipsigis purchases were made possible not only by the earnings of local and migrant labor above the needs of hut and poll tax, but by the mounting sales of hides, skins, meat and, especially, maize. It is apparent that the Kipsigis, having been introduced to the uses of cash, and capitalizing on their fortuitous placement with regard to the large tea plantations, as well as the relatively high fertility of their lands, would continue to expand their cash-cropping endeavors. If traditional practices with regard to land use tended to impede expansion in this direction, there was bound to be some adjustment. The market conditions for encouraging that adjustment already existed. Nine trading centers were in operation by 1925. Hides, skins, and maize were brought to these centers and sold for cash, which was spent on cloth, beads, salt, blankets, etc. The gross sales for these centers in 1925 is reported by the District Commissioner as 361,188 shillings; in 1926 it is 590,508 shillings. Ten shopkeepers in the centers report total sales in 1928 of 674,541 shillings. And in Kericho alone, a check of eight of the larger shops shows the following gross income: in 1928, 529,875 shillings; in 1929, 637,500 shillings; and in 1930, 825,000 shillings. The latter figure becomes particularly important when we discern that the price paid for hides and skins in 1930 was less than half of what had been paid in 1929, and there was a "corresponding" decline in the price paid for maize.[14]

THE PLOW AND LAND TENURE: A BRIEF CASE HISTORY

In 1931 a young, mission-trained Kipsigis in the vicinity of Cheborge in Buret Location acquired a plow and prepared about five acres of land for maize on the slope below his hut. Contravening accepted practice, he did not fence his newly planted field. When his neighbor's animals wandered into the field, he threatened the owners with court action. Individually, and with the authority of the *kokwet* elders sup-

(14) District Commissioner's Reports for these years.

porting them, they tried to persuade the young man to put a fence around his plot. They even offered to assist him in its construction. But he was adamant and suggested they could avoid difficulties with him if they planted their own plots of millet right up to the borders of his maize. In this way their animals would be kept out of his fields. The neighbors finally complied, and the following year—as was customary—they abandoned their plots after they had harvested their crops of millet. The mission-trained Kipsigis promptly extended his maize cultivation into the areas just cleared of millet. There were no grounds for objecting, for such fields were customarily abandoned and let to lie fallow for several years after which they reverted to the use of anyone who wanted them for the planting of millet.

By 1935 the young man had enlarged the area of his maize cultivation to something over 25 acres, fenced off the earliest areas of cultivation for a paddock—thus reviving the soil through natural manuring—and in subsequent years, by a judicious expansion of fencing, maize cultivation, and rotation of paddocks, he had amassed and enclosed between 250 and 300 acres of land. The pattern of permanent, individual tenure, which had in this particular case been established largely through use of the plow and cultivation of maize as a cash crop, soon spread throughout the Reserve until today there is virtually not a square foot of unclaimed land.

Meanwhile the mission-trained Kipsigis had built two water mills for grinding maize, one on the river below his fields and another at Chemosit on the main road between Sotik and Kericho, some ten miles from Cheborge. He sold the maize he himself grew to Asian traders and to the tea estates. For grinding the maize of other Kipsigis he charged a fee in the form of a small percentage of the shelled maize. He bought a wagon for transporting his grain to the trading centers and markets and built a road to help him get it there. Later he acquired a truck for the transport of his grain. Within recent years he bought a passenger car and has built on the site of his old hut a brick house with several rooms and casement windows of glass and steel. He wears western suits, good shoes, shirts with necktie, and owns a warehouse and two general merchandise shops which are run for him by hired employees.

He uses his money to educate his children and for the purchase of up-to-date equipment and farm machinery. The fruits of his enterprise are material comfort and prestige. The neighborhood of which his farm is a part includes a high percentage of "better farmers" (a term used by the District Agricultural Officer to designate and honor those who practice advanced methods of cultivation, house betterment, etc.) who have certainly learned from his example. And he is one of several outstanding Kipsigis leaders in the Reserve whose activities not only reflect the growing importance and use of money but who have served, by their example, to accelerate the tempo of emulation, to increase cash-mindedness, and to speed the drive for acquisition of Western commodities among their tribesmen.

Many of the demands of the more prosperous Kipsigis like this one can no longer be met by shops on the Reserve or in the trading centers. For these they must go to the shops of Kericho or—in some cases and for certain needs—those of Nairobi, 200 miles away, with its population of more than 225,000 and its hundreds of shops and other businesses.

WAYS TO ACQUIRE CASH OTHER THAN BY WAGE LABOR

It would, I believe, be no exaggeration to say that the Kipsigis have become the acknowledged "show tribe" of Nyanza Province—or even of Kenya—because of their rapid shift from horticultural usufruct and communal grazing areas to individual tenure in land and to an increasing dependence upon market income, and that these developments were facilitated by proximity to the tea estates and their ready market for maize and maize flour.[15] The practice of earning and spending cash has been ingrained and the enlargement of the market economy continues. The Kipsigis have come to interpret their future almost exclusively along those lines which will allow the further development of cash-producing activities.

From their initial ventures into "cash cropping" through the sale of sheep hides and skins, the Kipsigis moved rapidly to the sale of cattle and then to maize. Although cattle still retain first place in value among commodities *exported* from the District by the Kipsigis, there is no question that the total cash value of the annual maize crop has, at least during the last 25–30 years, far exceeded that of cattle or any other product. This may be accounted for by the relatively large but unrecorded intra-District sale of maize and maize flour as compared with the unrecorded but relatively light intra-District sale of cattle. Other commodities like potatoes, onions, black wattle bark, charcoal, honey, wheat, etc. are also produced and sold by the Kipsigis, but they are of relatively minor importance as compared with maize and cattle.

But to today's Kipsigis the most exciting prospect for prosperity in cash terms is tea cultivation. A limited number of Kipsigis have been permitted by the European administrators to plant some tea and

(15) Note also that the African shops adjacent to large farms and tea estates do a thriving business with the resident laborers on these European holdings, especially on week-ends. The estates thus often account for as well as support many Kipsigis shops.

small amounts of coffee. By 1959, 126 Kipsigis had been approved for tea planting. Starting with a third of an acre each they were to be allowed a maximum of one acre after three years. Since they have no processing facilities of their own (the cost of constructing a modern tea processing plant in Kenya is estimated at something in excess of half a million dollars), the Kipsigis tea growers will sell their crop to local European processors who are also engaged in the African and overseas marketing of tea. There is a smaller number of restricted coffee growers among the Kipsigis.

It should be noted that no land in the Kipsigis Reserve may be planted to tea or coffee without the express permission of the District Agricultural Officer. Thus far, two separate and limited areas have been "gazetted" by the administration for the cultivation of tea, and a small number of individual producers has been allowed to purchase seedlings for transplanting on plots prepared by them. No one on land which is not gazetted to tea or coffee may plant these crops. No one within a gazetted area who has not been given specific permission may do so. And no one may put in an amount of either of these crops in excess of the acreage prescribed by the administration.

The administration says that they employ these restrictions because they fear the Kipsigis may become monocrop cash crop producers if they are allowed to plant as much tea or coffee as they like. This would place them completely at the mercy of cash for survival and satisfaction of basic food requirements. It would open the door to severe hardship in the event of crop failure or a sharp decline in prices. The administration cites the difficulties of some Gusii coffee growers who have devoted all or most of their land to that crop and have little or no land left over for the cultivation of food crops or pasture for their animals. The District Agricultural Officer says he fears that the Kipsigis would do the same thing. He has encouraged diversified, balanced farming geared primarily to providing subsistence in grains and vegetables, along with adequate pasture for cattle. Fencing, and rotation of paddocks with tilled areas insure controlled fertility.

Another explanation offered by the administration for regulating the planting of tea is that the surrounding tea factories of the Europeans are neither prepared for nor especially desirous of processing *large* amounts of Kipsigis leaf. In the absence of adequate processing facilities or the wherewithal to construct their own, it would be foolish and harmful, the administration says, to allow or to encourage the indiscriminate planting of tea.

The same argument does not hold as well for coffee since the purchase of simple processing equipment would be within the reach of a cooperating group of producers. And if the coffee is sold as *buni—*

less desirable than the processed product but saleable nevertheless—it would require no processing whatsoever. Nevertheless, the administration exercises the same kinds of restrictions on the cultivation of coffee by the Kipsigis as of tea.

The first harvest from each of these crops is expected to take place in 1960. Of the two new cash crops, tea is vastly preferred to coffee. This seems natural enough when we recall that the Kipsigis have before them the example of the wealthy tea estates whose annual profits are known to be large and regular, while coffee has undergone drastic price fluctuations and is far more subject to loss through disease than tea.

The Kipsigis are also keenly interested in tapping the large market for the sale of milk—*to other Kipsigis.* To this end they have been engaged in a running war with the European administrators for permission to acquire the high-milk-yielding European-type cattle (Ayrshire, Holstein-Friesan, Jersey, etc.). The administration has been firm in its insistence that the Kipsigis stay with their native cattle as these are bred "up" by crossing with Sahiwal humped cattle. It insists that acquisition of European-type (called grade) cattle by the Kipsigis could prove catastrophic. There are at least two diseases of infertility to which grade cattle are subject which seem not to affect native cattle. Although another disease (epivaginitis) does affect native cattle, they recover from an attack while grade cattle are left permanently sterile. The other infections cause a mechanical sterility which may be counteracted by artificial insemination. In any case, the administration says that it could not cope with a widespread epidemic of the many infections which might follow the indiscriminate introduction of grade cattle and grade-crosses into the Reserve.

The District Veterinary Officer maintains that the Kipsigis would do much better with the Sahiwal crosses than they would with grade or grade-crosses. The Sahiwal, he says, will "do as well as the grade with good management and better than the grade with the poor management the Kipsigis are likely to give them." In short, the administration's position is that the Kipsigis cannot "cope" with the more delicate European-type cattle. Nevertheless they are even unwilling to approve the purchase of these cattle by Kipsigis who have demonstrated their capacity for taking good care of their animals. The European settlers generally side with the administration in opposing the right of the Kipsigis to acquire grade cattle. However, a few have reported that they can see some advantage to the sale of their calves to the eager Kipsigis. Some members of the administration suspect that these Europeans are less anxious to help the Kipsigis than they are to dispose of some of their culls.

In any case, as in the matter of tea and coffee restrictions, the Kipsigis interpret the administrations's interference with their right to plant what they wish or take their chances with "those sickly European cows that give so much milk" as a conscious effort to restrain the development of potential competitors of the European producers.

They point out that in 1958 the Kipsigis spent more than £18,000 for milk. All but a small part of it was produced by European dairymen. Only 114 Kipsigis were known to be selling milk, mostly in quantities of a few pints each. The Kipsigis would like to be free of the need for buying milk from the Europeans or, to put it another way, since milk buying is not going to terminate while available grazing land contracts, numbers of Kipsigis would like to appropriate all or at least a good part of the tribal market for milk to themselves.[16]

THE GROWTH OF MARKETS

Pre-contact exchange with Gusii, Luo, and Masai followed the announcement of a *kalyet* (literally peace, but also the word used for barter) and this was, in turn, generally arranged only when famine or other circumstances of severe want induced trade. There was no regularity or schedule of barter. The Kipsigis would exchange skins and hides for grain with the Gusii; six goats could be bartered for about 60 pounds of husked millet. The Kipsigis sometimes exchanged tobacco with the Masai for cattle. One goat was exchanged for a spear, the same for a hoe or an axe. All barter was conducted on the shores of a river boundary between the normally hostile tribes. The major precontact sites of this *ad hoc* barter were Kibaraa (presently Sondu) Kibirech, Chebwenge, Sanet, Kapsorok, and Kamulgelwo.

The casual local trade in cash of the first few post-contact years assumed a greater regularity in 1912 when two Kipsigis, arap Komuilong and arap Marinyo of Buret, organized the buying of skins and hides from Kipsigis and sold them to Indian traders who had located at Chemororoch (Litein) to establish the first trading center within the Native Land Unit (Reserve). By 1914 other Asians had set up shop at Kipsonoi. And by the end of the first World War there were over 50 shops in and around the Reserve, none of them owned or run by Kipsigis. It was not until 1925–26 that Nyamburugi arap Rotich established the first Kipsigis-owned shop, at Chemosit.

So-called open barter markets, that is, space for itinerant peddlers

(16) Before the end of 1960 the Kipsigis had won this battle with the administration and were allowed to acquire grade cattle freely. As this goes to press (early 1962) the results are generally very good, although initially, it is reported, there were some fairly heavy losses until the Kipsigis exercised greater care in spraying their animals.

to display and sell their wares for cash, developed alongside the shops and regular markets.[17] Ordinarily, each of these "barter" markets was held on a particular day of the week, the day varying from market to market, largely to allow the professional hawker to make his rounds with as little difficulty as possible. With the implementation of more precise government controls over markets in 1946, this staggering of the market days was formalized.

Although the barter markets thus have a cyclical nature which is superficially like that described for the Maya, Berbers, and Dahomeans (Silverman 1959), the Kipsigis markets do not serve as these latter do to interrelate specialist communities or "sections." There is no internal specialization of any importance within the Reserve. The only specialist commodities offered for sale in the Reserve markets come from outside; for example, pots from the Luo. The Kipsigis "barter" markets resemble those described by Silverman primarily in the staggered scheduling, less in respect of the function of this scheduling. At these markets cattle, rope, pots, beads, bangles, millet, ochre, tobacco, maize, and other items were offered for sale— for cash. Barter, of course, occurred, but it became increasingly rare as time went on. Even today one may occasionally see a pot bartered for the amount of husked maize required to fill it. But this is the only item of common barter that occurs with any frequency in all of the markets I have examined.

By April of 1958 the number of market places in the Kericho District (all Kipsigis) had grown to 53.[18] In addition there were four trading centers—places where non-Kipsigis as well as Kipsigis are permitted by the administration to operate shops—and four centers for cattle auctions. There were 154 licensed produce buyers and 23 licensed stock traders functioning regularly in the shops and markets of the Reserve. In all there were over 450 Kipsigis-owned and operated shops in the Reserve as of that date.[19] Of these, approximately 10–15 per cent are individually operated; the remainder are run by groups of partners (called "companies"), usually three to six individu-

[17] *By-Laws of the Kipsigis African District Council*, p. 2, defines a 'barter market' as a "general market which includes an area allotted by the authority for the barter of native and non-native produce." It consists of an open grass space in the vicinity of the market shops. Although the word barter is used in all official communications and is employed by Africans and Europeans alike when referring to these open-air markets, it is clearly understood that those traders who function in these markets are hawkers or peddlers (p. 3). Barter in the generally accepted sense is rare, most goods in barter markets being exchanged for cash only.

[18] Mimeographed minutes of meeting of Marketing Committee, Kericho, April 26, 28, 1958.

[19] District Commissioner's Files. As this goes to press (early 1962) the number of market places has risen to 67, and the number of shops to more than 600.

als, but in about one-fifth of the "company" situations there may be as many as 10 to 20 people involved. The overwhelming majority of shops is in the hands of renters, approximately 80 per cent to 90 per cent of African-run shops on the Reserve being rented for amounts varying btween 20 and 125 shillings per month.[20] In addition to the shops *in the Reserve*, there are 54 African-run shops in Kericho, 12 in Sotik, and 7 in Lumbwa, most of them run by Kipsigis and all of them coming under the supervision of the Nyanza County Council. Besides these, the Council supervises an additional 343 shops owned by Europeans and Asians in the townships and on the farms and estates surrounding the Reserve.[21] The vast majority of these shops cater exclusively, or almost so, to the African trade, to the Reserve Kipsigis and to the estate laborers and "legal squatters."

The fact that marketing and trade have developed largely as male-dominated enterprises among the Kipsigis does not signify the absence of females. Most women in the open barter markets, however, are minor hawkers of eggs, chickens, vegetables, etc. The shops are owned and run almost exclusively by men. There were in 1959 only two shops in the entire district run by women—both of them widows. While non-Kipsigis are prohibited from owning shops in any of the 53 markets in the Reserve, they may own shops in any of the four trading centers. Trade in these centers is dominated by Asians. Anyone may hawk in the open "barter" markets. In them, each hawker pays a fee to the market master, who is an employee of the Kipsigis African District Council. The fees for use of the space are geared to the value of the marketer's commodities and range from 10 cents upwards.[22] In the larger, open, "barter" markets, like those held in Kericho and Kapsuser, there may be as many as several hundred hawkers present, their wares ranging from matches and razor blades to dried fish. Here Luo, Gusii, Kamba, and other tribes will be represented in sizable proportions.

The fees that are collected in the Kipsigis African District Council-supervised, open, "barter" markets are turned over to that agency through the Markets Inspector who is under the charge of the Executive Officer, a European appointed by the European administration. The entire marketing staff—Kipsigis—is under direct supervision of the Markets Inspector, and it is their responsibility to look after the cleanliness of markets as well as to collect fees. At present there are

---

(20) Personal Communication from the Market Inspector for the KADC.

(21) From the files of the Nyanza County Council, Kericho.

(22) There are 100 cents to a shilling. Produce valued under 2 shillings pays the ten cent tariff; for each additional two shillings of value, the hawker must pay another ten cents.

twelve market masters, each of whom has four or five markets under his supervision. Staggering of market days enables this relatively small staff to carry on its work without too much difficulty. The Kipsigis African District Council realizes about £100 a month from fees collected at all open barter markets. Plot rents, premise licenses, and slaughter fees account for about another £85 per month. The total annual revenue to the KADC from markets thus comes to around £2200. Salaries, uniforms, travelling expenses, fencing of barter areas. and so on, usually run a little above the revenue figure so that a small annual subsidy from other KADC funds is required.[22A]

While it is impossible to know with any accuracy the total cash value of sales carried on in all of the open, "barter" markets—just as it is impossible to get accurate figures for the gross volume of sales in the shops—it is conservatively estimated by the market inspector that the average is a round £35 per market per month or, roughly £21,000 a year for all of the "barter" markets inside the Reserve. The average for the weekly market in the Nyanza County Council supervised plot at Kericho is given officially as £20 per week. I have attended this market on a number of occasions at different seasons of the year, and on the basis of informal computations would place the average weekly sales volume at something closer to five times that figure.

The volume of sales in the shops in the Reserve market places is estimated at many times the amount figured for the "barter" markets, but I am unable to supply accurate data on the total involved. Some of the market places, like those at Kapsuser and Ainabkoi which are on the road across from large European tea estates are believed to have weekly gross sales in all of their shops of well over £200.

The shopkeepers reckon the relationship between themselves and the barter market advantageous to them, for much of their sales revenue on market days comes from the casual peddler (one who generally produces his own sale objects) who quickly exchanges the cash he gets for the sale of his maize flour, rope, chickens, etc., for items sold in the adjacent shops.

The market itself usually consists of an arc of buildings off the main road to which it is adjacent. A few of the larger and more modern markets have their buildings arranged in parallel lines facing each other across a plaza, or with shops arranged on three sides of a rectangle. Each of the buildings is constructed of the same materials and has the same general outward appearance as the others, but the type varies within limits from market to market. The poorer and more isolated markets consist of mud and dung buildings with thatched

(22A) By the end of 1961, the income figure had risen to about £135 and £100 respectively per month, or about £2800 per year.

roofs; and then there are those that are made of brick with tin roofs, or others of concrete blocks and tin roofs. While the design and style of architecture for each market is internally uniform, the scheme is to improve the buildings whenever possible. Thus when the shop owners are willing to better their facilities, they usually construct the new building directly behind the old one. When all of the new ones have been completed, the old buildings are demolished and the new arc of shops stands ready for use.

Sometimes a market place may have only six shops surrounding it. Some of the larger markets, like the only at Kapsuser, include as many as 24 shops. Most of these are referred to as "general" of "sundry" shops, meaning that they sell a variety of everyday commodities like blankets, foodstuffs, housewares, soda pop, and so on. Other special shops—and most of the markets do not include all categories of these— are butcher, hotel (tea shop), carpenter, shoe repair, hardware, and bicycle repair. There is at least one sewing machine in at least one of the general shops in virtually all of the markets. But the tailor him- self is likely to be Gusii or Luo, just as the carpenter and the shoe repair man (in contrast to the bicycle repair man) are almost certain to be non-Kipsigis employees.

Most of the African-run shops in the Reserve or township areas are owned and/or operated by men whose homes and land are in the same general vicinity. They continue to rely upon their farms for a large part of their subsistence and possibly for income as well. Some of the men engaged in these businesses have an interest in more than one shop; or they may have a part interest in some other money- making enterprise.

As far as I could discover, many of the shops seem to have been built by indivuals or "companies" with the intention of running them themselves. But in the majority of cases the effort to amass the money needed to put up the building seems to have exhausted the reserves of the builders and forced them, in the absence of cash or credit resources for stocking the shop, to rent them after completion. Some shops were, of course, built with the purpose of rent-income clearly in mind. Some others are in fact operated by the men who put them up.

Most of the shopkeepers whom I knew or interviewed were small farmers, although a few had sizeable land and cattle holdings in addition to their commercial activities. But there is an apparently growing number of men involved in shopkeeping who have expanded their activities to other forms o fbusiness enterprise, many others who are hoping to do so as savings permit or if credit becomes available. There are, thus, a number of traders who own trucks which they rent out or use to transport commodities for a fee. There are others who are part-owners of tractor companies which plow and harrow land for Kipsigis at anywhere from 50–80 shillings an acre.[23]

CREDIT AND THE COOPERATIVE

Despite the government's early and continuing interest in the expansion of trade among the Kipsigis, it has been only in the past few years that even a small amount of government credit has been made available to shopkeepers. The new source of credit is extended in the form of loans to those shopkeepers who have a going business and wish to expand it or branch out into new enterprises. It is not available for simple inventory purchases. Moreover, procurement of one of these Loans to African Traders is hedged around with considerable red tape, including the requirement that an applicant spend six weeks at a central boarding school learning how to keep records and accounts and being instructed in a variety of merchandising skills. In 1958 these loans bore an interest of $5^1/_2$ per cent. Only 15 of them had been made, and the total amount involved was £8900.

Bank loans are almost entirely out of the question because the borrower so rarely possesses anything that he might put up as collateral. Without formal title or the right of alienation to an outsider, the Kipsigis' land or Reserve shop is useless as security. And private lenders or banks, of which there are three in Kericho, would be unwilling to accept cattle for security, since these could prove most elusive to a creditor who wanted to seize them for sale.

In the early years, the activities of Asian traders and shopkeepers largely kept pace with the Kipsigis demand for sale of their own produce and purchase of processed and manufactured commodities. Thus, while expansion of trade and the multiplication of wants were closely related to growing labor requirements in the District during the first three decades of contact, there was no need for the government to entice Kipsigis into marketing activities on their own. In fact, it seems clear that the incentives to increasing participation in the cash economy—of which the emerging markets were one aspect—came from the Kipsigis themselves. Once the Pandora's box of the material

(23) In 1958 there were 88 Kipsigis-owned trucks in the Reserve and 24 tractors. A number of these were out of commission because their individual or collective owners could not find the money to make the necessary repairs that would keep them in operation. After they have invested everything they have in the purchase of the vehicle they are often left without resources to meet the cost of repairs. If they have not been fortunate enough to have earned and put aside a fund for such eventualities, they may lose the vehicle or, if it is fully paid for, they may just let it sit and rust. I myself saw seven or eight tractors and trucks "unnecessarily" abandoned in this manner.

allurements of industrial civilization was opened, the Kipsigis began to seize upon any device that would make available to them a greater amount of these objects. Because the items which stocked the Asian shopkeepers' shelves were so attractive, it followed that some Kipsigis would appreciate the income-yielding potential of their own proprietorship of a shop.

Since loans were unavailable, the usual road to proprietorship or shopkeeping lay through individual accumulation, especially by sale of cattle, labor to the Europeans and, to a lesser extent, the sale of agricultural produce. In today's period of market expansion,[24] the techniques for becoming a shopkeeper and/or owner are the same, for no important new sources of credit for the purpose have opened up. The chief source of *operating* (merchandise) credit for the Kipsigis shopkeeper is the Asian trader. Despite the existence of the Kipsigis Traders Cooperative, a European-run but Kipsigis-owned enterprise, about 80 per cent of all goods sold by Africans in the Reserve are purchased at wholesale from Asians who extend credit on relatively generous terms and for comparatively long periods—and without collateral.

The absence of long-term KTC credit, an avowed suspicion of the European management, the fact that the Asian traders have been striving to destroy the competition of the Coöperative by beating its prices as well as by supplying goods on credit, all together account for the failure of the Cooperative to wrest wholesale trade in the Reserve from the Asians in the nine years of its existence.

In 1958 the Cooperative had 183 Kipsigis members, each of whom had contributed at least £25 for the purchase of a single share. Although the monthly average of sales throughout the Reserve was around £7500 in that year, the Coöp had so often been on the verge of collapse that it was decided by the management to hand over the operation of the enterprise to the United Africa Company. Several loans, one from the Kipsigis African District Council and another from the Colonial Government, had managed to keep the Coöperative going during the fifties, but by 1958 it appeared to the European director that the only way to insure survival of the enterprise was to place its management in the hands of a group which had the staff, the equipment, and the experience to meet the Asian competition. The circumstances of the transfer looked attractive to the membership, for they had been perennially fearful that the cooperative would collapse, and they voted supervision of the activity to the UAC.

(24) In 1958 the administration set aside 13 new plots for shops in the trading center at Litein. The plots were finally awarded by the drawing of lots, since several hundred Kipsigis had submitted applications.

It is interesting to note that the government, in its latter-day eagerness to encourage the Kipsigis Traders Cooperative and thus build Kipsigis participation in and responsibility for the growth of markets and marketing in the Reserve, made this the only "closed" Reserve in Kenya. This means that aside from a few "reputable traders" who are granted licenses by the District Commissioner, no peddlers other than the KTC are permitted to enter the Reserve. In practice, of course, there is a good deal of illegal hawking carried on which the administration says it is powerless to stop. The new UAC management now inherits this virtual monopoly of trade in return for 50 per cent of the net profits.[24A]

The Government has, from time to time, launched other cooperatives among the Kipsigis, like the Hides and Skins Cooperative. None has had the financial backing of the KTC, and all have, so far, been singularly unsuccessful.

CONCLUSION

While the fate of individual shopkeepers and even the continued existence of some clusters of shops in Kipsigis country may be in doubt, there is no question about the overall growth of commercial activities in and around the Reserve in the years ahead. The inevitable increase in cash-cropping, and the certainty that ever-larger numbers of Kipsigis will become dependent upon wage labor as tea and coffee cultivation expand and population growth presses on the remaining land, are guarantees of this development. Although a part of the growth in marketing volume will thus be a consequence of land shortages, as well as of new kinds of land use, the trend and involvement are inescapable because of the increasing needs for money income. The new wants can only be satisfied through cash purchase, and they are bound to multiply. If one means of acquiring cash income dries up the Kipsigis will have to make use of others. Even the limited record of the past 30 years reveals such accommodation. As yet, the Kipsigis have not been forced into the labor market in the numbers of their Luo and Gusii neighbors whose lands are generally poorer and more crowded. But if tea cultivation is denied them or allowed only in small scale by a powerful European administration; or if low prices and disease destroy the value of coffee crops in the years to come, many more Kipsigis will have to turn to wage labor to

---

(24A) In 1961 the operation of the KTC passed from the UAC to Dalgety's, a private enterprise with branches in several Commonwealth countries. Although the KTC did not declare bankruptcy, it is clear that if they were to liquidate all of their current assets, their obligations would be far greater than the cash they could realize.

provide them with the material items the growing markets around them are prepared to sell. The simple, almost completely subsistence lifeways that are still followed by a tiny minority of the 175,000 Kipsigis on this Reserve of 1001 square miles is about to disappear even for these few.

The District Agricultural Officer in 1958 estimated that 496,383 of the total 640,640 acres in the Reserve were suitable either for grazing or cropping. This represents 77.48 per cent of the land. Even if these figures are accurate—and one cannot be sure whether they are more or less generous than they ought to be—it gives us a situation at present of approximately 2.8 acres per capita. In an economy where herding is still very important this is not an overly large amount. Even if herding declines in importance in years to come, population expansion is almost certain to continue. Under these circumstances subsistence farming must inevitably suffer. Survival in the present and future world of Western inspired wants and needs will require more and more cash income.

In 1958, the District Agricultural Officer estimated the average annual expenses of a "better class Kipsigis farmer" to be 1368 shillings (about £ 68.)[25] While the figure given may be somewhat generous and subject to considerable individual variance even among "better farmers,"[26] it reflects the wide range of items for which cash is required and suggests the potentially growing need for money income, not only as prices rise but as more and more Kipsigis come to demand ever-increasing participation in the Westernized material universe that is being shown them.

If we assume no radical change in the land-owning status of the settlers during the next few years, then agricultural wage labor will be one of the important ways in which cash can be earned in the period ahead. When and if profound political changes do take place in Kenya, the picture of peasant vs. plantation cultivation may undergo serious alterations for the Kipsigis. However, this kind of forecasting is not our concern at the moment. Nothing can halt the growth of commerce and internal (Kenya) exchange. Increased peasant pro-

(25) Poll tax, 20 shs.; KADC rate (or tax), 20 shs. parents' clothes, 224 shs.; childrens' clothes, 113 shs.; blankets, 159 shs.; school fees, 53 shs.; meat, 189 shs.; salt, 27 shs.; vegetables, 21 shs.; medicines, 66 shs.; boots and shoes, 93 shs.; soap, 58 shs.; kerosene, 44 shs.; cooking fat, 44 shs.; miscellaneous 227 shs. It should be noted that the tax rates have risen in the intervening two years; school fees have been advanced very sharply, especially in the intermediate grades; and the prices of other commodities continued to rise.

(26) In 1958 there were 1011 Kipsigis farmers in the Reserve entitled to enjoy this designation. An uncertain proportion of these are classified by the District Agricultural Officer as "better class farmers" in terms of the foregoing budget.

duction and the growth of a middle class of professional, artisan, and service personnel, along with the burgeoning of internal trade and commerce are ways other than wage labor in which money incomes can be acquired. All of these involve mutually reinforcing activities which yield cash to the individual and simultaneously excite the expansion of goods, services, and other devices for the disposal of the cash so earned.

CHAPTER 20

Wealth and Power in Gusiiland

BY ROBERT A. LEVINE

Gusiiland, known in Kenya as Kisii Highlands, is located in South Nyanza District,[1] 50 miles south of the equator and 25 miles southeast of the Kavirondo Gulf of Lake Victoria. Geographically, the area is a southwestern extension of the White Highlands, but it is inhabited exclusively by the Gusii,[2] a Bantu-speaking people of more than a quarter of a million who are the seventh largest tribal group in Kenya and constituted just under five per cent of the total African population in the 1948 census.

There are two major ecological regions of Gusiiland: a northeastern region adjacent to the Kericho highlands in the east and the low country of Central Nyanza in the north; and a southwestern region which abuts on the lake shore lowlands. The northeastern region is high (5500 to more than 7000 feet above sea level); wet (rainfall averages 66 to 101 inches a year in different spots); and hilly. The southwestern region is lower, with elevations as low as 4500 feet; dryer (approximately 60 inches a year); and somewhat more level. The northeastern region is more orthodox in its Gusii culture and currently more densely populated (1948 population densities ranged up to 524 per square mile), while the southwestern region has been more influenced by the culture of the lake-shore Luo (a Nilotic-speaking people) and is less densely populated. Gusiiland, especially in its northeastern region, has the climate for which the Kenya highlands are well-known: cool temperatures and two clearly defined rainy seasons. The field study on which this article is based was carried out in northeastern Gusiiland; thus primary attention will be paid to conditions in that region.

(1) South Nyanza District was the administrative unit which contained Gusiiland in 1955–57, when the author carried out a field study there on a fellowship granted by the Ford Foundation. In 1958 the Kenya Government announced its intention to divide South Nyanza into two districts along ethnic lines, with Gusiiland becoming a separate administrative unit retaining the headquarters in the township of Kisii. The material presented in this article refers to the administrative arrangement which existed in 1955-57.

(2) The Gusii are commonly known as Kisii, which is a Swahili version of their name, and refer to themselves collectively as Abagusii. The term "Gusii" is an ethnographic convention formed by dropping the Bantu prefix.

THE TRADITIONAL GUSII ECONOMY

Like many other Kenya Bantu peoples, the Gusii traditionally combined agriculture and animal husbandry. Cattle herding, however, was more important to them than it was to any other Kenya Bantu group except the linguistically related Kuria, and it tended to overshadow cultivation in social significance, if not actually in subsistence importance. Residential units were dispersed across the hillsides, and each homestead cultivated eleusine on several strips of land running down the hill from the house. Land was abundant, property rights to it were vaguely defined, and lineage groups moved around considerably within the highlands rather than being fixed to a particular piece of land. Economic aggrandizement was seen primarily in terms of the acquisition of large herds of cattle through breeding, and raids on neighboring Gusii clans and on other cultural groups such as the Luo. Each homestead had a young man (single or married) living in the cattle-village *(egesaraati)* of its local lineage unit. In these cattle-villages, the young men herded collectively and plotted raids on neighboring clans. Women were not allowed into the cattle-villages, and children were sent from the homesteads to fetch milk. Some cows were always kept in a kraal just outside the traditional house, and when the Government abolished cattle-villages in 1912 (to reduce the bellicosity of the Gusii), the family herds were relocated there. The importance of cattle for the Gusii is illustrated by the fact that they retain cattle as the primary object in bridewealth, although cash is as much in general use as it is among many Kenya groups which have abandoned cattle for cash bridewealth. So elaborate are traditional Gusii regulations concerning bridewealth transfer of cattle and other goods, and the related problems of cattle inheritance and cattle debts, that a monograph (Mayer 1950) has been written on the subject. Land tenure, however, until recently was so vaguely defined that the contemporary system of land inheritance has been largely patterned after the older cattle inheritance customs. Thus the Gusii are a people whose economic traditions emphasize the value of cattle as a commodity and animal husbandry as an occupation, although agriculture has always been important in subsistence.

The traditional productive unit among the Gusii was the polygynous extended family, typically composed of a male homestead head, his wives (each occupying a different house), his married sons and their wives, and the unmarried children of both adult generations. There might also be some older people such as the mother or paternal uncle of the homestead head residing there in a separate house. Work was organized according to age and sex. Women and middle-aged men worked the fields; young men lived out in cattle-villages to herd and raid; uninitiated children herded sheep and goats; old men discussed cattle and settled local disputes. Agriculture was primarily woman's work and thus less prestigeful than the care and disposal of cattle, a male activity. Most work of a routine nature was done by women and children, while adult males concentrated on activities that required concerted effort and decision-making skills. In the authority system of the family-homestead unit, leisure and work were a function of sex and age. Men had more leisure and performed more prestigeful duties than women, but old men had the most leisure (being relieved of productive activities) and performed the most prestigeful duties, particularly those of a judicial and political nature. Old men could order about younger persons and men could order women about. Children, at the bottom of the age-hierarchy, were ordered about by everyone and used as messengers and handservants. The young men living in the cattle-villages were the only exception in the age-hierarchy, since they sometimes disobeyed the elders in their military adventures against other clans. A concept basic to Gusii family life is that persons of higher status have more leisure, perform less routine activities, and can order those of lower status to do laborious chores for them.

Although there were (and are) work groups involving inter-homestead cooperation, a Gusii family lived off the crops, milk, and meat of its own herds and land and was in large measure economically self-sufficient. Subsistence in the fertile highlands was not a problem for anyone, but homesteads varied in their possession of prestige goods, particularly cattle. Cattle were transferable for the other major symbol of wealth—wives. A rich homestead was one with a large herd of cattle and numerous women married to the homestead head. The wives in turn produced sons to defend the herds and daughters to bring in more cattle through their marriages. A poor homestead featured a monogamous homestead head and only a few cattle for family needs. Variations in the wealth of the homesteads resulted from a number of factors: the number of cattle a man inherited from his father; the number of uterine sisters he had whose bridewealth cattle were not used as bridewealth for other males of the paternal homestead; and the number of cattle obtained in raids on the Luo and other Gusii clans. If a man acquired a relatively large number of cattle in his youth, he might acquire a permanent advantage by marrying several wives whose daughters brought in many bridewealth cattle. On the other hand, a preponderance of sons might dissipate this advantage through their own marriages unless they were active raiders. The wealth of the rich polygynist might have to be divided among so many sons that none of them would inherit the economic advantage of their father. Social classes based on wealth did not develop; any particular lineage or local group would contain a few rich home-steads and many others of less wealth.

The social status of a homestead head and his influence in community affairs were largely dependent on his wealth. A rich man *(omanda)* was respected and listened to, while a poor man *(omoraka)* was despised, at least covertly, and ignored. This pattern of invidious distinction is most explicit in Gusii terminology used for referring to these two categories of men. The word *omonguru*, literally "man of power" and used in Gusii versions of the Bible to mean "the Lord," is invariably defined by informants as a big polygynist with many wives and much cattle. For monogamists there are several terms of abuse. One of these is *omworo*, "weak man." Another is *nyakekemo*, "one basket," referring to the fact that he has only one wife to prepare a basket of food to offer visitors when they come. Every wife prepared a basket of dry porridge for the main meal, so that a polygynous home-stead would have abundant food for guests, while the monogamist shared his single basket with them. A rich man would also slaughter a bull to feed visitors from far away, while the average person would slaughter a goat or sheep—and a poor man, merely a chicken. These differences in capacity to entertain guests were among the most important economic differences within a community, for the lavish hospitality of the wealthy polygynist attracted many guests, particularly lineage elders *(abagaaka begesaku)* who would congregate at his homestead to eat and adjudicate disputes. The wealthy host often dominated such judicial proceedings and people would bring their cases to him because of his dominant position. Thus was wealth translated into power in the local community.

The rich man exercised power in other ways as well. The leader of the young men in a cattle-village was often a son of the richest home-stead head represented in the cattle-village, since his cattle formed the largest part of the joint herd. A wealthy elder with many sons was often feared and respected because of the retaliatory power of his sons as a military force. There are indications that the wealthy used their power to dominate and exploit others in a local area. This is expressed in the Gusii proverbs; "The property of the poor man is used by the rich man"; and, "The property of the *omworo* is grabbed by the *omonguru*." Furthermore, there was rivalry between wealthy home-steads in a given area ("Rich men fear each other") resulting in the emigration of one or more of them, leaving one homestead head in undisputed dominance over the area. In the large tribe of Getutu, which alone among Gusii tribes developed a hereditary chieftainship, the military-judicial power of the chief was solidly rooted in great wealth. Bogonko, most famous of the chiefs, who lived in the 19th century, is said to have had fourteen wives and many sons. A song still sung boasts of Bogonko's herds of cattle so great that many men were needed to herd them without losing any. His descendants claim that Bogonko would slaughter four bulls just to feed his sons to make them strong in warfare. The association of wealth, as indicated by polygyny and cattle, with political power was a pronounced characteristic of the traditional Gusii social system.

Traditionally, the Gusii had no general medium of exchange and no organized markets. They did engage in exchange of various kinds involving goods and services, with each particular kind being carried on within a specifiable social grouping. The local community can be defined as the maximal group of contiguous homesteads which recognized the mutual obligation to exchange work for beer.

This form of group is known as *risaga*, with the maximal group being called *risaga rinene* (big *risaga*), and each of its subdivisions, *risaga riike* (small *risaga*). When a man had some agricultural work to get done in a hurry, he would prepare beer and send out the call to members of his large or small *risaga*. Each homestead in the group that was notified had to send women to do the work while men came to drink the beer. Sometimes men did some of the work also. Although the group participating in *risaga* were ordinarily agnatic kin and close to one another in many ways, there is no doubt that *risaga* was thought of as a transaction involving an exchange of goods for services. For example, people would grumble if too little beer were prepared, and the host would grumble about families whose representatives drank a lot of beer but performed too little work. Ultimately, however, *risaga* meant not only a single exchange of work for beer but a reciprocal obligation to provide manpower in exchange for beer when another member of the local group needed it.

A second kind of economic transaction was the lending of livestock among agnatic kin for bridewealth, sacrifice, or payment of specialists. Repayment was ordinarily in kind and did not include interest.

A third kind of exchange, carried on only between exogamous patrilineal clans, was bridewealth, or the payment of a specified number of cattle, sheep and goats by a bridegroom or his father to the father of the bride. A good deal of bargaining concerning the quantity and quality of the cattle went on, and the marriage was called off if an agreement could not be reached. Bridewealth rates fluctuated according to the supply of cattle and the fear of girls' fathers that the rates would rise (Mayer 1950 : 39–56).

A fourth type of transaction could be carried on between any Gusii regardless of territorial or kin ties, although it was carried on locally when possible. This was the hiring of specialists to provide services or goods that a household could not provide for itself. The specialists who provided services were medicine men, head surgeons, sorcerers, diviners, removers of particular kinds of curses, witch-smellers or witch-detectives, circumcisers, clitoridectomizers, and rainmakers. Specialists who provided goods included smiths and hide-dressers. They were paid with livestock and grain.

The final type of transaction to be mentioned was carried on between Gusii and other peoples, primarily the Luo. The latter people, inhabiting the semi-arid lake shore region, suffered frequently from drought and subsequent famine. They came to rely on food obtained from the Gusii at such times. Making use of the scant resources of the lake shore, Luo would exchange salt which Gusii needed for their cattle in return for eleusine grain. The Luo are also good potters and would also bring pots to exchange for Gusii grain. The amounts of goods to be exchanged were arrived at by bargaining between individuals; there were no permanently established markets. An obvious limitation on the extent of such transactions was the Gusii fondness for raiding Luo cattle, disrupting peaceful relations between the two groups. It was Gusii cattle raids on the Luo that brought the former to the attention of British authorities in 1905 and led to the British administration of Gusiiland.

ECONOMIC CHANGE IN GUSIILAND

There are many respects in which the contemporary Gusii economy and the sociopolitical attitudes associated with it are as they have been described above, even after half a century of contact with Western civilization. Insofar as this is the case, it is due to the isolation of Gusiiland (more than 75 miles from the nearest railway station and even farther from large urban centers and areas of substantial European settlement) and to the relative lack of economic pressure toward urbanization. Nevertheless, Gusiiland has undergone an economic transformation; the seven changes outlined below are of greatest prominence.

1. The establishment of British administration, beginning in 1907. This was the beginning of economic development in Gusiiland, and had several immediate effects. One was the cessation of interclan feuding and of warfare and cattle raiding between the Gusii and Luo. Peaceful trading became possible. A second effect of British administration was the imposition of taxation and the introduction of Western-type money as a medium of exchange. Following this came the

introduction of Western consumption goods, brought by Indian and Somali traders.

2. The shift to intensive agriculture and production for export. Since 1907 the quality and quantity of Gusii agriculture has changed drastically. Maize, requiring less arduous cultivation than the traditional staple of eleusine, has become a very widespread crop, and sweet potatoes, bananas, legumes, and tomatoes are also more commonly grown than they were 50 years ago. The cattle epidemics of the 1890's, the cessation of cattle raiding in 1907, and the abolition of the cattle-villages in 1912 favored a greater emphasis on agricultural activity, and the development of a cash market for maize (and eleusine) provided the motivation for more intensive cultivation. Gusiiland remained the breadbasket for the peoples of the lake-shore lowlands, but crops could be sold for cash, and the cash could be used to buy Western consumption goods as well as cattle and goats. Nowadays, large quantities of Gusii maize and eleusine are exported to various parts of Kenya, and much of it is sold illegally at two to three times the prices set by the Government's Maize Control Office.

Since World War II, several non-subsistence cash crops have been introduced into Gusiiland. Coffee (arabica) is the most important of these, although black wattle, pyrethrum, and tea are also grown. Coffee production has progressed rapidly in Gusiiland, so that by 1957 Gusiiland was second among African areas in Kenya in the value of clean coffee produced. There is a Kisii Farmers Coöperative Union, consisting (in 1957) of 28 coöperative societies with 10,626 members. Although each member receives, on the average, no more than £10 for his annual crop, coffee cultivation has brought considerable amounts of cash income into Gusiiland and represents a relatively fast-growing part of the economy.

3. Population growth. The population of Gusiiland has been growing rapidly and is now about three times as great as it was before the British conquest. Land was abundant ín the area half a century ago, and new lands, fertile but previously uninhabited because of Gusii-Masai hostility, have been opened up for settlement by Gusii as recently as 1930. In fact, as late as 1935, there was enough free land in Gusiiland for Kikuyu and Logoli people from overcrowded areas in other parts of Kenya to be invited to settle on it. (The Kikuyu were removed during the Emergency caused by the Mau Mau rebellion.) Continued population growth has changed this situation drastically: land scarcity is now a problem, despite the new lands which have drained off settlers from older areas during the past 30 years. Agricultural officers in South Nyanza estimated an average of seven acres per extended family homestead in 1956, but there is great variability

within Gusiiland. In some of the newly settled areas homestead land holdings are much larger than that, while in the older, densely populated areas the average holding may be as low as three or four acres.

The increasing scarcity of land in Gusiiland has had several notable economic effects: (1) the stabilization of settlement, since there is no longer unoccupied land to move to; (2) a lessened interest in cattle-breeding (but it is still too intense to satisfy the Agricultural Department), since land is too valuable to use for pasturage; (3) increased attention, guided by the government, to increasing agricultural productivity through soil conservation measures (such as terracing) and the cultivation of cash crops; (4) attempts by Gusii men to find non-agricultural sources of income, primarily in the form of wage employment outside the district.

4. Labor migration. Increasing numbers of Gusii men have been leaving South Nyanza temporarily for employment on European plantations and in urban areas. In the 1948 census, 18,078 Gusii (out of a total population of 255,108) were found to be living outside of South Nyanza District, and it can be assumed that all of them were employed or the dependents of employees. The largest cluster of emigrants was in Kericho District (just adjacent to Gusiiland), where 9,783 Gusii were living and working in and around the tea plantations of that area. The remainder were widely scattered throughout Kenya, with concentrations in urban centers such as Nairobi and Kisumu.

In a survey of a small community in eastern Gusiiland, 24 of the 28 adult males in the community were found to have been employed outside of South Nyanza at some time in their lives, most of them no farther than Nairobi but a few as far as Egypt and the Belgian Congo. A majority of those who had emigrated had returned home either permanently or until they felt the economic pressure to leave again. Over an 18-month period the community experienced continual departure and return of men from outside employment; few of them intended to settle permanently outside of Gusiiland. The few who did had jobs with the Kenya Police and, unlike the others, tended to have all or part of their conjugal families living with them at work. Not represented in this community are the Gusii supervisory personnel of Kericho tea plantations, who establish relatively permanent family residences at their place of work.

Most Gusii males go off to work on the Kericho tea plantations for varying periods during their adolescence. Such sojourns have become as expected a part of a male life history as living in the cattle-villages was 50 years ago. In Kisii township there are labor recruiters for the tea plantations, who provide bus transportation to Kericho for a young man who agrees to become employed. In the small community mentioned above a man has only to walk down the hill to the road and hail a tea plantation bus to be transported 60 miles to a job in Kericho District. Like life in the cattle-villages, working in Kericho is viewed as simply a phase of a young man's life, terminated by his return to the community or by his seeking more lucrative employment in the cities.

Local officials in Nairobi report that Gusii stay in the city for shorter periods than groups such as the Luo, and that they exhibit a greater nostalgia for their home country which makes them disdainful of city life. In spite of this centripetal tendency it is clear that more and more Gusii are taking up employment outside of South Nyanza, and bringing (or sending) part of their earnings back to Gusiiland in the form of cash. There is no doubt that this has become a significant part of the cash economy of Gusiiland.

5. Craft production for the tourist market. In western Gusiiland a handicraft industry has developed which produces decorated "Kisii stools" and figurines from locally available soapstone, which are sold for high prices to tourists and others in Nairobi and other cities. The work is organized on a family basis, and the finished products are sold to middlemen, mostly Africans from North Nyanza, who sell them in the city. The cash payments made to Gusii artisans for their wares by the middlemen are alleged to be a small fraction of the retail prices for which they are sold.

6. Markets. Although Kisii township—the only town in South Nyanza—has the largest concentration of shops and the largest open market place where food is sold and bartered, there is an extensive network of local markets throughout Gusiiland. One feature which distinguishes the local market shops from the shops in Kisii is that the latter are owned and operated largely by Indians and Somalis, while the former are almost entirely owned and operated by Gusii. The local markets were introduced by the government and have no traditional counterpart; many of them are less than 15 years old. The government plans them, issues licenses for the shops, and controls a good deal of their overall operation. The shops are invariably arranged in a rectangular pattern, and plans for the construction of a building must be approved by government officials. Most markets have a day when cattle sales are conducted in a certain section of the open space, often in the middle of the rectangle formed by the shops, and when all the shops are open and trade flourishes. Government coördination staggers the market days so that markets near one another are not in operation simultaneously.

Markets are now an important part of the landscape as well as of the economy of Gusiiland. Although a fuller account of their role in

Gusii life appears below, it is appropriate at this point to indicate their ubiquity. In Nyaribari, an eastern Gusiiland administrative location with a population of approximately 50,000 and an area of 100 square miles, there are 13 markets. These range in size from Keroka, officially a "trading centre" rather than a market, which has a section of Indian-run shops and one of African shops, and which serves the main Kisii-Kericho road with a petrol pump, to small, isolated markets with but a few simple shops. Distributed fairly evenly over the area of the location, the markets are situated so that no one lives more than a few miles from a source of European consumer goods, an outpost of the growing cash sector of the economy. Many persons, however, do not trade entirely at the nearest local markets but attend the larger markets on their trading days, go into Kisii on Thursdays (the big trading day there), and even travel to markets at the Luo border for trade in special items discussed below. This mobility is facilitated by a fairly adequate network of dirt roads throughout Gusiiland, and by privately owned buses which travel over the roads carrying people to and from town and markets.

7. Rising standards of consumption. With the use of money and with cash income from the sale of crops, the production of craft objects, and employment, many Gusii have cash incomes in excess of their bare subsistence needs. In fact most are still growing their own food, building their houses with the aid of coöperative labor, and paying local specialists in livestock, so that their "need" for cash, from a traditional viewpoint, is slight. But the economic forces which have provided them with sources of cash income have also introduced a variety of ways of spending the cash, creating many new needs. Most Gusii now feel a need for cotton clothing, woolen blankets, kerosene lamps, tea, sugar, and a folding chair or two, all of which must be bought with cash. Many of them also desire cash for school fees, bicycles, and more elaborate clothing and furniture. The most sophisticated want gramophones, European beer, and even motorcycles. There is no end to the catalogue of wants introduced with Western economic values, and it is familiar to the reader. In addition to the desire for consumer goods must be mentioned the extreme litigiousness of the Gusii, a characteristic which consumes large quantities of their cash in court fees and fines. (The revenue goes to the African District Council which spends some of it on local projects). All in all, the affluence of the Gusii relative to other African groups is accompanied by increasing needs for cash which in turn spur them to pecuniary activities.

A GUSII MARKET AND ITS SOCIAL FUNCTIONS

The market to be described is Keumbu, third largest of the 13 markets in Nyaribari Location. It is situated on the main road (actually
a dirt road which in the rains is sometimes closed to heavy traffic)
running eastward from Kisii to Sotik and ultimately to Kericho and
Nairobi. Keumbu is eight miles out of Kisii township. Three miles
closer to town, on the same road, is a smaller market called Kegati
("the middle"), and three miles farther from town than Keumbu
is another smaller market called Birungo. Keroka, the "trading
centre" and largest concentration of shops in Nyaribari, is six to seven
miles east of Keumbu (about fifteen miles from town) on the same
road. Since buses run along this road several times a day and distances
of fifteen miles are not considered excessive for walking, it is obvious
that people living near Keumbu are not entirely dependent on it.
They can go eight miles into town or seven miles to Keroka if they
want a larger market, and some of them may find the smaller markets
of Birungo or Kegati more convenient. However, Keumbu market
has several unique features from which it derives considerable benefits. One is that it is located just across the road from the Chief's Camp,
consisting of the office of the Chief of Nyaribari, the assembly hall for
the location, quarters for a few tribal policemen, and a prison cubicle.
Also clustered around the Chief's Camp are the houses of an African
agricultural officer and a public health officer. Just up the hill from
the Chief's Camp is a Roman Catholic primary and intermediate
school with about 400 pupils and a number of Gusii teachers. The
Chief's Camp brings Keumbu market the trade of policemen, sub-
headmen, and litigants trying to see the chief, as well as the large
number of elders who attend the Monday *baraza* (assembly); the
school brings the resident teachers and large numbers of pupils as
consumers. In recognition of its constant importance, Keumbu
market does not have a special day when large crowds come; it does
a less spectacular but steady business throughout the week.

The shops of Keumbu form three sides of a large rectangle, with
the road as the fourth side. The interior of the rectangle is a grassy
expanse, larger than a soccer field, cropped short by grazing sheep.
Most of the 19 to 21 shops (some closed and others were built during
1955–57) are whitewashed mud and wattle structures with thatched
or corrugated iron roofs. They contain the following specialized shopkeepers: a butcher, who slaughters a cow daily and sells the meat; a
baker who baked loaves of bread before going out of business in 1956
(he was not replaced); a young carpenter, trained in mission schools,
who builds simple furniture, mostly chairs, beds, and tables. The

other businesses at Keumbu market include less specialized retail shops and wholesalers; they fall into three general categories: (1) produce middlemen, who buy grain, eggs and vegetables from local Gusii farmers; (2) restaurants; (3) purveyors of varied consumption goods, including cloth, candy, vegetables, kerosene, blankets, sugar, tea, head scarves, tobacco, bananas, soft drinks, soap, etc.

The middlemen who buy grain and eggs from the surrounding farms are supposed to sell what they buy to the Government Maize Control Office, whose official prices are posted on the outside of the buildings of the middlemen at Keumbu market. There are inspectors who come by to see that all such trade is legally performed. In fact, however, the middlemen sell a great deal of their maize and eleusine privately, at high black-market prices which can be gotten in town and near the lake shore, and the inspectors are bribed heavily to overlook this illegal trade. One middleman at Keumbu is an entrepreneur of many talents: he regularly combines being an egg dealer with professionally dressing cowhides (for use as mats on which to dry grain) and was also, in 1957, learning to become a professional sorcerer.

The restaurants at Keumbu all have tables and chairs and serve refreshments. One of them, right at the road, does a thriving business serving cooked food (dry corn porridge, meat and vegetables in gravy), bread, hot tea and coffee, and Pepsi-Cola. Cigarettes are also sold there, and in a back room there are several beds on which travellers can sleep for a fee. Another establishment in this category is a beer shop, having an exclusive franchise on the sale of bottled beer in Keumbu. The beer is sold in bottles and also served at tables.

One of the most succesful variety shop owners has a treadle-operated sewing machine in front of his shop. He sells the cloth and sews men's shirts and women's dresses for those who order them. He grows numerous vegetables at his nearby homestead and sells tomatoes and onions, along with household goods such as soap, in his shop. Under the terms of a contract with a European school in Kericho he supplies it with vegetables he grows himself, including lettuce, carrots, and beans, and one of his wives manages the shop when he is away. The shop, like others of its kind, is decorated with colorful commercial calendars and posters. Soft drinks from a bottling plant in Kisii are also sold there.

In addition to the housed shops and wholesale establishments at Keumbu, a certain amount of trading goes on in the open. Cattle are bought and sold in a crude compound on the interior of the rectangle, and near the road women sometimes sell oranges they have grown. Because of its daily character, however, and the fact that it does not attract large crowds at any one time, this trading in the open is not as pronounced at Keumbu market as it is at other markets in Nyaribari.

The people who come to Keumbu to buy, sell, and watch are varied as to age, sex, and occupation. Young men, 16 to 30 years old, come to play soccer on the field in the middle of the market. Nyaribari Location is proud of its champion soccer teams, and they often practice at Keumbu market, although persons who are not team members play there also. The young men come to market for another reason: to seduce girls from other clans. From the beginning, markets in Gusiiland were popular as places where young men and woman could meet free from interclan hostility and parental supervision. Until 1937, when there was a mass outbreak of rape among the Gusii, traditional dancing was a common feature of Gusii markets, but after the outbreak it was prohibited and has never returned. Boys and girls still meet at the market, however, and the shops benefit considerably from the courtship patterns in which the girls must be bribed and flattered to entertain the idea of sexual relations or marriage with the eager young men. The latter buy the girls food at the restaurants and present them with gifts of head scarves, bananas, and various trinkets from the variety shops (LeVine 1959 : 965–990).

Older men, particularly homestead heads, come to the market for recreation and also to buy and sell cattle. Many of them can be seen in the restaurants and beer shop gossiping over food and drink. For many, eating at Keumbu is necessary because they have come from a distant part of Nyaribari to see the chief or participate in the *baraza*; for others, especially the more affluent, it is simply a pleasant way of spending time with other elders.

Women from the communities surrounding Keumbu come to market with perhaps the most serious intent. They are most frequently the ones who bring maize, eleusine, and eggs to sell to the middlemen, and they are likely to use the money to purchase soap, kerosene, or an article of clothing for themselves or the children. In many homesteads, grain is stored until a need for cash arises, and if no cash is forthcoming from other sources, then the grain will be put into kerosene tins and taken to the market to sell for cash.

For children, the market is a place of excitement where one can get sweet things to eat. Those who attend the nearby school come to the market at noontime, particularly if they have relatives in the market who will feed them or some money with which to buy bananas. The school is a day-school with no facilities for feeding the pupils, and parents do not give the children lunches to take even when they must walk eight or ten miles to school. In consequence, many go without food all day and the more fortunate ones use the money their parents gave them to buy bananas. Aside from school children, other children living nearby wander about the market watching the soccer games and the trading. They beg their parents to give them pennies with which to buy candy. They are sent by their parents to the market to sell a few eggs or to buy small household items. Girls from the age of nine on are sent to the market on fairly important buying and selling missions which they enjoy greatly, taking their friends along with them. Children in general spend as much time at the market as their many assigned chores and parental supervision will allow.

The non-farming residents of Keumbu—teachers, tribal policemen, and the few other government servants—are quite dependent on the market, since they are unable to produce all of their own food, but do have cash with which to buy a variety of consumption goods. They are customers of a wide range of shops in the market but have nothing to do with the produce buyers. The schoolteachers, who live with their families next to the school, have garden plots, but must buy many food items at the market. Such people are also more likely to buy furniture and bottled beer at Keumbu. The teachers come down to the market in the late afternoon to drink European beer and discuss the day's news and gossip with other educated men and with elders. For the teachers and other men whose schooling lasted eight years and longer, the market represents the nearest outpost of the Westernized culture which attracts them. On weekends they go into town for contact with a fuller and more authentic version of that culture.

One other category of market consumer that should be mentioned is the traveler. He may be a market inspector, Kenya Policeman, sub-headman or other government official; he may be a relative of a shop-owner or someone else in the neighborhood, or a bus-driver waiting for riders. Such persons stop at the market, spend some money at the shops and, perhaps most importantly, act as sources of news and information for people of the Keumbu area. Adult men are attracted to the market in part because of opportunity to talk with these itinerants. Many local people come to Keumbu because the busses stop there; crowds of them waiting for busses can be seen there every day. All of this adds to the attractiveness of the market as a place where large numbers of people from isolated homesteads are gathered in a sociable mood.

Keumbu market may be seen as fulfilling four social functions in terms of the general population: (1) It acts as a specialized economic institution where some crops may be sold for cash and various non-agricultural goods may be purchased. The inroads that this economic specialization has made on the homestead economy can be illustrated by the case of meat, which in the past was eaten only when an animal owned by the family was slaughtered for food but which is now eaten (in many cases) only when the family has the money to buy a few pounds of meat from the butchery at Keumbu. (2) The market gratifies the desire of many, especially the young, to have daily contact with the appurtenances of Western culture, through the purchase of articles such as cigarettes, bottled drinks, and sweets and also through interaction in a relatively sophisticated commercial atmosphere. (3) The market is a meeting-place where, in the absence of traditional feelings concerning homestead privacy and interclan hostility, elders may gather, heterosexual liaisons may be initiated, local people can come into contact with those who are passing through the area, gossip may be passed on, and people may watch or participate in athletic activity. In this sense the market place is viewed as less regulated and freer than the local community of homesteads. (4) The government uses the market as a focal point for some of the services it provides. Adult literacy and community development programs operate at Keumbu, and, in 1957, local inhabitants were required to bring their cattle there to be branded as a safeguard against interdistrict stock theft.

It should be emphasized that none of these functions are fulfilled for local people exclusively by Keumbu market; their mobility is too great. In a small adjacent community studied, many people go to Kisii township to sell vegetables and purchase consumption goods. One group of women walks weekly to a market called Nyakoe which is ten miles away at the border of Luoland. There they trade eleusine grain for Luo-made pots which they carry home. A few days later the women take the pots to Keroka market on its trading day and sell them for cash. Some goods are even sold for cash within the local community without recourse to a formal market. Native beer is the item most frequently traded in this manner. Coffee is marketed through coöperative societies.

Another point worth mentioning is that markets which have trading days, especially those farther from town, are the scenes of activities not found at Keumbu. On the market day at Nyanturago, which is a few miles from Keumbu and the main road, large crowds congregate and trade. On one such day I saw a man dressed and painted according to ritual prescription, dancing publicly to do penance for a Kipsigis he had killed whose spirit was making his child ill. People in the crowd were throwing coins at him which he gratefully picked up. At another market an Indian doctor comes on market day to administer injections of "penicillin" to anyone who can pay the price.

MARKETS AND THE POLITICAL ELITE

On the whole, shop-owners and middlemen are considerably wealthier than the average Gusii farmer. This is partly due to their being drawn from the ranks of the wealthier Gusii farmers, who have large land holdings and herds of cattle, and the capital necessary for trade because their crops bring in so much cash, and who can afford to lose money in business (which some of them do). Some Gusii traders however, do very well in commerce and become much wealthier. Virtually all of them have more imported goods, furniture, and decoration in their houses than the average Gusii. Therefore, being in commerce is associated with wealth and prestige.

Wealth is still considered a requisite for political power among the Gusii, even though the political system now consists of institutionalized positions hierarchically arranged. There is a circle of cumulative causation such that a wealthy man is more likely to be considered a serious candidate for a political position, while a political incumbent uses his power and influence to make himself wealthier. Wealth is conspicuously displayed by plutocrats in their clothing, vehicles, houses, and wives. If a man is appointed location chief (there are seven in Gusiiland) by the Provincial Commissioner, he attempts to increase his wealth by building lucrative market shops (often beer shops) and power mills to grind maize. As a chief, he can obtain loans from the African District Council, wealthy partners who will provide capital, and capital of his own from bribes if he has no other source. Most chiefs do own shops and/or wholesale establishments which are run for them by kinsmen or employees. The same is true of the presidents of African Tribunal Courts and of the sub-headmen who take their orders from the chief. All such individuals, if they are not already wealthy, have access to easier credit than the average Gusii, and they use this advantage to become traders in the markets or owners of power mills. The profits obtained thereby are used to support the conspicuous display worthy of a Gusii leader: polygyny (only one chief was monogamous in 1957; another had fourteen wives; court presidents at that time had two to five wives), an automobile (for a chief), formal western clothing, a house with a corrugated iron roof, etc. Even sub-headmen are clearly marked off from ordinary Gusii by wearing large rubber boots and pith helmets.

The chiefs use their power and influence to establish their close kinsmen as market traders. In one location, for example, most of the beer shops (each with an exclusive franchise on beer in a market) are owned by sons and brothers of the chief and by the chief himself. The same is true of power mills, also with local monopolies, in that location. Since trade is developing in Gusiiland and cash income available for consumption expenditure is growing, the chiefs are able to get themselves and their relatives advantageous shop sites, the capital to exploit them, and some degree of monopolistic advantage. The effect of this would be an increasing concentration of economic and political power in certain families were it not for the fact that men who have been educated beyond secondary school, many of them from relatively poor and non-chiefly families, have increasing political influence and constitute a source of countervailing power. These men are able to command relatively high salaries in bureaucratic jobs, and some of them establish shops and power mills on the side to reinforce their elite position. In the future of Gusiiland, rapid economic and political development may dwarf economic advantages established at this early date, but the association of wealth, based in part on the marketing economy, with political power seems likely to persist.

CHAPTER 21

Zande Markets and Commerce

BY CONRAD C. REINING

The 750,000 Azande (singular: Zande) live in the Republic of the Congo, the Central African Republic, and the Republic of the Sudan, in the territory where the three countries meet. The information in this essay pertains to the time of my observations, between August 1952 and August 1955, and is about Zande District of the Sudan, where most of my research was carried on.

The Azande probably did not have markets in pre-European times. The household, consisting of a man with his wife or wives, their children and other dependents, was largely self-sufficient. However, even though there were no market places where goods were bought and sold, some exchange probably has always been carried on among households and clusters of households. Probably such exchange was only in small quantities and was accomplished in the sphere of gifts and social obligations, for there are two kinds of exchange among the Azande.

They distinguish a thing which is given *(fu he)* and received *(di he)* from one which is bought *(ngbe he)* or sold *(baga ha)*. The two different kinds of exchange are accompanied by different patterns of behavior and expectations and by different relationships. The giving of gifts is what one does with a relative or with a friend with whom one has a continuing relationship, whereas selling is an action generally done with a person with whom one has only an ephemeral relationship. And since a gift should be a token of esteem, there should be no haggling in the gift exchange. In selling, Azande are not precise, in a western sense, for they are content with estimates and rough judgments of quantities involved. But even so, there is in buying and selling a much more precise calculation of *quid pro quo*. In gift giving the quantities involved and time of return should not be specified. If gainful accounting does take place, it is politely hidden.

MARKETS

Markets became a regular feature of Zande life under colonial administration. The first District Commissioner of Zande District in the Sudan considered the instituting of markets to be his idea. Zande markets are the result of the administration's establishment of towns, with a specialized population which was partially dependent upon the rural cultivators for food and craft products. The ability to travel freely under *Pax Britannica* and the introduction of currency helped to make markets feasible.

Markets were held daily in the two largest centers, Yambio, the district headquarters, and Nzara, the factory town built to process the cotton products of the development scheme, while at the smaller centers one day a week was designated as market day. The administration specified the location of the market, the hours, and other details, such as the location of the beer sellers in a special place away from the rest of the market. In Li Yubu, the women vendors were required to be on one side of the road and the men vendors on the other. Each of the towns had a designated market area near its center, where there were no buildings; the goods were displayed on the ground under shade trees. The areas were large enough to accommodate the several hundred people who might congregate at the markets.

The idea of markets caught on among the Azande because spontaneous markets, which had no connection with the administration, occurred wherever there was a gathering of any size. Markets of varying significance were observed at cotton markets, in chiefs' courts, at meetings, and at the sites of large-scale fishing operations, for example. These were not held regularly and were not usually under any administrative regulation.

The three main categories of articles sold were food, craft objects, and imported goods. In the regular town markets there was an emphasis upon foodstuffs, while in the smaller, spontaneous markets, craft objects were proportionately in greater supply, since the markets outside the towns were for the rural Azande who rarely bought food products.

Women most often were the sellers of the food products, because they are the processors of food. Very occasionally a man would be selling food for a wife or a female relative. On the other hand, the craft items were almost without exception sold by men, because crafts, except for pot making which is done by women, are exclusively in the male province. Almost all imported goods at the markets were sold by men, since the peddlers were invariably men.

Most of the goods sold in markets were ready to use and were intended for local consumption. The craft items were invariably finished and also intended for use by the local inhabitants, since tourist trade was small and was centered in the two hospitals, where some woodcarving, ornamental pottery, and basketry was done under European supervision.

Beer, flour, and dried meat and fish were the goods most sought after and most often found at the markets. In addition there were leafy vegetables of several kinds; peanuts, usually in the shell; bananas; sweet potatoes; eggs; yams; rice, usually unhulled; corn on the cob; okra, fresh or dried according to the season; Bambara groundnuts, either shelled or unshelled; beans, shelled or unshelled, dried or partially dried; sesame seed; oil seed pastes, such as peanut butter, sesame butter, and squash seeds; cassava root and sweet sorghum stems. Wild food products were erratic in supply and most often consisted of termites, caterpillars, and mushrooms of various kinds. Cooking oils of any kind were always in great demand and seemed always to be in extremely short supply.

The only imported food items regularly sold at the markets were salt and onions. The salt was a coarse product obtained from the Red Sea coast of the Sudan and had been imported into the district for a long time. Onions will not grow to bulb form in Zande country, although a few enterprising gardeners grew and marketed scallions. Bulb onions were imported from the northern Sudan in considerable quantities. They were not of much consequence to the economy of the ordinary Azande, because of their expense, and were consumed primarily by townspeople.

When flour was sold in the markets, it represented more than food, for an important service was also being sold. Only women learn to use the grinding stones upon which flour is prepared; therefore, properly processed food is extremely important for consumers who do not have the services of women. A considerable part of the workers in the towns, especially at Nzara, were men without the usual household. Men without women preferred to attach themselves to the household of a relative or friend to obtain necessary services and food, but such was not always possible. Men can do some cooking in a pinch, but not the grinding process which is required for the preparation of flour and oil seed pastes, such as peanut butter.

Flour sold in the markets was almost always of either eleusine grain or cassava root, or a mixture of the two. Eleusine was the traditional staple food and was still a great favorite, while the more easily prepared and processed cassava was considered a substitute to be used when eleusine was scarce.

Flour was rarely available in sufficient quantity, and particularly in the larger centers it was chronically in short supply. Workers and clerks from Nzara bought flour at small markets 15 miles and more from Nzara. The administration augmented the food supply with grain from outside Zande District, but the employees still had to travel into the countryside, usually by bicycle, to buy food. The effort of the Nzara workers to find food in the countryside—a situation less prevalent around other towns—was cited by the people as a manifestation of the poor supply arrangements for Nzara. I was not able to detect any regular patterns in this search for food, other than that some of the workers frequented certain areas fairly regularly. There did not appear to be regular buyer-vendor relationships, because the vendors were far from regular in their appearances in these little casual market places.

Town-dwellers must always have needed to buy food in the countryside, judging from the frequency of complaints about the far greater difficulty in buying food after the people had been resettled away from the roads. Many times I heard that it used to be much easier to find food to buy when the people lived along the roads. I, among others, followed this pattern of foraging for food when it was short in the Sudan by driving or cycling into French territory. Although there was much less formal marketing, people lived along the roads and also had the reputation of having more time for the production of food.

The dried meat was from various kinds of wild birds and animals including elephant, buffalo, wild pig, water lizard, antelope and buck of several varieties, cane rat, and guinea fowl. The meat was always dried and smoked in pieces ranging from about half a pound to five pounds or more. Fish were of all varieties and sizes, also dried and smoked. Occasionally salted dried fish commercially imported from outside the district was sold, but it was usually more expensive than the local product.

Fresh meat from cattle was available in the larger centers, butchered and sold under the supervision of one of the larger merchants under government concession. The cattle were usually imported on the hoof from the Dinka herds to the north of Zande District, and more rarely, as at Nzara, locally raised cattle were available from special herds raised under European supervision. The meat was usually too expensive for the ordinary Azande and was consumed largely by the European and northern Sudanese and urban southern Sudanese population. Very occasionally an enterprising small group of Dinka entered Zande District with a herd of cattle which they slaughtered one by one and sold, as they moved from place to place. This meat was consumed by the local Zande, since it was sold in very small pieces, and was usually somewhat cheaper than the fresh meat in the markets.

Beer was the supreme item of the market place and in a category by itself. In some of the large markets it was given a place of its own and in the larger towns beershops, open daily, were being established at the time of my observations. As with flour, the sale of beer rendered an important service as well as refreshment, for the brewing of beer is women's work. If a man does not have a wife or a female relative who will brew for him, he is dependent upon the hospitality of others and upon the beer for sale in the markets. Moreover, beer is much more than food and drink, for it is the universal social lubricant, without which hospitality is not possible and convivality difficult. A household's influence depends upon its ability to give beer to its guests. Traditionally a chief or any important man had to have an unlimited supply of beer and food for visitors. Even now a man is judged by the amount of food which he can afford to give away. As one old man put it, when I commented upon the extraordinary size of his granary, "If a man has a lot of beer to give to people, they will come to listen to his good advice."

Beer was regarded as the best way to convert subsistence produce into money income. When people complained about the nuisance of growing cotton as a cash crop, I would ask how they could better earn the money they wanted; they most often replied they would like to be able to grow food crops in sufficient quantity to sell a surplus in the markets. And, repeatedly, I was told that the best possible way of doing this was by brewing beer, because grain would bring several times the money in the form of beer that it would in any other form. Women regarded beer brewing as the best means of augmenting their personal incomes; since each woman had her own fields and granary, she had a great deal of control over the grain she used for sale. Arrangements about how much to take for her store of grain and the disposition of the money obtained were matters to be approved by their husbands and varied widely with personalities.

Most of the food items sold in the market were for cooking at home, but some of the foods were ready to eat. This category consisted mainly of the fruits, typically bananas, pineapples, mangoes, various citrus fruits, and occasional wild fruits, along with certain other items such as sections of sweet sorghum stems. The oil seed pastes were also ready to eat but were not eaten by themselves, since they were relishes to be eaten with porridge. Similarly, cooking oil required no more processing, but was an ingredient for cooking at home.

Beer, of course, was ready to consume on the spot and was usually the only thing other than fruit which was available for consumption in the market. Very occasionally an enterprising trader sold little fried cassava cakes spread with peanut butter for eating in the market. An important non-food item seen often was locally grown tobacco.

The craft items most often found were sleeping mats of various types, pots of many sizes, baskets of many types and sizes, plaited sieves, cups made of gourds, and locally made iron implements. Less frequent in appearance were brooms of the local pattern, wooden basins, barkcloth, wooden furniture on the traditional patterns, such as stools carved out of a single block of wood, or chairs, stools, and beds made of wooden poles doweled together. Fairly frequently were seen craft items of more recently learned techniques and materials; these included wooden boxes made of boards—either from packing crates or adzed out of logs—secured with nails and equipped with metal hinges and hasp, either imported or locally manufactured on the imported pattern. Other new items were folding deck chairs with seats of woven cane or animal skins, and, occasionally, chairs, tables, or beds made with boards and nails.

At every market were found vendors of minor imported goods, most often hardware. Nails, strips of steel from packing crates, beads, thread, needles, bottles, bobby pins, hinges, hasps, locks, soap, perfume, and cigarettes were some of the more common items.

A tacit rule of the market was to arrange most things in quantities to sell for the smallest coin in use, the *tarifa* (five millemes in Egyptian currency, equal to about one and one half U.S. cents). Bundles of vegetables, handfuls of beans or peanuts, measures of flour or beer, and so on, were most often sold for a *tarifa*. The imported goods in the markets were also broken down into smaller units in order to sell them in units for a *tarifa;* this breakdown was, indeed, the only advantage which a peddler could offer over the nearby shops which sold all his goods and much more. Two Congo-made cigarettes or one English cigarette, five nails, two needles, or a one-inch cube of Lux or Palmolive toilet soap are examples of items selling for a *tarifa*. However, meat, cooking oils, and other more expensive items were usually sold in larger units, and large items of produce, such as pineapples, pumpkins, and squash, were usually sold entire and for more than a *tarifa*. Craft items were always more expensive, ranging up to 25 piastres (about 70 U.S. cents) for a good sleeping mat or a bed frame.

Although there were no explicit purposes associated with markets other than the primary one of material exchange, there is no doubt that other purposes were in fact served. The roar of the market at Li Yubu and the hundreds of people who gathered there each Sunday, left no doubt that the markets served as centers for social communication. Many persons went there with no purchases in mind, simply because everyone else was there.

There was no social organization within any market, other than that imposed by the administration, and there was no organization among markets, their only connections being the tenuous ones of the peddlers on their bicycles.

Except for some of the cooking oil, which was produced in the northern parts of the district and carried by bicycle to the southern parts where most of the markets were held, virtually all the items sold at the markets were produced within a few miles of the markets.

The marketing activity was, for the bulk of the population, still of relatively little significance. The money incomes from cotton as a cash crop and from wages were greater, despite low levels of payment. But the idea of market exchange was important, as shown by some of the tendencies which it had started.

An appreciable number of farmers around the towns were beginning to raise produce especially for the markets, rather than depend upon chance surpluses. A number of people expressed a preference for this way of earning money. In this tendency can be seen the beginnings of specialization which might lead in time to a growth in exchange economy accompanied by other important changes.

Another change was noted in the increased purchases of food items by ordinary Azande. Although they deviated little from the principle that money should not be "wasted" on food for ordinary use, they were relying more and more on money and market goods for social purposes. As their cash incomes increased, they tended to save more for social emergencies and to use money in lieu of produce or services in meeting social obligations, such as contributions to memorial feasts sponsored by relatives. The money given to a relative instead of, say, flour or beer, could be used to buy flour or beer at the market. Again, here was the beginning of increased local market exchange.

The persons most affected by marketing were the few—less than five per cent—who had taken full-time wage employment: the clerks in the offices of the administration agencies, the shop assistants in the larger shops, the school teachers, policemen, and the technicians and the dressers in the dispensaries and hospitals who rarely managed to produce any significant part of their food. They were also dependent largely upon what they could buy in the shops or at the markets for clothing and household equipment, unless they could arrange for someone to make things to order.

SHOPKEEPING AND PEDDLING

There were other exchange activities—shopkeeping and peddling—which were much more important than market places because they were the means by which the Azande obtained imported goods. While only about five per cent of the Azande were dependent upon the local produce sold in the markets, virtually everybody bought imported goods in some quantity. The monetary value of those exchange transactions involving imported goods was undoubtedly many times that of market-place exchange of local produce.

The shopkeepers and peddlers were not producers of the goods they sold, but merely middlemen. They tended to regard their trading activities as a means of livelihood, in contrast to the sellers in the markets, who were almost always members of the household which had produced the goods being sold and who were seldom regularly engaged in selling for more than supplementary income. Few of the peddlers or small shopkeepers were actually able to make a living from their trading activities and had to depend partially upon the subsistence activities of their households for necessities. Only the largest of the merchants of the towns made their entire livelihood from shopkeeping.

World commerce in the Zande scene is represented by the shops which buy local produce for export, primarily chillies, honey, beeswax, and, occasionally, grain or cassava flour; and which sell imported goods, principally cloth and clothing, blankets, household utensils, bicycles, salt, soap, oil lamps, matches, simple hardware, cigarettes, and kerosene. Zande participation in world commerce has always been very small, even though it started about one hundred years ago with the trade in ivory. This ivory trade of the nineteenth century seems to have been a monopoly of the chiefs who received firearms, cloth, and other goods in return from Arab traders. This trade was interrupted for a long period around the turn of the century, following the Mahdist uprising in the north. The territory was reconquered by the British in 1905, but little occurred for the first few years of the British regime, when payments for labor were made in goods from the government military storehouses. We are told that money was introduced about 1914 and that Greek and northern Sudanese merchants soon followed. They bought ivory, a goodly supply of which had been hidden away in the previous, disturbed years, and sold cloth and other products. After the stockpile of ivory was gone, the trade in Zande District remained at a low level for many years. The killing of elephants was controlled strictly by the administration and all ivory had to be registered with the administration at time of sale. While ivory remained a relatively significant item of income for some chiefs, it dropped into insignificance for the district as a whole.

Motor transport penetrated to the district in the early 1920's, and rapidly supplanted human porterage. By the middle of the 1930's, 1500 miles of all-weather roads had been constructed in the district, largely by men working on the roads in lieu of paying taxes. The lateritic soil and gravel make remarkably mud-free road surfaces. The administration and medical service, which made frequent inspections of the population for sleeping sickness, were motorized as soon as possible, and by 1934 there were, in addition, over a dozen private motor vehicles in the district, mostly trucks belonging to the merchants of the towns.

In the early 1930's, a rapid increase in the export of chillie peppers took place, increasing from 70 tons in 1930 to 600 tons in 1934. The number of shops also increased sharply with the influx of cash and imports to the district. In 1931, there were only six of the small shops, usually known as bush shops, outside the towns where the Greek and northern Sudanese merchants had their larger shops. The number of bush shops increased to seventeen by the end of 1932, and to over one hundred by the end of 1934. These bush shops were owned by the merchants of the towns and were operated by Zande agents who received a small monthly wage. Some of the Azande who were sent by the merchants into the remote regions to buy chillies began to ask the help of the administration to set themselves up in business in small shops of their own.

The world economic depression, however, caused a drop in the prices of peppers and a general decline in commerce. In 1936, the value of produce purchased from the populace amounted to about $12,000. The low level of commerce drew unfavorable comments both from the inhabitants and from the northern Sudanese. The Sudan Azande could compare themselves with the Azande in the Belgian Congo where cotton as a cash crop had been started in the 1920's. Proposals were made for the introduction of cotton as a cash crop into the southern Sudan, but only experimental trials were made until after the war when the Zande development scheme was started in 1946.

The Azande, along with the people of the entire province, experienced an increase of cash income in the payments for labor and services during the early war years when the Mediterranean and Red Sea shipping routes were cut off, and Juba, the province capital and the southernmost port on the Nile, was the focus of various land routes across Africa. In 1942 alone, 2,400 laborers were provided from Zande District and others joined the armed forces.

An increased cash income had been received by the Azande for their produce during the war, principally chillie peppers, beeswax, rubber, and ivory, in that order of importance. Rubber was gathered only during the war emergency. After the war, peppers, honey, and beeswax remained in demand and prices were favorable. Construction work for the development scheme meant enlarged cash income, and cotton began to be a major source of cash sales.

By 1950, the total paid for produce to the Azande was about

$340,000. Although the per capita cash income was still very small, there was a considerable increase in imports and in the number of shops. In 1953, there were about 300 shops of all sizes in the district, of which about forty were owned by Azande.

The thirty merchants who were required by the administration to pay business profits tax conducted the bulk of the business of the district. Among them they owned over two hundred bush shops, each managed by a Zande agent. The largest of the businesses declared, for tax purposes, gross profits of $10,000 and more a year, from the commerce in peppers, honey, and beeswax alone in contrast to small Zande merchants who handled only a few hundred pounds of peppers or a few tins of honey a year, yielding in some cases no more than $50 gross annual income. Most of the large merchants were Greeks or northern Sudanese; fewer than ten were Zande or the offspring of Zande mothers and expatriate fathers who had been merchants before them.

There was constant friction between the merchants and their bush-shop agents. The agents, who were paid between $3.50 and $7.00 a month by the merchants in 1953, were accused of being as much as $150.00 short in their accounts in the frequent court cases initiated by the merchants. These difficulties were not confined to foreigners and their Zande agents, for Roberto, the largest Zande shopkeeper, had an agent imprisoned for being $60.00 short in his accounts. Usually, however, he simply fired agents with shortages, for he said it was too much trouble to bring cases against them for small amounts of money.

In general, the non-Zande merchants kept aloof from Zande society and displayed a rather contemptuous attitude toward the people who came to their shops. The general attitude of most of the non-Zande merchants was an exploitative one which was exemplified by the remark of one of them during a discussion of various qualities of cloth: "Cloth is cloth and the cheapest is good enough for the Zandes." The Azande were sensitive to these attitudes and tended to favor the merchants who were exceptions to the general rule; one northern Sudanese and one Greek merchant who had shops in different towns were known to be pleasanter and fairer than the others and enjoyed popularity which enabled them to conduct two of the largest businesses in the district. The educated Azande were particularly apprehensive of the non-Zande merchants, consistently complaining that the profit from Zande commerce was being drained out of the district by the foreign and northern merchants. They had asked for discriminatory rulings against the merchants from the outside for many years; the administration had done little in response other than to ask the large merchants to use Zande agents whenever possible, and to allow Zande merchants to set up businesses whenever they could.

Many Azande aspired to ownership of small shops. An example was a hospital dresser named Jerimino, who told me that his capital was about $375 saved over ten years, and that he had ordered $350 worth of goods from Cairo, from a firm suggested by one of the larger Zande merchants in the area. He had ordered by mail because costs were lower than if he bought from the merchants of Zande District. The list of items ordered consisted mostly of sweaters, blankets, dresses, shirts, trousers and the large squares of cloth used by the women as a wrap. He said that there was no use in buying piece goods until the second-hand sewing machine which he had bought could be repaired.

At the time I met him his shop was just being finished after a construction period of seven months. The total cost of the mud and thatch building, with one room about 12 feet by 12 feet inside and a veranda of similar size, had been about $17. The other major expenditure had been for the shop license, which cost $23.50 annually. The location of the shop had been chosen for him by the District Commissioner. When approval for the shop had been requested, the District Commissioner had specified that the shop was not to be near the center containing the hospital where he worked, but was to be about six miles out, where there were no shops and where it would be of service to the populace which had been resettled in that area. Jerimino was worried because at the time there was no cash crop in the area and little money.

While waiting for the shop to be finished, Jerimino had set up a small stand in front of his house in the town, where a boy sold cooking oil, salt, sugar, and soap which Jerimino had purchased from the local large merchants and from an itinerant wholesale merchant, a northern Sudanese, who occasionally came through the area, selling goods from his truck to the shopkeepers along the roads.

I helped Jerimino move his stores from his house to the shop when it was finished and hauled goods for him from the district headquarters, about 140 miles away. I also supplied him with stamps from the nearest post office, 120 miles away, since he could not get them from the mail truck which picked up and delivered mail once weekly.

His brother agreed to live at the shop and to manage it. He had helped Jerimino before, by bringing cooking oil by bicycle from 100 miles or so to the north where the Belanda people produced edible oil from sesame and from the seeds of wild trees. Jerimino found his performance satisfactory, although his not being able to read or write left all the accounts and correspondence to Jerimino. When I last saw the shop, it was in modest operation, selling perhaps $100 worth of goods a month.

At the other end of the scale of Zande shopkeepers stood Roberto, the first Zande merchant, who had started his own shop in 1936 with the help of a loan of money from the large Catholic mission station where he had been a driver and tailor, and finally, the sub-chief. The Father Superior approved of the idea of having a shop at hand, but decided not to make it a mission enterprise and helped Roberto instead. Roberto had started business with $50 of his own and the $200 loan. He was able to buy his supplies of cloth, salt, soap, iron tools, and spearheads from Wau, with the aid of mission transport.

His shop was the largest of the Zande enterprises, comparable with some of the shops of merchants of the towns in variety of goods for sale, and probably in turnover. His own shop and his six bush shops were well-stocked except for bicycles which were generally in short supply. He was fortunate in having mission transport, and also the use of the pickup truck of a brother, the chief of the area, who was the only Zande in the Sudan who owned a motor vehicle at the time of my observations. Roberto was of the opinion that his business would not warrant having a truck, since he bought and sold only about 50 sacks (about 100 lbs. each) of peppers a year, compared with 500 by some of the large Greek enterprises.

The greatest obstacles to success for the small shopkeepers—which included virtually all the Zande shopkeepers—were the lack of transport facilities, the lack of wholesale facilities, and the lack of capital. The Zande shopkeepers generally had full control over only one means of transport: their own bicycles. On these they carried as much as 100 pounds of goods up to 200 miles. But, by and large, they were dependent upon the trucks of the large merchants who were their competitors; when the large merchants serviced their own bush shops, they also sold goods to independent shopkeepers and bought produce which they had collected. I often heard complaints from the independent shopkeepers that they had to buy goods at retail prices, or slightly under, and that they were not able to sell their peppers and other produce at the prices obtainable in the centers. Also, they often could not get the kind of goods they wanted and sometimes were not able to obtain certain goods at all because they did not have access to the wholesale agencies. Some of the small, independent merchants used the postal system to order large portions of their goods from Khartoum or even Cairo.

All the small shopkeepers were handicapped by a severe lack of capital. Jerimino's case was typical of the small amounts of money with which they attempted to operate. They resorted to all sorts of devices to obtain goods on credit or to borrow money with which to buy goods. I was approached a number of times for loans to pay for parcels which were lying unclaimed in the post office. In the time I was there, few of the large merchants would give credit to the Zande shopkeepers and claims in court were common by the merchants against small shopkeepers who had not paid for goods obtained on credit. Because Roberto was more substantial than the others, he was able to obtain goods on credit occasionally.

Besides unavailability of capital, another inhibitor of commercial expansion was the long-time period involved in receiving goods after they had been ordered. Even the largest merchants had difficulties in this regard. A Greek merchant once told me that most of his considerable capital was invested in goods which were still sitting on the docks in Port Sudan, 1500 miles away. Delays of 18 months between order and delivery were not uncommon.

Although most Zande shopkeeping efforts were marginal, the Azande were keenly aware of the more favorable situation in the Sudan, compared to French Equatorial Africa or the Belgian Congo. In these territories there were no shops owned by Azande. The shops tended to be large ones, owned by foreigners, and widely spaced. The bush shop was unique to the Sudan portion of Zande country. In the Belgian Congo the Azande expressed particularly strong resentment against the foreign, mostly Greek, shopkeepers. In French territory, where there were few shops of any kind and prices were high, people were said to walk two and three days to the Sudan, preferably, or to the Congo to buy imported goods.

The peddling activities of the Azande overlapped both the marketing and shopkeeping activities. Some of the Zande shopkeepers had started their careers as peddlers; they often continued to engage in some peddling and appeared with goods at certain markets. The cotton markets, which were usually located away from towns and shops, were visited by large numbers of merchants who brought goods to sell to the people who had just sold their cotton; temporary stalls were set up along the approaches to cotton markets with colorful goods, mostly clothing, on display. An indeterminate number of enterprising Zande men, usually on bicycles, ranged throughout the area, especially in the remote regions, selling imported goods and buying peppers, honey, and beeswax.

A variety of peddling, which was probably the most lucrative of all Zande pursuits, was the trade across the international frontiers. Differentials in prices of imported goods in the three territories made the transport and sale of such items across the borders a profitable, if hazardous, venture. The most common form of this international trade was to move bicycles from the Sudan to the Congo, where they were more expensive, and to return with American and Congo cigarettes, which were cheaper than the British cigarette sold in the Sudan. This trade supplied most of the cigarettes consumed by the Zande in the Sudan. Sometimes clothing from the Sudan was sold in the Congo and occasionally chillie peppers were carried from the Congo to the Sudan, since there was no market for them in the Congo.

The three different kinds of money involved caused the Azande considerable difficulty, for most of them did not know the official rates of exchange. One of the Greek merchants in the Sudan was said by the people to be taking advantage of the exchange of French currency into Egyptian currency, which was then being used in the Sudan. They said that he gave the people from French territory less for their money when they bought things from him than they received when they changed Egyptian into French currency at his shop in order to pay their taxes. Egyptian coinage was used far into French territory where there was only paper money, even for the smallest denominations. I could not determine what was going on in this exchange of currency, because of the reticence of the merchants to discuss it and vagueness of the Azande in their computations.

The currency exchange situation between the Sudan and the Congo was clearer, because the piastre and the franc were equated by the merchants in the Congo, although the official rate was about 1.4 piastres to 1 Congolese franc. Most of the Sudan Azande assumed the parity of the franc and the piastre to be correct, which caused the prices in the shops and the cotton prices in the Congo to appear higher than they would have been at official exchange rates. Only in the larger towns of the Congo was I able to obtain the correct exchange rate, and the Sudan Azande with me assured me that they had never heard of this being done by a Zande.

MONEY

Money (Reining 1959) has been introduced relatively recently. Probably very small quantities of coinage came with the Arab traders at the end of the last century, but only since the 1920's has coinage become widely used.

Zande country is one of the least developed regions in Africa because of its remoteness and its poverty in exportable commodities, and there has been little labor migration. When taxes were introduced in the early 1920's in Zande District of the Sudan, most men were not able to pay the annual tax (then about 25 cents) and worked on the roads for five days each year in lieu of cash payment. The development of a small trade in wild pepper soon brought in enough money for most families to pay taxes in cash.

Work for the administration and sale of forest produce were the major sources of cash income until the recent introduction of cotton as a cash crop. The cash income of the Azande was still relatively low, even by African standards. A rough average figure was about $10 per year per family, while a $50 annual income was a relatively high one. A laborer, working regularly, earned about $50 per year in 1955.

Nonetheless, the Azande have been using money for about 40 years and they were universally familiar with it as a medium of exchange. Virtually all economic transactions among themselves, as well as those with the outside world, involve money. But money had a different role, or more accurately, a different set of roles, than it does in industrialized societies.

The Azande saw money primarily as a special item necessary to acquire in shops certain commodities which could not be manufactured in their subsistence economy—clothing, blankets, various household utensils, bicycles, and guns. These things were not indispensable, but they had been a part of Zande life for a long time. They invariably answer questions as to why food and other articles were being sold in the markets or why individuals were working for money wages in terms of the need for money to obtain desirable imported goods. When I asked a woman why she was selling flour in a market, she replied, "I am selling it for money." When asked why she wanted money, she pointed to the shops and replied that they were full of things she needed. The Azande did not resent the intrusion of imported goods into their lives; on the contrary, they resented only that they were not able to obtain a greater quantity and variety of these goods. Everybody wanted more money because he wanted more manufactured things.

Despite the preoccupation with money and imported goods, these goods satisfied only a small part of a family's total needs. The subsistence economy was still extremely important and the productive activities of the individual household had changed relatively little in contrast to the pervasive changes in the political organization and the territorial distribution of the Azande. By far the greatest portion of the subsistence goods consumed by any family was produced by its members, and most of Zande productive economy was not involved in any market exchange, or other money transaction. Since the subsistence economy still produced most of the things required for daily life, we can say that the Azande had a "pin-money" economy. They wanted money primarily to buy extras, not to live on. A consistent characteristic of Zande cash expenditures is that almost nothing was spent for daily subsistence, even among families with members earning regular wages. This principle was verbalized by the Azande, who stated that they did not like to spend money on food or shelter. Even town laborers regarded money spent merely to live as "wasted."

This, then, was the Zande view: money was a special commodity, a sideline to ordinary life. But this special role was only a part of the story of money in Zande economy. Money also played an important role in the subsistence economy which was not grasped clearly by the Azande themselves. No family was found which spent all of its cash income for goods in the shops. In my investigations of cash expenditures, the first responses were always about the amounts spent for taxes and for imported goods and further probing was usually necessary to bring out the existence of expenditures for marriage payments, contributions to feasts, and gifts. A distinction was implicit between the subsistence goods used for ordinary life within the household and those which are required for broader social purposes. Money should not be used for ordinary living, but could be expended to meet social obligations.

Along with this distinction we can note a certain hierarchy of exchangeability in the Zande use of money (Bohannan 1955 and Steiner 1954). They believed it commendable to convert subsistence goods into money, but they did not want to reverse the process. Money could be freely exchanged for imported goods but not for subsistence goods, unless—and this is important—these were needed for some social obligation. This same sort of limited exchangeability can be seen in the former use of spears for marriage payments. The father, who received the spears in the marriage of a daughter, could exchange them for subsistence goods for his own use, but he was in fact morally bound to use them for arranging other marriages, especially if he had sons. If he squandered the spears he met with the disapproval of the community. However, an alternative approved use for spears was the purchase of food and beer for a funeral feast or for some other social obligation (Seligman 1932 : 513).

Money had been substituted for marriage spears, but the money payments were still referred to as "spears." However, money cannot be said to be a simple substitute for spears, for it has a much wider range of exchangeability and is much more generally available. Not only were spears scarcer than money, but they also tended to pass more exclusively through certain channels. In effect, spears had a narrower range of uses than money, which is a common denominator to all kinds of exchanges. This more general nature of money had had far-reaching implications; for example, the introduction of wages and the substitution of money for spears as marriage payments had contributed to profound changes in certain family relationships, particularly the father-son relationship. Sons were no longer dependent upon their fathers to provide the means for making marriage payments. Spears were formerly available largely through the father, who received them in the marriage of a daughter, but at the time of my study almost anyone could earn enough money to make the necessary payments. While the position of the father was still morally strong, it had been perceptibly weakened by the removal of this special economic control. We are aware, of course, that such changes derive from a complex of factors resulting from European administration, of which money and wages are only a part.

Money has another quality, different from anything else in the Zande economy in the relative ease with which it can be accumulated and stored away; spears were scarcer, were socially marked, and could not be hoarded as readily as money. Nowadays surplus money is converted into silver coins and buried, and such hoards are not destroyed upon the death of individuals. When families were questioned about the disposition of their cash incomes, they mentioned savings only at the very last. Almost all families were found to save money when possible; some said they were saving for large purchases, usually bicycles, and others explained that they saved for future social emergencies. Savings seem to have become markedly greater as cash expenditures in the shops have not risen as fast as the recent increases in cash income reported for the district in general.

Increased savings seemed to be accompanied by increased use of money for social purposes. Contrary to all expectations, including those of the Azande, increased cash income had not resulted in corresponding expenditures for imported goods. The Azande themselves assumed that they would simply buy more European goods if they had more money and thereby become more like the Europeans. Instead, there seemed to be a distinct tendency to substitute money for goods and services required for social obligations.

The special nature of money was clearly illustrated in that it had become a preferred form of gift to relatives and friends. In any relationship in which gifts were exchanged, a small present of money was considered to be appropriate. The chiefs expected presents of money from their followers, and money seemed to be given and accepted in the same spirit as services or gifts of goods. What might seem to be bribes to the European were regarded as justifiable gifts by the chiefs and as wise precautions by the chiefs' followers. Similarly, money was often given in lieu of beer or food contributions to feasts sponsored by relatives, so that the sponsor could make the necessary purchases to provide for the feast. In some instances in my knowledge, money contributions were specifically solicited, particularly when meat was required and could be obtained most readily by purchase, either from the butchers in the towns or from the Azande of French Equatorial Africa who had more time for hunting and greater surpluses of meat. Another use of money for social obligations appeared when a man came to borrow money from me, explaining that he had not attended the funeral of a relative of his wife and therefore had been "fined" 20 piastres by his father-in-law for failure to perform the obligatory duty as son-in-law. Such obligations can weigh heavily on the Azande and they find it convenient to have reserves of cash with which to meet emergency social obligations.

The increased use of money for subsistence items in the social sphere meant that there was increased internal trade, which might ultimately have far-reaching implications. As of 1955, however, the acceptance of money as a medium of exchange had not resulted in money economy becoming dominant, for Zande usage imposed constraints on money usage, especially in its not being used to acquire everyday subsistence items. Therefore, despite an increase of trade in subsistence goods in connection with social obligations, there was little occupational specialization, and the subsistence economy remained one of the least altered aspects of Zande life under European administration.

COTTON MARKETING

Azande regarded cotton marketing in a category by itself, something very different from ordinary marketing. Cotton had to do with the government: its cultivation was compulsory, it had to be brought to special places—usually apart from shops and ordinary markets—at specific times for sale to the European representatives of an organization designated by the government as the sole buying agency. From the Zande point of view, cultivation and marketing of cotton was simply a variant on draft labor for government projects, or taxes.

In the Belgian Congo, after a beginning period which involved severe compulsory measures, cotton growing had become lucrative for many Zande families especially with the rise of cotton prices after World War II. Even women, children and old people cultivated cotton voluntarily in fields apart from the compulsory community fields tended by the men. In the Sudan, however, initial enthusiasm on the part of the Azande had been dulled by unfavorable prices for the cotton in comparison to those in the Congo. To the Azande in the Sudan, cotton became a nuisance, and production dropped from a record yield in 1949 until, in 1955, the future of the development scheme was jeopardized by the low yield.

The planners of the Zande Scheme hoped that the Azande would absorb the cultivation of cotton into their subsistence economy, but the Azande considered activities associated with cotton to be different from their normal activities. The compulsory aspect of the cotton program confirmed the view that in growing and selling cotton, special services were being rendered to the government officials. The Azande felt that they were entering new relationships, as clients of the officials, with the beginning of the development scheme; they expected to be repaid for their work, their co-operation, and their respectful attitude. They were not selling their cotton, they were receiving their reward for their participation in a relationship. Since the only tangible rewards were the cash payments at the time of sale, and the bonus payments later, the amount of these payments indicated to the Azande the esteem in which they were held by their patrons. The money reward had a distinct value in terms of what it would buy in the shops, but it also served as an indicator of the generosity of the patron.

The cultivators were virtually unanimous in the expression of their resentment against the administration for not giving sufficient rewards for cultivating cotton. The poor return for the work which was required by the government had the effect of showing poor regard for the Azande, as individuals.

That they did not see the cash crop activities as commercial transactions is shown by the frequency with which rewards were estimated in terms of needs rather than production. The most frequent type of complaint about the returns for cash crops was that the administration was not "taking care" of its people, as behooved a good and infinitely powerful patron.

The personal element in the administration had been represented for many years in the District Commissioner, who was regarded as a sort of paramount chief; but with the advent of the development scheme he became more distant and identification of a patron was not easy. The British Inspector of Agriculture of the locality was responsible for the cultivation of cash crops, he visited cotton cultivations from time to time and was present at all cotton buying. Very often he was the only European seen by the cultivators and he served to give some amount of personality to the administration.

There was a noticeable drop in enthusiasm after the second sale of cotton, say the Azande, in each of the regions. The first time they were disappointed, but thought there would be suitable adjustment later. After the second season of poor cash sales, they began to suspect that there might be no greater rewards.

The Azande would, of course, have reacted immediately, had they received no money for their cotton at a market. Their final reaction to what they considered inadequate rewards, was delayed because they hoped for adjustments in the rewards, because they believed the British to be good patrons who would, in time, make amends. The British, in spite of what the Azande saw as their unprogressive ways, were the best liked of the three kinds of European administrators because of their personal attitudes and, therefore, assumed the Azande, they would be the most generous in the rewards for cultivating cotton. Lack of effective communication made the situation hopeless, for there were not, in fact, the personal relationships to which the Azande were accustomed. And, in applying their personalized criteria to the foreign situation, they were disappointed, which feeling was heightened because they had waited so long for the proper return.

Out of the stabilization fund for cultivators, the Europeans on the cotton board decided to award in 1951 a bonus of 75 piastres to each cultivator who had followed instructions concerning cultivation and the cleaning up and burning of the cotton stalks after the harvest. The purpose of this bonus, which was voted in lieu of a price increase, was to encourage good cultivation and to stimulate cotton production. There were signs that it had the reverse effect.

The bonus payments were particularly confusing and irritating to the Azande, who considered them to be gifts from the government officials for the trouble of growing cotton. As one young chief put it: "The money at the market is for the cotton, but the bonus is for their [the people's] tiredness." The bonus payment was taken to be a gift in the manner of patronage, which was not too much at variance with the administration's notion of it as an "appreciation payment." A separate payment was taken by some Azande as admission by the administration that the proper price had not been paid for the cotton and the bonus was accepted as a bribe to keep them quiet. The dissatisfaction of those who did not receive it or who received less than others was far greater than the satisfaction of those who received the full amounts. As the bonus system was altered, in attempts to make it into a medium for punishing laggards, the negative effects became stronger. Alterations and reductions in the amount of the bonus produced hard feelings, which culminated with the handing back of the bonus to the Inspector of Agriculture in some parts of Tembura Sub-District; the people explained afterwards that they had been incensed at the pittance, about 20 to 40 piastres, which had been given to them as bonus. They believed that they had been shabbily treated, for not only had they been consistently underpaid for their cotton, but they had also been consistently offended by the smallness of the bonus "gifts". The bonus payments, in adding to the confusion, probably helped to delay the final reaction of the cultivators, which led to serious consequences for the scheme.

LABOR

Another means of getting cash income was by labor; the adminis·tration was the largest employer by far, for work on the roads, bridges, and public grounds and buildings.

The Azande did not conceive of their labor in the same way as the European members of the administration, for the notion of labor as a marketable commodity was unknown to the Azande. Instead, they dealt with the labor situation in terms of specific types of re·lationships; as in the cotton marketing discussed above, the Azande saw themselves in special personal relationships with their employers, involving factors aside from the money paid, and labor performed. The money paid in return for labor was regarded as only part of the rewards involved. This idea was enhanced by the smallness of the pay—about $.15 per day, without food, in 1955—and by the fact that the pay for porters in 1911 had been almost as much as the pay for laborers in 1955, while the prices of the goods in the shops had risen many times over.

The laborers were universally resentful of the insufficient rewards for their participation in the relationship with their employers. The ordinary Zande was still willing to forego much money in return for intangible benefits, such as security and social standing, afforded to him by his chief and the administration. But he was not as devoid of a "sense of money" as some members of the administration assumed him to be; he had a precise knowledge of prices for things which he needed in the shops, and he used these prices as a rough gauge to determine what he should be getting for his participation in the employee-employer relationship. But this gauge did not have the precise nature of the comparison with the cotton prices across the border in the Belgian Congo. Volunteer laborers in the stations had been raised in pay during the development scheme, from one and one-half piastres per day (about $1.30 per month) to five piastres per day (about $4.30 per month), but they were still utterly dissatisfied with their wages in 1955 and said that they were being ruthlessly exploited. The argument of the administration that the wages had been increased several times over was rejected by the Azande who pointed out that in the days when they had been paid one piastre a day it had been for public service labor for the administration, which had been compulsory and which they had performed as a sort of tax.

The laborers worked for reasons other than earning a livelihood and they tended to regard their money wages as tokens of the personal esteem in which they were held by their employers. When they were asked how much they thought they should be earning, they gave amounts from three times to one hundred times as much as they were earning; the most common figures were fifteen to twenty-five times the amount they were earning. When they were asked where the vast amount of money would come from, they were extremely vague in their answers, usually indicating a belief in the infinite ability of the government to coin money.

When one laborer stated a particularly large sum as his idea of a fair wage, I asked him what he thought I earned each month, since the amount he had cited was considerably more than my monthly pay. He waved at three large piles of peanuts spread to dry in his courtyard and stated that the pounds I must be earning each month were as numerous as those peanuts. I could not help smiling at the notion of the thousands of pounds implied, but he was hurt that I should be amused, for he had been quite serious. The great social gap between the Europeans and the Azande and the lack of effective communication between them left the Azande with little basis for effective comparison and allowed the belief in the inexhaustible wealth of the Europeans and the government to persist.

When pressed to give some basis for the desired wages, the laborers would always cite the high prices of goods in the shops. Often they would add that they should be paid at least enough to buy adequate clothing and bedding for themselves and their families and to have a little in reserve for meat and other special things such as tea and sugar. Here the stress was on the duty of the employer to care for the needs of his employees, especially for blankets and clothing.

The educated and widely traveled Azande had more definite bases for the wages they wanted and they also gave less fantastic figures for ideal wages than did the laborers. Clerks and artisans, earning between $10 and $30 a month, indicated they considered fair wages to be from two to five times their current wages. When asked why they should receive more money, they compared their wages with those of the northern Sudanese in the factory town built for the development scheme, and with wages of comparable persons in Uganda and the Belgian Congo. They also cited the costs of goods in the shops as reason for higher wages, and their estimated cost of needs for food, clothing, bedding, and other needs coincided fairly well with the amounts given as desired wages. They, as well as the cultivators and unskilled workers, consistently pointed out how little they could buy at the shops for what they earned. The more educated persons felt the pinch more acutely since they were more dependent upon purchased food than the others and because they had learned to want certain things which were still in the class of dispensable luxuries for the others.

The more experienced persons were also more cynical of the value of relationships involving patronage than were the unskilled laborers and, particularly, the cultivators. The resistance to patronage came out most clearly at the factory town where there was the greatest concentration of the clerical and skilled workers and of permanent laborers. They realized more clearly than the bulk of the population that the protection of kin or patron was no longer vital and they based their hopes on small, regular increases in pay which they had been promised. They were most apprehensive of any form of patronage which might take the place of these increases in pay.

In 1953, a canteen was started to provide one free meal daily for the workers at Nzara; it was modeled on a successful one in a large ginnery in the northern Sudan. At first, the project was a success, for the workers, who had difficulty in finding prepared food, were able to get one large meal per day there. The cost of the food was a good deal more than had been anticipated by the management, which felt, however, that the project was worthwhile because of the noticeable improvement in working efficiency, particularly in the latter hours of the working day. After some weeks of operation, the canteen was suddenly boycotted; no one dared to go near to it and it had to be closed. A deputation received by the management had no complaints to make about the food, but only asked that the workers be able to receive money instead of the food. This was not possible, decided the management.

Afterwards, it was explained to me by the Azande that the trouble had started with the married men who did not benefit as much from the free meals as did the unmarried men. The married men preferred to eat at home and wanted to have the money instead, so that their families could benefit too. There was, also, the more general fear that these free meals would result in the loss of future increases in pay.

The management's refusal to give money in lieu of free meals resulted in a complete boycott of the canteen; those men who wanted to eat there were kept away by threats from the others. As in the case of the bonus payments which were rejected by cultivators, the workers were willing to do without something in order to show their disapproval. The promise had been made that the food would not be taken from their pay, either present or future, but the men were fearful that the canteen would place them at a disadvantage and they chose to forego the food which some of them undoubtedly appreciated and needed.

The fear of patronage in lieu of pay came out most clearly when, in June of 1955, the new Sudanese General Manager at Nzara, who had just replaced the British General Manager, called an open meeting to discuss a social center. The workers were generally hostile to the idea. They asked where the money would come from for the building and equipment; when they were told that the Board would pay for this, they asked that they be given the money, individually, instead. The General Manager explained that the amount would be very little if prorated to each worker in Nzara; he used the example of the radio which was to be the first piece of equipment. It would cost about £45 and, if the money were divided up among the 1500 workers, each would get about three piastres. One man replied that he would rather have the money, with which to buy cigarettes, than to have a share in a radio. This voiced the general sentiment of the crowd: they did not want any free services for fear of prejudicing their future wages. They expressed themselves as being tired of being fobbed off with paltry gifts instead of the money they had worked for.

Here we can see the beginnings of awareness of the European standards by a small part of the population and the disillusionment with the promises made on the basis of a patronage relationship. While the cultivators were withdrawing their services from an unfavorable relationship, the more sophisticated persons were trying to avoid getting involved again in this sort of relationship. They were willing to try to earn their livelihood from their labor, but were frustrated by the scale of wages, which was in actuality derived from the implicit assumption by the administration that the worker obtained most necessities from the subsistence activities of his household.

There was a tendency for those who had become wage earners to revert to subsistence agriculture, as they grew older. Often the educated persons were disappointed in the standards of living which they could attain by means of their wages and a number of cases were known in which educated men resumed a traditional way of life, with several wives who cultivated the usual crops and produced a marketable surplus that could be used for social purposes. A number of men told me that they had been trained to expect things which they were not able to achieve by earning wages, and that they could live more satisfactorily in the Zande manner. I noted, however, that in no case was the reversion a complete one, for the educated men would always try to augment the income of their households, usually as traders or by continuing to work for wages occasionally.

CHAPTER 22

Trade and Markets among the Lugbara of Uganda

BY JOHN MIDDLETON

THE TRADITIONAL ECONOMY

The traditional economy of the Lugbara of northwestern Uganda was a subsistence one, and the basic residential and productive units were large self-sufficient lineage groups, in and between which there were only minimal differences in standards of living.[1] Lineage-groups produced virtually all they consumed, and consumed all they produced; both goods and labor services were exchanged in terms of mutual obligations between kin and neighbors, without the use of currency. Today local domestic groups are no longer self-sufficient and have decreased in size, and differences in wealth have become considerable. With these changes has come the growth of a cash economy, which involves the use of money and markets for the exchange of both some (though not all) goods and some (though again not all) services; neither money nor markets existed in pre-European days. In this paper I show the ways in which these developments have been interrelated.

The Lugbara are a Sudanic-speaking people, numbering 183,000 in Uganda and 60,000 in what was formerly the Belgian Congo. In the center of the country the density of population is about 240 persons to the square mile, but the total average density for all Lugbara-land is about 90 to the square mile since there is much almost empty bushland on the edges of the country. Most of the Lugbaraland lies at about 4,000 feet above sea level. Rainfall is well distributed throughout the year and is between 40 and 60 inches per year. There are many permanent streams and rivers. The dry season is a short one of two or three months only, and seasonal differences are not sufficient to lead to any marked disturbance of settlement or economic life (Greenland and Chancellor 1958).

The staple crops are millets, sorghums, cassava, various pulses,

(1) Field work among the Lugbara was carried out for 24 months between December 1949 and April 1952. It was financed by the Worshipful Company of Goldsmiths of the City of London and by the Colonial Social Science Research Council. The material was written up with aid from the Wenner-Gren Foundation for Anthropological Research, New York. I wish to express my gratitude to these bodies for their assistance.

sweet potatoes, simsim and—of less economic importance—maize and plantains. A variety of gourds, hibiscus and other plants is grown for the sake of calabashes, string and similar materials. There are many varieties of these plants known, grown in different areas with local differences in soil fertility, acidity and structure, and rainfall. Nevertheless, it may be said that the subsistence economy of all Lugbara areas is essentially very similar. Many other materials, such as wood for fuel, clay for potmaking, ochre for decoration, mud for housebuilding, are found in all parts of the country. Today wood is scarce in the more densely populated areas, but this is a recent phenomenon. Alluvial iron occurs sporadically. Cattle, goats and sheep are kept everywhere and provide certain materials of domestic importance. There are certain resources which are economically important which do not occur everywhere; these include good quality iron for smelting, most of which is found in the Congo to the west; oracle poison, found also in the Congo; fish (other than small river fish), which are obtained from the neighboring Madi to the east in the Nile valley; and papyrus which is found mainly in the north of Lugbara, on the Sudan border. All these objects are obtained by trade, and have always been so obtained.

The largest politically independent group, which I call the tribe, is an aggregate of population clustered round an agnatic sub-clan.[2] It averages some 4,000 people. Formerly, the homesteads of a tribe were grouped fairly close together, with their fields providing an unsettled zone between them and neighboring tribes. Fighting occurred regularly between tribes, and these zones of fields provided protection. Traditionally each wife was given three types of field: the "home fields" (*amvu akua*), which were near the homesteads and between them; the "outside fields" (*amvu amve*), which were in the intertribal zones; and "riverine fields" (*yimile*). Only the "outside" fields were under a system of shifting cultivation, the others being cultivated either permanently or for long periods with mixed stands of crops; the outside fields were used for single stands of crops for only a year or two and were then left fallow. Riverine fields were cultivated permanently, and were under a system of irrigation. A woman with all three types of field could provide her homestead with all its foodstuffs, including salt which was made from the ashes of certain grasses (Middleton and Greenland 1954).

The traditional situation may be summed up by saying that each local community was economically almost self-sufficient. Only certain goods had to be obtained from outside the local community. The degree of self-sufficiency was well described by Stigand, an acute

(2) For a description of the traditional political system, see Middleton 1958.

observer, who visited the country as its administrator in 1912. He wrote:

To the south of Wati (Mount Eti) ... there are an immense number of little communities, some under petty chiefs having only a few dozen followers, and some under no chiefs at all ... The disorganization of this part of the country was so complete that it was absolutely unparalleled by anything I have seen elsewhere, or heard about ... On pitching camp near a village, people would come out and stand in a group about two hundred yards or more distant and watch proceedings. Every time anyone approached them, or shouted to them to come and speak to us, all would turn and fly, coming back later when they found that they were not followed. It was generally only on the second day that they became so bold as to come near enough to speak to, and not until the third day that one was able to buy food from them. As the community was very small, this meant only a few little baskets of flour. On moving to another village only a mile or two away, one would have to go through the whole of this exasperating game again, as there was seldom any communication between neighboring villages. Each little group was perfectly isolated. (Stigand 1923 : 89)

There was, however, exchange of certain goods, in certain circumstances. Within the tribe local gifts of grains and other objects were made among kin, and wives who visited their natal kin in tribal areas other than those of their husbands took gifts of foodstuffs. Most exchange was between co-wives or wives of closely related men, and it was not a formal market transaction. There were no established markets until the late 1920's. This kinship distribution of food did not entail the use of any currency, nor was it barter; return gifts of approximately the same size would be made on later occasions.

There was some external trade in fish with Madi, iron ore and oracle poison with the Congo, papyrus mats with northern Lugbara and Kakwa, and possibly other objects. These trading transactions were organized by both men and women. Women were able to travel freely, even moving between groups which were fighting one another; they, and men who went for iron and poisons, moved along lines of kinship from one tribe to another. It is now difficult to estimate the extent of these trading journeys, but I do not think that they were ever very considerable in number or in distance; rather the objects themselves were exchanged between members of neighboring tribes, and so might move along the line of kinship in this respect. They were exchanged either for goats or, less commonly, for iron objects (lumps of iron ore, hoes and spears), which were also used for bridewealth transactions. An account of one expedition into the Congo, to a tribe about 30 miles away, was given to me by an old man, and from his account it was clear that exchange was by barter, fine iron being obtained for goats and lumps of rough iron ore.

A third kind of exchange that traditionally took place was that of women for grain at times of famine. There were periodic famines, which can be dated by the marriages of wives for grain instead of for iron objects or livestock. At these times a man would move with his sisters or daughters into those areas with enough food, and would exchange the women for food for himself; he would usually be attached to his hosts as a client, and be given a wife by his hosts in exchange for one of the women he had brought with him. Clients were also given wives in exchange for service. We might include ordinary bridewealth transactions as part of the traditional exchange system, rights in women being exchanged for iron objects—cattle were first used for bridewealth only at the very end of the last century.

The use of iron was limited to certain situations only: it was never an object of currency. Special arrows, spears and hoes, all of types not used as weapons or tools, were payments made between affines at marriage and mortuary ceremonies. They were tokens of affinity and kinship and not used in commodity exchange. These objects were obtained from Ndu smiths, who were scattered throughout Lugbaraland and who made them from iron ore or old iron objects supplied by the client. A man could therefore transform one iron object into another according to his needs at a given time. A man who had no iron to start with could easily acquire it by his own efforts since ore was available in several parts of the country and anyone was permitted to take it: the local community claimed no rights of ownership over it.

CHANGES IN LUGBARA ECONOMY

The traditional pattern has altered considerably with changes in several economic, ecological and political factors. Many, though by no means all, exchanges are made through the medium of money, and markets and traders are important institutions in Lugbara life, being found in almost every part of the country. The principal factors of change include the introduction of money and the growth of a need for it, especially for payment of taxes, for purchase of imported consumer goods, and as a form of capital. Changes in the traditional patterns of farming and settlement have made it difficult for individual family-groups to be economically self-sufficient. Changes in the system of status and authority have also occurred with an increase of movement of individuals and of independence of younger men of their seniors; thus the scale of social relations has become wider and small kin-groups are socially less self-contained than formerly.

Certain far-reaching changes in the economy took place in the early years of this century. The Belgians set up an administration in northern Lugbaraland in 1900. They established chiefs, and these men were paid in cattle taken by the Belgians' troops as part of tribute from the Lugbara, the tribute consisting of cattle and grain. The chiefs became extremely rich by Lugbara standards, and it is said that they were the first men regularly to marry their wives with livestock instead of with iron objects. (It should be noted that Lugbara do not regard the acquisition of livestock as conferring prestige.) In using their wealth to acquire wives, they were, of course, following Lugbara values in establishing large families as a sign of prestige and high status.

The stages by which the Lugbara were introduced to a cash economy cannot now be traced in detail. Neither the Belgians nor the Sudanese introduced taxation (as apart from tribute in kind) while they administered the area that is now West Nile District of Uganda—the Belgians from 1900 to 1908 and the Sudanese from 1911 to 1914 (there was an interregnum from 1908 until 1911). The area became part of Uganda in 1914, although the western part of Lugbaraland has remained part of the Congo to the present day. Taxation in currency was introduced by the Belgians in the Congo part of the country in 1912, and by the British in the Uganda part in 1918. In 1915 it was estimated that there were 45,000 potential taxpayers in West Nile District but that:

before taxation can be thought of, means must be given to the people to provide their tax. At present their only means is the sale of their livestock and a small trade in hides. (Report of Provincial Commissioner for the Northern Province of Uganda, 1915)

A critical need for money made itself felt in the 1920's, and its mention has been a recurrent feature of annual administrative reports ever since. Various cash crops were introduced into the area (simsim, groundnuts, chillies, sunflower, coffee and tobacco, only the last being successful in the last few years). But the district has had to rely upon labor migration to obtain cash.

The first traders reached Arua by 1915, bringing salt and cloth; the first shop was opened in Arua by a Baluchi in that year, the second at Aru in 1919. Arab and Indian shops have since spread throughout the country at the smaller trading centers.

In the years following the setting up of the European administration, several disasters occurred which considerably hastened the changes. There were severe droughts and crop failures in 1918 and 1922. There were outbreaks of rinderpest in 1917 and 1924–25, the latter being particularly severe and carrying off over half the total Lugbara cattle; in 1923 the livestock had already suffered what the District Commissioner's report described as "colossal" mortality from East Coast Fever. There was an influenza epidemic in 1922. The great losses of cattle removed the most obvious means by which Lugbara could pay their taxes, and labor migration became the only way for most of the people to acquire money.

The opening of Lugbara was accompanied by its increasing involvement in the economic development of the rest of Uganda. Large-scale railway construction took place in southern Uganda in the early 1920's; Lugazi sugar works was opened in 1924. Other large employers who have relied on Lugbara labor began to operate later in this period: Kakira sugar works and the Masindi sisal estates in 1929, the Bunyoro tobacco factories in 1931. Timber, rubber and other European- and Indian-owned estates flourished in Bunyoro throughout the 1920's until the 1931 depression. The large employers of labor usually used Lugbara laborers on contract, there being many recruiters in the area until 1948, when a single recruiting organization was formed. In the early days only Alur and a few Madi went south from the district, but by 1924–25 Lugbara laborers were also going, and by the early 1930's Lugbara formed the majority of laborers emigrating from the district. Detailed or reasonably accurate figures are not available until 1932, when 1,700 Uganda Lugbara went south. The numbers increased steadily and in 1951 over 5,000 Uganda Lugbara and over 2,500 Congo Lugbara crossed Lake Albert southward. The peak year was 1947, with over 8,000 Uganda Lugbara and 2,500 Congo Lugbara crossing the lake.[3]

The 1951 absentee rates for laborers from the Uganda Lugbara counties are set forth in Table 37, the figures being those of the

TABLE 37

Absentee Rates for Lugbara Laborers

County	Absentee Rate	Density of Persons to the Square Mile
Maraca	26.5%	240
Ayivu	20.9%	239
Terego	17.8%	80
Vura	13.7%	65
Aringa	12.4%	16

(3) 1932 figure from *Annual Report of the District Commissioner, West Nile District*; other figures from returns submitted by the steamer clerk, Butiaba, to District Commissioner, West Nile.

absentees as percentage of adult males of each county. The absentee rate is correlated with the degree of population pressure.[4]

Details of cash income for Lugbara are very difficult to obtain and are not very reliable. But some indications are available. My estimates for 1951 cash income per head of population from the sale of animal products, tobacco, sunflower seed and cotton are given in Table 38.[5]

TABLE 38

Cash Income per Head of Population

County	Shillings
Maraca	10/60
Ayivu	7/10
Vura	4/80
Terego	16/40
Aringa	13/90
Average:	10/60

In 1951 I estimated the earnings of labor migrants. Migrants return after a year or two in southern Uganda with money and goods, the latter usually being cloths and blankets. In addition, money is usually sent home during the migrant's absence. The average amount of money brought home by a single migrant was about Shs. 35/00; the average value of goods brought home was about Shs. 24/00. It may be accepted that the total cash value of money and goods brought and sent home by any migrant is about Shs. 60/00 for a single year's work in southern Uganda. This figure takes into account the fact that migrants who go south to work for Nyoro and Ganda cotton-farmers earn rather more than those who go on contract to the sugar and sisal estates, for whom the figures quoted above are applicable. A very approximate estimate of the annual income per head from labor migration is about Shs. 19/00. The total cash income per head from both sale of produce and labor migration is therefore about Shs. 30/00. This figure tallies with that obtained from various small income surveys made during 1950. The cash income per head is higher in those areas with a high labor migration rate than in those with a low one. I wish to emphasize that these figures refer to income per head of population, and not merely to those men who go south as labor migrants. It does not include money acquired by wage labor within

(4) Figures computed from Sleeping Sickness Records, West Nile District, 1951. Congo figures are rather lower. The density figures for Terego, Vura and Aringa are deceptive as these counties include large areas of almost empty bush. The central part of Terego averages about 150 persons to the square mile, and that of Vura 140.

(5) Details of these figures, and for those of laborer absentee rates quoted above, are in Middleton 1952.

the district or by sale of crops or livestock to other Lugbara, but only to money income acquired in the form of earnings or of money receipts for crops or livestock sold to traders who export them. And since 1951 the income from tobacco growing has increased very considerably.

The average Lugbara elementary family consists of 4.5 persons; the average elementary family income is therefore Shs. 135/00 from extra-district labor or cash sale. Wage labor and sale of crops and livestock within the district probably amounts to about Shs. 100/00 for an average elementary family. The amount of foodstuffs exchanged by barter cannot be known with any degree of reliability, nor can that exchanged by gift between kin. The latter is certainly very important, since men who earn wages or who grow a considerable surplus of food are expected to distribute much of their earnings and surplus among their closer kin. There is considerable variation in the incomes of families; with such a relatively low average cash income, an extra Shs. 40/00 a year represents a considerable addition to a family's income. A few labor migrants return after three or four years with up to Shs. 1,000/00, and many men earn wages which may amount to Shs. 200/00 or 400/00 a year. Although I have included these high-money incomes in the figures given above, I wish to make the point that these earnings are usually distributed among kin and neighbors. And the same point applies to any extra large amounts of foodstuffs grown. The institutions that affect this distribution are markets and kinship feasts.

It is not possible to compute with any accuracy whether or not the amount of home-produced supplies consumed by the household is greater or less today than it was before European impact. The density of population is greater and today there is virtually no unused land; but previously there was considerable unused land, and of land long fallow. Today the acreage used for cash crops has presumably lessened that available for food crops, but it may be assumed that the average acreage per head has not diminished to any marked extent. The fact that some modern crops have higher yields than some traditional ones (see below) is significant here. It may, I think, be said that including home-produced income the average total income per head is greater today than it was formerly, but the amount cannot be stated with accuracy.

PRESENT-DAY LUGBARA ECONOMY

Before considering details of present-day Lugbara domestic economy, it should be emphasized that the broad patterns of exchange are very different from those of half a century ago. Money is now an accepted medium of exchange; consumer goods are imported into the area and can be obtained only by money; taxes can be paid only by money; returning labor migrants bring money back with them. Exchanges of foodstuffs between kin, and of women between lineages in marriage, are very rarely made by means of money. But most other exchanges are so made, usually at markets; to buy food or goods with money in a person's homestead is not considered a proper thing to do, except in the case of beer-selling, as mentioned below.

Before discussing markets, I shall consider the position of traders. Indian and Arab traders import goods into Lugbaraland, mostly from southern Uganda; a small amount of goods comes from the Congo. In the Uganda part of Lugbara there are Indian and Arab traders with shops in the main township of Arua (about 40 shops, although some are extremely small) and in the smaller townships of Yumbe, Omugo, Terego and Maraca (only Yumbe having more than four shops). These shops sell cloth, cigarettes, kerosene, small lamps and a vast array of other goods from cases of whiskey for a rare European traveler to matches by the half-dozen and small packages of salt. Lugbara is not a cotton-growing area and shopkeepers make little profit compared to that made by those in the cotton-growing areas of Uganda; also there are no through roads to bring in travelers. Almost all traders supplement their incomes by tailoring the clothes they sell, buying tobacco, vegetable oils, hides and skins, and so on, usually as middlemen for other concerns; until 1948 many of them were also labor recruiters; and some of them go out as hawkers at the tobacco-buying season where there is plenty of ready cash about. I have been informed by many traders that these activities produce greater income than the ordinary trading, but actual figures are virtually impossible to obtain.[6]

In the smaller centers, those not gazetted as townships, there are African shops even smaller than those owned by Indians and Arabs. Their range of goods is more limited, as the demand is less in the smaller settlements and African traders have to buy goods at retail prices. Wholesaling is in the hands of Indian traders, most of whom refuse to sell to African traders at wholesale rates.[7] Most African shops are small buildings with one room for trading, a storeroom and the trader's living quarters behind, the whole being mud and wattle with a tin roof. They sell cloth, soap, salt, sugar, tea, kerosene, matches, tobacco, beads and other cheap commodities. Most African

(6) One hawker I knew made about Shs. 90/– profit a day, but only for a couple of weeks in the year.

(7) This was the position in 1952.

traders are also tailors or employ tailors—the treadle sewing machine is the usual mark of a shop. Again, details of income are difficult to obtain; one shopkeeper whom I knew well made about Shs. 20/00 a week, and the average is probably slightly higher.

Other African shopkeepers deal primarily in cooked food, tea and beer; their shops are usually known as *hoteli,* whereas an ordinary shop is known by the Swahili word *duka. Hoteli* depend on passing travelers along the few roads, and if they are to keep going, they tend in the evenings to become beerhouses for local inhabitants. Their mark is a blaring gramophone rather than a sewing machine.

Traders, whether Indian, Arab or African, play certain important economic roles in Lugbara. They provide imported consumer goods, certain skills (especially tailoring), and to a less extent they cater to the welfare of a few travelers along the roads. Many of them also buy the less important cash crops, providing a means for purchase of these goods and so a source of cash to the local population. Many African shopkeepers provide many of the services provided elsewhere by banks—the supply of cash, credit, holding money deposits.

Traders are patronized by women as well as by men, women buying cloth and household commodities. But it is felt that women who go to traders' shops—and especially those who go to loiter and chat there— are doing something outside traditional women's behavior. I was told by a respectable married woman:

> Shops are were you find loose ("mad") women. Shops are bad places. Our girls go there to look at clothes and then they do not know their brothers. There, too, they meet strangers who entice them away and seduce them. Shops are the places of strangers.[8]

This view, which is a very common one, does not arise only from the fact that the goods sold by traders are new and imported and stand for strange and foreign ways. It is due also to the fact that the traders themselves are usually strangers. Of a sample of twenty African shop-keepers among the Uganda Lugbara in 1951, twelve were Lugbara, and of these only four had their shops in or very near to their natal homes. Five were Congo Lugbara and three were Lugbara from areas distant from their shops. However, six of the twelve had married local girls, and two of these and two of the others had uterine kin in the neighborhood. Of the other eight shopkeepers, five were Kakwa and three Alur, all of them from Uganda and all of them from Arua

(8) "Strangers" are seen as the bringers of the bad things of modern life. The reference to "knowing brothers" is to the popular Lugbara belief that today people who wear clothes forget their lineage affiliation and can no longer tell their own kin and so commit incest.

township and not from Kakwa or Alur counties. Of the Kakwa, three were Muslims and so counted as "Nubis." Of the twenty traders, fourteen had been soldiers during the last war and after it had all worked as lorry-drivers, assistants in Indian shops or in various government departments (forestry, agriculture, etc.) All had worked at least three years as labor migrants in southern Uganda. All were literate, seventeen of them having attended a Christian, three a Muslim school. All were accepted as being members of the class known as *'Ba odiru* ("the new people"), a class composed of government officials, school teachers and so on.

Besides shops there are also full-time peripatetic traders, who move around the countryside. They are mostly "Nubis" from Arua town. The town consists largely of Nubis, who are said to be the descendants of Emir Pasha's Sudanese troops who were settled in various parts of this region after the Mahdi revolt and the Uganda mutiny. Today, however, there are very few pure-blooded Arab or Sudanese Nubis in Arua, most of them being Lugbara, Kakwa or members of other tribes who have become Muslims and married into Nubi families. They control the hide and skin trade, and deal in other goods in which the profits are too small for larger traders. In addition they control the illicit gin trade in Arua, perhaps the most profitable trade in the district. (I was informed on good authority that several Nubi women each make some Shs. 5,000/00 annually from sale of gin).

Besides a large permanent central market at Arua town, open daily and containing many permanent stalls kept by Nubis, there are many small markets scattered about the countryside. The market *(cu)* is now a recognized Lugbara institution, but the first market seems to have been opened about 1925; before then exchange was carried on solely by traditional means. Markets are all organized in a similar way, and are found near all sub-county headquarters and at a few other places. They are open one or two days a week only, and are attended regularly by most people, especially by women. A market is surrounded by a hedge or fence, with a porch in which sits the "owner" of the market, who has "bought" or "eaten" that particular market. With him are his assistants with usually the sub-county policeman and a few hangers-on. Markets are licensed to market-owners by the African Local Government for an annual sum.[9] The owner has the right to levy an entrance fee on anyone entering the market to sell, the levy ranging from two to twenty cents depending on the produce brought for sale; this gives the owner a handsome income, and market-owners are becoming extremely wealthy men.

(9) I am here describing the situation as it was in 1952. There have been several changes in the licensing system since then.

The owner is responsible for the upkeep of the market, for insuring that its fence and gateway are kept in good repair, that it is kept clean and swept, that stalls are provided if necessary; with the help of the sub-county police, he is responsible for maintenance of peace in the market. Almost all market-owners in 1952 were men who had been government clerks, police and other minor officials who could satisfy the Local Government of their reliability and ability to maintain the market properly; most of them neither came from nor lived in the area of the market, and some of them were owners of more than one market.

There are always two categories of sellers in the market. One category is the men who sell knives, razor blades, salt, tea, soap and other cheap consumer goods; they are either local shopkeepers or their assistants, or wandering hawkers. Even in a large market of 500 people there are rarely more than half a dozen of these men. The second category consists of women who sell grain, beans and other foodstuffs, and pots, grinding stones, gourds and other products of domestic industry. There are usually several women outside the market fence, either because they refuse to pay the market fee (in which case they may be turned away by the market-owner) or because they are selling grinding stones and other bulky articles for which they need considerable space. The women who sell pots, stones and similar products use the money they get for them to buy foodstuffs; they are specialists and grow less food than nonspecialists. But the majority of women come with foodstuffs and return home with other foodstuffs, using money as a medium of exchange, although at any particular market most women also either bring money with which to buy food or return home with money after having bought what food they require.

There are also a few women traders, almost always foreigners (either Nubis or women from the Congo, distinct in dress and language from Lugbara) who both sell and buy to make cash profits and also make a profit from buying and selling Uganda and Congo currencies; they are usually considered to be rogues and whores by Lugbara, and are outside the market system proper. Lugbara women do not come to markets alone, but in groups, each consisting of the wives and unmarried daughters of lineage-groups. They sit together, taking turns watching over one anothers' baskets and babies while the others wander round the market buying what they need.

The average number of tickets sold for market-fees at six markets in different parts of Lugbara in 1951 was just over 500. At the height of the market, about mid-morning, there were usually some 250 people present. Relatively few women go to a market solely to buy, and so most of them pay entry fees. On the average there were also

15 women selling goods outside the market fence who did not pay entry fees. Women come from long distances to those markets at which some of the goods sold are found only in a particular region, such as the papyrus mats sold along the northern part of the Uganda-Congo border. But the great majority of women come from a radius of five miles; to travel more than that distance to a market is something of a special occasion and is done only by women who wish to sell produce in an area of temporary shortage or to buy cheaply in an area of temporary plenty.

All transactions in markets are in money. I was told that "we women have no money; we go to markets to get it. How else can women get things made by Europeans?" (the "things" refer to money). A county chief told me that people could not pay their taxes if there were no markets. Money is still scarce in Lugbara and enters from only a few sources. Much of it is removed again in the form of taxes. All adult men must have cash for taxes, but not all adult men can acquire cash themselves—they do so through their wives' transactions in the marketplace.

MARKETS IN THE SOCIAL ECONOMY

Markets have several functions in present-day Lugbara economy. They are the means by which small amounts of local foodstuffs are distributed in a neighborhood of those households which do not supply themselves wholly from their own gardens or manufacture. They transact locally produced commodities such as pots and gourds; they are a source of money income to the local population; and they are a distributional channel for imported consumer goods. These functions are related to the recent changes in farming and settlement patterns as well as to changes in domestic economy of the Lugbara household. Moreover, such economic changes impinge on the traditional system of status and authority within the lineage.

During this century there has developed an ever-increasing pressure upon the land. The traditional pattern of the compounds of a tribe, with their "home" fields being surrounded by a zone of "outside" fields under shifting cultivation has by now vanished in every part of central Lugbara. Instead there is virtually continuous settlement across the countryside, the former inter-tribal zones of "outside" fields being filled with homesteads and "home" fields. Formerly there was a continual slow movement from north to south by a process of migration-drift, and also a continual readjustment of inter-tribal boundaries by warfare. The traditional optimum population to a given area of land was thus maintained. After the establishment of

British administration, however, chiefs and sub-chiefs were set in control of tribal and smaller areas, and the boundaries between them were demarcated. Movement of groups across these boundaries was no longer permitted, although individuals could become tenants on the land of matrilateral kin elsewhere. The fixing of boundaries in the places where they happened to be about 1914 has led to an increasing disparity between population and the carrying capacity of an area of land. This has been mitigated, though only to a small extent, by individual emigration to outlying areas, and by labor migration from the more densely crowded areas.

In almost all cases, and particularly in the densely settled areas of central Lugbaraland, the consequence of disparity between population and carrying capacity of the land has been that the traditional distribution of types of fields between women of the settlement can no longer be made, and also that the rarest type of field, the irrigated riverine field, is no longer available to be worked at all by a large number of women, especially the wives of junior men. There have been changes in traditional crop rotations and also in types of crops grown. With the increase in labor migration and the consequent absence of many young men, fields are cultivated for longer periods than they would have been traditionally, and crops that involve lighter labor and bring heavier yields have been substituted for the traditional staples. Today cassava has the greatest acreage of any crop planted in the district, although it is disliked by Lugbara as a food; yet it is not even mentioned in a list of crops grown in 1931.[10]

Maize was introduced into the area about 1925, and today has a large acreage, as has sweet potato, another crop of recent introduction that has largely taken the place of traditional crops.[11] Cassava and

(10) Information from District Medical Office, West Nile, 1952.

(11) Acreages planted in 1951 were estimated as follows by the Agricultural Office, West Nile. Although liable to some distortion due to the fact that many crops are grown in mixed stands, the figures do give an idea of the proportions of crops, and also agree with sample figures taken by myself in various areas.

Crop	Acres	Yield per Acre
Cassava	30,000	13,500 lb.
Beans	30,000	450 lb.
Eleusine	23,000	650 lb.
Sweet potatoes	21,000	6,000 lb.
Maize	18,000	900 lb.
Groundnuts	12,000	800 lb.
Peas	11,000	400 lb.
Sorghums	9,000	700 lb.
Simsim	5,000	250 lb.

The acreages are approximate only. Most crops are grown in mixed stands. A good deal of the eleusine grown is taken to the government famine stores at sub-county headquarters and not consumed by the growers.

sweet potatoes are ideal crops for families many of whose men are absent on labor migration. They have the largest yields of any crops and need comparatively little weeding. Maize is used mainly for beer-making, in place of the traditionally used white sorghum, *ijio*. Both maize and *ijio* are grown mostly in riverine plots, however, which are scarce, and so are not grown in quantity by many wives, especially in the crowded central areas of Lugbara.

Traditionally the domestic economic unit was a family cluster. This is a cluster of from five to eight elementary and compound families, most of the male heads of which are related as members of a small patrilineal lineage. There may be a few attached families also. The whole is under the authority of a single elder, the genealogically senior man of the core lineage. He was and still is to a large extent, responsible for the allocation of the groups's resources—women, land and livestock. Within the group, component families and individuals possess individual property—tools, huts and money—but all are under the general supervision of the elder. Traditional working groups in the fields are the men and women of an entire family cluster. Although each wife had fields of all the types I have mentioned, there was considerable exchange of produce between those of a single man or set of brothers. This is the traditional pattern, and is still observed where it is possible to do so. But in most areas this pattern has changed. The domestic economic unit is now the compound and often the elementary family (only 37 per cent of Lugbara men have more than one wife). The consequence is that a woman finds it more difficult to insure a regular supply of all types of foodstuff that she may normally need. Whereas in the past she and her co-wives could draw upon one another's supplies (although each wife had control of her own stores) nowadays she is much less likely to be able to do so, both because of the greater separation and independence of the wives, and also because of the greater financial independence of their husbands. Men may earn money from labor migration and sale of cash crops, and the tendency is for them to keep their own earnings and not share them among other members of the family cluster. A wife must therefore obtain extra supplies of particular foods, and supplies for unforeseen occasions, from markets. Today wives find it more and more difficult to obtain all types of fields; as they tend to substitute cassava for the traditional grains which are grown mainly in "outside" fields (which are today scarce), it becomes more difficult for any wife to supply all her own needs. However, not all foods are in equal demand at markets. The grains sold most frequently are maize and white sorghum. These are used almost entirely for beer-making, and the demand for beer is the most difficult to foresee of any. Beer is needed in almost all religious rites and for a large number of ceremonial occasions, as well as for casual visiting of kin. It is also brewed by women for sale at beerdrinks, both in their own homes and at beer-clubs. Since births, deaths, marriages and visits by kin cannot be foreseen, maize and sorghum for the essential beer has usually to be obtained from the market. Any beer left over is usually sold for cash at beerdrinks, the woman keeping the money for herself. The appearance of maize, the scarcity of irrigated land, and the use of markets are certainly interconnected.

In addition, women exchange cassava for those other foodstuffs which are preferred, especially as relishes, but which are often difficult for a woman to grow herself under present conditions of land shortage; these are particularly groundnuts, peas, beans and simsim. Cassava is bought by poorer women and those who lack fields: it is considered rather shameful to give a guest cassava, and it is eaten mainly by large families in which many children have to be fed. It is also bought by women who sell the rarer foodstuffs and buy cheaper food in exchange, and have a profit in cash from the transaction as well as food for their families.

The market may thus be seen as an accomodating institution that is a response to the changes in the size of the basic residential group and in patterns of farming to enable the Lugbara to avoid drastic changes in their way of living. The large, self-sufficient family-clusters of traditional Lugbara society can give way smoothly to the smaller, non-self-sufficient households of today only if frequent exchange of small local surpluses is possible and can be relied upon by a housewife; this has been achieved through the use of the small local market.

Although most women who go to a market both enter and leave it with foodstuffs, they also bring away money. They may keep this money in order to buy maize when they next need to brew beer, to buy knives, pots and other domestic utensils, or to buy their children clothes. But in addition they also hand over some of it to their husbands and their brothers. Traditionally a bachelor had a special garden, called *lomere,* which he cultivated with the aid of his unmarried sisters; he exchanged the crops for goats or other livestock to get part of his own bridewealth. Today men need money for taxes, consumer goods and also for the purchase of bridewealth cattle. Formerly, a young man had a formally defined status, which became higher when at marriage he changed from being a "youth" to a "big youth" and later, after the birth of children, to a "man behind" (behind the more senior men). This status was associated with his age, his marital status, his genealogical position in his lineage, and with factors of personality and influence. Today he may increase his status, influence and prestige, or more accurately may hasten its increase, by the acquisition of money. He may then acquire a wife or a second wife before his fellows, he may buy beer for his seniors and so acquire influence, and he may become more independent of the authority of his elders, an authority which used to derive from his economic dependence upon them for bridewealth cattle. The commonest way for a man to get money is to go to southern Uganda as a labor migrant or to grow cash crops, mainly tobacco. But labor migration has certain disadvantages. Men prefer to stay in their own homes, since their women and kin are there; if they are away for too long they become "lost" and may lose chances to acquire high status in their lineages. Many do not regard the cash rewards as commensurate with the disadvantages. Another way of acquiring money is for a man to be given it by his sisters or his wives; the former is extremely common, the latter less so because the wives have other financial responsibilities, especially towards their children. Almost all unmarried girls make money at markets and give it to their brothers, who are expected to make small gifts in return. In addition they look after their sisters generally, acting as go-betweens for them in their love affairs which usually last three or four years before marriage. A lover gives a small gift to a girl whom he has visited, and these gifts are usually given by the girls to their brothers. With land pressure, bachelor gardens are now rare, and the money made by sisters at markets has taken the place of income formerly derived from these gardens.

The desire for a higher, or at least a more independent, status than their traditional one is a reason why many women trade at markets. Women can earn money to buy themselves clothes and ornaments, so that they are seen as "progressive" and desirable to young men who have been to southern Uganda and seen the relatively "advanced" peoples there. This applies mainly to unmarried girls and to divorced women. The latter are frequent in Lugbara society, and supply most of the women who visit markets to make money rather than to acquire foodstuffs for their households.

It is significant that the goods which are traditionally exchanged by men are not important in market transactions; they are the concern of more senior men who continue to deal in them as they have always done. These are mainly iron objects (especially those used as token of kinship and affinity rather than as tool or weapons), livestock, and women, who are still largely under the control of heads of family clusters. Although most markets today have an itinerant seller of women's knives who is a middleman between the smiths and the women who buy their products, most iron objects other than imported hoes are still made by smiths. These objects include knives of various kinds, spears, arrows of various types, earrings, armlets and legrings. The smith is given either raw iron or old iron objects, and makes new objects in return, charging grain or livestock for his skill. Smiths do take money, but it is much more usual for them to be paid in kind— partly as a result of their client-like status within the lineage group in whose territory they live. As mentioned earlier, they are Ndu, the only foreigners traditionally accepted into Lugbara communities without being absorbed into Lugbara family clusters. Livestock are needed by men, especially by senior men, for sacrifice and bridewealth payments. They may be bought for money, but are far more usually acquired by direct exchange, a bull for so many goats, and so on. In short, objects which are used in transactions that concern changes of status in the kinship system are still outside the system of market-exchange.

In place of a formerly largely self-sufficient series of small and almost independent communities bound together only by ties of interpersonal kinship and common clans and myths, there has emerged a society in which small local communities are no longer economically self-sufficient, and in which considerable movement of people across the country is possible. Until very recently there were few differences in wealth, few people with marked political authority and little incentive for the acquisition of wealth. But today government chiefs and other people associated with the administration or the missions, and people such as traders, are markedly more wealthy than their neighbors. A distinction is appearing between these people (known as the "New People"), who marry among themselves and enjoy a different standard of living from the ordinary, and the mass of the peasantry. The introduction of consumer goods made outside Lugbara has provided both the means of conspicuous consumption by the "New People" and those who wish to emulate them, and a new standard of "necessary" luxuries for ordinary people. With the introduction of these goods, and with the changes in domestic economy brought about by local disparity between population and the carrying capacity of the land, traditional forms of exchange have been found inadequate to provide either the necessities of life or the luxuries, and new forms of exchange have come into being.

CENTRAL AFRICA

CHAPTER 23

Rural Rhodesian Markets

BY ROBERT I. ROTBERG

In Northern Rhodesia the concept of selling or exchanging commodities within fixed or circumscribed bounds is from all evidence a recent phenomenon, and one related closely to the assumption of Western ways and practices by tribal peoples. Although there are some reports of inter-group or inter-tribal trade in pre-Western times,[1] it was neither regular, institutionalized nor devoted to a wide range of commodities (Colson 1951 : 107–108). On the basis of what little information is available, it would seem that pre-European trade was usually barter for salt, for weapons, or for food in times of seasonal hunger or prolonged famine.[2] There was a lucrative trade in ivory and slaves, which was controlled and directed by foreign entrepreneurs, with profits neither invested in the country nor stimulating tertiary trade or regularized marketing.[3] Traffic in skins or feathers was also developed for international markets, but indigenous proliferation of local feeder groups was unknown. Considerable variation in the level of societal chaos made knowledge of local conditions of paramount importance to the trader or exploiter, whether he dealt in slaves, ivory, or feathers, but it did not lead immediately to any important forms of marketing.[4] Trade in pre-European times was then a prolegomena to the economic development of Northern Rhodesia; as such it did not, by itself, bring about the growth of markets.

This essay will discuss the historical development and present

[1] For purposes of this study the year 1885 may be taken as the date of effective Western penetration into what is now Northern Rhodesia. This contact was limited and tenuous before 1910. Before 1885 the only contact with the West had been with Lusitanian travelers, English traders, half-caste Arabs, and David Livingstone and other British and Middle-European explorers. *Vide* Gann, 1958; Hanna 1956.

[2] See reports of Val Gielgud, an administrator sent to Northern Rhodesia in 1900, for interesting accounts of the different forms trade could take. Public Records of Northeast Rhodesia, A 3/8/1; National Archives of Rhodesia and Nyasaland, Lusaka. William Watson, *Tribal Cohesion in a Money Economy* (Manchester 1958) Ch. 1.

[3] The best discussion of the slave trade is Gann 1954 : 27–51. Also correspondence between Blair Watson and Henry Hamilton Johnston, 18 May 1895 in district notebooks at Mporokoso.

[4] There is a discussion of these subjects in correspondence from Northern Rhodesia and Nyasaland in the Foreign Office records, FO 84, and FO 2, 1889–1900, in Public Record Office, London.

organization of markets in rural Northern Rhodesia. It will indicate that the growth of markets is essentially a result of government efforts exerted during the last 30 years, and that Africans themselves have only occasionally organized markets or encouraged the territorial or tribal authorities to grant necessary facilities or permission. Later sections will indicate the location and distribution of markets. They will discuss the commodities and comparative prices found in the various markets. Vendors are discussed according to their age, sex, and education. An impression of their motives for entering the market arena is advanced, and the methods of pricing and weighing are examined. A short section is devoted to the parallel development of state-run cooperative markets.

THE HISTORY OF MARKETS IN NORTHERN RHODESIA

There is no evidence to support a contention that African markets existed in Northern Rhodesia, or on its borders, much before 1930.[5] All anthropological research indicates an absence of markets or marketing activities before the arrival of Europeans, and government records and reports document the period 1901–40. Gluckman denies the existence of African markets and notes his surprise that this should have been so (Gluckman 1941 : 77–82; *in litt* 17 July 1959). Colson (1951 : 107) and Smith and Dale[6] concur with regard to the Ila-Tonga people. Apthorpe and Argyle both report a lack of indigenous markets among the Soli, Nsenga, and Kunda.[7] To the north, Watson found no evidence of marketing activities by the Mambwe or Lungu.[8] Richards' writings (1939 : 22 ff. and 1951 : 167), as well as local information, confirm this for the Bemba and for the related tribes of the Luapula Valley. Melland, Doke, Torrend, and others agree on a lack of markets for the Kaonde, Lamba, Swaka, Lenje, and cognate peoples of the lower Katanga and Broken Hill regions.[9] In the northwest White has found little evidence of pre-European

(5) *Vide* J. Moffat Thomson Chief Secretary, 31 Jan., 18 May, 25 Sept., 1933, Public Records of Northern Rhodesia, ZA 1/9/165, National Archives Lusaka.

(6) Smith and Dale, London 1920, omit any references to marketing organizations. This absence is also confirmed in Smith's papers, now contained in the Methodist Missionary Society archives, London.

(7) Personal information, Raymond J. Apthorpe, W. J. Argyle. Cf. Barnes 1951 : 244.

(8) William Watson, *in litt* 17 March 1960.

(9) Julius Torrend, S. J., makes no mention of markets in his diary (1914–21) at Kasisi Mission, Northern Rhodesia, or in his papers and correspondence, at Campion House, Salisbury, Southern Rhodesia. Melland 1923 makes reference to markets as do the Melland Papers now at the Rhodes-Livingstone Museum. Doke 1931 records many items other than market activities. Charles Foster, a missionary among the Kaonde since 1917, confirmed the lack of markets for the Kaonde, personal information.

marketing activities for Luvale, Lunda, or Luchazi (White 1959 and personal information). Continuous independent attempts to unearth recollections of marketing activities from tribal chiefs or traditional councilors throughout the territory failed to produce any reports which would tend to disagree with the anthropological evidence.[10]

Explanations for such a widespread absence of market activities can, at best, be tentative. Further study of the country's ecological conditions, and of the economic organization of Rhodesian society in pre-European times, is necessary before any hypotheses about the lack of markets can be advanced with complete confidence. Nevertheless it is well to assume that the character and distribution of Northern Rhodesia's small population limited the possibility of economic diversification and any large degree of regional specialization. Only about 500,000 to 800,000 Africans lived in Northern Rhodesia before the arrival of Europeans.[11] Many parts of the country—either because of inhospitable terrain, the unavailability of water, or the infertility of the soil—were without inhabitants.[12] Overall population density was therefore low (in some cases an average of one person per square mile) while large numbers of tribesmen clustered about available water or built villages only on the riparian reaches of permanent streams.

Demand for foreign articles has come about only with the growth of European influence in the last 75 years. Before missionaries and traders arrived in Northern Rhodesia, Africans wanted little they could not produce themselves, and they sold little.[13] Only after the arrival of these foreigners did Africans appreciate that a temporary surfeit of grain could purchase colorful clothes, trinkets, or other items of interest.[14] Missionaries preached against "heathen" undress

(10) I am grateful for the careful assistance of M. Rodgers Mumbi, Simon C. Katilungu, Leshomwa Sheba Muuka, Edward Mbewe, and Humphrey Maunga.

(11) These figures are based on estimates collated from the early records left by administrators and found in district notebooks throughout the territory.

(12) Average annual rainfall ranges today from 16 inches in the Zambezi Valley to 64 inches in the Lake Bangweulu region. The nitrogenous content of most soil is between 0.38 and .110 per cent.

(13) Traders from Benguella and Lobito Bay were frequent visitors to Barotseland and the Katanga. George Westbeech and George Blockley were active in southern Barotseland during the period 1875–1885, and the African Lakes Company established a store at Kituta on Lake Tanganyika in 1888. Missionaries arrived with trade goods as early as 1879, but for practical purposes only after 1886.

Vide Westbeech's diary for 1885-8, in Rhodes-Livingstone Institute, Lusaka; Childs 1949 : 190–215; and correspondence of the London Missionary Society, LMS archives, London.

(14) By 1902 the annual import of trade goods by the LMS exceeded 15 tons; Kawimbe mission was stocked with 1,600 fezes, 4,300 fancy scarves, 1,850 pounds of soap, 5,400 yards of red calico, 39,000 yards of sheeting, 2,000 pounds of beads, and large amounts of

and encouraged both men and women to obtain shirts, dresses, and other foreign objects.[15] Calico and cowrie shells became currency and symbols of status.[16] But at first this new demand did not unleash any propensities for African market organization. Most new African economic activities were not unnaturally directed towards the satisfaction of European needs, for it was only by obtaining European employment, or selling to Europeans, that new goods could be purchased by Africans.

The growth and development of African markets in Northern Rhodesia was, therefore, a concomitant of Western influence. It was only with the growth of European towns and administrative centers, and the consequent concentration in urban areas of Africans who were divorced from subsistence agriculture, that a new demand for African foodstuffs was created. One of the by-products of industrialization and African migration to the towns was the beginnings of indigenous market organizations. Africans increasingly assumed entrepenurial roles and many assimilated the European's concept of a cash crop (Turner 1955 : 19–25). These new activities were basically foreign to the African agriculturalist, but during the 1930's a new African town labor force demanded staples and relishes and eventually obtained them. Urban employers, particularly on the Copperbelt, and government administrators contributed to these developments by encouraging, providing land for, and demarcating the initial markets.[17] An increasing European population also provided a market for the door-to-door sale of pulses and fruits in mining townships and isolated administrative centers.

Rural markets, with which this essay is primarily concerned, were subject to a haphazard evolution in the 1930's before legislative action and administrative direction recognized the need for such rural markets and attempted to assist in their orderly development.[18] In Fort Jameson (Eastern Province), for example, vendors used a roughly circumscribed area near the main African location to sell grains and pulses as early as 1939. Trade with Europeans was based on ambula-

---

cheap jewelry, watches, umbrellas, salt, and necklaces. Wright-Thompson, 23 Jan. 1903, LMS archives. Robertson, diary ii, 2 May 1923, Abel Papers.

(15) "A few people are beginning to respect themselves by pulling on Sunday clothes." Chapman-Pickett, 14 Sept. 1906, MMS archives. "All our servants are already neatly dressed and have assumed a civilized [sic] appearance." Hemans-Thompson, 11 July 1891, LMS archives.

(16) See Desmond Clark's note Quiggin 1960 : 14.

(17) Thompson-Chief Secretary, 31 Jan. 1933, Pub. Recs of N.R., ZA 1/9/165 National Archives, Lusaka.

(18) The first market ordinance was Cap. 21 (30 Nov. 1937) *The Laws of Northern Rhodesia*. It has been amended frequently.

tory hawking during this period and until 1956. Both of these early developments were tolerated by government, although lack of proper facilities and supervision precluded any efficient rationalization of the existing methods of marketing. A 1939 ordinance providing for assistance in the establishment of markets was implemented in Fort Jameson in 1942 when the market was allotted a plot of land, and a building was constructed. Additions were made to the market after World War II, and an entirely new market place was constructed by government in 1953.[19] In 1956 a separate and smaller market was built for hawkers who sold to Europeans, and all door-to-door sales were prohibited.

The Fort Jameson market indicates the prevailing pattern of development for rural markets. In the urban centers, government was prone to take an earlier initiative, especially on the Copperbelt, while in the smaller rural centers government activity in this sphere was almost nonexistent before 1954. Although some kind of market existed in Fort Rosebery, Lundazi, Kasama, Abercorn, and Mongu before 1948, it has only been since that time that shelters have been constructed and the seasonal sales put on a regular year-round basis. Rural markets have been actively promoted for only 14 years, then, and only more recently has it been accepted government practice to stimulate new markets. Within the last four years administrators have sometimes built markets before buyers or sellers were available or interested. In other localities the opening of new markets has been preceded by publicity and fanfare in order to encourage Africans to take up the arts of buying and selling at a market. Government intended that Africans should rely for food more on locally produced staples than on canned goods from the shelves of Asian- or African-owned shops. In addition, the administration in recent years has attempted to rationalize single-commodity trade by building specialized markets where middlemen can operate more efficiently than formerly. Fish markets near principal ports or coöperatives to deal in ground nuts or sorghum, have been logical institutions for a developing country.

PRESENT-DAY MARKET PLACES

In late 1959 organized African markets were situated throughout Northern Rhodesia. Along the railway, where the concentration of African population is heaviest, one or more markets existed in all the main towns except Kalomo. Livingstone had two markets, Lusaka three, Broken Hill two, and there were 21 markets in the seven towns

(19) *Vide* The Fort Jameson district notebooks, at Fort Jameson.

comprising the Copperbelt. In the rural area, recognized markets existed in Fort Jameson (two) Fort Rosebery (two), Abercorn, Kasama, and Lundazi. Smaller markets were operating at Serenje, Isoka, Chavuma, and Kawambwa. There were irregular markets at Petauke, Rufunsa, Mununga, and Mwandi, and small market stations along bus and truck routes in the heavily populated Luapula Valley, along the Zambezi River between Seoma and Katima Mulilo, and between Kachalola and the Luangwa Bridge along the Great East Road.[20]

Except for those markets along the transport routes, all are sited at centers of European influence or control. The Mwandi, Chavuma, and Luapula markets are also well-situated to serve large numbers of rural Africans. In other rural districts of Northern Rhodesia, markets are being started by government officers at Senanga and Luwingu, and possibly at Sesheke. At Chinsali two markets proved failures and were closed. In the remaining 11 administrative divisions no markets —and presumably no demand for markets—exist, although in certain cases government-sponsored coöperative societies now buy primary products, without engaging in the exchange of retail commodities. Cash obtained by selling produce to a coöperative is therefore spent in the stores of traders, who have outlets in most rural parts of Northern Rhodesia.

Most rural markets are similar in physical appearance. A typical small market building is merely a shelter for simple protection against the elements during Northern Rhodesia's wet season. A corrugated iron or thatch roof on metal or wooden supports covers one or more rows of brick or concrete stalls. The markets are usually rectangular and long, unlit, and without side-walls. Floors are pounded earth. Vendors rent stalls in these markets for fees varying from 1d to 6d per day per stall. Or they may squat around the market in the open, displaying their wares on mats or on the ground. As a rural market grows in popularity, government may build additional shelters, or merely erect shelters to demarcate new boundaries for the squatters. The administration has also recently introduced a prefabricated market shelter of lightweight aluminum and tubular steel supports; it way serve to standardize the appearance of smaller markets.

Urban market buildings show more variation. The Lusaka main market is closed on all sides except one. It is built of brick with an asbestos roof and a concrete floor. Two Copperbelt markets look more like their rural counterparts, however, for they have high corrugated iron roofs supported on steel girders. Concrete floors are the rule. The stands in Copperbelt markets and in Lusaka are concrete sup-

(20) All the markets mentioned were visited at least once during 1959.

ported by brick pillars, the stall size being 3′6″ x 4′6″.[22] Stall fees are 6d. on the Copperbelt and 1/- in Lusaka[23]. Most rural and many urban markets do not open for business officially until 7:30 or 8:00 a.m., but vendors are usually present much earlier during the warm months. Activity in the rural centers, but not the urban markets, declines in the afternoon and vendors and buyers return to their fields or their homes. Larger markets are open seven days a week, although missionary influence may force closing on the sabbath.[24]

COMMODITIES AND PRICES

In those markets studied intensively,[25] a wide variety of commodities were offered for sale at different seasons of the year (see Table 37). Staple crops, the basic items in any African's diet, and relishes to be used on the prepared staples, were the primary foodstuffs sold.[26] Cassava, maize, and millet can be considered the important staples, although in urban areas bread is now sold in large quantities (Thompson 1954 : 5 and Nyirenda 1957 : 49–50). Fresh and dried fish is also sold in large quantities in areas where Africans are accustomed to make it the central ingredient in their diet. It may also be sold as a relish for *nsima* or *bwali*, the African grain porridge.[27] As Table 39 indicates, approximately one-third of all vendors in the sample were selling conventional staples except at Fort Rosebery, where fish is the more important food. Again excepting Fort Rosebery, about one-third of all vendors dealt in some variety of vegetable relish. There were few esoteric commodities sold in the rural markets, except for strips of car tires offered at Fort Jameson, fresh eggs in Abercorn, local sponges in Fort Rosebery, and rubber stamps made-up to individual requirements at Fort Jameson. There was a surprising absence of caterpillars and similar relish delicacies in the rural markets.

(22) Peter Stutley, "Report on a Visit to African Urban Markets in Northern Rhodesia," unpub. typescript (March 1959) contains a comparison with conditions in Basutoland.

(23) After stall fees in Lusaka market were raised in 1956 to 1/6 per stall, per day, a boycott by African traders resulted. After protracted negotiations the stall fees were returned to a 1/- figure. Ackson Nyirenda, "A note on the Recent Boycott," *Rhodes-Livingstone Journal,* xxii (1957) pp. 57–63, discusses the boycott and its effect.

(24) In Barotseland missionary influence closes the Mongu markets on Sunday. *Vide* Colson 1958 : 59.

(25) Mongu, Isoka, Serenje, Fort Jameson, Fort Rosebery, Kasama, Abercorn, Lundazi.

(26) Colson, 1958 : 54 ff. has a discussion on the preparation of porridge and relish. *Vide* Thompson 1954 for a discussion of food preparation in Lusaka and Serenje.

(27) *Nsima,* pronounced in various ways, is the Cinyanja, Citonga, and Luvale-Lunda form. *Bwali* is the Chibemba usage.

Robert I. Rotberg

Services to suit different demands were also supplied in the rural markets. One could have a bicycle repaired, shoes mended, or a watch fixed. One could buy tea and scones or, at Mongu, eat cooked rice with sour milk and sugar in it (3d a mug). At Fort Jameson cooked

TABLE 39

Number of Vendors by Commodity (Northern Rhodesia)

	Abercorn	Fort Jameson A	Fort Jameson B	Fort Rosebery	Kasama	Lundazi
Cassava	3	0	3	3	5	1
Cassava meal	9	0	0	1	7	0
Maize	3	3	4	0	0	3
Maize meal	0	1	8	1	0	2
Millet	4	2	1	2	2	0
Millet meal	3	0	0	0	1	0
Rice	0	1	2	0	4	0
Dried fish	9	4	6	6	5	2
Fresh fish	0	0	0	1	0	0
Raw nuts	9	3	5	1	7	0
Fried nuts	0	1	0	1	7	0
Tobacco	5	0	0	0	3	0
Snuff	0	1	3	4	3	0
Tomatoes	0	1	2	2	0	0
Beans	10	1	6	2	8	0
Onions	3	0	3	1	2	0
Oranges & lemons	0	3	0	0	2	0
Bananas & plantains	4	1	2	0	0	3
Cowpeas & Grndpeas	0	1	1	0	2	0
Dried Vegetables	0	1	7	0	0	0
Cabbages	0	1	3	0	0	0
Guavas	0	1	0	0	0	0
Malt	0	0	3	0	0	0
Cane sugar (misale)	1	2	2	0	1	0
Water Melons	0	1	0	0	0	1
Sweet potatoes	0	1	0	0	0	0
Pumpkin	0	1	0	0	0	0
Fat cakes	0	0	1	0	1	0
Charcoal	0	0	0	1	0	0
Musks	0	0	0	0	0	1
Curry powder	0	0	0	1	1	0
Eggs	2	0	0	0	0	0
Cooked cassava	0	0	3	0	0	0
Rice	0	0	4	0	0	0
Potatoes	0	0	2	0	0	0
Maize	0	2	0	0	0	0
Baskets & Sponges	0	5	0	1	0	0
Car tire strips	0	1	0	0	0	0
Cooked meat	0	0	4	0	0	0
Wood	0	0	0	0	0	1
Doughnuts	0	1	0	0	0	0

porridge, rice and meat, or cassava were available for consumption in the market or at home. These services are also common in urban markets, where in addition there may be barbers, illicit beer, and prostitutes.[28]

Prices in rural markets are determined on various grounds, which appear to be somewhat more casual than they are. The operation of the supply and demand mechanism is given somewhat more latitude because the motivations that move marketers are sometimes more diffuse than in our own society. For example, if the vendor is at market for a short time—that is, if he is not a regular dealer—the price of his produce may be dependent upon some specific sum, such as the cost of a bicycle he desires. He may, also, set his price by guesswork, his mood of the moment, or a convenient monetary denomination (1d, 3d or 6d).

Prices in the urban markets are created by more overt reference to supply and demand, a situation which also penetrates the larger rural markets in some degree. There is in the local markets, however, little conscious desire to undersell a competitor and to increase volume—in part, no doubt, because a source of supply may be remote or limited. It is common for a vendor to sell a load he himself has carried from a distance, then return home to catch more fish, harvest more grain, or pick more vegetables.

There is increasingly a trend for urban dwellers to assume an entrepreneurial role in this situation, buying from a recognized source of supply (either from relatives in a rural village or a local coöperative depot). There is also some evidence that a type of mail-order buying is used in Lusaka and Fort Jameson: a vendor writes to his relatives at home and asks them to forward a replenishment of his stocks, which are carried to him by bicycle or sent by bus.

African vendors, at least in the rural markets, tend not to compute costs and prices in the way that traders do in Western society. They often set prices according to their own trading skill and initiative. Prices, thus, follow supply and demand, but the elements entering into a man's decisions about selling price are more diverse than they are in market-oriented societies.

The comparable commodity prices for five rural markets are set forth in Table 40. Although there was a surprisingly high correlation of prices for commodities sold in the same way in different markets, this may not be significant. Most produce was sold by the item, or by a small measure of weight, making minimal prices dependent upon coin denominations. Traders in Rhodesia often complain that they

(28) There are butcheries at Isoka, and one at Fort Jameson. Prostitutes are available in most urban markets, and at Fort Rosebery and Mongu. *Vide* Wilson, 1942 : 66–69.

TABLE 40

Commodity by Price and Method of Calculation (Northern Rhodesia)

	Abercorn	Ft. Jameson A	Ft. Jameson B	Ft. Rosebery	Kasama	Lundazi
Cassava	2d.–5d. @	1d. @	1d.–2d. @ 1b	1d. @	1d.–5d. @	1d. @
Cassava meal	3d. @ b	—	—	4/- @ t	3d. @ b	—
Maize	3d. @	5/- @ t	5/- @ t	—	—	3d. @ 2 ear
Maize meal	—	1d. @ p or 3d. @ 8 oz.	1d. @ 2–3 oz., 4/- –4/6 @ t	6d. @ pt.	—	1d. @ p
Millet	3d. @ b	4d. @ p	3d. @ 1b	10d. @ t	3d. @ b	—
Millet meal	3d. @ b	—	—	—	3d. @ b	—
Rice	—	3d. @ heap	3d. @ 8 oz.	—	6d. @ b	—
Dried fish	3d., 6d., 2/6 @ b	3d., 8d., 1/- @ heap	3d. @ 2 oz. 1/- @ 3 oz. 1/9 @ lb	1/- @ heap	3d. @ s	6d. @ 8 fish
Fresh fish	—	—	—	1/ @ lb	—	—
Raw peanuts	3d. @ b	3d. @ heap	3d. @ 3–4 oz.	3d.–6d. @ heap	3d. @ b	—
Fried peanuts	—	1d. @ heap	—	1d. @ heap	1d. @ s	—
Tobacco	3d. @ piece	—	—	—	1d. @ piece	—
Snuff	—	1d. @ tsp.	1d. @ tsp.	1d. @ tsp.	1d. @ tsp.	—
Tomatoes	—	3d. @ heap	3d. @ 1¼–2 lb	6d. @ 3 or 6d. @ lb	—	—
Beans	3d. @ b	3d. @ 1½ oz.	3d. @ 3 oz. 6 oz., 1 lb	6d. @ heap	3d. @ b	—
Onions	3d. @ bunch	—	6d. @ 2 lb	3d. @ bunch	3d. @ bunch	—
Oranges & lemons	—	1d. each	—	—	1d. each	—
Bananas, etc.	1d. @	1d. @	1d. @	—	—	1d. @ 4
Peas	—	3d. @ heap	3d. heap	—	3d. @ s	—
Dried vegs.	—	1d. @ p	3d. @ 1, 2 oz.	—	—	--
Cabbages	—	3d. @	9d. @ 3 lb or 6d. @ 3½ lb	7½d. @ lb	—	—
Guavas	--	1d. @ 4	—	—	—	—
Malt	—	—	3d. @ 4, 14 oz.	—	—	—
Sugar cane	2d. @ 2	3d. @ 2	1d. @ 4 lb	—	2d. @ 2	—
Water melons	—	8d. @	—	—	—	1d. @
Sweet potatoes	—	8d. @ 6 lb	—	—	—	—
Pumpkin	—	6d. @	—	—	—	—
Fat cakes	—	—	1d. @	—	1d. @	—
Charcoal	—	—	—	1d. @ b	—	—
Husks	—	—	—	—	—	3d. @ bask
Curry powder	—	—	—	1d. @ tsp.	1d. @ tsp.	—
Eggs	2d.–4d. @	—	—	—	—	—
Cooked staples, meat	—	--	3d. @ portion	—	—	—
Baskets etc.	—	2/-, 3/- @	—	1d. @ (sponges)	—	—
Car tire strips	—	3d. @ strip	—	—	—	—
Wood	—	—	—	—	—	5d. @ log
Doughnuts	—	1d. @	—	—	—	—

@ = each; p = plate; b = shallow bowl; t = paraffin tin (4 gal. size); s = small tin must price products sold to Africans in readily visible denominations. The penny, the tickey (3d) and the sixpence are common coins, and an item retailing for an odd combination of these coins (say 5d, or tickey and two pennies) will not sell as well as the same item for six-pence. Within markets, as well as between different markets, there was rarely knowledge of the range of prices available for one com-modity. Indeed, prices changed on succeeding days, or, less frequently, during the hours of a single day. Vendors did not sell at a lower price when stocks were depleted, neither to enable themselves to leave for home earlier, nor to replenish their supplies more quickly. And more often than not buyers purchased from "A" instead of from "B" be-cause of tribal or linguistic affiliation, or on the basis of closer kinship ties, rather than after a period of careful and diligent comparison of the various prices.

Measurements by vendors and buyers were usually inexact. Scales, except in the larger urban markets, were almost unknown. Produce tended, as Table 40 indicates, to be measured in terms of heaps, shallow or deep bowls, four-gallon paraffin tins, smaller tins, baskets or by guesswork. Sometimes cassava meal is sold in a large tin, some-times by the pound weight, sometimes by heaps of variable sizes, or sometimes by the bowlful. Teaspoons are also used as measuring devices, as are plates. Tobacco is sold by the piece,[29] although a vendor will often add an extra amount if his pieces are smaller than usual. An extra banana or orange may also be added when they are sold indi-vidually. But without proper scales, or any real desire to calculate costs closely, there is little incentive to be exact in measurement, and buyer and seller are probably equally short in the long run.

MARKET VENDORS

From impressions gathered after a tour of Rhodesian markets, and after an analysis of the available data, it seems evident that there is increasing professionalization of market skills with increasing market size. This inference also emerges from data on the sex of sellers and their ages (see Table 41). In the larger markets investigated (Abercorn, Fort Jameson, Fort Rosebery, Kasama, Livingstone, and Lusaka[30]) the majority of vendors were men in their working years. On the basis of individual case studies, it appears that men were con-tent to make a living from regular or intermittent selling in the markets. But in the smaller centers—Lundazi, Mongu, and Isoka—the

[29] Sun dried Turkish or Burley tobacco. It is not Virginia leaf.
[30] Livingstone and Lusaka were studied for comparative data, and to supplement or complement the research done by Nyirenda and Miracle.

TABLE 41
Age of Market Vendors (Northern Rhodesia)

	Under 17	17–22	23–29	30–40	41–50	Over 50
Fort Jameson						
Male	5	5	10	14	9	1
Female	3	4	3	12	5	1
Fort Rosebery						
Male	–	4	4	4	2	9
Female	–	–	–	–	1	–

majority of the vendors were women, although men continued to sell fish, wood, or bananas, which were products of their own labor. Women reported that they made only a little money from the markets, but that vending had become a way of life for them. For most women, market vending was only a part-time occupation, although one woman had made 30/- a week selling cooked rice at 3d. a bowl in Mongu market ever since it opened in 1958.

The distribution of market vendors by ages also bears out a conclusion of professionalization. More than one-half of the male vendors were in the 23-40 age group, while only one-fourth were over 40 (see Table 41). Some form of vegetable produce was the most common item sold by the younger vendors: a 12-year-old boy at Fort Jameson dealt in dried vegetables, a 16-year-old boy also sold dried vegetables and entranced customers with tunes from his mouth organ, a 17-year-old marketed onions, and an 18-year-old sold bananas. Two 21-year-old men were selling cooked cassava and cooked rice and meat, and a 20-year-old dealt in maize meal. At Fort Rosebery, however, the men under 23 all specialized in fresh or dried fish. They had caught it themselves, or were selling it for kinsmen. One boy of 18, however, was Fort Rosebery's only watch repairer; he filled an occupation usually reserved for older men.

Older men at Fort Jameson sold vegetables (dried and fresh), cooked rice, bananas, cooked potatoes, dried fish, and similar commodities, but at Fort Rosebery they tended to specialize in snuff. They also participated equally with other age groups in the sale of fish. Older men dominated the secondary trades there, however; one was a shoe repairer, a second man was a blacksmith, and a third repaired cycles. In the urban markets this pattern was repeated, particularly where a wide rage of services were offered.

Distribution of female vendors according to commodity followed that of men at the larger markets. At Fort Rosebery—the prominent exception—there were only two women vendors (one sold maize gruel, another sold snuff; both were over 50). This disproportion of male to female vendors is easily understood once it is realized that Fort

Rosebery market's main commodities are fish, and that men not unnaturally choose to sell their own catch. At Mununga, near Lake
Mweru, where women take part in some fishing activities, they then
sell their catch on equal terms with men.

At the other markets women sold maize meal (which they themselves prepare), snuff, and malt. They also sold varieties of vegetables,
cooked rice and meat, and fat cakes. There were few significant differences with regard to commodities and the ages of female vendors at
Fort Jameson. Both the youngest and the oldest women sold maize
meal and vegetables. The oldest woman at Fort Jameson (50 years,
widowed) was the only one selling finger millet. She had walked 100
miles to sell her millet at 3d. for three pounds. At Abercorn the only
egg vendor in the entire sample was a woman. No women sold bananas or *misale* (a type of sugar cane), those commodities being reserved for men. This was also true of tobacco sales at Kasama. In
Mongu, women specialized in cooked rice or beans sold to workers
for breakfast or lunch, while men devoted themselves to fish vending
and the roasting and selling of groundnuts. An informal division of
commodities sold, by sex, seems to take place in most markets. It is
evident that men tend to specialize in those commodities which
promise a high profit per load or a more rapid turnover. Nyirenda's
study of Lusaka main market bears this out, for he found males dealing only in sales of snuff and bread, and females only selling porridge
and cooked rice and green relishes (Nyirenda 1957 : 43).

It is hardly surprising in a country with only limited educational
facilities for Africans that an examination of the educational background of market vendors should reveal that almost all are either
without any formal schooling, or of little literacy (see Table 42).
From the inadequate statistics available, where only those collected
in Fort Jameson were in any way complete,[31] a tiny proportion of the
sample had been educated beyond standard Sub-B, or second grade.
A smaller proportion of the women were functionally literate; the
others were unable to write their names or to read them when
printed. In the urban areas, more men and women were literate or
had attended schools, but Nyirenda notes that only 30 per cent of his
sample had progressed beyond Standard I (grade three), and that
almost 40 per cent of his sample had had no formal education
whatsoever. (Nyirenda 1957 : 44)

It is rare for an educated Northern Rhodesian African to enter a
trade occupation, except where he is employed by a European. The

---

(31) Edward Mbewe was able to obtain information on educational backgrounds
whereas at other centers too many vendors evaded this question, making returns from
these markets unreliable.

educated tend, as in pre-independence India and Egypt, to take bureaucratic positions where their educational attainments are visibly more important. Educated women are few in the society, and they likewise are rarely to be numbered among any entrepreneurial group. Thus, it is not surprising that the educational background of African vendors, particularly in the rural areas, should be so low.

TABLE 42

Educational Attainments of Market Vendors (Fort Jameson)

	Literate	Illiterate	Stds. I,	II,	III,	IV,	V,	VI
Males	14	10	1	1	0	1	0	1
Females	3	10	None					

TABLE 43

Marital Status of Market Vendors (Fort Jameson)

	Single	Married	Divorced	Widowed
Males	9	33	1	0
Females	3	21	1	2

Vendors were regular in attendance at the venues of their choice. The average length of continuous selling by all vendors was one year and four months in the Fort Jameson market (see Table 44). Men had an average duration of two years and 20 days; women, seven months. The conclusion that women tend only to sell for a short period, or for part of the year when extra money is required, is also borne out by an examination of returns from the other rural markets.[32] At Fort Jameson more than one-half of the female vendors sold for less

TABLE 44

Duration of Market Vending Experience (Fort Jameson)

	Less than 1 wk.	Less than 1 mo.	6 mos.	12 mos.	2 yrs.	5 yrs.	10 yrs.	More than 10 yrs.
Males	16	2	7	2	2	7	3	2
Females	16	2	2	2	3	3	–	–

than one week, and nine of the sample sold for only one day and failed to return to the market on subsequent occasions. The woman with the longest continuous vending experience had been selling for only two years. Two of the three women with the longest experience sold malt, the third sold maize meal.

In contrast, more than one-half of the men sold the same commodi-

(32) The full statistical evidence for other markets was not as complete on this point as were the returns from Fort Jameson.

ties in the same market for two months or more. The man with the longest service had been selling for 17 years at the same market. He was literate, sold unmilled grain, and was only 40 years old. A man with continuous experience as a vendor dealt in dried fish and rice, was 49 years old, and had been educated to Standard I. Both of the men who had been vendors for seven years sold bananas. One was 42, while the other claimed to be only 17 years old. The latter had started Standard VI (grade eight); the former was uneducated. Some of the other men with long years as vendors had worked previously as small traders or vendors in other markets. At Serenje a marketer had sold by the side of the Great North Road for more than 16 years before a realignment put him out of business. He then came to Serenje's small market to sell vegetables, bananas, and guavas. Earlier he had worked on the gold reef in South Africa and had accepted casual employment.

The most regular vendors at Abercorn, Fort Rosebery, and on the Copperbelt are those who catch, transport, and sell fish, either dried or fresh. These traders are almost always men, and they spend perhaps one of every four weeks on the Copperbelt, or perhaps two of four weeks at Fort Rosebery or Abercorn, where the source of supply is not as far away.[33] During the other weeks the vendors seek their catch and transport it to market. In 1959 the government attempted to rationalize the marketing of fresh fish from Lake Mweru on the Copperbelt, but its scheme failed after opposition from middlemen who feared competition from a government-sponsored coöperative.[34] The government also has been seeking to improve commercial fishing on Lakes Mweru and Tanganyika by introducing new methods from overseas.[35]

Vendors characteristically travelled considerable distances if it was believed necessary to do so in order to sell their wares at a profit. Often other markets were bypassed by vendors in order to reach a particularly favored center. Table 45 contrasts two medium-sized markets at the same time of year. In Fort Rosebery, the smaller center, almost

(33) Information on the Kafue flats fishing industry is currently being obtained by Charles la Muniere.

(34) The Northern Province Development Commission desired to institute a central buying and selling arrangement for the Copperbelt trade. It was prepared to underwrite the scheme. An ice plant was built at Nchelenge on Lake Mweru, and a storage facility was contemplated on the Copperbelt. Two refrigerated lorries were available. The African traders felt, however, that the proposed coöperative was a threat to their existing methods of trade. They therefore opposed the scheme. The body of their objections is contained in "Record of a meeting between the Deputy Development Commissioner ... and the Committee of the Copperbelt African Fish Traders' Association held at Kitwe boma on 15 April 1959," mimeographed. Also, personal information, A. P. Bathurst-Brown, then Western Province Cooperative and Marketing Officer.

(35) All commercial fishing rights in Northern Rhodesia are reserved to Africans. *Vide* Thompson (Livingstone 1930) and MacLaren 1958.

all vendors were local men; two who came from some distance away resided at Fort Rosebery while they sold their fish. In Fort Jameson, a more general market with a wider range of goods for sale, the majority of the vendors came from more than ten miles away from the

TABLE 45

Distance from Market Occupation (Northern Rhodesian Vendors)

Miles	Fort Jameson	Lundazi	Fort Rosebery
Under 1	14	0	5
1–3	13	8	11
4–10	4	0	5
10–20	20	0	0
Over 20	21	1	2

market. More than one-quarter of the sample travelled 20 miles. One woman walked 100 miles to this market. Almost all had chosen the Fort Jameson market in preference to other possible markets because they believed higher profits would be obtained (transport costs were rarely considered) or simply because friends or kin resided there. Two men who could easily have marketed their fish in Fort Rosebery cycled the much longer distance from Lake Mweru to Abercorn instead. They did so because they expected better remuneration for their 180-pound bundles of dried fish in Abercorn, despite heavy depreciation on their cycles, and despite a four-day journey to Abercorn. Western considerations failed to alter their belief that such market behavior was "sensible" and thoroughly "rational." In such case, as in so many others, the individual market's reputation did more to influence a choice of venue than any rigid calculations of costs.

Motives for the sale of particular commodities, or for entering the market arena at all, were unexpectedly varied. Few agreed that they sold because vending was their only means of livelihood. One spinster sold vegetables in order to obtain money with which to buy bracelets and necklaces, and thus to "look beautiful." One man grew tomatoes and sold them for three weeks solely in order to raise funds to pay his son's school fees. One boy became a vendor because his mother's brother, a chief clerk at a nearby administrative center, supplied him with pumpkins and ordered him to sell until he had rid the uncle's farm of pumpkins. A woman sold *misale* ostensibly to purchase soap, but most of her time in the market was spent gossiping with three friends who accompanied her daily to market. A young boy was sent by his father to sell bananas in order to raise money with which to pay an elder brother's school fees. A 30-year-old man sold fish and claimed that he did so only because he could find no other employ-

ment. Two sold fish and snuff because they "did not like to work for
Europeans." A 52-year-old fish vendor sold because he was "too old"
to do "hard work." Others sold fish "for a change" or between periods
of employment by Europeans or on the copper mines. Women had
become vendors when they were widowed or divorced and had no
other ready means of support.

The case of the gossiping spinster is illustrative of behavior observed in all the markets studied. Buyers and sellers often spent long
hours discussing the events of the day or week instead of haggling
over the price and quality of commodities. Politics, tribal activities,
and world affairs are all discussed in regular course during a market
day. Those vendors who dealt in cooked meals or teas became focal
points for gossip and discussion, particularly during the winter
months. There seemed to be a stronger bond between people mutually drinking tea or eating cooked rice and meat than there was between people shopping for a good bunch of raw cassava or a handful
of caterpillars. In the rural areas without a local beer hall, the market
is the place of social intercourse and political activity. In larger towns
where beer halls open in the late afternoon, the market is the center
of ordinary communication until such time as beer begins to flow.
In all the markets the number of persons who are neither buying nor
selling is often greater than the number of those who are. This is
especially true in Lusaka and Fort Jameson, where the main markets
are centrally located and serve as a crossroads for the African community.

THE MARKET NETWORK

Rural markets are only linked together tenuously, making reputation
that much more an important consideration in the vendor's selection
of a market. There is no accurate information about prices and commodities in any given market, and indeed there are few visible ties
between the various markets.[36] Consequently there is little exchange
of commodities between markets. A vendor does not normally buy
maize in Lundazi, where it is less expensive, and transport and resell
it in Fort Jameson where it is dearer. There is some evidence that
this occurs in the urban areas, however.

Commodities are generally home-grown or produced, although
cooked meals may consist of material purchased from a shopkeeper
or a coöperative depot. In Mongu, rice meals are sold when rice itself

(36) Marvin Miracle has noted interesting links between rural Tonga markets and
Copperbelt centers, personal information.

is out of season, the vendors buying uncooked rice from European traders. The man who sold rubber stamps at Fort Jameson purchased his materials locally, and ultimately from Lusaka. The vendors of groundnuts at Abercorn and Livingstone purchased their supplies from the coöperatives. Others buy local tobacco or fish from producers and sell it themselves. Middlemen are not common. The majority of vendors who sold home-produced grains expected to grow enough both for their own subsistence needs and in order to make reasonable profits in the market place.

COOPERATIVES

Rural markets serve local and social and economic functions, but they are not linked in any significant way to the world economy. The development of retail producer-consumer markets, with which this essay has been concerned, proceeded alongside a corresponding development of producers' coöperative marketing societies and territorial marketing agencies. In Northern Rhodesia, therefore, government-directed coöperative channels have provided an alternative means of obtaining the cash crops of primary producers, and of organizing the efforts of scattered rural entrepôts. It has meant that markets, which began at about the same time as coöperatives, have been by-passed in areas where there is a well-run coöperative. Large buyers do not depend on a proliferation of local markets to supply them with basic commodities, and the rural markets therefore are restricted to serving parochial ends.

In an attempt to encourage and stimulate African production of cash crops, and thereby to contribute to the orderly economic development of the then neglected rural areas, government in 1948 established its first coöperative and marketing organization and its first local societies. At this time traders—or more accurately, shopkeepers—of whom the majority were of Asian descent, existed primarily as retail outlets. They were therefore unaffected by the growth of cooperatives.[37] At the same time the few existing rural markets lost their own direct ties to the world economy.

Coöperatives have developed unevenly in the various regions of Northern Rhodesia, although their essential organization has remained the same since 1948. They act as a funnel for produce from the individual producer to the territorial marketing board responsi-

(37) Most rural trading stores are owned as part of a chain. African traders are prevalent in the Southern Province, Europeans in the Northwest Province and Barotseland, and Asians in the majority of the rest of the country.

ble for a particular commodity, or as a channel to more parochial markets.[38] In regions where there is a substantial agricultural carrying capacity for a certain crop, a producers' society is formed. Each society has a given number of specified market places, each with a *capitao* or head-man. Individuals bring maize, groundnuts, or beans to the market place, which is usually little more than a clearing with a scale, some sacks for produce, and possibly a shelter. The individual is paid a fixed price per bag or per pound, determined centrally at the start of each season by the provincial coöperative teams or the territorial marketing boards. Periodically the collected produce is transported to the headquarters of the local marketing union, the central organization for a number of small local producers' societies. There, bookkeeping and other services are performed, the produce is stored, and later shipped to the central marketing board depot or disposed of locally. Such is the rural African's only important relationship with the world economy, particularly so since Northern Rhodesia is agriculturally underdeveloped, with little immediate likelihood of an economic resurgence based on the land. The main cash crop is groundnuts, with yellow maize (African-grown maize is differentially discriminated against in relation to that grown by Europeans) and a few specialities also important.[39] Beans and sorghum, and formerly cassava, are bought by the cooperatives and returned to the local economy by sales to traders or individual market vendors in the different regions.

CONCLUSIONS

The markets of rural Northern Rhodesia are recent in origin, many having been established only within the last five or ten years. There is no evidence of pre-European markets. They serve as centers for the retail exchange of goods or services, but a connection with the world economy is tenuous because of the parallel development of state-run producers' coöperatives. All bulk trade in foodstuffs is carried on through the latter channels; consequently rural markets play important, but essentially local, roles in a regional economy.

Within the rural markets, both men and women are vendors, although men more generally consider their roles as regular and full-

(38) The quarterly and yearly reports of the various provincial coöperatives and marketing officers give a realistic picture of the coöperative program in practice. The ideal form is discussed in Boyd Wilson 1952.

(39) In 1958 shelled groundnuts worth £72,185 (4,006 short tons) were marketed cooperatively. The respective figures for maize were £953,126 (47,757 short tons) and for sun dried tobacco £1,739 (18,042 short tons).

time ones. There is a rough division of items offered for sale by sex of the vendor; women deal characteristically in staple grains and men in relishes and fish. Such a division of labor follows the expected pattern in Rhodesian society. Most vendors had little formal education, were in the 23–40 year old age bracket, and obtained the products offered for sale by the fruit of their own labor. There were few links between the rural markets, and little African awareness, from one market to the other, of differences in the character of each market.

CHAPTER 24

Trade and Wealth among the Tonga

BY ELISABETH COLSON

People speaking dialects of language known as *ciTonga* occupy most of the Southern Province of Northern Rhodesia and extend over the Southern Rhodesian boundary into Sebungwe, Wanki, and Urungwe districts. They call themselves BaTonga, their country BuTonga, and their language ciTonga. These terms have been anglicized by omission of the prefixes, and I shall follow this practice here. The language belongs to the Central Bantu group and is related most closely to the languages of the Subiya, Totela, Ila, Sala, Soli and Lenje of Northern Rhodesia.

Altogether the Tonga probably number somewhere in the neighborhood of 250,000 at the present time. Numerically they are the strongest group in Northern Rhodesia, though their lack of a centralized political organization and the absence of powerful indigenous chiefs have minimized their importance and influence in the political life of the country. Today they are organized into three tribal divisions: the Plateau Tonga of Mazabuka and Choma districts, the Valley Tonga of Gwembe district, and the Toka-Leya of Kalomo and Livingstone districts. Each of the tribal divisions is administered independently of the others under its own Native Authority.

This account deals only with the Plateau and Valley Tonga since I have no first hand knowledge of the people of the Toka-Leya division. In 1946–47 and 1948–1950, I carried out field work among the Plateau Tonga, in 1956–57 among the Valley Tonga.[1] Since 1957, the Northern Rhodesian Government has resettled some 35,000 Valley Tonga due to the building of Kariba Dam and the formation of Lake Kariba which now covers much of their former territory. Here, however, I shall ignore the changes brought about by the formation of the lake and the resettlement of the people.

Since so much has already been written about the Plateau Tonga as cash crop maize farmers, I shall also very largely ignore this aspect of Tonga economy save insofar as it impinges upon ideas about exchange. This article is based on my own field work, and it seems

---

(1) Under the auspices of the Rhodes-Livingstone Institute. In the study of the Valley Tonga, I was associated with a colleague, Mr. Thayer Scudder.

pointless to provide footnote references to the various published
works now available on the Tonga.

Environment and Population.

   The Plateau Tonga occupy the high savannah country of the
Northern Rhodesian Plateau, living at an altitude of some 3000 to
4000 feet above sea level. On the northwest their territory extends
into the flood plain of the Kafue River, which provides magnificent
pasturage for cattle and herds of game. Here the Tonga adjoin the Ila,
whom they emulate and with whom they share the deep attachement
they have for their cattle. To the east lies bush savannah, where the
soils are good by the standards of Africa and where agriculture rather
than cattle raising predominates as a valued way of life. Rainfall
averages some 30 inches per year, concentrated in a single rainy
season which lasts from mid-November to the end of March. Arable
soils and surface water are sufficiently well distributed so that the
population is relatively evenly distributed across the country. Today
average density is in the neighborhood of 60 to the square mile. In
the nineteenth century it was much less, but at that time many people
had found refuge in the hills to escape the raiding parties of Ndebele
and Lozi who periodically swept the area. Communication between
neighborhoods is easy, and few neighborhoods have any natural
boundaries.

   On the east, the Plateau breaks into a zone of very rugged hills,
locally known as the Escarpment, carved by tributary rivers running
down to the Zambezi River where it flows through a narrow fringing
plain some 1300 feet above sea level. In the hills, although the average
annual rainfall is higher than either on the Plateau or in the Zambezi
Plain, there is a shortage of arable soils. Spurs of hills usually cut off
one small tributary valley from the next. Travel is difficult, and much
of the country is uninhabited. Average density is probably no greater
than two to the square mile. Small isolated neighborhoods center
around the alluvial soils of the tributary valleys.

   In contrast to this is the densely populated Zambezi Plain, where
the density in places rises to around 300 to the square mile. Populous
neighborhoods center around deposits of alluvial soils formed along
the banks of the Zambezi or in the deltas where the tributaries join
the great river. Although rainfall averages only 25 inches in the
Zambezi Plain, it is sufficient to support agriculture. In addition,
many fields adjoining the river can be cultivated twice a year: during
the rains and again in the cold season after the annual inundation of

the Zambezi River. When the waters begin to fall, the people plant on the river banks, gradually extending their cultivation down the slopes as the waters continue to subside. The Tonga of the Zambezi Plain can therefore expect two harvests each year.

The Tonga practice mixed farming. Crops are annual ones. Sorghums and bulrush millet were the staple crops in the nineteenth and twentieth centuries although maize was already of considerable importance, especially in the Zambezi Plain. Today maize has become the staple, and almost the only grain crop upon the Plateau; elsewhere the other grains continue to be of at least equal importance. Subsidiary food crops consist of groundnuts, groundpeas, sweet potatoes, sesame, and various cucurbits grown for their leaves as well as for their fruit. Fruit trees have been planted in this century in imitation of the European settler: mango and papaya trees are found in many homesteads and in the little valleys of the hills the riversides may be planted in bananas. A few cultivators have also begun to grow European vegetables, and the advanced farmers of the Plateau grow beans and sunnhemp as part of their crop rotation. Tobacco is the only important non-food crop. Small amounts are grown everywhere, but the chief tobacco growing region is on the Zambezi Plain. The tobacco is of a native type which is not sold on the regular European market.

Distribution of livestock is less general. In the nineteenth century, most of the cattle herds of the Plateau were lost to raiding parties or in the rinderpest epidemic at the end of the century. During the present century, the herds have increased rapidly throughout the Plateau, but the largest herds are still to be found among the western Tonga near the Kafue River. Here the people have few other animals except hunting dogs and the inevitable chicken. Other Plateau people keep goats as well as cattle, and since the 1920's they have begun to raise pigs to sell to European buyers. The Tonga of the hills and the Zambezi Plain have large flocks of sheep and goats. Wherever tsetse fly is absent, they also have small herds of cattle. In most of Gwembe District these are recent introductions since until about 1950 much of the district was tsetse country.

Indigenous Organization.

Today the peoples of the Zambezi Plain and hills are joined together in one tribal division as the Valley Tonga; the Tonga of the Plateau form another. The divisions and their governing bodies have been created by the British Administration and date only from the 1930's. They do not represent cultural or linguistic distinctions recognized by the Tonga themselves, nor do they conform to any previous tribal units. The indigenous territorial organization was in terms of small independent neighborhoods.

A neighborhood might have no more than 200 inhabitants; the largest probably had no more than 1,000. Occasionally a man who had the ability to attract followers was able to dominate a neighborhood or a series of neighborhoods. People deferred to his wishes, followed his leadership, and looked to him to settle their disputes. But his status was a personal one created by himself. He did not occupy an institutionalized office which could be passed to a successor. He might be called *mwami,* the term today used for the official chiefs introduced by the British Administration, but in Tonga parlance it originally meant no more than "rich man" or "important man." There might be several such men within a neighborhood, or there might be none. Their power was ephemeral, but while it lasted such men, if they would, could give protection to strangers. With one another or with lesser men they formed alliances known as *bulongwe,* "bond friendship." Thus they expedited communication between independent neighborhoods and assisted in the exchange of goods and services. Their alliances, however, like their power, were personal, and created no stable continuing organization. They had no general right to tribute, though on occasion they were able to make good their claim to specified portions of certain game animals if killed within the areas where they exercized power.

Institutionalized leadership within the neighborhoods rested on a more secure basis. Each neighborhood has its own shrine, or sometimes a number of shrines, for community rituals. The shrine was under the guardianship of a hereditary priest whose authority was limited to the ritual sphere. A few shrines became famous and from time to time supplicants from many miles around might visit them to appeal for rains and good harvest or for protection from epidemics or other disasters. The priests of such shrines might have a wide reputation, but this was not accompanied by any spread of secular authority. The people of the priest's own neighborhood brought him first fruits and had the obligation to provide animals for sacrifice at the shrine if so ordered. Refusal to comply or infringements upon the ritual were punished by fines, paid either to the shrine or used for a community feast of reconciliation. Distant visitors brought gifts to the shrine which were left to disintegrate about it. They also brought gifts to the priest. He in turn provided his visitors with small quantities of grain which they mixed with their own seed to give it potency and ensure a good crop. Famous shrines provided a kind of focus for movement about the countryside, but the organization which they provided was again minimal. They could not give safe conduct which would take their visitors through intervening neighborhoods; nor could they coördinate the arrival of missions from various quarters. Appeal to the shrine from those outside the neighborhood was voluntary and sporadic. No priest had the right to receive tribute: the material rewards which he received were minimal.

The shrines, therefore, important as they were in providing a permanent anchorage for neighborhood organization, did not become centers for any form of exchange system. No markets grew up around them, and indeed the idea of any regular market place was alien to the Tonga. Visitors to distant shrines might engage in trade with the people of the neighborhoods through which they passed, but usually they were in a hurry to complete their mission and to return to report to their own neighborhood leaders.

Community shrines and their priests provided an organization for ritual activities and for the regulation of the agricultural work of the neighborhood. Leadership in other spheres fell to other men. There were prophets who spoke under possession by spirits which had some control over natural phenomena. They could make innovations in ritual and occasionally command in other fields. There were diviners who sought to find the cause of misfortune or to predict the outcome of some meditated action. There were men recognized to have power, either magical or through the gift of some spirit, for success in warfare or hunting. Any of these men might exert leadership in the sphere for which he was noted, though in others he had no special role and in turn accepted the guidance of the appropriate experts. Finally there were the heads of homesteads, the elders of the community, who formed an informal council for the settlement of disputes and the discussion of neighborhood affairs.

Loyalty to a territorial group did not extend beyond the neighborhood. Though the Tonga recognized that they all spoke a common language and shared much the same culture, they saw this as no reason to outlaw war among themselves. A stranger, although he was recognized as a fellow Tonga, might be considered fair game, and the man who ventured into an area where he had no kinsmen or friends did so at his own risk. Usually a neighborhood tried to maintain the peace with others in its immediate vicinity with whose members its own residents came in frequent contact. Beyond this range, it might raid—for grain in a hunger year, for livestock when it seemed desirable, and for slaves. The last became more common after the middle years of the nineteenth century when the Tonga came into contact with foreign slave traders from Angola and Mozambique who set neighborhood against neighborhood and provided a market for the spoils.

That the Tonga could move as freely as they did was due to the importance which they gave to kinship ties which overrode neighborhood boundaries. A man was a member of small corporate matrilineage as well as a resident of a neighborhood. In many circumstances, lineage membership was considered more important than residence in determining allegiances. Lineage members had the right to inherit one another's property and the obligation to assist one another in times of dearth or other misfortune. It was the lineage which had primary responsibility to assist a man in collecting and paying debts and compensation for injury; in the event that a claim was not met, the lineage had the obligation to take vengeance. Equally, it was held jointly responsible for the act of any of its members.

Despite its corporate character and the occasional need for united action, members of a lineage did not share a common residence. Usually they were scattered throughout a vicinage of neighborhoods. They intermarried with the other residents, acquiring at the same time claims upon them and their lineage mates. These in turn had ties of kinship with those in more distant neighborhoods. If a man moved along the chain of kinship, he could travel safely for considerable distances provided he exercised caution in avoiding areas which had unsettled quarrels with his own neighborhood or lineage, or with those of his sponsors.

Those who wished a further safeguard could initiate a "bond friendship" with prominent men along the route or at the place of destination. The man who accepted such a pact agreed to guarantee his friend's person and property while he remained within the neighborhood. An attack upon either was considered an attack upon the host who could then summon kinsmen and supporters to retaliate against the offender. The "bond friendship" was initiated and maintained by an exchange of gifts, and was a favorite channel for trading activities. At the same time it was more than a commercial arrangement. Transactions were phrased in terms of gifts. When a "bond friend" gave, he did not expect an immediate return. That would be the height of discourtesy, indicating that the recipient viewed the transaction as one of direct trade and had no desire to maintain a permanent relationship. At some later date the recipient should either visit his friend carrying valuables to him, or he should summon him to receive his gift. Months and sometimes years might elapse between gift and counter-gift. Each partner to the pact had to be satisfied that it was to his long-term benefit and therefore that he received roughly equivalent value for what he gave, but bargaining was outlawed by the very nature of the pact.

Where kinship or "bond friendship" linked men together in a permanent relationship, they were expected to subordinate their cupidity to the advantage of the many other facets of their long-term association. At the same time, it was the obligations of kinship, the institution of bridewealth, and the existence of "bond friendships," all of which were mediated through gifts and payments, which provided much of the incentive behind the circulation of goods and services. Otherwise, men were willing to exchange their possessions only if they themselves had an immediate need. The Tonga were not traders at heart. Their ideal was the self-sufficient family unit which relied upon outsiders only in an emergency or for the occasional item which it could not produce for itself.

The Ideal of Self-Sufficiency.

Subsistence was based on agriculture. Each family had its own fields, where it grew the grain and vegetables which formed the staple diet. This was supplemented by wild produce gathered in the bush by the wife and by game and fish provided by the husband. In some areas, livestock provided a substantial contribution to the diet in the form of milk and butter, but they were valued primarily because of their utility in meeting social obligations or because in an emergency they could be exchanged for food or other necessities. Stock owners frequently kept few of their animals by them. Instead they dispersed their herds by lending animals to kinsmen, "bond friends," and to others with whom they wished to form alliances. By so doing they minimized risk of loss from raids or epizootics, while at the same time they retained their right to recall their animals when the need arose. When an animal was killed, it was usually for a ceremonial occasion, and then the meat was distributed according to set patterns to those participants who had the right to receive.

Labor for assisting in the clearing of fields and in weeding and harvesting could be obtained through work parties drawn from the neighborhood. These were rewarded with beer or a meal, and participants could expect their hosts to give their labor in their turn. Work parties also assisted in the building of homesteads, though most of the work fell upon the occupants.

Local craftsmen produced most of the tools and utensils required by the Tonga, although they were dependent upon outside sources for iron. In the distant past, iron may have been smelted locally. In the nineteenth century, the Tonga depended upon traders from western Northern Rhodesia who imported hoes in return for slaves, cattle, ivory, or skins. Local craftsmen reworked scraps of old iron into spears, axes, adzes, and other metal articles. They carved the drums, the wooden mortars and pestles, and the stools. Along the Zambezi and Kafue, they made dugout canoes as well. Men were craftsmen in iron and wood. Women produced pots and baskets. Both men and women made woven mats.

Craftsmen were specialists, but their primary occupation was still farming. They did not expect to exchange their manufactures to meet their subsistence requirements nor did they necessarily produce for a market. Not everyone was expected to learn a craft; indeed, it was believed that a craftsman could be successful only if he had been chosen by the shade *(muzimu)* of some ancestor who in life had worked in the craft. The shade endowed its chosen successors with the skill and at the same time required them to use it. The recalcitrant could expect to suffer from the anger of the shade, who was assumed to have the power to send illness and other evils to its descendants. Craftsmen were therefore under an obligation to work in their crafts even though they had no immediate customers in view. They gave their products to friends and kinsmen knowing that they would eventually receive a return in some form or another. Customers who found them with stock on hand could usually effect a trade. They could also commission an article unless the craftsman was prohibited by some taboo from promising a product in advance. It might be months before the order was filled, since the craftsman worked at his leisure and when the spirit moved him. Only the blacksmith was likely to prove more amenable to his customers' urgency, for here men took old pieces of iron to the smith and stood about the forge, helping in the rough work, while the smith fashioned the pieces into the articles required. In return for his work, he retained unused scraps of the metal which provided him with material for his own purposes. This was his only payment when he filled an order. Craftsmen rarely sought a customer and then only when they felt the pinch of hunger. At such times they produced as much as they could and peddled their wares about the countryside in return for food.

Other specialists, such as diviners and herbalists, worked only for a fee—the amount depending upon the seriousness of the case. Medicinal plants and other substances, and red ochre for ornamentation were desired articles, as was tobacco. Salt, game, fish, wild fruit and vegetables, honey, garden vegetables, and grain were all in demand upon occasion and could be exchanged for other goods. In hunger-years people would sacrifice all other possessions to obtain grain which was the staff of life.

Natural features also ensured some degree of specialization between neighborhoods. Some areas had an abundance of fish and game, while others had little or none. Tobacco was produced most abundantly on the alluvial soils of the Zambezi Plain. Groundnuts did poorly on the Plain but flourished in the hills and on the Plateau. Certain species of wild fruit and wild roots had a limited area of distribution, as did some of the medicinal plants. Salt deposits and outcrops of red ochre were found only in a few places. Villages close to sources of good potting clay produced pottery for areas less well endowed. The wooded areas of the Plateau provided wooden utensils for those who lived on the treeless portions of the Kafue flats.

The ideal of self-sufficiency was therefore only an ideal, but it was a potent one in determining the way in which the Tonga viewed trade and the way that they conducted it.

THE IMPACT OF THE EUROPEANS

The coming of the Europeans altered Tonga life, although the people of the Plateau were drawn into the main currents of change more rapidly than were their compatriots who lay behind the barrier of rugged hills. Explorers reached the region in the 1850's. They found the Tonga already in touch with Bisa traders in the northwest and with Mambari traders in the southwest. Through them they received cloth and other goods brought from the coast, but the traders had arrived so recently that ivory was still commonly used for posts at the local shrines. The explorers also found the Tonga in a state of turmoil which ended only with the 1890's, for the Tonga's lack of centralized organization left them fair game to Lozi and Ndebele war parties.

At the end of the nineteenth century the Tonga came under British Administration. This had an immediate impact throughout the region, for the Administration now guaranteed the peace and provided protection to the traveler. It also sought to develop a new form of political organization in the form of a hierarchy of chiefs given power to hold courts and to rule their people. In the late 1930's, the Native Authority system developed to provide an organ for local government. Such changes affected all the Tonga alike, wherever they lived, as did the imposition of a head tax payable annually by every able-bodied man.

Other changes centered on the Plateau. When the Rhodesian railway was built in 1906 it cut through the country of the Plateau Tonga. This, combined with the fertile soils and the absence of tsetse fly and relatively temperate climate, attracted European settlement. Blocks of land on either side of the railway were taken for European farms. The Tonga were moved into reserves. Even in the most remote portion of the reserves, none lived more than 30 to 40 miles from the railway and the small trading hamlets which began to grow up along it and the highway which came to parallel it. Missionaries were early attracted to the Plateau. By the 1920's some seven different denominations had mission stations in the region and schools began to proliferate. In the 1930's, the Plateau was chosen as the site for the bases of the Agriculture and Veterinary Departments of the Northern Rhodesian Government. Technical assistance was immediately available to the ambitious Tonga farmer, who could also seek the advice of European farmers or of the missionaries.

In the early days, the Plateau people had little opportunity to earn the cash they needed for tax or for other purposes except by going out to work as labor migrants. With the development of the Rhodesian copper mines in the late 1920's and early 1930's and the creation of a demand for grain and other foodstuffs, the Plateau people took advantage of their good soils and their proximity to transport to develop into cash-crop farmers. They turned to ploughing, purchased wheeled transport in the form of carts and wagons, and under guidance from agricultural officers accepted a system of crop rotation. By 1950, some had invested in lorries and one or two in tractors whose services they rented to their neighbors.

Most of the people lagged behind their more progressive leaders. Probably no more than one per cent of the cultivators can be considered large farmers, but these expect to sell over 100 bags of maize per year and a few in 1950 had gross cash incomes of over £1000 from the sale of produce. Most of this comes from the sale of maize, but there is also a good trade in chickens and eggs and some sale of livestock as well as of other crops. Perhaps some 14 per cent to 20 per cent of the producers are in the class of small holders, who must be content with smal returns. The rest are termed subsistence cultivators, but they too expect to trade their produce in sufficient quantities to provide minimum essential cash purchases and payments.

The Government has encouraged them to expand their production and at the same time to maintain soils in good condition by sponsoring an improved farming scheme and paying bonuses to those who meet the standards set. It has trained and paid Agricultural demonstrators to work among the people and demonstrate new methods.

As a result of the influx of cash into the region, trading stores proliferated, and some Tonga now devote themselves primarily to shopkeeping. Specialists have appeared who work at house-building, carpentry, or other trades when they are free from farm work. Hawkers ply the countryside on bicycles. After the harvest when the crop is sold, people throng to the railway townships where the stocks of goods reflect an increasing sophistication of taste modeled on that of the European.

These developments end at the point where the Plateau breaks into the Escarpment. Beyond its barrier, the people of the hills and Zambezi Plain have continued to live a life of self-sufficiency. They need cash for tax and for a few luxuries and this they have obtained over the years through labor migration. In any one year 41 per cent of the able-bodied men are away at work, but until recent years they could bring few goods with them on their return. No roads entered the Valley until 1950–51. The populous Zambezi Plain was 60 miles or more from the nearest trading store, a three-day climb over rough footpaths, which defeated even the bicycle. All transport was upon the back or head. Cultivators grew tobacco for export, but they usually preferred to move it through "bond friendship" pacts with men of trading tribes from western Rhodesia who visited the region annually. In return they received blankets or other goods in gift from the traders in the following year.

No Europeans lived in the region. The few schools took children only through the first four years. It was the rare child who went on to boarding school. Few could read or write, and few wished to do so. Their interests were centered in their homeland.

With the first roads came trading stores, an increase in mission activity, the building of schools, and a general stir of activity. Immediate access to European goods gave the people a new desire for money. Export of their cash crop, tobacco, was simplified, and they began to find some sale for sheep and occasionally for groundnuts or other crops. Nevertheless, these changes occurred so recently that they had no time to alter fundamental patterns of life before the building of Kariba Dam brought even more drastic change in its wake.

THE DUAL ECONOMY

Despite the radical change in their circumstances, the Tonga of all regions, with the exception of the most advanced of the Plateau people, still cling to the ideal of the self-sufficient household unit which grows its own food and provides for most of its necessities. To this extent, they can still be considered primarily subsistence cultivators; though where conditions are favorable they also raise a deliberate surplus for sale. On the Plateau especially they count upon the surplus, but they are not willing to subordinate all other interests in order to obtain it. Neither has all exchange been drawn into the field of commerce, to be governed by the profit motive. Many of their products and some of those supplied by Europeans circulate among themselves in accordance with the old emphasis upon the importance of maintaining ties with kinsmen, neighbors, and "bond friends."

Men continue to lend their livestock rather than raise them for the market. When they exchange goods among themselves, even where no long-term association is at stake, they are likely to operate in terms of traditional Tonga ideas of wealth and the roles of buyer and seller.

Thus the Tonga of all regions are involved in a dual economy in which their exchange transactions are carried out through two different systems. The first, the internal system, encompasses those transactions where conditions of trade are defined by the Tonga. The second, the external system, covers exchanges ultimately regulated by reference to controls stemming from aliens. Hill and Zambezi Tonga are the more firmly bound to the first system which still dictates their basic attitudes toward production and exchange. The progressive farmers and shop-keepers of the Plateau are absorbed almost completely by the second system. Their compatriots, though involved perhaps equally in both, associate themselves in their thinking more closely with the internal system. Even the most progressive must deal with it and be governed by it on occasion.

Each system interacts upon the other. Goods may move from one system to the other, although some appear almost exclusively in one. Tonga craftsmen still ply their skills and their products are still desired by their fellows. Wooden bowls and certain types of pottery are almost the only local products which have been completely replaced by European manufactures. Craft products, goats and pigeons, game and dried fish, and various other local foodstuffs circulate only in the internal system. Eggs, cattle hides, sunnhemp seed are local products aimed solely at the external system. Grain, groundnuts, tobacco, cattle, sheep, and chickens as well as European goods and money belong to both. So does the pig, for Tonga trade breeding stock with one another, although they claim to produce them only for sale to European buyers.

The external system is dominated by money; it has its trading centers where most transactions take place. The internal system depends upon no centers to facilitate trade, and although money circulates within it many transactions are carried on through direct barter. Ideally it has no middlemen and depends upon direct personal dealings between buyer and seller, but on occasion middlemen who are working primarily in the external system also operate within the internal system. Because of the different ways in which goods are evaluated within the two systems, the man who can operate in both finds it profitable to do so.

The Tonga concept of "wealth" appears to be ruled by the internal system.

"Wealth" is a free translation of the term *lubono,* which in ordinary speech also has two secondary meanings. When a man uses the term, he may be referring specifically to bridewealth payments or to livestock, or to "wealth" in general. In the last sense, it includes cattle, sheep, goats, chickens and pigeons, and today probably pigs. Among western Tonga, where a good hunting dog may be exchanged for a cow, dogs are also classed as *lubono*. Tools, weapons, household equipment, clothing and ornaments also belong in this category. Today money is also regarded as a form of *lubono*. Fields, houses and granaries, stores of grain and other food stuffs are not considered to be *lubono*. Mr. M. Chona, a Plateau Tonga trained in law, is of the opinion that the word derives from the term *ku-kona*, to inherit, and that it applied only to such property as could be inherited. If so, the term has not been adapted to the widening scope of inheritance. In the Zambezi Plain, river gardens and stocks of grain have been subject to inheritance for generations, yet neither is considered *lubono*. On the Plateau, fields, grain, and homesteads have begun to be inherited in recent years, but no one calls them *lubono*. On the Plateau the sale of homesteads and the illegal sale of land have also made their appearance, and the greater proportion of all income is derived from the sale of maize. Men may call a farmer who cultivates many acres and sells many bags of maize a rich man, *muvubi*, but his "wealth" consists of his farm equipment, his livestock, his household furnishings, his clothing, and his money. Grain can become *lubono* only by being converted into some other category of goods.

I believe that the basic concept underlying the term is that of goods which can continue to circulate as identifiable objects. In the past, at least, grain and other food might be exchanged but they were obtained for immediate consumption by one of the partners to the exchange; they did not circulate further. Items of *lubono* could be exchanged again and again, and their utility was beyond that of immediate consumption.

Lubono therefore referred to goods which entered freely into exchange, and where the demand for them was in part created by their exchangeability. This is still true. Today grain is freely exchangeable among the Plateau Tonga, but this is because of the external market rather than because the Tonga themselves desire it as grain. They therefore do not classify it as *lubono*, although on occasion they use it almost as though it were currency.

Items of *lubono* were not of equal value, nor are they today. In the past, the Tonga had no way of stating prices. Certain categories of *lubono* were classed together, as having equivalent value, for exchange purposes. Thus slaves, hoes, livestock, and *impande* shell ornaments could be quoted in terms of one another, but not in terms of other items considered to be *lubono*. Over the years there might be a change in the terms affecting this class of items, but it had no obvious effect upon the terms at which other items were exchanged since they fluctuated independently. Today the common use of money within the internal system does make it possible to have a price structure, but the Tonga in many instances prefer to ignore it.

Frequently they treat money as though it were an equivalent of some other valuable, at least in certain circumstances. Throughout the 1940's, the Plateau Tonga maintained the ruling that damages in cases of adultery should consist of £4 or two cattle. By 1949, cattle were selling at from £7 to £8 per head. Men grumbled, and few were willing to pay in cattle. If necessary they sold a beast, and paid the £4. The successful claimant swore that he was being cheated. Nevertheless, there was widespread resistance to any attempt to alter the ratio in terms of current prices. When men buy at the trading store, they plan their expenditures in terms of prices, as "a pot that is the 10/-kind," "a blanket that is 25/-kind," "bread for 3d." Price changes disturb them, even when these are in their favor. A man who has planned to pay 25/- for a blanket, may not be pleased to find it on sale for 22/-. He wants a blanket equivalent to his 25/-, and a blanket selling at 22/- is only equivalent to 22/-. This, however, is not a sign that they are completely unconscious of differences in value and unaware of the advantage of seeking the lowest price for a particular ware. They know that they get more for their money in the shops in Bulawayo than they do at the trading stores on the railway line and that these in turn have lower prices than trading stores away from the line of rail. This they accept; fluctuation in price is another matter.

Money is also not yet accepted as standard of value through which other items can be equated. Men may be prepared to sell both a chicken and a watermelon for two shillings, but this does not mean that they consider a chicken equivalent to a watermelon or that they would ever trade on these terms. In the trading stores in the reserves, a four-gallon tin of maize may be worth 10/-, yet it may be exchanged for a child's dress which sells at 7/6, without the purchaser feeling that he has been cheated. In his view he is trading grain for the dress, and the money value of each may be irrelevant.

It is also possible for the money price to be set in terms of the object which a person hopes to buy with the proceeds of his sale. This is particularly true of the Zambezi and Hill people who have least acquaintance with a full-scale money economy. A woman on her way to the trading store to buy a blouse worth 5/- may try to sell her chicken en route for this sum. This may be exorbitant in terms of local exchanges, but she is not concerned with this. She does not want money as such; she wants her blouse. If she cannot obtain her 5/-, then there is no point in selling her chicken. If on the other hand her intended purchase will cost only 3/-, then she will sell her chicken for 3/-.

This last example highlights the fact that the Tonga in large part still see themselves engaged in trade because they want some particular item or items. In this sense they are target traders. It also governs the way they view the role of buyer and seller and the direction of trade.

To develop this point, I shall discuss the trade in grain, for this is probably the most important commodity at the present time.

In the past, the Tonga did not plan their production of grain to provide a surplus to be disposed of through sale to other Tonga, and it is doubtful if they would do so today. This would mean planning upon the misfortune of others since in general people do not expect to purchase grain except when misfortune strikes. The man with large fields and big harvest is still suspected of sorcery, the brunt of the ill-will of his neighbors, although on the Plateau this is minimized by the knowledge that he is growing grain for the external market rather than in an expectation of profiting from his fellow's misery. In times of shortage, the man with grain has a first obligation to share with kinsmen and friends who have a right to receive assistance from him. Nevertheless, the man fortunate enough to have grain when others are hungry has always been able to derive some profit from it.

He does not seek a buyer, for he does not envisage himself as the person who desires an exchange. In transactions between Tonga, it is left to the one who desires a commodity to take the initiative. He is the buyer and therefore the supplicant. The one who meets his need is the seller and is in a position to control the terms of the exchange. If there is a permanent association between the two, the seller is expected to be merciful. If there is none, he may extort what he can. Although the Plateau Tonga are thoroughly involved in maize production for a cash market, this rule still applies. When a man sells grain in a hunger-year or in an emergency to a kinsman, a "bond friend," or to someone of his village or neighborhood, he is likely to take much less than the price he would receive if he sold his grain through the Maize Board. But when he deals with strange Tonga from a distance, he demands the full market price.

Grain-rich areas in a hunger-year attract customers from grain poor areas. The producer does not need to sell, and it is not for him to undertake a rigorous journey and the problems of transporting grain. He might carry grain to a "bond friend" or kinsman, but that is a different matter.

Regular exchanges also take place between certain regions, but the flow of trade depends upon who undertakes the role of buyer. Cultivators of river gardens along the Zambezi, and to a minor degree along the Kafue, yearly grow green maize, cucurbits, and cucurbit leaves in their winter gardens at a time when residents in other areas have none. Some of the produce is given to kinsmen and friends; some is traded. The direction of the traffic depends upon the current needs in the different regions. If the river dwellers are short of grain, they carry their vegetables to neighborhoods where they can expect to find grain. If they have sufficient grain, they wait for inland dwellers to seek them out. They are then in a position to sell their vegetables, whereas before they were in the position of buying grain.

All trade in the internal system follows this same pattern. It has already been noted how the Tonga craftsman waits for customers to visit him and only attempts to peddle his wares if he feels some pressing need.

When the average Tonga, even of the Plateau, is involved in the external system, he tends to adhere to the pattern of the internal. He envisages himself as a buyer rather than as a seller. Because he wants particular goods, he is willing to buy money with grain or other produce, with which in turn he can buy the goods he wants. Then he is prepared to make the effort to market his surplus. If his wants are not pressing, he sees no reason to exert himself. If a buyer appears, he will sell, but it is not for him to seek out a purchaser.

The expanding range of goods now available in the trading stores is continually raising the standards of living desired by the people. More and more of their efforts are going towards finding means whereby they can continue to buy. But only the big farmers of the Plateau and the shop-keepers have learned to envisage themselves as sellers, who must dispose of their goods. They sell even though they have no immediate need to meet, and they use the proceeds to finance new businesses. A few have also put money in savings schemes. The majority of the Tonga like to have a little money on hand—"It can help you in time of trouble." For the most part, however, they prefer their "wealth" to be in other assets, in goods which can be used as well as exchanged.

CHAPTER 25

Bridewealth and other Forms of Exchange among the Herero

BY GORDON D. GIBSON

The Herero are of great interest for a comparative study of African economic systems because, like other Africans, they are beginning to sell their labor and their ritually important domestic animals in market-like transactions. Before European contact they transferred cattle at marriage, in the form of bridewealth. However, unlike most other African examples, bridewealth among the Herero has not undergone inflation. This matter is worthy of detailed attention, and this paper sets out to review the history and to comment upon the economic aspects of Herero exchange, including bridewealth payments.[1]

The Herero in South West Africa, like many other pastoral peoples of sub-Saharan Africa, must have been nearly self-sufficient in pre-European times. The available records indicate that, in contrast to many African peoples who lived in large settled communities and who developed specialized crafts, each Herero extended family itself produced nearly all of its material cultural inventory. However, contacts with other cultures in the century or so prior to European penetration apparently had generated certain needs that were not readily satisfied by the techniques known to the Herero, and in consequence some trade with outsiders had developed, chiefly in metals, tobacco, and glass beads.

Early accounts are in agreement that at the time of European contact the Herero cultivated no crops, with the possible exception of tobacco (Alexander 1838a : II 167). Calabashes, apparently in general use for the churning and storing of milk, must therefore have been obtained through trade. It is possible that dagga, also, was obtained in trade from cultivators, but the record is extremely scant with respect to trade in this narcotic; J. Hahn (1868 : 216) records the smoking of wild Cape dagga (*Leonotus leonurus* and *L. orata*) by the Herero, but does not mention the cultivated variety (Indian hemp).

The family-level self-sufficiency of the Herero fitted well with their

(1) The author is grateful to the Social Science Research Council of New York for support of his field work among the Herero in 1953, and to the National Science Foundation for support of his research in the literature in 1957–58.

pattern of pastoral mobility in a sparsely occupied territory, and fits well today with the widely scattered residential units and cattle posts of Herero in Ngamiland (Gibson 1956). Doubtless this self-sufficiency is also a factor in their well-known independent and self-reliant attitude. It is not to be assumed, however, that self-sufficiency on the family level prevented the Herero from banding together in larger groups; indeed, they did congregate under wealthy headmen, some of whose herds are said to have numbered over 10,000 cattle, with comparable numbers of small stock (J. Hahn 1869 : 237). But this banding together was for the economic, political, and military advantages which derived from pooled efforts, and not for the exchange of the products of specialized skills. In these larger aggregates, labor was traded for food and protection, and perhaps sometimes for cattle, but the labor and food and cattle were not produced by specialists.

The great differences of wealth in cattle among Herero families did not lead poor Herero to develop other skills; poor Herero only hired themselves out to their richer relatives, or retired to the areas where a living could be obtained from hunting and gathering. Markets, therefore, were entirely lacking among the Herero in pre-European times. Yet among these people who traded few if any material goods of their own production among themselves, the transfer at marriage of domestic animals from the family of a bridegroom to that of the bride was a standard practice. This paper will compare the record of trade among the Herero in early historic times in South West Africa with observations made during field study in recent times in Ngamiland; and particularly will attempt to determine the extent to which the exchange of cattle and women in Herero marriage may be considered a matter of sale and purchase.

HERERO TRADE IN HISTORIC TIMES

The Linguistic Evidence.

If it can be shown that the Herero had specific words for buying and selling, it may be assumed that the practice was known to them. Meyer, a secondary source, asserts that the Herero language lacked a proper word for "buy" and implies that the form *randa* later used by the Herero for this concept was adopted in post-contact times (Meyer 1905; 73). However, none of the extant bilingual dictionaries of Herero and German or English confirm this; all list the verb stem *randa* as meaning both "buy" and "sell," and none mentions that it is a newly adopted term (C. H. Hahn 1857 : 178; Kolbe 1883 : 73, 435; Brincker 1886 : 258; Irle 1917 : 198, 378). Cognate forms are listed in the dictionaries of several other southwestern Bantu languages;

thus *landa* means "sell" in Kwanyama Ambo (Tönjes 1910 : 76), and in Kwambi, Ganguela, Nyaneka, and Ndonga (Homberger 1925 : 72, 83). Meinhof relates these forms to a reconstructed Ur-Bantu form *landa*, "to follow" (Meinhof 1932 : 208). Homburger reconstructs *danda, dandisa*, "buy, sell" as the proto-forms for languages of the southwestern Bantu group (Homburger 1925 : 108). From this evidence there can be no doubt that Herero *randa* "buy, sell" is a cognate of the corresponding terms in other southwestern Bantu languages. If it was indeed lacking in Ociherero when Whites first arrived (after 1835) it must have been adopted before 1857 when Hahn's dictionary appeared, and probably it was adopted from a neighboring southwestern Bantu tongue rather than from a European language. Portuguese *vende* "he sells" is a possible original source, but the surmised shift of *v* to *l/r* and of *e* to *a* makes it only a remote possibility.

Two other terms, *pimba*, "exchange" and *pimbasana*, "barter" are also listed in dictionaries of the Herero language. The distinction between *pimba* and *randa* is not clear, however. Cognates of *pimba* have not been identified in the dictionaries of the other southwestern Bantu languages examined to date; Homburger does not list the form; Meinhof's reconstruction for "buy, barter" is *ula*. At any rate, it seems clear that in the early days of European contact, if not before, the Herero had adequate terms to describe the process of the exchange of goods, and that these were distinct from terms used for giving (*pa*, "give") and begging (*ningira*, "beg").

Giving and Begging.

Gift giving and begging for gifts are patterns that were well established for the Herero at the time of first white contact, and it seems likely that such transfer of goods as did occur took place more often by the process of giving than by that of buying and selling. Meyer has summarized the literature on giving, and concludes that Herero made gifts without expectation of return within the family, or to an *oupanga* (wife-lending) partner, to an age mate, to a lover, or to sick people to express sympathy (Meyer 1905 : 76). This list may be extended a bit: Alexander, who travelled in Hereroland in 1837, records that a Herero would give a calf to a Hottentot during times of peace with the understanding that peace would be preserved as long as the calf lived (Alexander 1838a : II 171). Irle records that food was shared with all persons present, presumably whether they were members of the family or not (Irle 1906 : 61 ff.). Irle, a missionary, and H. von François, a first lieutenant in the German colonial forces, disagree with respect to gifts outside the family circle. Irle declares that Herero often gave white settlers cows, goats, or sheep as presents, and often gave him presents without begging anything in return, though begging for a return gift was also a common and honorable practice (Irle 1906 : 61). Von François denies that the unilateral giving of domestic animals was conceivable to the Herero, and asserts instead that they were traded in exchange for goods (von François 1896 : 178). Von Zastrow, who compiled information from questionnaires circulated among European residents in the Herero area, concludes that in general things were given away only under the specific assumption of an equivalent reciprocal gift. Missionary Brincker, says von Zastrow, received a gift of 5 wethers as an indication of respect, but soon after was so annoyed by begging with reference to the gift that he had to make a counter gift far beyond the value of the animals received (von Zastrow 1930 : 261 f.).

Trade with Other African Peoples.

Trade differs from reciprocal gift exchange in the type of interpersonal relations involved, and is fostered by specialization in the production of desired commodities or in the rendering of desired services. Trade for the products or the services of specialists in preEuropean times was not unknown to the Herero, though it appears to have been relatively uncommon and not very important in the distribution of wealth within the Herero nation. Doubtless the most extensive trade for commodities was carried on with outsiders who could provide metals in exchange for domestic animals. Early reports on the Herero indicate that they knew neither how to smelt nor how to forge iron. Baines, who travelled through Hereroland in 1861, records that the Herero "could not even make an assegai, but bought their weapons and the iron for their ornaments from the Ovampo" (Baines 1864 : 40). Vedder (1938 : 136) recounts a legend which indicates that the Herero lacked iron-pointed arrows in pre-European times, and only adopted them after being severely beaten in a battle with the Ambo who possessed such superior weapons.

Frances Galton, who travelled through Hereroland to Ovamboland in 1851, noted that the Herero were trading with the Ambo who came south for the purpose: "Two Ovampo caravans, each consisting of from twenty to thirty men on foot, came here (Okamabuti, located by Galton at 19° 31' S, 18° 30' E) with beads, shells, assegais, woodchoppers, and such like things, which they exchanged for cattle. They obtain the beads and some of the assegais from the half-caste Portuguese traders who frequent their northern frontier." Galton himself accompanied a trading party of Herero going to Amboland, driving cattle and carrying ornaments of ostrich eggshell to sell; he estimated the annual export of Herero cattle to the north at that time to amount to 800 head (Galton 1891 : 105, 121). Even earlier, Alexander noted that the Herero were trading with Portuguese north of an inlet on the coast, at about 17° S (probably Tiger Bay), exchanging cattle for iron, copper, knives, and calabashes (Alexander 1838a : II 170). Thus when contact with them was first established by English and Dutch from the south, some Herero had already established trading relations with the Portuguese in Angola on the north.

McKiernan, who travelled about in South West Africa from 1874 to 1879, reports that Ambo blacksmiths were, at that time, to be found all over Hereroland:

> They bring with them a small stock of iron and copper and travel about from village to village, making knives, arrow-heads, spear-heads, beads and rings, for which they receive sheep and goats which they again trade for cows where they can; and after a year or two they go back with a small herd, most of which they are required to give to their king. (McKiernan 1954 : 74)

Apparently in post-contact times the Bergdama acquired the art of forging iron, and served the Herero as smiths (Vedder 1938 : 28, 43); they are variously called servants or serfs, and were paid in food for their services (Gr. Br. 1918 : 108). Irle (1906 : 122 ff.) reports that the Herero bought iron wire at a high price and had it fashioned into spears, shears, knives, axes, armbands, and iron beads by the Bergdama.

Every Herero woman wore anklèts heavy with iron beads, iron beads fastened to her leather clothing, and a leather headdress ornamented with many iron beads, including a long wide tail of iron beads reaching halfway down her back. The trade in iron, therefore, must have been considerable. There is one report (Mattenklodt 1931 : 194) that the Herero passed iron arrow and spear points on to the Bushmen in exchange (very likely for ostrich eggshell beads), and thus acted as middlemen as well as ultimate consumers.

In addition to raw and finished metal, the Herero traded for other commodities which they did not produce themselves. Von François (1896 : 168) reports that calabashes were obtained from the Bergdama, who presumably cultivated them, and also that the tubular drilled stone tobacco pipes used by the Herero were obtained from the Bergdama.

Pottery also, according to von François (*ibid*), was acquired from the Ambo, but Irle (1906 : 124) asserts that pottery vessels were found in every Herero home, and does not indicate that they were not locally produced. J. Hahn (1869 : 247) includes in his inventory of the equipment of Herero huts clay cooking pots which he reports were often so large that the small doorway had to be partially torn away to permit their entry. It seems unlikely that pots of such size were imported.

Unfortunately there are very few records of the exchange equivalents in the trade between the Herero and other African peoples in this early historic period. Not only are we ignorant of how much iron might be received in exchange for an ox, we also do not know whether prices were standardized or subject to bargaining. With respect to tobacco, however, we do have some information on exchange values. Irle (1906 : 115) records that some Herero had tobacco cultivated for them by their servants (probably Bergdama), and that this they sold at a high price, a 5-pound roll bringing a fat sheep or a 2-year old ox in exchange.

It will be noted that the trading relations described above were largely confined to two peoples: the Ambo living to the north, with whom the Herero must have had contact over a considerable period of time, since their route of migration carried them past Ambo country, and the Bergdama, who were often attached to the Herero as serfs or servants. I have found no report of extensive trade with the Nama Hottentot in the south, who apparently had little to offer the Herero that they could not obtain elsewhere under more favorable conditions. The earliest trade with the Tswana in the east is dated at about 1895, when some Herero are said to have acquired horses, guns, and ammunition from them in exchange for cattle at camps along the Omuramba Omatako (Eggers 1900 : 185).

Trade for goods among the Herero themselves is almost unmentioned in the literature. It is not unlikely that certain Herero were part-time specialists in the carving of wooden milk pails, ladles, funnels, bowls, spoons, and beads. Among the Herero of Ngamiland today these utilitarian and ornamental objects, which are to be found in every household, are not made by all men, and must be obtained in exchange with those who are skilled in their manufacture. Almost every large homestead, with 30 to 50 inhabitants, includes among its members one or two such craftsmen who produce objects of this sort as needed. The method of distribution of carved wooden objects among the households, however, is unrecorded.

Markets were established under mission influence in Herero territory as early as the 1850's. Vedder (1938 : 232 ff.) mentions those at Otjikango and at Windhoek, and that Herero living close to these centers were encouraged by the missionaries to grow tobacco and calabashes for sale.

Herero were well acquainted with those types of exchange of services for goods, in which the laborer either received a gift payment or worked on a contract basis. Meyer (1905 : 85) records that medicine men were paid for their services with "gifts," thus suggesting that the fee was not fixed in advance. It was the common practice for a poor man to herd cattle for a rich chief or relative, being compensated with the milk of the herd and an occasional animal for his own. Galton on his journey between Schmelen's Hope and the Omatako Hills records that he:

> ... passed by a great many kraals, in few of which there were more than ten houses, generally only five or six—probably one hundred head of cattle and not more, belonged to each kraal. Of these, twenty or thirty were the chief's own property, taken care of by the people who occupied the huts, together with the other oxen which were their own. The perquisites for taking care of the chief's cattle consisted of the milk of the cows, and occasionally a calf or lamb. (Galton 1891 : 88)

And many Herero, after fleeing into Bechuanaland to escape from the German troops in the war of 1904, went to work themselves as herdsman for the Tawana (northwestern Tswana) cattle farmers (Streitwolf 1911 : 32).

In attemping to determine the relative importance of cattle to the Herero for food, ritual, trade, and other purposes, we are confronted with some apparently contradictory statements. J. Hahn lists the many uses of cattle, specifically mentioning that they were kept

> ... to defray the costs of alliance, of marriage, of purchase, etc., and of many religious ceremonies. Whoever owns no cattle counts as nought according to their tribal values... The herds are both capital and the chief means of nourishment and trade of the Herero. (Translated from J. Hahn 1869 : 245 ff.)

On the other hand, Irle (1906 : 61) states that, in contrast to the Nama whom he considered spendthrift, the Herero saves his animal herds for his sacrificial feasts. Doubtless the amount of use made of cattle in trade varied with place and time, but on the whole I am inclined to the view that trade was a minor use of cattle—that several times as many animals were sacrificed as were sold and transferred in marriage. As for "alliances," I take it Hahn refers to the temporary loan of cattle to others for herding in return for the use of the milk.

Trade with Europeans.

For the early days of European trade in Hereroland there are some records of the equivalents of exchange of European goods for Herero livestock. Doubtless the scarcity of the former accounts for the inordinately high prices received for them. In the 1830's we have the report of Alexander (1838a : II 170) that an axe was exchanged for an ox. In the 1850's Galton (1891 : 84), more to give examples of the nature of trade than as actual records of transactions, mentions that a "nine shilling gun" might be exchanged for five fine oxen, and that two sticks of tobacco would be exchanged for one sheep. In a publication some 40 years later, when European goods were presumably more common, von François mentions that an iron tar barrel would be exchanged for one to two sheep, and an ox wagon for from 50 to 60 oxen (von François 1896 : 168).

Trade with Europeans is also recorded for other commodities, but without mention of the equivalents of exchange. Alexander (1838b : 19) mentions that knives were traded for sheep, a cotton handkerchief for sheep, shawls for bullocks, and needles for milk, but fails to supply details with respect to the quantities involved. Farini, who visited Ngamiland before 1885, records that the Herero supplied ostrich feathers and skins as well as cattle in exchange for European goods (Farini 1886 : 147–8). Norton, reporting information secured from an old resident who entered South West Africa in 1872, says the Herero traded ostrich feathers and ivory for guns (Norton 1919 : 457). McKiernan records that in 1879 his party traded iron wire, beads, and powder for sheep, goats and ostrich feathers (1954 : 182), and says in another place the Herero were eager to trade sheep and goats for ammunition (*ibid.*47). However, most Herero apparently were often ignorant of the relative value of goods offered for sale by Europeans, for Schwabe reports that the Herero were regularly swindled by European traders in the early days (Schwabe quoted by Farson 1941 : 49).

Herero Bridewealth in the 19th Century.

There are two remarkable features of Herero bridewealth, namely that it is ideally a standard amount, and that it is a relatively small amount in relation to the size of the cattle herds held by many Herero. Gluckman has summarized the difference in marriage payment between patrilineal peoples and peoples with matrilineal or double descent in Africa:

> ... in patrilineal societies of the Zulu type the marriage payment permanently transfers the woman's procreative capacity to her husband's lineage. Therefore, relative to the society's wealth the payment tends to be large.

On the other hand,

> ... there are several African peoples who had large herds of cattle but did not use them for marriage payments, and they are all peoples with

mother-right or an unspecified or double descent system of succession. The Lozi fall into this category, as do the Ovambo and the Herero. (Gluckman 1950 : 200, 192)

Gluckman offers the explanation that since in matrilineal society the woman's procreative capacity is not transferred permanently to her husband's lineage, divorce is easy, and high marriage payments are therefore not the custom—in other words, a high marriage payment in a society where divorce is frequent would not be sensible. In view of the differences in marriage payment customs, Gluckman suggests that it may no longer be suitable to name the common institution of transferring goods by a single term (marriage payment, bridewealth, or bride-price), for the functions may be different in various societies (Gluckman 1950 : 200).

Not only is the marriage payment generally large in the purely patrilineal African societies where there is considerable wealth in cattle, but it is usually also subject to negotiation to permit adjustment to the wealth of the bridegroom's family, the social position of the bride, the history of relations between the families, etc. But among the Herero the bridewealth is small, and the amount of variation permitted is narrow. The available reports on Herero bridewealth in the nineteenth century are few and sparse in detail; some of the more explicit reports are given here: Chapman reported that the marriage price varies from two to ten head of cattle (Chapman 1868 : I 341). Brincker (1886 : 217) defined *otjitunja* as a "gift or purchase price," and added that it consists of a cow and several sheep. Viehe declared that the marriage payment was always the same, consisting of an ox, a young cow, a sheep, a sheep with a lamb, and a young ewe. This, he added, did not include the cost of the wedding, which was born by the bride's father. Since, however, "the same gifts are required of rich and poor, they should not be viewed as a purchase price" (translated from Viehe 1903 : 307). He also rejects the interpretation that the Herero marriage payments are made to compensate the father of the bride for his expense in rearing his daughter, for the payment is too small (Viehe 1883 : 400). Irle in 1906 speaks of a purchase payment ("Kaufpreis") which he defines as a kind of morning gift which the parents of the bridegroom bring to those of the bride to arrange the marriage. He stipulates that the gift consists of six head of stock, namely a heifer, an ox, a wether, two ewes, and an ox to be killed. Although this "engagement gift is always the same," Irle says that "rich people often ask several head in addition for their daughter ... At divorce the animals must be returned" (translated from Irle 1906 : 106).

The discrepancies between the above accounts of marriage payments may be due to local or temporal variations in tribal custom, or to the inclusion by some reporters of animals donated for the wedding feast, or to variations in family resources in spite of the statements that the payment is always the same. However, it would appear that the nineteenth-century observers with the longest experience among the Herero are in general agreement that the marriage payment is relatively small and is standard in amount. Irle's qualification concerning the daughter of a rich person probably refers to a dowry given to a daughter, and not to the marriage payment made to her parents.

Some clarification of the nature of the marriage payment may be derived from an examination of the rules governing divorce and widowhood. Viehe declares that the previous husband of a divorced woman is entitled to claim the usual wedding payment from her next husband when she remarries (Viehe 1883 : 400). But T. Hahn says that if a wife runs away from her husband without reason, he can reclaim the cattle from her father or guardian. Also, he says, a married Herero woman whose husband dies becomes the property of his brother (T. Hahn 1883 : 253 ff.). Viehe concurs, saying a deceased husband's heir inherits his wife as property (Viehe 1883 : 400). And finally, if a wife dies, her brother or parents give her sister to the same husband, but only if he had treated the deceased wife well enough (Dannert as reported in Meyer 1905 : 105).

It would appear, then, that among the Herero certain rights in women are acquired by the marriage payment, and that those rights may be transferred to another male through a kind of resale, or can be inherited. Evidently, the rights so acquired do not invariably remain in one woman, for another can be substituted. The nature of the rights acquired at marriage has been analyzed in another place (Gibson 1958). The economic aspects of the marriage transaction will be discussed at greater length after the introduction of data on bridewealth in modern Ngamiland.

HERERO TRADE IN MODERN NGAMILAND, BECHUANALAND PROTECTORATE

Herero in Ngamiland in 1953 raised cattle for sale as well as for food and ritual purposes. With the exception of the purchase of milk vessels (pails, ladles, and funnels), which still retain a ritual association, and some ornaments, from part-time specialists who carve these items out of wood, Herero did little trading among themselves. For most goods bought, Herero patronized stores established by European merchants in various villages, chiefly along the road between the

Tawana tribal administrative centers at Maun and at Shakawe near the northern border of the District. South African currency was the medium of exchange. The items purchased comprised finished clothing, yard goods, maize, sugar, tea, salt, tobacco, household utensils, soap, matches, paraffin, and sundries. Prices on most utilitarian commodities were controlled by law (a 33-1/3 per cent profit above the delivered cost was allowed on goods imported from outside the Protectorate). On luxury items, such as women's fringed shawls of silk or rayon in bright colors, controls were lacking, and prices were set much above cost. However, the shawls were a standard part of Herero women's costume, almost every Herero woman owning at least one. The European residents (numbering fewer than 200 in all Ngamiland) who traded at the same stores were generally granted a discount on the price established for Africans. Europeans were privileged to enter the stores from the rear and to conduct their business behind the counters, while African customers entered by the front door and had to remain in front of the counters.

Herero custom in trading with the storekeepers was to offer an animal for sale whenever in need of cash, but not to sell more than enough to provide for cash needs over the next few weeks. Herero needed cash not only to make purchases from the stores, but also to pay taxes (the proceeds being divided between the Tawana tribal treasury and the Protectorate government). A basic annual tax of £1.8.0 was assessed on every male aged 18 or over, unless still in school. In addition, an annual graded tax on cattle holdings as recorded in the tax register was due. The tax register had not been revised for several years in the case of some individuals and some were several years in arrears in their payments. The cattle tax amounted to 5s for each 10 head up to 80 head, £3 for holdings of over 80 head plus £1 for each 50 head over 100 up to 200, £7.10.0 for 201 to 300 head, and £10.0.0 for herds numbering over 300.

Statistics on cattle holdings are not available for the separate peoples in the Reserve. This is doubtless because the tribal groups in Ngamiland occupy no large areas exclusively, but live in relatively close proximity to groups of people of different cultural background; in addition to Herero there are Tawana, Yei, Kalakgadi, Mbukushu, Bushmen, and others. Since, however, the Herero are preeminently a cattle people, and all of the other peoples of the area depend more upon grain or upon hunting and gathering, it may be assumed that the Herero cattle holdings are above rather than below the average for the area. The estimated human population and the livestock holdings by direct count of the Sehitwa area (comprising the N. Lake, S. Lake, and Dautsa districts) in Ngamiland for 1952 were as shown in Table 46 (from unpublished official records). We may assume, therefore, an average of at least six head of cattle for every Herero in the area, plus smaller numbers of sheep and goats.

In order to raise cash, residents of the Sehitwa area in 1952 had applied for and been issued 2049 permits for the sale of cattle. According to law, cattle could be sold only by permit. On the average, each permit pertained to one and one-third head of cattle. If all permits issued during 1952 had resulted in sales (a few cattle offered to

T A B L E 46
Human and Animal Population of Sehitwa

Humans	Cattle	Sheep	Goats	Horses	Donkeys	Poultry	Dogs
5000	28,605	2,970	10,780	498	638	475	342

the traders were not acceptable to them), an estimated 2732 head or less than 10 per cent of the stock holdings would have been sold. Clearly, stock are not raised primarily for sale.

Of the 5000 inhabitants of the Sehitwa area, the Herero are estimated to number between 1000 and 1500. For this group in the month of January 1952, permits were issued for the sale of 137 head of cattle. (In January more permits were issued than in any other month of 1952, the January rate being 53 per cent above the average number of permits a month for the year as a whole). The 137 Herero cattle were described on the permit records as 17 oxen, 37 trek oxen, 74 tollies (young steers), 3 bulls, 2 cows, 1 calf, and 3 unspecified. Records of prices at which European traders in Sehitwa bought cattle in January 1952 were not available, but during January 1953 a European trader in Sehitwa paid the prices for cattle bought from Africans shown in Table 47.

T A B L E 47
Prices paid for Herero Cattle

	Range	Mean
Oxen and trek oxen	£ 5 to 20	£11.1s
Tollies (young steers)	4 to 7	6.10s
Bulls	11 to 12	11.10s

Taking into account the month-to-month variation in numbers of cattle offered for sale (cows could not be sold legally, except under unusual circumstances, before March 1953), the figures in Table 45 permit an estimate of annual per capita cash income for Herero in this area from about £9.14s to £14.4s. Although a few Herero grow maize, very few have a surplus to sell. Therefore, cattle sales may fairly be assumed to be the only substantial source of cash income for the Herero in the Sehitwa area.

The practice of hiring cattle herders, usually relatives, and paying them with the milk of the cows and an occasional animal, continues in Ngamiland among Herero. Younger brothers or more distant relatives often herded for elder relatives under such arrangements. In addition, a few Herero kept members of other nations (Bushman, Yei, etc.) as "servants," providing food, shelter, and some clothing in return for services rendered.

Few Herero worked for non-Herero in 1952. When they first arrived in Ngamiland—most coming in flight from German South West Africa in 1904—the Herero came without cattle or other means of support, and many hired themselves out at remote cattle posts to Tawana owners, having the use of the milk and being paid at the rate of one animal a year. Fifty years later most of these immigrants and their descendants had built up their own herds and had become independent. That many Herero in 1953 controlled herds of over

TABLE 48

Labor Recruits from Herero as Compared with Other Tribes

	Population	Number of Recruits	Recruits per 1000
Non-Herero	36,069	462	12.8
Herero	5,798	17	2.9
Total	41,867	479	11.4

100 head of cattle was variously ascribed by the Tawana and European residents to their better herding practices and to theft.

Ngamiland is an area in which the Witwatersrand Native Labor Association conducts an active recruiting program for mine workers. In 1953–54 the program was much more successful among members of some tribes than others, the Herero being one of the people in the area among whom it was least successful. Table 48 gives a summary of all WNLA recruits from the Tawana Reserve passing through Maun, Ngamiland, in the period Aug. 11, 1952, to Aug. 10, 1953, as recorded in the governmental District Office at Maun where copies of the labor contracts are kept on file. The rate of recruiting for Herero is less than a quarter of that among non-Herero in the area (including about 3700 Bushmen who also very rarely go to the mines); the observed difference between the recruiting rates of Herero and non-Herero has a high statistical significance, the probability that the difference is due to sampling error being less than .0001.

Herero questioned about work in the mines replied that it is chiefly poor Herero who have neither cattle nor close relatives with cattle who sign up for work in the mines. However, some who had returned from the mines indicated that they valued the experience and might sign up for another contract period.

Only a few Herero in Ngamiland had ventured beyond the range of trading outlined above. Two men, in different parts of the region, had become merchants in hides, buying the dried but otherwise untreated skins of slaughtered animals for transport to European markets outside the Protectorate. In each area of Herero settlement one or two women brewed beer. The brewing of beer is not a traditional part of Herero culture (McKiernan 1954 : 85), and I was told that Herero chiefs may not drink beer today, because it would make them foolish. The manufacture of beer is said to have been acquired from the Hottentot. Herero beer *(ocikariha* from Nama *kari)* is sometimes made from the fruits of wild plants, but more often it is made from fermented peas and sugar, both of which are purchased from the local storekeepers. It is sold, by the women who brew it, at 6d for a large cup (about half an imperial pint). Relatively few Herero men patronized the beer huts in 1953.

From the foregoing survey of trade among the Herero of Ngamiland in recent times, it is clear that the people are well acquainted with the use of money and are accustomed to trading. Some bargaining is practiced in the sale of cattle; most other items are exchanged at prices set by the traders within legal limits, but nevertheless subject to change from year to year. The price of maize fluctuates widely, dependent upon the season and the crop. It seems, therefore, that price is largely determined by supply and demand for the abovementioned commodities, though other factors such as government control and racial discrimination do intervene. Let us now turn to a consideration of the economic aspects of bridewealth in modern Ngamiland.

Bridewealth among the Herero of Ngamiland.

The basic principle of Herero bridewealth *(ocitunya)* in Ngamiland today is that upon marriage a bridegroom contracts to pay a standard amount for a previously unmarried woman, and a reduced amount for a woman who has been married before. The reduction is not applied because the bride is pregnant or because she has borne children, unless she has also been previously married. This rule, expressed as an ideal by those Herero questioned, is carried out with a high degree of consistency in practice, insofar as one may rely upon verbal reports of the amounts of bridewealth concerned. Certain substitutions are generally recognized, however, as well as the possibility of marrying "on credit," with transfer of all or part of the pledged amount to be made later, often, it develops, after a long period of time. Table 49 shows the amount of bridewealth pledged or actually paid in relation to the premarital status of the bride in a sample of 146 marriages contracted among Ngamiland Herero over a sixty-year period.

The traditional bridewealth for a previously unmarried woman is one ox, one heifer, and four sheep. This is identical with the marriage gift reported by Viehe (1903 : 307), and also with that reported in 1957 for the Herero living in the Okahandja Urban Area in South West Africa (Wagner 1957 : 73). Irle (1906 : 106 fn.) notes that the heifer is said to symbolize purity and the ewe fertility; the symbolism of the other animals is not reported. Ngamiland Herero explain that the ox is to be killed for the wedding feast, and the other animals go to the bride's father, to distribute as he wishes. Substitution of another heifer for the four sheep is common, particularly within the Mbanderu sub-group. While sheep are generally included only in the bridewealth of previously unmarried women, the substitution of a heifer for the sheep does not necessarily indicate that the woman has been married before, and it does not indicate that her value is otherwise impaired—for example, it does not indicate that she is married as a junior wife, or that she has previously borne children, or even that she is not virginal. The ox, however, is an essential part of the bridewealth, and should not be omitted in any transfer in which animals alone are involved. A cow, a trek ox, or a tolly is occasionally substituted for the heifer or the four sheep; bulls and goats are never part of the bridewealth.

When money is substituted, it first replaces the ox, and may be substituted for part or all of the remainder of the bridewealth. The amount of money substituted varies, perhaps with the current market price of cattle; usually £8 to £15 is substituted for the ox, which corresponds well to the range of prices paid for oxen by European traders in Ngamiland in 1953, though large steers occasionally sold for prices up to £20.

When the bridewealth pledged for a previously unmarried woman is below the standard amount, whether paid in animals, money, or both, an explanation is due; my field data permit some cases of this sort to be explained. In one instance, a man's mother's brother agreed to the marriage of his daughter to his sister's son with no transfer of bridewealth at all "because he loved his nephew," but this was by no means customary in mother's brother's daughter marriages in general. In another case, when the bridewealth consisted of one ox and a heifer but no sheep, it was explained that the ox was unusually large; in three other cases, when fewer than the traditional number of animals was given, the husbands volunteered the information that the payments were not yet complete, and indicated what payment still remained to be made. Cases of the latter sort have been entered in Table 49 under the total bridewealth rather than under the amounts

TABLE 49

Herero Bridewealth and Premarital Status of Bride

Bridewealth	Not Previously Married		Divorcee		Widow			Premarital Status Unknown	Total
	No Premarital Pregnancy	Premarital Pregnancy	No Children	Children	No Children	Children	Children Unknown		
OHS_4	17	3	2*					9	31
OH_2	16+2*	1	1	1				12	33
OHTr								2	2
OToC								1	1
OHS_3		1						1	2
O_2								1	1
O(large)								1	1
OH	5	2	1			1		6	15
O				4			1	1	6
HS				1					1
H				1					1
C				1	1			1	3
$L_{8/9}HS_4$	1							1	2
$L_{23}H$		1							1
$L_{15}H$								1	1
L_{18}	1							1	2
L_{15}		1						1	2
L_{12}	1+1*							1	3
L_{10}		1	1					1	3
L_8				1					1
On credit	1	2	2					5	10
Zero	4		3		2	9	3	3	24
Total	49a	12	5	14	3a	10a	4	49	146

Bridewealth symbols: O = ox, H = heifer, S = sheep, Tr = trek ox, C = cow, To = tolly (young steer), L = pounds sterling; subscript numbers indicate number of units. Starred figures are "on credit" marriages at indicated pledged amounts; amounts pledged for other "on credit" marriages are unknown.

a) Of the 49 marriages of women not previously married and without premarital pregnancies, 3 were sororal, no bridewealth being transferred. Of the 3 marriages of widows with no children, two were leviratic, a cow being given as bridewealth for one and no bridewealth for the other. Of the 1 marriages of widows with children, 5 were leviratic and no bridewealth was transferred.

paid to date. I suspect that in some of the other cases of under-payment, full payment was originally intended, but the remainder has either been postponed indefinitely, or the debt has been forgiven.

In divorce in which the woman is judged at fault, Herero law permits the bridewealth to be reclaimed by the injured husband; but in all those cases of divorce which I collected, at least a partial payment had been made and was not returned. Therefore, the question whether reduced bridewealth is related to the termination of marriage must be studied further. Among seventeen women married for the first time for whom less than the full traditional bridewealth or its equivalent has been pledged, eleven were current marriages and six had been terminated by divorce or death. In all six terminated marriages a partial payment had been made. This difference, in this sample, has a .07 probability of being due to sampling error, assuming that on the average in the population as a whole the value of the bridewealth is not affected by termination of the marriage. The average duration of the terminated marriages in this sample, however, was greater than the average duration of the current marriages, and this most likely accounts for the fact that some payment had been made in more terminated than current marriages. We may safely conclude, then, that these data do not support the proposition that, in the case of women married for the first time, nonpayment or reduced payment of the bridewealth is generally to be explained by subsequent termination of the marriage.

The empirical evidence does not show that the number of children born to a woman, either within or outside marriage, bears any relationship to the amount of bridewealth pledged for her in a subsequent marriage.

As a rule, reduced bridewealth is pledged for women who have been previously married. Table 50, in which bridewealths have been assigned monetary equivalents, exhibits the data on bridewealth in relation to the premarital status of the bride. It will be observed that for widows, the bridewealth is usually omitted altogether, or reduced to a small token payment. Similarly, there is no additional bridewealth in true sororate (when a substitute bride is provided by the family of a woman who has died or who has proven sterile), for bridewealth was already pledged or transferred for the expected childbearing capacity.

As a rule, sheep are omitted from the bridewealth of a woman who was previously married. Table 51, which summarizes the data on the inclusion of sheep in the bridewealth in relation to the previous marriage of the bride, shows that sheep were pledged in only 3 out of 34 remarriages, as opposed to 22 out of 58 first marriages. The three exceptions to the rule, unfortunately, remain unexplained. In the leviratic remarriage of a widow, a sheep is killed by the bridegroom to symbolize the establishment of connubial rights, but this is not considered a part of the bridewealth. The reduced bridewealth pledged for a widow corresponds to her inferior status as a wife. It has been shown previously (Gibson 1958) that among the Herero of Ngamiland, widows never are remarried as first wives, and rarely become senior wives (except in the case of leviratic remarriage).

TABLE 50

Value of Bridewealth and Premarital Status of Bride (Herero)

Value of Bridewealth in £	Never Married and Never Pregnant (sororate)	Never Married but Previously Pregnant	Divorcee	Widow	Total
15	37	0	7	4	0	48
10–14	7	0	3	2	1	13
5–9	0	0	0	6	1	7
0–4	1	3	0	5	15	24
Total	45	3	10	17	17	92

(Marriages "on credit" in which the amount pledged is unknown and marriages for which the premarital status of the bride is unknown have been omitted.)

Divorced women, however, do occasionally remarry as first wives.
The value of the bridewealth pledged in the remarriage of divorced women is less consistent than in the marriage of women who have not been divorced, but it can be shown that the average value of bridewealth pledged for a divorcee is below that pledged for a previously

TABLE 51

Inclusion of Sheep in Bridewealth (Herero)

Premarital Status of Bride

Bridewealth	Previously Unmarried	Previously Married	Total
Includes sheep	22	3	25
No Sheep Included	36	31	67
Total	58	34	92

P = .0017 by direct computation.

(Marriages "on credit" in which the amount pledged is unknown and marriages for which the premarital status of the bride is unknown have been omitted.)

unmarried woman. In our sample, the mean value of bridewealth pledged for divorcees at remarriage is £8.97 and for previously unmarried women (excluding sororal marriages) it is £16.32, this difference being statistically significant at the .001 level. There appears to be a low negative correlation between the age of divorcees at remarriage and the value of the bridewealth pledged for them, but the number of cases collected is too small to give this correlation any statistical significance.

It appears to be true, also on empirical evidence, that a divorced woman who has borne a child to an earlier husband commands less bridewealth upon remarriage than a divorced woman who has borne no children, if she is still young—a woman in the latter category is remarried with a bridewealth of at least an ox or £10. In the remarriage of a woman past the age of childbearing, whether a widow or divorcee, no bridewealth is pledged. It appears, therefore, that the ox, or its monetary equivalent, constitutes compensation for the first legitimate child which a woman will bear, and this compensation is usually given in advance.

In the marriage of a previously unmarried woman who has become pregnant premaritally, or who has borne a child out of wedlock, the bridewealth pledged is generally equal to that pledged for a woman married for the first time, whether or not her husband is the genitor of her premarital child. In certain cases of premarital pregnancy, the parents of the girl agree to her marriage "on credit" in order to encourage the marriage; indeed, such marriages account for 26 per cent of all marriages contracted "on credit" in the sample.

TABLE 52

Equivalent Value of Bridewealth and Husband's Marital Order (Herero)

| Bridewealth | I | Husband's Marriage | | All |
		II	III+	
£15–19	44	17	17	78
£10–14	10	8	4	22
£ 5–9	1	3	3	7
£ 0–4	2	8	18	28
Total	57	36	42	135

For the 2 × 2 table shown by the dashed lines chi-square $= 15.24$. $P < .001$

("On credit" marriages in which the amount pledged is unknown have been omitted.)

Among marriages in the sample which were contracted "on credit" and were not yet wholly paid up, more were marriages of junior than of senior wives. It would appear also that a man gives more for his senior wife than for junior wives, on the average (Table 52). However, when the data of Table 52 are stratified according to the premarital status of the bride (Table 53), the relationship of the amount of bridewealth to the husband's marital order disappears, and it becomes clear that the average bridewealth pledged for later wives is less than that for first wives only because the later wives are more often women previously married.

TABLE 53

Bridewealth, Husband's Marital Order, and Premarital Status of Bride (Herero)

Bridewealth	Husband's Marriage			Total
	I	II	III+	
A. *Women Not Previously Married*				
£15–19	29	9	6	44
£10–14	6	3	1	10
£ 5–9	0	0	0	0
£ 0–4	1	0	0	1
	—	—	—	—
Total	36	12	7	55
Mean	£16.25	16.25	16.67	16.32
B. *Divorcees*				
£15–19	0	3	1	4
£10–14	0	0	2	2
£ 5–9	1	1	3	5
£ 0–4	1	1	3	5
	—	—	—	—
Total	2	5	9	16
Mean	£ 5.00	12.50	8.05	9.06
C. *Widows and Women Married Sororally*				
£15–19	0	0	0	0
£10–14	0	1	0	1
£ 5–9	0	1	0	1
£ 0–4	0	6	12	18
	—	—	—	—
Total	0	8	12	20
Mean	£	4.37	2.50	3.25

The data at hand have enough time depth to permit some investigation of trends of substitution in bridewealth, at least insofar as Herero residing in Ngamiland are concerned. Money, of course, was not used in pre-European times, but the data do not indicate that the substitution of money for animals has increased significantly since 1900. On the other hand, the substitution of other animals for sheep in the

TABLE 54

Animals and Money in Bridewealth (Herero)

	Before 1900	After 1900	Total
Animals only	5	92	97
Money all or in part	1	14	15
	—	—	—
Total	6	106	112
	P = .817		

full bridewealth does show a significant increase in this century, but the meaning of this trend remains obscure. The relevant data and the probabilities that the differences are due merely to sampling error (computed directly rather than by chi-square) are shown in Tables 54 and 55.

TABLE 55

Sheep and Other Animals in Full Bridewealth (Herero)

	Before 1900	After 1900	Total
Sheep included	5	31	36
Other animals substituted for sheep	0	36	36
Total	5	67	72
	P = .027		

CONCLUSION

To ask whether marriage payment is part of an economic exchange or a token of good faith and sincerity on the part of the husband and a pledge of security for the wife is a needless dilemma—clearly it is both. As Gray (1960 : 45) has pointed out, anthropologists in seeking the latent functions of marriage payments have tended to emphasize the symbolic, non-economic aspects of the marriage payment, but in so doing the material aspects should not be ignored. This is not to say that the two functions are equally important, however. Let us attempt to assess the relative importance of the marriage payment in the exchange and symbol systems of the Herero.

Among the Herero, with their relatively large herds of domestic animals, the transfer of two cattle and four sheep at marriage cannot be considered a very important factor in the distribution of wealth. Certainly the division among the heirs of a rich cattle farmer of herds numbering hundreds of animals constitutes a much more significant distribution. As to market transactions in recent times, I estimate that there is roughly an annual sale of about one head of cattle per person —man, woman and child—among Ngamiland Herero today. At this rate a 40-year old man would have sold about 40 head of cattle in his lifetime, whereas if he has married twice (about average) with full bridewealth in the same period, he would have yielded up for this purpose four head of cattle and eight sheep.

It cannot be held for the Herero that their chief object in acquiring cattle is to use them in obtaining wives. At the standard full rate of marriage payment, a man with 100 head of cattle could acquire and maintain at least five wives; yet Herero men, some of whom held herds of up to 1000 head of cattle, averaged only 1.44 wives each. No man

could count more than three wives for whom he had paid full bridewealth, and only one man in a random sample of 71 men aged 18 or
over had more than three current wives (Gibson 1958 : 14). Certainly
the use of Herero cattle for food, to increase political strength by
attracting relatives as subordinate herdsmen, and even for sacrificial
purposes, outshadow their use in the marriage payments.

As a token of sincerity, Herero bridewealth may be compared to
the gift of an engagement ring in modern Euro-American culture,
which, even though measurable in monetary terms, is not considered
primarily a purchase price. Herero bridewealth distinguishes a legal
marriage from a concubinal relationship, and establishes the patrilineal affiliation of children born to the woman in the *oruzo*, "patri-
clan," of their father. Without transfer of the bridewealth, the
children are ascribed to their mother's father's patrilineal group and
must abide by its prohibitions. To illustrate the strength of the
relationship so established, consider the case of a married woman who
had become separated from her husband in the war of 1904. She
escaped to Bechuanaland with some of her relatives, and there,
presuming herself a widow, entered into a second marriage in which
no bridewealth was transferred, and bore children by her new husband. After the death of the second husband, the woman's relatives
decided that her children really belonged to the first husband because
he had made the only marriage payment for her. Her children, therefore, had to learn and observe the proscriptions of their mother's first
husband's patrilineage, and to regard its members as their relatives.

From the foregoing it appears that among the Herero the marriage
payment for previously unmarried women fluctuates little, has an established maximum, is relatively low in proportion to the average
wealth of the Herero, and is certainly no measure of the economic
value of a woman in the cattle-raising economy. Custom has held the
marriage payment constant and has not permitted a significant shift
from animals to money for well over half a century during which
period the Herero have been adjusting otherwise to a market
economy.

In Herero society, polygyny is desired and practiced by most men.
This is possible because women tend to marry on the average eleven
years younger than men (Gibson 1958 : 18–19). The cattle which
Herero men hold do vary in number from family to family and from
time to time, and it is sometimes not possible for a man to supply the
animals or the equivalent cash required to marry a maid. In such a
situation the Herero man seeking a mate has three alternatives:
marriage on credit, marriage to a widow or divorcee with the marriage
payment reduced or eliminated, or concubinage with no marriage

payment. Only in times of great scarcity of cattle have marriages of previously unmarried maids without pledge of bridewealth been considered valid.

When we attempt to treat Herero bridewealth as an economic matter, we must assert emphatically that the laws of the market do not apply. In spite of the great desire for wives, Herero men apparently do not compete for them by raising the amount of bridewealth offered to their parents. The symbolic significance of the bridewealth animals even today outweighs their economic significance. Within the narrow range of bridewealth pledges permitted, we might imagine that the proportion of men willing to offer the standard full amount determines the proportion of women who will mate as wives rather than as concubines. This proposition, however, remains to be tested; even if the proposition could be demonstrated, bridewealth would certainly be secondary to other factors in determining whether a woman becomes wife or concubine.

We have seen that Herero trade has developed from an occasional event for the acquisition of metals, calabashes, and luxury items to a regular practice, fostered by the imposition of taxes and the prestige value of certain kinds of European food and clothing. Money transactions have become commonplace, and a few Herero even have hired out their labor for money, or have become small scale entrepreneurs. But throughout this period of economic development, Herero bridewealth payments, in Ngamiland at least, have remained low, relatively constant, and have not been increasingly translated into money, apparently because the ritual rather than the economic significance of the payment remains dominant.

CITIES AND INDUSTRIAL COMPLEXES

The Marketing of Staple Foods in Kampala, Uganda

BY A. B. MUKWAYA

Those familiar with both East and West Africa have often commented on how few Africans in the East engage successfully in commerce. In West Africa nearly everyone engages in trade, be they full-time traders, farmers, clerks or laborers. By contrast, East Africa seems largely devoid of what Adam Smith described as "man's natural propensity to truck, barter, traffic and exchange." Much of the commerce is left to Indians. It is, therefore, of some interest to find a trade, that of supplying Uganda's largest town with staple food for the African inhabitants, in which non-Africans play no part at all and which has developed as a purely African response to the growth of an urban market. It is this trade which the rest of this paper seeks to describe and analyze. First, the sources of supply of some of Kampala's staple foods will be described; next, the ways in which these foods are brought to the consumer.

The nature of the demand for food in Kampala distinguishes the town in two respects from others both in Africa and elsewhere. In the first place, many of those who work in Kampala are able to grow for themselves at least a part of the food they need, either in suburbs where they have small plots, or because they live on small holdings at some distance from the town. What proportion of the food requirements of the town are provided in this way has never been established. However, it may well be more than half, and probably constitutes as much as two-thirds of the fresh produce consumed within the area. The proportion varies with the size of the harvest. When the rains are good and there is an abundance of beans, fresh maize, and sweet potatoes, the price of plantains and sweet potatoes falls to an extent that cannot be accounted for by the increase in marketed quantities alone.

In the second place, the demand for food is highly diverse. The population of Kampala is cosmopolitan in the extreme, and the dietary habits of its inhabitants are almost as varied. Not only do the dietary habits of its African inhabitants vary with the part of East Africa from which the inhabitants have come, but there are Europeans and Asians who make for still greater diversity. The diversity can, however, be exaggerated. A rise in the standard of living of many

Africans and changes in their habits of life have, for instance, popularized the consumption of bread, hitherto a purely European food. Recent steep rises in the price of plantains have also caused a marked switch from this traditional staple to sweet potatoes and cassava, which were hitherto regarded as food only for the poorer immigrants.[1] Nevertheless, the demand for food remains complex, and we have decided for the sake of clarity to restrict the scope of this article to the supply of three basic foodstuffs which enter into the diet of the majority of Africans, who in themselves constitute the majority of the town's inhabitants. These basic foodstuffs are plantains, cassava, and sweet potatoes. They constitute, moreover, the principal foodstuffs sold in the markets. Their relative importance is shown in Table 56 which relates to Kampala's largest African market place.[2]

TABLE 56

Weekly Quantities of Foodstuffs in Katwe Market (Kampala)[a]

Week Ending	June 20th cwts.	June 27th cwts.	July 4th cwts.	July 11th cwts.	July 18th cwts.
Plantains	750	960	1070	890	550
Sweet potatoes	120	110	100	130	100
Cassava root	35	35	30	30	40
Cassava dry	20	15	25	25	15
Total	925	1120	1225	1075	705

[a] For five weeks in 1953.

Food has been sold in Kampala for many decades. Even before Kampala became the commercial capital of Uganda it was the seat of the Buganda Government and as such already attracted a population greater than the food production of the town area itself could support. The rapid growth of the town in recent years did not therefore create a new problem of food supply, but merely accentuated it.

The Production of Fresh Vegetables for the Kampala Market.
The growth of the supply of food for sale must be seen in the con-

(1) "The most striking change in the pattern of food expenditure from previous Kampala surveys was the substitution of maize meal for plantains as a main food item. Often in the past expenditure on plantains alone accounted for 25% of the total food expenditure. In the present survey plantains came fourth in order of importance." (Uganda Protectorate 1953.)

(2) Three other staple foods, maize, rice and bread are sold in shops, while meat and fish are sold in both shops and market places. An outline study of the entire food supply of Kampala was made by N. D. Oram in 1952. His report, which was made to the Department of Labor, has not been published.

text of the development of other cash crops. A report of the Department of Agriculture describes the system of agriculture in Uganda as follows:

To date agricultural development in Uganda has taken the form of superimposing on traditional methods a system of cash crop economy in varying degrees and the modification of the accepted system of land use to make this possible. (Uganda Protectorate 1947 : 1)

The same conclusion has been reached by a recent and careful study:

Nearly half the cultivated area is devoted to economic crops, including maize, which take about two-thirds of the labor and four-fifths of the male labor employed in agriculture. The original subsistence basis, however, has remained intact. No cultivator, however commercially-minded, would dream of dispensing with the plantain garden. (Wrigley 1953)

The Ganda peasant producer has expanded the range and amount of his production by supplementing the labor of his wives with his own and that of immigrants. He has also enlarged the area of production partly by taking up unused land within the areas already occupied, but mainly by expansion into hitherto unoccupied parts of the Kingdom. Around Kampala, land is now largely occupied, but in the counties of Buddu and Bugerere for instance, there are still areas where expansion is possible and, in fact, taking place. C. C. Wrigley (1953) states that of the men over 30 now living in one Buddu village, only one had been born there, and that only a few years ago there were more buffaloes than men. This transition is visibly continuing in other areas, especially in the county of Bugerere. Evidence is provided by the increase in population in the *gombololas* covering the fertile Sezibwa basin on the Bugerere side. The population was given by the 1948 census as 12,926. Since then, the figures collected by the chiefs show the following annual increases by immigration into the area:

TABLE 57

Immigration into Bugerere

1949	4,870
1950	4,938
1951	5,906
1952	9,626
1953	9,154

About two-thirds of the immigrants come from other areas of Buganda and only a third from neighboring tribes. It appears that more Ganda have settled in the area since 1949 than before (Fortt 1953 : 103).

The process of expansion has also taken the form of agricultural diversification. The earliest and most important addition to cash crops in most areas was cotton, which was introduced in Uganda a decade before the first World War. Cotton is well suited for an *extensive* type of agriculture. It yields a crop within eight months, and requires a great deal of labor for only a short period of the year; moreover, it is sold without being processed. The cotton plot is required for only part of the year, and can be cleared after the harvest to make room for a food crop. Another cash crop that has gained importance in recent years is coffee, which, however, requires a more permanent occupation of one area; the soil has to be carefully selected, and the trees, which yield fruit only after three years, require tending throughout, though coffee growing is lighter work than cotton growing.

The adoption of these and other cash crops was not left to the spontaneous play of demand and supply. Vigorous and persistent Government propaganda reinforced by the chiefs with their traditional methods of persuasion and coercion has accompanied their introduction and development. Such effort, coupled with scientific research on the selection of seeds, types of soil, planting dates and methods of cultivation, has made cotton and coffee production an essential part of the economy of the country.

While the Government actively promoted the growing of cotton and coffee, it showed little concern about the production of food for sale. Until quite recently, the Department of Agriculture was content to report annually that the food situation was good or not so good, by which was meant that there was no famine or that there was. The policy began to change during the second World War, especially when it was considered necessary for Uganda in particular, and East Africa generally, to be self-supporting in food requirements. The Annual Report of the Department of Agriculture for 1950 apologetically explains the changed policy as follows:

While the general policy of the Department continued to be directed towards obtaining an improvement in the traditional farming systems and also, where possible, towards introducing more modern methods, the first and fundamental aim was again to ensure the production of an adequate supply of food both for rural and urban populations. It is necessary to place particular emphasis on this part of the work of the Department since it is impossible for an undernourished or underfed peasant community to work with that vigor which is necessary if a general advance in their farming economy, and an overall and gradual improvement in standards of living, are to be achieved. (Uganda Protectorate 1950 : 2)

An added need for change was the policy of industrialization launched in 1946. Supplies of food were required not only because the population was growing, but also because a growing proportion of the population ceased to produce its own food.

The necessary knowledge for the pursuit of a vigorous food-growing campaign is perhaps lacking, for hitherto the policy has not been backed by as much propaganda or coercion as that of the growing of cotton. Even the comprehensive Buganda Agricultural Law of 1946 did not provide rules for the growing of food crops. In contrast to cotton and coffee, therefore, the production of food for the Kampala market has grown with the stimulus of the market itself in combination with improved and improving transport facilities. What is available for market sale depends on two factors: first, the existence of a surplus above consumption requirements of food products primarily produced for home consumption—such a surplus is sometimes fortuitously created by favorable changes in the weather, but may be deliberately created by the producers—growing more than their household requirements—or alternatively, the producer *may* abstain, especially when the prices are good, from consuming such products as plantains or sweet potatoes, and content himself with lower quality foods such as cassava; the other possibility is so to rearrange production that food crops become a main or subsidiary cash crop.

The last ten years have seen a rapid expansion of plantain production in North Kyagwe and Bugerere as the main cash crop. Though in some areas it is being supplanted by coffee, many a big or small grower will still proudly show you his plantain garden as the source of his wealth or his regular income. Nearer to Kampala, within a radius of 10 to 15 miles, sweet potatoes are grown specially for the market. Until ten years ago, Kampala was mainly dependent on supplies produced in the area itself and within a few miles radius. The first marketing from a distance was organized by contractors who supplied big institutions such as hospitals and prisons. For example, in 1945, when the Bugerere Growers Association was formed, it depended almost entirely on these institutions to buy all its supplies.

Plantains require a heavy fertile soil naturally covered by forest or dense elephant grass. To start production on a large scale a farmer has to employ laborers. He can do so only if he already has money from another source. If he has not, the only course open to him is to build up his plantation gradually over the years. In the first year, and sometimes in the second, the trees are interplanted with annual cash crops such as cotton, beans, or groundnuts which may help to pay for part of the other costs of the establishment, or more likely for the cost of incessant weeding required in the first two years.

Beginning with the second year, the dead matter from the trees is available for mulching, thereby providing patches or portions that do not require so much weeding. The unit cost of producing plantains for the market is greater than that of producing for the household alone because the normal household refuse is inadequate to cover the larger area and also because the peels are now taken away with the produce instead of being used for mulching.

The actual cost of maintenance is difficult to assess without more intensive studies. Farmers questioned in Bugerere thought that a man and his wife could keep three to four acres in good condition if they did not grow any other cash crops. But very few growers concentrate on plantains alone, and paid labor—both regular and occasional—is readily available.

The trees begin to bear fruit in the second year, though the heavy crop begins only in the third year. Part of the produce is commonly used as payment in kind to casual laborers who are employed throughout the year on weeding and similar tasks. In praise of their gardens, growers point out that, in contrast to cotton and coffee, a plantain garden pays something every month.

The size of production units varies a great deal. In the vicinity of Kampala, the portion of the holding reserved for plantains has tended to become smaller and smaller partly because of the exhaustion of the soil but mainly because it has ceased to be the main source of household food requirements. Because of the low food yield per acre of plantains, people have become more and more dependent on sweet potatoes and cassava which they supplement with occasional purchases of plantains. In the newer and more distant areas such as North Kyagwe and South Bugerere, six acres of plantains are above the average and anyone with more than ten acres is regarded as a big grower. In the Gombolola of Mumyaka, Bugerere, which is the biggest producing area of plantains in the county, about 40 growers were considered by the chief to be big plantain growers. Of the 22 of these growers who were interviewed, the average stated area of plantain garden was 10.2 acres. Fifteen had ten acres or less and only seven had between eleven and twenty-five acres each. The tax-paying population of the area was 4,917 in 1953.

The yield per acre is reported to be between three and six tons. Table 58 illustrates what farmers consider to be their production average figures:

TABLE 58

Reported Average Sales of Plantains (Kampala)

Number of Bunches	Number of Farmers
Up to 100	9
101–200	7
Over 200	3
None	3
	22

This gives a figure of 2.3 tons per acre per year and should be compared with the figure of 4.3 tons per acre calculated from data collected in the same area by N. D. Oram (1952 : 8). The difference in yield may reflect the difference in the weather; 1952 was a good year, 1953 a bad one.

Even in this area, the big grower is the exception. Most of the growers are small peasant farmers. The rarity of the large grower can be illustrated if not proved from the books of one buyer in the area. Out of the 48 growers from whom he bought in the first four months of 1954 only one could count as a big grower. Of the 48, six were his regular suppliers and these sold on the average 32 bunches per month, or about 1000 lb. Their income would be about Sh. 600/00 to 800/00 per year at a price of Sh. 1/50 to 2/00 per bunch.

It is of far-reaching consequence that once the plantain garden has been established the grower has very little control over the quantities which he can offer for sale at any particular time. Given sufficient care and favorable weather conditions, the trees will produce regularly over a long time. Unlike the coffee grower, the plantain grower cannot withold his produce from the market for more than the 30 days between the time when a bunch reaches maturity and the time when it begins to ripen. Even if there is a glut and prices are at their lowest the grower cannot withold his produce from the market; the wealthy grower is in no stronger position than his poor neighbor. What applies to the grower applies equally to the trader; his scope for speculating on a rise in prices is strictly limited.

The plantain is both bulky and perishable. These characteristics determine the methods of collection and transport. Once harvested, plantains begin to deteriorate on the third or fourth day. If handled carefully and kept fairly cool they will last about a week before they begin to ripen or to dry, depending on the condition at harvest. But under the usual marketing conditions, plantains last four to five days. Therefore, they must be transported to the distributing markets as soon as they are harvested.

Where the trade is well organized and the roads are good the following practice is usual: The trader goes to each of the growers a day before the harvest and asks him how many bunches he can offer and what price he is willing to accept. Having made sure of a full lorry load, the trader hires a lorry (if he does not own one himself); next morning his men cut the plantains down and stack them at convenient points. The lorry then collects them the same morning or later in the evening. They are hauled that day or night so that they are available for marketing and retailing the next morning, the second day after picking. The retailers, thus, have two to three days to sell the plantains in fresh condition.

There are variations on this practice. The resident trader may employ a cutter on monthly terms and send him out with instructions to offer a certain price to the growers. The cutter cuts and stacks the plantains and informs his employer when they are ready for collection. A lorry owner may, on the other hand, employ three or four cutters and go round the village with his men, bargaining with the growers and collecting on the same day. In any case it takes the best part of a day to collect a full load.

The cost of collection is normally borne by the trader: the grower sells the fruit on the tree. In Bugerere and North Kyagwe the charge for cutting is five cents a bunch and for carrying and stacking at a convenient point, ten cents a bunch. To this must be added the cost of transporting the fruit in a lorry on small secondary roads to the main roads.

There are three types of dealer: (1) The farmer who combines farming with trading, has a big or medium-sized farm and lives in the neighborhood. His home is the center of his trade which radiates in all directions. He buys primarily from the small producer. (2) The specialized trader who often owns his own lorry which, if he lives in a plantain growing area, he uses mainly for the plantain trade. If, however, he lives in the town where opportunities are more varied, he may engage in the plantain trade only at times when other business is slack. His geographical area of activity is usually wider. Sometimes he forms permanent connections with a few farmers but more often he buys wherever the plantains are cheapest. He often underestimates his own transport costs and is therefore more likely to go to remote places which those who hire their transport usually avoid because their costs are immediate. (3) The market seller with cash to spare but who rarely owns a lorry himself. He believes that it is an advantage to buy directly from the grower and thus by-pass the middleman. Like the specialized trader, he buys wherever it is rumored there is plenty, and he may go to any county. He normally buys from the big producer or from the villages in which big producers are reputed to reside. Table 59 illustrates the proportion in which these three types of traders appeared in Katwe market between Feb. 15 and March 11, 1954.

TABLE 59

Number of Lorry Loads Delivered in Katwe Market

	Total	Own Lorry	Hired Lorry	Not Stated
Grower/Trader	26	15	9	2
Specialist/Trader	21	16	2	3
Market seller	42	5	37	–
Not stated	2	–	–	2
Totals	91	36	48	7

The period covered was a time of relative abundance when anyone could go out and buy sufficient quantities from growers to make the load pay. But at a time of scarcity the trade is pursued solely by the grower/trader and the lorry owner, since the first can utilize his knowledge of local conditions and the latter can minimize the transport costs, or utilize his transport to the best advantage.

There is also a division as to the type of grower from whom the different traders buy. The local grower/trader may combine with two or three other growers, but normally he buys alone from small growers. They come to him and tell him when their harvests will be ready, while he, on his unhurried rounds, can approach them and ask them when they expect to sell. "Not next week, but the week after, I will have forty to fifty bunches." The books of one trader illustrate this type of trade. In four months, January to April, 1954, he bought 2635 bunches from 48 different growers involving 107 transactions. All the 48 lived in two villages; only one was a big grower who contributed to three out of the eleven trips. Seven out of the 48 were his regular suppliers, but six out of these seven had connections with him other than the commercial ones. A feature of this trade is the absence of credit or advances except very rarely.

The specialist trader, on the other hand, prefers to deal directly with big growers who can offer him a load or half a load at a time and thus minimize transport and collection costs. The big grower himself prefers such selling because he is in a stronger bargaining position because the trader has no other immediate sources. As a result, the big producer gets relatively higher prices than the small one.

The areas nearer Kampala where production is on a very small scale are served by cyclists who roam the villages searching for and collecting anything saleable, from eggs to plantains. The bicycle can go anywhere, and the running costs are very small. The loads these cyclists carry have to be seen to be believed. The cyclists sometimes pile on as much as five bunches at a time. They perform two functions: they collect from the small peasant producers who do not live in the same villages as the big producers and also from those who have an occasional bunch or two; and they sell to consumers who are far from the marketplaces. On the Kasawo road, extending as far as 20 miles out, the cyclist begins to sell his loads a bunch at a time and then cycles along till he is stopped by yet another consumer. He would consider it an unfortunate day if he were to cycle as far as Kampala, partly because he would have to cover a greater distance and partly because he would have to accept a lower price in the more competitive conditions of Kampala.

The bicycle is also used for collecting plantains in small quantities for sale on the roadside or at dukas on the road. There is one such roadside market in Bugerere, two miles out from the bridge, where motorists stop to buy a bunch or two to carry with them to Kampala.

Transport.
As we have seen, many of those who engage in the plantain trade do not own lorries but hire them. Lorries can be hired from Indians or Africans in the producing areas as well as in Kampala. The trader who resides in a producing area will naturally hire his lorry locally. But even the trader who resides in Kampala may prefer to go to the area, buy from the growers a sufficient quantity of plantains, and then make arrangements with a local lorry owner for collection and transport. Alternately, he may instruct a partner to make arrangements with a lorry owner in Kampala to go out to the producing area the day after he collects the load. Sometimes he will bring a lorry with him if he is sure of procuring a full load in a single day.

The cost of hired transport is relatively heavy, but the work is laborious and time consuming. Collecting plantains takes a lorry owner the best part of a day whether the distance travelled is 60 or 100 miles. In Bugerere, which is 40 miles from Kampala, the rental rate is Sh. 120/00 to 160/00 depending on the size and condition of the lorry. Many buyers prefer to hire a new lorry at a rate slightly higher than the minimum. In any case, the stated distances are at times deceptive. One would need to add at least ten miles of secondary roads for collecting in the villages, and another ten miles for distributing the load in the Kampala markets. The total is therefore about 100 running miles of which 60 miles are loaded. The rate per mile for a three-ton lorry is therefore 60 to 80 cents per ton.

For the lorry owner, the costs are difficult to assess because so few African traders keep accounts. The average running cost for one very old three-ton lorry was found to be 1/19 per mile or 00/41 cents per ton mile and that for a new five-ton lorry 00/64 per mile or 00/13 cents per ton mile. No great reliance should be placed upon these figures, but if they are at all accurate, then it is clear that the owner of an old lorry stands to gain little by hiring it out to a plantain buyer. The element of risk in transport costs is of course considerable, though it is smaller now than it was in 1952 when Oram made his investigation. There was no evidence of lorry loads of plantains rotting on the roadside because the lorry had broken down. The position has improved tremendously since 1952 because of purchases of new lorries, and improved servicing facilities.

Production and Collection of Sweet Potatoes and Cassava.

Neither sweet potatoes nor cassava roots have come to the status of a main economic crop in any one area. There have been sporadic attempts by a few individuals to produce them on a commercial scale, but unless the producer has an assured market, such as a contract with a big institution, they are very risky mainly because the demand for them is extremely variable, and the price, therefore, uncertain.

If new ground is opened up, the cost is relatively high. But often sweet potatoes are planted in rotation with cotton or maize and then the cost is only that of making the mounds. From calculations made in Kyadondo it would appear that the initial cost of establishing sweet potatoes is between 60/00 and 100/00 per acre. They mature in five to six months and during this time they require little further attention.

Judging from four villages of Kyadondo, the plots are very small; a five acre plot must be considered big. Sometimes the plot is planted all at once and is expected to mature all at the same time, but some growers space out the times of planting so as to spread out the time for harvesting and marketing.

The yield of sweet potatoes is said to vary between three and six tons an acre (three to five tons in the case of cassava) and anything above four tons per acre is considered good. This would give a return of from 240/00 to 300/00 per acre to the grower if the crop is sold in the village, at 10 cents per pound.

Most of the sweet potatoes consumed in Kampala are grown in its immediate neighborhood in patches and strips dotted around the hillsides, and even in the swamps. Some come from further afield, but few are brought in from more than 20 miles away. All are grown within bicycling range of the town. Within this wider area, two sub-counties, Musale and Mut. I Kyaddondo of Ssabagabo in Busiro, supply more than others.

A grower may dispose of his crop in one of the following ways. He may take it to Kampala himself on his bicycle. This is heavy work and only a strong young man can carry from 140 to 160 pounds on a bicycle for ten to fifteen miles. He may, alternatively, hire a cyclist to carry the load and to sell it for him. If the grower provides the bicycle, the cyclist is paid 45/00 to 50/00 a month. If the cyclist uses his own bicycle, the rate of payment is reported to be 2/50 to 3/00 a bag.

If the grower is old and unable to make his own arrangements, he may sell the crop, either by the bag or still in the ground. In the latter case all the labor of digging up the crop is the responsibility of the buyer and the price paid is low, ranging from 60/00 to 100/00 the acre. It is a highly speculative undertaking as the size of the crop can only be gauged after the harvest. If the grower sells by the bag, he himself bears the expense of digging and packing. The price paid per bag, judging from information obtained in Kyaddondo, is between 5/00 to 10/00 lower than the price ruling in the Kampala markets.

Disposal of Fresh Vegetables in Kampala.

The crops which we are considering are distributed in Kampala in public market places. Originally, markets here as elsewhere were places where producers offered their produce directly to the consumers, but now the organization of the Kampala markets has become more complex. Except in the case of cassava and sweet potatoes it is rare for the producer to be in direct contact with the consumer. We have already seen how, in the case of plantains and other crops, middlemen have taken on the tasks of collection and transport and have come to provide the finance for the crops from the time of harvest to the time when they reach Kampala. We must now describe how the crops are distributed to the consumer once they have reached the town.

Unlike many towns which are served by a central wholesale market or exchange from which the produce is distributed to a series of retail markets or shops, Kampala has a number of markets in which fresh vegetables are sold both at wholesale and retail. Not one of Kampala's 20 or so markets is concerned solely with retail; neither is any significant quantity of fresh vegetables sold in shops. The explanation for this pattern of distribution is dual. First, a stall holder in the market needs less capital than a shopkeeper. Second, the combination of wholesale and retail trade "under one roof" reduces transport costs. The consumer may have farther to go to do his shopping but he gains by getting his vegetables more cheaply. In a country in which food expenditure forms the largest item in most household outlays, this is an important consideration.

The location of the markets in Kampala has not been determined by any deliberate plan. Markets grew up at random and prospered if they satisfied a need. The markets themselves differ greatly from each other; only two of them, Nakasero Market (owned by the Municipal Council) and Wandegeya Market (owned by the Buganda Government) are properly set out and built-up places. In all of them there is a small building, in varying states of repair, which houses one or two meat stalls. This building is normally located near a road or a road junction. Adjacent to it are a number of shelters made of odds and ends of all types of building materials and erected by the market sellers themselves. Usually each seller erects a reed bed or arranges a number of boxes to make a stand on which to display his wares. The plantains and sweet potatoes are laid on the bare ground, spread out or heaped. Most of the markets are open all day, every day except Sunday.

A description of Katwe Market, which is the biggest and which handles more than half the plantains entering Kampala, will make the picture clearer. It is held every day except Sunday. With the break of day, regular sellers begin to arrive, primarily to make early purchases from cyclists and lorry owners, but also to sell to such buyers as "hotel" owners who like to collect their daily supplies as early as possible. By nine o'clock the market is full of sellers and several lorry owners have disposed of their loads and gone. For the rest of the day there is a steady stream of buyers who come and go, having collected their supplies or having refused to buy at the prices current. There are two peak periods in the day, one about ten o'clock when local residents, especially women, buy their daily supplies. The other period is after four o'clock when employees from the town come to buy vegetables to carry away on their bicycles. At this time also, a number of laborers come to buy cooked food and meat delicacies which they eat in the market, probably in place of an evening meal.

Like most of the Kampala markets, it is a drab and dirty little place lacking the colorful variety of country markets or the orderly arrangement of the municipal market. There is an impression of crowding, due as much to lack of planning as to actual confinement. The ground covered is a little over half an acre, and plantains take up a lot of room.

The market was built at the present site in 1937 in the heyday of the meat trade. That is why the meat stalls occupy the most favored position. They are housed in a long building which also contains a store. Next to it is the only other building, erected by the owners. It contains an office for the market master and two stalls permanently occupied by regular traders, selling skins and native medicines. The area between the meat stalls and the road is covered by shelters erected by the regular sellers whose ownership is recognized so long as they continue to occupy them; all except two are built from bits and ends of every kind of building material. The two exceptions are timber huts, one where tea and maize porridge are sold, and the other occupied by a small shopkeeper. An empty space covering about 450 square yards is reserved specifically for the sale, both wholesale and retail, of plantains. Behind the office building there is an area reserved for dry and fresh fish and roasted and cooked meats.

Most of the markets sell fish, both fresh and dry. All of them sell beef and goat's meat. In addition to the staple vegetables, markets sell maize, beans, potatoes, onions, oranges, tomatoes, groundnuts and pawpaws.

The range and variety of the produce offered in any one market reflects the eating habits of those who frequent it. In Nakasero market, where the non-African population is catered to, a large variety of vegetables and fruits is offered; in the smaller market serving the African population, onions and tomatoes are often the only non-staple vegetables offered for sale. Table 60 illustrates the distribution of the sellers in Katwe Market by the commodities they sold in June 1953.

TABLE 60

Distribution of Market Sellers in Katwe Market by Commodities Sold

Food and vegetable sellers	71
Meat and fish sellers	18
Sellers of other commodities (mainly hardware and old clothing)	51
	——
	140

The source of most of the vegetables, fruits and roots are the villages within bicycling range surrounding Kampala. For some commodities they extend as much as 20 miles. Plantains, however, are brought in on lorries from a distance of between 40 and 100 miles; while in times of dearth they come in from as far as Ankole and Bukoba districts, 200 miles and more distant. Table 61 shows the estimated importance of plantains delivered in Katwe Market by place of origin.

By far the most important item of food sold in the Kampala Markets whether measured by the volume or by value is plantains, as is illustrated by Table 62.

We have already seen that the organization of the cassava and sweet potato trade is very simple. The plantain trade, however, is not. Since plantains form the largest single item in the markets, it may be of interest to describe in some detail the ways in which this trade is handled. First, as we would expect to find in a loosely organized

TABLE 61

*Percentages of Plantains Delivered in Katwe Market by Sources*a

	June/July 1953	February/March 1954
North Kyaggwe and Bugerere	56	71
South Kyaggwe	–	11
Buddu	21	11
Ankole and Bukoba Districts	21	–
Bulemezi	–	4
Ssingo	–	3
Other areas	2	–
	100	100

a June/July 1953 was a period of scarcity. Feb./March one of plenty.

trade, nearly all transactions are in cash. Credit is given only in times of glut and then only for a few hours or for the day. Although this means of trading requires that a trader be in constant possession of liquid cash, it also minimizes the risk of buyers being tied to particular sellers.

TABLE 62

Quantities and Values of Three Principal Foodstuffs Sold in Katwe Market

	June 15/July 11 '53		Sept 12/Oct 3 '53		Feb 15/Mar 11 '54	
	Weight cwt	Value £	Weight cwt	Value £	Weight cwt	Value £
Plantains	6700	6810	5290	6440	14430	9930
Sweet potatoes	1540	2050	1960	2020	3660	2700
Cassava (root)	440	400	190	130	120	70
Cassava (dry)	130	390	60	120	130	180
Totals	8810	9650	7500	8710	18340	12880

Secondly, the number of times that plantains change hands between retail traders themselves is very great. The chief reason for this fact is that retailers like to spread their risks. A subsidiary reason is that in selling a commodity as little standardized as plantains, retailers cannot employ assistants and are restricted in the amount they themselves can sell. They therefore buy in bulk in order to be able to buy cheaply. But they rely on being able to resell part of their purchase to another trader at a price lower than that which consumers customarily pay. This practice is known as *okugobesa* "giving a profit." Furthermore, the turnover is slow. Consumers buy in small quantities and haggle for a long time before they buy. As a result, the number of retailers is large in relation to the quantities sold. In February 1954 an average of 17 retailers selling in quantities of less than a bunch in Katwe Market sold about six bunches each per day. During the period of shortage in 1953, the average was even smaller.

Thirdly, there are a number of unwritten but widely accepted rules of trade. When a lorry arrives in the market, several of those regularly engaged in the trade (and some others) rush to the trader or the lorry owner. If he is a regular supplier he will be able to distinguish the *bona fide* trader from the outsider and will not hesitate to choose one of the former. In this case, the others stand aside and look on until the two agree or fail to agree. The seller will name a price, usually a flat rate per bunch to cover all sizes and qualities of bunches. If agreement is reached after a certain amount of haggling, the buyer will pay a deposit equal to about one-fifth to one-third of the price. This deposit is recoverable if the deal falls through. The agreed price is apparently not binding on the buyer though it is considered binding on the seller. The plantains are unloaded at the expense of the seller, who still owns them and they are arranged and stacked according to size. There usually follows yet another haggle about the price, and when agreement is reached, payment is made in full and ownership of the plantains passes to the buyer.

At any point during the negotiations, which can last up to one hour, disagreement may arise. For example, the seller may refuse to unload until the full price is paid because he knows that the buyers will always try to beat down the price; but if the price is fully paid, ownership passes to the buyer and no responsibility for quality is accepted by the seller. If the seller persists and the buyer refuses to make a firm offer before he has inspected the whole lot, then the deposit will be refunded. The seller then either starts negotiations with another buyer, or takes his lorry load to another market. If, after an inspection, the buyer demands a reduction in the price or the refund of his deposit, and if the seller chooses the latter course, the buyer is under an obligation to reload the plantains onto the lorry. Sometimes the buyer will therefore refuse to take back his deposit and insist on having his way. In such a case the trader has the right to complain to the market master or his assistant; if the buyer still refuses to take back his deposit, the trader can leave it with the market master and proceed with the sale of his plantains either to another bulk buyer or retail to consumers. Each of the parties is free to open a case at the court of Omukulu we Kibuga, but it is considered proper that the plantains should be sold immediately.

The transaction completed, the buyer, who is himself a wholesaler, proceeds to resell the plantains to one or more of three other types of buyers. First, there are the other wholesalers to whom he usually sells at a rate of a few cents above his own purchase price. This rate ranges between 30 cents and one shilling per bunch. He is prepared to sell his lorry load in this way if he can get a profit of between 50/00 and 100/00 on the load. If he cannot secure at least 50/00 in this way he will sell to one of the other types of buyers. The second type are the retailers, who are mainly women and small boys. They buy on the basis of a discount from the current retail price. Normally they take one bunch at a time and pay for the previous one as they buy the next one, paying any balance in the evening. Finally, there are the consumers. Few wholesalers are engaged exclusively in wholesaling; most of them are willing on occasion to sell direct to the consumer. The line between wholesaler and retailer is as we have seen, difficult to draw. The only clear distinction which can be made is that few of the women and boys in the market engage in anything but retail trade while few of the men confine themselves to retail trade.

The quantities in which consumers buy and the nature of the commodity sold determine the methods of retailing. The one requires that vegetables be sold in very small quantities. The fact that plantains in particular are difficult to standardize means that it is easier to fix a standard price and make changes in the quantities sold at that price than to pursue the more conventional course of fixing a unit of weight or measure and determining the price at which it shall change hands. Moreover, this method makes it easier for the seller who knows little or no arithmetic to calculate his profit, and obviates the need for expenditure on scales. The bunch of plantains or the bag of potatoes or cassava is divided up into as many heaps as will give the retailer a profit. For example, a bunch costing him 6/00 would be divided up into nine heaps sold for 1/00 each. One heap would normally be used to give extras to persistent buyers or would bring in an extra shilling above the expected profit of 2/00 a bunch.

A bag of sweet potatoes costing 30/00 would be divided up into 42 to 45 heaps of 1/00 each. In the course of the day, some heaps would become smaller through shrinkage or rejections of bad potatoes and some of the heaps would be used to give extras. The resulting profit would be about 10/00. A bag of dry cassava would cost about 40/00 to 45/00 and the profit expected is also about 10/00. This is a slow selling commodity and a bag may take as many as four to six days to retail.

The Cost of Marketing.

Before we can arrive at some estimate of the cost of marketing, we must discuss the range of price variations in the course of one day, from one day to another, and over a longer period of time. An accurate assessment of prices is not easy, partly because there is no standard measure in the trade and partly because few traders keep accounts. Prices may be quoted per bunch of plantain, but bunches vary in size and quality. If they are quoted per heap, the same applies. Nor is it easy to classify the quality of plantains—county of origin, size of each individual fruit and the degree of ripeness all affect quality, and the two latter factors can vary even in one bunch. Accurate price assessment is therefore not possible. The investigator dare not even bring his own scales for any weighing device is associated with controlled prices and hence with courts. The open bargaining or haggling over prices is, however, some compensation to the investigator for the absence of written records of account; retail prices at least are easily observed.

The Labor Department collects (and correlates) prices of certain foodstuffs. Table 63 gives the prices for six foodstuffs, for the year 1953.

TABLE 63
Average Retail Price of Three Types of Foodstuffs

Cents per Pound in:	Jan.	Feb.	Mar.	Apr.	May	June	July	Aug.	Sept.	Oct.	Nov.	Dec.
Plantains	8	12	18	20	21	24	24	24	26	22	20	19
Sweet potatoes	14	18	19	20	25	22	25	19	16	16	14	10
Cassava root	10	14	16	17	19	20	21	21	17	14	16	18
Cassava dried	23	31	37	39	39	46	40	39	33	32	31	36

As this collection constitutes a regular, consistent and permanent record the facts given in this section may be taken as a commentary upon it.

The average prices noted in Table 63 are made up of prices collected in different markets at different times of the month. Tables 64 and

TABLE 64
Range of Retail Prices[a]

	1953: Sept. 7th	8th	9th	10th	11th	12th
Plantains in Katwe	25	25	22	23	26	22
Sweet potatoes in Bakulii	16	16	19	19	20	19

a In cents per pound.

65 illustrate the range of variation compressed into these averages. In any one market there are three fairly distinct pr ces at which plantains are sold: (1) The price at which a lorry load is sold to a wholesale buyer in the market; this is usually expressed as a flat rate

TABLE 65

*Range of Retail Prices in five Markets (Kampala)*a

	Plantains	Sweet Potatoes
Katwe	22	19
Wandegeya	22	22
Mulago	26	22
Kawempe	25	21
Bakuli	25	19
Makawa	20	

a On Sept. 12, 1953, in cents per pound.

per bunch. (2) Retail prices by the bunch, expressed as so many shillings for each individual bunch. (3) Retail prices by the heap which is either 1/00 or /50 per heap, the size of the heap depending on the ruling prices on the day. For sweet potatoes and cassava there

TABLE 66

*Prices of Plantains and Sweet Potatoes (Kampala)*a

Date 1953	Plantains			Sweet Potatoes	
	Wholesale	Retail per Bunch	Retail per Heap	Wholesale per Bag	Retail per Heap
June 15	15	18	27	18	25
16	–	22	31	20	26
17	15	21	32	22	30
17	15	21	32	22	30
18	14	15	27	24	30
19	12	18	–	19	29
20	15	19	–	19	24
22	12	16	–	–	–
26	12	17	25	17	22
27	–	18	30	–	21
29	15	17	–	–	–
30	14	19	24	18	22

a In cents per pound.
– No price recorded.

are only two prices: (1) Prices per bag; and (2) prices per heap. We have converted these prices into cents per pound, and Table 66 shows the relationship between different prices on particular da ys.

For the calculation of the value of the commodities offered per day we have used, in the case of plantains, the retail price per bunch, and in the case of the sweet potatoes and cassava, the retail price per heap. In other words we have used a consumers' price. It is clear from these tables that the price range is not large. There appears to be a consistent gap between the prices ruling in Katwe and those in the smaller markets, which may be due to the fact that most loads are brought to Katwe first. Nakawa market, where plantains are sold by the pound, is an exception; throughout September 1953 the price remained steadily at −/50 cents per pound and throughout February 1954 at −/10 cents per pound. Nor do prices fluctuate violently from day to day; they move up and down, but the range of fluctuation in

TABLE 67

Cost and Profit of Plantains Grown in Bugerere[a]

	Price Paid to Farmer	Cost of Collection and Transport	Mark-up of Wholesaler
January 1953	7.90	4.11	2.54
February	8.58	4.48	1.50
March	8.34	4.44	2.90
April	13.74	5.30	2.24
June	12.05	3.19	1.59
November	6.93	2.64	0.56
December	8.00	2.64	1.30
Average for 7 months	9.04	3.96	1.30

[a] In shillings per cwt.

any one week or even month is not great. One would not expect it to be otherwise, so long as supplies remain fairly constant over a period of a month or so. Over short periods of time, retailers tend to keep the price relatively constant so that a drop in wholesale price is not passed on to the consumer immediately, but is taken up as increased profit.

We are now in a position to consider the actual cost of marketing. To quote Clark and Weld "marketing is a part of production. In other words, the total cost of production is made up of two parts—the farming cost and the marketing cost, including the cost of transportation and that of performing all the other marketing operations" (Clark and Weld 1932 : 182).

All these costs together make up the price at which a commodity is retailed. The cost of production, collection and transport have already been discussed. Suffice it here to recall that the data available are not sufficiently complete and accurate to warrant an analysis of the relative importance of each cost item in the determination of prices.

Taking the price received by the grower as indicative of his costs, or at least as sufficient to induce him to grow and offer for sale that particular commodity, Table 67 illustrates the relation between three of the components which go to make up the final price—the price paid to the farmer, the cost of collection and transport, and the mark up of the wholesaler in the market.

Table 67 covers the cost up to the time when the plantains are delivered to the retailer. To this must be added the very heavy cost of

TABLE 68

"Marks-ups" from a Few Recorded Items (Kampala)

No. of Bunches	Bought Wholesale	Sold Wholesale	Sold Retail	Margin	%
3	17/50	22/00	–	4/50	25.7
203	913/50	974/40	–	60/90	6.7
24	120/00	–	157/00	37/00	30.8
42	190/00	–	272/00	82/00	43.2
200	950/00	1050/00	–	100/00	10.5
200	1100/00	1145/00	–	45/00	4.1
50	325/00	–	343/00	18/00	5.5
34	142/80	–	203/00	61/20	42.9
102	400/00	473/80	–	73/80	15.6
88	510/40	–	619/80	109/80	21.5
160	709/50	809/50	–	100/00	14.1
95	612/50	–	737/50	125/00	20.4

retailing itself. Much of the trade is done in very small amounts at all times of the day to hundreds of buyers. In the plantain trade for example, on a certain day in February 1954, more than half of the traders were selling in quantities smaller than one bunch. The heavy cost of retailing may be illustrated by the figures of Table 68, recorded in Katwe in June/July 1953.[3]

These margins refer to that part of the retail trade which is done in bunches; where retailing is done in quantities smaller than bunches the margin is likely to be considerably greater.

A subject of perennial interest in agricultural marketing studies is the proportion of the final retail price received by the grower. Table 67 shows the prices received by the growers in relation to the wholesale prices over some months in 1953. Table 69 illustrates the percentages received by the grower, transporter, wholesaler and retailer at four different periods, on plantains grown in Bugerere.

(3) See also **Table 66** for increase in the cost of retailing in small quantities.

The most obvious aspect of the price structure is that any benefit in the rise of prices is passed to the producer almost immediately. This may be due to the proximity of the market to the producing area and to the fact that plantains do not pass through any manufacturing process before they are marketed. Changes in the prices ruling in Kampala markets are known the same or the next day in Bugerere. Consequently, most of the farmers asked were satisfied with the prices they received by selling the plantains on the tree. They were all agreed that they could not get better prices by selling the produce in the market themselves. Some of the reasons given to explain their reluctance to sell direct to the consumers were: (1) that lorry owners know the exact prices that can be received in the markets and there-

TABLE 694

Percentage Breakdown of Retail Price of Plantains

	% of Retail Price Received by Grower	Transportation and Collection	Wholesaler	Re-tailer	Retail Price per Bunch (Shs)
June 1952[5]	29.8	40.3	12.3	17.5	2.85
June 1953	50.1	15.–	13.4	21.7	6.00
September 1953	53.2	13.3	13.3	20.0	7.50
February 1954	44.4	20.0	11.1	24.4	4.50

fore raise and lower their offers accordingly; (2) that the buyers in the market combine against the growers because they work in the same place, whereas the growers come from all parts of the country; (3) that retailing is time consuming and there are many thieves in the markets who cause such losses as to nullify any profits that can be made through retailing.

Some of the above reasons may be exaggerated. For example, the transport charges are well-known and almost fixed by common practice. But being a fixed charge, the percentages change inversely in relation to the rise and fall of the retail prices.

(4) The percentage received by the growers compares favorably with those given by Clark and Weld (1932 : 456) as ruling in the U.S.A. in the 1920's.

	% of Retail Price Received by Farmer
Grains	70
Potatoes	50
Other vegetables	30
Fruits	30

(5) Calculated from figures given for deliveries from Bugerere by N. D. Oram (1952 : appendix III). The figures have been adjusted to allow for transport costs where the lorries were owned.

Perhaps the other most significant factor revealed by the above figures is that the percentages received by the wholesalers and retailers have a very narrow range; the first varying between eleven and thirteen and the other between eighteen and twenty-four.[6]

There is no measure of the absolute cost of any marketing process or service to show by comparison whether the process or service is unduly expensive. There are, however, at least two relative standards. One of these is the income of the people engaged in the trade as compared with earnings in similar occupations.

We found no indication that market wholesalers or retailers earn more than other people engaged in comparable activities. Indeed, it would be surprising if they did, considering the reported occupational mobility among the urbanized section of the population, and considering further that monopolies are very difficult to create under the existing agricultural and commercial conditions. In time of plenty, the number of retailers rises almost in proportion to the increase of the quantities marketed.

Even if the earnings of those engaged in the trade are not very great, the marketing services might still remain expensive if it could be shown that the organization itself was relatively inefficient. Other standards of efficiency can be arrived at considering alternative forms for providing the same service. Here and there, shopkeepers have combined trade in piece goods or other commodities with the sale of plantains. In two or three cases, shopkeepers specialize in this trade. The comparative costs have not been studied, but the retailers in the markets have two well-known advantages: low overhead expenses and no fixed capital investment. It is very unlikely that in the prevailing stage of economic development, any other form of distribution could compete successfully with the present organization. This does not mean that the present organization is satisfactory from every point of view. Consumers often have a long walk to the nearest market. A retail shop in their immediate neighborhood would save them time, but increase retail price.

A more hopeful approach might be to encourage the growth of additional markets as the town expands. This is already happening to

(6) An example of the percentages received on a perishable fruit in America is given by Clark and Weld (1932 : 451):

Distribution of Dollars Paid for Citrus Fruit by Consumer

Retailer	25.4
Jobber	7.5
Transportation	15.1
Selling, including advertising	1.4
Picking, Packing	8.8
Fruit on tree	41.8

some extent when the occasional lorry load of plantains is delivered not to one of the existing markets but direct to a suburb which at present is remote from the older markets.

We saw earlier that one of the heaviest costs in bringing plantains to the Kampala consumer is the cost of collection and transport. Improvements in the number and roadworthiness of lorries, and to a lesser extent in the state of repair of the roads, have already reduced this element considerably in the years since Oram made his investigation. Further improvements along these lines would no doubt further reduce both the running costs of lorries and the element of risk in bringing plantains from a distance. An increase in the number of transport contractors engaged in this business would insure that the ensuing reductions in cost would be passed on to the consumer. Improvements in the ease of transport would also enlarge the area from which collection could profitably be made and this would in turn insure a larger and more stable supply for Kampala. Finally, the extension of the area of supply would probably result also in an increase in the proportion of Kampala's food supply which was grown as a cash crop. It is a more certain source of supply than that which results from accidental surpluses of peasant producers.

CHAPTER 27

The Koforidua Market

BY DANIEL F. McCALL[1]

The purpose of this essay is to present the facts about economic activities of traders, the organization of Koforidua market in what is now Ghana, and to analyze the complex of marketing[2] in the area which has its center in the town of Koforidua.

Koforidua is the fifth largest town in the Gold Coast, after Accra, Kumasi, Sekondi-Takoradi and Cape Coast. In the 1948 census, three years before our field work, it was credited with a population of 17,715 although a survey by the Sanitation Department found it to have a much larger number of residents—nearly 30,000.

THE KOFORIDUA MARKET

The market is just about in the center of Koforidua, both socially and geographically. Koforidua, as a town, is the result of the convergent growth of three villages, Soldai, Betum and Oguaa.

The original villages are definable today as sections within the town (see Map 18). Betum and Oguaa are on the western side of the Accra-Kumasi highway which runs through the town to provide its

(1) The research on which this paper is based was conducted in what was at that time the Gold Coast, from late 1951 through the first quarter of 1953, the principal part of which time was spent in the town of Koforidua. The research was made possible by a grant from the Social Science Research Council and a small supplementary grant from the Horace Moses Smith Fund.

I was aided by my wife, who carried out all of the interviews with traders in the market. I also had a team of local young men, all recent graduates of Standard VII. Their tasks were mainly enumerating the number of persons who enter the market, the number of headloads of produce, etc., as well as simple and brief interviews about point of origin of commodities. All interviews were conducted in Twi. Wherever the words "we" and "our" occur, they are true plurals and not editorial singulars. I am alone responsible for the design of the research and the interpretations.

Nearly 100 interviews were obtained from traders in Koforidua market. Some of the information has been published in McCall 1959.

(2) In this paper the word "market" means the market-place in the town; the term "marketing area" means the area dependent on the town. There are many other senses in which "market" has been used. The word "marketing" involves two things: (1) the production and distribution of goods (predominantly but not solely foodstuffs) for local consumption, and (2) the export and import of commodities which form part of the network of world trade.

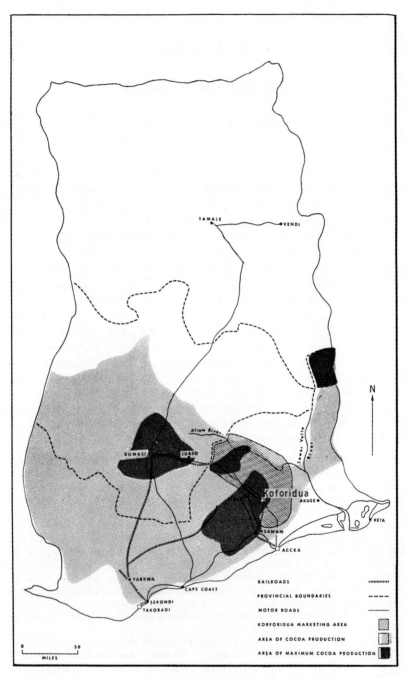

TAMALE   •VENDI

N

Afram River

KUMASI   JUASO

Lower Volta River

Koforidua
AKUSE•

KETA

NSAWAM

ACCRA

•TARKWA

CAPE COAST

SEKONDI
TAKORADI

RAILROADS	
PROVINCIAL BOUNDARIES	
MOTOR ROADS	
KORFORIDUA MARKETING AREA	
AREA OF COCOA PRODUCTION	
AREA OF MAXIMUM COCOA PRODUCTION	

0   50
MILES

FIGURE 17
Koforidua and its Hinterland

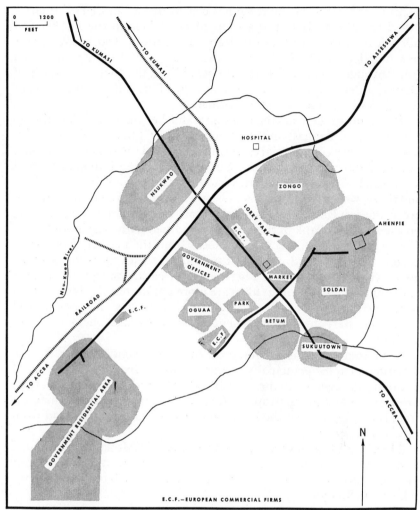

FIGURE 18
Schematic Map of Koforidua, Showing Land Use

main street. Betum is Southeast of Oguaa and the two are separated by a wide paved street which crosses the highway and runs up to the Ahenfie, or Omanhene's palace. Soldai is to the south of this street on the eastern side of the highway. The market, a walled enclosure a good city block in size, is located at the northeastern corner of this crossways. This spot where the two streets meet is so important that it is the only intersection in town that has a name—*Nkwantanam,* which means "four corners."

Another section of the town has grown up: a "strangers" quarter called the *Zongo*. It begins a short distance behind the market and fills out the northweastern quadrant of the town. Another relatively new neighborhood, *Nsukwao*—so called because of the stream which runs through it—occupies an area straddling the highway, north of Oguaa, squeezed in a curve of the railway. This is the only section of the town which does not abut the market.

The main street bears the through traffic between Accra 53 miles to the south and Kumasi and the remote north. This street is lined on both sides with commercial establishments.[3] On the easterly extension of the side street from the Four Corners were three Indian stores and a few small African shops. On various back streets of the town, here and there, were other African enterprises. Barclay's Bank and Leventis are on Station Road opposite the railroad station. This street, running on the southern flank of the railway, was lined with warehouses.

The railway station is several blocks from the market; *kaya-kayas*, porters who headload merchandise, compete with taxis to transport goods when a train arrives. There is a lorry-park, just to the northeast of the market; goods and traders are more apt to come by lorry, which is more convenient to the market and also cheaper. *Kaya-kayas* and taxis wait here for lorry passengers with baskets, sacks or other packages.

A number of paths converge on the town from all sides. In the morning, people—principally women—come in from farms and small out-lying villages with their headloads of produce for the market. From all these sources, people and commodities arrive in the market: from the railway, from the lorry-park, from the forest paths and from the town itself.

The Koforidua market is open every day, but Mondays and Thursdays are the busier days and Sunday is very quiet. Saturday, too, tends to be less busy, and it is the day when a trader goes to tend to the farm if he or she has one.

The market is trapezoidal in shape; the main street side is 400 feet long but its opposite side is only 250 feet long. The other two sides are 500 and 450 feet long. There are five gates, as shown in Map 20.

The aisle running from the main gate to the gate opposite is the widest and has a number of trees shading it; there are five other transverse aisles as well as twelve lengthwise. The aisles are formed by the placement of rows of stalls. These are the open stalls, the closed stalls being built against the walls. If one enters by the main gate,

(3) Paterson & Zachonis, the Bank of British West Africa, G. B. Olivant, SCOA, CFOA, UAC and John Holt, all European concerns, as well as three Syrian shops and an African-owned drug store.

there are more stalls on the left, not only because this is the longer side of the trapezoid, but also because considerable space in the narrower end is occupied by the meat-house.

Certain commodities tend to be located in certain parts of the market but since it has become overcrowded, sellers have to take any space they can get. Dry goods, hardware and clothing, cloth, tailors and seamstresses fill the closed stalls as shown in Map 19. The open stalls encircled by the closed stalls are also mainly occupied by textiles, drugs and other dry goods, but the stalls on the other side of the main aisle are filled primarily with foodstuffs. Fish, palm-oil, shea butter, rice, gari, onions and a great variety of other comestibles are to be found. There is even a restaurant in a shed near the main entrance. The aisles throughout the market are spread with neat piles of vegetables and fruits, especially peppers, onions, plantains and cassava. In some places, principally in the main aisle, small tables have been put up for a better display of products.

The market opens at 6:00 A.M. and by noon most of the women who sell vegetable produce have sold their supplies and are heading back home. The sellers of cloth and dry goods stay on, but by 4:00 P.M. many have drifted away and the market is noticeably less crowded. Gradually the five gates, one after another, are closed until before six o'clock all are closed. On Friday, August 29, 1952, when I had a team of enumerators watching each gate, gate 5 closed at 4:20; gate 2 at 4:30; gate 3 at 4:35; gate 4 at 5:12; and gate 1 (always the last to be closed) at 5:35. That day a total of 28,632 persons went into the market (see Table 70). On Monday, August 18, 1952, a total of 37,871 persons entered the market (see Table 71). These figures would include some persons who entered more than once, but as even the lower figure is larger than the resident population of the town, it gives an indication of the market as a center of activity. Not all of these people were necessarily customers; some were friends or children of the traders. The Monday market had 2800 sellers, but at the Friday market there were only 1370 sellers.

The market used to be regulated by the Oman, but now comes under the Urban Council. There are 15 employees who run and maintain the market. There is a Senior market clerk who has an office within the market where he collects fees for market stalls, makes change for sellers or checks money thought to be counterfeit. He has an assistant market clerk who takes over in his absence or relieves gate ticket sellers when necessary. There is a market inspector who reports on the sanitation and sees that every seller has a ticket. He makes a complete round of the market every day, which takes about $2^1/2$ hours. He reports people to the police if they do not keep the

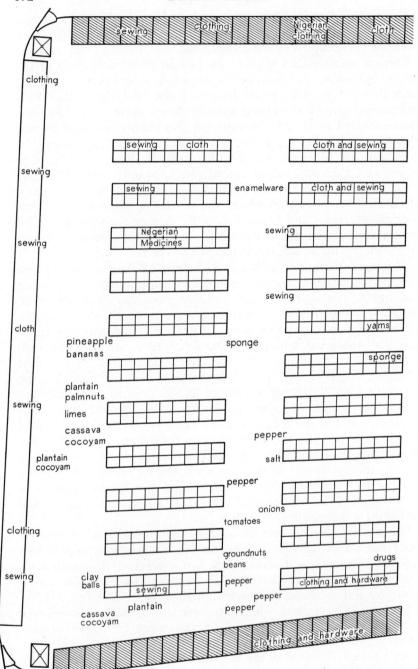

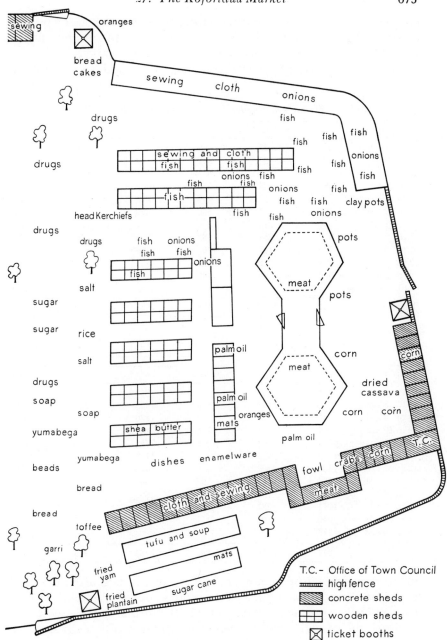

THE KOFORIDUA MARKET

FIGURE 19

market clean. If he finds someone selling without a ticket, the person is required to pay double the first time, triple for the second offense and, for a third offense, is forbidden the use of the market.

In addition there are five ticket sellers, one on each gate, and four

TABLE 70

Number of Persons Entering Koforidua Market on Non-Marketing Day

Hours	Gate 1	Gate 2	Gate 3	Gate 4	Gate 5	Totals
6 to 7 A.M.	246	38	106	234	215	839
7 to 8 A.M.	829	151	322	549	230	2081
8 to 9 A.M.	1193	492	349	963	547	3544
9 to 10 A.M.	1153	587	548	1062	902	4252
10 to 11 A.M.	957	516	443	878	642	3436
11 to 12 A.M.	875	313	332	320	710	2550
12 to 1 P.M.	687	278	359	671	420	2415
1 to 2 P.M.	503	264	483	535	485	2270
2 to 3 P.M.	760	141	367	675	840	2783
3 to 4 P.M.	993	252	292	587	220	2344
4 to 5 P.M.	600	118	163	712	159	1752
5 to 6 P.M.	255			111		366
Totals	9051	3150	3764	7297	5370	28,632

TABLE 71

Number of Persons Entering Koforidua Market on a Market Day

Hours	Gate 1	Gate 2	Gate 3	Gate 4	Gate 5	Totals
6 to 7 A.M.	431	39	87	240	40	837
7 to 8 A.M.	739	142	313	455	220	1869
8 to 9 A.M.	1033	543	484	1870		3930
9 to 10 A.M.	1924	661	1216	3469		7270
10 to 11 A.M.	1071	551	1072	2445		5139
11 to 12 A.M.	1245	445	820	1717		4227
12 to 1 P.M.	1406	262	697	1445		3810
1 to 2 P.M.	731	263	297	1550		2841
2 to 3 P.M.	650	190	305	925	805	2875
3 to 4 P.M.	1011	237	434	1095	505	3282
4 to 5 P.M.	640	100	111	225	345	1421
5 to 6 P.M.	370					370
Totals	11,251	3,433	5,836	15,436	1,915	37,871

market sweepers who remove all refuse in the late afternoon and early morning when the market is not occupied. A painter works continuously painting the sheds and walls. The place, in consequence, is clean and attractive and as there are a number of trees growing in the market which give a pleasant shade, strangers coming to this market for the first time usually remark favorably on its appearance as well as on the turnover of goods.

In the market there are: 118 concrete stalls (large) which rent at 6/8 per month (these are built against the market walls); 44 concrete stalls (small) which rent at 2/- per month (these are near the meat-house); 350 wooden stalls which rent at 4/- per month (these are in rows between the walls); 10 wood and concrete stalls which rent at 2/- per month (these are near the meat-house). In the meat-house there are 12 slabs. (There are two chief butchers each of whom rents one side for £4.0.0 per month and rents out five slabs at 7/- per month for each.) Thus, counting the slabs in the meat-house, there were 534 stalls and at the time of this study all were rented. This should have produced a monthly revenue of £123.2.8 from stall rents.

In addition to the people who rent stalls on a monthly basis, other sellers buy tickets at the gate which permit them to sell for the day. On August 18, 1952, 1498 tickets at 2d. each were sold at the five gates. On the same day 1020 tickets at 1d. each were sold for children or assistants of the trader who take some of the goods and wander through the aisles of the market hawking their merchandise while the trader settles in a place between the rows of stalls. Thus on one of the big market days the income from tickets was £16.14.6. The sale of the tickets stops at 2:00 P.M. and the senior market clerk takes the daily receipts to the bank and deposits them in account of the Urban Council. Each Friday the account book is taken to the District Commissioner's office to be checked. At the end of the month, bank deposit slips are handed over to the Urban Council Treasurer. A government auditor checks books and receipts twice a year. The revenues average between £400 and £500 a month.

This money is more than enough to pay the market employees, the cost of tickets, paint and other maintenance expenses. In fact, half of it must be available to the Urban Council to dispose of for purposes other than maintenance of the market.

This is *the* market, but there are in addition two other small unwalled markets. One is adjacent to the lorry-park and is authorized by the Urban Council and a clerk is stationed there to sell tickets. Firewood and charcoal are sold here but otherwise the place is not as busy as the main market. The United Africa Company had some stalls which it rented to a few traders who were their customers. It was located near one of the UAC warehouses and some lorries stopped there so that it was called UAC Park. Both of these smaller markets were quite close to the main market so that a person could conveniently go from one to another if he chose to do so.

The Koforidua market is one of at least 30 and perhaps as many as 50 markets in the Koforidua Marketing Area, in various towns and villages, but it is of course the largest one.

The many women who hawk in the streets must buy a Hawker's License for 2/6 per month from the clerk at the Lorry Park. We made the market itself the focus of our investigation, but there were about as many women selling outside the market as inside.

In Koforidua there was no organization of market women, although such organizations have been reported elsewhere in West Africa.

Goods Obtainable in the Market.

Sellers are apt to offer a variety or a surprising combination of goods. Though a trader will sell what is available for sale, there is nevertheless specialization in certain lines by most traders. The categories indicated below do not mean that the sellers included in them did not also carry other goods.

In our sample there were on a single day 54 sellers of foodstuffs: 28 were sellers of vegetables of various kinds; 9 were sellers of prepared foods; 6 were sellers of fish; 3 were sellers of meat or fowl; 2 were sellers of snails; 3 were sellers of salt; 2 were sellers of refined sugar.

In our sample there were 42 sellers of commodities other than food: 14 were sellers of cloth or clothing; 10 were sellers of dry goods; 5 were sellers of hardware; 2 were sellers of pots or clay; 5 were sellers of drugs; 3 were sellers of soap of local manufacture; 1 was a seller of African medicines; 1 was a seller of bulk tobacco; 3 were sellers of beads or gold jewelry.

The food is almost entirely of local origin but a few imported items are to be found. The imported foods are less frequently to be found in the market than they are with the sellers who set up small tables in the streets, particularly just outside the European stores where the products were obtained. The list of such items is not long: canned pilchards; tomato paste; canned milk, and cube sugar.

1) Vegetables: Small vegetables such as peppers, tomatoes, garden eggs (eggplant) and onions were the commonest offering by the sellers of vegetables. Plantains, palm nuts, shea butter, ginger, sugar cane, corn, yam, gari (cassava flour), beans, okra, palm oil, palm wine, bananas and other vegetables and vegetable products were in the market. This and the following lists cannot be made exhaustive.

2) Prepared foods: Those on sale included bread, boiled yam, *ampesi* (rice with fish and tomato and oil sauce), *kenky* (fermented ground maize) and sauce *corndu* or *kafa* or *agidi* (fermented corn for making *kenky*) "fried balls" or "sweet-bad" (fritters about an inch and a half in diameter), groundnuts (sometimes boiled), tigernuts, and peeled oranges. Sugar cane is also sometimes eaten on the spot by the purchaser who peels away the outer fiber to suck and chew the pith.

3) Fish: Both fresh and smoked fish was available. Four people of our sample sold fresh fish and two sold smoked fish.

4) Meat: Butchers sold beef, goat and mutton. The beef cattle had to be walked down from the north and therefore had little fat. Goats and sheep were able to live in this forest country and could be fattened up and were preferred by many purchasers. Chickens, guinea fowl, and occasionally turkeys were sold. Pickled pig's feet, imported in vats, were also sold. Our sample included one butcher, one seller of chickens and one vendor of pig's feet. Only the latter was a woman, meat being normally considered a man's concern; the men who deal in meat are predominantly from the north, the grazing country. Pig's feet are processed and imported, which no doubt accounts for the fact that a woman was selling them.

5) Snails: These, found in the woods, were sold in both instances by women.

6) Salt: Two of the salt sellers had mounds of rough, grey salt which had been mined in the Sahara and brought south. The other salt seller had both the rough salt and imported, refined salt. In general one may say that foodstuffs are predominantly of local origin, and that goods other than foodstuffs are predominantly of foreign origin.

The sellers who offered commodities other than food displayed many objects that had been imported but some things of local fabrication were also included.

7) Cloth and clothing: Of our fourteen sellers of cloth or clothing, seven were men and seven were women. Of the men, four were tailors who made up a desired piece of clothing to order, one was a seller of imported clothing, mainly "singlets" (undershirts), one sold cloth by the bolt, and one sold native cloth and garments made from this material. Of the women, four were seamstresses, two of whom had apprentices working with them; one four, the other two. One just sat waiting for someone to bring her something to sew and had no cloth to sell, and one sewed only the bright-colored brassieres which are used by some young women as an upper garment. One woman sold cloth in bolts, and two sold *dukus* (headkerchiefs).

8) Dry Goods: Of the ten sellers of dry goods, nine were women and one was a man. The category is what is locally called *niema-niema* or "things" reduplicated to emphasize the variety. Some of the items were ladles, plastic cups, magnifying glasses, dolls and a few other toys, oil lamps, thread, small enamel pans, patent medicines, tobacco, blankets, starch, schnapps, brandy, warm beer, eyeglasses, machetes, shoes, matches, singlets, kerosene, canned milk, canned corned beef, men's caps, towels, soap, and fine sieves. The *niema-niema* women

have some items from most of the other categories; there is no predicting what a particular seller will have.

9) Hardware: Of the five sellers of hardware in our sample, four were women and only one was a man, but our impressions are that this does not represent the actual proportions in the market; a fair proportion of the men in the market are engaged in selling hardware; the percentage of the total hardware sellers is certainly more than one-fifth. Items sold include clocks, buckets, electric torches (flashlights), iron cooking pots, enamel pails and pans, kerosene lamps, nails of various sizes, hammers, hinges, locks, bolts, knives, knife sharpeners, pliers, scissors, and picks.

10) Pots and Clay: The clay pots for sale were of African manufacture. They ranged from 4″ across to 15″ across and 2′ high. Different shapes are for different purposes. Clay pots compete with enamel and iron cooking pots. Clay pots have the advantage of being cheaper; one can afford to break many pots and still have invested less than in the purchase of a single imported enamel pot. Clay pots are made in sizes convenient for local uses and preferences, and for some there are no imported equivalents. For instance, a small shallow pot is made with concentric circular ribbing on the inside. This is used for crushing peppers which is done with the underside of a wooden ladle. No imported piece of enamelware will do the job and yet scarcely a meal can be prepared without peppers. Large water pots are also designed for local conditions. They are unglazed and therefore porous to allow a little seepage which in evaporating on the surface of the jug absorbs heat thereby cooling the jug and its contents and therefore the water jug is known as a "cooler" and is ideally suited to this area.

One woman sold lumps of red clay, of rough, sandy texture, about 4″ long by 2″ in width. They are called *ntroma* and are used for cleaning charcoal stoves. She also sold plantains.

11) Drugs: Of five sellers of drugs, four were women and one was a man. When men sell drugs, they usually do not do so in the market. The man in our sample was sickly which accounted for his presence. Many of the drug pushers are itinerants going out to the villages. Drugs and patent medicines form one of the largest categories of advertising in the newspapers. The drugs found here included liniments, cough syrups, aspirin, laxatives, milk of magnesia, "blood purifier," "heart tonic," cod liver oil, Optrex Eye Solution, Esten's Syrup (for male virility), sulphate tablets, "kidney and bladder pills," Dr. Lynn's Specific (for painless menstruation), iodine, A.P.C. Tablets. Cosmetics were sold by the same vendors: pomades, perfumes (called "lavenda," or lavender, in local parlance), talcum powder, hair grease, hair straightener.

A Yoruba woman sold "medicines" which were of almost infinite variety—a complete list would be too long to give here. The majority of her things were of African provenience but a few items were bought from drug stores in Accra and elsewhere. Some of these items were medicine in the sense we ordinarily use the word and others were medicine in the sense the word is sometimes used in Africa—that is, magic.

A Ga woman sold *yomobega*, a very black heavy liquid of a pasty consistency that is sold in small bottles to blacken grey hair. In the Ga language, *yomobega* means "There are no old women in Accra." Its composition is a trade secret ardently sought because of the profits the knowledge would entail. This woman gets it from a man in Accra who, she says, imports the ingredient from Germany, prepares it and sells it at a "big, big" profit because, she alleges, he is the only source of *yomobega* in the country. We knew a male school teacher who imported some likely substances and attempted to duplicate the manufacture of this hair dye without success.

12) Tobacco: Bulk tobacco was sold from a large vat. Strings of tobacco leaves, known as "twist," could be cut to a desired length.

13) Soap: The soap is made in the town by certain men. The women buy large blocks of it and cut it into smaller cubes for sale.

14) Beads: Beads are not a luxury; every woman wears beads as a necessary part of her costume. Strands of beads around the waist hold up the *amusa* which is perhaps best described as a red loincloth and which most of the women still wear although many of the younger women, particularly those who have been to school, wear "drawers." Quite a few of them still wear waistbeads, said to be exciting to their sweethearts. The beads come from Europe, especially made in sizes, shapes and colors for the African market.

Goldsmiths have a number of outlets. Their wives sell their jewelry in the market, but this probably accounts for only a small part of their sales.

15) Local and imported goods. Certain reflections on the competition of European and African goods arise from this survey of goods that move through this market. Textiles are the biggest item of import, yet cloth is perhaps also the most profitable item of local manufacture. Cloths from England, Holland, Switzerland and elsewhere are made specifically for the West African market; one of the most active pieces of market research done in the area is testing local tastes in regard to colors and designs. Words and pictures of famous people are printed on some cloths which may have a large sale for a limited time while the subject remains topical. Kente cloth, the most famous of the local cloths, is now woven of imported silk threads of

brilliant colors, but the intricate geometrical designs are traditional, and each has a name and a meaning. Twelve yards, the length necessary for a man's cloth, worn toga fashion, may cost as much as £60. Kente is usually commissioned to a weaver and therefore is not generally sold in the market. Cloths of African cotton, white or died with indigo or a red "Moroccan" color, and made up in stripes, are found in markets. Local styles ensure an outlet for local textiles.

Organization of Supply.

Regulations of the markets specify that produce being brought into the town for sale must be brought directly to the market. At one time traders used to walk out on the paths and try to buy things cheaper because the farm woman then would not have to carry the load so far. This "forestalling" had been deemed unfair competition in old English legislation and the restriction was introduced into the colony. A policeman sometimes watches the paths to prevent this practice.

On July 24, 1952, I had three of my assistants tabulating the loads coming into the market by the three main paths. Results are set out in Table 72.

TABLE 72

Use of Paths Approaching Koforidua Market

	Accra Rd. Path	Assessewa Rd. Path	Densu Rd. Path	Total
No. of loads	310	207	282	799
pts of origin	24	28	28	80

We did not check a few smaller paths, for instance, one coming down the mountain from Eti Kwami. Allowing for what was missed, there were perhaps 1000 loads.

There were 45 items but 9 items were represented by only one headload each whereas some items were represented by over 100 loads (see Table 73). The most common item was dried cassava, of which there were 137 loads. Next was clay pots with 123 loads, and then cocoyam with 94. The weight of these loads varied a great deal, but I had no equipment to weigh them nor did I wish to upset the flow of traffic as this would have done. Baldwin[4] found the following weights carried five miles from the village of Akohia to the Assessewa market: bush-yams, 126 pounds; bush-yams, 80 pounds; garden eggs, 56 pounds; pepper, 46 pounds; pepper, 44 pounds; pepper, 32 pounds; plantain, 91 pounds; tomatoes, 33 pounds; tomatoes 28 pounds. These weights are, no doubt, representative of those we counted.

(4) From a ms. of K.D.S. Baldwin.

TABLE 73

Number of Loads per Item per Path (Koforidua)

Item	Accra Rd. Path	Assessewa Rd. Path	Densu Path	Total
Bananas	1	16	4	21
Brodobe			10	10
Brooms	3			3
Cassava	60	28	49	137
Dried cassava		11	8	19
Cassava & plantain		2		2
Cocoyam	59	4	31	94
Coconut	1	1	2	4
Corn	14	1	16	31
Charcoal	26	7	3	36
Clay pots	2		10	12
Firewood	27	46	50	123
Gari	4		8	12
Garden eggs		9		9
Guava		1		1
House mats			3	3
Kernel oil	5	6		11
Kenky		1		1
Konkonte	52			52
Kola		1		1
Lime	1			1
Leaves (spinach)		3	1	4
Leaf (wrapping)		2		2
Oranges			1	1
Pears (avocado)	2			2
Pestle (wooden)	5			5
Pineapple	1		1	2
Plantain	5	40	9	54
Palm kernel	21	8	15	44
Palm wine	11	1	46	58
Palm oil	6		1	7
Palm frond			1	1
Pepper		4		4
Sponge (fiber)		1		1
Sugar cane		8	6	14
Snails			2	2
Tomatoes		3		3
Vegetables	4		5	9
Yams		2		2
Plantain & firewood		1		1
Total	310	207	282	799

The heaviest traffic of portage along the paths was between 8:00 and 10:00 A.M. and transport was virtually stopped by 11:00 A.M. (see Table 74). I had hoped to be able to tabulate the distances of portage but as the names of the points of origin appeared on no map

TABLE 74

Number of Loads Per Path Per Hour

Hours	Accra Rd. Path	Assessewa Road Path	Densu Path	Total
7 to 8 A.M.	34	38	17	89
8 to 9 A.M.	67	95	160	322
9 to 10 A.M.	176	74	80	330
10 to 11 A.M.	33		23	56
11 to 12 A.M.			2	2
Total	310	207	282	799

and porters' estimates of distances were unreliable, and as I had no time to pace them all out, I had to give it up. I don't believe any loads came from further than ten miles; most came from a good deal less. However, Baldwin found at Assessewa that people came from 15 and more miles to market. It can be shown that there was some specialization of production in some of the villages.

We made an attempt to ascertain how many traders and how much merchandise came in by lorry and by railway. This was more difficult than checking the forest paths. When a lorry came into the park the passengers were anxious to go about their business. They could not all be interviewed, but we interviewed as many as possible and nearly all the drivers. When two lorries came in at about the same time, the interviewers sometimes failed to get an interview with any of the passengers of one of them. However, relatively few were completely missed. The registration plate number of the lorry is recorded in the Lorry Park Office, and a fee of 1/- per lorry and 1/6 per trailer (of which there are few) is collected. The average number of lorries per day according to the man in charge of the park is: 300 on Mondays (market day), 150 on Tuesdays, 200 on Wednesdays, 250 on Thursdays (market day), 350 on Fridays, and 200 on Saturdays. The total, then, is 1450 lorries per week. The figure given us for Fridays seems suspiciously high and may be an error, but even if cut down, the total would be about 1200 lorries per week.

Our sample consists of 79 lorries which originated from 40 different places; 68 of them had Koforidua as their destination and only 11 were continuing on to other towns. Nine came from Somania, eight from Suhum, six each from Accra, Assessewa, and Adukrum. Some of the lorries made more than one trip a day. The largest number of trips made by one lorry was 10, but the average was 2.1 and the length of time of the trips varied from 20 minutes to 11 hours and 20 minutes. About two-thirds of the drivers ran the same route every day and the others had alternate routes which they followed on other days.

In Assessewa, Baldwin found that out of every 20 lorries 6 went to Koforidua. This was more than to any other place even though Koforidua is in a different "native state." Five went to Odumase; three each to Akuse and Accra; one to Kumasi; and one elsewhere. He says that the absolute number varies from 10 in the slack season to 100 or 200 in the main cocoa season.

The 79 lorries in our sample brought in 1700 passengers. This was in the slack season and the number during the cocoa season would probably be about seven times as high. On that basis, the cocoa season lorry passenger arrivals would be nearly 12,000 persons per day. We were able to interview 91, or approximately 20 per cent of the passengers. Of the 91 passengers, 56 came to Koforidua to buy or to sell. If our sample was typical of the whole group of passengers, 62 per cent of the people arriving by lorry do so for purposes of trading.

Five persons brought loads of firewood and the same number brought foodstuffs to sell; four brought bags of maize; two brought cassava and two brought palm oil; one brought palm wine in tins, and two brought baskets of fish. That is, at least 22 of our sample of 91 carried a load of goods for sale, but in the rapid movement of unloading we could not get all the items or reliable estimates of quantities.

Of those who were coming to buy, one specified iron sheets for a house he was building, another mentioned clothes, one drugs, one kerosene, and four came to buy fish—freshly arrived from the coast. Thus at least eight passengers came with specific purchases in mind.

Of the passengers arriving by train, we were able to get only a much smaller number of interviews in proportion to arrivals; it is impossible to say what percentage of the total train passengers our 148 interviews constitute. The day of our interviews was July 29, 1952. There were certain noticeable differences between passengers from the south and those from the north. Whereas 55 persons or 37 per cent of our sample of 148 came to buy or sell, of 89 northbound passengers 42 (or 57 per cent) came to trade, but of 59 southbound passengers, only 13 (or 22 per cent) came for trade. One explanation is that no one from the south need come to Koforidua for hospital treatment since there is a larger hospital in Accra, but eight persons (or 13 per cent) of the southbound travelers came for this reason.

Five baskets of fish came by train, and also bananas, yams, palm wine, 3 packages of drugs, and one load of iron bars. But no adequate survey of commodities, quantities, or destinations could be attempted under the conditions.

Seven persons were on the train hawking food or other goods while the train was in movement.

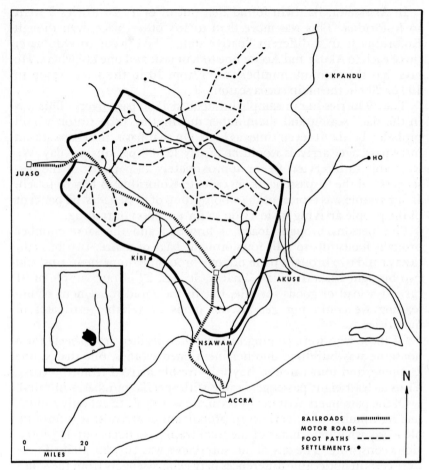

FIGURE 20
The Koforidua Marketing Area

From other sources we were able to add to the picture of the provisioning of the market from distant areas. A resident of Koforidua told us that a relative who worked in the Northern Territories bought up yams at 1d "a stick" and hired a lorry to send them to Koforidua where another relative of our informant sold them. The buying price cited by our informant perhaps is not accurate and he did not know how much was paid for transport or how the profits were divided. K. A. Busia in his *Social Survey of Secondi-Takoradi* gives some information on the transport of foodstuffs by railway which would indicate that Sekondi-Takoradi and Koforidua actually compete for the yams grown along the upper length of the railroad between Koforidua and Kumasi.

KOFORIDUA MARKETING AREA

Koforidua market draws its customers and goods from an extensive area, shown approximately on Map 20. It is impossible to determine with accuracy either the exact size or population within the area, but computing from the 1948 census and the maps, a reasonable estimation of 165,000 persons in 2000 square miles can be arrived at. This area lies mainly within the forest zone, but also includes some of the arid zone of the Volta Valley to the east of Koforidua, and a portion of the Akwapim Hills.

The products of the forest and the open country are naturally different; but the most important in this case is that cocoa is grown in the forest and, with the income derived from its sale, food from the valley lands on the other side of the hills can be bought by the people in the cocoa area. Thus, Assessewa in the Volta Valley is a part of the Koforidua Marketing Area and is important in supplying the market place in Koforidua with vegetable foods.

At Koforidua and Nkawkaw there are breaks in the escarpment of the Akwapim ridge permitting easy movement through the hills. The favorable placement to access to the transmountain valley region was undoubtedly a factor in the growth of the town.

Before the railroad (which arrived in 1915, over a decade before the motor road), there were two alternate routes for produce going south. One was by head porterage through the gap to Akusi on the Volta and then downstream to Ada on the coast and then along the coast by canoe to Accra. The other was by head porterage to Dodowa on the plains and then large barrels were rolled eight miles to Pram-Pram and the sea near Accra.

Koforidua was aided in its growth by the railway which for several years went no further north so that Koforidua became a collecting center for the transport of cocoa.

The annual money income for this area at the time of the study was estimated by the manager of one of the largest firms to be more than £3,000,000. Much of this will be spent in Koforidua or in stores under the management of Koforidua offices, he claimed. He gave the figures set forth in Table 75 for the annual purchase of products in the Koforidua area.

In addition to this income to local producers, there is a substantial local payroll. Because some managers and department heads had different ideas about what was confidential information or perhaps

were of different inclinations to coöperate with my investigation, I
was not able to get the payroll figures for all the companies and
government departments, but I got enough to be able to estimate the

TABLE 75

Estimated Annual Purchases in Koforidua Area

14,440 tons Cocoa @ £150 per ton	£2,166,000
2,000 tons Palm kernels @ £29 per ton	58,000
55,000 gals. palm oil @ 5/– per gal.	13,750
650,000 cu. ft. timber @ 6/– per cu. ft.	195,000
1,200 tons maize @ £60 per ton	72,000
15,000 tons firewood @ £2 per ton	30,000
Total disbursed by firms in purchase of products: £2,534,750	

remainder: six companies out of twelve, and five departments out of
nine (see **Table 76**).

This is for employees resident in the town of Koforidua itself, but
the payroll for the employees in the Koforidua marketing area would
be about double, and the estimate of the government payroll is, if
anything, on the low side, so that £20,000 per month or £240,000 per
annum are paid out each year in the area. The money put out for the
purchase of produce (£2,774,750) plus the salaries and wages of commercial and government employees (£240,000) gives a total of
£3,014,750, which is in keeping with the estimate given.

The economy of the Koforidua marketing area has some characteristics that are typical of the country as a whole, but some things, such
as mining, which affect the economy of other areas in the country,
are not found here.

TABLE 76

Estimated Monthly Payrolls (Koforidua)

Estimated monthly payroll for 12 European firms	£5,300.0.0
Estimated monthly payroll for 9 gov't depts	4,500.0.0
Monthly payroll for 2 African firms	96.9.3
Estimated total payroll in 1952:	£9,896.0.3

The prosperity of the Koforidua market area rests primarily on the
sale of cocoa. Cocoa is solely a cash crop, and many cocoa farmers did
not know of the connection between cocoa beans and the chocolate
sold in the shops. Cocoa production has affected the traditional system
of collective land tenure. Permanent stands of cocoa, as opposed to
shifting cultivation for other crops, has introduced a tendency towards a freehold system of land tenure which encroaches more and

more on the traditional system. *Ipso facto,* land has entered the market.

Labor has also entered the market. It is needed mainly for the harvest, of which there are two in a year although one is much smaller than the other, and they are not spaced so that a laborer can expect to be gainfully employed for the greater part of the year. Labor comes mainly from the Northern Territories and the French areas. A floating rural proletariat has grown up.

The distribution of cocoa income follows a very intricate pattern. Land owners may have rent collectors who take a slice between tenant and owner. The owner must contribute to the local chief and he to the Paramount Chief. There may be more than two in the hierarchy, and each may have a collector who has to be paid. Sharecropper-grown cocoa money is even further decimated. Cocoa brokers also take a cut.

When a crop is sold by numerous small producers, a marketing system which can cope with the problem of collecting small, scattered loads is necessary. Trading companies employ African brokers who, in turn, have sub-brokers to buy up the cocoa. Competition forces firms to advance money to farmers through the brokers before the crop is ready in order to insure its delivery to a particular firm. Many brokers succumb to the temptation to use the firm's money for other purposes than buying cocoa and set themselves up as short-term, high interest money-lenders or speculative house builders.

Each year some brokers are not able to liquidate their investments or collect their debts as needed.

The managers of European firms continuously complain of the corruption of this brokerage system. The year previous to this study, Koforidua firms lost a considerable amount of money in this manner. One firm, according to its manager, lost £1,800 that year and had lost £3,000 the previous year, and another firm lost £4,000 the year of this study. This loss was considered normal.

The produce-buying firms also sell merchandise and they handle this in a way which is analogous to the purchase of produce. They give large amounts of credit to certain traders who distribute it in wholesale amounts to other traders who parcel it out to retailers. The European managers never complain about this part of this business. On the contrary, they eulogize the honesty of the women traders, who have an astounding record of meeting their commitments on time and in full (McCall 1955).

The foodstuffs that come into the market are often said to be the surpluses of the subsistence farmers. That this is too simplistic a view can be seen from the Agricultural Statistical Survey carried out in

1952 by the Office of the Government Statistician under the direction of William Booker. In Report No. 1 for June of that year he gives the net surpluses, that is, sales less purchases for 53 households in 5 villages not far from Koforidua. In Report No. 2, for July, similar information is given for six different villages in the same general area, while Report No. 3 reports for August on 69 households (see Table 77).

It can be seen that certain crops, notably corn, are produced in much greater quantity than they are used. These samples of farm households averaged better than two farms per household and much of the clearing of extra farms must be intended for deliberately producing for the market.

TABLE 77

Proportion of Crop Disposed of by Sale

June

172 lbs. of Cassava	or 30% of crop disposed of in sales
68 lbs. of Cocoyam	or 20% of crop disposed of in sales
62 lbs. of Corn	or 60% of crop disposed of in sales
62 lbs. of Plantain	or 20% of crop disposed of in sales

July

296 lbs. of Cassava	or 40% of crop disposed of in sales
52 lbs. of Cocoyam	or 20% of crop disposed of in sales
515 lbs. of Corn	or 95% of crop disposed of in sales
36 lbs. of Plantain	or 20% of crop disposed of in sales

August

301 lbs. of Cassava	or 48% of crop disposed of in sales
98 lbs. of Cocoyam	or 33% of crop disposed of in sales
61 lbs. of Corn	(sold from storage, no production this month)
63 lbs. of Plantain	or 26% of crop disposed of in sales
5 lbs. of Wateryam	or 45% of crop disposed of in sales
6 lbs. of Yam	or 8% of crop disposed of in sales
98 lbs. of Palm Fruit	or 43% of crop disposed of in sales

That this is so is further indicated by an examination of the household budgets of these farm families. In June, £4.0.1 out of a total of £5.12.7 in their average monthly income was derived from the sale of farm produce. In July, £3.15.11 of a total of £5.11.5 came from this source, and in August, £3.8.0 of a total of £5.7.10 came from the sales of their farm products. It can hardly be claimed that they are indifferent to the exchange economy or that they do not purposely produce foodstuffs for the market.

The fact is that under certain conditions, the income derived from maize may actually exceed that from the same acreage of cocoa. Kenneth Baldwin, in a manuscript which he allowed me to copy, shows that with the possibility of getting two crops annually with fallowing four years out of six, or even two years out of four, in certain years maize income per acre exceeded that of cocoa. He also pointed out that the prices of certain foodstuffs have risen in close equivalence to that of cocoa. For example, between 1930 and 1948 the price of cocoyams, per given weight, rose 292 per cent compared with 300 per cent for cocoa.

Nevertheless, the food farmer does not usually profit as much from the use to which he puts his land as does the cocoa farmer. There are more difficulties for the food producer than for the cocoa farmer, whose work falls mainly in four months out of the year.

Sellers' Sources of Goods.

The differentiation of the roles of farmer and trader is obvious in that only two of the 28 sellers of vegetables got them from their own farms. Eight bought the vegetables at the market from farm women who brought them in from out-lying farmsteads. Two bought them at the lorry park where they were brought from other towns. Six went by lorry to the market at Assessewa to purchase them. Two went to Jumapo and two to Sekesua to buy in the markets there. Kumasi, Keta, Kwamboso, and Yendi were visited by one each. In other words, 12 obtained their supplies locally from three different sources (the market itself, the lorry park, or their own farms), while 14 get their supplies from out of town, from eight different towns. Most of these

TABLE 78

Types of Firms From Which Commodities Were Obtained

Commodity	E.F.K.	E.F.A.	A.F.U.	S.F.A.	A.F.K.	A.F.A.	I.F.A.	Total
Cloth	3	8		6			1	18
Dry goods	2	3	3	1				9
Hardware	5	6						11
Drugs	2	3			2	1		8
Beads	2							2
Tobacco	1							1
Total	15	20	3	7	2	1	1	49

E.F.K. = European Firm, Koforidua; E.F.A. = European Firm, Accra; A.F.U. = Accra Firm, Unspecified; S.F.A. = Syrian Firm, Accra; A.F.K. = African Firm, Koforidua; A.F.A. = African Firm, Accra; I.F.A. = Indian Firm, Accra.

out-of-town sources were nearby. Yendi, Keta and Kumasi were the farthest away—411, 147 and 130 miles, respectively. These towns all furnished less perishable items such as yams and shea butter.

The sellers of prepared foods for the most part bought their supplies right in this market. Six did so, but two went to Assessewa and one to Mangoase. And the baker of bread bought the flour at the UAC in Koforidua.

Fish, of course, comes from the coast. Five of the six sellers interviewed received supplies from Accra, and one from Togoland. One went to get the fish; five had mothers or sisters who arranged the transport.

The butcher bought his animals at the lorry park, took them to the slaughterhouse at the northern end of the town to be killed and returned with the carcasses to the meat-house to cut them up for sale. The seller of chickens made a trip to Yendi for his supplies.

The African salt was purchased by two of the sellers at this market in sacks about the size of a cocoa bag. One went to Keta to get supplies; this may have been seasalt, but I am not sure. The seller of refined salt bought it from UAC and UTC. The imported sugar was also obtained from the local stores. Those who dealt in goods other than foodstuffs bought either from local stores or went to Accra to the stores there, or divided their purchases between the two towns. The European stores in Koforidua are all of the same companies as those in Accra. However, the stores in the capital have a wider selection of items. The sellers may have personal arrangements with personnel of the Accra stores, and the women sometimes simply like to make the trip for the change of scenery. Also, there are a few additional companies in the capital but none of these are major firms.

For all imported goods, sellers bought from a total of seven Koforidua firms, five of them European and two African (both drug stores). One of these was mentioned fourteen times; one eight; one twice; and the others once each.

Eleven European Accra firms supplied imported goods to sellers in the Koforidua market; one was mentioned sixteen times; one was mentioned ten times; one was mentioned six times; one was mentioned two times; six were mentioned once.

One African and one Indian store were mentioned, once each, but Syrian stores, never specified by name, were mentioned seven times.

African commodities, foodstuffs and other things came from sixteen towns besides Koforidua itself (see Table 79).

Forty-nine sellers in our sample made trips to obtain supplies. Mothers, sisters, friends, husbands and unspecified persons were also mentioned as arranging for the transport of goods, either by bringing them or sending them. The lorry was the most popular means of transport, but train, airplane and steamship were also used:

Three towns were reached by train—Mangoase mentioned once; Nsawam mentioned once; Accra mentioned eleven times.

Eleven towns were reached by lorry—Accra mentioned seven times,

Assessewa mentioned six times, Sekesua mentioned three times, Kumasi mentioned twice, Jumapo mentioned twice, Kwamboso mentioned twice, Yendi mentioned twice, Addokwanta mentioned once, Akwisi mentioned once, Odosu mentioned once, Keta mentioned once. One town (Lagos) was reached by plane (from Accra). One town (Lagos) was reached by steamship (from Accra); it was mentioned twice.

The following fares include the charges for accompanied freight: The highest fare paid was £5 one way (Lagos by steamer); the lowest fare paid was 9d one way (Addokwanta); by train the highest fare was 8/- one way; by train the lowest fare was 1/7 one way; by lorry the highest fare was £1.5.0 (Yendi) one way; by lorry the lowest fare was 9d one way; by steamer the highest fare was £5 (Lagos); by steamer the lowest fare was £3.10 (Lagos); by plane the only fare was £5 one way (Lagos).

TABLE 79

Towns Supplying Produce to Koforidua Market

Town	Distance from Koforidua	Visited by	Commodity
Assessewa	26 miles	9 sellers	vegetables
Accra	53 miles	7 sellers	fish
Sekesua	25 miles (approx.)	2 sellers	vegetables
Addokwanta	5 miles (approx.)	1 seller	snails
Jumapo	5 miles	2 sellers	vegetables
Kumasi	130 miles	2 sellers	yams, "medicines"
Keta	147 miles (approx.)	3 sellers	salt
Kwamboso		1 seller	
Yendi	411 miles (approx.)	2 sellers	chickens, shea butter
Mangoase	13 miles (approx.)	1 seller	oranges
Togoland	200 miles (approx.)	1 seller	fish
Lagos	278 miles (approx.)	1 seller	African cloth, African medicines
Densuagya	5 miles (approx.)	1 seller	clay pots
Tinkong	28 miles (approx.)	1 seller	clay pots
Odosu	7 miles (approx.)	1 seller	clay balls
Akwisi		1 seller	

The frequency of trips varied a great deal, the longer and more expensive trips being quarterly, or at most monthly trips. Shorter trips were sometimes weekly or even in a few instances more than one trip per week.

Forty-five sellers hired *kaya-kayas* to headload goods to the market either from their homes, the lorry park or the train station.

The largest amount paid to a *kaya-kaya* was 10/-. This amount was paid only once; the next highest amount was 6/-. This does not give the whole story because the amount was usually given per load and sometimes a trader might have several loads. The smallest amount paid to a *kaya* was 2d. This was paid only once; the next lowest amount paid was 3d which was paid by 9 of our sellers.

Several women were contemptuous at the suggestion that they would bother to hire a *kaya*; many carry their own supplies habitually but hire a *kaya* when they have more than one load. Seamstresses with apprentices, girls usually from about 12 to nearly 20, have them carry the loads. Some women also had young daughters help them; the older daughters usually having their own trade, with consequent headloads, to care for.

Sales Revenue.

The figures on sales revenue by particular traders in the market are difficult to obtain because, aside from meeting more suspicion on this point than elsewhere in the questioning, they do not keep daily records. The business varies from day to day as well as seasonally, and not being in the habit of thinking in such terms it is difficult for many of them to furnish the investigator with a reliable average. We met this difficulty as best we could by asking how much was sold on a good day, how much on a bad day, and at a different point in the interview, how much was sold the previous day. Some probably perceived the intended check and brought their statements into coördination, but some discrepancies emerged. Six women revealed that the previous day they had taken in less than what they had given as their lowest rate. In general there seemed to be a tendency on the part of some traders to exaggerate the volume of their business: A vegetable seller who gave as her low 8/-, yesterday got 6/-. A vegetable seller who gave as her low £1, yesterday got 4/-. A fish seller who gave as her low 16/-, yesterday got 3/-. A bread seller who gave as her low £1, yesterday got 16/-. A boiled yam seller who gave as her low £2, yesterday got 30/-. A snail seller who gave as her low £10, yesterday got 5/-.

The highest turnover claimed by any trader for a single good day was £40. This was claimed by two individuals, one a seller of hardware and the other a seller of dry goods. The next highest turnover claimed was £14, claimed by a seller of cloth and by a seller of vegetables. The latter case is palpably a gross exaggeration considering the prices of her items for sale.

Sales the previous day did not come close to these exalted amounts but it should be kept in mind that this was "off-season"; that is, that the income from cocoa crops had not yet been received, and many commented, or complained, during the interview about the slowness of business at this period. Aside from the alleged turnover of £14 worth of vegetables, the highest value of goods sold by a single seller on the previous day was £8 (see Table 80).

TABLE 80

Monetary Value of Goods Sold per Day per Seller

Vegetable Sellers
  (discounting the one exorbitant claim)
  Low ranged from 6d. to £1
  High ranged from 4/- to £6
  Yesterday ranged from 1/6 to £2.10

Prepared Food Sellers
  Low ranged from 2/- to £2
  High ranged from 4/- to £3
  Yesterday ranged from 5/- to £4

Fish Sellers
  Low ranged from 16/- to £1
  High ranged from £2 to £5
  Yesterday ranged from /3 to £3.5

Meat Sellers
  Low given as £2
  High ranged from £8 to £10
  Yesterday (not disclosed)

Snail Sellers
  Low ranged from 10/- to £2
  High ranged from £1 to £10
  Yesterday ranged from 5/- to 10/-

Dry Goods Sellers
  Low ranged from 0 to £2
  High ranged from 10/- to £40
    (next highest £12)
  Yesterday ranged from 0 to £8

Hardware Sellers
  Low ranged from 0 to £2
  High ranged from £1 to £40
    (next highest £3)
  Yesterday (not disclosed)

Cloth Sellers
  Low ranged from 0 to £6
  High ranged from £1 to £14
    (next highest £10)
  Yesterday ranged from 0 to £5

Individually, these amounts are not very impressive, but aside from the fact that this survey was taken at the slack season, it should be remembered that these are the petty traders and that there are others who do not sit in the market but supply those who do. These bigger traders, fewer in number, have substantially larger turnover of goods. Also, considering the number of sellers in the market, the figures show considerable movement of goods, for despite the fact that certain sellers pass the day without a single sale, some sellers in every category (where disclosed), except snail sellers, managed to sell more than £1 worth of their commodity. Yesterday's high point of transactions, except for snail sellers, ranged from £2.10 to £8. The only sellers who ever go a day without a sale are those who have the expensive commodities so that a single sale will sometimes make up for a day or two without sales.

Cash Income and Outgo.

It is a difficult task to determine the income of a sample of traders. We made an attempt. We persuaded ten sellers of our sample to agree to give us daily a record of every pound, shilling and penny taken in or given out and the purpose of the transactions. We did not require

them to write this down for many could not do so but we visited each
one every morning and obtained the information for the preceding
day. Even this became boring or annoying to many of them; one did
not even finish a week, and others tired before we had a long enough
run to determine profits. With those that were left, the sample would
have been so small as to be without sufficient spread to be representative even if we had continued. Therefore, we did not get a picture of
the pattern of profits in the various lines of commodities. Despite the
reticence of many traders and the exaggeration of others, I believe
that it would be possible to get some traders to persist long enough
to get results, and this is necessary to understand this group fully. If
we had been persistent on this point, we might have acquired the
information, but by the time that we realized how much time was
required to follow it up, we were too involved with other informants
on other subjects. The way this should be done, we now feel, is to
select a sample that would include traders with each category of goods,
and follow each through the monetary phases of the movement of
one consignment or purchase of trade goods. The outlay for this
quantity of goods plus the inventory on hand at the time of purchase, if any, subtracted from the sum of the sales proceeds and the
inventory on hand at the time the consignment was sold, if any, would
give the profit or loss on the transaction. The time required would
vary for traders with different kinds of goods.

For nine sellers during one week, expenditures exceeded receipts
for the group as a whole and for five of the individual traders. The
excess of expenditures for the week ranged from 3/- to £48.5.1 but
each of these five had invested more that week in trade goods than
they were out of pocket; whereas, of the four who showed an excess
of receipts, three did not invest any money that week in trade goods.
Thus, only for one trader did we get what appears to be the income
for the week: this was a young girl who sold "fried-balls" for her
mother, giving £3.15.0½ to her mother who bought her supplies, and
yet having a profit which she retained of £1.10.0½. This may be an
interesting case of an "apprentice" trader under her mother's guidance, but in itself it is certainly not indicative of trading profits. The
excess of receipts over expenditure of the other three ranged from
£5.6.5 to £17.8.3.

The most important information from these records is a list of
categories of revenue and expenditure. All revenues were from sales.
Expenditures (it is impossible to keep household budgeting separate
from marketplace transactions) broke down in this manner: Food
was the most constant expense; clothing—only once in our sample,
but it is an important item; fuel—firewood, kerosene, charcoal;

business expenses—trade goods, transport (train, lorry, *kaya*), tickets to market, payment of guard for goods, a tailor bought machine oil; family obligations: mother, child, wife, visitors, and "friend" were specifically mentioned; a beggar received alms, gifts were given at funerals; health (hospital fees), church and debt payments; indulgences—cigarets (men only), kolas (small but popular), beer, whiskey (once), chewing gum, candy, cinema, concert, boxing match.

In sum, necessities accounted for 12 per cent of the expenditure; business expenses for 80 per cent (including 78 per cent investment). Indulgences accounted for 5 per cent, and all others for 2 per cent.

Market and Society in Koforidua.

The conditions of trade change, but trade has in one form or another been an important part of social life to the people of this area for as long as we have any information on them.

Linguistic analysis shows how deeply imbedded trade is in their culture. The word "to buy" is *tɔ* and the word "to sell" is *tɔŋ*. Both words would appear to derive from the same root. The word for market, *ogua,* I was told derived from *gua,* a bench, because people wait in the marketplace on little benches until they find the person looking for the items they have to exchange.

The people in this region have been accustomed to using a medium of exchange for several centuries. Gold dust was given names for weighed amounts—*akie, perigun*—and the famous gold weights were used for this purpose. Small change could be made with cowrie shells. Strings of fives and twenties as well as loose shells were used. According to an eldery informant, cowrie shells were still in use in his youth, and four cowries were equated to one farthing at that time. The farthing has followed the cowrie into oblivion.

The coins now in circulation are those of the British West African Currency Board; all have names in Twi. Some are corruptions of English (*sireng* for shilling) some have the names of weight-values in the older system (*taku* for sixpence). Others were derived in other ways: *manang,* penny, comes from the word for four because a penny was four farthings. *Taku ne fa,* sixpence and a half, is used rather than ninepence, and in the same way, fourpence is designated threepence and one, *tro ne manang.*

Traders keep their accounts in their heads, including credit and debit items with a number of individuals; everyone who has had anything to do with them has commented on their remarkable facility.

The market place plays an extremely prominant part in the life of Koforidua. Besides being the source of food and clothing for the family, it is the place where the wife and mother spends most of her waking day. The market place is largely a woman's world. Except for the small percentage of traders who are men, the processes of trade are said to be mysteries to men. Men often seem uncomfortable in the market; they prefer to send a woman or a child to make purchases for them, and avoid entering it if possible.

For women, the market place is not only a place of business but of leisure as well. Sales are sometimes slow and women chat and josh with each other. The younger children, those still carried on the back, are kept with the mothers and nursed when necessary even during the transacting of a sale. Older children come to visit the mother while she is selling.

The occupational system and the family system are functionally interrelated, and the family structure, as I have shown elsewhere, has changed as a result of this adoption of trading as a full-time role for town women and their rejection of the old occupation of farming.

The conditions of the marketing area are no less important in defining the life circumstances of Koforiduans. The economy of the marketing area determines the status of the majority of its inhabitants. Cocoa farmer, cash-crop food farmer, cocoa broker, cocoa grader, trader, storekeeper, commercial clerk, watch-man, lorry owner, lorry driver, and many other occupations are closely integrated in the economy of the marketing area and although occupation is not the only factor determining status, it is one of the most important.

The particular economic arrangements in this area are relatively new. Cocoa began to be exported in the later part of the last century but it is only for about a generation that it has dominated the economy. Before that, palm oil and palm nuts were the largest earners of income. The demand on a large scale for the oils of West African palms goes back to about the 1830's. Before the rise of palm oil exports, the dominant export was slaves, a trade that was suppressed in the early years of the 19th century, but which had been prominent on the Coast for three centuries. Thirty forts on the coast testify to the trade activity of that period.

Each of these trade arrangements tended to reorganize the society it found—to modify the pre-existing societal structure in such ways that would contribute to the more efficient functioning of the trade roles of whatever groups in the society were involved in furthering the typical exchange of the period. But despite all of the earlier changes the majority of the population remained within the subsistence section of the economy.

Each of these periods, furthermore, has been characterized by a somewhat different culture contact situation. The European society has been developing in a revolutionary way during the centuries of contact with West Africa. But acculturation has always been limited to the selection of European types—hardly representative of Western Culture as a whole—that frequented the coast. Pertinent here are the slave trader who gave way to the "palm-oil ruffian" who was replaced by the cocoa buyer, and now the hydro-electric engineer seems to be a forerunner of the future.

In the beginning, the chiefs and "caboceers" were the most important people in the trade, but individual traders outside the chief's control early arose on the coast, and *mulattoes* and *mustees,* children of European traders and African women, were important in this group.

At the present time, the chiefs have largely lost control over trade; this fact is no doubt of as great an importance in their decline as the political change implicit in colonialism. Where chieftancy is still relatively strong—as in Ashanti—revenue from cocoa lands help to support it.

Men were once more prominent in trade than women when the high-value commodities for export were slaves, gold, ivory and monkey furs. But the social circumstances defining these things, as well as the demand for them, have changed, and women now far outnumber men in the field of trade.

The economy of this area is likely to change considerably in the near future with the implementation of the various development plans, particularly the Volta Scheme which will bring a number of changes to Koforidua itself and to its marketing area. The situation described in this paper is therefore a transitory rather than a permanent one.

CHAPTER 28

African Markets and Trade in the Copperbelt

BY MARVIN P. MIRACLE[1]

In the zone characterized mainly, but not entirely, by copper mining, that is shared by the Congo and Northern Rhodesia and is usually referred to in Central Africa as "The Copperbelt,"[2] live roughly half a million Africans[3] who are largely non-self sufficient in food production, and who have a relatively high per capita purchasing power—probably the highest for any single group of urban Africans in tropical Africa. The Copperbelt has come into being largely within the second quarter of this century and has created what is unquestion-

(1) In addition to the literature cited, and personal observations in Copperbelt markets June 20 to 25, September 12 to 18, and December 6 to 12, 1959, this paper is based on field work done in the vicinity of Gandajakia June 9 to 19, the same year; along the Kafue River (between Namwala and the railroad, approximately), in Areas I, G, and L (Map 21), and in central and southern Nyasaland July 29 to December 1; and on interviews with 475 Africans in Rhodesian Copperbelt markets carried out in September and December by my assistants, James K. Lutaka and Harry Nyondo, using a questionnaire described in a later section.

The research resulting in this paper was done while under a fellowship granted by The Ford Foundation; however, all conclusions, opinions, and other statements presented are, of course, those of the author, and not necessarily those of The Ford Foundation. I should like to thank William O. Jones, Bruce F. Johnston, and Thomas T. Poleman, Jr. of the Food Research Institute, Stanford University, for their helpful comments on portions of earlier drafts of this article.

(2) In the Rhodesias and the Union of South Africa, the term "The Copperbelt" is typically used to refer only to the area of copper mining along the northern boundary of Northern Rhodesia. I use the term to include the adjacent area of the Congo since both regions are part of a single economic complex of which a dominant characteristic is copper mining.

(3) There are no precise population statistics, but in 1958 estimates placed the aggregate African population of the Northern Rhodesian portion of the Copperbelt at 215,000 (Fed. of Rhodesia and Nyasaland 1959); this checks well with the 1956 census of employment which lists the number of Africans employed in the same area as 120,099 (N. Rhodesia 1956). On the Congo side, the population seems slightly larger. Official estimates are that in 1958 there were 376,335 Africans in the three *territoires* which jointly contain the Congo segment of the Copperbelt (Belgian Congo 1959). Most of these were thought to be in urban areas, and if so, would have been in the Copperbelt as defined herein, *viz.*, the following towns and cities and their suburbs: Jadotville, Kambove, Elisabethville, Kipushi, Kasumbalesa, and Sakania, in the Congo; and Bancroft, Chingola, Nchanga, Chambishi, Mufulira, Kitwe, Nkana, Ndola, and Luanshya in Northern Rhodesia. Administratively it is included in Ndola District of Northern Rhodesia and Kambove, Kipushi, and Sakania *territoires* of the Congo.

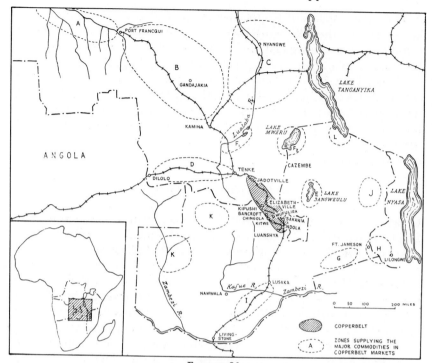

FIGURE 21

The Copperbelt and its Hinterland

ably the largest market complex in Central and Eastern tropical Africa, with markets that draw a good portion of their commodities from 600, and notable amounts from as much as 900, miles distant.

The Copperbelt is particularly interesting, too, because to African entrepreneurs of roughly two-thirds of Northern Rhodesia and a quarter of the Congo (Kasai and Katanga Provinces) it stands out as one of the two major business opportunities. Storekeeping is still mainly the preserve of foreigners, and many Africans know from bitter experience that it requires (1) considerably more capital than that at their disposal; (2) knowledge of at least rudimentary bookkeeping; and (3) the goodwill of Asian and European competitors, who are prone to turn to "gentlemen's agreements," price wars, and the like, when faced with a new rival. What remains, then, is selling in local markets or in the Copperbelt; and the opportunity as well as the profitability of the latter are well known even to those who have never been there, through the tales traders or migrant laborers tell.

The main aspects of Copperbelt market places and commerce to be treated in the following pages are these: historical patterns of commerce; physical, social, and economic characteristics of Copperbelt market places (including techniques of selling, the amount and kind of competition found, economic characteristics of the major commodities sold, and their geographical origins); the magnitude of net imports relative to Copperbelt production (for the commodities for which there are reasonably reliable data); the organization of marketing, the scale of operations, and the major sources of capital on which traders draw.

HISTORICAL TRADE

Creation of a huge food-deficit population which has become dependent on purchased food is a recent development in the Copperbelt, as are markets themselves; there is no record of places for regular and frequent exchange prior to firm establishment of European rule.

Lacerda in 1798 described commerce of the area adjacent to the Copperbelt on the east, but he does not speak of market places (Burton 1873 : 129. A little over a decade later, Baptista traveled within what is now the Copperbelt (Burton 1873 : 222) and mentioned that people there dug copper; but the narrative does not refer to market places.

In 1831 Monteiro visited Cazembe, one of the kingdoms adjacent to the Copperbelt, but his discussions of trade focus on external traders and do not mention market places (Portugal 1937 : 316). Cameron passed through the area immediately to the northwest of the Copperbelt and at one point reckoned he was no more than fifty miles from copper mines, but he makes no hint of market places (Cameron 1877). Presumably he would have commented on them had they been encountered, for he had recently found very large and colorful markets some 400 miles north, at Nyangwe.[4]

About a decade later, Arnot, in an account of his first two years of mission work (1886–1888) in the northern Copperbelt, discusses trade without reference to market places (Arnot 1889 : 231–236). Neither Crawford in 1890, Molony, nor Capello and Ivens mention them (Crawford 1912 : X–XVII; Moloney 1893 : Ch. X; and Capello and Ivens 1866 : Ch. XX and XXI).[5] The memory of the Rev. John M. Springer, who visited the area in 1907, and the accounts given by two elderly Africans confirm what the records of travelers suggest.

(4) Cameron (1877 : 5–6) and Livingstone (in Waller 1874 : 112–126) describe Nyangwe market colorfully and in some detail.

(5) Two years before Arnot, the Copperbelt was visited by Paul Reichard, but this report was not available to me.

There was trade, however. In addition to slaves, ivory, and items exchanged for them (principally sea shells, beads, cloth, fire arms, and copper), trade involved salt, iron and iron goods, goats and goat skins, honey, beeswax, and perhaps other items.

Baptista, talking of an area between the Lualaba and Cazembe, which seems certainly to have included the northern portion of the Copperbelt, commented in 1810:

> There is nothing they can make use of for dress; men clothe themselves in Mussamba basts, and women buy strawcloth from the people before named [Pumbo] in exchange for salt; that is, in the dry season. In the rainy season when the salt traders do not come, they are put to great straits, and the traders cannot obtain the salt at such times, the river-plain itself being flooded. In order to get the salt they cut the straw and burn it; after which they dissolve the ashes in water, and throw the lye into small pans which they make; they boil it, and this they exchange for what they consider wealth, namely, woolen cloth, Indian tissues, beads, and strawcloths. The smiths (Ferreiros) also exchange their bars for flour and other provisions that are valued. (Burton 1873 : 223)

Traders came not only from neighboring African kingdoms, but from both the East and West African coasts and from some 800 miles to the north and possibly from as far south.

When Cameron in 1875 passed through the area ruled by the notorious Mshiri, which included most of the Copperbelt, he noted what he was told about the organization of trade:

> Mshiri has collected around him large number of Wanyamwesi and malcontents from amongst the lower order of traders from the East Coast, and obtains supplies of powder and guns by trading both to Benguella and Unyanyembe.
>
> Caravans commanded by half-caste Portuguese and slaves of Portuguese traders have visited him for over twenty years and furnish numerous recruits to his ranks. Ivory being scarce, his principal trade is in slaves and copper. The latter is procured on the spot from the mines at Katanga; but for slaves he has to send far and wide ... His trade with Bihe and the West Coast is rapidly increasing. (Cameron 1877 : 140–141)

Just over a decade later (1886–1888), Arnot described in some detail the origins of traders he found frequenting Mshiri's headquarters:

> At Msidi's [or Mshiri's] capital I have met with native traders from Uganda; the Unyamwesi country; the Ungala, to the east of Lake Tanganyika; the Luba country almost as far down as the Stanley Falls [now Stanleyville]; the basin of the Zambesi; Zumbu; Bihe, and Angola, as well as Arab traders from Lake Nyasa and Zanzibar [At another juncture he also mentions Portuguese traders]. Copper, salt, ivory, and slaves are the chief articles of commerce. In exchange for these Msidi purchases

flint-lock guns, powder, cloth, and beads, besides many other curious things these native and Arab traders bring. (Arnot 1889 : 235)

Although it is not clearly stated by either of these writers, inter-tribal trade appears to have been of considerable significance. Informants say so, and it is what one would expect a priori, for the Copperbelt peoples were relatively rich in iron, copper, salt, beeswax, and rubber, but seem to have been relatively short of such things as materials for body and bed coverings, domestic animals, and various foodstuffs; conditions could have hardly been more favorable for exchange.

The most complete account I have been able to obtain is from the Lamba, who seem to have been the major tribe in what is now the Copperbelt during the last of the 19th century. Slaves, ivory, and sometimes iron implements were exchanged for guns, gunpowder, beads, sea shells, and cotton cloth with Mbunda, Swahili, and Chikunda (Thompson 1893 : 112 and Doke 1931 : 79), who, in turn, traded them to Portuguese and Arabs.[6]

The Mbunda, at least, also bought beeswax and wild rubber collected by the Lamba. Salt was bought from the Yeke with bark cloth and iron implements. And at one time or another during times of food shortage, foodstuffs seem to have been purchased from, or sold to, nearly every neighboring tribe. Whether the Lamba bought or sold was determined by the size of Lamba supplies relative to those of adjacent peoples.

Guns (muzzle-loaders) and gunpowder were desired not only for defense and conquest, but for killing elephants and other game, for which purpose they were considered vastly superior to traditional techniques.

At least two types of beads were brought by the slave traders: one was about two inches, and the other some two-thirds of an inch, in diameter (Doke 1931 : 79). Sea shells of roughly corresponding diameters were also traded. The large one, called *impande* in the vernacular, was a conical, white shell from the Indian ocean which came in varying sizes—a popular one was two inches in diameter at the base. It was the base, separated from the vertex by filing, which was traded. Lamba wore them, usually singly, on the side of the head, on the forehead, around the bicep, or suspended around the neck. They could be worn only by those with rank or wealth. The *impande* was often given as a gift at the conclusion of a bargain by the slave trader—as something extra to close the deal or to create good will.

(6) Some of the Swahili traders may have been mere agents for Arabs, but others—and all of the Chikunda and Mbunda—seem to have been independent middlemen.

Cowries were also brought by the slave traders. The Lamba made them into necklaces and sometimes used them to pay fines arising out of disputes. They seem not to have been generally used as a medium of exchange, however.

Calico was greatly demanded because it was stronger and more durable than the bark cloth upon which the Lamba had traditionally relied.

Salt could be obtained locally by burning certain grasses, but this process was laborious and yielded a product inferior to earthen salt which could be, and was, imported from the Yeke and Kaonde (Doke 1931 : 79).[7]

The Lamba say they were not venturesome and typically waited for caravans or smaller parties to visit them; but they did take the initiative at times, particularly when they were short of food. When a group of traders arrived, they usually went directly to the chief for his permission to trade, possibly for lodging, and for trade itself, since he was usually the most important Lamba trader of the area, if for no other reason than that he got half the yield of elephant tusks from his area and controlled the sale of slaves. His compound was the focal point for trade between visiting foreigners and local commoners; although trade could take place at other locations, visiting traders commonly seem to have resided in the chief's village and waited there for those interested in trading.

Usually both partners to a transaction gave the chief a "present" for the privilege of trading. The chief, in turn, distributed among his people much of what he acquired, directly or indirectly: a chief was expected to be generous.

Trade was by barter, with cloth serving as the standard of value, but not always as a medium of exchange; that is, price is said to have always been stated in terms of units of cloth although payment was not necessarily made in cloth. Cloth was easy to measure and could readily be divided into extremely small units, if bargaining dictated. And, the units commonly used—finger tip to elbow; to shoulder, to chest, to opposite shoulder, etc.—were easily visualized and did not give a visiting trader much latitude for cheating. Moreover, cloth was one of the major items of trade, if not the most common one.

Prices varied considerably according to skill in bargaining, among other things; it is impossible to establish what were typical rates of exchange, as several informants were quick to point out.

I have not discussed historical trade with a large enough number

(7) Doke mentions only the Congo Lambas and the Kaonde as suppliers of earthen salt; but my informants, both Lamba and Yeke, mention the Yeke as a source.

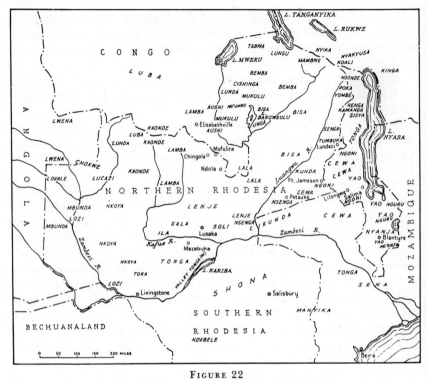

FIGURE 22
Location of the Major Tribes Trading in the Copperbelt[a]

(a) After Mitchell, 1957. Tribal boundaries are those found and fixed by the European Administration; they are roughly the boundaries of the post-1895 period.

of elderly Yeke or Swahili, the other major tribes that appear to have resided in the Copperbelt in the latter part of the last century, to be confident that the information thus far obtained is reasonably complete or accurate; but material in hand suggests that they too imported food in times of hunger (exchanging slaves for grain). In addition, the Yeke stress that they sold salt far and wide, and remember trading salt with the Luba, Bemba, and Lamba especially (see Map 22 for location of tribes). The first two, but not the latter, also remember exporting copper. Besides their slave, gun, and ivory trade, the Swahili tell of buying salt from the Bemba and cattle from the Lenje.

The Influence of European Colonization on Patterns of Trade.

Firm establishment of European rule at the beginning of the present century profoundly altered traditional patterns of trade. Most obvious was suppression of the slave trade, but indirect effects were of equal significance. European hunter-traders began to tour the country, living off the land and trading such items as hoes, salt, blankets, cloth, beads, other ornaments, and meat of the game they shot. For these they got grain, other foodstuffs, and, when they could be found, elephant tusks, cattle, and hides.

African traders could not withstand the competition. Europeans supplied, at reasonable terms, the *mainstays* of *traditional commerce,* or a substitute (and often one of superior quality). The African trader who formerly had made long expeditions on foot to buy hoes, salt, etc. not available at home, was nearly extinct by the time European settlers, administrators, and missionaries came in numbers.[8] It is not surprising that the reports most of them sent the world of this new land they were civilizing give no hint of Africans having a mercantile bent.

During the first decade of the twentieth century, with the first serious European efforts at mining (Union Minière 1956 : 80 and Bradley 1952 : 53 and 72), foodstuffs were badly needed to feed the miners. Problems of supply seem to have been left largely to European traders who may have introduced the use of market places. Five of my informants remember that these traders tried to keep to a schedule, that each village they visited was told approximately when the trader or his African representative would visit it, in an effort to be sure to find people assembled and prepared to trade. Alternatively, days were fixed for Africans to bring their produce to mining centers. If these accounts are true, and these practices were widespread, they suggest the first use of market places in the Copperbelt.

However that may be, it was not long before the Administration decided market places would facilitate commerce, and decreed their establishment in many areas.

(8) There is a fragment of evidence which suggests that Africans were quick to recognize the mining areas as a market. In 1908, an administrative officer stationed about 150 miles south of Ndola commented in his annual report: "Tobacco is also cured in the valleys and a considerable trade is carried on the natives taking their tobacco to the mines and to where they can find a market at some of the native stores. Fishing is carried on along the principal rivers by means of drag nets and weirs, the "catch" being generally dried and cured and then taken to barter with the Mine Natives ("Annual Report for the Year Ending 21st March, 1908, Mukushi Sub-District," Unpublished Manuscript, Central African Archives, Salisbury).

If trade of this sort was general, it would, of course, have offset some of the loss of traditional trade; however, it would have been restricted to items such as fish, meat, wild greens for relish, and tobacco: starchy-staple foods and some meat were provided in rations given by employers. It is very unlikely that such could have been of enough consequence to compensate for the loss of the salt, ivory, iron goods, cloth, and slave trade.

CURRENT MARKETING

The Market Place.

Market places vary greatly in size and shape. Some accommodate fewer than 50 sellers, others as many as 2000. All are "open air" for many sellers—sometimes most—sell without a roof over their heads (some Congolese provide their own umbrellas, often of a bright red hue), and their shelters are always without walls, though the bounds of the market place are often marked off by a fence, and sometimes a wall. Fish and meat sellers seem always to be provided with a roof, and in Northern Rhodesia, most of the other sellers, as well. In the Congo, only fish, meat, and sometimes charcoal, sellers have shelter.

All sellers pay a daily fee for use of the market; usually the charge is 3d or 6d or 2.5 Congolese francs, depending on the area.

Sellers tend to locate near others selling the same item. One finds a row of meal sellers, a cluster of vegetable vendors, the meat and fish sector, the charcoal area, etc. A number of vendors display three or four commodities, sometimes more; others have only one or two.[9] In general, the number of items a vendor sells seems to vary inversely with the volume of sales. Sellers of things for which there is a steady stream of customers—e.g., meat, fish, poultry, starchy-staples and their derivatives, pulses, sugar cane, or tobacco—usually specialize in only one or two items. Those with wild greens, vegetables, condiments, and the like often deal in small quantities of several items.

A few sellers use scales, but despite efforts by both governments, selling by weight has been strongly resisted. Each seller arranges his wares in small heaps before him, or in one large heap, with a spoon, tin cup, bowl, or something similar for measuring, if the commodity lends itself to scooping.

Usually the price can be ascertained only by query, although in the Congo, a few vendors, especially those with scales, have prices displayed on a scrap of paper or a piece of slate. There is little haggling over the price quoted, but actual prices sometimes can be altered through bargaining over quantity.

Most sellers strive to divide their merchandise into units worth the lowest common monetary unit (three pence in Northern Rhodesia, one franc in the Congo).[10] With fluctuations in supply or demand, or

(9) In a survey of 473 Rhodesian Copperbelt vendors in September and December 1959, described on the following pages, 63 per cent of the marketeers displayed only one item; 20 per cent had two; and 17 had three or more.

(10) Storekeepers say African consumers prefer to buy small quantities rather than to store foodstuffs. In Northern Rhodesia, for example, they sell sugar, salt, oil, fish, kerosene and most other items in three-penny lots.

both, stated prices tend to remain fixed, but the size of the measure or heap is varied. One reason for this is that the quantity sold in African markets is, for many commodities, so large relative to the smallest monetary unit that price changes dictated by economic conditions, or bargaining, often can be achieved only through altering the quantity offered. (For fish and meat, commodities for which the quantity sold is comparatively small relative to the amount of money demanded, price adjustment in the Copperbelt tends to be through a change in the amount of money demanded for fixed quantity). A second reason probably is that sellers can more easily conceal price changes if the adjustment is through quantity.

Besides direct adjustment of the unit of measure (by changing the tin used in measuring the size of the heaps displayed) the quantities offered can also be altered through varying the amount of *basela* (*matabish* in the Congo), an extra amount given by the seller at the end of a transaction. The primary function of *basela* seems to be to provide scope for bargaining, or to make possible a hidden price reduction in situations where an overt price reduction would risk retaliatory action by one's competitors. Whether it is given, and its size, depends on one's skill in bargaining, the commodity,[11] conditions of supply and demand, the kind of competition one faces, and whether the buyer is known or liked.

There is ample scope here for misinterpretation of economic behavior by the casual observer: the apparent price offered may be fixed while the actual offer varies because of changes in the unit of measure. Even the actual price offered may seem not to respond to changes in conditions of supply or demand; but the price ultimately given, as distinct from the one offered (that is, the one after allowance is made for *basela*), usually does.

Competition in Marketing.

Selling is characterized by both pure monopoly and pure competition, and by almost all of the species of competition that lie between these two extremes. In Northern Rhodesia, maize, millets, sorghums, grain meals, salt, sugar, coffee, and tea (and possibly a few other items) cannot legally be sold in most market places or hawked by Africans. For the grains and grain products, such prohibitions enforce a statutory government marketing monopoly which appears to have been designed to disguise a subsidy to European farmers. Restriction of the sale of other products is designed to protect storekeepers who

(11) For commodities for which the size of the smallest natural unit is large relative to price—tomatoes, eggs, or onions—*basela* is usually not given because it is not possible to obtain a small fraction—say approximately less than a third—of the unit sold.

commonly assert that without limiting competition, some of them
would go bankrupt. The officials say they must cater to the demands
of the store owners because they pay a disproportionately large share
of municipal taxes. There appear to be no official restrictions in the
Congo sector, but the development of cartels is permitted, if not
encouraged.

Many commodities found in market places are sold competitively
often approaching the classical pure competition with many sellers,
no one of whom can affect price through his activities alone. But the
degree of competition varies considerably with the commodity; for
fruit, condiments, and sugar cane, for example, there are often only
a few sellers and collusion is relatively easy. Attempts to corner the
market for some commodities are not unknown (I saw the sugar
cane market cornered for a day in one Elisabethville area). At Ndola,
an association of African charcoal producers seems to exist mainly
for price regulation and restriction of competition.[12] An African
hawkers association near Kitwe appears to have a similar *raison d'être*.

Markets appear to present no barriers to entry, other than the
official limitations of commodities that can be sold, and the small
market fees which have already been mentioned; and evidence suggests that for most commodities the number of sellers fluctuated
widely (see Figure 23).

Markets are held daily on the Congo side, but in Northern
Rhodesia they usually close one or two days a week. In Ndola, markets
close Wednesday afternoon and all day Sunday. (The half-day on
Wednesday is possibly in imitation of European merchants, most of
whom close on Wednesday at noon.) But in some areas only Sunday
is a day of rest.

Market activity fluctuates within the year, month, week, and day.
As Rhodesian data illustrate (Figure 23), they are most active towards
the end of the dry season when supplies are plentiful and farm labor
light, least active near the end of rains when fields must be prepared
and crops planted.

During the dry season, following harvest, there are few agricultural
tasks to be done and many farmers try their hand at marketing. A
seasonal abundance of produce strengthens this movement; from
July to November not only is there the new harvest in, but fish—
probably the most important commodity marketed, quantitatively
and in terms of the number of sellers—are the most plentiful.

Within the month it is buyers who account for the major fluctu-

_____

(12) One of their recent activities, I am told, is to plead with the Government for the
elimination of European competition on the grounds that Africans do not have, and
cannot easily get, enough capital to compete with whites.

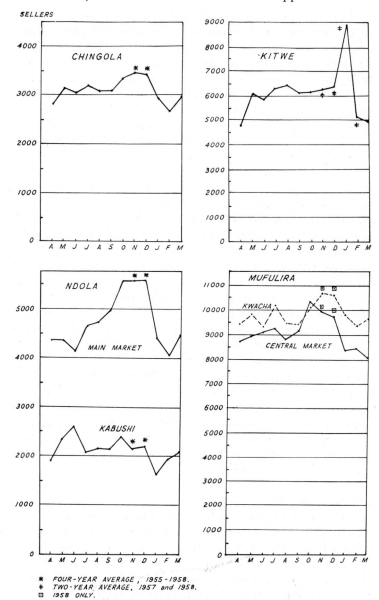

FIGURE 23
*Average Seasonal Variation in the Number of Sellers
in Selected Rhodesian Copperbelt Markets*[a]

(a) Data are from the municipal administrations of the towns represented and are the recorded number of sellers paying market fees; hence, they should be accurate and complete. The length of the average is as follows (in years): Nodla and Chingola, 5; Kitwe, 3; and Mufulira, 2.

ations. The greatest number are found towards the month's end, reportedly because this is when monthly wages are paid. The end of the week, too, is a time of notably increased activity, as consumers buy for weekend entertaining and feasting (and in parts of Northern Rhodesia, at least, to tide them over Sunday, when markets are closed). Monday, too, is a day of greater than average attendance: people are possibly replenishing stocks depleted over the weekend.

Within the day, fluctuations are less marked in the Rhodesian portion of the Copperbelt than in the Congo. Selling begins as early as 7:00 A.M., and there is a notable mid-morning peak, after which activity gradually diminishes until about 5:00 P.M. or so when the market closes. There are no sudden changes in the pace of selling during hours when marketing is allowed.

Fluctuations are more pronounced in the Congo. There selling begins about an hour earlier with a few individuals; activity gradually increases as the main body of sellers arrive, and the market often is in full swing by 8:00 A.M. About 11:00 A.M., activity begins to diminish as both buyers and sellers go home to prepare, or eat, midday meals. By noon, only fish and meat sellers, and a handful of people with manufactured goods and specialities remain, and the cleaning crew has already begun to dispose of rubbish left behind by departed vendors. In the early afternoon a number of sellers return, but the morning peak is never again reached.

Explanation of this contrast between Northern Rhodesia and the Congo seems to lie partly in the character of the vendors. Congo market sellers appear more frequently to be housewives who buy from a wholesaler and combine a morning's shopping with an attempt to do some selling. Northern Rhodesian vendors seem more typically to be people who rely on market sales as a major source of income. But there are important geographical variations.

Extra-marketplace sales.

Near most market places—often adjacent to them—are establishments selling alcoholic beverages (bars in the Congo; much larger and less elegant beer halls in Northern Rhodesia), tea rooms (Northern Rhodesia) or coffee bars, and stores. In the Congo, especially, one frequently sees goods displayed in front of homes, and the front rooms of many houses seem to serve as shops. In the Congo one also frequently sees individuals—mainly women—sitting under a tree near a road or a place of employment with food for sale. This is rarely permitted in Northern Rhodesia. Hawkers are to be found in most communities in both countries, but what they are allowed to sell varies with the municipality, in Northern Rhodesia, at least. Some towns restrict their wares to manufactured goods; in other areas, hawking foodstuffs is considered a useful service and is encouraged.

Characteristics of Rhodesian Copperbelt Vendors.

The only quantitative data available on Copperbelt traders as individuals is part of a survey I made of selected Northern Rhodesian and Nyasaland markets in the last half of 1959. A pilot survey of 12 per cent of the sellers in the Main and Kabushi markets of Ndola was made in September. It was followed in December by an approximately 25 per cent sample of those same markets, and a 100 per cent sample from the following: the small Ndola vegetable market (comprised mainly of African vendors and European or Asian buyers); the two African markets in Chingola, and Chingola's vegetable market; plus one of the two African markets in Mufulira, and Mufulira's vegetable market. Markets chosen were selected because of their location (to get a wide geographical sample), and because preliminary investigation showed them to be the principal markets referred to by traders in the hinterland in discussions of their activities in the Copperbelt. They also represented divergent municipal policies regarding market regulations, especially those which limit competition.

In total, 473 vendors (probably something like one-third of the total sellers in the Rhodesian Copperbelt) were surveyed by two African assistants, using a questionnaire which asked for the vendor's tribe, age, sex, level of education, marital status, previous occupation, and previous experience as a market vendor; a list was made of the commodities currently being sold and the price at which they were offered; vendors were also asked where they had obtained their commodities, how they had been transported thence to the market place, and the amount of time spent in obtaining, transporting, and selling the commodities; additional questions covered supplementary sources of income, the reasons for selling in the market, and the number and relationship of assistants. Most of the vendors were either completely coöperative or refused to give any information at all. Only in the Main market, Ndola, and the Central market, Mufulira (the one not surveyed) was there general resistance, and it was for this reason that the survey was discontinued in those markets before a 100 per cent sample was taken. I doubt that there was much deliberate falsification of information; most vendors seem simply to refuse to answer questions if they prefer not to reveal the truth.[13] Neither

(13) I am told by an officer in the Central African Statistical Office, Salisbury, that this is also characteristic of Africans interviewed in social and agricultural surveys in Southern Rhodesia.

names nor addresses of informants were taken, in an effort to encourage coöperation and discourage distortion.

A little over half of the sellers (59 per cent) were male; almost
three-fourths (71 per cent) were married; and the typical seller was
fairly young, about 40 per cent being under 30 (but I suspect many
can give their age accurately only within five years). Nearly three-

TABLE 81

Estimated Tribal Size and Per Cent of Surveyed Rhodesian Copperbelt
Vendors Belonging to Each Tribe[a]

Tribe	Per Cent of Sellers in Markets Surveyed	Tribal Size (Thousands)	Tribe	Per Cent of Sellers in Markets Surveyed	Tribal Size (Thousands)
Bemba	24.6	144.4	Ngoni	1.1	66.5
Lamba	11.0	35.1	Lungu	1.1	38.0
Bisa	9.4	50.8	Lenje	0.8	42.7
Aushi	7.8	43.2	Henga	0.6	d
Cisinga	4.6	28.7	Kaonde	0.6	42.3
Lovale	4.4	40.0	Shona	0.6	d
"Kasai"[b]	3.6	d	Lozi	0.6	54.6
Mukulu	3.2	20.8	Ngonde	0.4	d
Lunda	3.0	122.1	Chewa	0.4	127.8
Lala	2.5	55.9	Soli	0.4	19.2
Tumbuka	2.7	25.3	Kawendi	0.4	9.3
Nsenga	2.3	73.6	Nyika	0.2	d
Tabwa	1.7	15.3	Sukuma	0.2	d
Nyanja	1.7	d	Ila	0.2	17.7
Tonga[c]	1.7	166.4[e]			
Chokwe	1.5	11.3			
Ng'umbo	1.3	28.0			
Unga	1.3	9.2			
Mambwe	1.3	21.4			
Lucazi	1.3	21.4			

(a) Tribal sizes are from Brelsford 1956 : pp. 124–125, and are for 1953; they are based
on administrative reports, and probably are only rough estimates. For tribes which
extend into other countries—mainly the Chokwe, Bemba, Lamba, Lunda, Kaonde,
Tumbuka, Nsenga, Ngoni, and Chewa, of the tribes listed above—they refer only to the
portion of the tribe in Northern Rhodesia. See Map 22 for location of tribes.

(b) People from Kasai province, Congo, call themselves, and are known as, "Bakasai"
(people of the Kasai); the majority are probably Luba.

(c) The Plateau Tonga of Northern Rhodesia, most of whom trade seasonally (see
following pages). Had the bulk of the survey been done in the dry season, rather than
at the beginning of the rains, they would have been considerably better represented.

(d) No data available at the time of writing.

(e) Includes the Valley Tonga.

quarters had no education, but 18 per cent reported three or more years of school.

Thirty-four tribes were represented, and only five accounted for five per cent or more of the sellers; the majority (75 per cent) were from tribes located in that part of Northern Rhodesia lying to the north and east or due west of the Copperbelt; eight per cent came from Northern Rhodesia to the south, four per cent came from the Congo, and two per cent were from Nyasaland.

Only 28 of Northern Rhodesia's eighty-odd tribes were encountered; some of the larger tribes—the Tonga, Chewa, Ngoni, Lozi, and Senga, for instance—were very infrequently represented.

Many tribes are said not to participate actively in trade because of tradition or lack of enterprise. Substantial support cannot be marshalled for this position as regards Northern Rhodesia. The evidence definitely indicates that the Plateau Tonga, Soli, Chikunda, Nsenga, Chewa, Senga, and Lozi—all fairly large tribes and all poorly represented in Copperbelt markets—have a strong trading tradition. And there is nothing to suggest that they are notably lacking in enterprise. I suspect careful research would reveal the same to be true for the bulk of the remaining Northern Rhodesian tribes.

The answer to the riddle of the disproportionate tribal distribution among the Copperbelt vendors surveyed seems to lie more in economic alternatives. The Rhodesian tribes northeast and due west of the Copperbelt (which together account for three-fourths of the vendors interviewed), have a relatively unfavorable environment for agriculture and the little physical yield that can be obtained with present techniques is further reduced when translated into economic yield (that is, money value) because of the high transport costs that must be deducted from the price received when the commodity is marketed. The Bemba and most of their neighbors find agriculture relatively unattractive; and trading enterprise or working in the mines is the major option. Surveys of the origin of Rhodesian Copperbelt labor since 1940 have consistently shown the dominance of the portion of Northern Rhodesia northeast and due west of the Copperbelt (according to Mitchell 1956 : 112, these two regions accounted for the following proportions of Rhodesian Copperbelt mining labor: August, 1940, 61.2; December, 1944, 58.4; December, 1949, 53.9; and December, 1954, 52.6 per cent).

In our market survey, seven per cent of the vendors reported mining as a previous occupation; another 40 per cent were women, most of whom were wives of laborers of the same tribe.

TRADING AS A PROFESSION

Most African vendors do not consider the question "Why have you selected your occupation?" worth the asking; they assume it is as obvious to others as it is to themselves that there is no alternative way of earning a comparable income. But since the quest for leisure and the desire to gossip have been stressed in some of the scant literature on Central African markets, the question is worth examining.

Both Nyirenda (1957) and Brelsford (1947) slight the question of income, and the latter takes an extreme position:

> It is not undesirable for an African to make money, but the danger lies in the second fascination of marketeering, for added to the financial reward is the attraction of a leisurely way of life. The man is his own master; he does not have to follow the grind of monotonous labour; and chatting and gossiping in between sales is a way of life that has compensations even in cases where the cash receipts are not as big as from labor. In a great many cases this desire for the leisurely life has developed into loafing, paid loafing, for there are a few shillings profit to be made . . . Such profits are not deserved, and they are earned by a lazy man or unemployed worker at the expense of the consumer . . . I think we have reached the stage when marketing and trading generally should be a full-time job for an efficient man, and not an easy way of earning a few pounds by rooking the consumer . . . I shall have more to say about the reduction in the number of marketers. (Brelsford 1945 : 34–35. In a later section he recommends that the number of marketers be cut roughly in half.)

Brelsford seems to be laboring under the false assumption, not uncommon among British colonial administrators, that middlemen are nothing more than parasites who exploit both producers and consumers. But if they did not provide a service demanded, as is evidenced by the fact that people are willing to pay for it, they could not earn enough to make their profession worthwile—consumers would seek out producers or vice versa, and the middleman would be circumvented. Only when selling or buying is not competitive—a situation fostered by administrative orders limiting the number of middlemen —can there be consumer exploitation.

As for the hypothesized laziness of market vendors, our survey suggests that greater rewards for effort was the magnet rather than less work for the same reward.

Approximately 40 per cent of the traders surveyed (the women), because of their illiteracy and unfamiliarity with spoken English, had no other way of earning income, except possibly prostitution. Less than one per cent of the women vendors surveyed had previously been employed.[14]

The reasons given by vendors for selling in the market also gives some indication of motivation. Only one per cent (mostly women) reported non-economic motives, such as boredom, loneliness, etc.; 31 per cent expressly stated they were dependent on trade for their livelihood; 7 per cent said they were trying to accumulate capital to start another business; 4 per cent (nearly all women) were trying to earn money for new clothes; another 4 per cent were working to defray the expenses of schooling for a relative; 3 per cent said they were trying to supplement the family income; 1 per cent reported they were in quest of a little pocket money; and nearly half (49 per cent) gave no reason (most of these seemed to be professional traders and thought it was a silly question).

Professional and Non-Professional Traders.

There appears to be a distinct dichotomy between professionals and people with a specific goal or target for which they are trying to accumulate money. Professionals, defined as people regularly in the market, can be further divided into relatively large scale operators, most of whom are men trading fish, and housewives who ply their trade fairly continuously but on a much smaller scale.

It was not possible to determine accurately market attendance; a majority of vendors were so vague on this point that their answers could not be trusted. Another indicator, the number of years of market experience, is somewhat more reliable, although many may not have reported all of their earlier experience. Almost a third (29 per cent) claimed to be new at selling in the market. At the other extreme, a fifth reported over five years of experience, and probably most of another 14 per cent, the "no information" category, should

[14] About 40 per cent of the men had tried employment.

Previous Employment Reported	Per Cent of Men Surveyed	Previous Employment Reported	Per Cent of Men Surveyed
None	42	Servant	5
Mining	12	Professional asst.[b]	4
Professional[a]	9	Other[c]	2
Laborer	8	No information	18
	71		29

[a] Teachers, tailors, policemen, clerks, storekeepers, carpenters, painters, bricklayers, and drivers.

[b] Sales assistants, medical orderly, veterinary assistant, survey assistant.

[c] Foreman; watchman; and paint, bus, and mail boys.

We were not able to get a satisfactory account of the reasons for leaving previous employment or the proportion of these who had held more than one job previously.

be grouped in the over five years interval, for it represents mainly people who had been selling several years, but could not remember how many.

TABLE 82
Experience of Market Vendors (Copperbelt)

Number of Years of Some Experience as a Market Vendor	Per Cent of Sellers	Number of Years of Some Experience as a Market Vendor	Per Cent of Sellers
One or less	29	Seven	2
Two	22	Eight	2
Three	9	Nine	2
Four	3	Ten	4
Five	3	Over ten	10
Six	0	No information	14
	66		34

Consumer Purchasing and Commodities Marketed.

Patterns of consumption in the Northern Rhodesia and the Congo sectors seem to be similar in terms of broad categories, but vary considerably in detail. For neither area do we have complete statistics; in fact, for Northern Rhodesia there are none sufficiently reliable to merit attention. Nevertheless, something can be inferred from data on agriculture and diet of Rhodesians and Congolese.

Engle's law leads us to expect societies at a relatively low level of consumption per capita to spend a large proportion of their disposable income on food and foodstuffs; and Copperbelt families undoubtedly do. According to two surveys of African families in Rhodesian Copperbelt towns (one of 55 families in 1953, and the other of 74 families in 1954), well over half of the monthly expenditure of most families was for food and foodstuffs, although there was considerable variation by income group. The range in the first survey was from 80 per cent for food among the lowest income group to 29 per cent for the highest (Nyirenda 1957 : 35) and in the second was from 63 per cent to 37 per cent (Richardson 1954 : Figure 10). M. K. Bennett finds in an analysis of the world's diets that the "starchy-staple ratio"—defined as the proportion of caloric intake represented by cereals, roots, and starchy fruits—is negatively correlated with per capita disposable income. He concludes that we can expect the starchy-staple ratio to fall—we can expect people to substitute relatively expensive calories for cheap ones (starches are generally the cheapest source of food energy)—as levels of living rise (Bennett 1954 : 213–227). We should accordingly expect relatively cheap sources of calo-

ries to loom large in the diet in the under-developed countries generally, and certainly in diets of Copperbelt Africans.

The cheapest calories in the Copperbelt, as in most, if not all, the
rest of tropical Africa, come from the starchy-staples. Of these, maize
seems usually the cheapest in the more humid areas of the Copperbelt
hinterland where soils are reasonably fertile; elsewhere it is commonly manioc, and occasionally millets-sorghum.

Quantitative data on consumption are not available for Northern
Rhodesia, but net imports to the Congo Copperbelt show starchy-
staples to be easily two or three times as important as all other categories (Figure 24), although the exact position is obscured by the
incompleteness and probable inaccuracy of production statistics. The
representation of commodities in market places is considerably different from that shown in Figure 24, because the two dominant starchy-
staples—maize and manioc—are marketed through Government stores.
In the market places, fish seem to rank first quantitatively, with
vegetables second, possibly followed by meat and poultry.[15]

Table 86 lists the major items observed in market places during the
dry season and the beginning of the rainy season, 1959, or reported
to be available at other times by sellers. Over one hundred major
items are listed, and in all probability the list is incomplete particularly as regards manufactured goods.

In one characteristic—the predominance of foods and foodstuffs—
Copperbelt markets are like their counterparts in small towns and
villages. But they differ in the greater diversity of products found,
which stems both from greater per capita purchasing power in the
Copperbelt and from the Copperbelt's greater ethnic diversity. A
large portion of its inhabitants are Bemba or Luba, but sizable numbers of the 200 odd tribes of Northern Rhodesia and what was the
southern Belgian Congo are to be found, and adjacent countries are
also well represented. Consequently, there is a demand for all the
foods and foodstuffs special to each tribe represented. Hinterland

---

(15) The following percentages were shown by the Rhodesian Copperbelt market
survey:

Commodity	Per Cent Selling	Commodity	Per Cent Selling
fish	40%	tobacco	5%
vegetables	39%	wild roots	4%
pulses	21%	insects	4%
charcoal	8%	poultry	3%
fruit	7%	condiments	1%

Total more than 100 because many vendors sold more than one article. Since there
is no measure of sales volume, the quantitative importance of each commodity cannot
be computed from these data unless one can assume each seller has roughly the same
turnover.

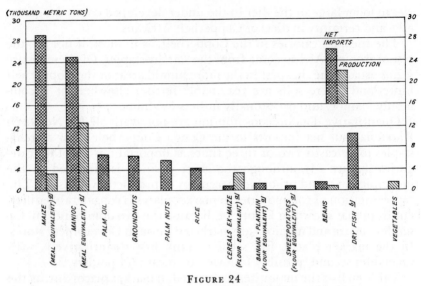

FIGURE 24

*Production and Net Imports of the Major Commodities
Marketed in the Belgian Congo Sector of the Copperbelt*a

(1) Data are from Affaires Economiques, Annual Reports, Katanga Province, various years. Production statistics are a 1957–1958 average of estimates for Kambove, Kipushi, and Sakania *territoires* aggregated. Except for fish, net imports are a five-year average of rail shipments (1954–1958). For fish, data are estimates of quantities sold in 1958 to wholesalers from the areas supplying the Copperbelt. All the import data are total imports and therefore include quantities destined for European and Asian consumption; these populations, however, are relatively small—not more than 10 per cent of total population —and their per capita consumption is insignificant for all these products, save wheat, rice, and vegetables.

(a) Ideally, all commodities should be reduced to a common unit for purposes of comparison. If satisfactory price data existed, one could use money values represented by the imports of each commodity. Lacking reasonably trustworthy prices, one must approach value indirectly. One adjustment should be made for water content, since water in foods is of very little, if any, nutritional value. Even the dry content of foods and foodstuffs is of varying worth, depending on the proportions of starch, fat, protein, vitamins, and minerals. No satisfactory index taking all of these into account has yet been devised, but adjusting for water content probably goes a long way towards reducing commodities to comparable units. For the major starchy-staples, a caloric index has been used to achieve this—that is, tonnages have been multiplied by:

$$\frac{\text{calories per unit of commodity}}{\text{calories per unit of maize}}$$

The following caloric count per 100 grams "as purchased," were used: maize, 360; manioc, 109; rice, 359; cereals, ex-maize, 345; banana-plantain, 75; and sweet potatoes, 97. Vegetables would require a complex index weighted by the importance of each of the several kinds of vegetables found.

(b) To convert fresh fish to dry basis, the Belgian conversion factor of 3.3 fresh units per dry unit was used.

markets, on the contrary, need only cater to the culinary needs of one or two tribes, at most.

Figure 24 compares production of the major commodities in the Congo sector with its net imports.[16] Production data are official estimates and may contain sizeable margins of error. However, unless they very grossly underestimate production, or their accuracy varies greatly from commodity to commodity, they illustrate the importance of regional imports compared with local production as well as the relative importance of the major commodities and commodity groups in commerce. Import data are considerably more reliable. Except for fish and vegetables, imports come from areas too distant to be economically tapped by road, hence the statistics used—amounts shipped by rail—should be a close approximation of trade.[17] These data are recorded shipments, and should be fairly precise.

Northern Rhodesian areas supplying the Copperbelt are, in the main, considerably closer to markets, and are served by hard surface, all-weather roads more frequently, by rail less. Most of the major zones of supply can be, and are, reached efficiently by truck as well as by rail; figures for rail shipments alone, therefore, are inadequate to portray total quantities. It is not possible to make even a rough guess of quantities moving by motor vehicle. (Tables 85 and 86 show the geographical origins of the principal commodities found in Copperbelt markets, based on the quantitative data available, and supplemented by qualitative information.)

In the Congo, only two major commodity groups—vegetables and fuel—are of predominantly local origin, but possibly a large proportion of cassava consumed should also be so classified (Figure 25). Fish come from areas as much as 150 miles away, but rarely farther. Wheat, rice, and beans mostly come from districts 150–200 miles distant. Most of the poultry and eggs travel at least 400 miles. Most maize, manioc, and their products, palm nuts and palm-nut oil, palm oil, groundnut oil, and tobacco, are transported 500 miles or more. More than half the palm oil and notable quantities of groundnut oil, coffee, rice, and maize were shipped as much as 800 miles to market.

In the Northern Rhodesian part of the Copperbelt, transport distances are roughly the same, save for maize, poultry, and eggs, most

(16) Actually production figures are for the three *territoires* which contain the Congo portion of the Copperbelt, an area somewhat larger than the Congo Copperbelt itself.

(17) For fish, the data used are quantities sold to wholesalers at the main river and lake points the Belgian fisheries officials believed to be supplying the Copperbelt. No reasonably trustworthy data are available for the quantity of vegetables marketed, most of which seem to come from areas within trucking distance of the markets.

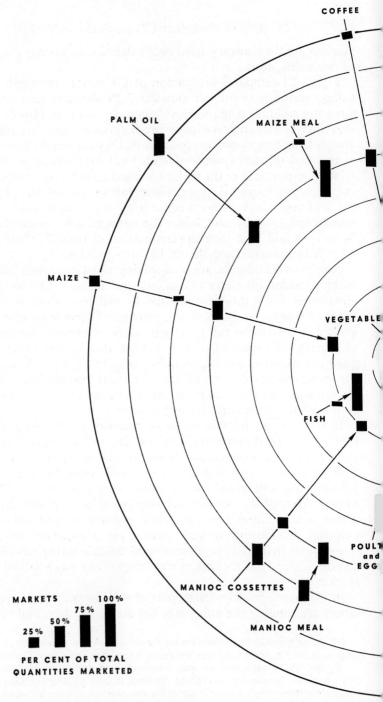

COFFEE

PALM OIL

MAIZE MEAL

MAIZE

VEGETABLE

FISH

POULT
and
EGG

MARKETS

25% 50% 75% 100%

PER CENT OF TOTAL
QUANTITIES MARKETED

MANIOC COSSETTES

MANIOC MEAL

FIGURE 25

Proportion of Major Imports to Congo Copperbelt from Principal Zones of Supply

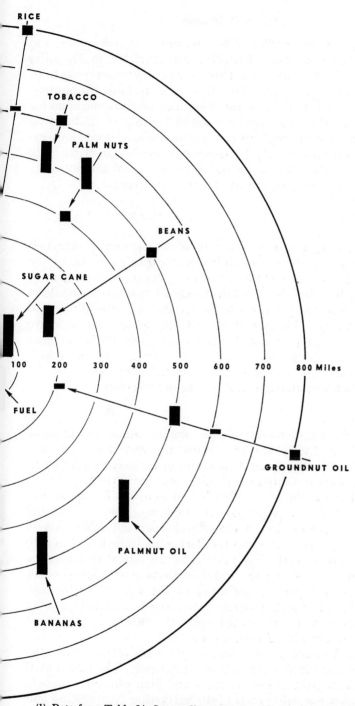

RICE

TOBACCO

PALM NUTS

BEANS

SUGAR CANE

100   200   300   400   500   600   700   800 Miles

FUEL

GROUNDNUT OIL

PALMNUT OIL

BANANAS

(1) Data from Table 84. Commodity percentage blocks are not necessarily placed in their true direction from markets. For indentification of the actual areas where commodities originate, and the exact percentage of total supplies, by commodity, coming from each supply zone, see Map 21 and Table 86.

of which come from areas 100 to 200 miles nearer the consumer; and
fish, rice, and palm oil, most of which must travel 100 to 300 miles
farther (see Table 88). Small quantities of rice and pulses come from
Southern Nyasaland, roughly 1800 rail miles away. Only for poultry,
palm oil, and some fish do both countries draw on the same areas for
supply; and generally there appears to be little prospect of obtaining
goods more cheaply through international trade. Conspicuous exceptions are maize and rice: the Congo could probably get maize more
cheaply from Northern Rhodesia and Rhodesia could get rice more
cheaply from the Congo were it not for import barriers.

THE ORGANIZATION OF TRADE

In general, there appear to be no connections between Copperbelt
markets and those in the hinterland: commodities go to one or the
other, but not first to one and then the other. An exception is poultry;
Congolese retailers often buy fowl in Rhodesian markets for resale in
Congo towns, presumably because Rhodesians are not allowed to
trade in the Congo. The result is that Rhodesians are unaware
of prevailing Congo prices and often offer their birds at retail
for less than the Congo wholesale price (minus transport costs).
Congolese wholesalers exploit such situations, when they arise, by
buying in the Rhodesian sector and selling in their own.

Starchy Staples.
In the Congo, the dominant starchy staples, maize and manioc,
are marketed by Europeans or Asians at every stage but the
last (see Table 83). Rural merchants, almost entirely non-Africans,
buy from producers and ship to the Union Minière in the Copperbelt
on contract. Thence, the commodity is sold to urban European and
Asian storekeepers (or, in years past, but no longer, issued to mining
families as part of their ration). Urban storekeepers sell either directly
to the consumer or to the African retailers, who, in turn, sell to consumers in African markets. That Africans can buy at retail, add a
margin, and still sell only a few hundred yards away appears to be
possible because shoppers do not mind paying a premium for convenience and because they get more courteous treatment in the market
than from European or Asian storekeepers, as a rule, and are allowed
more freedom in examining what is for sale.

In Northern Rhodesia, the starchy-staple is maize and little else,
and legal marketing is by a Government monopoly. The differential
between the price paid to the producer and final consumer price is
designed to cover operating costs of the marketing organization and

TABLE 83

Middlemen Involved in the Marketing of Selected Commodities Sold in the Copperbelt, 1959

Commodity	Area	Number of Middlemen Involved	Sequence of Sales	Predominant Ethnic Group of Middlemen
Maize	Congo	3–4	Producer, rural storekeeper, Union Minière, urban storekeeper, consumer or African retailer.	European
	Rhodesia	2	Producer, Government marketing monopoly, urban storekeeper, consumer.	European
Fish	Congo	3	Producer, European or African wholesaler, retailer, consumer.	Mixed; African & European
	Rhodesia	1–2	Producer, African collector, consumer or African retailer.	Mixed; many African tribes
Poultry	Congo	2	Producer, African collector, African retailer, consumer.	Luba
	Rhodesia	1–2	Producer, African collector, consumer or African retailer.	Plateau Tonga
Vegetables	Congo Rhodesia	0–1	Producer, consumer or African retailer.	Mixed; many African tribes
Fruit	Congo	1–2	Producer, African retailer, consumer. Or, producer, European wholesaler, European retailer, African retailer, consumer.	Luba / Mixed; African & European
	Rhodesia	3	Producer, European or Asian wholesaler, European retailer, African retailer, consumer.	Mixed: African & European

also to provide Governmental revenue to be used to improve African agriculture. (In 1959, maize grain was bought from African producers at $27^1/_2$ shillings per 200 pound bag, and maize meal was sold for 42 shillings per bag of the same weight). The Government sells maize meal to shopkeepers (principally European) in Copperbelt towns where it is retailed. Resale of maize in African markets is illegal, nor can beer made from maize, millet, or sorghum, be sold in the towns except in Government-regulated beer halls.

In actual fact, blackmarket transactions are common. African farmers sell to storekeepers, who usually pay for maize with manufactured goods.[18] Africans like to sell to storekeepers because they pay immedi-

[18] Occasionally, the merchant also gains because of imperfect knowledge among Africans. Especially at the beginning of the crop year when the price the Government is paying has not been known long, a considerable number of Africans seem to know less well than the merchants how the official price (quoted for units of 200 pounds) translates into the $33^1/_3$ pound measure typically used at the store in buying. Therefore, sometimes they accept goods worth less—valued at stated store prices—(or less money for that matter) than they could get for the same quantity of maize at the official buying station.

ately, as opposed to the Government, which accepts maize at its depots at any time within the official buying season (roughly July to October, with local variations), but pays only once a month or so. Storekeepers often exploit their bargaining position by purchasing maize only if the seller will accept merchandise for part of all of it. By so doing, the storekeeper reasons he increases his volume of sales. Beer and stronger drink is also made by the farmer and sold illegally.

Fish.

Congolese fish traders deal in fresh, dried, smoked, or salted fish. Only freshly dried and smoked fish are sold in Rhodesia. Whether a trader deals in fresh fish depends mainly on the capital at his disposal and his attitude towards bearing risk. Because fresh fish is perishable, it is left for traders with considerably more capital than the average—those with enough capital to buy extra equipment needed for cooling and for rapid transport.

If fresh fish are packed in ice and rushed to market by truck, losses are small; but any sort of truck breakdown in transit can cause almost total loss of the cargo. (Traders say that perhaps 10—at most 20—per cent of a large load can be cut open, cleaned, and dried or smoked before it spoils, in case of a breakdown.) The probability of a lengthy delay appears to be great. Most African traders can afford only well-worn second-hand vehicles.

In both the Congo and Northern Rhodesia, fish traders operating trucks often work in teams of three to five, which may include fishermen as well as the truck owner's assistants. Usually members of a team are related and are in the employ of the truck owner; frequently they are his younger brothers.[19]

(19) In my survey of Rhodesian vendors, 66 per cent of those who bought fish at the fisheries had no assistants; 23 per cent had one; 7 per cent had two; 3 per cent had three; and 1 per cent had over three. Of those who bought fish from Copperbelt wholesalers, 83 per cent had no assistants; 14 per cent had one; and 3 per cent had three.

The majority of assistants were related to the informant; the relationships were as follows (per cent of assistants):

Traders Who Frequented Fishheries	Non-Related	Spouse	Child	Parent	Brother	Cousin	Nephew	Uncle
	18	9	36	5	18	9	2	2
Traders buying from wholesalers	0	59a	0	6	29	0	6	0

(a) (Typically the wife sells while her husbands is on a trip to procure supplies.)

Just over half of the fish sellers (52 per cent) bought their wares from local wholesalers; only 12 per cent were fishermen. Thirty-three per cent used bus transport and 20 per cent employed a truck. Thirteen per cent (or 65 per cent of those using a truck) had hired the vehicle used; the remainder said they owned their own vehicle.

In the Lake Mweru area there are a few European fishermen (largely Greek) and about twice as many European fish buyers.

Europeans own over three-quarters of the trucks employed. Most of the European traders, like the non-African fishermen, are Greek. As a rule, they buy fish at the lake and sell in urban centers to European storekeepers catering to African trade and to African retailers selling in markets.

Fish trade in Area F1 (see Map 21) is entirely in the hands of Africans. Fishermen were estimated by the Department of Agriculture of Katanga to number some 3,000 in 1958, but no estimate of the number of middlemen is available. Like the Lake Mweru area, wholesalers usually have African retailers they supply regularly. Not infrequently they extend short-term credit to their customers.

TABLE 84

Fishermen and Buyers, Lake Mweru, 1958

	Fishermen	Trucks	Licenses to Buy Fish
European	29	62	57
African	2805	18	160
Total	2834	80	217

(Data from Brelsford 1945)

In September, 1959, the same prices prevailed in both Congo areas; they were those set forth in Table 85.

In Northern Rhodesia, the organization of commerce is roughly similar to that in Area F2, Map 21, for Lakes Mweru and Tanganyika: fish are typically bought in bulk at lakeside by African traders, trans-

TABLE 85

Sale Price of Fish (Copperbelt)

(Sales Price in Belgian Congo Francs per Kilogram)

Seller	Fresh fish	Dried and Salted	Smoked
Producer	4–5	9–10	13
Wholesaler	9–10	13–15	26–28
Retailer	15	20–25	40–60

(Data from personal communications from the Department of Agriculture, Province of Katanga, 1959).

ported to the Copperbelt by truck or bus, mainly the latter, and there sold to market retailers.

Around Lake Bangweulu according to Fryer (1958 : 486), bicycles are important in fish transport. He implies that a decade ago they were much more important, and an earlier study by Brelsford suggests they may formerly have been the primary means of transport (1945 : 110–116); but introduction of regular bus service in 1950 led to a decline in their use. They are probably of only very minor significance now; in fact, in the Rhodesian Copperbelt markets surveyed in December, 1959, Lake Bangweulu was the most common source of fish reported, but not one of the Bangweulu traders listed a bicycle as his means of transporting his commodity. (But it is possible some traders may have been using the bus only temporarily because of rain.)

According to Fryer's account of the Bangweulu fish trade in 1958, fish are sought in swamps which lie to the east of the lake, and there gutted, cleaned, dried or smoked, and packed into "large rectangular packages wrapped in dried reeds or perhaps even the paper from an old cement bag, the whole being in a light frame made from wooden twigs and reeds (Fryer 1958 : 483)." These bundles are reported usually to range in weight from 60 to 130 pounds. It is not clear how much of the processing is done after the fish are sold to the middleman, but it is certain that middlemen penetrate the swamps and transport the packages of dried fish by canoes to the bus depot—distances up to 80 miles (Brelsford 1945 Ch. VIII; Fryer 1958 : 483). At the mainland, fish are loaded on to buses (formerly bicycles) and carried to the Copperbelt. The description Fryer gives of cyclists he saw is perhaps worth repeating:

> Each bicycle usually carries two large bundles, one on the rear carrier and one in front of the handle bars. An ingenious wooden bracket made to serve as an accessory front carrier is often to be seen supporting the foremost bundle ... each bundle may weigh up to 70 or 80 lbs., and ... each is often surmounted by the cyclist's bedding, food, and cooking utensils ... (Fryer 1945 : 486)

On the Kafue river, besides the fairly large-scale traders with trucks (estimated to number at least 100 in Baxter 1958), there are a number of small traders whose only investment in equipment is a bicycle. At least 300 of these were thought to be operating in September, 1958 (Baxter 1958), buying dried and smoked fish, cycling them to the nearest railway station, and shipping them to the Copperbelt, where typically the trader retailed them in person. Most seem to be sporadic traders who make a few trips and then turn to something else. Many are farmers who trade fish only in the slack agricultural season.

In September, 1958, the following prices were reported in the Kafue area (Baxter 1958), price per pound of dry fish: at the Kafue River, 0.5d.; in the Rhodesian Copperbelt, 1.6d. to 1.9d.

In September, 1959, fresh fish cost about the same as in 1958 at the river, but sold for about a shilling per pound more in Rhodesian Copperbelt markets.[20]

There is a notable difference in buying between areas F1, F2, E, and the Kafue River (see Map 21 and Table 87). In area F2, buyers rarely, if ever, barter for fish, while in Area F1, E, and along the Kafue, barter is fairly common.

In the latter zones, fishermen are isolated and seem to prefer to have their necessities delivered if they can arrange it; hence, they often insist on barter as the mode of trade, exchanging fish for salt, matches, cigarettes, and other common items of daily use.

The conditions under which barter takes place are shown in Figure 26. Assuming the size of the catch to be constant, whether barter will take place, and, if so, the rate of exchange, is a function of the stock of imported commodities the fisherman has on hand.

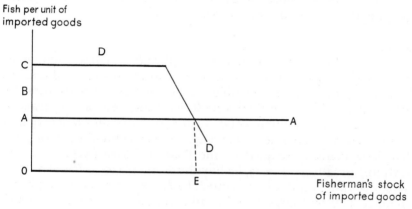

FIGURE 26

Conditions for Barter of Fish (Copperbelt)

On Figure 26, OA is the average price of the goods at store or village X (the nearest one that can provide what the fisherman needs); AB is average transport costs per item purchased from point X to the fisherman; and BC is an additional amount the fisherman is willing to pay per item purchased to avoid making the journey to point X. It might be called a convenience premium. Curve DD may be re-

(20) Area K (Map 21) is of slight importance as a supplier of fish for the Rhodesian portion of the Copperbelt, but unfortunately I have no information on how the trade is organized or the structure of prices.

garded as the fisherman's demand schedule, and shows the highest price he is willing to pay in fish for trader's goods; at rates of exchange above OC he will not barter at all, but will make a trip to the nearest store or village. OA is the minimum price the fish buyer will accept for the goods he has brought.

Providing the fisherman has OE or less of imported commodities on hand, there is scope for finding a mutually agreeable rate of exchange somewhere between OA and OC, through haggling. If the fisherman's stock of imported goods exceeds OE, the fish buyer will find there is no barter demand for his commodities at a price above OA, and that he must accept considerably less than anticipated, or buy fish with money—at rate OA. (I have heard of traders who brought goods to barter and had to wait two or three weeks to dispose of them at cost.)

I have no data on the actual magnitude of the preference premium (BC), except for the Kafue area. In September, 1959, both a penny sweet and a three-penny package of cigarettes would buy a six-pence size fish at several points on the Kafue River.

Poultry.

The Congolese poultry trade moves through channels similar to those used by the Congo fish trade; but in terms of the capital invested in equipment, it resembles the non-motorized portion of the Rhodesian fish trade on the Kafue River. Congolese poultry traders, nearly always Luba, often work in pairs; one stays in the Rhodesian Copperbelt and the other makes trips to the section of the Northern Rhodesia Plateau occupied by the Plateau Tonga (Area I); there, traveling usually by bicycle, he buys birds in villages, a few at a time. When working capital is exhausted, he crates the chickens, typically in units of 20, and ships them by rail to his partner (usually his wife) in the Rhodesian Copperbelt, who gets them through customs and sells them to a retailer, or possibly retails them directly in Congo markets. Alternatively, birds may be shipped to a Congolese wholesaler in the Rhodesian Copperbelt, who in turn sells them to Congolese retailers there.

In early September, 1959, prices were roughly as follows in Congolese francs per hen, European breed, of average quality: in the Plateau Tonga villages, 21–23; in the Rhodesian Copperbelt, 77; in the Rhodesian Copperbelt (retail), 91; in the Congo Copperbelt (retail), 130–140.

A few Rhodesian traders operate much like the Congolese, but the great majority trade sporadically, making a trip or two—perhaps several—in the slack agricultural season, then giving up the trade for farming as the time for plowing approaches.[21] But only a small minority seem to have partners or commercial contacts in the Copperbelt. Therefore, after getting their fowls on the freight train they must follow on the passenger train to receive them, and then personally sell them in some Copperbelt market, or to a wholesaler.[22]

For such ventures, Tonga not only draw on their kinsmen for capital (as do traders in every sort of Copperbelt trade), but also use income from maize farming, which they receive just before and during the period they are free from farming duties. (Maize is sold July to September, usually, and trading ventures are mostly August to November).

The motive for trading is usually to supplement one's income, and particularly to purchase something specific—a farming implement, a radio, or an article of dress, for example. Only a few of the Rhodesian regular traders appear to depend primarily on the income from such activity.

Charcoal.

Without data of quantities marketed, it is difficult to assess the economic importance of charcoal, but a number of local Government officials regard it as a major activity of Copperbelt traders. It certainly seems to be a form of commerce that has grown rapidly in recent years.

In the Rhodesian sector of the Copperbelt, probably almost no charcoal was sold as late as 1946 (Brelsford 1947 does not mention charcoal in his study of Copperbelt marketing in late 1945 and early 1946). In 1954, charcoal was mentioned for the first time in the annual report of the Northern Rhodesian Forestry Department, and the wording suggests that charcoal may have been a new development:

African town dwellers took to charcoal as their principal fuel. There seemed never enough to satisfy their demands... an average of 459 burners on the Copperbelt plied their trade throughout the year, many of them working in informal or tribal cooperatives under the guidance of a sort of headman (p. 8).

In each of the next three years, the report carries a statement to the effect that charcoal use was increasing, but no quantitative evidence is given, and it is possible—and from the similarity of the

(21) A few chickens are transported in trucks by fresh-fish traders who have failed to get a full load of fish; but this trade appears to be small compared with quantities sent by rail by either the Tonga or the Congolese.

(22) Egg marketing appears to be identical in organization to poultry marketing, both among Congolese and Rhodesians; it is, in fact, a part of it, although a small part. Traders complain about breakage spoilage, and the lack of demand, and comparatively few bother with such an unprofitable and uncertain commodity.

phrasing, likely—that each of these statements simply repeats the 1954 evidence without further investigation. By 1959, however, charcoal was a conspicuous item in markets on both the Rhodesian and Congo sides.

Few middlemen participate in the trade; the market vendor typically is also the producer. Production, on the other hand, is relatively well organized, with most producers belonging to more or less informal association. Probably most assume more managerial functions than the average vendor, for commonly an assistant or two is employed to cut wood and keep heaps smoldering while the owner of the business sells.

Vegetables.

Vegetables are the only major kind of commodity for which the organization of trade appears to be identical in the Congo and Northern Rhodesia. Some vegetables are sold directly by urban producers from their gardens or by producers living within cycling distance of towns (as far as 25 miles). Alternatively, retailers visit producers in the periphery of towns and buy directly. In Northern Rhodesia, at least, it is not uncommon for Africans to buy from European farmers as well as from Africans, and some of the former send their African employees to sell vegetables in the African market. Some retailers buy from urban wholesalers. In our survey of the Rhodesian Copperbelt, only 13 per cent of the sellers were also vegetable growers (see Table 89).

Pulses and Fruit.

In Congo, pulses and fruit typically seem to be ordered by mail from an acquaintance or a relative in the hinterland who sends the consignment by rail to the Copperbelt town specified, where it is received by the retailer who ordered it. Some also purchase from European storekeepers and resell in African market places.

In Northern Rhodesia, purchase from European retailers is common, as is buying directly from producers near towns. That Africans can buy fruit at retail, add a margin, and still sell in African markets appears to stem not only from reasons of convenience and the preference for dealing with Africans, already discussed, but also because ripe fruit is a handy snack, and a tempting one, even if one knows the same product can be obtained more cheaply at a store a few hundred yards distant. And of course, there are always neighboring vendors selling something else who buy because they cannot leave their wares.

If our survey of Rhodesian markets is fairly representative, probably none of the cultivated fruit is sold by producers, and not more than five per cent of the pulses. Almost half of the wild fruit, however, was sold by people who had collected it.

Tobacco.

Our Rhodesian survey indicated that tobacco is nearly always bought directly from the grower. Most of the vendors interviewed had made long trips initially by bus, then by bicycle to isolated valleys specializing in tobacco, to make their purchases.

Insects.

Caterpillars were the only insects in season during our survey, and 42 per cent of the vendors said they had collected and dried their produce. Some said they collect, but do not sell, caterpillars when they are abundant (the rainy season) because the price is low. They prefer to sell something else and hold their caterpillars until the price rises in the off season. Perhaps this practice is widespread; it certainly is possible, for when caterpillars are processed—squeezed, smoked, and dried—they will keep for several months.

In the Northern Rhodesian Copperbelt at the time of the survey, 57 per cent of the caterpillar sellers were Lovale and 31 per cent were from the tribes adjacent to them. Eighty-eight per cent procured their supplies from Area K.

African Crafts.

A very small but fascinating commerce in African crafts is conducted by a handful of Senegalese who sell to the Europeans of Elisabethville. The main market place for these traders is in the sidewalk in front of the Elisabethville post office, which they use from 5:00 to 8:30 P.M. daily.

Merchandise ranges from Moroccan leather goods to ivory and ebony carvings and grass baskets. Most of it comes from areas more than 3,500 air miles away, which is in all probability the longest trade distance conducted solely by Africans anywhere on the continent. Typically, wares are ordered and received by post, but occasionally a trip is made to the nearer sources of supply, such as the French Cameroons or Stanleyville, to replenish stock.

During the day these, and others whose countries of origin are somewhat nearer (Nigeria or Kenya, for example), hawk their wares on bicycle. In the evenings they display their goods on the sidewalk and wait for passing tourists or local residents downtown for an evening's entertainment.

Kinsmen and Business.

Often relatives are employed as assistants, more from necessity than choice: most traders are partly responsible for the support of younger brothers, nephews, and possibly other kinsmen who are less prosperous. In return, dependents are often put to work as assistants, sometimes with unfortunate results. A number of the more articulate traders have pointed out that assistants who are relatives are difficult to control and sometimes help themselves to stock or money as if it were their own. (Another observer confirms this for Lovale traders: see White 1959 : 42).

There is a further drain on profits by kinsmen not involved in the trade, which perhaps explains why Copperbelt African storekeepers seem, on the whole, more successful than their counterparts in the African reserves: in the Copperbelt a merchant is less accessible to most of his relatives. (The possibility of regularly supplementing the working capital needed for a store by mine employment or other jobs, is probably of equal importance).

But if affinal obligations hinder the African's economic success in commerce, at the same time they also make a vital contribution. The trader who must support a younger brother or nephew, can call on an elder brother or uncle for capital and get it without interest.

A relatively small proportion of traders rely on non-relatives for working capital and shun their kin as employees or partners.

Abnormal Economic Behavior.

Copperbelt traders, like businessmen everywhere, often are not articulate about why they operate as they do, but there is no evidence, contrary to what has often been alleged for Africans in general,[23] of failure to follow a maximizing behavior any more than their western counterparts.

It is true that Copperbelt traders sometimes seem to ignore areas where supplies are relatively cheap, or markets where prices are relatively high, but this may be no more than reflection of lack of information, or imperfect knowledge. And people reportedly sometimes frequent markets to buy a commodity they earlier sold from their fields or granaries for a lower price, whereas what most Europeans would regard as normal behavior is, of course, to anticipate a post-harvest price rise, and to market only what is surplus to one's expected needs. But even if Africans could accurately estimate needs, (and this would involve knowing how many of their kinsmen would make extended visits, a common, but irregular, phenomenon), there

(23) See Jones 1960 for a summary and criticism of some of the literature on alleged abnormal economic behavior by Africans.

is an additional explanation of why people sell cheaply only to buy back dearly; shortage of money and lack of a banking tradition mean many Africans often have little to turn to when funds are needed quickly, except sale of a domestic animal or something from the granary.

The allegation that the forces of supply and demand are inoperative seems often to be based on the observation that quoted prices are the same in the post-harvest and pre-harvest seasons, times when conditions of supply and demand are usually different. As has been noted herein, measurement of the quantity offered for the quoted price, or the amount of gift given with a purchase, is enough to cast doubt on this myth.

Perhaps a more fruitful question to ask than whether African economic behavior is normal is why do many who generalize about the behavior of Africans so readily and uncritically accept evidence that superficially suggests African economic behavior is basically abnormal?

TABLE 86

The Principal Commodities Appearing in Copperbelt Market, 1959[a]

Commodity	Botanical name or Description
Sold mainly by women:	
Cassava or manioc[b]	*Manihot utilissima,* fresh roots
Manioc cossettes[b]	Leached, dried chunks of manioc roots; white and chalk-like in appearance
Manioc flour	Pulverised cossettes
Manioc,—(?)[b]	Fermented manioc wrapped in wild leaves
Manioc,—(?)[b]	Cooked, mashed manioc; looks like rice from a distance
Boiled manioc	Boiled whole roots
Maize[b]	*Zea mays;* whole, dry grains
Maize meal[b, c]	Finely ground meal; almost a flour
Maize fritters	Small cakes of maize dough deep fried in vegetable oil
Maize-manioc	Small cakes of maize and manioc meal, mixed in varying proportions, and deep fried in vegetable oil
Kaffir corn	*Holcus Sorghum;* whole, dry grain
Kaffir corn meal	Finely ground meal; flour-like
Bulrush millet	*Pennisetum,* sp; whole, dry grain
Finger millet	*Eleusine coracana;* whole, dry grain
Rice	*Oryzae sativa;* whole, dry grain
Cooked rice	Boiled whole grains
Potato	*Solanum tuberosum;* whole, fresh tube
Sweet potato	*Ipomola Batatas;* whole, fresh roots
Cooked sweet potato	Boiled whole root
Bread[b, c]	Wheat loaves and buns
Wheat fritters	Wheat dough deep fried in vegetable oil
Plantain[b]	*Musa paradisica;* fresh fingers
Lumanda[a]	Leaves of *Hibiscu acetosella;* whole raw

TABLE 86 (continued)

Commodity	Botanical name or Description
Sold mainly by women:	
Mulembwe[a]	Wild leaves; whole raw
Munkoyo[a]	Leaves of the *munkoyo* bush; whole raw
Lenga-lenga[a]	Wild leaves; whole, raw
Masuka[a]	Leaves of *Uapaca kirkiana*; whole, raw
Bean leaves	Variety unknown; whole, raw
Cow-pea leaves	Leaves of *Vigna unguiculata;* whole raw
Salt[b, c]	White table salt
Curry	Finely ground Indian curry
Palm oil[b]	Oil from the fruit of the oil palm tree *(Elaeis guineenis)*
Palm fruit	Whole, fresh
Groundnut oil	Oil from the seed of *Arachis hypogaea*
Sprouted maize	*Zea mays* grains with sprouts $1/4$ to 1 in. long, usually
Sprouted kaffir corn	*Holcus sorghum* grains with sprouts as much as $1/2$ inch long
Sprouted bulrush millet	*Pennisetum* grains with sprouts up to $1/4$ inch long
Sprouted finger millet	*Eleusine corcana* grains with sprouts up to $1/4$ in. long
Munkoyo or "African tea"	A sweet, almost nonalcoholic beer made of *munkoyo*-root extract and maize[d] or a combination of maize and manioc[b]
Cucurbits	Predominantly pumpkins; whole, raw
Pumpkin leaves	Variety unknown; dried
Asparagus	Variety unknown; whole, raw
Wild greens	Leaves of various wild species; whole, raw
Wild greens	Dried leaves of various wild species; dried
Roasting ears	Boiled or roasted immature ears of *Zea mays*
Chikanda	A spongy cake-like preparation made from a wild starchy tuber
Pumpkin seed	Roasted seed of pumpkin, variety unknown; roasted
Sponge	A wild sponge-like growth used in washing pots and pans
Broom	Bundles of palm-frond ribs used for sweeping
Termites	Fried in vegetable oil
Manioc leaves[b]	Variety unknown; whole, raw
Sold mainly by men:	
Tomatoes	Variety unknown; whole, raw
Onions	Both yellow and white are found; whole, raw
Cabbage	Variety unknown; whole, raw
Beef	All cuts, including the offal; raw
Barbel and bream	*Clarias,* sp. and *Tilapia,* sp.; fresh fish
Dried fish	*Clarias* and *Tilapia;* dried
Dried fish	Small, sardine-like fish; dried
Smoked fish	Smoked *Clarias* and *Tilapia*
Salted fish[b]	Salted *Tilapia*
Chickens	Small African breeds; alive
Chickens	Large European breeds and African-European crosses, alive

TABLE 86 (continued)

Commodity	Botanical name or Description
Sold mainly by men:	
Ducks	Breed unknown; alive
Pigeons[b]	Breed unknown; alive
Hen eggs	Various sizes; fresh
Hen eggs	Various sizes; boiled
Caterpillars	Species unknown; dried
Locusts	Species unknown; dried
Haircutting	
Sold by both: Neither sex Predominates among Sellers:	
Groundnuts	*Arachis hypogaea;* whole, dry seed
Groundnuts	Roasted, salted seed of *Arachis hypogaea*
Cow peas	*Vigna unguiculata;* whole, dry seed
Beans	Many sizes and colors; varieties unknown; whole dry seed
Chilles	*Capsium futescens* small, hot red peppers; varieties unknown; whole, dry
Apples	Variety unknown; whole, fresh
Oranges	Variety unknown; whole, fresh
Lemon	Variety unknown; whole, fresh
Bananas	Variety unknown; whole, fresh
Mangoes	Variety unknown; whole, fresh
Pineapple	Variety unknown; whole, fresh
Paw paw	*Caricu papaya;* whole, fresh
Sugar[b, c]	White, table sugar
Sugar cane	Two types; varieties unknown, whole stalks, fresh
Sweet sorghum	A sweet-stemmed variety of *Holcus sorghum;* whole stalks, fresh
Honey	Wild honey
Munkoyo	Several kinds of wild roots and tubers used in making light beer; whole, fresh
Lettuce	Variety unknown; whole, raw
Mushrooms	Variety unknown; whole, raw
Coffee[c]	Coffee brewed Belgian style
Lump tobacco	Used in pipes; variety of tobacco unknown
Leaf tobacco	Cigarette material
Snuff	
Wood	Whole logs
Charcoal	
Kerosene	
Combs	Carved of wood by Africans
Combs	Plastic, European manufacture
Hair oil	European manufacture
Matches	European manufacture
Bottled soft drinks	Orange flavor mostly; European manufacture
Jewelry	European manufacture
Perfumes	European manufacture
Wooden[d] mortars	African manufacture
Baskets	African manufacture
Pots	Clay, African manufacture

TABLE 86 (continued)

Commodity	Botanical name or Description
Sold by both: Neither sex Predominates among Sellers:	
Pots	Metal, European manufacture
Pans	Metal, European manufacture
Drinking glasses	Glass, European manufacture
Spoons	Wooden, for cooking, African manufacture
Rubber	Rubber strips cut from a tire tube for tying bundles behind a bicycle
Sewing thread	European manufacture
Mirrors	European manufacture
Wire meal sieves	African manufacture
Charcoal braziers	Tin, African manufacture
Furniture[d]	African manufacture
Shoes	African manufacture
Tailoring and mending	
Bicycle repairing	

(a) Unless otherwise specified all terms in the venacular are Chinyanga.

(b) Sold predominantly in the Congo.

(c) Barred from most Rhodesian markets to protect Government marketing monopolies or storekeepers.

(d) Sold predominantly in Northern Rhodesia.

(e) Not observed, but reported available in the rainy season.

TABLE 87

*Proportion of Major Imports to Congo Copperbelt from
Principal Zones of Supply*[a]

Commodity	Local (50 Miles)	Zone F_1 (150 Miles)	Zone F_2 (150 Miles)	Zone D (200 Miles)	Zone I (400 Miles)	Zone B (500 Miles)	Zone C (600 Miles)	Zone A (800 Miles)	All Zones
				(per cent)					
Fuel[b]	100.0	0.0	0.0	0.0	0.0	0.0	0.0	0.0	100.0
Vegetable	100.0	0.0	0.0	0.0	0.0	0.0	0.0	0.0	100.0
Sugar cane		100.0	0.0	0.0	0.0	0.0	0.0	0.0	100.0
Fish	0.0	34.0	60.0	5.0	0.0	1.0	0.0	0.0	100.0
Wheat	0.0	0.0	0.0	100.0	0.0	0.0	0.0	0.0	100.0
Beans	0.0	0.0	0.0	84.5	0.0	12.1	3.4	0.0	100.0
Coffee	0.0	0.0	0.0	55.1	0.0	29.9	0.0	15.0	100.0
Rice	0.0	0.0	0.0	68.5	0.0	0.0	5.5	19.4	100.0
Poultry & eggs	5.0(?)	0.0	0.0	0.0	95.0(?)	0.0	0.0	0.0	100.0
Palm-nut oil	0.0	0.0	0.0	0.0	0.0	100.0	0.0	0.0	100.0
Bananas	0.0	0.0	0.0	0.0	0.0	99.9	0.1	0.0	100.0
Maize meal	0.0	0.0	0.0	1.0	0.0	89.9	9.1	0.0	100.0
Palm nuts	0.0	0.0	0.0	25.1	0.0	74.7	0.2	0.0	100.0
Manioc meal	(?)[e]	0.0	0.0	0.9[e]	0.0	52.1[e]	47.0[f]	0.0	100.0
Groundnut oil[c]	0.0	0.0	0.0	11.5	0.0	48.0	15.5	25.0	100.0
Palm oil	0.0	0.0	0.0	1.7	0.0	41.7	0.4	56.1	100.0
Manioc cossettes	(?)[e]	0.0	0.0	25.8[e]	0.0	20.4[e]	53.8[e]	0.0	100.0
Maize	0.0	0.0	0.0	27.0	0.0	48.2	4.8	20.0	100.0
Tobacco	0.0	0.0	0.0	0.0	0.0	77.4	22.6	0.0	100.0

(a) Data from Affaires Economiques, Annual Reports, Katanga Province, various dates, and all five-year averages (1954–1958). Zones referred to are demarcated on Map 21. Distances are approximate and were measured from the center of zones to the center of the Congo sector of the Copperbelt. Zone A is defined as all the river stops between Leopoldville and Port Francqui; Zone B is all the rail stations between Port Francqui and Kamina; Zone C is all railway stations north of Kamina; and Zone D is those between Diolo and Tenke.

(b) Charcoal and wood.

(c) Oil from the seed of *Arachis hypogaea*.

(d) Author's rough estimate based on reports from informants and the type of chickens and eggs found in markets.

(e) Per cent of imports by rail; local production unknown and possibly sizable. See Table 84 for description of manioc cosettes.

(f) Derived from quantities sold to wholesalers at the major river and lake points Belgian fisheries authorities believe are supplying the Copperbelt.

TABLE 88

Principal Zones Supplying Major Imports to the Northern Rhodesian Copperbelt, 1959[a]

Commodity	Local (50 Miles)	Zone E (100 Miles)	Zone F_1 (200 Miles)	Zone K (200 Miles)	Zone L (300 Miles)	Zone I (300 Miles)	Zone G (400 Miles)	Zone H (500 Miles)
Fuel[b]	X							
Vegetables	X							
Fish		X	X			X		
Insects				X				
Poultry & eggs						X		
Maize						X		
Sugar cane							X	X
Groundnuts[c]							X	
Rice								X
Tobacco								X

(a) From information provided by informants and rough estimates of production made by the Northern Rhodesian Department of Agriculture. Zones referred to are demarcated on Map One.

(b) Wood and charcoal.

(c) *Arachis hypogaea.*

TABLE 89

Number of Sellers and Assistants Surveyed, by Major Commodity Groups, Selected Rhodesian Copperbelt Markets, 1959[a]

Commodity Group	Number of Sellers Surveyed	Origin of commodity			Sellers with assistants			
		Produced by Seller	Pur- chased	No Info.	0 asst	1 asst	2 asst	No Info.
		(per cent)			(per cent)			
Vegetables	185	13	83	4	82	12	1	5
Pulses	97	4	96	0	88	11	0	1
Fruit (cultivated)	25	0	100	0	72	16	8	4
Fruit (wild)	11	45	55	0	100	0	0	0
Tobacco	24	13	87	0	88	8	0	4
Caterpillars	19	42	58	0	79	21	0	0
Wild roots	17	35	59	6	94	0	0	0

(a) Data from the survey described pp. 711–713.

BIBLIOGRAPHY

ADANSON, M.
1759 *A Voyage to Senegal, the Isle of Goree and the River Gambia (1749–53)*. London: J. Nourse.
ALEXANDER, J. E.
1838a *An Expedition of Discovery into the Interior of Africa*. 2 vols. London: Henry Colburn.
1838b "Report of an Expedition of Discovery, through the Countries of the Great Nom Aquas, Boschmans, and the Hill Damaras in South Africa," *Journal of the Royal Geographical Society of London*, Vol. 8, pp. 1–28.
ALEXANDRE, P. AND BINET, J.
1958 *Le Groupe dit Pahouin*. London: International African Institute.
ALLAN, W., GLUCKMAN, M., PETERS, D. U., AND TRAPNELL, C. G.
1948 "Land Holding and Land Usage among the Plateau Tonga of Mazabuka District," *Rhodes-Livingstone Papers*, No. 14.
AMES, D. W.
1955a "The Use of a Transitional Cloth-Money Token among the Wolof," *American Anthropologist*, Vol. 57, No. 5.
1955b "The Economic Base of Wolof Polygyny," *Southwestern Journal of Anthropology*, Vol. 11, pp. 391–403.
ARNOLD, ROSEMARY
1957 "A Port of Trade: Whydah on the Guinea Coast," in *Trade and Market in the Early Empires* (K. Polanyi, C. W. Arensberg, and H. W. Pearson, eds.). Chicago: The Free Press.
ARNOT, F. S.
1889 *Garenganze*. Chicago, New York: F. H. Revell.
ASTLEY, THOMAS (PUBLISHER)
1745 *A New General Collection of Voyages and Travels*. 2 vols. London: Printed for T. Astley.

BACON, R. H.
1897 *Benin, the City of Blood*. London: Edward Arnold.
BAINES, THOMAS
1864 *Explorations in South West Africa*. London: Longmans.
BALANDIER, G.
1952 "Actualité du problème de la dot en Afrique Noire," *Le Monde Non-Chrétien*, No. 21.
1954 *Conséquences sociales de l'industrialization et problèmes urbains en Afrique: étude bibliographique*. Paris: Bureau International de Recherche sur les Implications Sociales du Progrès Technique.
1955 *Sociologie Actuelle de l'Afrique Noir*. Paris: Presses Universitaires de France.
BANTON, M.
1957 *West African City*. London: Oxford University Press.
BARNES, JOHN A.
1951 "The Fort Jameson Ngoni," in *Seven Tribes of British Central Africa* (E. Colson and M. Gluckman, eds.). Manchester: Manchester University Press.
BARTH, HENRY
1857 *Travels in North and Central Africa*. London: Ward Lock (Edition of 1890).
1859 *Travels and Discoveries in North and Central Africa*. New York: Harper and Brothers.

BAUER, P. T.
1954   *West African Trade.* Cambridge: Cambridge University Press.

BAXTER, W. B.
1958   "A Report on the Fishing Industry on that Part of the Kafue River Lying within Lusaka District." (Mimeographed.)

BEAUMINY, A. DE
1919   "Le Pays de la Boucle du Niger, Étude Économique", *Revue géographique et commerciale de Bordeaux,* Vol. 6, pp. 71–78.

BENEDICT, RUTH
1956   "The Growth of Culture," in *Man, Culture and Society* (H. Shapiro, ed.). New York: Oxford University Press.

BENNETT, M. K.
1954   *The World's Food.* New York: Harper and Brothers.

BINET, J.
1956   "Budgets familiaux des planteurs de cacao au Cameroun," *L'Homme d'Outre-Mer,* No. 3.
1957   "Une élite rurale: conseilleurs municipaux de Cameroun," *Le Monde Non-Chrétien,* No. 42.

BINGER, CAPTAIN LOUIS A.
1892   *Du Niger au Golfe de Guinée par le Pays de Kong et la Mossi.* Paris: Librairie Hachette et Cie.

BOEKE, J. H.
1953   *Economics and Economic Policy in Dual Societies.* New York: Institute of Pacific Relations.

BOHANNAN, LAURA, AND BOHANNAN, PAUL
1953   *The Tiv of Central Nigeria.* London: International African Institute.

BOHANNAN, PAUL
1955   "Some Principles of Exchange and Investment among the Tiv," *American Anthropologist,* Vol. 57, pp. 60–69.
1959   "The Impact of Money on an African Subsistence Economy," *The Journal of Economic History,* Vol. 19, pp. 491–503.
1961   "The Tiv Market Place." (Unpublished manuscript.)

BONNET-DUPEYRON, M. F.
1945   Maps (showing animal husbandry in West and Central Africa). Paris: O. R. S. T. O. M.

BOVILL, E. W.
1958   *The Golden Trade of the Moors.* Londen, New York: Oxford University Press.

BOWDITCH, T. E.
1819   *Mission from Cape Coast to Ashanti.* London: J. Murray.

BRADLEY, K.
1952   *Copper Venture.* London: Mufulira Copper Mines.

BRELSFORD, V. W.
1946   "Fishermen of the Bangweulu Swamps," *Rhodes-Livingstone Papers,* No. 12.
1947   *Copperbelt Markets.* Lusaka: Government Printer.
1956   *The Tribes of Northern Rhodesia.* Lusaka: Government Printer.

BRINCKER, H.
1886   *Wörterbuch und Kurzgefasste Grammatik des Otgi-Herero.* Leipzig: T. O. Weigel.

BRUSH, J. E.
1953   "The Hierarchy of Central Places in Southwestern Wisconsin," *Géographical Review,* Vol. 43, pp. 380–402.

BULTOT, F.
1954   *Saisons et Périodes Sèches et Pluvieuses au Congo Belge et au Ruanda-Urundi.*
        Bruxelles: Publications de l'Institut National pour l'étude agronomique du
        Congo Belge.
BURTON, R. F.
1873   *Lacerda's Journey to Cazembe in 1798.* London: Royal Geographic Society.
1910   *First Footsteps in East Africa.* New York: E. P. Dutton.

CAILLIÉ, R.
1830   *Travels Through Central Africa to Timbuctoo.* Paris: Impr. par autorisation
        du Roi à l'Imprimerie royale.
CAMERON, V. L.
1877   *Across Africa.* London: Doldy, Isbister.
CAPELLO AND IVENS
1886   *De Angola a Contra Costa.* Lisbon: Imprensa nacional.
CERULLI, E.
1956   *Peoples of South-west Ethiopia and its Borderland.* London: International
        African Institute.
CHAPMAN, JAMES
1868   *Travels in the Interior of South Africa.* London: Bell & Daldy.
CHILDS, MURRAY GLADWIN
1949   *Umbundu Kinship and Character.* London: International African Institute.
CLAPPERTON, HUGH
1829   *Journal of a Second Expedition into the Interior of Africa, from the Bight of
        Benin to Soccatoo.* London: J. Murray.
CLARK, FRED EMERSON AND WELD, LOUIS DWIGHT HARVELL
1932   *Marketing Agricultural Products in the United States.* New York: The Mac-
        millian Company.
CRAWFORD, DANIEL
1912   *Thinking Black.* London: Morgan & Scott, Ltd.
COLSON, ELIZABETH
1951a   "The Plateau Tonga of Northern Rhodesia," in *Seven Tribes of British Central
        Africa* (E. Colson and M. Gluckman, eds.). Manchester: University of Manchester
        Press.
1951b   "The Role of Cattle among the Plateau Tonga," *Rhodes-Livingstone Journal,*
        Vol. 11, pp. 10–46.
1958a   "Plateau Tonga Diet," *Rhodes-Livingstone Journal,* Vol. 24.
1958b   *Marriage and the Family among the Plateau Tonga of Northern Rhodesia.*
        Manchester: University of Manchester Press.
1960   *Before Kariba: The Social Organization of the Valley Tonga.* Manchester:
        University of Manchester Press.
CROZAT, DR.
1891   "Rapport sur une mission au Mossi," *Journal Officiel de la République Fran-
        çaise,* 5–9 October.
CURLE, A. T.
1937   "The Ruined Towns of Somaliland," *Antiquity,* Vol. 11, pp. 315–27.

DEANE, P.
1953   *Colonial Social Accounting.* Cambridge: Cambridge University Press.
DIAGNE, A. M.
1919   "Un pays de pilleurs d'épaves: Le Gandiole," *Bulletin du Com. d'Études His-
        torique et Scientifique de l'A.O.F.*

DILLEY, M. R.
1937   *British Policy in Kenya Colony.* New York: T. Nelson.
DOKE, CLEMENT
1931   *The Lambas of Northern Rhodesia.* London: George G. Harrap.
DORJAHN, V. R.
1959   "The Organization and Functions of the Ragbenle Society of the Temne," *Africa,* Vol. 29, No. 2, pp. 156–70.
DOUGLAS, MARY
1951   "A Form of Polyandry among the Lele," *Africa,* Vol. 21, pp. 1–12.
1954   "The Lele of the Kasai," in *African Worlds* (D. Forde, ed.). London: Oxford University Press.
1957   "The Pattern of Residence among the Lele," *Zaïre,* Vol. 11, pp. 818–43.
1958   "Raffia Distribution in the Lele Economy," *Africa,* Vol. 28, pp. 2 ff.
1959a "Age-Status among the Lele," *Zaïre,* Vol. 13, pp. 386–413.
1959b "The Lele of the Kasai," in *The Church and the Nations* (A. Hastings, ed.). London: Sheed & Ward.
——   "Blood-debts among the Lele," *Journal of the Royal Anthropological Institute,* forthcoming.
DRAKE-BROCKMAN, R. E.
1912   *British Somaliland.* London: Hurst & Blackett, Ltd.
DUBOIS, CORA
1936   "The Wealth Concept as an Integrative Factor in Tolowa-Tututni Culture," in *Essays in Anthropology Presented to A. L. Kroeber* (R. H. Lowie, ed.). Berkeley: University of California Press.
DUPIRE, M.
1957   "Les Forages dans l'Économie peule" (Mission chez les Peuls nomades du cercle de Linguère, Sénégal), in *Eléments de politique sylvo-pastorale au Sahel sénégalais* (P. Grosmaire, ed.). Gouvernement du Sénégal, Service des Eaux et Forêt. Pt. 2, Fas. 14.
1962   *Peuls pasteurs, Étude descriptive des Wodaabe nomades du Sahel Nigérien.* Paris: Institut d'Ethnologie, Musée de l'Homme.
DUPUIS, JOSEPH
1824   *Journal of a Residence in Ashantee.* London: H. Colburn.
DURAND, J. B. L.
1806   *A Voyage to Sénégal.* London: R. Phillips.

EGGERS, (LEUTNANT)
1900   "Bericht über eine Reise nach dem Okavargogebiet," in *Mittheilungen (für Forschungsreisenden und Gelehrten) aus den Deutschen Schutzgebieten,* Bd. 13, H. 3, pp. 185–88. Berlin: G. S. Mittler und Sohn.
ELLIS, A. B.
1883   *The Land of Fetish.* London: Chapman and Hall, Ltd.
EVANS-PRITCHARD, E. E.
1954   "Introduction," in *The Gift* (by Marcel Mauss). Chicago: The Free Press.

FAGE, J. D.
1958   *An Atlas of African History.* London: E. Arnold.
FALLERS, LLOYD A.
1956   *Bantu Bureaucracy.* Cambridge: W. Heffer, for the East African Institute of Social Research.
FARINI, G. ANTONIO
1886   *Through the Kalahari Desert.* London: Sampson, Low.

FARSON, NEGLEY
  1941 *Behind God's Back.* New York: Harcourt, Brace.
FERRANDI, U.
  1903 *Lugh. Emporio commerciale sul Giuba.* Rome.
FEUNTEUN, L. M.
  1955 "L'élevage en A. O. F., son importance économique et sociale," *Revue d'élevage et de médecine vétérinaire des pays tropicaux.*
FIRTH, RAYMOND
  1951 *Elements of Social Organisation.* London: Watts.
  1958 *Human Types.* New York: Mentor Books.
FORDE, D.
  1937 "Land and Labour in a Cross River Village," *Geographical Journal,* Vol. 40, No. 1.
FORDE, D. AND JONES, G. I.
  1950 *The Ibo and Ibibio-speaking Peoples of Southeastern Nigeria.* London: International African Institute.
FORDE, D. AND SCOTT, RICHENDA
  1946 *The Native Economies of Nigeria.* London: Oxford University Press.
FORTT, J. M.
  1953 in *Economic Development and Tribal Change* (A. I. Richards, ed.). Cambridge: Heffer and Sons.
FRYER, G.
  1958 "Mwamfuli's Village: The New Fulcrum of the Bangweulu Fish Trade," *The Northern Rhodesia Journal,* Vol. 3, No. 6.
FURNIVALL, J. S.
  1939 *Netherlands India, A Study of Plural Economy.* Cambridge: Cambridge University Press. (Edition used—New York: The Macmillan Company, 1944.)

GABUS, J.
  1955 *Au Sahara.* Neuchatel: A. la Baconnière.
GALBRAITH, J. K.
  1955 *Economics and the Art of Controversy.* New Brunswick: Rutgers University Press.
GALETTI, R., BALDWIN, K. D. S., AND DINA, I. O.
  1956 *Nigeria Cocoa Farmers.* London: Oxford University Press.
GALTON, FRANCIS
  1891 *Narrative of an Explorer in Tropical South Africa.* London: Ward, Lock and Bowden.
GAMBLE, D. P. G.
  1949 *Contributions to a Socio-Economic Survey of the Gambia.* London: Colonial Office.
  1955 *Economic Conditions of Two Mandinka Villages: Kerewan and Keneba.* London: Colonial Office.
  1957 *The Wolof of Senegambia.* London: International African Institute.
GANN, LEWIS
  1954 "The End of the Slave Trade in British Central Africa, 1889–1912," *Rhodes-Livingstone Journal,* Vol. 16, pp. 27–51.
  1958 *The Birth of a Plural Society.* Manchester: University of Manchester Press.
GENEVIÈRE, J.
  1950 *Le Commerce des Kountas.* Bulletin I. F. A. N. Dakar.
GIBSON, GORDON D.
  1956 "Double Descent and its Correlates among the Herero of Ngamiland," *American Anthropologist,* Vol. 58, pp. 109–39.

1958   "Herero Marriage," *Human Problems in British Central Africa*. Vol. 24, pp. 1–37.

GIELGUD, VAL

1900   Reports in the Public Records of Northeast Rhodesia, A 3/8/1; National Archives of Rhodesia and Nyasaland, Lusaka.

GLUCKMAN, MAX

1941   "Economy of the Central Barotse Plain," *Rhodes-Livingstone Papers,* No. 7.

1950   "Kinship and Marriage among the Lozi of Northern Rhodesia and the Zulu of Natal," in *African Systems of Kinship and Marriage* (A. R. Radcliffe-Brown and Daryll Forde, eds.). London: Oxford University Press.

GOLDSMITH, K. L. G., AND LEWIS, I. M.

1958   "A Preliminary Investigation of the Blood Groups of the *Sab* Bondsmen of Northern Somaliland," *Man,* Vol. 58, pp. 188–90.

GOODFELLOW, D. M.

1939   *Principles of Economic Sociology.* London: G. Routledge & Sons, Ltd.

GOUROU, P.

1951   *Notice de la carte de la densité de la population au Congo Belge et au Ruanda-Urundi.* Bruxelles: Institute Royal Colonial Belge.

1955   *La Densité de la population rurale au Congo Belge, etc.* Brussels: Acad. Roy. Sci. Col. Mem. 8, 1, 2.

GRAY, J. M.

1940   *A History of the Gambia.* Cambridge: The University Press.

GRAY, R. F.

1960   "Sonjo Bride Price and the Question of African 'Wife Purchase,'" *American Anthropologist,* Vol. 62, pp. 34–57.

GRAY, W., AND DORCHARD

1825   *Travels in Western Africa (1818–21).* London: J. Murray.

GREAT BRITAIN

1902   Northern Territories of Gold Coast, Report of 1901. London: H. M. S. O. (Cd 788–27, No. 357).

1905   Northern Territories of Gold Coast, Report of 1903. London: H. M. S. O. (Cd 2238–6, No. 429).

1918   Report of the Natives of South West Africa and their Treatment by Germany. London: H. M. S. O. (R 9146). (Parliamentary Papers 1918, Vol. 17, p. 491).

GREENBERG, J.

1955   *Studies in African Linguistic Classification.* New Haven: Compass Publishing Company.

GREENLAND, D. J. AND CHANCELLOR, R. J.

1958   "West Nile District: Some Soil and Vegetation Types," *Uganda Journal,* Vol. 22, March.

GREGORY, T. E.

1933   "Money," *Encyclopedia of the Social Sciences,* Vol. 10, pp. 601–2.

GULLIVER, P. H.

1955   *The Family Herds: A Study of Two Pastoral Tribes.* London: Routledge and Kegan Paul.

HAHN, C. HUGO

1857   *Grundzüge einer Grammatik des Herero (im westlichen Afrika), nebst einem Wörterbuch.* Berlin: W. Hertz.

HAHN, JOSAPHAT

1868   "Das Land der Ovaherero," *Zeitschrift der Gesellschaft für Erdkunde zu Berlin,* Vol. 3, pp. 193–224, 493–507.

1869 "Die Ovaherero," *Zeitschrift der Gesellschaft für Erdkunde zu Berlin,* Vol. 4, pp. 226–58.

HAHN, THEOPHILUS

1883 "Answers to questions on Criminal and Civil Law, marriage and inheritance, land tenure and self-government." *Cape of Good Hope Reports and Proceedings with Appendices of the Government Commission on Native Laws and Customs,* Part 2, Appendix C, pp. 248–58. Capetown.

HANNA, A. J.

1956 *The Beginnings of Nyasaland and North-Eastern Rhodesia.* London: Oxford University Press.

HANNA, M.

1958 "The Lebanese in West Africa," *West Africa,* April 19, p. 369; April 26, p. 393; May 3, p. 415; May 17, p. 463; and May 24, p. 487.

HARRIS, M.

1959 "The Economy Has No Surplus?" *American Anthropologist,* Vol. 61, No. 2, pp. 185–200.

HERSKOVITS, MELVILLE J.

1938 *Dahomey.* New York: Augustin.

1941 "Economics and Anthropology: A Rejoinder," *Journal of Political Economy,* Vol. 49, pp. 269–78.

1952a *Economic Anthropology.* New York: Knopf.

1952b "The Problem of Adapting Societies to New Tasks," in *The Progress of Underdevelopted Areas* (B. F. Hoselitz, ed.). Chicago: University of Chicago Press.

HEWETT, J. F. N.

1857 "On the Jolloffs of West Africa," *Royal Geographical Society Proceedings,* Vol. 1.

HIGGINS, B.

1956 "The 'Dualistic Theory' of Underdeveloped Areas," *Economic Development and Cultural Change,* pp. 99–115, January.

HILTON-SIMPSON, M. W.

1911 *Lands and Peoples of the Kasai.* London: Constable & Co., Ltd.

HODDER, B. W.

1959 "The Yoruba Rural Market Ring," *Research Notes,* No. 12. Ibadan, Nigeria.

HOMBURGER, L.

1925 "Le Group Sud-ouest des Langues Bantues." *Mission Rohan-Chabot,* Tome 3, Fasc. 1. Paris: Imp. Nationale.

HORNER, GEORGE R.

1950 "La littérature orale: Une étude du folklore des tribus Bulu et Bassa du Cameroun." Unpublished doctoral thesis, University of Paris, Sorbonne.

HORRABIN, J. F.

1960 *An Atlas of Africa.* New York: Praeger.

HUNTLEY, SIR HENRY

1850 *Seven Years' Service on the Slave Coast of Western Africa.* Vol. 11, *Twelve Months in the Gambia.* London: T. C. Newby.

HUTT, W. H.

1939 *Theory of Idle Resources.* London: J. Cape.

IRLE, JAKOB

1917 *Deutsch-Herero Wörterbuch* (Abhandlungen des Hamburgischen Kolonialinstituts 32). Hamburg: L. Friedrichsen.

1906 *Die Herero.* Gütersloh: Bertelsmann.

JARRETT, H. R.
   1954   "Freetown, A Study in Space Relationships." *Sierra Leone Studies,* N. S., No. 2,
         pp. 98–108, June.
   1955   "The Port and Town of Freetown," *Geography,* Vol. 40, pp. 108–18.
JENSEN, A. E. (ed.)
   1936   *Im Lande des Gada.* Stuttgart: Strecker und Schröder.
   1954   *Mythes et cults chez les peuples primitifs* (M. Metzger and J. Goffinet), Paris: Payot.
JOBSON, R.
   1932   *The Golden Trade or a Discovery of the River Gambia, and the Golden Trade
         of the Aethiopians (1620–21).* London: The Penguin Press.
JOHNSON, C.
   1956   "African Farming Improvement in the Plateau Tonga Maize Areas of Northern
         Rhodesia." *Northern Rhodesia Agricultural Bulletin,* No. 11. Department of
         Agriculture.
JONES, W. O.
   1960   "Economic Man in Africa," *Food Research Institute Studies,* Vol. 1, No. 2.

KARP, M.
         See Lorimer, Frank.
KENYATTA, JOMO
   1938   *Facing Mount Kenya.* London: Secker and Warburg.
KNIGHT, FRANK
   1941   "Anthropology and Economics," *Journal of Political Economy,* Vol. 49, pp.
         247–68.
KOELLE, REVEREND S. W.
   1854   *Polyglotta Africana.* London: Church Missionary House.
KOLBE, F. W.
   1883   *An English-Herero Dictionary.* Capetown: J. C. Juta.
KRAUSE, ADOLPHE
   1887–88   "Krause's Reise," in *Petermann's Mitteilungen.* 1887, pp. 57, 92, 152 and 217;
         1888, p. 88.
KROEBER, A. L.
   1948   *Anthropology.* New York: Harcourt, Brace.

LARRAT, R.
   1954   "Problèmes de la viande," in *A. O. F. Zones de production. II. Niger.* Paris:
         Editions De l'Outre-mer.
   1958   "Etat actuel de la production, de la collecte, du transport, de la transformation
         et de la distribution des divers laits et produits laitiers dans les pays chauds."
         Paris: Commission internationale pour la laiterie dans les pays chauds.
LAWRIE, J.
   1954   "Frankincense," *The Somaliland Journal,* Vol. 1, pp. 26–30.
LESSER, A.
   1959   "Some Comments on the Concept of the Intermediate Society," in *Intermediate
         Societies, Social Mobility and Communication.* Seattle: American Ethnological
         Society.
LEVINE, ROBERT A.
   1959   "Gusii Sex Offenses: A Study in Social Control," *American Anthropologist,* Vol.
         61, pp. 965–90.
LEWIS, I. M.
   1955–56   "Sufism in Somaliland. A Study in Tribal Islam," *Bulletin of the School of
         Oriental and African Studies,* Vol. 17, pp. 581–602; Vol. 18, pp. 146–60.

1958   *Modern Political Movements in Somaliland.* International African Institute Memorandum 30. London: Oxford University Press.

1959a   "Somalia, United Nations Trusteeship Territory: Pastoral and Party Politics," in *From Tribal Rule to Modern Government* (proceedings of the 13th conference of the Rhodes-Livingstone Institute [R. Apthorpe, ed.]), pp. 157–73.

1959b   "Clanship and Contract in Northern Somaliland," *Africa,* Vol. 29, pp. 274–93.

LEWIS, R.

1954   *Sierra Leone: A Modern Portrait.* London: H. M. S. O.

LEYS, SIR NORMAN

1924   *Kenya.* London: Hogarth Press.

LINTON, RALPH

1940   "A Neglected Aspect of Social Organization," *American Journal of Sociology,* Vol. 45.

LIPSON, E.

1949   *The Economic History of England.* 10th Edition. London: A. and C. Black.

LITTLE, K. L.

1951   *The Mende of Sierra Leone.* London: Routledge and Kegan Paul, Ltd.

LLOYD, P. C.

1952   "A Comparative Study of the Political Institutions in Some Yoruba Kingdoms." Unpublished thesis submitted for the Degree of B. Sc., Oxford.

LONSDALE, CAPTAIN R. LA T.

1882   in *Parliamentary Papers,* 46 (C. 3386) No. 42, En 2. London: H. M. S. O.

LORIMER, FRANK (ed.)

1960   *Seminar on Populations in Africa.* Boston: Boston University Press.

LUGARD, SIR F. D.

1929   *The Dual Mandate.* London: Blackwood.

MABOGUNJE, A.

1958   "Abeokuta." Unpublished thesis submitted for the Degree of M. A., London.

MACBRIAR, REVEREND R. M.

1861   *The Africans at Home, being a popular account of Africa and the Africans,* etc. London: Longman, Green, Longman, and Roberts.

MACLAREN, P. I. R.

1958   *The Fishing Devices of Central and Southern Africa.* Livingstone: Rhodes Livingstone Museum, No. 12 N. S.

MALINOWSKI, BRONISLAW

1922   *Argonauts of the Western Pacific.* London: Routledge and Kegan Paul, Ltd.

MANGIN, FR. EUGÈNE

1921   *Les Mossi.* Paris: Augustin Challamel.

MARC, LUCIEN

1909   *Le Pays Mossi.* Paris: Emile Larose.

MARX, KARL

1867   *Capital.* Edition used—New York: Modern Library.

MATTENKLODT, WILHELM

1931   *Fugitive in the Jungle.* New York: Little, Brown & Company.

MAYER, PHILIP

1950   "Gusii Bridewealth Law and Custom," *Rhodes-Livingstone Papers,* No. 18.

MEINHOF, CARL

1932   *Introduction to the Phonology of the Bantu Languages.* (N. J. v. Warmelo, tr.). Berlin: D. Reimer & G. Vohsen.

MELLAND, FRANK

1923   *In Witchbound Africa.* London: Seeley, Service & Company.

MEYER, FELIX
 1925   "Wirtschaft und Recht der Herero," in *Jahrbuch der Internationalen Vereinigung für vergleichende Rechtwissenschaft und Volkswirtschaftslehre zu Berlin*, Vol. 8. Berlin: J. Springer.

MIDDLETON, JOHN
 1952   "Labor Migration Among the Lugbara." An unpublished report submitted to the Colonial Office, London, and the Government of Uganda.
 1958   "The Political System of the Lugbara of the Nile-Congo Divide," in *Tribes Without Rulers* (J. Middleton and D. Tait, eds.). London: Routledge and Kegan Paul.

MIDDLETON, JOHN, AND GREENLAND, D. J.
 1954   "Land and Population in West Nile District, Uganda," *Geographical Journal*, No. 120, December.

MINTZ, S.
 1959   "Internal Market Systems as Mechanisms of Social Articulation," in *Intermediate Societies, Social Mobility and Communication*. Seattle: American Ethnological Society.

MIRACLE, M.
 ——   "Plateau Tonga Entrepreneurs in Historical Inter-Regional Trade," *Rhodes-Livingstone Journal*, forthcoming.

MITCHELL, C.
 1956   "Tribes in Towns," in *The Tribes of Northern Rhodesia* (W. V. Brelsford, ed.). Lusaka: Government Printer.
 1957   "Tribal Distribution in the Federation of Rhodesia and Nyasaland." Map. Salisbury: University College of Rhodesia and Nyasaland.

MOLLIEN, G.
 1820   *Travels in Africa, to the Sources of the Senegal and Gambia in 1818*. London: Sir R. Phillips, and Company.

MOLONEY, J. A.
 1893   *With Captain Stairs to Katanga*. London: S. Low, Marston and Company.

MONOD, TH.
 1951   *Description de la Côte Occidentale d'Afrique (Sénégal au Cap de Monte, Archipels) par Valentim Fernandes (1506–10)*. Bissau: Centro de Estudos Portuguesa.

MOORE, FRANCIS
 1738   *Travels into the Inland Parts of Africa*. London.

MURDOCK, G. P.
 1959   *Africa, Its Peoples and Their Culture History*. New York: McGraw-Hill.

MURPHY, R. F. AND STEWARD, J. H.
 1956   "Tapper and Trappers: Parallel Process in Acculturation," *Economic Development and Cultural Change*, Vol. 4, No. 4.

MYRDAL, GUNNAR
 1957   *Economic Theory and Underdeveloped Regions*. London: G. Duckworth.

McCALL, DANIEL F.
 1955   "Family Structure and Changing Economic Activities of Women in a Gold Coast Town." Unpublished doctoral thesis, Columbia University.
 1959   "Trade and the Role of Wife in a Modern West African Town." Paper read at International African Institute Conference, Kampala, Uganda.

McCULLOCH, M.
 1950   *Peoples of Sierra Leone Protectorate*. Ethnographic Survey of Africa, Western Africa, Part II. London: International African Institute.

McKIERNAN, GERALD
    1954   *The Narrative and Journal of Gerald McKiernan in South West Africa 1874– 1879* (P. Sheraton, ed.). Capetown: The Van Riebeeck Society.

NADEL, S. F.
    1947   *The Nuba.* London: Oxford University Press.
NICOLAI, H.
    1952   "Problèmes du Kwango," *Bulletin de la Société Belge d'Études Géographiques,* Vol. 25, No. 2.
NICOLAI, H. AND JACQUES, J.
    1954   *La Transformation du paysage Congolais par le Chemin de Fer, L'Exemple du B.C.K.* Acad. Roy. Sci. Col. Brussels, Sect. des Sci. Natu. et Med. Mem. in 8, XXIV, L.
NIGERIA (Federal Information Service)
    ——   *The Nigerian Farmer's Diary.* Lagos, Nigeria. (Published yearly.)
NIGERIA (Census Superintendant)
    1953   *Population Census of the Eastern Region of Nigeria, 1953. Bulletin No. 4, Ogoja Province.* Port Harcourt.
NORTHERN RHODESIA
    1956   "Geographical Distribution of Population." Mimeographed tables.
NORTHERN RHODESIA (Forestry Department)
    1954   *Annual Report.* Lusaka: Government Printer.
NORTON, W. A.
    1919   "The South-West Protectorate and its Native Population," *The South African Journal of Science,* Vol. 16, pp. 452–65.
NYIRENDA, A. A.
    1957   "African Market Vendors in Lusaka with a Note on the Recent Boycott," *The Rhodes-Livingstone Journal,* No. 22.

ORMSBY-GORE, W.
    1925   *Report of the East Africa Commission.* London: H. M. S. O.
ORAM, N. D.
    1952   "The Food Supply of Kampala." Unpublished report made to the Department of Labor of the Uganda Protectorate.
OTTENBERG, PHOEBE VESTAL
    1958   "Marriage Relationships in the Double Descent System of the Afikpo Ibo of Southeastern Nigeria." Unpublished Ph. D. dissertation, Northwestern University.
    1959   "The Changing Economic Position of Women among the Afikpo Ibo," in *Continuity and Change in African Cultures* (William R. Bascom and Melville J. Herskovits, eds.). Chicago: University of Chicago Press.
OTTENBERG, SIMON
    1957   "The System of Authority of the Afikpo Ibo of Southeastern Nigeria." Unpublished Ph. D. dissertation, Northwestern University.
    1958   "Ibo Oracles and Intergroup Relations," *Southwestern Journal of Anthropology,* Vol. 14, No. 3, pp. 295–317.

PALMER, H. R.
    1908   "The Kano Chronicle," *Journal of the Royal Anthropological Institute,* Vol. 38, pp. 63–98.
PARK, MUNGO
    1799   *Travels in the Interior Districts of Africa.* (Reissued in Everyman's Library, 1907).

PEDLAR, F. J.
  1948   "A Study of Income and Expenditure in Northern Zaria," *Africa,* Vol. 18, pp.
         259–70.
PEDLER, E.
  1955   *Economic Geography of West Africa.* London: Longmans, Green.
POLANYI, KARL
  1944   *The Great Transformation.* New York: Rinehart.
  1947   "Our Obsolete Market Mentality," *Commentary,* Vol. 13, pp. 109–17, September.
  1957   "The Economy as Instituted Process," in *Trade and Market in the Early Empires*
         (K. Polanyi, C. W. Arensberg, and H. W. Pearson, eds.). Chicago: The Free Press.
PRÉSIDFNCE DU CONSEIL
  1951   "Le Sahara des nomades" (map). *L'economie pastorale saharienne.* Paris: L'Insti-
         tute des Études islamiques.

QUIGGIN, A. H.
  1949   *Trade Routes, Trade and Currency in East Africa.* Livingstone: Rhodes-Living-
         stone Museum.

REDFIELD, ROBERT
  1956   *Peasant Society and Culture.* Chicago: University of Chicago Press.
REINING, CONRAD C.
  1959   "The Role of Money in the Zande Economy," *American Anthropologist,* Vol. 61,
         No. 1, pp. 39–43.
RICHARDS, AUDREY
  1939   *Land, Labor, and Diet in Northern Rhodesia.* London: International Institute
         of African Languages and Cultures.
  1951   "The Bemba of North-Eastern Rhodesia," in *Seven Tribes of British Central
         Africa* (E. Colson and M. Gluckman, eds.). Manchester: University of Man-
         chester Press.
RICHARDSON, E. M.
  1954   "Preliminary Account of the Standard of Living of Africans on the Copper Belt,
         Northern Rhodesia." Unpublished manuscript in the Rhodes-Livingstone Insti-
         tute.
ROBINSON, JOAN
  1954   "The Impossibility of Competition," in *Monopoly and Competition and Their
         Regulation* (E. H. Chamberlin, ed.). London: Macmillan.
ROPER, J. I.
  1958   *Labour Problems in West Africa.* London: Penguin Books.
ROUCH, JEAN
  1956   "Migration au Ghana," *Journal de la Société des Africanists,* Tome 26, Fasc.
         I-II. Paris: Musée de l'Homme.

SAUGNIER, M.
  1792   *Relations de Plusieurs Voyages à la Côte d'Afrique, à Maroc, au Sénégal, à
         Gorée, à Galam, etc.* London: G. G. J. & J. Robinson.
SCUDDER, T.
  1961   *Before Kariba: The Human Geography of the Gwembe Valley.* Manchester:
         Manchester University Press.
SELIGMAN, C. G. AND SELIGMAN, B. Z.
  1932   *Pagan Tribes of the Nilotic Sudan.* London: G. Routledge and Son, Ltd.
SHOBERL, R. (ed.)
  Ca. 1821–25   *The World in Miniature. Africa.* London: R. Ackermann.

SIERRA LEONE
1959   *Report for the Year 1957.* London: H. M. S. O.
SILVERMAN, S. F.
1959   "Some Correlates of the Cyclical Market," in *Intermediate Societies, Social Mobility and Communication.* Seattle: American Ethnological Society.
SKINNER, ELLIOT P.
——   "Conflict and Flexibility in Succession to Political Office among the Mossi." Unpublished.
SMITH, E. W. AND DALE, A. M.
1920   *The Ila-Speaking Peoples of Northern Rhodesia.* London: Macmillan & Co.
SMITH, M. G.
1952   "A Study of Hausa Domestic Economics in Northern Zaria," *Africa,* Vol. 22, pp. 333–47.
1955   *The Economy of Hausa Communities of Zaria.* Colonial Research Studies No. 16. London: H. M. S. O.
1957a   "The Social Functions and Meaning of Hausa Praise-singing," *Africa,* Vol. 27. pp. 26–45.
1957b   "Cooperation in Hausa Society," *Information,* UNESCO, No. 11, pp. 1–20.
SMITH, MARY
1954   *Baba of Karo.* London: Faber.
STEINER, FRANZ
1954   "Notes on Comparative Economics," *British Journal of Sociology,* Vol. 5, pp. 118–29.
STIGAND, C. H.
1923   *Equatoria: The Lado Enclave.* London: Constable & Co., Ltd.
STREITWOLF, K.
1911   *Der Captivizipfel.* Berlin: W. Susserott.
STUTLEY, PETER
1959   "Report on a Visit to African Urban Markets in Northern Rhodesia." Unpublished.

TALBOT, P.
1926   *The Peoples of Southern Nigeria.* London: Oxford University Press.
TAUXIER, LOUIS
1912   *Le Noir du Soudan.* Paris: Emile Larose.
1917   *Le Noir du Yatenga.* Paris: Emile Larose.
1924   *Nègres Gouro et Gagou.* Paris: P. Geuthner.
TESSMAN, G.
1913   *Die Pangwe.* Berlin: E. Wasmuth.
THOMAS, N. W.
1916   *Anthropological Report on Sierra Leone, Part I, Law and Custom.* London: Harrison and Sons.
THOMPSON, B. P.
1954   *Two Studies in African Nutrition.* Lusaka: Rhodes-Livingstone Museum.
THOMPSON, J.
1893   "To Lake Bangweolo and the Unexplored Region of British Central Africa," *The Geographical Journal,* Vol. 1, No. 2.
THOMSON, J. MOFFAT
1930   *Report on the Native Fishing Industry.* Livingstone: Rhodes-Livingstone Museum.
THURNWALD, RICHARD
1932   *Economics in Primitive Communities.* London: Oxford University Press.

TONJES, H.
N.D. Wörterbuch der Ovambosprache. Lehrbücher des Seminars für Orientalische Sprachen 25. Berlin: G. Reimer.

TORDAY, E.
1925 *On the Trail of the Bushongo.* London: Seeley, Service & Co., Ltd.

TRAUWBORST, A. A.
1956 "Vee als Voorwerp van Rijkdom in Oost-Afrika." Unpublished Ph. D. thesis, University of Leiden. (Resume in *Zaïre,* May, 1956.)

TURNER, V. W.
1955 "Money Economy among the Mwinilunga Ndembu," *Rhodes-Livingstone Journal,* Vol. 18, pp. 19–25.
1957 *Schism and Continuity in an African Society.* Manchester: Manchester University Press.

UGANDA PROTECTORATE
1947 *Annual Report of the Department of Agriculture.*
1950 *Annual Report of the Department of Agriculture.*
1953 *The Pattern of Income and Expenditure and Consumption of African Unskilled Laborers in Kampala, September 1953.*

UNION MINIÈRE
1956 *Union Minière du Haut Katanga, 1906–1956.* Brussels.

UNITED NATIONS
1954 *Enlargement of the Exchange Economy in Tropical Africa.* New York: UN, Department of Economic Affairs. (E/2557 ST/ECA/23. Sales No.: 1954, II.C.4).

UNITED STATES DEPARTMENT OF AGRICULTURE, FOREIGN AGRICULTURAL SERVICE
1959 *Notes on the Agricultural Economies of the Countries of Africa: Central and Western Africa.* M-64, September 1959.

VAN DEN PLAS, A.
1947 *La Température au Congo Belge.* Pub. Minis. Colon., pp. 33–38.

VANSINA, JAN
1954 "Les Valeurs Culturelles des Bushong," *Zaïre,* No. 9, pp. 900–910, November.
1955 "Initiation Rituals of the Bushong," *Africa,* Vol. 25, pp. 138–52.
1956 "Migration dans la Province du Kasai," *Zaïre,* pp. 69–85.
1957 "L'État Kuba dans le cadre des institutions politiques Africaines," *Zaïre,* Vol. 11, pt. 1, pp. 485–92.

VEDDER, HEINRICH
1938 *South West Africa in Early Times.* London: Oxford University Press.

VERGER, P. AND BASTIDE, R.
1958 "Le Leseau des marchés Nago (Dahomey)," in *Proceedings of the N.I.S.E.R. Conference, Ibadan, Nigeria.*

VIEHE, G.
1903 "Die Ovaherero," *Rechtsverhältnisse von Eingeborenen Völkern* (S. R. Steinmetz, ed.). Berlin: G. Fischer.

VIEILLARD, G.
1939 *Notes sur les coutumes des Peuls au Fouta Djallon.* Paris: Larose.

VON FRANÇOIS, HUGO
1896 *Nama und Damara.* Magdeburg: G. Baensch.

VON ZASTROW, B.
1930 "Die Herero," in *Das Eingeborenenrecht* (E. Schultz-Ewerth and L. Adam, eds.), Vol. 2, pp. 213–68. Stuttgart: Strecker und Schröder.

WAGNER, GÜNTHER
1957   *A Study of Okahandja District (South West Africa).* (Oswin Kohler, ed.) Ethnological Publications No. 38. Pretoria: Union of South Africa.
WALLER, H. (ed.)
1874   *The Last Journals of David Livingstone.* London: J. Murray.
WATSON, BLAIR, AND JOHNSTON, HENRY HAMILTON
1895   Unpublished correspondence in District Notebooks at Mporokoso.
WATSON, WILLIAM
1958   *Tribal Cohesion in a Money Economy.* Manchester: Manchester University Press.
WHITE, C. M. N.
1959   "A Preliminary Survey of Luvale Rural Economy," *Rhodes-Livingstone Papers,*
No. 29.
WILSON, GODFREY
1942   *An Essay on the Economics of Detribalization in Northern Rhodesia.* Living-
stone: Rhodes-Livingstone Institute.
WILSON, J. L. BOYD
1952   *A Cooperative Digest.* Lusaka: Government Printer.
WITTFOGEL, CARL
1957   *Oriental Despotism, A Comparative Study of Total Power.* New Haven: Yale
University Press.
WOODWARD, E.
1902   *Precis of Information Concerning Uganda Protectorate.* London: H. M. S. O.
WRIGLEY, C. C.
1953   "Agrarian Structure in Buganda." Report of the Second Joint Conference on
Research in the Social Sciences in East and Central Africa.
WYNDHAM, H. A.
1935   *The Atlantic and Slavery.* London: Oxford University Press.

ZAHAN, D.
1954   "Notes sur les Marchés Mossi du Yatenga," *Africa,* Vol. 24, No. 4.

A

Acculturation (also see change, cultural): viii, ix, xi, xiv, 697
Adja: 89
Administered trade: 13
Adultery: 614
Advertising: 97
Affinity, as a basis for trading relationships: 435
Afikpo (Ibo): Chapter 5 (pp. 118–169)
Afikpo Trade Union: 155, 158–9
Age sets: 119, 227, 230, 410, 423, 433, 442, 475
Agricultural activities, rhythm of: 116, 521, 526
Akasa (cornstarch paste): 89–93, 99–100
Alcohol: 36, 47, 710
Alms: 49, 57, 59, 311, 382
Alur: 566, 570, 571
Amhara: Chapter 14 (pp. 386–408), 411, 420, 425, 426
Amulets: 46, 50, 57, 59, 117
Apprentices: xi
Arabs: 317, 367–9, 381, 389, 400, 402, 403, 406, 408, 550, 565, 569, 570, 571, 702
Arbitrage: 56, 262–3, 572
Aro (Ibo traders): 123, 124, 125, 126, 128, 160
Arusha: 21–2, Chapter 16 (pp. 431–456)
Ashanti: 240, 242, 247
Asians: 406, 408, 439, 449, 452, 463, 466, 501, 504, 512, 528, 529, 565, 569, 570, 571, 598, 699, 711, 722
Auctions: 489–90
—, cattle: 466
Azande (see Zande)

B

Bambara: 36, 40, 48, 241
Banking: xii, 62, 88, 102, 406, 733
Barabaig: 458, 459, 461, 465
Barbers: 106, 115, 143, 163
Bargaining (see haggling)
Barter: viii, 10–11, 30, 31, 44, 61, 123 ff., 125, 128, 191, 216, 262–3, 346, 348, 373, 418, 454, 564, 570, 581, 619, 703, 727, 728
Barter markets: 511–13
Bathurst: 33, 34, 35, 36, 42, 48, 49, 56
Bee hives: 473, 476, 485
Beef: 65, 66, 149, 163, 656

Beer: 22, 73, 163, 264, 266, 275, 277, 453, 483–4, 540, 541, 553, 575, 576, 577, 589, 607, 630, 710, 723, 724
Bemba: 704, 717
Bembe: 582
Bergdama: 621–22
Bicycle: 7, 51, 80, 81, 129, 726
—, increase in use of: 137
—, repairing of: 129, 146, 163, 164
—, traders use of: 158, 651–2
Biscuits: 44, 46, 50, 51, 117
Black market: 723
Blood feuds, Bulu: 172
Bloodwealth: 12, 367 ff., 379, 381, 383
Body marking: 122
Bookkeeping: 695, 697, 699
Bori ritual: 306–7
Bornu: 303-4
Boycotts: 196
Bride wealth: ix, x, 7, 12, 30, 37, 43, 51, 58, 84, 87, 102, 173, 174, 177–8, 181–3, 187, 192, 337, 383, 398–99, 469, 475, 478, 488–9, 491, 521, 522, 524, 552, 553, 563, 564, 565, 569, 576, 578, 607, 617, 624 ff., 630 ff.
Brokers: 195, 305, 308, 348, 381, 402, 687
Budgets: 49 ff., 102, 312, 325-6, 332, 688, 694
Bulk produce buying: 113
Bulk selling: 115
Bulu: Chapter 6 (pp. 170–189)
Bus line: 135
Bushmen: 629
Bushong: 22, 23, 24, Chapter 7 (pp. 190–210), Chapter 8 (pp. 211–233)
Butchers: 146, 265, 336, 338–9, 453, 520, 540, 690

C

Calories: 716–17
Cameroon: 170
Capital: 95, 151, 217, 223, 548–9
Capital equipment: 216
Caravans: 240–1, 243, 244, 245–6, 249, 308, 309, 352, 369–71, 386, 387, 388, 432, 703
Carpenters: 131, 143, 145, 163, 164, 165, 530
—, itinerant: 115
Cash crops: 2, 20, 21, 35, 36, 462, 507, 526, 541, 543, 565, 584, 646
Cash income: 21, 551, 552, 567, 568
Cash trade: 86
Caste: 47, 48, 59, 381 ff., 387, 391, 405, 408, 423, 474

Cattle: 5, 10, 14, 15, 24, 29, 35, 36, 43, 46, 47, 56, 58, 65, 66, 119, 129, 160, 238, 251, 280, 290, 297, 350, 458, 460 ff., 494, 507, 562, 602, 612, 614, 618
—, European: 509
—, Fulani: 301, 339, 359
—, herding: 521
—, property of men: 336
—, sales: 528, 531, 532, 628
—, slaughter of: 133–4
—, villages: 521, 522, 523, 527, 528
Cattle markets, government: 453
Ceremonial: 25, 86, 87, 124, 128, 131, 162, 312
Chagga: 435, 436, 439, 443, 454, 463, 467
Change, economic: 177, 188, 328 ff., 362, 405, 442 ff., 564–5, 577–8, 647 ff., 697
—, resistance to: 362
Charcoal: 729
Chewing sticks: 117, 148
Chiefs: 39, 47, 49, 80, 119, 121, 133, 185 ff., 229, 266, 280, 360, 458, 535, 541, 544, 565, 574, 578, 601, 604, 609, 646, 693, 703
Choice: 339–40
Christianity: 180–1, 230, 255
Christians: 410
Chukchee: 43
Church: 388, 390, 396, 397, 403–4
Cigarettes: 46, 51, 56, 58, 65, 72, 82, 93, 117, 148, 151, 531
Circulation of goods: 360
Circumcision ceremonies: 274
Cisterns: 389
Civil servants: 90
Clans: 124, 368, 377, 384, 477
Clientage: 480
Clients: 314, 381, 479, 555
Climate, attitudes toward: 211–12
Cloth money: 37 ff., 42, 43, 247
Clothing: 51, 114
—, used: 142, 148, 163
Cloves: 56
Clubs: 453
Coco yams: 116, 119, 122, 125, 132, 149
Cocoa: 10, 106, 173, 176 ff., 273, 685, 686 ff., 688, 696
Cocoa farming: 104, 110
Cocoa harvest: 116
Coconuts: 56, 122, 148
Coffee: 49, 81, 280, 446, 450, 463, 508, 526, 645, 646, 647
Coins: 84

Cokwe: 221, 230
Commercial agents: 123
Commercialization, increase of: 134
Commission: 308
Commodities, origins of: 680 ff., 689, 691
Commodity money: xi, 30
Communications: 15–17, 273
Competition: 97, 114, 264–5, 705, 707
—, restriction of: 225-6
Concubinage (see also *ngady*): 192 ff., 638
Consumer demand, shift in: 160
Consumer population: 135
Consumption habits: 51
Contract: 368
Contractors: 165
Conversion: x, 5 ff., 14, 24
Conveyances: 5
Cooking implements: 51, 72
Cooperative work: 404
Cooperatives: 193, 317, 449, 450, 516–7, 598 ff.
— as alternatives to markets: 598
Copper: 698, 701
Copperbelt: 585, 586, 595, Chapter 28 (pp. 698–738)
Cosmetics: 94, 129, 678
Cost: 95, 591, 662 ff.
Cotonou: 89, 90, 92, 94
Cotton: 117, 238, 463, 541, 554, 555, 556, 646, 647
Cotton cloth: 31, 41, 74, 86, 129
Country Cloth: 84, 87
Courts: 126, 374 ff., 480
Courtship: 309
Cowrie shells (cowries): ix, xi, 19, 41, 124, 192, 194, 197 ff., 223, 247, 248, 260, 261, 262, 266, 274, 304, 584, 695, 703
Craft organizations: 57, 226, 305, 311, 392
Crafts: 29, 47, 147, 190, 191, 219, 296, 314, 315, 326, 330, 335–6, 381, 391, 392, 416, 421, 422, 423, 435, 484, 494, 528, 538, 541–2, 607, 617, 622, 731
Craftsmen: 46, 115, 608, 612
Credit: xii, xv, 30, 50, 52, 53, 61, 67, 72, 75–6, 81, 86, 88, 92, 95, 100 ff., 315–7, 418–9, 515–6, 535, 549
— in bridewealth transactions: 635
Cross cousins: 349
Culture change: 129, 141, 175, 184 ff., 425 ff.
Culture traits: 471
Cushites: 409, 427
Customs: 253

D

Dagomba: 237
Dahomey: 15, 19, 89–102
Days, associated with markets: 306, 395
Debts: 51, 53, 80, 100, 405
Development, economic: 215, 404 ff.
Dhows, Arab: 369
Dia (Somali blood wealth payments): 366 ff.
Diamond mining: 75, 80
Diets: 218, 643 ff., 716 ff.
Digging sticks: 475
Dillali (Fulani term for "broker"): 348 ff.
Dinga: 216
Dioula: 243, 286, 287, 289, 290, 292, 293, 295, 296, 347, 357
Disputes: 121, 196, 604, 605
District officer: 133
Divorce: 633, 634–5
Dogs: 173
Domestic animals: 173
Dual economy: ix, 25, 611 ff.
Ducks: 139
Dye: 56

E

Economic behavior, rationality of: 358–9
Economic man: vii
Education: 176–7, 180, 394, 444, 462, 593, 600
Eggs: 65, 85, 113, 139, 149
Employment agency: 164
Entrepreneurs: 47, 61
Epizootics: 339, 344, 436, 461, 467, 509, 565–6, 603, 607
Equivalences: 85, 614, 615, 622, 624
Eritrea: 406
Erosion: 467
European firms: 315
European goods: 531
European trade: 19, 32
Exchange, forms of: 524–5
Exchange rates: 261, 358
Exchange, rules of: 781, 782
Exchange-value, reckoning: 346, 472
Expeditions, long distance trading: 317-18
Exports: 353

F

Factors (traders): 76–77

Factors of production: 9, 188–9, 686-7
Factory workers: 90
Falasha (Ethiopian Jews): 391, 392
Fang: 89, 101, 170
Festivals, influence on markets: 115
Feuds: 172, 227–8
Fighting: 291, 562
Fines: 87, 101
Fish: 34, 36, 48, 49, 55, 56, 61, 66, 67, 68, 69, 74, 76, 87, 89, 90, 91, 94, 97–8, 100, 112, 113, 114, 118, 119, 120, 122, 124, 127, 132, 137, 141, 147, 148, 158, 168, 217, 587, 593, 595, 596, 607, 608, 612, 690, 706, 707, 708, 717, 719, 722, 724–8
Flax: 504
Flour: 91, 93, 540
"Forestalling": 680
Freetown: 61, 81
Friendship: 410, 442, 606–7, 611, 615
Fringe markets: xiii
Fruit: 93, 94, 95, 116, 125, 148, 149, 541, 730–1
Fulani: 14, 32, 40, 45, 46, 48, 51, 54, 65, 66, 244, 296, 299 ff., 309, 314, 318, 328, Chapter 12 (pp. 335–364)
Funerals: xiv, 191, 275
Furniture: 163
Futures: 316–17

G

Galla: 390, 409, 411, 417, 427
Gambia: 29–59
Ganda: 645 ff.
Generosity: 59, 541
Germans: 175, 176, 186, 436, 437, 458
Gerontocracy: 118
Gift-exchange: ix, 174, 311, 314, 332, 537, 563, 568, 619–20
Gifts: 342, 563, 568, 606, 619, 623
Gin: 86, 128, 168, 571
Goats: 22, 29, 44, 46, 49, 50, 112, 116, 148, 173–4, 175, 238, 251, 336, 339, 398, 450–1, 454, 458, 469, 472 ff., 475, 486–88, 494, 562, 563
Goat's milk: 482–3
Gold: 19, 30, 31, 32, 36, 40, 41, 290, 679, 695, 697
Goldsmiths: 115, 393
Grazing, rights to: 366
Greeks: 544, 545, 546, 548, 549, 550, 725
Ground nuts (see peanuts)

Guilds (see craft organizations)
Guinée: 65
Gums: 368, 371, 377
—, gathering of: 361
Gunpowder: 15, 19, 40, 41, 112, 122, 123, 142, 148
Guns: 15, 35, 40, 123, 701-2
Gunu: 89, 101
Guro: 14, 15, 19, Chapter 10 (pp. 279-298)
Gusii: 19, 482, 494, 503, 508, 510, 512, Chapter 20 (pp. 520-536)

H

Habe (Hausa): 299-300
Haggling: 86, 97 ff., 114, 132, 201, 401, 434, 658, 660, 703, 707, 728
Hardware: 90, 94, 129, 542
Hausa: 14, 48, 240, 242, 243, 246, 247, 264, 296, Chapter 11 (pp. 299-334), 336, 353
Hawkers: 47 ff., 62, 96, 130, 549, 584-5, 610, 683, 705, 708, 711, 712, 731
—, women: 676
Headloading: 111, 112, 120, 129, 165, 670, 691-2
Herds, composition of: 339
Herero: Chapter 25 (pp. 617-639)
Hierarchy: 59, 179-80, 360
History, attitude toward: 447
Hoe: 29, 117, 122, 131, 175
Homicide: 367, 379
Honey: 473, 476, 480, 484-5, 494, 546, 549, 608, 701
Honey beer: 473, 491
Horses: 31, 36, 38, 40, 160, 238-9
Hospitality, obligations of: 173
Hotels: 152, 163, 164
—, bars and restaurants: 138, 153
Hottentots: 622-3, 630
Households: 333
Housing: 217-18
Hunting: 190, 215, 220, 226, 238, 280, 285, 415, 422, 459, 554, 607, 705
Hut tax: 58, 499

I

Ibo: 18, 19
Incentives: 441
Income: 693 ff.
—, annual per capita (Hausa): 325 ff.
—, annual per capita (Fulani): 337

—, seasonal influence on: 116
Indigo: 54
Inflation: 198 ff.
Inheritance: 360, 422, 613
— of cattle: 337, 342
— of trading businesses: 318
Initiation fees: 87
Initiation payments: 84
Injections: 401, 402
Inter village group trade: 124, 130
Interest: 52, 100, 315-6
International trade: 89-90
Intra-tribal trading: 122
Inventories: 71-2, 75
Iraqw: 5, 14, 436, Chapter 17 (pp. 457-468)
Iron: 122-3, 130, 162, 175, 285-6, 562, 563, 701-2
Iron ore: 61, 474, 494
Iron ware, indigenous: 148
Ironworkers: 29, 36, 39, 46, 47, 106, 113, 122, 123, 131, 143, 146, 469, 474, 494, 621
Irrigation: 237, 433, 470, 471 ff., 476, 478 ff.
Islam: 29, 38, 47, 306, 311, 368, 376, 382, 389, 391, 402, 408
—, introduction to Hausa: 303
—, attitude toward charity: 313
Ivory: 30, 173, 175, 194 ff., 290, 292, 462, 544, 581, 607, 609, 697, 701, 702, 731

J

Joking relationships: 275, 349
Jolloffs (see Wolof)
Jukun: 301

K

Kakwa: 570, 571
Kamba: 512
Kampala: Chapter 26 (pp. 643-656)
Kano: 303-4, 305, 316
Kano Chronicle: 302-3
Kanuri: 301
Katanga: 699 ff., 725
Kaur: 32-3, 40, 49, 51, 55-6
Kikuyu: 481, 526
Kinship: vii, 8, 73, 171, 185, 271, 311, 333, 345, 384, 410, 438-9, 563, 569, 596, 606-7, 611, 615, 629, 732
— as an element in trade: 380
— behavior: 270-71
—, obligations of: 87

—, obligations toward: 82–83
— terminology: 171
Kipsigis: 14, 22, Chapter 19 (pp. 493–519)
Knives: 51, 86, 117, 122
Koforidua: Chapter 27 (pp. 667–697)
Kola nuts: 44, 45, 46, 48, 53, 56, 58, 65, 70, 81, 82, 85, 110, 111, 114, 115, 116, 148, 242, 246, 247, 249, 251, 259, 264, 272, 273, 277, 285–6, 287, 289, 290, 293, 296
Konso: 8, Chapter 15 (pp. 409–428)
Kuba (see Bushong)
Kula: 3–4, 5, 10–11, 13
Kuria: 521

L

Labor: 2, 10, 188–9, 190, 199–200, 202, 223, 391, 414, 416, 474 ff., 496 ff., 557 ff., 618, 645, 647–8, 687
—, division of: 172, 216, 217, 264, 387 ff., 392, 408, 476, 521–2, 600
—, forced: 280, 554
—, organization of: 215 ff., 421
—, sexual division of: vii, xiii, 186, 195, 226–7, 280, 311, 330, 475, 538, 572, 592 ff.
—, skilled: 405–6
—, wage: 21, 188, 311, 331, 336, 359, 393, 421, 441, 445, 452, 463, 497–8, 501–2, 517, 518, 560, 567–8
Labor market: 21, 557-8, 665
Labor migration: 54, 253 ff., 273, 408, 489–90, 527, 565, 566, 567, 568, 574, 575, 577, 611, 629–30, 687
Laborers: 82, 106, 504
—, juvenile: 502–3
Laibon: 501 ff.
Lamba: 703
Land: 2, 22, 171, 173, 188–9, 408, 413–4, 425 ff., 439, 444 ff., 471, 478 ff., 481, 485–6, 491, 505 ff., 521, 527, 573, 574, 602–3, 686, 689
Leather: 472
Leather workers: 36, 50, 55, 57
Lebu: 36, 56
Leisure: 714
Lele: 6, 22-24, 193, Chapter 8 (pp. 211–233)
Livestock: 38, 47, 51, 114, 142, 524
Loans: 78, 461
— of livestock: 343, 607
Local government, development of: 154
Locust beans: 55
Logoli: 526

Lorry transport (see trucks)
Lozi: 609, 713
Luba: 195, 215, 230, 717
Lubono (Citonga word for wealth): 613–14
Lugbara: 14, Chapter 22 (pp. 561–578)
Lulua: 194
Lungu: 582
Luo: 494, 503, 510, 512, 520, 521, 525, 528, 529, 534

M

Madi: 562, 563, 566, 571
Maize: 111, 115, 116, 122, 129, 161, 238, 458, 459, 501, 506, 507, 526, 531, 562, 587, 643, 645, 656, 719, 722, 729
Mambwe: 582
Mandingo: 36, 48, 52 ff.
Manillas: ix, xi
Manufacturing: 407, 416
Mark up: 201
Markets, absence of: x, 618
—, association with day names: xiii, 423
—, associations with government: 125, 582, 584–5
—, cornering of: 708
—, distance to: xii, 681–2, 684–5, 698–9
—, establishment of: 465, 537–8, 705
—, expansion of: 20, 188, 543
—, motivation for attending: 331, 354–5, 403
—, night: xiii, 102, 257
—, seating arrangements in: 263–4
—, social functions of: x–xi, 133, 292, 309, 332, 532, 533, 534, 535, 542
Market controls: 132, 151, 155, 422–3
Market courts: 18, 154
Market economies: 9, 88
Market fees: 63, 671, 675, 706, 708
Market networks: xiii, 19, 105–6, 119
Market officials: 64, 112, 136, 139, 140, 147, 150, 153, 154, 155–6, 196, 255–6, 268–70, 307 ff., 671
Market organization: 124, 133, 136, 153, 402 ff., 465, 542
Market peace: 17-18, 572
Market place: viii, 1, 9, 15 ff., 25, 26, 31, 47, 55, 63, 88, 94, 254, 257, 376, 388, 416, 655, 705
Market police: 125
Market principle: viii
—, distinguished from market place: 1

—, as a basis for society: 2–3, 4, 8–12, 25–6
Market restrictions: 125, 132
Market stalls: 111, 138–9, 152–5, 586–7
Market tolls: 120
Marketing boards: 319
Marketless transactions: 193, 403, 423
Marriage: 183, 227, 271–2, 274–5, 280, 289, 291, 292, 297, 311–12, 337, 341, 360, 469, 475, 638–9
Masai: 14, 22, 431 ff., 458, 459, 461, 465, 467, 470 ff., 490, 493, 494, 501, 510
Mat makers: 131
Matches: 46, 49, 51, 65, 72, 86, 112, 148, 151
Matrilineal groups: 117
Mau Mau: 526
Mayoso: 71–2, 74, 76, 78–81
Mbugwe: 458, 459
Measures: 98, 308, 591, 659, 665, 707
Medicine: 46, 48, 51, 56, 72, 90, 93, 113, 117, 129, 148, 397, 678–9
Mende: 70, 85
Mercenaries: 123
Metal rods: xi, 41, 43, 124, 125, 286, 287, 289, 296
Middlemen: 90, 93, 94, 113, 116, 142, 175, 544, 598, 714
—, increase of: 144–45
Migration, Afikpo: 130
Miners: 80
Missionaries: 175–6, 277, 443–4, 548, 583–4, 587, 622
Money: ix, x, xi, xv, 6–7, 10–12, 20, 37, 57, 59, 94–5, 102, 124, 346–8, 490–1, 525, 550, 551–2, 553, 557, 614 ff., 695
Money-barter: viii, 38, 43, 83
Money lender: 46, 102
Moneyless exchange: 418, 561
Moors: 30, 31
Mortars & pestles: 140, 149
Mortgage: 478
Mossi: 18, Chapter 9 (pp. 237–278), 294
Mourning ritual, influence on marketing: 91
Multicentric economy: 3, 5, 6, 12, 20, 26

N

Nagots (see Yoruba)
Nandi: 493, 499, 501
Narcotics: 617
Ndebele: 609
Ndorobo: 432

Nigerian Motor Workers Union: 158–9
Ngady (Bushong concubinage): 192 ff.
Nubi: 571

O

Oracles: 123
Overstocking: 467
Ownership: 477

P

Palm nuts: 100
Palm oil: 44, 45, 48, 65, 70, 72, 76, 77, 84, 85, 93, 111, 115, 116, 119, 122, 123, 125, 130, 132, 140, 144, 146, 719
Palm oil mill: 119, 167
Palm products: 90, 93, 120, 127, 696
Palm wine: 69, 101, 111, 119, 131, 148, 162, 163, 164, 222
Pariah: 474
Pastoralism: 361, 617 ff.
Patronage: 381, 538
Pawn broking: 81
Pawned goods: 79, 80
Pawning: xv, 494
Pawpaws: 140, 143
Pax Britannica: 36, 47, 70, 79, 538
Pay rolls: 685–86
Payments: 191, 435
Peanut oil: 45, 157
Peanuts: 34, 35, 36, 40, 42, 43, 45, 49, 50, 51, 53 ff., 58, 65, 70, 72–4, 79, 84, 89, 90, 92, 98, 116, 132, 140, 143, 144, 147, 148, 149, 158, 161, 173, 353, 539, 656
Pende: 214, 230
Peppermints: 46, 56
Perfume: 46, 51, 56, 94, 163
Peripheral markets: 2, 3, 7-10, 25
Peulh (see Fulani)
Phonographs: 80, 81
Photographs: 163, 164
Pinmoney economy: 10, 551–2
Planning, economic: xiv
Plantains: 112, 113, 116, 643, 644 ff., 647 ff., 650, 651, 655 ff., 678
Pledge, of land: 478
Plow: 413, 504–5, 610
Polygamy: 47, 58, 182, 226–7, 228, 488, 523, 524, 535, 563, 576, 638
Population density: 127, 445, 583
Population growth: 526

Poro society: 87
Portuguese: 30–32, 390, 391
Potlatch: 5, 174–5
Pottery: 29, 47, 48, 84–6, 111, 117, 120, 122, 124, 127, 129, 130, 131, 139, 146, 147, 149, 174, 470, 474
Prestige: ix, x, xv, 59, 191, 200, 224, 288, 296, 297, 313, 359, 384, 480, 506, 535, 565, 577, 639
Prestige goods: 25, 165, 172, 280, 522
Price: xv, 1, 2, 8, 9, 53, 54, 74, 86, 87, 96, 98, 101, 126, 132, 196, 199 ff., 247, 248, 260, 288, 320–22, 347, 352, 357–8, 359, 380, 383, 401, 419 ff., 422, 451, 464, 488, 510, 558, 589–91, 613–14, 622, 627, 653, 659, 660–2, 703, 707, 722, 727, 733
Profit: 95, 112, 128, 265, 313, 596, 658, 694
Property: 132, 477
Prostitutes: 163, 164, 307, 397, 589, 714
Purdah: 270, 314, 331

R

Raffia: xi, 174, 197, 222–3, 224–5, 229
Raiding: 431, 455, 458, 461, 469, 471, 521
Ramadan: 29
Reciprocity: 4, 19, 20, 343
Redistribution: 3, 19, 20, 312
Regulation, government: 508
Religion, association with markets: xiii–xiv, 125, 137–8, 267, 255–6, 306, 534
Residence: 341
Rice: 36, 40, 45, 47, 48, 50, 58, 65, 69, 73, 74, 75, 76, 78, 79, 82, 90, 112, 116, 119, 120, 122, 131, 141, 144, 148, 161, 162, 166–7, 285, 539, 589, 722
Rites de passage: 30, 44, 59
Ritual: vii, 101-2, 127, 132, 273-4, 460, 604
River traders: 120, 168
Royal Africa Company: 32
Rum: 40

S

Sacrifices: 256, 260, 269, 336, 341, 344, 479, 603
Sales revenue: 692 ff.
Sales techniques: 96
Salt: 32, 36, 43, 48, 50, 51, 56, 65, 73, 82, 83, 84, 85, 87, 98, 112, 113, 116, 122, 145, 148, 190, 194, 244, 259, 266, 292, 295, 350, 352, 358, 371, 417, 418, 419, 425, 474, 539, 544, 565, 581, 608, 609, 677, 690, 701, 703, 704
Savings: 360, 452, 553, 616
Scales: 261, 591, 659, 660, 706
School books: 129
Secret society: 119
Sedox (see *alms*)
Self-sufficiency: 495–6
Servants: 629
Services: 128, 343
Settlement patterns: 108, 237, 378–9
Sewing machines: 36, 51, 70, 400
Sharecroppers: 54
Sharing: 185, 360
Sheep: 29, 48, 112, 116, 148, 173, 174, 238, 251, 336, 340, 398, 399, 458, 471, 562, 612, 631
Shells (other than cowries): 702
Shifting cultivators: 170
Shopkeepers (see storekeepers)
Shops (see stores)
Shrines: 604, 605
—, women's: 155
Silver: 41
Silversmiths: 393, 407
Slash-and-burn: 172
Slaves: 6, 14, 19, 30, 31, 32, 36, 38, 40, 89, 90, 123, 124, 127, 162, 170, 175, 192, 194, 195, 243, 247, 265, 267, 274, 286, 288, 290, 304, 308, 318, 349–50, 368, 458, 462, 469, 497, 581, 605, 607, 697, 701–2, 703, 704, 705
Slum areas: 164
Smuggling: 251-2
Somali: 12, Chapter 13 (pp. 365–385), 426, 436, 439, 454, 466, 490, 538
Sonjo: 5, 6, Chapter 18 (pp. 469–492)
Spears: 175, 552-3
Specialists: 525, 592, 682
Specialization: 112, 143–4, 371
Speculation: 47, 102, 649
Spheres of exchange: 427
Squatters: 499, 503
Standardization: 657
Starch: 65
Status symbols: 24, 51
Storage: 219
Storekeepers: 90, 543 ff., 569, 570, 616, 722, 723–4, 730
Stores: 96, 105, 138, 143, 160, 163, 193, 452, 463, 500, 505, 507, 513-4, 531, 535, 569 ff., 585, 610, 611, 614, 626–7, 699, 710

Stratification, social: 478 ff., 696
Suk: 493
Suku: 214
Supply and demand: xi, 73, 96, 101, 199 ff.,
    357, 420, 451, 589, 646, 649, 653, 733
Surplus: 13, 14, 175, 424
Susu: 66
Swahili: 436, 504, 520, 702, 704
Sweet potatoes: 45, 50, 55, 73, 95, 473, 483,
    562, 643, 653, 659
Syrians: 61, 62, 64, 66, 78, 81, 293, 315

T

Tailors: 49, 51, 70, 106, 115, 129, 146, 163,
    164
Target traders: 7, 615
Target workers: 83, 499
Tax: 7, 21, 33, 36, 51, 77–8, 99, 102, 246,
    248, 252, 260–1, 265–6, 267, 338, 354, 358,
    406, 426, 462, 489, 490, 497, 499, 518, 544,
    546, 550, 554, 564, 565, 566, 569, 573, 576,
    611, 627, 639, 708
Tea: 48, 56, 82, 501, 504, 507–8, 517, 527–8
Temne: Chapter 2 (pp. 61–88)
Terracing: 413
Thaler, Maria Theresa: 406–7, 418–9
Timbuktu: 239, 242, 243, 250
Tithes: 311
Title societies: 119, 124, 139
Tiv: 6
Tobacco: 46, 51, 65, 85, 117, 123, 163, 319,
    541, 591, 679, 731
Tonga: 7, 582, Chapter 24 (pp. 601–616),
    713, 729
Town crier: 101
Towns: 186, 373–4, 389, 448–9, 452, 540
Trade, attitudes toward: 200, 388, 401
Trade friends: 87–88, 172–4
Trade guilds: 114
Trade routes, for cattle: 352–3
Trains: 683
Transhumance: 336, 351, 354, 361
Transport: 47, 61, 649 ff., 652 ff., 724
Tribute: 193, 229
Trobriand Islands: 3, 4, 5, 6, 13
Trucks: 66, 68–69, 70, 75, 80, 129, 135, 683,
    719, 724, 726
Tse-tse fly: 65, 173, 467
Tswana: 623

Tuareg: 302, 303, 317, 336, 342, 348
Turks: 390

U

Umbrellas: 80
Underemployment: 113
Unicentric economy: 20, 26
Upward mobility: 152
Urbanization: 110, 112–3, 118, 584

V

Volume measures: 84–5, 98, 148

W

Wages: 123, 165, 377, 394, 557–8
Wangara: 32
War: 120, 226, 283, 369, 408, 472, 605
Wax: 30, 40
Wealth: 23–24, 57, 60, 132, 172, 224, 535,
    616
Wealth, attitudes toward: 185, 191, 313,
    337–8, 342, 383–4, 419–20, 479, 523–4,
    612–3
Weavers 29, 47, 393, 679–80
Weights: 695
Wholesalers: 64, 92, 111, 659
Widows: 377, 597, 633
Wine: 73, 82
Wives, salaried temporary: 403
Wolof: Chapter 1 (pp. 29–60)
Women, rights to: 227, 625–6
Women, traders and venders: xi, xii, xiii,
    8, 55, 56, 88 ff., 104, 110, 111, 112, 114,
    120, 123, 124, 129, 131, 145, 147, 150, 295,
    376, 532, 538, 592, 593, 594, 687, 696, 710,
    714
Work parties: 404, 607

Y

Yoruba: 10, 19, 89, Chapter 4 (pp. 103–117),
    264, 304, 315, 679

Z

Zande: Chapter 21 (pp. 537–560)
Zande scheme: 555–57